TACKLING PRECARIOUS WORK

Tackling precarious work has been described by the United Nations (UN)'s International Labour Organization (ILO) as the main challenge facing the world of work. In this ground-breaking book, leading applied research scholars, advocates, and activists from across the globe respond to this challenge by showing how Industrial and Organizational (I/O) psychology has a significant contribution to make in humanity moving away from precarious work situations toward sustainable livelihoods.

Broken down into four key parts on Sustainable Livelihoods, Fair Incomes, Work Security, and Social Protection, the book covers a multitude of topics including the role of poor pay, lack of work-related security, social protection for human health and wellbeing, and interventions and policies to implement for the future of work. The volume offers a detailed look into useful and effective ways to tackle precarious work to create and maintain sustainable livelihoods. This curated collection of 22 chapters considers the broader relationships between previous research work and issues of human security and sustainability that affect workers, families, communities, and societies. Each chapter expands the present understandings of the world of precarious work and how it fits within broader issues of economic, ecological, and social sustainability.

In addition to I/O psychologists in research, practice, service, and study, this book will also be useful for organizational researchers, labor unions, HR practitioners, fair trade, cooperative, and civil society organizations, social scientists, human security analysts, public health professionals, economists, and supporters of the UN SDGs, including at the UN.

Stuart C. Carr is UNESCO Professor on Sustainable Livelihoods and a Professor of Psychology in the School of Psychology at Massey University, New Zealand. Stu's research, service, and teaching focus on transformation from insecure, precarious work to sustainable livelihoods, under the aegis of the UN Sustainable Development Goals.

Dr. Veronica Hopner is Senior Lecturer in the School of Psychology, Massey University in New Zealand. Her research interests include modern slavery, occupational health psychology, and violent extremism.

Darrin J. Hodgetts is Professor of Societal Psychology at Massey University where he researches issues of human [in]security, including urban poverty. Darrin has held various academic positions in Canada, the United Kingdom, and New Zealand, and his work is increasingly focused on the Asia Pacific region.

Megan Young is Assistant Lecturer in the School of Psychology at Massey University, New Zealand. With an undergraduate degree in English Literature, she is particularly interested in the different ways that research can be communicated to a broader audience where it may benefit professionals and lay people alike.

SIOP Organizational Frontiers Series

The Organizational Frontiers Series is sponsored by the Society for Industrial and Organizational Psychology (SIOP). Launched in 1983 to make scientific contributions accessible to the field, the series publishes books addressing emerging theoretical developments, fundamental and translational research, and theory-driven practice in the field of Industrial-Organizational Psychology and related organizational science disciplines including organizational behavior, human resource management, and labor and industrial relations.

Books in this series aim to inform readers of significant advances in research; challenge the research and practice community to develop and adapt new ideas; and promote the use of scientific knowledge in the solution of public policy issues and increased organizational effectiveness.

The Series originated in the hope that it would facilitate continuous learning and spur research curiosity about organizational phenomena on the part of both scientists and practitioners.

The Society for Industrial and Organizational Psychology is an international professional association with an annual membership of more than 8,000 industrial-organizational (I-O) psychologists who study and apply scientific principles to the workplace. I-O psychologists serve as trusted partners to business, offering strategically focused and scientifically rigorous solutions for a number of workplace issues. SIOP's mission is to enhance human well-being and performance in organizational and work settings by promoting the science, practice, and teaching of I-O psychology. For more information about SIOP, please visit www.siop.org.

Using Industrial-Organizational Psychology for the Greater Good
Helping Those Who Help Others
Edited by Julie Olson-Buchanan, Laura Koppes Bryan, and Lori Foster Thompson

The Psychology of Workplace Technology
Edited by Michael D. Coovert and Lori Foster Thompson

Facing the Challenges of a Multi-Age Workforce
A Use-Inspired Approach
Edited by Lisa M. Finkelstein, Donald M. Truxillo, Franco Fraccaroli, and Ruth Kanfer

Big Data at Work
The Data Science Revolution and Organizational Psychology
Edited by Scott Tonidandel, Eden B. King, and Jose M. Cortina

Understanding the High Performance Workplace
The Line Between Motivation and Abuse
Edited by Neal M. Ashkanasy, Rebecca J. Bennett, and Mark J. Martinko

Autonomous Learning in the Workplace
Edited by Jill E. Ellingson and Raymond A. Noe

The Self at Work
Fundamental Theory and Research
Edited by D. Lance Ferris, Russell E. Johnson, and Constantine Sedikides

Workforce Readiness and the Future of Work
Edited by Frederick L. Oswald, Tara S. Behrend, and Lori L. Foster

Vocational Interests in the Workplace
Rethinking Behavior at Work
Edited by Christopher D. Nye and James Rounds

Creativity and Innovation in Organizations
Edited by Michael D. Mumford and E. Michelle Todd

Social Networks at Work
Edited by Daniel J. Brass and Stephen P. Borgatti

The Psychology of Entrepreneurship
New Perspectives
Edited by Michael M. Gielnik, Melissa S. Cardon, and Michael Frese

Understanding Trust in Organizations
A Multilevel Perspective
Edited by Nicole Gillespie, Ashley Fulmer, and Roy J. Lewicki

Age and Work
Advances in Theory, Methods, and Practice
Edited by Hannes Zacher & Cort W. Rudolph

Data, Methods and Theory in the Organizational Sciences
A New Synthesis
Edited by Kevin R. Murphy

Neurodiversity in the Workplace
Interests, Issues, and Opportunities
Edited by Susanne M. Bruyère and Adrienne Colella

Expatriates and Managing Global Mobility
Edited by Soo Min Toh and Angelo DeNisi

Senior Leadership Teams and the Agile Organization
Edited by Stephen J. Zaccaro, Nathan J. Hiller and Richard Klimoski

For more information about this series, please visit www.routledge.com/
SIOP-Organizational-Frontiers-Series/book-series/SIOP

TACKLING PRECARIOUS WORK

Toward Sustainable Livelihoods

Edited by
Stuart C. Carr, Veronica Hopner,
Darrin J. Hodgetts, and Megan Young

Routledge
Taylor & Francis Group
NEW YORK AND LONDON

SIOP
SOCIETY for INDUSTRIAL and ORGANIZATIONAL PSYCHOLOGY
SCIENCE FOR A SMARTER WORKPLACE

Cover image: © Getty Images

First published 2024
by Routledge
605 Third Avenue, New York, NY 10158

and by Routledge
4 Park Square, Milton Park, Abingdon, Oxon, OX14 4RN

Routledge is an imprint of the Taylor & Francis Group, an informa business

Library of Congress Cataloging-in-Publication Data
Names: Carr, Stuart C., editor. Title: Tackling precarious work : toward sustainable livelihoods / edited by Stuart C. Carr, Veronica Hopner, Darrin J. Hodgetts, and Megan Young.
Description: Abingdon, Oxon ; New York, NY : Routledge, 2024. |
Series: SIOP organizational frontiers | Includes bibliographical references and index. |
Identifiers: LCCN 2023021674 (print) | LCCN 2023021675 (ebook) |
ISBN 9781032576633 (paperback) | ISBN 9781032576657 (hardback) |
ISBN 9781003440444 (ebook) Subjects: LCSH: Precarious employment—Psychological aspects. | Work. | Labor. | Economic security.
Classification: LCC HD5857 .T327 2024 (print) | LCC HD5857 (ebook) |
DDC 331.25/729—dc23/eng/20230512
LC record available at https://lccn.loc.gov/2023021674
LC ebook record available at https://lccn.loc.gov/2023021675

ISBN: 978-1-032-57665-7 (hbk)
ISBN: 978-1-032-57663-3 (pbk)
ISBN: 978-1-003-44044-4 (ebk)

DOI: 10.4324/9781003440444

Typeset in Times New Roman
by codeMantra

We dedicate this book to the memory of Dr. Bimal Arora (1970–2022),
a passionate visionary and interdisciplinary scholar who rather uniquely straddled the worlds of academia and practice and dedicated his life to tackling precarity in workplaces and beyond.

True to his name, which translates to 'pure' in the English language, Bimal carried on with an unflinching commitment for a kinder world in the face of all hurdles. Those whose lives he touched will forever remember him as a beautiful human being who walked the path alongside us and the work, he accomplished in this journey, which was cut short too soon, will continue to inspire all of us. Some reflective cases of his work have been included in this volume including a biography which serves as an inspiration to us all.

Biography of Dr. Bimal Arora written by Divya Jyoti

In 1947, a line was sketched on the map of the Indian subcontinent. This line (referred to as the Radcliffe Line after its creator, Sir Cyril Radcliffe) formed two nations, India and Pakistan, from what was previously one country, and forced millions of people to leave their lives behind and cross over the line. Bimal was born to one such couple who had been forced to leave their home in Rawalpindi. They eventually settled in Lucknow in the state of Uttar Pradesh in Northern India. Bimal was born nearly two decades after his parents had migrated, but the scars and trauma of the family's social, cultural, and economic life, built up over generations, being suddenly and arbitrarily uprooted persisted and manifested itself in his childhood as multiple financial, psychological, and physical insecurities and scarcities. Losing his father to a sudden heart attack while he was travelling for precarious work when Bimal was a teenager generated emotions and reflections which shaped Bimal's being and guided his work for decades to come. He had developed a nuanced understanding of precarity, long before he identified and analyzed the phenomenon academically. His childhood lived experience became a significant pathway in his work confronting and tackling precariousness and prompted him to set up a not-for-profit organization right after completing his undergraduate studies, at the age of 21, where he worked with vulnerable children living on the streets in India

Having worked closely with government and development agencies in his early career, Bimal noted the potential in the private sector for tackling the development, propagation and persistence of precarious workplaces, which motivated his journey into issues of corporate responsibility. He worked with companies of various sizes, examining narratives and organizational structures, and ultimately embarked on doctoral studies on the topic at the International Centre for Corporate Social Responsibility (ICCSR) at the University of Nottingham.

Bimal's father had worked for a small, local, family-owned clothing business as a contract salesperson where he was paid a percentage on the sales and was responsible for all expenses, including his travels across the country to sell the garments. This meant that often even the candy floss and toffees that young Bimal demanded his mother buy for him were purchased through loans from the father's employer, and sometimes on credit from tradespeople. These were later paid off, often only partially, against the household income. His formative years were characterized by an intriguing mix of both exploitative and humane experiences associated with small enterprise, which later contributed invaluable insights about small businesses and the informal economy and enabled Bimal's scholarly self to develop unique perspectives on both corporate responsibility and tackling precarity.

Bimal's PhD journey enabled him to develop a wider understanding of the issues of development and corporate social responsibility from a global perspective. Keen to enact an informed approach to reform, and to translate his learning and insights into public good, Bimal moved back to India with the intention and vision to establish an institution to navigate the socioeconomic and cultural differences and other divisive barriers in our society in order to inspire action to create a kinder, more inclusive and sustainable world. This vision became the founding intellectual pillar of what is today the Centre for Responsible Business (CRB) in New Delhi. At CRB, and indeed throughout his professional life, he deployed what he referred to as "disruptive questioning and awakening" to challenge norms, hierarchies, and processes; and created forums and spaces for representation and dialogue, with a specific focus on including those at the margins who often remain unheard, unseen, unknown, left out, and overlooked. He worked with many national and international governments, agencies, corporations and charities; served on various committees; and presented at various local and global forums. His work and efforts were widely respected, and he was recognized as a leader and as an inspirational and authoritative voice on inclusive and sustainable development.

Having established CRB, Bimal was keen to share insights generated through his practice with his academic colleagues and students and moved back to the UK. There he worked with the Universities of Manchester, Cambridge, and Aston, and Manchester Metropolitan, in various roles. On the insistence of CRB's Governing Body, who appreciated his vision and passion, he remained the Chairperson of CRB, while also devoting his time to challenging academic norms and theories, disciplinary boundaries, and methodological silos. He secured a research grant for a project[1] and used it to bring together an eclectic mix of scholars under one umbrella by establishing a distinctive cross- and multidisciplinary multimethods research network on sustainable value chains, which also integrated policy actors. The outputs of this network were at various stages of development and publication when the thread of his life was unfortunately cut short in March 2022. Nevertheless, his legacy will live on through CRB; his publications; and his mentees, colleagues, and friends.

The suddenness and randomness of Bimal's departure in some ways epitomizes his mantra of the "magic of maybe"; that is, we do what we can to the best of our abilities with a conscious awareness of the multitude of factors beyond our control. Bimal suggested we do not allow such factors to overwhelm us or become an excuse for inaction; instead we remember that in them lie possibilities for both hope and despair, and we leave scope in our actions and decisions for the "magic" of life to unfold. Both his life and departure will continue to serve as a reminder of the "maybe" which arises from life's fragility and tentativeness. Bimal's refusal to "settle down" when more remained to be done to make a better world created various personal and professional challenges in his life, but he continued to strive, dared to dream, and overcame hurdles with inspirational grace. His was an ordinary life lived extraordinarily, in many ways. In just a short period he laid the foundation for conversations which continue, forged partnerships which have prospered, established institutions which carry forward, expanded a vision for an inclusive society, and inspired those whose lives he touched to make a difference in our own small ways. May we together create a kinder world.

Note

1 A brief summary, in Bimal's words, of the project's focus on sustainability and value chains in India was captured in a 2019 interview. The author expresses gratitude to the network and its founding organizations for this interview and making the excerpt publicly available.

CONTENTS

ACKNOWLEDGMENTS

We thank the School of Psychology and College of Humanities and Social Sciences at Massey University New Zealand for your kind support of this project. We would like to thank Priscilla Cameron for her professional copyediting time and skills in the preparation of this manuscript. Thank you to all our peer reviewers who have provided their insights and feedback to make this volume possible and to bring its contributions into the light of day.

CONTRIBUTORS

Bimal Arora, Aston Business School, University of Manchester, Manchester, United Kingdom.

Sarah Bankins, Department of Management, Macquarie University, Sydney, and Rotman School of Management, Toronto, Canada. Australia.

Mary O'Neill Berry, Global Organisation for Humanitarian Work Psychology, New York City, United States of America.

Donald Jay Bertulfo, Department of Psychology, Ateneo de Manila University, Quezon City, Philippines and Faculty of Technology, Policy and Management, Delft University of Technology, Delft, The Netherlands.

Stuart C. Carr, EPIC (End Poverty & Inequality Cluster), School of Psychology, Auckland, Massey University, New Zealand.

Shemana Cassim, EPIC (End Poverty & Inequality Cluster), School of Psychology, Auckland, Massey University, Aotearoa New Zealand.

Jose Antonio R. Clemente, Department of Psychology, University of the Philippines Diliman, Quezon City, Philippines.

Anna Crawford, Department of Psychology and Behavioral Sciences Louisiana Tech University Ruston, LA USA.

J. Crentsil, Centene Corporation, Dallas, TX USA.

Annamaria Di Fabio, Department of Education Science and Psychology, University of Florence, Florence, Italy.

Jean-Yves Gerlitz, SOCIUM Research Center for Inequality and Social Policy, University of Bremen, Bremen, Germany.

Yannick Griep, Behavioural Science Institute, Radboud University, Nijmegen, The Netherlands and Stress Research Institute, Stockholm University, Stockholm, Sweden.

Patrick Gunnigle, Department of Management, University of Limerick, Limerick Ireland.

Jarrod Haar, Massey Business School, Auckland, Massey University, New Zealand.

Samantha D. Hansen, Department of Management, University of Toronto Scarborough and Rotman School Management, Toronto, Canada.

J. Hernandez, Department of Psychology, University at Albany, SUNY Albany, NY USA.

Darrin J. Hodgetts, EPIC (End Poverty & Inequality Cluster), School of Psychology, Auckland, Massey University, New Zealand.

S. Hohmann, Team Development Solutions, Hyde Park, NY, USA.

Veronica Hopner, EPIC (End Poverty & Inequality Cluster), School of Psychology, Auckland, Massey University, New Zealand.

Dusadee Yoelao Intraprasert, Graduate School, Srinakharinwirot University, Bangkok, Thailand.

Lixin Jiang, Faculty of Science, Psychology, University of Auckland, Auckland, New Zealand.

Divya Jyoti, Management School, Lancaster University, Lancaster, UK.

Maureen E. Kenny, Department of Counseling, Developmental, and Educational Psychology, Lynch School of Education and Human Development. And the city is Boston, USA.

Katharina Klug, Faculty of Business Studies and Economics, University of Bremen, Bremen, Germany.

Johannes M. Kraak, KEDGE Business School, Bordeaux, France.

Kristine M. Kuhn, Department of Management, Information Systems, and Entrepreneurship, Carson College of Business Washington State University, Pullman, Washington, United States of America.

Jonathan Lavelle, Department of Work and Employment, Kemmy Business School University of Limerick, Limerick Ireland.

Molefe Maleka, Office of DVC: Teaching and Learning, eMalahleni Campus, Tshwane University of Technology, eMalahleni, South Africa.

Juliet McMahon, Department of Work and Employment Studies, Kemmy Business School, University of Limerick, Limerick Ireland.

Ishbel McWha-Hermann, Business School, University of Edinburgh, Edinburgh, UK.

Mary Beth Medvide, Psychology Department, Suffolk University, Boston. USA.

Ines Meyer, School of Management Studies, University of Cape Town, Cape Town, South Africa.

A. F. Miles, Department of Organizational Sciences & Communication, The George Washington University, Washington D. C., USA.

Kanu Priya Mohan, Behavioral Science Research Institute, Srinakharinwirot University, Bangkok, Thailand.

Caroline Murphy, Department of Work and Employment, Kemmy Business School, University of Limerick, Limerick Ireland.

Katharina Naswall, School of Psychology, Speech and Hearing, University of Canterbury, Christchurch, New Zealand.

Mike O'Brien, Department of Management & Marketing, Kemmy Business School, University of Limerick, Limerick Ireland.

Deirdre O'Shea, Department of Work and Employment, Kemmy Business School University of Limerick, Limerick Ireland.

Michelle O'Sullivan, Department of Work and Employment, Kemmy Business School University of Limerick, Limerick Ireland.

José Maria Peiró, IDOCAL Research Institute, Universitat de Valencia, Valencia.

Walter Reichman, Emeritus Professor of Psychology, Department of Psychology, Baruch College and the Graduate Center of the City University of New York, New York, United States of America.

J.R. Roman, Kennesaw State University Business Administration (Management Concentration), Coles College of Business, Kennesaw, GA USA

Jeffrey M. Saltzman, CEO OrgVitality, Pleasentville, New York, USA.

Raymond Saner, Raymond Saner, Economics and Management Department, University of Basel, Basel, Switzerland.

Mahima Saxena, Department of Psychology, University of Nebraska, Omaha Nebraska, USA.

Rosalind H. Searle, Adam Smith School of Business, University of Glasgow, Glasgow, UK.

Eva Selenko, School of Business and Economics, Loughborough University. Loughborough, UK.

Christian Seubert, Department of Psychology, University of Innsbruck, Innsbruck, Austria.

Lisa Seubert (née Hopfgartner), Department of Psychology, University of Innsbruck, Innsbruck, Austria.

Ultan Sherman, Department of Management & Marketing, Cork University Business School, Cork, Ireland.

Piyada Sombatwattana, Behavioral Science Research Institute, Srinakharinwirot University, Bangkok, Thailand (Retired)

Charles L. Tchagneno, Laboratoire de Psychologie Universitê of Franche-Comtê and University Grenoble Alpes, Besançon France.

Mendiola Teng-Calleja, Ateneo Center for Organization Research and Development (CORD), Department of Psychology, Ateneo de Manila University, Quezon City, Philippines.

./Steven Toaddy, Department of Psychology and Behavioral Sciences Louisiana Tech University Ruston, LA, USA.

Donald M. Truxillo, Department of Work and Employment, Kemmy Business School University of Limerick, Limerick Ireland.

J. Tuason, You and Better Work, San Francisco, CA, USA.

Thomas Turner, Department of Personnel and Employment Relations, Kemmy Business School, University of Limerick, Limerick Ireland.

Edwin A. J. van Hooft, Edwin A.J. van Hooft, Work & Organizational Psychology, University of Amsterdam, Amsterdam, The Netherlands.

Greet Van Hoye, Greet Van Hoye, Department of Marketing, Innovation and Organisation, Ghent University, Ghent, Belgium.

Xiaohong (Violet) Xu, Carlos Alvarez College of Business, The University of Texas at San Antonio, San Antonio. United States of America.

Lichia Yiu, President, Centre for Socio-Eco-Nomic Development (CSEND), Geneva, Switzerland.

Megan Young, EPIC (End Poverty & Inequality Cluster), School of Psychology, Auckland, Massey University, New Zealand.

Lorraine Ryan, Department of Work & Employment Studies. University of Limerick, Limerick, Ireland.

SERIES FOREWORD

As the world of work continues to change, it is not always noted that, for some people, these changes have not been positive. In fact, an increasing number of working people around the world live an existence where they cannot always rely on keeping their jobs and/or being paid a living wage. These individuals face challenges to find decent work for decent wages, in jobs that are secure. These are issues that are not often discussed by I/O psychologists, but they are issues that we must all face and for which we need to find answers.

Carr, Hopner, Hodgetts, and Young have assembled a distinguished group of academicians and practitioners from around the world, to try to help us understand what precarious work really means, the toll it exacts on people and society, and how we might make work more sustainable. This group of authors begins discussing the general topic of precarious work and refers to various world organizations that are trying to make work both decent and sustainable for everyone involved. Chapters then address specific issues associated with "fair" incomes and wage inequalities, as well as problems of job insecurity and underemployment. Attention then moves to the various attempts of scholars and practitioners to find practical ways to make work more sustainable and more meaningful for workers.

When Kevin Murphy and I took on the role of series editors, it was our goal to make I/O psychologists aware of a broader set of social issues related to work, and to expose them to new voices who have a different perspective on the problems we face. *Tackling Precarious Work* is exactly the kind of volume we hoped we could produce, and we hope that our field pays attention to the issues raised in this volume and begins to focus more on research that can help resolve some of them.

Angelo DeNisi
Tulane University
Series Co-Editor

1

FROM PRECARIOUS WORK TO SUSTAINABLE LIVELIHOODS

Introduction to the Volume

Stuart C. Carr, Darrin J. Hodgetts, Veronica Hopner, and Megan Young

A Great Unfreezing

The 2020s are not just a new decade; they mark a new chapter in the world of work. The United Nations (UN) agency mandated to assess the state of the world of work is the International Labour Organization (ILO). According to ILO Director-General Guy Ryder, "As the COVID-19 pandemic enters its third calendar year, the global employment and social outlook remains uncertain and fragile" (ILO, 2022a, p. 3). In a word, the entire world of work is today *precarious* and poses a serious threat to human security that has been a long time in the making and which has been exacerbated by the present pandemic (Hodgetts, Hopner et al., 2022). According to the ILO (2012, p. 28), in everyday working life, this precariousness often means: (1) being poorly paid and unable to fully support a household; plus (2) facing work insecurity; (3) having little, or zero, social protection: all of which result in being subject to increased material and psychological stress and strain. This new Society for Industrial and Organizational Psychology (SIOP) volume broaches discussion of these combined threats to humanity and thus a frontier to be addressed, in research and practice, with a concerted, integrated, humanitarian response (Hakel, 2013). The responses that comprise this volume are anchored in, but not simply confined to, one particular discipline and profession: Industrial and Organizational (I/O) psychology. Collectively, they tackle the human insecurities that stem from precarious work, thereby advancing humanitarian work psychology closer toward supporting sustainable livelihoods.

The purpose of the book series is to push the frontiers of research in I/O psychology. Therefore, the foci of all volumes point to new areas and avenues of

DOI: 10.4324/9781003440444-1

research. The series' core focus is not on policy or actions to address issues such as precarious work. However, I/O psychology—like other areas of engaged or applied scholarship—has always been about praxis and employing research to inform efforts toward positive real-world impacts. As such, this volume moves beyond documenting precarity and hardship to consider research evidence regarding how we might respond in ways that help workers. Our relational ethics do not allow us to extract knowledge from workers through research and not reciprocate by working on solutions to the problems they face (Hodgetts et al., 2022; Hopner & Liu, 2021). Hence, each chapter in the volume reviews the substantive research on their respective topics: some reflecting on their own seminal work and many discussing applications of research including future directions.

The breadth of this frontier is immense, and some statistics may help illuminate the scale of precarious work today. The last time the world of work was anywhere near stable enough to reliably freeze-frame with global statistics was 2019. After decades of labor markets racing to the bottom on wages and other work conditions, almost two-thirds of the world's 3.3 billion people in the workforce were working informally, mainly self-employed and on their own means (ILO, 2019). The majority of the remaining one-third who actually had a formal job were struggling to make ends meet (International Trade Union Confederation [ITUC], 2018). Sounding global alarm bells, the ILO (2019) singled out "poor work conditions" as the "main global employment challenge" for the world of work. Chiming with that tocsin, the UN's World Bank Group (2019) warned the world was entering a time to "protect people, not jobs"—implying that job precariousness was actually the nub of the challenge. Underscoring that point regarding the precarity of work, the year of 2020 opened with another UN agency announcing a pandemic (World Health Organization, 2020). Throughout 2020 and 2021, the COVID-19 pandemic was a great disruptor. In 2022, a third seismic event—the Russian Federation's invasion of Ukraine—created a perfect storm involving precariousness, a pandemic, and shattered peace. In the face of this conflagration, the global labor market went into "reverse gear" in 2022, regressing from a tentative recovery during 2021 in some countries and economic and societal disasters in others to levels back at the 2019 baseline nadir for jobs, wages, and work precarity (United Nations, 2022).

Precarity notwithstanding, disruptors can bring opportunities as well as threats. *Tackling* precarious work and promoting increased equity is one such opportunity. Revisiting Kurt Lewin (1947), today we are living in a great *un*freezing moment (Burnes, 2020). Core everyday assumptions about "where" we work, "how" we work, and even "who" pays our wages (employer, government, or people who pay us for our goods and services) have been challenged and, for many people, re-imagined. For example, we have seen mass furloughs with government wage subsidies for public and private sectors and the movement of many workers from traditional office work-places to increased reliance where possible on "place-less" digital platforms and automated artificial intelligence

(AI) systems—and in some cases back to the office again. We have also heard serious policy proposals for a universal basic income (UBI) that would help protect society's most vulnerable in the wake of devastating job losses (United Nations Development Programme [UNDP], 2020). For most of us, ideas such as UBI would have been radically unthinkable prior to the 2020s. Today these are ethical, normative challenges to rethink the world of work—and with it, the ways we practice, theorize, and teach I/O psychology.

In the spirit of making the unthinkable thinkable, the idea for this volume came from SIOP. In 2020, the team of editors and editorial Board of SIOP's Organizational Frontiers series identified precarious work as a timely topic for this prestigious series. This book stands on the shoulders of previous contributions in the humanitarian space (e.g., McWha-Herman et al., 2016; Olson-Buchanan et al., 2014; Reichman, 2014; Rupp & Mallory, 2015). It was envisioned by the editorial team and the SIOP Board that a new volume should examine specifically the nature and effects of precarious—poorly paid, insecure, and unprotected—work on individuals, organizations, and communities. This demarcates the domain of the current volume from more established fields in IO, such as business enterprise training and development (see Frese et al., 2016; Satzman et al., Chapter 2), enterprise selection (Klinger et al., 2013), and newer fields (for I/O psychology) such as social enterprise development (Nguyen et al., 2021). In each of these fields, I/O psychology has contributed to and is contributing toward tackling poverty (Carr, 2013). This volume continues and builds on that tradition. Crucially, the remit for this particular volume was not solely to document work-related misery and hardship. More importantly, it was to shift discussion toward tackling and reforming precarious work.

Toward what end? An impending challenge for I/O psychology as for work—by definition their shared frontier—is how to move the needle from unstable, low-paid work to work that is more decent, protective, and, in a word, *sustainable* for people, organizations, and the communities that support them (Bal et al., 2019). With the promotion of—and transformation to—more sustainable livelihoods in mind, this volume brings together a range of pioneers in their related specializations. It contextualizes their contributions, setting the scene for the volume as a whole in relation to the changing world of work and the ILO goal of "decent work and economic growth" for all. This goal is officially designated as SDG-8 of the 17 2016–2030 UN Sustainable Development Goals (SDGs). UN SDG-8 is operationalized across the volume and links this volume to the rest of the Organizational Frontiers series with its ethos of ethical practicality, and humanity.

This volume further anchors often-abstracted, global ideas like "universal decent work" within local situations, everyday work practices, and lived experiences. Relatedly, a historical strength of I/O psychology has been its focus on the diversity of sociocultural values and norms in the workplace, including at national, organizational, and individual levels (for a review, see Carr, 2013). This chapter builds on, but also constructively away from, those foundations. Specifically, this chapter—like the contributions that follow—adds to these sociocultural considerations. We do so by including diversities associated with the various socioeconomic situations of different groups that are omnipresent at the hard edges of the wage, work security, and wellbeing spectra (Carr, 2023). Finally, this chapter and book take a deep dive into "who" has been systematically *ex*cluded from decent work in the past, and how they might be systemically *in*cluded in our collective and sustainable futures.

Volume Structure

Based on advice from the SIOP board and series editors, and resonant with the facets of decent work identified by the ILO (2012), this volume explores four interrelated dimensions of a precarious work-scape. The first and foundational is Sustainable Livelihoods. The adjective "sustainable" links the volume conceptually to the future and thereby to new frontiers. Sustainability is also the core focus in global policy for world development, for example, at the UN and the ILO. The second term, "livelihoods," radically expands the older idea on which work policies and IO alike have placed much stock-in-trade faith: "the job." An inconvenient truth is that "the job" has not reduced but instead exacerbated poverty and inequality for many people in the world (World Bank Group, 2019). Clearly, the world, and IO with it, needs a much more expansive, inclusive, and durable concept than "finding a job" to alleviate poverty. This is because increasing numbers of jobs are poor quality and do not pay a liveable wage sufficient to lift people out of poverty. Sustaining a livelihood through decent work is thus a more substantive, salient, and aspirational goal in life for large swaths of the human population globally.

The remaining three sections of the volume—Fair Income, Security, and Social Protection— are named after specific elements in the ILO's (2012) definition of decent work, which the ILO proposed precisely to tackle precarious work. In policy terms, they represent the antithesis of work precariousness—which includes (1) poor pay, (2) lack of work-related security, and (3) poor social protection. According to the ILO (2022b, p. 1, emphases added):

> Decent work sums up the aspirations of people in their working lives. It involves opportunities for work that is productive and delivers a fair income, security in the workplace and social protection for families, better prospects for personal development and social integration, freedom for people to express their concerns, organize and participate in the decisions that affect their lives and equality of opportunity and treatment for all women and men.

A key challenge (and opportunity) for I/O psychology, operating as it does mainly at micro/group levels, is finding ways to translate these often-abstracted ideas of fair income and work security into lived work experiences. As an organization with accredited special consultative status at the UN and joined by other associations like the International Association for Applied Psychology (see Saltzman, Reichman & O'Neill Berry, Chapter 2), SIOP has recognized this need to expand our subdisciplinary horizons to include everyday lived experiences of human development goals for over a decade (Scott, 2011; see also, Bal et al., 2019). This volume takes another step forward in that professionally responsive direction.

Sustainable Livelihoods

For much of its first 100 years, I/O psychology has been critiqued for following and contributing to the primacy of managerial and economic perspectives on work, rather than those of workers, their families, and communities. In other words, I/O has tended to serve power rather than empowerment (Baritz, 1960; Brief, 2000; Carr, 2007) and "efficiency" rather than humanity (Lefkowitz, 2017) and the broader human relations that are impacted by work. In recent decades, a figure-ground reversal has been building between efficiency and humanity. In a case in point, humanitarian work psychologists have made the case that we need to pay more attention not only to work that focuses on humanitarian issues (for example, in aid agencies and food banks) but also to making work conditions more humanitarian (Carr et al., 2012; McWha-Hermann et al., 2016; Olson-Buchanan et al., 2014; Reichman, 2014).

In the 2nd century of I/O, calls to tackle poor working conditions to protect people from precarious jobs and their personal and relational impacts foreground how much further we need to go in the human security and wellbeing direction. One way for us to advance that frontier would entail defining, articulating, and embracing a new, more expansive—and inclusive—superordinate goal for I/O psychology. We as co-editors contend that this goal should include sustainability. Sustainability science "tackles effects of globalization on the [world's] fragile ecosystems and economies" (Kates et al., 2001, p. 642). Embracing that ethos, the aptest focus for I/O psychology— transcending precarious jobs and work in general—becomes sustainable livelihoods that foster human security (see later section).

Arguably, the concept of a sustainable livelihood is an ancient one, having been around for as long as people have had to sustain themselves as a species on this planet. In the late 1980s, the modern English term *sustainable livelihood* was coined. It appeared in a report on environmental sustainability in economically poor rural communities located in the so-called developing world

(World Commission on Environment and Development, 1989). Subsequently, the term was defined in a manner that resonates with the concept of decent work:

> [A] livelihood comprises the capabilities, assets… and activities required for a means of living, a livelihood is sustainable which can cope with and recover from stress and shocks, maintain or enhance its capabilities and assets, and provide sustainable livelihood opportunities for the next generation; and which contributes net benefits to other livelihoods at the local and global levels and in the short and long term.
>
> *(Chambers & Conway, 1991, p. 6)*

During the 1990s, the ambit for sustainable livelihoods widened, by extending from a focus on rural work to include considerations pertaining to urban environments where most of the world' s population now lives and works. In the 2000s, it was expanded yet again with a focus on how to buffer work from the impacts of natural and humanmade disasters. In the 2010s, the importance of sustainable livelihoods featured at the landmark 2012 United Nations Conference in Rio de Janeiro, wherein it was now linked to the broader issue of sustainable development. Among the first outcomes to be defined as deliverables from a sustainable livelihood perspective were: (1) generating a decent amount of income and (2) protecting people's everyday wellbeing (Department For International Development, 1999). Anchorage points like these connect the concept to humanitarian concerns in IO, including humanitarian work psychology and the emphasis placed on promoting the wellbeing of workers and those around them through decent work practices. Policywise too, the 2012 Rio Conference Declaration highlighted the need for a concerted plan, more comprehensive and coordinated than any predecessor, for all countries to break free of poverty by grappling with the complexities of the world of work and the need for decent employment. It is also crucial that IO responds to broader plans for economic, material, social, and psychological inclusion through work and communal life.

Out of Rio emerged the current, most widely consulted, grand plan for human development: the 2016–2030 SDGs. Unlike their predecessors the 2000–2015 Millennium Development Goals, which focused on aid to lower income countries, these SDGs have a much wider and more inclusive ethos. Their primary goal (SDG-1) is eradicating poverty "in all its forms, everywhere." Supporting this primary goal are 16 other goals. In these, we see an integrated framework that overtly signals links between decent work (SDG-8) and opportunities for people to develop and realize their potentials in life. These links include access to decent nutrition (SDG-2), healthcare (SDG-3), and education (SDG-4); equal opportunities for women (SDG-5); and access to clean water and energy (SDGs 6 and 7). Decent work in turn also supports the other SDGS from nutrition and health to sustainable industrialization (SDG-9); income equality (SDG-10); safe cities and decent housing (SDG-11); sustainable consumption (SDG-12); climate action (SDG-13) on water (SDG-14) and on land (SDG-15); and by promoting human security (SDG-16). All 16 of these are implemented through one final process goal, partnerships for development (SDG-17).

The concept of decent work and the related conceptualization of SDG-8 invoke a win-win situation in terms of combining decent work conditions *and* economic development (see above) which will be familiar to I/O psychologists. What is probably newer, and more resonant with HWP, is the concept of sustainable livelihood. In the past, we have placed much of our trust in making work decent in one institution at a time: "the job," an institution within the formal economy. Job analyses, job descriptions, job evaluations, job selections, job placements, job design, job performance, job training, and job wellbeing have been IO stocks-in-trade. Yet today, as we have seen, a full two-thirds of the world's 3.3 billion workforce *do not have a formal job at all*, while the remaining one-third that do have one are mostly *struggling to make ends meet*. Hence, now is the time not to ditch jobs completely (if you have one, and it is sustainable, good luck to you!) but rather expand our conceptual horizon of what decent work can and must deliver for people, regardless of sector.

Sustainable livelihoods provide us with a conceptual foundation for the rest of the volume, including its foci on tackling (1) poor pay, (2) lack of work-related security, and (3) poor social protection. Such considerations must include the over 2 billion people who work in the informal sector and who may not want to join the formal economy or pay taxes to regimes that they may experience as oppressive, for example. Instantiating and incorporating life-worlds of work, chapters in the foundational section, Sustainable Livelihoods, span a range of ways that IO can readily rethink the world of work and respectfully engage in partnerships with diverse stakeholders (under SDG-17) to tackle the problem of precarious work. These ways are fundamentally future-oriented, interconnected, intergenerational, and human-relational.

Chapter 2 (by Saltzman et al.) documents the extent and nature of precarious work. The authors identify the psychological foundations of decent work and extract key lessons learned when advocating for it at the UN. Chapter 3 (Di Fabio, Medvide, & Kenny) reviews and advances the leading vocational theory on the psychology of working, incorporating elements from the Decent Work Agenda and linking these to the psychology of sustainable livelihoods. Subsequently, Chapters 4 (Searle & McWha-Hermann) and 5 (Saner & Yiu) function in concert to articulate I/O psychology evidence-informed policy shifts toward more sustainable livelihoods in practice and some new I/O psychology diplomacies for monitoring progress on SDG-8. These contributions invite I/O psychologists to consider forms of organization—and different stakeholder groups—that may help promote sustainable livelihoods, from for-profit digital conglomerates to local social enterprises and classic management-directed entities to worker cooperatives.

The final chapter in this section, Chapter 6 (by Jyoti & Arora), gives substance to this invitation. It details, as interorganizational cases, a series of ground-breaking initiatives to bring diverse, and often competing, perspectives to the policy table, at regional and supply-chain levels. This chapter also links humanitarian work psychology to the SDGs, through the perspectives of NGOs and other stakeholders engaged in partnerships for development (SDG-17).

Fair Incomes

Being poorly paid and unable to support a household is a core facet of precarious work conditions (ILO, 2012). The ILO's definition of decent work, which implies *tackling* precarious work, includes *fair income* (ILO, 2022b), including sufficient income(s) to support a worker and their families' material sustenance. This encompasses, for example, having access to nourishing food (SDG-2) and healthy housing (SDG-11). Moreover, as the term "fair" implies, the incomes from wages also have to be socially equitable: part of addressing inequality within and between countries (SDG-10). Wages are a part of that equation. For example, wage budgets for chief executive officers (CEOs) can and do impact wage budgets for the shop floor (ILO, 2013). Accordingly, this section of the book focuses on what kinds of remuneration models, including both absolute and relative wage levels, help to sustain livelihoods materially and socially.

This section is particularly important to our subdiscipline because I/O psychology has arguably yet to have a serious conversation about wages psychology (Furnham, 2019). Yes, we do already have a long-standing specialization in IO, "job evaluation," which was partly designed to promote pay fairness. Unfortunately too, however, job evaluation has not prevented most working people from experiencing in-work poverty and waged precariousness (ILO, 2019; World Bank Group, 2019). Additionally, one of the earliest promises of job evaluation was to help eradicate gender wage gaps (Figart, 2000). Today though, these gaps still exist.[1] Women continue to be not just underrepresented in better paid leadership roles but are also overrepresented in precarious work (ILO, 2018b; also see SDG-5—Gender equality).

Job evaluation is implicated in these continuing inequities because it relies on what "the market" is paying to set wages for any given job (using regression-based wage trendlines). Insofar as the market pays women and men different rates of pay for work with the same "job size," job evaluation can end up perpetuating the very inequities it was meant to dissolve (Carr, 2023). Women are still paid less for doing the same-sized jobs as men, and they remain significantly overrepresented in poorer paying jobs compared to men—who in turn are overrepresented at the other end of the wage spectrum (Carr, 2023). Markets cannot be left to regulate rates of pay because markets regularly fail to deliver equitable outcomes. Initiatives for market interventions, such as sector-wide fair-pay agreements, are important for tackling precarious work.

Likewise, job design theories, notably the job characteristics model (Hackman & Oldham, 1974), barely mention and do not seriously consider wages (Williams et al., 2006). These theories have focused instead on more purely psychological variables, for instance, hypothetical constructs like "identity," as if the wage did not/does not matter. Mass precariousness foregrounds the importance of wage income for groups of people who may or may not recognize themselves as members of an emergent precarious class (Standing, 2011). Indeed, even the fundamental "meaning of work" is still researched (Sharabi & Harpaz, 2019) by analyzing what people talk about when financial necessity is *removed* from the equation, i.e., as if pay is simply a "confounding variable." This *figure-ground reversal* is often done by using the lottery question ("Would you work or not if you won a massive lottery, and why?"). Lottery (question) research does open up some nonfinancial meanings of work, but it has again arguably omitted to tackle the financial realities of mass economic necessity, including a massive lack of fair income due to precarious wages (Bergman & Jean, 2015; Gloss et al., 2017). The reality is that at lower wage levels, money still really matters (George & Brief, 1989; Shaw & Gupta, 2001).

Tackling broken wage-setting processes, and their links to ill-being, is a massive gap in previous scholarship in I/O psychology. Slavery wages, from tipping, internships, and sex trafficking, for example, exist as daily realities for many people in all corners of the world from tea plantations to unregulated construction work to fishing fleets (ILO, 2018a, 2021a). Where then is our I/O psychology for documenting and working to abolish slavery wages? Likewise is with minimum wages, which predate the formation of the ILO over 100 years ago, but which until relatively recently have remained almost completely overlooked by scholars and practitioners in I/O psychology (Smith, 2015). Today, wage structures are clearly broken. They fail to enable many workers to make ends meet, even on the minimal promise of subsistence (Carr, 2023; ITUC, 2018).

Outside of I/O psychology itself, some influential economists continue to claim that initiatives to alleviate poverty and precarity, such as raising minimum wages to subsistence levels or paying living wages, will cost jobs or lead to business closures. These assertions are made without due diligence or regard for decades of IO evidence for the upsides for work justice and work engagement or the downsides for wellbeing of keeping jobs that are poor in quality (Carr, 2023; Neumark & Shirley, 2021). Using jobs as a proxy for either productivity or wellbeing fails to recognize the huge public health costs to humanity and society from indecent, precarious work that features inequitable remuneration (Kaufman et al., 2020; Leigh et al., 2019). Ultimately, the logical conclusion of the current course in many low-wage economies of keeping wages as low as possible, no matter the costs to worker wellbeing against returns to shareholders, is economic slavery. We are certain that this is an end-state to which very few I/O psychologists would ever subscribe.

The next level up from a precarious or at best minimal wage is a living wage (King & Waldegrave, 2012). Often confused with each other and both hotly debated in public deliberations regarding economic sustainability (Hodgetts et al., 2022), these two wage measures differ in at least three main ways. First is their wage value. Ideally, both minimum and living wages would have one and the same value, but in reality, the living wage usually aims higher than the minimum wage (King & Waldegrave, 2014). The second is who sets them. Minimum wages are set by legal statute: either national, regional, or municipal, while living wage values tend to be set by national agreement or through more local campaigns and agreements between particular employers and unions. This means, third, that they differ in legal status. Minimum wages are normally legal requirements. Living wages are more aspirational, recommended by nongovernmental bodies like unions, certain NGO foundations, and likeminded employers, and thereafter adopted by choice by some employing organizations.

What both concepts have in common, however, is that they are each paid by an employer to workers. As such, employers and their agencies may have a perceived conflict of interest, at least in the massive private sector, between (1) paying a decent wage and (2) the perceived financial viability of the organization.[2] Additionally, the systematic dismantling of tripartite (employer, union, and government) approaches to wage-setting in many nation states has resulted in an imbalance of power relations between employers and workers and contributed to increases in unliveable wages globally (see Carr, 2023, for a recent review).

In psychological terms, and as the UN SDG-8 (Decent work *and* economic development) implies, "conflicts" of interest might be more illusory than real. In terms of productivity concerns, there will be some upper as well as lower limits to what levels of wage will persuade people "to" work as well as being fair enough to keep them engaged "at" work (ILO, 2019; Stiglitz, 1976). The actual challenge though, as well as an opportunity for IO to help address it, is identifying "where" that value, or value range, may be (Carr et al., 2016). In terms of financial viability for an employing organization, what is a wage figure that is fair and inclusive enough to help make the work itself decent as well as sustainable for employees and employers alike? (Carr et al., 2018).

Arguably, concern with where such balance points reside and how organizations can achieve them has been sorely lacking in the world of work since (at least) the Washington Consensus back in the 1980s (Bal & Doci, 2018). At the same time, however, I/O psychology has already charted precisely these kinds of linkages, for instance, between (1) organizational justice and happiness and (2) wellbeing and productivity (Fisher, 2009; Harrison et al., 2006; Harter et al., 2002;

Pérez-Rodríguez et al., 2019). Unfortunately, we know from personal experience here in Aotearoa, New Zealand, that this extant IO literature in psychology seldom makes it onto wage-policy radars, whether in the private or public sectors. A core function of this volume is therefore to help redress such lingering oversights, both locally and globally.

A further oversight from much of the debate, political and academic, about wages is that the spotlight is seldom shone at the top end of the wage table. This oversight persists despite the ILO calling, for almost a decade now, for wage restraint among the CEO class (ILO, 2013). By 2020, the world was facing a crisis of income inequality that remains "out of control"—and fuelled in significant part by a race to the *top* in CEO wages (Oxfam, 2020). The available research looking at the top of the wage-wellbeing spectrum indicates that allowing many CEO wages to become out of touch with the realities of wages on many shop floors is not at all good for corporate conduct, reputation, productivity, or social responsibility (Desai et al., 2010; Jacquart & Armstrong, 2013; Malmandier & Tate, 2009; Rupp & Mallory, 2015). If real corporate social responsibility begins at home, then perhaps it starts with committing to employee wellbeing (Erdogan et al., 2015; Rupp & Mallory, 2015). One way to help serve that wellbeing might be through the implementation of a maximum wage (Pizzigati, 2018). This should be a threshold ratio of the living wage (Carr, 2023). Thus, while CEO wages would still have "elasticity," they could only grow if the CEO can grow the shop floor's wages too (ILO, 2013), lifting the latter to, or better still from, a living wage.

Such interconnectedness is not perfect. After all, a fixed ratio means that the top grows more, in absolute terms, than the bottom. But it is still a primordial example of sustainable livelihoods, meaning your livelihood is connected to mine and mine to yours; yours to ours, and ours to yours. Wages in general, and fair incomes in particular, are one—fundamental—way in which connections are recognized and reflected in wage policy. Accordingly, the contributions (in the Fair Incomes section of this volume) all speak directly to relational interconnectedness in and through fair incomes. They include implementing decent wages along connected global supply chains, as a means of combating wage slavery (Jyoti & Arora, Chapter 6). In the chapter on living wages, Meyer and Maleka (Chapter 7) introduce an I/O psychology of living wages across the Southern African region through their co-leadership of Project GLOW (Global Living Organizational Wage). In doing so, the chapter's co-authors forge links between wages and human capabilities, which speaks to the ILO's Decent Work Agenda (International Labour Organization, 2022b). This agenda can be further expanded with an emphasis on capturing the capabilities and skills that matter most to people in their own life-worlds. This frontier, and its implications for both theory and practice, is explored in an innovative chapter by Teng-Calleja et al. (Chapter 8).

A complementary form of connection is between production and consumption, in which the fairness of an income, via a wage, can be seen in its capacity to deliver what people feel they need in order to live and work well in wellbeing. People themselves are the subject matter experts in determining this need. A ground-breaking chapter in this section, by Intraprasert, Mohan, and Sombatwattana (Chapter 9), thereby considers a potentially controversial balance between sustainable production and sustainable consumption. From its inception over 100 years ago, I/O psychology has included consumer behavior. Intraprasert and colleagues (Chapter 9) present a modern perspective on sustainable consumption that is informed by ancient Buddhist traditions and their fitness for the purposes of living in modern Thai society, workforce, and economy.

Underscoring the interconnectivity of wages and decent work, a final chapter in this section articulates an I/O psychology for tackling wage inequalities. The chapter's focus is deliberately not on the foot of the table, and the breadcrumbs on it, but toward the top of the table and the relationships between each end and in between. This metaphor of a shared table implies instituting threshold wage ratios, in this case between CEOs and wage floors. To reemphasize the point raised above, central to the concept of a maximum wage is that the top wage in any given organization or sector should not exceed a certain ratio of the lowest wage paid in that organization or sector. Further, the wage floor should be set at a living wage level (Carr et al., Chapter 10). Such thresholds would mean that the top wage cannot rise unless the floor rises too—thereby holding in check and possibly even reversing some of the runaway wage inequalities that characterize many workplaces today. As noted above for example, it might help to lift wage baselines to a living wage, or better still, start from it by making the living wage its denominator (Carr, 2023).

Work Security

Work security has been under increasing threat in many contexts from the casualization of many jobs, rapidly accelerated automation, variable gig work, and digital labor platforms (ILO, 2021b). In response, we urgently need to develop aspects of I/O psychology that intersect with human security psychology (HSP) to allow a broader perspective on how issues of economic and work security are related to a broader raft of personal, community, health, food, and global security concerns (Hodgetts, Hopner, et al., 2022). In this first scene-setting chapter for the volume, we approach work and economic security as a central dimension of human security, which (as noted earlier) also impacts other dimensions of human security whereby inadequate wages can lead to inadequate diets, housing, and participation in civic life, like ripples in a pool. That is, increases in work precarity and hardship ripple outward into other domains of life, including community, food, health, and additional dimensions of human security. As such, the concept of human security becomes invaluable for a contextually responsive and socially responsible/ive I/O psychology.

In an integrative review of this nascent HSP field, Hodgetts, Hopner et al. (2022) propose that psychology is a discipline long concerned with issues of human security and socioeconomic protection (see next section). We might date early engagements to Adler's (1925) individual psychology. Adler offered a contextualized perspective on human beings that features the importance of secure environments—featuring positive interdependence with others and decent work—in shaping experiences of [in]equity and fairness and in enabling people to access the psychological and material resources to flourish, live productive lives, and reach their goals and potential in life. Many of these sentiments were echoed in Maslow's (1942) development of humanistic psychology, which also offers a dynamic perspective on links between human security, flourishing, and potential as being shaped by socioenvironmental factors, including work and economic security. More recently, calls have been issued for I/O psychology to be more humanistic (Lefkowitz, 2017).

Many of the wider contemporary understandings of human security stem from a foundational report commissioned by the United Nations Trust Fund for Human Security (2014) and drawing on multidisciplinary scholarship from around the globe. Conceptually, and as used in this volume, human security remains a broad term that includes all risks to humanity: including from precarious work. Human security is "a multifaceted and somewhat aspirational state whereby everyone has the freedom from threats, restrictions, and discrimination, to go about their daily lives with dignity and without harm" (Hodgetts, Hopner et al., 2022, p. 4). Improvements toward realizing this state of human security for precarious workers require initiatives to address *in*securities associated with precarious employment conditions. As noted above, these include income, access to decent food and shelter, and political and environmental conditions that also support human flourishing.

The United Nations Trust Fund for Human Security's (1994) formulation included Personal, Health, Food, Economic, Community, Political, and Environmental dimensions of human security. Later, Carr et al. (2021a, 2021b) argued for, and measured, two more dimensions, Cyber and National, which together form a nine-step quasi-Guttman Scalogram. Hodgetts, Hopner et al. (2022) then drew on all nine dimensions and added a tenth: Global Human Security, to create a Human Security Staircase Scale. This is still by no means a definitive list of dimensions and steps and more work needs to be done to explore how the different dimensions interact to shape the lives of human beings in general, and for our purposes here, those of precarious workers. Further, whether work is precarious (insecure) or decent (secure) can influence all of the dimensions of human security noted above. In New Zealand, for example, Carr et al. (2021a, 2021b) found that being more secure in terms of being fully employed (versus part-time, casual, unemployed, or retired) was associated with a significantly higher overall score, on their Human Security Staircase Scale.

As noted already, two-thirds of the world's workforce participate in the informal economy, where many experience inadequate social protections, unliveable wages, uncertain hours, a lack of occupational health and safety provisions, and so forth. These workers experience varying degrees of security and autonomy at work, with some engaged in risky, "radical commerce" (Groot & Hodgetts, 2015) as a means of financing their lives and realizing personal aspirations toward self-determination, economic independence, and human flourishing. These work lives can have considerable negative consequences for the persons involved, but they can also feature positive aspects.

Forging and extending that frontier for I/O psychology, Saxena and Tchagneno (Chapter 11) consider the sector skills displayed within informal economies and how these skills can be leveraged to increase the security of the persons involved. In doing so, these authors challenge various stereotypes about informal sectors and demonstrate the utility of strengths-based orientations in I/O psychology toward precarious work. Their chapter also reveals how and why many people who work in the informal sector may not necessarily warm to the idea of becoming formalized. Such emergent positive scholarship does not mean that we can ignore the threats to personal and community security that come with precarious work. Rather, it demonstrates that a focus on the problems of precarious work needs to include any potential benefits, strengths, capacities, and agentive skills that emerge with such work and which foreground the potential and benefits of work across both formal and informal sectors.

In the gig economy, wages and income have inherent flexibility, and the challenge may be ensuring that the flexibility enables capability and does not morph into further precarity (Kuhn, Chapter 12). This section also considers the *psychological contract* and how that particular idea can be used to respond to the current global situation in the world of precarious work, including, for instance, becoming more focused on how wages sustain the livelihoods of employ*ees* as well as employers (Griep, Bankins, Kraak, Sherman, & Hansen, Chapter 13).

Reflecting the urgency for I/O psychology to address issues of fair and sustainable wages, Seubert et al. (2019) argued that wages have real consequences, and costs, for the wellbeing of workers, families, communities, and societies. Among the most immediate of these consequences are money worries, stress, a sense of work-related insecurity, and actual situations of material and social precarity. In their chapter, Seubert and Seubert (Chapter 14) foreground the importance of assessing precarious work from the perspective of workplace wellbeing. These authors offer a contextually orientated conceptualization of the multidimensionality of work precariousness that can be applied in formulating effective responses to address risks to workers and their communities.

Likewise, O'Shea, *Peiró*, and Truxillo (Chapter 15) consider some of the antecedents and mediators of underemployment. These authors propose that efforts to tackle or redress underemployment, for example, need to be sensitive not only to the employment security/precariousness continuum but also to the needs of different groups, including women and young people. Such issues are likely to become more pressing as the world moves through successive crises and to require increasingly interconnected, cross-level interventions and initiatives. In that respect, a team of contributors from Ireland point to how the rise of irregular and highly casualized contracts requires particular initiatives, including those at the level of labor laws and policy frameworks to promote the social protection of workers (Lavelle et al., Chapter 16).

Social Protection

Social protection is about preventing, mitigating, and resolving precarious work situations that negatively impact the wellbeing and broader life-worlds of workers (Kalleberg, 2018; Munyon et al., 2020; United Nations Research Institute for Social Development [UNRISD], 2010; World Bank, 2001). Related actions include the development of strategies, policies, and practices to reduce precarity and human insecurity through the promotion of effective and fair labor markets and wage-setting processes. This extends to centralized initiatives like minimum wages that are meant to reduce risks to workers. These risks include underemployment, inequitable and unliveable wages, unequal opportunities, and unsustainability livelihoods.

Social protections against these concerns have been evident since antiquity in the form of the *jubilee* in Mesopotamia and rudimentary welfare provisions (e.g., the grain dole) in Ancient Rome (UNRISD, 2010). Contemporary social protections have been expanded to include both the formal (with the present focus on welfare provisions, wage subsidies, work furlough schemes, public housing provisions, etc.) and informal economies (where workers are not covered by formal provisions, using initiatives such as social insurance schemes, cash transfers, or wage subsidies).

Social protection is an important aspect of this volume as it raises issues about what we are aiming to protect workers against, and how we might promote increased human security beyond the immediate workplace or employment space. Recent scoping reviews suggest that the health of precarious workers has been impacted the most negatively by the COVID-19 pandemic, as essential workers are more at risk of infection due to hazardous conditions of work that amplify risks to health (McNamara et al., 2021). McNamara et al. and others have accordingly concluded that the pandemic has exacerbated existing health risks associated with precarious work as well as created new risks that may pertain more to some countries than others, but which can also prove global in scale.

Research into the health impacts of precarious work is increasingly nuanced and is showing that different population groups who are at higher risk of being restricted to such work—including youth, women, and migrant groups—experience poorer mental health outcomes than workers in general (Gray et al., 2020). Scholars have also begun to test conceptually rich frameworks for advancing understandings of how precarious work generates stress that has negative health consequences for people experiencing precarious work- and economic-related insecurities (Scott-Marshall & Tompass, 2011). Such research is invaluable for identifying pain points that can be targeted for emancipatory change initiatives. Key elements identified in relation to precarious work included unliveable wages, unpaid overtime, and lack of benefits such as pension cover.

Relatedly, social protection initiatives enact efforts to improve socioeconomic inclusion, protection, and human rights (Cook & Kabeer, 2009) through the provision of decent work and more equitable distributions of resources in society (Hodgetts & Stolte, 2017). Further, access to social protective resources, in this case via decent work, is associated with increased wellbeing and reduced ill-health at the population level (Kennedy & Hallowell, 2021). Research also suggests that when welfare provisions, for example, are properly resourced, population health and associated dimensions of human security are improved (Hodgetts & Stolte, 2017; Kalleberg, 2018).

The contributions in this section of the volume start at the social level that is most familiar to many I/O psychologists: namely work-life balance (WLB) (Haar, Chapter 17). By definition, WLB involves protecting everyday social relations, and many work institutions and policies, from governmental to organizational, arguably should serve that function. During the pandemic, government organizations and employers alike implemented a range of such schemes (see above). From an I/O psychology point of view, Haar points out in his chapter that WLB research has struggled to include the majority of the world's workers whose situation is neither WEIRD (Western, educated, industrialized, rich, and democratic) nor POSH (professional, official, safe from discrimination, and higher income; see Gloss et al., 2017). At the intersection between sociocultural and socioeconomic ex/inclusion, this chapter is a call for I/O psychology to be more responsive to articulating the realities and localities of work-life imbalance for many people in precarious work.

While it is important that we document the negative consequences of precarious work, Jiang, Naswall, and Xu (Chapter 18) offer a compelling exemplar for the necessary next steps up in terms of how I/O psychologists can contribute to the tackling of job insecurity. The authors do so by drawing on multilevel analyses of societal moderators of extant links between income, work precariousness, and job burnout across various precarious occupations. Insights distilled from such multilevel analyses result in practical recommendations for addressing the causes and consequences of precarious work, and for increasing social protection by improving job security through organizational support at the midlevel, and by enabling decent housing conditions at the macro level. Such contributions exemplify the generalist orientation toward social protection as a multilevel phenomenon that produces practical efforts to help workers address issues of precarity.

Likewise, the contribution to this collection by van Hooft and van Hoye (Chapter 19) exemplifies how traditional areas of I/O psychology, including job loss and job search, can be renewed and enhanced through the provision of evidence-based advice to offer to people experiencing precarious work and employment conditions from discriminatory and uncivil hiring practices at the midlevel to more macro concerns such as unemployment stigma. This chapter also reflects on the importance of adopting a broader systems-based orientation to precarious work and the need to enhance human security through the provision of decent work. It thus links worker experiences and needs to organizational, societal, and global systems that shape the nature of work and life today.

A particularly important aspect of social protection from precarious work is global mobility as many move voluntarily or are forced to move via exploitative pathways to precarious work. Cassim (Chapter 20) considers links between the global mobility of many workers and issues of precariousness and social exclusion and how, despite moving with agentive intentions to find decent work, many become permanently stranded within precarious work situations. Cassim contextualizes these processes in relation to issues of the future of work that have been brought into stark relief by the COVID-19 pandemic, and which hold the potential to disrupt, or accelerate and deepen, work-related insecurities and inequities between stigmatized migrants and other groups in the receiving communities.

In their chapter in this section, Klug, Gerlitz, and Selenko (Chapter 21) draw on their longitudinal research to explore the physical and mental health consequences of precarious work. In doing so, they identify as a key factor how many precarious jobs constrain the agency of workers and undermine their sense of control. A sense of control is a key moderating factor in terms of how people weather precarity and whether they become ill or not (Bolam et al., 2003). Yet the chapter also goes much further upstream to consider the role of governments and government policy in regulating decent work conditions and their roles in protecting all, including and most especially people who are economically vulnerable, in low-paid and unpaid, e.g., reproductive, work.

In their chapter on jobless futures, Toaddy, Crawford, et al. (Chapter 22) invite us to envision the massive developments in, and acceleration of, AI and digitalization which are replacing conventional jobs and thereby threatening the security of the people who have traditionally performed them. Policy options like UBI, for example, are now seriously being debated and in some cases implemented in field trials around the world. I/O psychology has a role to play not just in keeping up with these changes but also—and more importantly—staying ahead of them. Humanitarian work psychology is responding to the need to tackle precarious conditions at work because of the broader implications of these for people's lives. It has the legs to contribute toward sustainable livelihoods.

Preview

Worth considering when reading this volume is the Inverse Care Law (Hart, 1971) whereby those who need help the least tend to consume the most attention and support from health systems. The law does not apply perfectly to work, since much of our attention in the past has focused on the middle ranks, not the very top echelon or the floor (Carr, 2023). Nonetheless, today most of the world's paid workforce, formal and informal, as well as many of its economic slaves, are in need of more supportive, and fairer, systems. These systems are multilevel and within our purview.

Overall, previous research and the contributions to this current volume, including suggested future research directions, support and, more crucially, advance the frontier assertion that precarious work is a key organizational determinant of everyday health and wellbeing. Work precariousness is associated with reductions in wellbeing and, conversely, increased job security, and decent work is associated with increased wellbeing (Carr, 2023; Hodgetts & Stolte, 2017; Kalleberg, 2018). Contributions throughout the volume consider the impacts of precarious work on physical and mental health, work-family life, and the viability of communities where the proportion of precarious work is especially high. From this platform of evidence-informed research and theory, a number of future research directions are either indicated or implied.

Future Research Directions

Sustainable livelihoods is a much broader, inherently interdisciplinary, and arguably deeper concept psychologically than either "work," "occupations," "jobs," or indeed "the organization." If we as a profession and discipline were able to embrace the concept, our research agendas would be enriched and expanded accordingly. For example, we would be asking questions about the interorganizational and cross-generational impacts of decent and indecent work on human security, wellbeing, flourishing, and sustainability. Such questions might extend to whether or not supply chains that respect humanitarian standards have healthier workforces and better educational outcomes for generations that follow compared to supply chains that do not respect such standards. We would, as this example suggests, take human rights at work more seriously: for instance, by researching the efficacy, on both organizational and everyday wellbeing, of standards like the Organisation for Economic Co-operation and Development (OECD) (2011) Guidelines for Multinational Enterprises, the UN Global Compact (see for example https://www.un.org/en/un-chronicle/un-global-compact-finding-solutions-global-challenges) and the SDGs themselves. Most importantly of all, if we adopted sustainable livelihoods as a key concept in our discipline and profession, we could begin seriously researching the links between livelihoods and the ecosystem. This could include the creation of a sustainability index for occupations ranging from worst to best globally and in different contexts (Bohnenberger, 2022). More broadly, IO research needs to ask where our contribution is toward sustainability science and sustainability more generally.

Just as we do not yet have an I/O psychology of sustainable livelihoods, we have not yet seriously and respectfully researched the psychology of *fair incomes* (Carr, 2023). Wages are about much more than money, but money also counts—meaning that we need to make more connections with circular or "doughnut" economics (Raworth, 2017).[3] It is important to engage with these progressive branches of economics that address the human consequences of mass poverty and mass working poverty wages: considerations that are often reduced to externalities in neoclassical economic praxis. Fair incomes imply an integration of IO's substantive history of researching workplace justice with contemporary issues like growing wage and income inequalities globally, regionally, and locally. Such an agenda is a response to the criticisms of IO research for focusing on relatively middle-class occupations, to the detriment and exclusion of working-class roles, informal and precarious sectors, and unfair wage distributions: as well as overlooking the unfairness of massive wages being paid to the very top of the wage hierarchy. Research questions here include vital topics like how do we calibrate unfair and fair wages in any workplace from organization to digital platform to multinational to global supply chain? What are the consequences of everyday wage unfairness, from all sides, in workspaces and roles? These kinds of research questions are tailor-made for I/O psychology in general and humanitarian work psychology (HWP) in particular.

Fair incomes include and extend to *work security* and through work roles to life-worlds and related insecurities in communities, health, civic participation, education, and so forth. HSP (Hodgetts, Hopner et al., 2022) is a nascent and formative integration of a number of branches of psychology including IO. From this perspective, researching the conditions of work that help to promote, rather than impede, human security becomes fundamental. Questions such as "How do we measure key aspects of human security, including economic security through work and fair wages?" are central. Research into such concerns has only just begun (Carr et al., 2021a, 2021b). The next step, however, is to research the applicability of techniques, e.g., behaviorally anchored rating scales, to help determine what each type of human security, from food to economic to environmental, looks like: and how HSP in general can be promoted by and through decent work conditions? Do raises in minimum and living wages, as well as capping ratios between maximum and living wages, improve people's everyday experiences of various [in]human securities?

Research questions like these take us into the domain of social protection. As it stands, we can ask of research, "Where is our theory and evidence base concerning the sustainability, for livelihoods, of policy options like basic income (BI), and other forms of wealth transfer, whether unconditional, conditional, or participative?" Shockingly, other social sciences have advanced their research agendas to address such questions, whereas I/O psychology has languished behind the proverbial eight ball. Despite this laggardness, in research, we are actually well-positioned to contribute toward answering important research questions such as, "What functions can, and should, a BI perform? Will a BI lead to wage depression, compression, or diversity, and what conditions need to be fulfilled in order to optimize the probability of each of these outcomes? How can wealth transfers and wages *combined* enable social protection in future worlds in which steady jobs are more the exception than the rule? What roles are there for state and organization, or digital platform, to work in partnerships to enable sustainable livelihoods?" Questions like these are inevitably going to become more and more germane as the climate crisis worsens; as costs of living spiral; as conflicts proliferate; as pandemics come and go; and as inequalities and inequities across ethnic, racial, gender, and class fault lines widen. At the same time, these crises are also disruptors, and disruptors can bring positive changes. This volume is firmly in that camp. While not shying away from the negative, it also accentuates the positive and contains a variety of research suggestions for tackling work precarity and addressing the needs of workers across a range of occupations.

In summary, as co-editors and co-authors, we welcome you to engage with the raft of issues regarding precarious work and how I/O psychology is responding, and can respond further, through well-crafted, conceptually rich, evidence-based, and praxis-orientated chapters. This curated collection of scholarly and applied work does not merely document work-related human misery. It also considers broader relationships between previous research work and issues of human security and sustainability that affect workers, families, communities, and societies. More importantly, the multilevel and joined-up orientation that is foundational to the volume is crucial in extending present understandings of the world of precarious work and how it fits within broader issues of economic, ecological, and social sustainability, alongside UN SDGs. Above all, this is a volume that is meant to be useful, and to-hand, when tackling precarious work to create sustainable livelihoods.

Notes

1 Gender wage gaps exist alongside a range of intersectional wage gaps, including ethnic, [dis]ability, and class wage gaps (see Carr, 2023, for a review).

2 Profit is not the only motive for organizations, e.g., NGOs need to pay living wages as well.

3 Doughnut economics is conceptualized as two interrelated concentric rings. The first ring relates to the social foundations whereby economic activity is structured so that everyone is included and has access to the essentials of life. The second ring relates to ecological ceilings to ensure that economic activities remain within sustainable levels and do not exceed and undermine planetary capacities to support life.

References

Adler, A. (1925). *The practice and theory of individual psychology* (1st ed.). Routledge.

Bal, P. M., & Doci, E. (2018). Neoliberal ideology in work and organizational psychology. *European Journal of Work and Organizational Psychology*. https://doi.org/10.1080/1359432X.2018.1449108, accessed June 8, 2022.

Bal, P. M., Doci, E., Lub, X. D., van Rossenberg, Y. G. T., Nijs, S., Achnak, S., Briner, R. B., Brookes, A., Chudzikowski, K., De Cooman, R., De Gieter, S., de Jong, J., de Jong, S. B., Dorenbosch, L., Ghoreishi, M. A., Hack-Polay, D., Hofmans, J., Hornung, S., Khuda, K., … & van Zelst, M. (2019). Manifesto for the future of work and organizational psychology. *European Journal of Work & Organizational Psychology, 28*(3), 289–299. https://doi.org/10.1080/1359432X.2019.1602041

Baritz, L. (1960). *The servants of power*. Wesleyan University Press.

Bergman, M. E., & Jean, V. A. (2015). Where have all the workers gone? A critical analysis of the under-representativeness of our samples relative to the labor market in the industrial-organizational psychology literature. *Industrial and Organizational Psychology, 9*(1), 1–30.

Bohnenberger, K. (2022). Is it a green or a brown job? A taxonomy of sustainable employment. *Ecological Economics, 200*, 107469.

Bolam, B., Hodgetts, D., Chamberlain, K., Murphy, S., & Gleeson, K. (2003) 'Just do it': An analysis of accounts of control over health amongst lower socioeconomic status groups. *Critical Public Health, 13*, 15–31. https://doi.org/10.1080/0958159031000100170

Brief, A. P. (2000). Still servants of power. *Journal of Management Inquiry, 9*, 342–351.

Burnes, B. (2020). The origins of Lewin's three-stage model of change. *The Journal of Applied Behavioural Science, 56*, 32–59.

Carr, S. C. (2007). I/O psychology and poverty reduction. *The Industrial Psychologist, 45*(1), 43–50.

Carr, S. C. (2013). *Anti-poverty psychology*. Springer.

Carr, S. C. (2023). *Wage and wellbeing: Toward sustainable livelihoods.* Springer.

Carr, S. C., MacLachlan, M., & Furnham, A. (2012). *Humanitarian work psychology*. Palgrave-Macmillan.

Carr, S. C., Hopner, V., Moh. Abdul Hakim, Hodgetts, D. J., Chamberlain, K., Nelson, N., Ball, R., & Jones, H. (2021). Scaling the security staircase. *Political Psychology, 42*, 575–595.

Carr, S. C., Maleka, M., Meyer, I., Barry, M. L., Harr, J., Parker, J., Arrowsmith, J., Yao, C., Hodgetts, D., Jones, H., Young-Hausner, A., Afeaki-Mafile'o, E., Rasmussen, A.-H. Alefaio-Tugia, S., Falealili, B., Mafile'o, K., Pikula, T., Wolfgram, N., 'Uhila, H. … Naithani, A. (2018). How can wages sustain a living? By getting ahead of the curve. *Sustainability Science*. https://doi.org/10.1007/s11625-018-0560-7

Carr, S. C., Parker, J., Arrowsmith, J., & Watters, P. A. (2016). The living wage: Theoretical integration and an applied research agenda. *International Labour Review*

(International Labour Organization: Geneva), *155*(1), 1–24. Special Issue "Wages: Determinants, Distribution and Livelihoods".

Carr, S. C., Young-Hauser, A., Hodgetts, D., Schmidt, W., Moran, L., Haar, J., Parker, J., Arrowsmith, J., Jones, H., & Alefaio-Tuglia, S. (2021). Research update: How decent wages transform qualities of living—By affording escape from working poverty trap. *Journal of Sustainability Science, 3*, 1–15.

Chambers, R. C., & Conway, G. R. (1991). *Sustainable rural livelihoods: Practical concepts for the 21st century*. IDS (Institute of Development Studies), Discussion Paper 296. University of Sussex.

Cook, S., & Kabeer, N. (2009). *Socio-economic security over the life course: A global review of social protection*. Institute of Development Studies.

Department for International Development. (DFID). (1999). *Sustainable livelihoods guidance sheets*. Department for International Development.

Desai, S. D., Brief, A, P., & George, J. M. (2010). Meaner managers: A consequence of income inequality. In R. M. Kramer, A. E. Tenbrunsel, M. H. Bazerman, & D. M. Messick (Eds.), *Social decision making: Social dilemmas, social values, and ethical judgements* (pp. 315–332). Routledge.

Erdogan, B., Bauer, T. N., & Taylor, S. (2015). Management commitment to the ecological environment and employees: Implications for employee attitudes and citizenship behaviours. *Human Relations, 68*, 1669–1691.

Figart, D. (2000). Equal pay for equal work: The role of job evaluation in an evolving social norm. *Journal of Economic Issues, 34*, 1–19.

Fisher, C. D. (2009). Happiness at work. *International Journal of Management Reviews, 12*, 384–412.

Frese, M., Gielnik, M. M., & Mensmann, M. (2016). Psychological training for entrepreneurs to take action: Contributing to poverty reduction in developing countries. *Current Directions in Psychological, Science, 25*, 196–202.

Furnham, A. (2019, November/December). Pay secrecy. *European Business Review*, 69–72.

George, J., & Brief, A. P. (1989). The economic instrumentality of work: An examination of the moderating effects of financial requirements and sex on the pay-life satisfaction relationship. *Academy of Management Proceedings, 1*, 209–213.

Gloss, A., Carr, S. C., Reichman, W., & Abdul-Nasiru, I. (2017). From handmaidens to POSH humanitarians. *Industrial & Organizational Psychology Journal, 10*, 1–41.

Gray, B., Grey, C., Hookway, A., Homolova, L., & Davies, A. (2020). Differences in the impact of precarious employment on health across population subgroups: A scoping review. *Perspectives in Public Health*. https://doi.org/10.1177/1757913920971333

Groot, S., & Hodgetts, D. (2015). The infamy of begging: A case-based approach to street homelessness and radical commerce. *Qualitative Research in Psychology, 12*: 349–366.

Hackman, J. R., & Oldham, G. R. (1974). Motivation through the design of work: Test of a theory. *Organizational Behaviour and Human Performance, 16*, 250–279.

Hakel, M. (2013). Homo economicus, industrial psychology, and the greater good. In J. B. Olson-Buchanan, L. L. Koppes Bryan, & L. Foster Thompson (Eds.), *Using industrial-organizational psychology for the greater good: Helping those who help others* (pp. 559–566). Routledge.

Harrison, D. A., Newman, D. A., & Roth, P. L. (2006). How important are job attitudes? Meta-analytic comparisons of integrative behavioural outcomes and time sequences. *Academy of Management Journal, 49*, 305–325.

Hart, J. T. (1971). The inverse care law. *The Lancet*, *297*(7696), 405–412. https://doi.org/10.1016/S0140-6736(71)92410-X

Harter, J. K., Schmidt, F. L., & Hayes, T. L. (2002). Business-unit-level relationship between employee satisfaction, employee engagement, and business outcomes: A meta-analysis. *Journal of Applied Psychology, 87*, 268–279.

Hodgetts, D. J., Hopner, V., Carr, S. C., Bar-Tal, D., Liu, J., Saner, R., Yiu, L., Horgan, J., Searle, R., Massola, G., Hakim, Moh., Marai, L., King, P., & Moghaddam, F. M. (2022). Human security psychology: A linking construct for an eclectic discipline. *Review of General Psychology*. Advance online publication. https://doi.org/10.1177/10892680221109124

Hodgetts, D., & Stolte, O. (2017). *Urban poverty and health inequalities: A relational approach*. Routledge.

Hodgetts, D. J., Young-Hauser, A. M., Arrowsmith, J., Parker, J., Carr, S. C., Haar, J. & Alefaio, S. (2022) Deliberating upon the living wage to alleviate in-work poverty: A rhetorical inquiry into key stakeholder accounts. *Frontiers in Psychology, 13*, 810870. https://doi.org/10.3389/fpsyg.2022.810870

Hopner, V., & Liu, J. H. (2021). Relational ethics and epistemology: The case for complementary first principles in psychology. *Theory & Psychology*, *31*(2), 179–198. https://doi.org/10.1177/0959354320974103

International Labour Organization. (2012). *From precarious work to decent work*. ILO.

International Labour Organization. (2013). *World of work report 2013*: *Repairing the economic and social fabric*. ILO.

International Labour Organization. (2018a). *Baseline research findings on fishers and seafood workers in Thailand*. ILO.

International Labour Organization. (2018b). *Global wage report 2018/19: What lies behind gender pay gaps*. ILO.

International Labour Organization. (2019). *World employment and social outlook—Trends 2019*. ILO.

International Labour Organization. (2021a). *Forced labour, modern slavery and human trafficking*. ILO.

International Labour Organization. (2021b). *The role of digital labour platforms in transforming the world of work*. ILO.

International Labour Organization. (2022a). *World employment and social outlook: Trends 2022*. ILO.

International Labour Organization. (2022b). *Decent work*. https://www.ilo.org/global/topics/decent-work/lang--en/index.htm

International Trade Union Confederation. (2018, December 2). *Global poll: Governments' failure to address low wages and insecure jobs threatens trust in politics and democracy*. https://www.ituc-csi.org/ITUC-Global-Poll-2018

Jacquart, P., & Armstrong, J. S. (2013). The ombudsman: Are top executives paid enough? An evidence-based review. *Interfaces, 43*, 1–27.

Kalleberg, A. (2018). *Precarious lives: Job insecurity and wellbeing in rich democracies*. Polity Press.

Kates, R. W., Clark, W. C., Corell, R., Hall, M. J., Jaeger, C. C., Lowe, I., McCarthy, J. J., Schellnhuber, H. J., Bolin, B, Dickson, N. M., Faucheux, S., Gallopin, G. C., Grübler, A., Huntley, B., Jäger, J., Jodha, N. S., Kasperson, R. E., Mabogunje, A., Matson, P. … Svedin, U. (2001). Sustainability science. *Science, 292*(5517), 641–642.

Kaufman, J. A., Salas-Hernandez, L. K., Komro, K. A., & Livingston, M. D. (2020). Effects of increased minimum wages by unemployment rate on suicide in the USA. *Journal of Epidemiological Community Health, 74*, 219–224.

Kennedy, K., & Hallowell, B. (2021). Peace building in practice: Creating shared security at all levels. *Behavior and Social Issues*. https://doi.org/10.1007/s42822-021-00052-4

King, P., & Waldegrave, C. (2012). *Report of an investigation into defining a living wage for New Zealand*. The Living Wage Campaign.

King, P., & Waldegrave, C. (2014). *Living wage Aotearoa New Zealand 2014 update*. The Living Wage Campaign.

Klinger, B., del Carpio, C., & Khwajal, A. I. (2013). *Enterprising psychology and poverty reduction*. Springer.

Lefkowitz, J. (2017). *Ethics and values in industrial and organizational psychology* (2nd ed.). Routledge.

Leigh, J. P., Leigh, W. A., & Du, J. (2019). Minimum wages and public health: A literature review. *Preventive Medicine, 118*, 122–134.

Lewin, K. (1947). Group decision and social change. In T. Newcomb, & E. Hartley (Eds.), *Readings in social psychology* (pp. 330–344). Henry Holt.

Malmandier, U., & Tate, G. (2009). Superstar CEOs. *Quarterly Journal of Economics, 124*, 1593–1561.

Maslow, A. H. (1942). The dynamics of psychological security-insecurity. *Journal of Personality, 10*(4), 331–344.

McNamara, C., McKee, M., & Stuckler, D. (2021). Precarious employment and health in the context of COVID-19: A rapid scoping umbrella review. *European Journal of Public Health, 31*(Suppl. 4), iv40–iv49.

McWha-Hermann, I., Maynard, D. C., & O'Neill-Berry, M. (2016). *Humanitarian work psychology and the global development agenda: Case studies*. Routledge.

McWha-Hermann, I., Searle, R. H., & Carr, S. C. (2021). Striving for more: Work and organizational psychology (WOP) and living wages. *European Journal of Work and Organizational Psychology*, 30(6), 771–776.https://doi.org/10.1080/1359432X.2021.1972972

Munyon, T., Lyons, M., Carnes, A., & Zettler, I. (2020). All about the money? Exploring antecedents and consequences for a brief measure of perceived financial security. *Journal of Occupational Health Psychology, 25*(1), 159–175.

Neumark, D., & Shirley, P. (2021). *Myth or measurement: What does the new minimum wage research say about minimum wages and job loss in the United States?* National Bureau of Economic Research, Working Paper 28388.

Nguyen, M. H. T., Carr, S. C., Hodgetts, D., & Fauchart, E. (2021). Why do some social enterprises flourish in Vietnam? A comparison of human and ecosystem partnerships. *Sustainability Accounting, Management and Policy Journal, 12*(6). https://doi.org/10.1108/SAMPJ-04-2020-0137

Olson-Buchanan, J. B., Koppes-Bryan, L. L., & Foster-Thompson, L. (Eds.). (2014). *Using industrial-organizational psychology for the greater good: Helping those who help others*. Routledge.

Organization for Economic Cooperation and Development. (2011). *Guidelines for multinational enterprises, 2011 Edition*. OECD.
Oxfam. (2020). *Time to care: Unpaid and underpaid care work and the global inequality crisis*. Oxfam.
Pérez-Rodríguez, V., Topa, G., & Beléndez, M. (2019). Organizational justice and work stress: The mediating role of negative, but not positive, emotions. *Personality and Individual Differences, 151*, Article 109392. https://doi.org/10.1016/j.paid.2019.04.047
Pizzigati, S. (2018). *The case for a maximum wage*. Wiley & Sons.
Raworth, K. (2017). *Doughnut economics: Seven ways to think like a 21st century economist*. White River.
Reichman, W. (Ed.). (2014). *Industrial and organizational psychology help the vulnerable: Serving the underserved*. Palgrave-Macmillan.
Rupp, D., & Mallory, D. B. (2015). Corporate social responsibility: Psychological, person-centric, and progressing. *Annual Review of Organizational Psychology and Organizational Behavior, 2*, 211–236.
Scott, J. (2011). SIOP granted NGO consultative status with the United Nations. *The Industrial-Organizational Psychologist, 49*(2), 111–113.
Scott-Marshall, H., & Tompass, E. (2011). The health consequences of precarious employment experiences. *Work 38*, 369–382. https://doi.org/10.3233/WOR-2011-1140
Seubert, C., Hopfgartner, L., & Glaser, J. (2019). Beyond job insecurity: Concept, dimensions, and measurement of precarious employment. *Psychology of Everyday Activity, 12*, 33–45.
Sharabi, M., & Harpaz, I. (2019). To work or not to work: Variables affecting non-financial employment commitment over time. *International Labour Review, 158*, 1–25.
Shaw, J. D., & Gupta, N. (2001). Pay fairness and employee outcomes: Exacerbation and attenuation effects of financial need. *Journal of Occupational and Organizational Psychology, 74*, 299–320.
Smith, L. (2015). Reforming the minimum wage: Towards a psychological perspective. *American Psychologist, 70*, 557–565.
United Nations. (2022, May 23). Global jobs market recovery 'has gone into reverse, warns UN labour agency. *UN News*. https://news.un.org/en/story/2022/05/1118812
United Nations Development Programme. (2020). *Temporary basic income: Protecting poor and vulnerable people in developing countries*. United Nations Development Programme.
United Nations Research Institute for Social Development. (2010). *Combating poverty and inequality: Structural change, social policy and politics*. United Nations Research Institute for Social Development.
United Nations Trust Fund for Human Security. (1994). *Human security in theory and practice*. https://www.unocha.org/sites/dms/HSU/Publications%20and%20Products/Human%20Security%20Tools/Human%20Security%20in%20Theory%20and%20Practice%20English.pdf
Williams, M. L., McDaniel, M. A., & Nguyen, N. T. (2006). A meta-analysis of the antecedents and consequences of pay level satisfaction. *Journal of Applied Psychology, 91*, 392–413.
World Bank. (2001). *Social protection sector strategy paper: From safety net to springboard*. World Bank.

World Bank Group. (2019). *World development report 2019* [PowerPoint slides]. http://pubdocs.worldbank.org/en/808261547222082195/WDR19-English-Presentation.pdf
World Commission on Environment and Development. (1989, March). *Our common future*. Brundtland Commission.
World Health Organization. (2020, March 12). *WHO announces COVID-19 outbreak a pandemic*. https://www.euro.who.int/en/health-topics/health-emergencies/coronavirus-covid-19/news/news/2020/3/who-announces-covid-19-outbreak-a-pandemic, accessed June 5, 2022.

PART I

Sustainable Livelihoods

2

FROM PRECARIOUS WORK TO DECENT WORK

Lessons from the United Nations and Humanitarian Work Psychology

Jeffrey M. Saltzman, Walter Reichman, and Mary O'Neill Berry

Humanitarian work psychology (HWP) is a subset of industrial and organizational (I/O) psychology focused on using I/O psychology to improve human wellbeing and address multiple global problems. These problems include the absence of decent work (and, by implication, the increase in precarious work), poverty, discrimination, and inequality/inequity. HWP involves two broad areas: (1) the application of I/O psychology to humanitarian work (sustainable development, poverty reduction, disaster relief, etc.) and (2) applying humanitarian principles to I/O psychology as a discipline (promoting fair and just working conditions for all workers, providing a living—not just a minimum—wage, and more.). As such, it focuses I/O psychology on organized efforts to enhance human welfare (McWha-Hermann et al., 2016). In this chapter, we explore the state of precarious work around the world and offer a roadmap to improve the quality of work for the most vulnerable.

The Way Work Should Be

Each worker should have a job that will provide a secure and satisfactory life for themselves and their families; this is a far cry from the world of the precarious worker, but it is an aspiration that I/O psychologists and those engaged with HWP want to achieve. We want each person in our world to have the requisite education, training, and opportunities to use their abilities and fulfill their interests and values as they perform work that gives a sense of accomplishment and contributes to the growth of society. We want everyone to be assured that as long as they perform their job satisfactorily, they will have constant employment, and if for some reason this is not possible, they will have the security of knowing

DOI: 10.4324/9781003440444-3

their needs will be provided for. As people contribute to their world, they will have opportunities to develop and expand their abilities and rise to the levels to which they aspire.

The Way the World of Work Actually Is

A news photograph taken in September 2021 perfectly illustrates the state of precarious work in countries like the United States. This photo, taken after the remnants of Hurricane Ida slammed into New York City (NYC), shows a food delivery worker pushing his bike through thigh-high water in the Williamsburg section of Brooklyn in the midst of the storm, with his delivery bag attached to the handlebars. The photographer, Johnny Miller, posted his picture, and by morning, it had garnered 10 million views and news organizations had paid Miller a total of $1700 to use the photo. Miller decided to track down the delivery worker to give him the money. His extensive search turned up empty until the posters he was using to locate the worker were translated into Bangladeshi, as many of the delivery workers in that area hailed from Bangladesh. It was then that other delivery workers recognized the man in the now-famous photo because they were headed to his memorial service, as he had been struck and killed by a car soon after the storm had passed (Lach, 2021). Just who are these delivery workers and what kind of conditions do they face?

In NYC, food delivery workers used to work as employees for restaurants, delivering food to workplaces and homes alike. But with the advent of food delivery apps such as Grubhub and DoorDash, their employment status changed. According to NYC Department of Transportation estimates, 65,000 delivery workers—a field dominated by immigrants (see Cassim, Chapter 20)—now work in the gig economy (see Kuhn, Chapter 12) as independent contractors, taking delivery jobs from the online apps rather than restaurants. Approximately 64% of these workers ride their bikes tirelessly, performing deliveries six or even seven days per week. During the COVID-19 pandemic lockdown, these workers were classified as essential and were out delivering food to people who were not leaving their apartments or homes. Yet despite risking their own lives to keep food flowing, and enabling restaurants to stay in businesses, fully 98.2% reported not receiving any extra pay during this period, and during 2020 and 2021 (as of October 2021), 16 delivery workers were killed while delivering food for an average net pay, excluding tips, of $7.87 per hour. With tips, wages are roughly $12.21 per hour but the workers only get paid for making an actual delivery. Some of the food delivery apps argue that the pay is much higher if you only count the actual time the worker spends on a delivery, and not the time that they spend between deliveries waiting for an order to come in (Figueroa et al., 2021). Whilst certainly not uniform, here are some of the sentiments expressed by the workers toward the delivery apps:

> There is a lack of respect for delivery drivers [on the part of] company and clients, the company doesn't take time to take care of us.
>
> They don't care for our safety. I had an accident once and instead of asking for my wellbeing, they asked if I had delivered the food.

Another example of precarious work comes from the other side of the globe where on April 24, 2013, in Dhaka, Bangladesh, a garment manufacturing building containing five manufacturing companies collapsed, killing at least 1,132 people, most of whom were women and young girls, and injured another 2,500 (International Labour Organization [ILO], 2021). That disaster focused the world's attention on how Bangladeshi companies were supplying Western consumers with cheap, ready-to-wear clothing. Pressure began to be applied to international fashion brands to improve working conditions in their supply chains. A question that arose from that tragedy was whether working conditions for the Bangladeshi garment workers would improve through regulation: much as they did in the United States after the Triangle Shirtwaist Company disaster in 1911, which saw women leaping to their deaths as the factory they were working in burned down with the fire escape doors chained shut, killing 149 people in 18 minutes (Cornell University, 2018).

Unfortunately, the treatment of these Bangladeshi workers has not improved since 2013. Fast forward to March 2020, at the start of the COVID-19 pandemic. Once many fashion brands realized the potential impact of the pandemic on their sales, they either refused to accept completed orders or demanded large discounts. An estimated $3 billion US dollars in payment was withheld for garment orders that had already been shipped. What happened to the more than 4 million Bangladeshi garment workers who had already labored to produce that clothing for a minimum wage of $96 per month? Only 14.8% reported being fully paid for their work in April 2020, putting many at risk for homelessness, while preserving profits for the manufacturers and fashion brands (Open Access Government, 2020).

In both examples above, the workers were employed under precarious conditions, working for low wages as contract workers with no benefits, job security, or protections. In 2019, there were 5.7 billion people of working age on the planet. Of those, 3.3 billion were working. But of those 3.3 billion, 61% or 2 billion were part of the informal sector workforce (United Nations [UN], 2020). According to a 2021 World Bank report, more than 70% of total employment is "informal" in emerging markets and developing economies (EMDEs). In other words, the majority of people who work are part of the informal, precarious workforce (Carr, Hodgetts, Hopner, & Young, Chapter 10; Jyoti & Arora, Chapter 6; Saxena & Tchagneno, Chapter 11).

While the treatment of precarious workers varies, there is a handful of motivations and justifications used to rationalize and legitimize the practice among the organizations utilizing precarious workers:

- The first motivation is simply greed: greed on the part of companies to maximize profit, on the part of app developers and venture capitalists looking to disrupt an industry and become the next unicorn, and greed on the part of politicians looking to cater to their big donors by limiting or eliminating social safety nets that require tax revenues.
- A justification is provided by ostracizing and dehumanizing a group as "other": as somehow different and not worthy of the same societal benefits accrued to those in the majority. The "other," whether they be immigrants; refugees; non-native language speakers; racial, ethnic, or religious minorities; members of a lower caste; or women, are discounted as different from the rest of us; they're portrayed as lazy, unworthy, or having it better than they would have elsewhere, as though relative morality is enough to justify any kind of treatment, from one in-group toward another out-group (Tajfel & Turner, 1979; see Cassim, Chapter 20).
- Holding self above others, another form of greed, is when a person or group lays claim to some exalted position or standing because of special or unique characteristics, accruing benefits to themselves that are denied others. Politicians, religious leaders, industry disrupters, narcissists (and those with various other mental illnesses), triumphant militaries, and new settlers easily spring to mind as falling into this category (Rylander, 2016). For instance, the new settlers who came to the Americas in earlier centuries displaced, rounded up, and even killed the indigenous peoples and justified their actions by declaring they were "heathens," who did not worship the correct deity.

It must be noted that not all independent or part-time work is dangerous. There are some workers who must work independently or part-time because of their legal status or other specific needs and/or circumstances. For instance, those needing flexible arrangements or returning to the workforce after an extended absence to start a family, raise children, or take care of elderly parents might need the ability to work part-time or on a temporary arrangement that can be precarious in nature. And not all organizations that utilize precarious workers treat them poorly (Figueroa et al., 2021).

The Conditions that Can Create Change

Creating change occurs when societies or organizations must adapt to changing conditions. During stable times, most societies and organizations lack either the political will or sense of urgency to radically change, so it is a relatively rare event. It is only when there is a clear and obvious need for change, a burning issue, that change is brought about. Kurt Lewin, in his famous Unfreeze-Change-Refreeze model, describes how once the need for change is recognized and brought about, new patterns of behavior, or a new social compact, must be frozen into place (Lewin, 2008). Other social psychologists describe societal change as occurring in four phases: stability, inertia, incremental, and dramatic social change (de la Sablonniere, 2017).

As examples throughout history, there have been events that have fundamentally reshaped civilization by unfreezing the rules governing society (see Chapter 1). For instance, the Black Death (believed to be bubonic plague) savaged Europe beginning in 1347, causing the deaths of millions of serfs and creating a shortage of workers to plant, harvest, and work the farms. One estimate is that up to 50% of the workforce died. For landholders, that resulted in an inability to pay the taxes they owed the crown (Jedwab et al., 2020). This situation gave the serfs new leverage to demand better pay and conditions. The labor shortage, as well as other precipitating factors such as overextended banks, monarchs refusing to pay their obligations, and marginal lands being used for agriculture, spelled the beginning of the end of feudalism. A question that arises is whether the gig workers of today and others working in precarious positions are the equivalent, status-wise, of the medieval serfs (see Kuhn, Chapter 12).

Social upheaval fundamentally reshaped France and was extensive in the run-up to the French Revolution, where severe economic and political instability collided, causing the proletariat to rise up and create a society based upon The Declaration of the Rights of Man and of the Citizen, which eliminated special rights for the nobility and clergy by stating: "All the citizens, being equal in the eyes of the law, are equally admissible to all public dignities, places, and employments, according to their capacity and without distinction other than that of their virtues and of their talents." (Encyclopedia Britannica, 2022).

Another example of social upheaval and dramatic change that forever changed the role of women in the United States occurred during World War II, when an unprecedented 5 million women entered the workforce, working in factories and construction (Goldin, 1991). These women were crucial to America's successful war effort, and once they had that hard-earned paycheck in their pockets, they experienced increased independence and freedom that they were loath to give up after the war, and the changes became enduring. This increased independence not only fundamentally changed society in the United States but also brought some social stability to women as they were able to exert more control over their lives and live with greater dignity.

Starting in early 2020, COVID-19 caused worldwide quarantines, created additional work-from-home options, saw travel restrictions implemented, and helped to gather the forces that can drive broader cultural shifts. When the world first began hearing reports of a new respiratory virus, most people did not expect it to drag on for as long as it did. While various countries took different paths in dealing with the pandemic, globally the impact was enormous. In the United States, schools and offices closed for weeks which dragged into months and then over a year, for some. China continued with a Zero COVID policy until December 2022, which closed down cities and sections of the country whenever an outbreak was detected. The death toll continued to rise and vaccines, while greatly reducing casualties, did not eradicate the virus or return life to "normal."

A return to formal working conditions as they were pre-COVID, with centralized in-office groups, face-to-face meetings, and other close-contact unprotected situations, is not likely to happen across the board—despite a desire by many people, organizations, and societies to do so (see Toaddy, Crawford et al., Chapter 22). Remote work has gained a foothold, millions have moved out of crowded and expensive cities, and there are those who no longer feel comfortable in large groups. Societies and organizations evolve with changing conditions; they do not devolve or return to a past that often is illusory in nature. There has been not only too much loss, too much suffering, and too much juggling of work while caring for sick relatives and children—but also a reprioritization of what matters to people. Many people (who could afford to because they were not paid precarious wage rates) welcomed the slow-down ushered in by the worldwide quarantine. As formal offices and schools reopened, many were hesitant to go back to the chaotic, rat-race–like conditions of pre-pandemic life. Some people, fortunate enough to have good homes and decent jobs, perhaps liked the idea of hybrid working conditions. Workers demanded better pay, treatment, and conditions. Parents wanted more time with their children—or, at least, the ability to take care of them well while working. In the United States, for instance, almost 6% of workers quit their formal jobs in August and September 2021 alone (Rosenberg, 2021). A significant formal-sector labor shortage developed, which gave its workers leverage to demand better conditions and better pay. Strikes, or threatened strikes, became widespread.

In countries with less access to modern healthcare and vaccines, and higher levels of work informality, COVID has done significant damage to the workforce, with uncertain long-term impacts (see Klug et al., Chapter 21). In Lusaka, the capital of Zambia, 90% of those in the city morgue were positive for COVID, suggesting gross official undercounts of the true impact of the disease. The Lancet undertook an examination of "excess deaths," meaning deaths beyond those expected country-by-country, and found some staggering results (Wang et al., 2022). As of December 2021, the true global death count due to COVID is likely around 18.2 million, not the officially reported 5.94 million. The largest numbers of excess deaths were found in South Asia, North Africa, the Middle East, and Eastern Europe. India was most impacted, with over 4 million excess deaths, followed by the United States, Russia, Mexico, Brazil, Indonesia, and Pakistan. The largest excess mortality rates per 100,000 of population were found in Russia, followed by Mexico. While COVID has been shown to have greatest mortality among older and more vulnerable populations, it is also impacting the working-age population, and the duration and long-term impact of long COVID are still largely unknown (Wang et al., 2022).

The pandemic, while changing certain aspects of how work gets done, is unlikely to change workers' expectations around what they fundamentally desire (e.g., respectful treatment) from the workplace (see Griep et al., Chapter 13). There is no reason to believe that the psychology of what precarious workers desire from working conditions is any different than the psychology that drives those in the formal workforce; after all, one thing they all have in common is their shared humanity. What is likely to change is how those fundamentals are delivered, how the work gets done, and how worker desires and needs are fulfilled. Many of the current patterns in the data collected from employee surveys and interviews during the period of COVID-19 are similar to patterns seen after 9/11 and during the Great Recession that began in 2007 (Saltzman, 2021), and many of the suggested ways to address worker concerns are similar as well.

The Responsibility of I/O Psychology to Alter Precarious Work

The discipline of I/O psychology has assumed a responsibility for improving the lives of workers around the world. This is evidenced by the accreditation of SIOP, the leading I/O psychology organization, to the Economic and Social Council of the UN and its involvement in the development and implementation of the Sustainable Development Goals (SDGs) of the UN. SIOP's acceptance of HWP and pro-social research for its publications and conference presentations attests to the growing concern for precarious workers around the world.

Directions for Future Research

With this responsibility, I/O psychologists must first develop research-based best practices to eliminate or at least reduce the detrimental effects of precarious work. Second, those in the field must prepare future generations of I/O psychologists to assume responsibility for the improvement of the lives of workers by giving them the tools for carrying out that responsibility. Graduate programs in I/O should prepare students to conduct research and promote applied research directed at improving the lives of workers. Such programs already in existence include research on the living wage (Carr et al., 2018), basic income (Hüffmeier & Zachar, 2021), precarious workers (Saxena, 2017), women workers and poverty (Schein, 2012), person-centric research (Weiss & Rupp, 2011), and descriptions of opportunities for applied research on poverty reduction (Olson-Buchanan & Vera, 2021). Additionally, students can find research ideas in this chapter (and across the volume as a whole, see *Directions for Future Research* sub-sections).

Some ideas for future research might include:

- Do workers in the formal and informal economy experience and handle stress differently?
- What are the expectations of precarious workers for securing permanent work in today's rapidly changing working conditions?
- What are the characteristics of the private for-profit organizations that are willing to eliminate precarious work in their organizations and under what economic conditions are they willing to do so?
- What are the expectations of the increasing number of political and economic migrants for work opportunities in their new homes? (Cassim, Chapter 20).

It is hoped that I/O psychology faculty interested in humanitarian work will promote master's and doctoral research theses and dissertations related to work and poverty reduction. We believe that such research will promote employee wellbeing in the future as well as increase the humanitarian scope of the discipline. If future I/O psychologists are to assume a responsibility for employee wellbeing and see their research translated into programs and policies, they will have to learn the skill of advocacy. Currently, I/O psychologists are involved with state, national, and international organizations, academic institutions, business, and not-for-profit organizations. In all instances, they have opportunities to advocate for the wellbeing of employees using research and best practices as their database. They must learn ways to advocate for the changes in policies and procedures that their research and experiences demonstrate will improve the lives of workers. The teaching of procedures for advocacy should be added to the education of I/O psychology students. The example of a method of research evidence-informed advocacy called the "new diplomacy" (Saner & Yiu, 2014) could be a starting point for teaching and incorporating advocacy into the repertoire of future I/O psychologists (Saner & Yiu, Chapter 5; Searle & McWha-Hermann, Chapter 4).

Fundamentals

The underlying human psychology that drives the fundamentals of what workers (precarious or not) want from the workplace (Beck, 1978) did not change during the COVID-19 pandemic; nor did it change after 9/11 or after the Great Recession, and it is very unlikely to change any time soon. What does and can change is how those fundamentals are fulfilled. We can illustrate a few here linked to tackling precarious work (Brooks & Saltzman, 2016).

First is restoring a sense of equity and fairness: that the workplace environment provides for an equitable arrangement; that for the effort I put in, I am given a fair return. For those in the formal workforce, that return is measured in terms of compensation and benefits. For those in the informal workforce, equity is still important though less often achieved. Benefits can be varied, and each person will put different weight on the value of certain benefits such as independence, the ability to travel or change jobs, job prestige or organizational mission, development opportunities or resume building, flexibility, retirement plans, and job security. Some people will seek and accept a formal job with lower compensation, such as in the civil service, if they can retire after 20 years with health insurance and a pension. Others may take a job, formal or informal, and work under less satisfying conditions if the organization is viewed as serving a higher purpose, such as those working for various non-profits. What combination people value in terms of compensation and benefits is varied and changes over time, sometimes driven by life stage and sometimes by the impact of significant events, such as technological advances, economic crises, attacks by foreign powers, or pandemics. So, after a pandemic, people still desire equitable treatment but the factors that create that equitableness can and will change, not necessarily for all, but at least for some.

The second fundamental is being treated with respect and dignity (Lucas, 2017). We defy readers to find a worker anywhere in the world, precarious or not, formal or informal, of any generation, from any culture, that doesn't want to be treated with respect and dignity, pathology aside. This does not change over time and is a constant.

Let us focus in on dignity for a moment. The concept of dignity has a long history and interesting origins. As a constitutional right, dignity today is often defined as a "person's freedom to write their own life story." Freedom to create one's life story requires freedom from oppression and has within that notion both rights and obligations. One right is of control over oneself and one's own body; an obligation is to take responsibility for your behaviors and actions, for your future. While respect is often thought about in absolute terms, dignity is thought about in relative terms (Barak, 2015). By this definition, precarious workers, with their low wages and lack of benefits, protections, or security, are being treated with less dignity than those in the formal workforce. Maintaining dignity in the world of work is a balancing act. If dignity is about the right to choose, entering an employment situation is giving up at least some dignity, in that you are working not necessarily for your own ends, on your own initiatives, but on organizationally defined goals and often on an organizationally defined schedule.

Now let us turn to respect. People in organizations are rarely treated the same. Some of the differences are there for motivational purposes, to give people something to strive for—more money, a promotion, access to training and developmental experiences. Sometimes this meritocracy is real and sometimes it is a false meritocracy, and employees can determine that in relatively short order. As a relational variable (see Chapter 1), when we ask someone, "Are you treated with respect and dignity?" their response is in relation to how they see others being treated both within and externally to the organization. And across a large number of people, we will in all likelihood receive a range of responses. Through statistical analysis we can determine which specific policies, practices, and processes enhance people's sense of dignity, such as by increasing a person's sense of agency; which diminish it; and which simply have no bearing on the matter. Ultimately, we can determine what policies, practices, and processes best improve people's sense of being treated with respect and dignity: human fundamentals.

A third fundamental is that people need organizational effectiveness, which is a responsibility of good leadership but also an expectation of being productive in one's work. One of the most potent factors that cause people to leave an organization is if they experience frustrations day-to-day in getting their work done. While there are always exceptions, by-and-large people want to work, they want to contribute, and they want to do a good job and be productive. One piece of evidence for this is that people who are overworked, creating more feelings of being valued by an organization, have higher levels of job satisfaction than people who are not given enough to do and feel less valued (Saltzman, 2012). Organizational effectiveness has both an internal component (how well is the place being run?) and an external component (does it offer products and services that are attractive and of high quality?).

Many of the frustrations employees experience come from ineffective internal systems and processes, through the application of unyielding policies and practices across the organization. For instance, organizational leaders like to create rules and apply them uniformly, or at least say they are applying them uniformly. This enables the organization to function with less effort, expending lower levels of energy day-to-day. These uniform rules may be designed to try and lift the "lower" end of the performance distribution, the normative exceptions, rather than the rest of the distribution, where most people are located. But this kind of focus does not maximize performance. Instead, what it often does is create a regression toward the mean, whereby some higher performers experience frustration when trying to deal with unbending rules and policies (Brooks & Saltzman, 2016). Eventually, such processes may render everybody's job and work precarious.

A fourth fundamental factor for tackling precarious work is that each employee wants to have a sense of personal future, a career path, and a sense of things to come. Precarious workers, such as contract workers for instance, often have little sense of future with the organization; hence, their loyalty to the organization will be lower than their less precariously employed counterparts. If and when any more stable and decent opportunities present themselves, these more precariously employed people will simply leave. Continuance compliance and churn like this might work for organizations in the short term, but in the longer term, they are not sustainable for either employees or employers. Organizations create all sorts of messaging to motivate workers to align with organizational goals. Ultimately, however, these messages will only work if employees see them as relating to their own and their families' future goals (Brooks & Saltzman, 2016). The more these goals can be aligned, the less precarious both will be.

Worker Stress

A core component of decent work is freedom from worry and stress, which in turn are core characteristics of much precarious work, wherever it is found. Based upon numerous employee surveys conducted by the authors in the formal sector, it can be stated that during the COVID-19 pandemic, stress levels among workers increased and for those without safety nets or benefits, and oftentimes without the ability to work remotely, it is very likely that stress levels have increased even further (Saltzman, 2021). Specifically, these employee surveys often asked whether stress levels were significant enough that they were impacting people's ability to get the job done. From this data, we found that, globally, work stress levels have been steadily increasing over the last decades, and during the pandemic, affirmative responses to this question rose to between 85% and 95% (Saltzman, 2021). In other words, the vast majority of the formal workforce is very stressed. An organization will not be able to eliminate stress, but it can help employees cope with it. One of the causes of stress during the pandemic was a lack of information about how the organization was going to deal with the COVID crisis. Alongside increased levels of fear driven by the unknowns of a novel disease, this increased employees' anxiety (Brewer, 2021). One mechanism to help with stress is to provide as much de-stressing information to the workforce as possible.

In times of uncertainty, ratings of the competence and trust in leadership can improve significantly, especially when there is effective, decisive leadership, and this points to a solution (Saltzman, 2021). Workers are generally willing to give leadership the benefit of the doubt, at least until proven otherwise. Having visible leadership that describes to workers the path the organization will be taking is another mechanism to reduce stress.

Another coping mechanism which helps workers through times of uncertainty is to get people as involved in solving issues and giving them as much control over their own environment as possible. As mentioned, agency is a path to dignity. After 9/11, for instance, those employees who were actively involved in restoring one company's operation located at Ground Zero saw dramatic increases in satisfaction, pride, and engagement compared to another group at the same company who were not involved (Sherman et al., 2003).

The UN and HWP Tackle Precarious Work

As described in the opening section, precarious workers experience stress and depression from their uncertain work schedules as well as from their economic difficulties. The stress and depression are related to physical and mental health difficulties (Saltzman, 2021).

Recognizing the effects of precarious work on the mental and physical health and wellbeing of such workers and their families, the UN has initiated activities to protect all workers as part of its mandate to improve the lives of people. The first initiative was the passage of the Universal Declaration of Human Rights in 1948 (UN, 1948) which includes four articles related to rights of workers. Article 22 describes the right for everyone to have the social and cultural rights needed for dignity and the free development of their personality. Article 23 states that everyone has the right to work, to free choice of employment, protection against unemployment, favorable working conditions, the right to equal pay for equal work, and the right to join trade unions for the protection of their interests. Articles 24–26 describe the rights to rest and leisure and a limitation to working hours, the right to a standard of living adequate to the health and wellbeing of the worker and their family, and the right to an education. This universal declaration is the keystone to all other principles and conventions issued by the UN and its affiliated organizations from that time onward. A brief review of these rights will serve as an introduction to a procedure for tackling precarious work and its consequences.

Guiding Principles on Business and Human Rights

The UN has created the position of a special representative on business and human rights, with a mandate to deal with human-rights abuses in business, and appointed John Ruggie to this role. This led to the international convention, the UN Guiding Principles on Business and Human Rights (UN, 2011), which calls for all businesses to avoid causing or contributing to adverse human-rights impacts through their own behaviors, address such impacts when they occur, and prevent or mitigate such impacts that are directly associated with their businesses. Businesses are to follow these principles, regardless of the human-rights situations in the nations in which they operate.

ILO

The Universal Declaration of Human Rights and the Guiding Principles on Business and Human Rights were preceded by the establishment in 1919 of the ILO as a part of the League of Nations, which was created as a result of the Treaty of Versailles which ended World War I. It existed as an independent organization until it became an affiliate of the UN in 1946. The member nations of the ILO each send a representative from labor, a representative from management, and two representatives from the government. The decisions of the ILO are achieved by consensus. The former director-general of the ILO, Juan Samovia, stated that reaching consensus takes time and effort, but when achieved, "it sticks." In 1981, the ILO issued the Principles and Rights at Work (ILO, 2022).

Over the years, the ILO has issued 189 conventions, the latest dealing with the rights of domestic workers. These conventions echo the Universal Declaration of Human Rights by calling for freedom of association and collective bargaining, and the elimination of forced labor, child labor, and discrimination in employment. The member nations agree to abide by these conventions. The ILO has also issued a Decent Work Agenda which has been a major influence on the work of the UN and its SDGs issued in 2015. The agenda calls for people to have work which provides opportunities to be productive, a fair income, security in the workplace, social protection, social interaction, prospects for development, freedom to express their concerns, and equality of opportunity (Ghai, 2003).

Global Compact

Global Compact is another affiliate of the UN that represents organizations, both private and public, and has 13,000 members who have voluntarily pledged to adhere to their ten principles. Among the principles relevant to precarious workers are: to eliminate all forms of forced, compulsory, and child labor; combat corruption; and uphold freedom of association and the right to collective bargaining. Member organizations must submit periodic reports on how they are supporting and implementing the principles, and there are cases in which organizations have been barred from continuing their membership (UN, 2000).

Organisation for Economic Co-operation and Development (OECD)

The OECD is mostly concerned with multinational organizations and provides guidelines for businesses operating across boundaries in this age of globalization (Ruggie &Nelson, 2015). Their OECD members are encouraged to respect the human rights of workers in each OECD country in which they operate and are urged to create employment opportunities and facilitate training opportunities for employees. In 2018, a number of organizations formed an Employment Working Group to ensure labor and social protections such as access to social security even if unemployed.

Moving Beyond Aspirations

We will be the first to admit to a lack of a crystal ball to see into the future, but if history is any guide, there will be little action on significantly improving the conditions of the global precarious workforce until there are conditions present that enable, or perhaps force, dramatic social change to occur, as described at the beginning of this chapter. Counting simply on the goodwill of humanity or the goodwill of individual countries is bound to lead to significant disappointment, even if there is some modest success. Nevertheless, we can consider conditions that could lead to the shifting of the business environment, to bring forth the necessary political will to allow an across-the-board improvement of precarious worker conditions.

One condition that could bring this about is the significant shift in the world's climate that is now underway. Climate change is indisputable. A wide variety of organizations are now taking mitigating actions to begin to shield themselves from the effects of climate change. Public and private enterprises, geopolitical entities, as well as not-for-profits are taking actions in an attempt to mitigate the effects on themselves, if not society more broadly. Some of those effects will include the risk that increasing severity of weather events brings, the rise in temperatures to the point where some locations will become uninhabitable, and significant pieces of once prosperous farmland becoming arid and unproductive. In 2016, just under 1.7 billion people lived in areas where temperatures are rising and will continue to rise to the point where they affect day-to-day liveability; the majority of these are in Asia and sub-Saharan Africa (Costley & Forster, 2021). In May of 2022, Jacobabad in Pakistan was named the hottest city on Earth, where workers toil in fields with temperatures exceeding 50°C (122°F) at times (Greenfield & Dickie, 2022).

At least some of the species that we count on for food, and other species that are critical to the planet's ecology, will not be able to survive. Potable water in some locations will become scarce or non-existent. Sea levels are rising as vast amounts of water that had been locked up in ice melt, flooding coastal areas and causing low-lying islands to disappear underwater. Global ocean currents, or gyres, in the North Atlantic, South Atlantic, Indian, North Pacific, and South Pacific Oceans will shift or disappear, causing even greater weather disruptions. This shift is already underway (Boers, 2021). Poorer nations will suffer disproportionately, and the billions of precarious workers within those nations will suffer even more.

Think of the millions of people from around the Middle East that fled the failures of the Arab Spring brought on by corruption and economic hardship in Syria, Libya, Egypt, Sudan, Algeria, Yemen, and others. Think of the number of refugees that attempt to enter into the United States each year, fleeing crime, violence, and economic hardship back in their own countries. By one estimate (as of 2021), there are 68.5 million people worldwide who have fled their homes because of conflict, unrest, or disaster. While the arrival of refugees and asylum seekers in Europe and the United States gets most of the media attention, 85% of the world's displaced people have fled elsewhere. Uganda hosts more than a million refugees from South Sudan, the Democratic Republic of the Congo, and other neighboring countries. Other conflicts and catastrophes have caused people in North Africa, Ukraine, the Caucasus, South Asia, and Latin America to flee their homes (Edwards, 2018). According to the UN, as of June 1, 2022, more than 14 million people have fled their homes since Russia's invasion of Ukraine.

Now think about what would happen if not millions but billions of poor people without access to sufficient water (Solomon, 2010), food, and liveable temperatures (Woetzel et al., 2020) went on the move, fleeing uninhabitable environments. While those living in rich countries might think they will be insulated from turmoil happening elsewhere, at that scale, no country, location, or economy will be insulated. Wars could be fought over water, farmland, and liveable conditions. One could speculate that this could bring about economic collapse on a scale not seen previously, causing the potential collapse of societies. Bringing together the various experts and professionals who are currently working on issues of climate change, precarious work, and economics to perform linkage research on how these areas relate and impact each other would seem to be a very worthwhile endeavor. The UN could help by facilitating such integrative work.

Over the centuries, there have been doomsayers who have predicted that the world's resources cannot feed the population, or that disease will wipe out humanity. Each time we have risen to the challenges we have faced and have overcome them. And today, again, there is a path forward that can potentially avoid the worst of these predictions. While we likely may not agree with all of their actions and thoughts, both Benjamin Franklin and Henry Ford made important contributions to the solution. Benjamin Franklin was certain that the path to a sustainable democracy lay though a large, well-educated middle class (Pangle, 2007). Henry Ford felt that his workers should be able to afford the cars they produced, and he paid them accordingly (Cwiek, 2014).

A well-educated middle class that has the financial resources to cope with the hardships that climate change will bring is more likely to be able to stay in place and adapt to the changing climate impacts that are occurring. They would be able to afford housing with air conditioning, water, food, and medical care. Precarious workers moving from teetering on the brink of financial ruin, hunger, and homelessness to becoming a resourceful middle class may stave off the worst of the displacement. In order for this to happen, however, many other things would need to fall into place as well. Vast amounts of non-polluting and cheap energy will be required to build a resilient society that can cope with the hardships to come. Technological breakthroughs will also drive advances in our ability to cope, and science needs to be front and center in our approach (European Environmental Agency, 2017). From a societal perspective, the UN SDGs provide guidelines that can be used to begin shifting precarious workers into a robust and resilient middle class.

The UN SDGs

The contributions of the UN and its affiliates to the issue of precarious work are that they provide aspirations and standards. Membership in all these organizations is voluntary, and their principles and conventions are not enforceable. At best, there are annual reports describing adherence, rules for expulsion from the Global Compact, and a process of lodging complaints against members of the OECD. But the years since the Universal Declaration of Human Rights (1948) have only increased the number of precarious positions in the world of work, and it is unlikely that any process for tackling the negative aspects of precarious work will be universally enforceable. It will be necessary for each nation to accept and enforce any solution to the issue. We can look to the work of the UN for ideas that are at least acknowledged as worthy, even if not enforced. It is a step in the right direction.

The SDGs are the United Nations' current blueprint for the viability of the planet and the future success of its people. They are a call for action by all countries, in all economic circumstances, to promote prosperity while also protecting the planet. The SDGs recognize that ending poverty must go hand-in-hand with strategies that build economic growth and that address a range of social needs including education, health, social protection, and job opportunities, while also tackling climate change and environmental protection. As such, and spanning the years 2015–2030, the SDGs constitute the sequel to the earlier Millennium Development Goals (MDGs) which covered the years 2000–2015. They are the product of work done by a number of bodies, especially the United Nations Open Working Group, which reviewed the MDGs and revised and expanded them, resulting in a total of 17 new goals (United Nations Department of Economic and Social Affairs, 2014). The scope of these goals is broad and includes many aspects of human endeavor, but the SDGs most relevant to precarious work are as follows:

- Goal 8: Promote sustained, inclusive, and sustainable economic growth, full and productive employment, and decent work for all.
- Goal 9: Build resilient infrastructure, promote inclusive and sustainable industrialization, and foster innovation.
- Goal 10: Reduce inequalities within and among countries.
- Goal 17: Strengthen the means of implementation and revitalize the global partnership for sustainable development.

The problems raised by the concept of precarious work have multiple implications, especially for the achievement of SDG 8, and vice versa. The establishment of decent work (Chapter 1) as the gold standard for the future demands the reduction of the current levels of precarious work or, at the very least, the mitigation of its negative consequences and the elimination of its most egregious factors. Precarious work, if allowed to continue in its present forms, presents considerable obstacles to the achievement of decent work. For example, work that is temporary, part-time, uncertain, and unpredictable, pays less than a living wage, or offers little to no control over working hours or conditions falls far short of a livelihood which enables workers to not only survive but also thrive and develop into a resilient middle class.

Many of the tools at our disposal in the field of I/O psychology and HWP are crucial components for moving precarious work into the realm of decent work and, by extension, creating a world in which all workers can enjoy full and productive employment. These include assessment/evaluation, recruitment/selection, job analysis, performance management, training/enterprise development, prohibition of discrimination, respectful treatment, and fair reward and recognition systems (Reichman & Berry, 2012).

As described above, the potential value of decent work and full and productive employment extends beyond the mitigation of the effects of precarious work. Through such measures as evidence-based interventions (for instance, self-efficacy training), unemployment can be shortened, and associated psychosocial issues can be reduced (Eden & Aviram, 1993). In addition, the benefits of decent work include the promotion of psychosocial empowerment, which in turn fosters self-worth and self-efficacy for those living in lower income contexts (Deshpande & Sethi, 2010). Along with reforms to the wage system itself, this can engender the resilience to rise above low incomes and achieve truly living wages—a sort of virtuous circle.

By continuing to focus on SDG 8, the world stands poised, potentially, to reduce the impact of precarious work, and the implications of this, for the greater development and prosperity of the workforce. By raising wages and making rewards fairer, reducing precariousness would also, by definition, help to reduce inequality: an aim of SDG 10.

SDG 9, which stresses innovation, brings an important perspective to bear on some of the solutions to precarious work. Some examples of innovation in practice include the use of technology to facilitate international development initiatives. One of these is the SmartAid project based at Otago Polytechnic in New Zealand in collaboration with Rotary International, which has the goal of developing teams of e-volunteers who can assist in various projects from a distance, enhancing the effective management of aid work and aid workers (Atkins & Thompson, 2012). Closely related to innovation is the burgeoning arena of entrepreneurship, which also plays a crucial role in addressing precarious work.

Moving from policy to practice is a major challenge for most organizations (Berry et al., 2016). SDG 17, with its emphasis on global partnerships, will play a key role in implementing the steps necessary to counteract precarious work and, indeed, significantly reduce or eliminate much of it. Such partnerships will become more and more vital in securing long-lasting improvements in the world of work, and we will detail our recommendations in this regard later in this chapter.

Eliminating Precarious Work from Our World

There is little doubt that the people of the world, and likely the world itself, would be better off if they had a secure way of working for a living for themselves and their families. It would be best if they had constant jobs with sufficient income and time off, and the confidence that these jobs would be available as long as one's performance was acceptable. The question is, how does humanity create an economy and a culture to guarantee this option? No single institution can accomplish this change alone. It will take a universal commitment, which should be instituted and monitored by the United Nations. A new department should be created within the UN with the singular purpose of reducing or even eliminating precarious work by means of the steps described below. This would be in keeping with the SDGs, especially Goals 1, 8, 9, 10, and 17, that focus on eliminating poverty while creating decent work, business enterprises, and collaboration among organizations.

The areas that are necessary to put into practice in order to reach the goal of eliminating precarious work are:

- Universal acceptance of a goal, before 2030, to end precarious work; the establishment of businesses able to provide full-time employment, which necessitates entrepreneurship plus the education necessary to become an entrepreneur and also an effective employee in newly created enterprises; the guarantee by governments to implement living wages and a social floor; governments guaranteeing workers the human rights set forth in the declaration, as well as the principles of the Global Compact, ILO, and in the UN Conventions; and
- Greater involvement of civic organizations that look out for the human rights and wellbeing of the citizens of their countries. Examples of such organizations are the NAACP and American Civil Liberties Union in the United States, the African Union in Africa, and international organizations such as Lawyers Without Borders. The process would be modeled on the tripartite agreement of the ILO to include representatives from labor in order to guarantee the right of workers to organize and allow these representatives to protect the human rights of workers; and representatives from business organizations to promote the necessity of business success and business growth, advise on educating people currently in precarious jobs to function effectively in permanent jobs, and take an active role in promoting entrepreneurship. In addition, there would be a renewed focus on encouraging the world of work to

recognize and reward the often-overlooked skills that many informal workers already have. Going forward, measuring the skills and abilities of precarious workers can be instrumental in making those workers eligible for decent forms of formal employment. Finally, there would be representatives from the governments who will have the responsibility to promote the establishment of these ideas within their nations and to develop a system to hold their countrymen accountable for implementing these activities with penalties for deviation from the process.

Universal Acceptance

This will require the collective action of the UN, labor, management, government, and civic organizations to promote the goal of terminating precarious work. Some of the same procedures used to promote the acceptance of the SDGs would be applicable here. Together, these organizations could advocate and promote national associations for the promotion of security in work in their countries, which would take on the task of influencing attitudes toward the promotion of secure jobs and an end to precarious work.

Entrepreneurship

There is evidence from the work of psychologists such as Michael Frese that entrepreneurship can be taught: people who complete his 12-week action-oriented program start successful businesses that then employ other people in decent jobs (Bischoff et al., 2014). This program taught students entrepreneurship principles, gave them experiences in putting the principles into action, and gave them feedback on their performance. One year after training, 51% of the students owned their own business (Bischoff et al., 2014). The proposed UN department would arrange for training instructors to teach businesses and non-profit organizations about forms of entrepreneurship around the world, while labor, management, and civic organizations would work with their constituencies and government to provide the financing and promotion of training for their precarious workforce. The department would also promote the development of collectives and consortia among the employers who provide the precarious work and among workers who engage in this precarious work.

Living Wage and Social Floor

A living wage is defined as the minimum income necessary for an employee to meet minimum standards of subsistence in their region and to ensure a sustainable quality of life and work (Carr et al., 2018). New Zealand has established this living wage level for its country, and there is research through Project GLOW

(Global Living Organizational Wage) which has co-determined the living wage necessary to sustain workers and keep the economy operating successfully (Project GLOW: Global Living Organizational Wage, n.d.). A proposed new UN department will work to encourage the development of algorithms to define living wages in different countries and regions. Once living wages are established, the tripartite group will work to see that it is included as the standard within their country. They will also promote the establishment of a social floor to provide payments for citizens who, as a result of mishaps in their lives or the faltering of the economy, do not have enough money to support themselves and their families.

Human Rights at Work

A primary focus of the government representatives would be to pass legislation that incorporates the Declaration of Human Rights and the ten principles of the Global Compact, along with penalties for businesses violating those principles. The representatives of labor, management, and civic organizations would also work to promote the legislation through political activities in their countries. The termination of precarious work and its benefits to humanity can only be accomplished through shared responsibility of labor, management organizations, civic organizations, and governments, under the auspices of the UN.

Acknowledgments

A special thank you to Amanda Dundas for editorial assistance and Martin Flores for research assistance.

References

Atkins, S., & Thompson, L. F. (2012). Online volunteers and smart-aid. In S. C. Carr, M. MacLachlan, & A. Furnham (Eds.), *Humanitarian work psychology* (pp. 266–292). Palgrave Macmillan.

Barak, A. (2015). *Human dignity, the constitutional value and the constitutional right*. Cambridge University Press.

Beck, R. (1978). *Motivation theories and principles*. Prentice-Hall.

Berry, M. O., McWha-Hermann, I., & Maynard, D. C. (2016). Humanitarian work psychology and the millennium development goals. In I. McWha-Hermann, D. C. Maynard, & M. O. Berry (Eds.), *Humanitarian work psychology and the global development agenda: Case studies and interventions* (pp. 205–217). Routledge.

Bischoff, K. M., Glelnik, M. M., & Frese, M. (2014). Entrepreneurship training in developing countries. In W. Reichman (Ed.), *Industrial and organizational psychology help the vulnerable: Serving the underserved* (pp. 92–119). Palgrave Macmillan.

Boers, N. (2021). Observation-based early-warning signals for a collapse of the Atlantic Meridional Overturning Circulation. *Nature Climate Change*, *11*, 680–699.

Brewer, J. (2021). *Unwinding anxiety: New science shows how to break cycles of worry and fear to heal your mind.* Penguin.

Brooks, S., & Saltzman, J. (2016). *Creating the vital organization, balancing short-term profits with long-term success.* Palgrave Macmillan.

Carr, S., Maleka, M., Meyer, I., Barry, M. I., Harr, J., Parker, J., Arrowsmith, J., Yao, C., Hodgetts, D., Jones, H., Young-Hausner, A., Afeaki-Mafile'o, E., Rasmussen, A., Alefaio-Tugia, S., Falealili, B., Mafile'o, K., Pikula, T., Wolfgramm, N., 'Uhila, H., … & Naithani, A. (2018). How can wages sustain a living? By getting ahead of the curve. *Sustainability Science, 13*(4), 901–917. https://doi.org/10.1007/s11625-018-0560-7

Cornell University. (2018). *Remembering the 1911 Triangle Factory Fire.* https://trianglefire.ilr.cornell.edu/story/introduction.html

Costley, D., & Forster, N. (2021, November 12). AP analysis: Exposure to extreme heat has tripled since 1983. *AP News.* https://apnews.com/article/climate-science-asia-pacific-africa-environment-and-nature-aef81a77175098d899eb77e751aa7f53

Cwiek, S. (2014, January 27). The middle class took off 100 years ago … thanks to Henry Ford? *NPR.* https://www.npr.org/2014/01/27/267145552/the-middle-class-took-off-100-years-ago-thanks-to-henry-ford

de la Sablonniere, R. (2017). Toward a psychology of social change: A typology of social change. *Frontiers in Psychology, 8,* 397. https://doi.org/10.3389/fpsyg.2017.00397

Deshpande, D., & Sethi, S. (2010). Role and position of women's empowerment in Indian society. *International Research Journal, 1*(17), 24–27.

Eden, D., & Aviram, A. (1993). Self-efficacy training to speed re-employment: Helping people to help themselves. *Journal of Applied Psychology, 78*(3), 352–360. https://doi.org/10.1037/0021-9010.78.3.352

Edwards, A. (2018). *Forced displacement at record 68.5 million.* UNHCR. https://www.unhcr.org/en-us/news/stories/2018/6/5b222c494/forced-displacement-record-685-million.html

Encyclopaedia Britannica. (2022). *French revolution.* https://www.britannica.com/event/French-Revolution

European Environmental Agency (2017). *Energy and climate change.* https://www.eea.europa.eu/signals/signals-2017/articles/energy-and-climate-change

Figueroa, M., Guallpa, L., Wolf, A., Tsitouras, G., & Hernández, H. C. (2021). *Essential but unprotected: App-based food couriers in New York City.* Los Deliveristas/Workers Justice Project.

Ghai, D. (2003). Decent work: Concept and indicators. *International Labour Review, 142*(2), 113.

Goldin, C. D. (1991). The role of World War II in the rise of women's employment. *The American Economic Review, 81*(4), 741–756. http://www.jstor.org/stable/2006640

Greenfield, C., & Dickey, G. (2022). In hottest city on Earth, mothers bear brunt of climate change. *Reuters.* https://www.reuters.com/investigates/special-report/climate-change-pakistan-women/

Hüffmeier, J., & Zacher, H. (2021). The basic income: Initiating the needed discussion in industrial, work, and organizational psychology. *Industrial and Organizational Psychology, 14,* 531–562.

International Labour Organization. (2021). *The Rana Plaza accident and its aftermath.* https://www.ilo.org/global/topics/geip/WCMS_614394/lang--en/index.htm

International Labour Organization. (2022). *Declaration on fundamental principles and rights at work and its follow-up.* https://www.ilo.org/wcmsp5/groups/public/—ed_norm/—declaration/documents/normativeinstrument/wcms_716594.pdf

Jedwab, R., Johnson, N., & Koyama, M. (2020). *The economic impact of the Black Death* (IIEP-WP-2020-14). Institute for International Economic Policy, Elliott School of International Affairs, The George Washington University. https://www2.gwu.edu/~iiep/assets/docs/papers/2020WP/JedwabIIEP2020-14.pdf

Lach, E. (2021, September 21). A search for the delivery worker in a viral Hurricane Ida video. *The New Yorker*. https://www.newyorker.com/news/our-local-correspondents/a-search-for-the-delivery-worker-in-a-viral-hurricane-ida-video

Lewin, K. (2008). *Resolving social conflicts & field theory in social science*. American Psychological Association.

Lucas, K. (2017). Workplace dignity. *The International Encyclopaedia of Organizational Communication, 4*, 2549–2562. https://doi.org/10.1002/9781118955567.wbieoc222

McWha-Hermann, I., Maynard, D. C., & Berry, M. O. (Eds.) (2016). *Humanitarian work psychology and the global development agenda: Case studies and interventions*. Routledge.

Olson-Buchanan, J. B., & Vera, D. R. (2021). Basic income, cognitive capacity, and the workplace: The role of I-O psychology in the interdisciplinary research agenda to reduce poverty. *Industrial and Organizational Psychology, 14*, 573–576.

Open Access Government. (2020, July 8). *The cost of fashion: 4.1 million Bangladeshi garment workers*. https://www.openaccessgovernment.org/bangladeshi-garment-workers/89939/

Pangle, L. S. (2007). *The political philosophy of Benjamin Franklin.* Johns Hopkins University Press.

Project GLOW: Global Living Organizational Wage. (n.d.). *Project GLOW.* https://projectglow.net

Reichman, W., & Berry, M. O. (2012). The evolution of industrial and organizational psychology. In S. C. Carr, M. MacLachlan, & A. Furnham (Eds.), *Humanitarian work psychology* (pp. 34–51). Palgrave Macmillan.

Rosenberg, E. (2021, October 12). A record number of workers are quitting their jobs, empowered by new leverage. *Boston Globe*. https://www.bostonglobe.com/2021/10/12/business/record-number-workers-are-quitting-their-jobs-empowered-by-new-leverage/

Ruggie, J., & Nelson, T. (2015). *Human rights and the OECD guidelines for multinational enterprises: Normative innovations and implementation challenges* (Corporate Social Responsibility Initiative Working Paper No. 66). John F. Kennedy School of Government, Harvard University.

Rylander, P. (2016). Coaches' bases of power and coaching effectiveness in team sports. *International Sport Coaching Journal, 3*(2), 128–144. https://doi.org/10.1123/iscj.2015-0046

Saltzman, J. (2012). *Drive to work and social safety nets*. Presentation to high level conference of the Economic and Social Council, United Nations July 9, 2012. https://jeffreysaltzman.wordpress.com/2012/07/09/drive-to-work-and-social-safety-nets/

Saltzman, J. (2021). *Decent work: Pandemic impact on employee expectations* [Video]. YouTube. https://www.youtube.com/watch?v=JwpdsYxQ1Lw

Saner, R., & Yiu, L. (2014). Designing learning systems for poverty reduction in least developed countries. In W. Reichman (Ed.), *Industrial and organizational psychology help the vulnerable: Serving the underserved.* Palgrave MacMillan.

Saxena, M. (2017). Workers in poverty: An insight into informal workers around the world. *Industrial and Organizational Psychology: Perspectives on Science and Practice, 10*(3), 367–370.

Schein, V. E. (2012). Women, work and poverty: Reflections on research for social change. In S. C. Carr, M. MacLachlan, & A. Furnham (Eds.), *Humanitarian work psychology* (pp. 249–265). Palgrave Macmillan.

Sherman, J., Smith, S., Mischkind, L., DelDuco, S., Sirota, D., Klein, D., Stathatos, P., & Saltzman, J. (2003). *Tornadoes, teaching and terrorism* [PowerPoint Presentation]. In 18th Annual Conference of the Society of Industrial Organizational Psychology, Orlando, FL, USA.

Solomon, S. (2010). *Water: The epic struggle for wealth, power and civilization.* Harper Collins.

Tajfel, H., & Turner, J. C. (1979). An integrative theory of intergroup conflict. In W. G. Austin & S. Worchel (Eds.), *The social psychology of intergroup relations* (pp. 33–47). Brooks Cole.

United Nations. (1948). *Universal declaration of human rights.* https://www.un.org./en/about-us/universal-declaration-of-human-rights

United Nations. (2000). *United Nations global compact.* https://www.unglobalcompact.org

United Nations. (2011). *Guiding principles on business and human rights.* https://www.ohchr.org/sites/default/files/Documents/Publications/GuidingPrinciplesBusinessHR_EN.pdf

United Nations. (2020). *The world of work and COVID-19.* https://unsdg.un.org/sites/default/files/2020-07/policy-brief-the_world_of_work_and_covid-19.pdf

United Nations Department of Economic and Social Affairs. (2014). *Open Working Group proposal for Sustainable Development Goals.* http://sustainabledevelopment.un.org/sdgsproposal.html

Wang, H., Paulson, K. R., Pease, S. A., Watson, S., Comfort, H., Zheng, P., Aravkin, A. Y., Bisignano, C., Barber, R. M., Alam, T., Fuller, J. E., May, E. A., Jones, D. P., Frisch, M. E., Abbafati, C., Adolph, C., Allorat, A., Amlag, J. O., Bang-Jensen, B., … & Murray, C. J. L. (2022). Estimating excess mortality due to the COVID-19 pandemic: A systematic analysis of COVID-19-related mortality, 2020–2021. *Lancet, 399*, 1513–1536. https://doi.org/10.1016/S0140-6736(21)02796-3

Weiss, H. M., & Rupp, D. E. (2011). Experiencing work: An essay on a person-centric work-psychology. *Industrial and Organizational Psychology: Perspectives on Science and Practice, 4*, 83–97.

Woetzel, J., Pinner, D., Samandari, H, Gupta, R., Engel, H., Krishnan, M., & Powis, C. (2020, November 25). Will India get too hot to work? *McKinsey Sustainability.* https://www.mckinsey.com/business-functions/sustainability/our-insights/will-india-get-too-hot-to-work

3

PSYCHOLOGY OF WORKING THEORY

Decent Work for Decent Lives

Annamaria Di Fabio, Mary Beth Medvide, and Maureen E. Kenny

Our sustainability in the 21st century is threatened by numerous global challenges that undermine collective and individual wellbeing. In this chapter, we focus on the challenges posed by poverty and growing levels of social and income inequality. We argue that the psychology of working (Blustein, 2006, 2013; Duffy et al., 2016) offers a heuristic framework for guiding research, policy, and practice in vocational and organizational psychology that can increase access to decent work and promote sustainable lives. Through its connection with the Decent Work Agenda of the International Labour Organization (ILO, 2008, 2013) and the United Nations Sustainable Development Goals (UN SDGs, United Nations, 2021), the psychology of working describes the psychological impacts that macrolevel social and economic challenges can have on individuals, organizations, and communities and suggests opportunities for individual and systemic intervention to increase access to decent work and build lives that are sustainable, and hopefully flourishing (Blustein, Kenny, Autin et al., 2019).

Blustein (2006, 2013) initially developed the psychology of working perspective as an inclusive alternative to traditional career-development theories that focused on the work lives of those with the most privilege. The psychology of working delineates the role of work in people's lives, particularly those at the margins of society who face substantial economic and social barriers in accessing work. These efforts build upon the work of 20th-century career theorists such as Super (1980) while also calling for a more substantive discussion of the sociocultural milieu in which individuals' work lives are nested. Whereas the dominant theories of the 20th century were largely focused on individual decisions within an ideal social environment, Blustein recognizes the impacts

DOI: 10.4324/9781003440444-4

of various forms of oppression in constraining people's vocational choices and foreclosing many pathways to meaningful work. Thus, the psychology of working perspective questions the taken-for-granted assumptions of prevalent theories with the goal of developing a more inclusive way to study work in people's lives and to develop avenues for individual and societal change.

Psychology of working theory (PWT) is guided by a number of central tenets (Blustein, 2013; Blustein, Kenny, Di Fabio et al., 2019). These tenets include: (1) work functions as a major context for individual wellbeing and the welfare of communities; (2) work contributes to wellbeing through its potential to satisfy fundamental human needs for survival and power, for social connection, and for self-determination; (3) access to decent work is inevitably shaped, constrained, and facilitated by one's context, including family background, cultural identity, and powerful social, economic, political and historical forces; (4) the labor market is changing and will continue to undergo rapid change; and (5) work includes efforts in the marketplace and in caregiving contexts and shares psychological space with many salient life domains. Furthermore, the study of working should be inclusive, encompassing everyone who wants to work, and should embrace multiple research epistemologies.

The tenets of this framework incorporate social justice values, highlighting the effects of social status, discrimination, marginalization, economic barriers, and low work volition in constraining access to decent work and wellbeing. Blustein's (2006, 2013) emphasis on social justice is aligned with a growing paradigm shift within the career-development literature, represented by the work of Richardson (1993, 2009) and other scholars, who are challenging traditional career narratives that have centered the experiences of those with the most privilege in society. Further, as discussed throughout this chapter, the psychology of working embraces the work of international organizations, such as the ILO (2008, 2013), which identified access to decent and dignified work as a basic human right. PWT extends the attention given by the ILO to the political and economic dimensions of decent work by highlighting the psychological experiences of the individual and the complex interplay of macrolevel and psychological factors in shaping the work lives of individuals (Duffy et al., 2016).

PWT was developed by Duffy and colleagues (2016) to extend the work of Blustein (2006, 2013) and empirically verify the claims drawn from Blustein's qualitative studies and conceptual papers. Consistent with Blustein's (2006, 2013) conceptual work, the empirical model foregrounds the social and economic conditions of work as major determinants of access to decent work. According to the PWT model, and consistent with Blustein's assumptions, decent work is associated with greater life satisfaction and wellbeing through its role in meeting human needs for survival, power, social connection, and self-determination. The model furthermore specifies social and economic conditions that influence access to decent work through their impact on mediating psychological factors.

In addition, the model specifies moderators hypothesized to reduce the influence of marginalization and economic constraints on access to decent work and wellbeing.

The PWT model has been evaluated through a growing body of research, with implications for interventions also emerging in the literature. The practice implications of PWT include interventions at the individual level, referred to as the psychology of working counseling (PWC), and interventions at the systems level, referred to as the psychology of working system intervention (PWSI) (Blustein, Kenny, Autin et al., 2019). PWC focuses on intervention with individuals to develop their psychological competencies, aligned with the mediators and moderators in the PWT model, which can facilitate access to decent work despite social and economic constraints. PWSI, however, focuses on dismantling structures and changing policies that sustain marginalization and inequality and thereby limit access to decent work. PWSI may entail social and political advocacy and work at the community, organizational, and government levels to develop new policies and structures and develop social capital to effect structural change. Sound research grounded in concepts related to PWT is important for informing PWC and for advancing PWSI efforts in social and political advocacy (see also, Jyoti & Arora, Chapter 6; Saner & Yiu, Chapter 5; Searle & McWha-Hermann, Chapter 4).

As part of our effort in this chapter to parse the components of the PWT model and discuss related concepts and research, we begin with a discussion of decent work, as defined by the ILO (2008, 2013), and as a focus of the psychology of working; we then present the PWT model, along with specified PWT mediators and moderators for access to decent work. After delineating the components of PWT, we discuss the importance of research in advancing a PWSI policy agenda for tackling precarious work, promoting policy to overcome poverty and inequality, and advancing the goals of sustainability, especially in light of the new work challenges in the post-pandemic world.

Decent Work and the Psychology of Working

Securing decent work is the central goal and outcome variable in the psychology of working (Duffy et al., 2016). PWT draws on the conceptualization of decent work developed by the ILO (2008, 2013), which, like PWT, emphasizes the importance of decent work for wellbeing. The ILO recognizes that decent work is an aspiration for people's working lives, whereby work can contribute to the social and economic advancement of individuals, families, and communities. PWT conceptualizes decent work as a multifaceted construct rooted in individuals' psychological experiences of working. In PWT, decent work is operationalized as encompassing working conditions that are safe and free from physical, emotional, or mental abuse, offering adequate compensation and opportunities for free time (Haar, Chapter 17), offering access to healthcare, and espousing organizational values that support family and social wellbeing (Duffy et al., 2016; Klug et al., Chapter 21).

PWT seeks to understand the working lives of everyone who would like to work by considering the direct and indirect influences of experiences of marginalization and economic constraints as primary determinants of decent work. These predictors reflect the effects of limited power in society and restricted access to the economic and social resources needed to survive and ideally thrive (Duffy & Dik, 2009; Duffy et al., 2012). Decent work is delineated in the PWT (Duffy et al., 2017) as helping to satisfy three basic human needs: survival and power, social connection, and self-determination (Blustein, 2006, 2013; Duffy et al., 2016). Survival and power needs relate to securing necessary financial resources, as well as building prestige and social status that provide a sense of influence and respect in the world. Social connection includes feelings of belonging in social relationships at work and a sense of connection to the larger social world through the contribution of one's work. Self-determination refers to the experience of meaning, competence, and autonomy by engaging in work that is interesting, meaningful, and advances one's goals. The fulfillment of these three basic needs contributes to overall satisfaction at work, and general wellbeing beyond work (Duffy et al., 2017; Haar, Chapter 17).

Decent work as an outcome in the PWT model is also impacted by intermediate variables that moderate and mediate the direct influence of marginalization and economic constraints. Mediating variables, such as work volition and career adaptability, capture individuals' abilities to reflect upon career decisions, to act with intention, and respond effectively to a changing world of work. Work volition is the perception of choice in career decision-making despite barriers related to marginalization and limited economic opportunities (Duffy & Dik, 2009; Duffy et al., 2012). Career adaptability refers to the presence of psychological resources for coping with current and anticipated future tasks in career development (Savickas, 2002) and to perceptions of one's capacity to manage and adjust to future changes in work (Rottinghaus et al., 2005).

The moderators specified in the PWT model include a proactive personality, critical consciousness, social support, and economic conditions. Proactive personality represents a trait or tendency to anticipate and take personal initiative or action to influence one's environment and circumvent challenges (Li et al., 2010). Critical consciousness has three dimensions: critical reflection on social and structural aspects of societal discrimination; political efficacy as the perceived capacity to act and effect social and political change; and critical action as the experience of taking action (individually or collectively) to reduce marginalization (Freire, 1993; Watts et al., 2011). Social support entails the perception that support is available from family, friends, significant others, and one's community, to cope with difficulties related to marginalization and economic constraints (Cohen & Wills, 1985). Economic conditions include the unemployment rate, accessibility of living wages, job advancement opportunities, availability of training, and other economic factors that impact access to decent work (e.g., ILO, 2008, 2013).

The PWT model described above drew from existing theory and research but was designed to stimulate further research on pathways to decent work by integrating economic, sociological, and psychological perspectives. Duffy et al. (2016) explicated the model in the hope it would be evaluated, modified, and expanded by researchers in varied contexts across the globe. Existing research has focused primarily on adults in the US and Western societies, especially those who are most vulnerable to marginalization due to social class and societal biases (e.g., Duffy et al., 2018). Duffy et al. (2018) tested the fundamental aspects of the PWT among employed adults across varied racial and ethnic identities, documenting hypothesized associations between economic resources, marginalization, work volition, and career adaptability in relation to decent work. A growing body of scholarship evaluating the PWT model is emerging in varied international contexts, including Turkey (Kozan et al., 2019) and Asia (i.e., Kim et al., 2019; Wang et al., 2019). Duffy and colleagues developed the Decent Work Scale (DWS; Duffy et al., 2017) to assess components of decent work from a psychological perspective. Recent research in the US and other nations (e.g., Di Fabio & Kenny, 2019; Duffy et al., 2020) has examined components of the scale and their relationships with work satisfaction and wellbeing. PWT research has also been published for groups who experience varied types of marginalization, including LGBTQ (Douglass et al., 2017), immigrants (Autin et al., 2018; Cassim, Chapter 20), young people (Kenny et al., 2022), and people with disabilities (Gilson et al., 2022). Fewer studies to date have focused on the role of the hypothesized moderating factors (Autin et al., 2021; Douglass et al., 2020; Kim & Allan, 2021; Wang et al., 2019).

With regards to intervention, PWC typically focuses attention on building PWT moderators, including social support, critical consciousness, and proactive personality, as means for reducing the negative impacts of social and economic constraints (Blustein, Kenny, Autin et al., 2019; see also, Jiang et al., Chapter 18). PWC also seeks to strengthen the hypothesized PWT mediators of work volition and career adaptability. Career-development education represents one mechanism for developing these capacities with high-school age youth (Kenny et al., 2019; Kenny & Tsai, 2020). The proposed PWT approach to career-development intervention focuses attention on the development of youth purpose, critical consciousness, social support, and proactive personality as resources for coping with marginalization and continuous change in the work context (van Hooft & van Hoye, Chapter 19). With regards to PWSI, Blustein, Kenny, Di Fabio et al. (2019) identified several possible research directions guided by PWT that might advance efforts to enhance decent work at the policy, organizational, and personal levels. These research directions include the impact of psychological and social protections in the context of precarious work and ways to make work more just. In the following sections, we highlight some of these research and policy initiatives and their implications for PWSI. We begin with a discussion of precarious work as a threat to decent work and review some research that has grown out of the PWT agenda suggesting the need for enhanced social and psychological protections in the context of precarious work (see Jiang et al., Chapter 18).

Precarious Work and the Psychology of Working

Although the availability of decent work has long been problematic for much of the world's population, newly emerging challenges in the late 20th century and the early 21st century have also transformed the world of work in ways that can empower or oppress individuals. Globalization, technological change, the global recession of 2007–2010, and most recently the global pandemic have not only increased underemployment (O'Shea et al., 15) and unemployment (O'Shea et al., Chapter 15) but also growing economic inequality (Carr, Hopner, et al., Chapter 10). These changes have also coincided with the rise in precarious work (Blustein, Kenny, Di Fabio et al., 2019; Blustein et al., 2020). Precarious work can be considered the absence of decent work as it lacks the qualities of decent work defined by the ILO (2008) and elaborated on by Duffy et al. (2016), including safe working conditions, adequate work-life balance, organizational support, sufficient pay, and access to benefits. PWT scholars (e.g., Blustein et al., 2020) have promoted research to understand the psychological dimensions of precarious work, in the belief that such research can inform both PWC and PWSI. Blustein et al. (2020) identified profiles of precarious work that highlight the ways in which precarious work fails to meet basic human needs and the standards for decent work. Allan et al. (2021) have proposed a psychological perspective that connects the literature on precarious work with research across other disciplines. Allan and colleagues have noted how the uncertainty of precarious work contributes not only to unpredictable job and wage continuity but also to restricted rights, protections, and freedoms, which then limit workers' capacities to advocate for organizational and social change, and thus for conditions of decent work (Allan et al., 2021).

By focusing on the psychological experience of insecurity, instability, and powerlessness related to one's work, Allan et al. (2021) identified three categories of work precarity: precarity *of* work; precarity *at* work; and precarity *from* work. Precarity *of* work focuses on the fears and uncertainty related to loss of employment, income, and social relationships, while precarity *at* work reflects uncertainty and unpredictability related to worker psychosocial and physical safety, including fear of bullying, discrimination, social rejection, and harassment. Precarity *from* work reflects uncertainty and insecurity related to low wages, and lack of need satisfaction from employment in a precarious work situation. These three types of work precarity illustrate how precarious work is in opposition to decent work.

Allan et al. (2021) have developed the work precarity framework to promote research on the antecedents and outcomes of precarious work. In line with the PWT decent work model (Duffy et al., 2016), economic conditions and policies, and social and economic marginalization are considered antecedents of precarious work. Since precarious work is associated with structural and historical changes in organizations, the economy, and labor markets, the PWT model, and associated research findings may be used to highlight the adverse psychological consequences of the absence of decent work. Aligned with a PWSI perspective, the model may also be used to advocate for policy and structural changes, which attend to psychological and social protections associated with worker safety and increased worker power.

The work precarity model also proposes negative associations between precarious work and attitudes toward work, engagement at work, and commitment to a work organization. Outside of work, precarious work can contribute to low self-esteem, depression, and anxiety. The model also proposes that mediating factors, such as work volition, social support, resources, and social capital, serve as psychological mechanisms that mitigate the deleterious effects of work precarity on work and personal life. From a PWC perspective, the work precarity model can also inform efforts to build resilience, with a focus on strengthening proposed psychological mediators, and efforts to alleviate the negative psychological impacts of insecurity, instability, and powerlessness related to one's work.

Overcoming Poverty in the 21st Century: Minimum Wage and More

The decline in decent work and the rise in unemployment, underemployment, and precarious work are associated with growing poverty and income inequality across the globe. Poverty is broadly connected to wellbeing through its connection to healthcare, education, exposure to environmental toxins, and opportunities for active participation in political, work, and social life (Carr, 2021). Research and intervention related to income equality and fair and sustainable wages are thus aligned with the PWSI concern for advancing research and policy, and enhancing social and economic protections that make work more just (Blustein, Kenny, Di Fabio et al., 2019).

The challenge of overcoming poverty in the 21st century represents a critical policy and research agenda for vocational and organizational psychology, particularly when considering the connections between poverty, lack of decent work, and work precarity. Carr (2021) highlights two perspectives in antipoverty policy and research: an econometric approach and a subjective approach, which are not generally connected conceptually or theoretically. The connections between the two approaches highlight the immediate and long-term consequences of economic policy for human survival and wellbeing. The minimum wage represents one policy consideration that connects the econometric and subjective approaches to poverty that could help to ensure enhanced quality of life for many people (Carr, 2021; Carr et al., 2018).

A fair and adequate minimum wage is a fundamental component of decent work that is associated with the wellbeing of individuals, organizations, and society (Duffy et al., 2017). The ILO (2020) describes the minimum wage as the minimum pay required to facilitate economic growth by enhancing the labor income distribution, encouraging domestic consumption, and creating local employment. A perceived decent level of remuneration and perceived justice in determining wages have been associated with individuals' motivation, performance, and productivity in the workplace (Carr et al., 2018). Carr et al. (2016) expand the consideration of a decent or living wage beyond economic subsistence to encompass the quality of life at work and outside of work and identify psychological considerations related to living wage levels for workers from a humanitarian perspective. These extend to participation in organizational and social life and include the following: empowerment (meaning, self-efficacy, self-determination, and sense of power to influence), justice at work, identity at work, job satisfaction, and general wellbeing.

To advance understanding of the humanitarian considerations of the living wage, Yao et al. (2017) conducted a qualitative study with New Zealand workers to explore perceived wage effectiveness. Their findings suggest that focusing on a specific living wage rate could be conceptually limiting in comparison with a living wage range. Specifically, a pivotal range emerges where individuals move from self-assessed "survival" to a "decent" income. Furthermore, a living wage seems to have not only a monetary effect but also enhances wellbeing based on subjective perceptions of freedom, job satisfaction, equity, and security. The findings by Yao et al. (2017) thus broaden evidence regarding the impact of a living wage that considers personal and family wellbeing and indicates the need for a more comprehensive approach to organizational policy which includes concerns for sustainability and wellbeing, as articulated by the United Nations (United Nations, 2021).

With the aim of analyzing the contribution of wages toward a sustainable work-life balance, Haar et al. (2018) quantitatively tested a moderated-mediated model for New Zealand workers where pay at the living wage level and pay fairness were hypothesized to correlate with work-life balance and job satisfaction (Carr et al., 2018). The results revealed that when individuals moved from working poverty to a living wage, pay fairness and work-life balance had a greater salience for happiness at work. These results appear to support UN SDG 8 of decent work and economic growth, which highlights the importance of fairness, work-life balance, and job satisfaction, in addition to the monetary aspects of income, for wellbeing (United Nations, 2021). The findings also support the PWT definition of decent work that highlights the need for not only fair pay but also adequate free time and support for social and family values.

In sum, the research of Carr (2021) and others (Haar et al., 2018; Yao et al., 2017) present an evolution in the way in which poverty is evaluated by considering access to resources beyond money, and the subjective evaluation of wellbeing. To advance this agenda, Carr suggests that further research could individuate the "poverty threshold" where "on any given income (and/or asset) spectrum, subjective quality of life [is] actually transformed, from in poverty to feeling free from it" (Carr, 2021, p. 32). An amount of money that enables this change in quality of life could inform policy by signifying the basic threshold to exit from poverty to a fuller life (Carr, 2021). Since PWT is especially concerned with promoting wellbeing and emphasizes the connections across work and other life domains, these advancements in the understanding of poverty and minimum wage could inform PWT research and advocacy. During the COVID-19 pandemic, and especially in the future post-COVID period, the possibility of individuating the thresholds where individuals recognize subjective changes in their everyday quality of life appears even more important (Carr, 2021).

Making Work More Just: A Consideration of Job Crafting

Job design, or job crafting, represents one possible workplace-situated initiative for enhancing decent work and making work more just. Based on a review of recent research, Svicher and Di Fabio (2021) have highlighted how job crafting could enhance the capacity of workers to meet essential needs and outcomes as outlined by PWT, such as self-determination and work meaning (Bakker & Oerlemans, 2019; Hornung, 2019; Lee & Song, 2019; Petrou et al., 2017; Tims et al., 2016), and could enhance individual attributes such as proactive personality (Rudolph et al., 2017; Zhang et al., 2018), career adaptability (Federici et al., 2019; Woo, 2020), and work volition (Cheung et al., 2020; Kerksieck et al., 2019; Vogt et al., 2016). Evidence reveals, furthermore, that job crafting has particular benefits for vulnerable workers, including older workers (Nagy et al., 2019; Kooij et al., 2020; Zacher & Rudolph, 2019), unemployed workers (Hulshof et al., 2020a, 2020b), workers with disabilities (Brucker & Sundar, 2020), and migrant workers (Arasli et al., 2019). Di Fabio and Svicher (2021) delineated a framework of assessment and intervention to guide job crafting, especially for vulnerable workers. By promoting autonomous changes that better align workers' jobs with their needs, abilities, and vocational preferences, job crafting might make work more just for all human beings. Knowledge of how job crafting can provide access to decent work for more workers can be a tool for advocacy and organizational change in work settings.

Integration of Psychology of Working with Other Perspectives

The heuristic value of PWT in guiding policy and research is expanded by its alignment with other contemporary theories and initiatives within and outside of vocational psychology, some of which we highlight briefly below.

Sen's (1999) Capability Approach

The psychology of working (Blustein, 2006, 2013; Duffy et al., 2016) emphasizes the role of decent work in meeting not only needs for survival and relationships but also in offering opportunities for expanding self-determination and thriving (Teng-Calleja et al., Chapter 8). Wellbeing is related to the satisfaction of basic human needs for survival, relationships, and self-determination. Sen's (1999) capability approach proposes that development is related to freedom, and freedom from precariousness is viewed as essential for poverty reduction and human thriving (Teng-Calleja et al., Chapter 8). Though PWT focuses on the importance of economic conditions and self-determination for wellbeing, it aligns with Sen's (1999) capability approach and makes theoretical integration viable for practice and policy decisions (Searle & McWha-Hermann, Chapter 4).

The capability approach presents an alternative to conventional economic perspectives through its emphasis on the deleterious effects of poverty and discrimination for human agency and development. The capability approach also highlights the value of human flourishing as reflected in the Aristotelian concept of *eudaimonia* (Nussbaum, 1990). According to Sen (1999), quality of life depends first on the available commodities and economic resources, and then what individuals can achieve with accessible goods and services. Sen has criticized traditional welfare economic theories for positing a simple correspondence between economic wellbeing (income and commodity command) and utility (happiness and desire fulfillment).

PWT (Duffy et al., 2016) affirms the perspective described by Sen (1993) that both security that is afforded by economic resources and opportunities for personal and political freedom are necessary for individuals to implement agency and achieve their life goals (Blustein, 2019). This perspective is also aligned with the previously discussed research on the minimum wage (Carr, 2021). For both Sen (1993) and Blustein (2019), the working lives and wellbeing of individuals are shaped by a complex interplay of political, social, and economic factors at the macro- and individual levels, through contextual affordances and psychological factors. In this regard, therefore, Sen's (1999) capability approach and PWT share a vision for poverty reduction and enhanced human flourishing in precarious realities.

The Psychology of Sustainability and Sustainable Development

The Decent Work Agenda of the ILO has been incorporated into the 2015 SDGs (UN, 2021). The SDGs highlight the broad range of human rights and antipoverty goals necessary for the sustainability of decent life, including environmental sustainability and social fairness to women, the poor, and others marginalized by race, ethnicity, disability, religion, gender, or gender identity. The psychology of sustainability and sustainable development integrates the field of psychology with sustainability concerns and aligns with PWT in various ways (Di Fabio, 2017a, 2017b; Di Fabio & Peiró, 2018; Di Fabio & Rosen, 2018). At a microlevel, decent work fulfills the three basic PWT needs that are relevant to sustainability initiatives: the need for survival and power, the need for social connection, and the need for self-determination (Blustein, 2006, 2013). In promoting the need for "an adequate minimum wage" for vulnerable workers (ILO, 2020), the psychology of sustainability and sustainable development (Di Fabio & Rosen, 2018) addresses the PWT need for survival. Regarding the need for self-determination, the psychology of sustainability attends to the importance of fostering meaning in work (Di Fabio & Blustein, 2016) while also emphasizing the importance of the PWT need for social connection. The psychology of sustainability also embraces macrolevel policies recommended by the ILO (2008, 2013), including the promotion of sustained social and labor protections, ongoing social dialog among governments, workers, and employers, and the realization of human rights at work (Di Fabio & Svicher, 2021). Developments in the psychology of sustainability and sustainable development may provide the basis for further PWSI research and intervention (Carr, Hodgetts et al., Chapter 1).

PWT and the COVID-19 Pandemic

The COVID-19 pandemic increased existing inequalities in the world of work and created greater urgency for addressing issues of poverty, decent work, and precarious work (Duffy et al., 2020). In this way, COVID-19 has added to the existing threats undermining decent work and sustainability posed by technology, economic recession, political instability, migration, and mobilization. For already marginalized workers, the COVID-19 pandemic exacerbated existing stressors and sources of insecurity and increased risk to psychological wellbeing (Blustein, 2019; Duffy et al., 2020). The devastating effects of this most recent global health, economic, and social crisis have prompted PWT researchers to seek to better understand the impacts in ways that can inform PWC and PWSI. Consistent with the premises of PWT, researchers and policy advocates can expect ongoing changes in the world of work and the broader life context that will impact access to decent work and life quality on a global level.

Concepts from the psychology of working, and empirical findings on decent work can be utilized to examine the effects of the COVID-19 pandemic and delineate opportunities for intervention for mental health workers, organizations, and policy makers (Autin et al., 2020). Areas of need include economic concerns, such as unemployment and employment disparities, as well as issues directly pertinent to workers' wellbeing, such as work-life balance and mental health. While the COVID-19 pandemic is undoubtedly a public health crisis with noteworthy effects on economic and social conditions, Autin et al. (2020) suggest that it can also be viewed as an opportunity to increase public commitment to workers' wellbeing, and to reinforce the importance of decent work as fundamental to the vocational lives of all individuals.

Drawing on previous research in PWT, and emerging data on the effects of COVID-19, Autin et al. (2020) have delineated policy and practice recommendations for organizations, career-development professionals, and policy across four areas: unemployment; worker mental health; the work-family interface; and employment disparities. The framework identifies possibilities for promoting the wellbeing of workers through person-level (PWC) and systemic interventions (PWSI). At the person level, for example, counselors need to be informed about unemployment policies, inform clients about their right and benefits, advise clients on processes for accessing benefits, offer interventions that are adequate for populations with limited work choices, integrate mental health and career counseling, and expand telehealth services.

At the policy level (PWSI), recommendations include furthering collective actions by organizations, offering extensive and continued economic support for workers without employment, increasing financial and healthcare assistance for unpaid care workers, offering support for communities with few resources, reinforcing protections for and increasing family and sick leave for essential workers, and providing social security networks, including remuneration assurance.

The above represent only some recommendations (Autin et al., 2020) but illustrate how the PWT framework can be applied in order to consider PWC and PWSI in the context of change and crisis. We suggest that organizations and policy makers consider the implications of these and other recommendations for their settings and spheres of influence, as we respond to emerging crises and change.

The COVID-19 pandemic can also center a discussion of race and racism in the workplace, with interventions needed for workers and organizations (Erby et al., 2021). From the organizational point of view, organizations must challenge and change policies, practices, and procedures that sustain White supremacy. Moon and Sandage (2019) suggest investment in training leaders to increase their competencies in examining internal policies and promoting antiracist initiatives. Career counselors should also be alert to the needs of racial and ethnic minority clients and the discrimination they may face in the workplace. Moreover, career-development research should focus more on the effectiveness of interventions for people of color and on the negative impact of racism on wellbeing at work, while advocating for policy changes and political action (Erby et al., 2021).

Conclusion

This chapter foregrounds PWT as a framework for inspiring and guiding research, policy, and practice to address some of the most compelling psychological, social, and economic issues of our time. The complex challenges of growing inequality and marginalization amidst rapid change in the world of work and across society call for multidisciplinary interventions at the personal, organizational, and systemic levels (Blustein, Kenny, Di Fabio et al., 2019). PWT has expanded from a series of assumptions to a theoretical model than can be empirically assessed and stimulate research to guide intervention at the personal and systemic levels.

With regard to research, a substantive body of evidence has verified the premises of the PWT model, and some research has examined interventions at the individual counseling or PWC level. Research is lagging however to guide interventions at the systemic level. In this regard, there is an opportunity for organizations to develop research-informed strategies to promote access to decent work. The development and evaluation of job-crafting interventions designed with a focus on promoting the mediating and moderating factors from the PWT model is a promising research area that may increase access to decent work for the people who are the most vulnerable in the workforce. The emerging research on work precarity from a PWT perspective should be extended so that organizations and government entities can better understand some of the advantages of temporary work, such as flexibility in hours, and identify policies that will avoid or reduce the disadvantages of temporary work, such as income insecurity and lack of access to healthcare. Research is needed to evaluate the risks and benefits of governmental and organization policies, such as guaranteed income, which could promote individual and societal wellbeing. Research is also needed to design and evaluate interventions at the individual, organizational, and governmental levels that will bring people together to work toward the common good with a sense of social responsibility, social inclusion, and with a commitment to sustainable development (Carr, Hodgetts et al., Chapter 1).

The current work, health, and environmental crises are an opportunity for researchers across disciplines to collaborate in finding solutions to these complex challenges. As the cadre of interdisciplinary scholars considering the PWT framework grows, the model, while remaining true to the basic assumptions outlined by Blustein (2006, 2013), is being assessed with new populations and modified to add new constructs and related models. Indeed, the power of the framework is augmented by its alignment with multidisciplinary scholarship in economics, such as Sen (1993, 1999), and its connection with the agendas of global organizations, such as the UN (2021) and the ILO (2013, 2020), that seek to reduce poverty and promote social justice and decent work toward a sustainable future. We have highlighted some recent research initiatives related to the PWT framework in the hope that this chapter will inspire further research, policy, and practice to promote access to decent work and decent lives for all.

References

Allan, B. A., Autin, K. L., & Wilkins-Yel, K. G. (2021). Precarious work in the 21st century: A psychological perspective. *Journal of Vocational Behavior, 126*, 103491. https://doi.org/10.1016/j.jvb.2020.103491

Arasli, H., Arici, H. E., & Ilgen, H. (2019). Blackbox between job crafting and job embeddedness of immigrant hotel employees: A serial mediation model. *Economic Research-Ekonomska Istrazivanja, 32*(1), 3935–3962. https://doi.org/10.1080/1331677X.2019.1678500

Autin, K. L., Blustein, D. L., Ali, S. R., & Garriott, P. O. (2020). Career development impacts of COVID-19: Practice and policy recommendations. *Journal of Career Development, 47*(5), 487–494. https://doi.org/10.1177/0894845320944486

Autin, K. L., Duffy, R. D., Jacobson, C. J., Dosani, K. M., Barker, D., & Bott, E. M. (2018). Career development among undocumented immigrant young adults: A psychology of working perspective. *Journal of Counseling Psychology, 65*(5), 605–617. https://doi.org/10.1037/cou0000280

Autin, K. L., Williams, T. R., Allan, B., & Herdt, M. (2021). Decent work among people of color: The moderating role of critical consciousness. *Journal of Career Assessment, 30*(3), 455–473. https://doi.org/10.1177/10690727211039811

Bakker, A. B., & Oerlemans, W. G. M. (2019). Daily job crafting and momentary work engagement: A self-determination and self-regulation perspective. *Journal of Vocational Behavior, 112*, 417–430. https://doi.org/10.1016/j.jvb.2018.12.005

Blustein, D. L. (2006). *The psychology of working: A new perspective for career development, counseling, and public policy*. Lawrence Erlbaum Associates.

Blustein, D. L. (Ed.) (2013). *The Oxford handbook of the psychology of working*. Oxford University Press.

Blustein, D. L. (2019). *The importance of work in an age of uncertainty: The eroding work experience in America.* Oxford University Press.

Blustein, D. L., Kenny, M. E., Autin, K., & Duffy, R. (2019). The psychology of working in practice: A theory of change for a new era. *Career Development Quarterly, 67*(3), 236–254. https://doi.org/10.1002/cdq.12193

Blustein, D. L., Kenny, M. E., Di Fabio, A., & Guichard, J. (2019). Expanding the impact of the psychology of working: Engaging psychology in the struggle for decent work and human rights. *Journal of Career Assessment, 27*(1), 3–28. https://doi.org/10.1177/1069072718774002

Blustein, D. L., Perera, H. N., Diamonti, A. J., Gutowski, E., Meerkins, T., Davila, A., Erby, W., & Konowitz, L. (2020). The uncertain state of work in the US: Profiles of decent work and precarious work. *Journal of Vocational Behavior, 122*, 103481. https://doi.org/10.1016/j.jvb.2020.103481

Brucker, D. L., & Sundar, V. (2020). Job crafting among American workers with disabilities. *Journal Occupational Rehabilitation, 30*(4), 575–587. https://doi.org/10.1007/s10926-020-09889-9

Carr, S. C. (2021). Setting 'poverty thresholds': Whose experience counts? *Sustainability Science, 16*(1), 31–36. https://doi.org/10.1007/s11625-020-00859-x

Carr, S. C., Maleka, M., Meyer, I., Barry, M. L., Haar, J., Parker, J., Arrowsmith, J., Yao, C., Hodgetts, D., Jones, H., Young-Hausner, A, Afeaki-Mafile'o, E., Rasmussen, A.-H., Alefaio-Tugia, S., Falealili, B., Mafile'o, K., Pikula, T., Wolfgramm, N., 'Uhila, H., … & Naithani, A. (2018). How can wages sustain a living? By getting ahead of the curve. *Sustainability Science, 13*(4), 901–917. https://doi.org/10.1007/s11625-018-0560-7

Carr, S. C., Parker, J., Arrowsmith, J., & Watters, P. A. (2016). The living wage: Theoretical integration and an applied research agenda. *International Labour Review*, *155*(1), 1–24. https://doi.org/10.1111/j.1564-913X.2015.00029.x

Cheung, F., Ngo, H. Y., & Leung, A. (2020). Predicting work volition among undergraduate students in the United States and Hong Kong. *Journal of Career Development*, *47*(5), 565–578. https://doi.org/10.1177/0894845318803469

Cohen, S., & Wills, T. A. (1985). Stress, social support, and the buffering hypothesis. *Psychological Bulletin, 98*(2), 310–357. https://doi.org/10.1037/0033-2909.98.2.310

Di Fabio, A. (2017a). Positive healthy organizations: Promoting well-being, meaningfulness, and sustainability in organizations. *Frontiers in Psychology. Organizational Psychology*, *8*, Article 1938. https://doi.org/10.3389/fpsyg.2017.01938

Di Fabio, A. (2017b). The psychology of sustainability and sustainable development for well-being in organizations. *Frontiers in Psychology. Organizational Psychology*, *8*, Article 1534. https://doi.org/10.3389/fpsyg.2017.01534

Di Fabio, A., & Blustein, D. L. (2016). Editorial: From meaning of working to meaningful lives: The challenges of expanding decent work. *Frontiers in Psychology. Organizational Psychology*, *7*, Article 1119. https://doi.org/10.3389/fpsyg.2016.01119

Di Fabio, A., & Kenny, M. E. (2019). Decent work in Italy: Context, conceptualization, and assessment. *Journal of Vocational Behavior, 110*(Part A), 131–143. https://doi.org/10.1016/j.jvb.2018.10.014

Di Fabio, A., & Peiró, J. M. (2018). Human capital sustainability leadership to promote sustainable development and healthy organizations: A new scale. *Sustainability*, *10*(7), Article 2413. https://doi.org/10.3390/su10072413

Di Fabio, A., & Rosen, M. A. (2018). Opening the black box of psychological processes in the science of sustainable development: A new frontier. *European Journal of Sustainable Development Research*, *2*(4), Article 47. https://doi.org/10.20897/ejosdr/3933

Di Fabio, A., & Svicher, A. (2021). The psychology of sustainability and sustainable development: Advancing decent work, inclusivity, and positive strengths-based primary preventive interventions for vulnerable workers. *Frontiers in Psychology, 12,* Article 718354. https://doi.org/10.3389/fpsyg.2021.718354

Douglass, R. P., Autin, K. L., Buyukgoze-Kavas, A., & Gensmer, N. P. (2020). Proactive personality and decent work among racially and ethnically diverse working adults. *Journal of Career Assessment, 28*(3), 512–528. https://doi.org//10.1177/1069072719894571

Douglass, R. P., Velez, B. L., Conlin, S. E., Duffy, R. D., & England, J. W. (2017). Examining the psychology of working theory: Decent work among sexual minorities. *Journal of Counseling Psychology, 64*(5), 550–559. https://doi.org/10.1037/cou0000212

Duffy, R. D., Allan, B. A., England, J. W., Blustein, D. L., Autin, K. L., Douglass, R. P., Ferreira, J., & Santos, E. J. R. (2017). The development and initial validation of the Decent Work Scale. *Journal of Counseling Psychology, 64*(2), 206–221. https://doi.org/10.1037/cou0000191

Duffy, R. D., Blustein, D. L., Allan, B. A., Diemer, M. A., & Cinamon, R. G. (2020). Introduction to the special issue: A cross-cultural exploration of decent work. *Journal of Vocational Behavior, 116*(Part A), Article 103351. https://doi.org//10.1016/j.jvb.2019.103351

Duffy, R. D., Blustein, D. L., Diemer, M. A., & Autin, K. L. (2016). The psychology of working theory. *Journal of Counseling Psychology*, *63*(2), 127–148. https://doi.org/10.1037/cou0000140

Duffy, R. D., Diemer, M. A., & Jadidian, A. (2012). The development and initial validation of the Work Volition Scale-Student Version. *The Counseling Psychologist, 40*(2), 291–319. https://doi.org/10.1177/%20001100001141 7147

Duffy, R. D., & Dik, B. J. (2009). Beyond the self: External influences in the career development process. *The Career Development Quarterly, 58*(1), 29–43. https://doi.org/10.1002/j.2161-0045.2009.tb00171.x

Duffy, R. D., Velez, B. L., England, J. W., Autin, K. L., Douglass, R. P., Allan, B. A., & Blustein, D. L. (2018). An examination of the psychology of working theory with racially and ethnically diverse employed adults. *Journal of Counseling Psychology, 65*(3), 280–293. https://doi.org/10.1037/cou0000247

Erby, W., Smith, C., Blustein, D., & Davila, A. (2021). Racism and the future of work. *Career Planning & Adult Development Network Journal, 37*(2), 167–170.

Federici, E., Boon, C., & Den Hartog, D. N. (2019). The moderating role of HR practices on the career adaptability-job crafting relationship: A study among employee-manager dyads. *International Journal of Human Resource Management, 32*(6), 1339–1367. https://doi.org/10.1080/09585192.2018.1522656

Freire, P. (1993). *Pedagogy of the oppressed.* Continuum.

Gilson, C. B., Sinclair, J., Whirley, M. L., Li, Y., & Blustein, D. L. (2022). "More than a job, it's a purpose": A psychology of working perspective for the working experiences for individuals with intellectual and developmental disabilities. *Journal of Career Assessment.* https://doi.org/10.1177/10690727211048898

Haar, J., Carr, S. C., Arrowsmith, J., Parker, J., Hodgetts, D., & Alefaio-Tugia, S. (2018). Escape from working poverty: Steps toward sustainable livelihood. *Sustainability, 10*(11), Article 4144. https://doi.org/10.3390/su10114144

Hornung, S. (2019). Crafting task and cognitive job boundaries to enhance self-determination, impact, meaning and competence at work. *Behavioral Sciences, 9*(12), 136. "https://apc01.safelinks.protection.outlook.com/?url=https%3A%2F%2Fdoi-org.proxy.bc.edu%2F10.3390%2Fbs9120136&data=05%7C01%7CV.Hopner%40massey.ac.nz%7C435e5c953567499aa25808db9b7a24c5%7C388728e1bbd0437898dcf8682e644300%7C1%7C0%7C638274721154513837%7CUnknown%7CTWFpbGZsb3d8eyJWIjoiMC4wLjAwMDAiLCJQIjoiV2luMzIiLCJBTiI6Ik1haWwiLCJXVCI6Mn0%3D%7C3000%7C%7C%7C&sdata=X0zc6o1G8QQJEqHeGX%2FiAWdldu8LByvLnR5GFvwdxzw%3D&reserved=0"https://doi-org.proxy.bc.edu/10.3390/bs9120136

Hulshof, I. L., Demerouti, E., & Le Blanc, P. M. (2020a). A job search demands-resources intervention among the unemployed: Effects on well-being, job search behavior and re-employment chances. *Journal of Occupational Health Psychology, 25*(1), 17–31. https://doi.org/10.1037/ocp0000167

Hulshof, I. L., Demerouti, E., & Le Blanc, P. M. (2020b). Re-employment crafting: Proactively shaping one's job search. *Journal of Applied Psychology, 105*(1), 58–79. https://doi.org/10.1037/apl0000419

International Labour Organization. (2008). *Measurement of decent work.* https://www.ilo.org/wcmsp5/groups/public/—dgreports/—stat/documents/meetingdocument/wcms_100335.pdf

International Labour Organization. (2013). *Decent work indicators: Concepts and definitions.* https://www.ilo.org/wcmsp5/groups/public/—dgreports/—integration/documents/publication/wcms_229374.pdf

International Labour Organization (2020). *Global wage report 2020–21: Wages and minimum wages in the time of COVID-19.* https://www.ilo.org/wcmsp5/groups/public/—dgreports/—dcomm/—publ/documents/publication/wcms_762534.pdf

Kenny, M. E., Blustein, D. L., Liang, B., Klein, T., & Etchie, Q. (2019). Applying the psychology of working theory for transformative career education. *Journal of Career Development, 46*(6), 623–636. https://doi.org/10.1177/0894845319827655

Kenny, M. E., Haase, R. F., Tsai, B. W., Medvide, M. B., & Davila, A. (2022). Applying the psychology of working theory for understanding adaptive career progress of youth. *Journal of Career Assessment.* https://doi.org/10.1177/10690727211067699

Kenny, M. E., & Tsai, B. W. (2020). Person- and system-focused prevention in preparing youth to navigate an uncertain work future, *1*(2), 155–182. *Journal of Prevention and Health Promotion.* https://doi.org/10.1177/2632077020965568

Kerksieck, P., Bauer, G. F., & Brauchli, R. (2019). Personal and social resources at work: Reciprocal relations between crafting for social job resources, social support at work and psychological capital. *Frontiers in Psychology, 10*, Article 2632. https://doi.org/10.3389/fpsyg.2019.02632

Kim, H. J., Duffy, R. D., Lee, S., Lee, J., & Lee, K. (2019). Application of the psychology of working theory with Korean emerging adults. *Journal of Counseling Psychology, 66*(6), 701–713. https://doi.org//10.1037/cou0000368

Kim, T., & Allan, B. (2021). Examining classism and critical consciousness within psychology of working. *Journal of Career Assessment, 29*(4), 644–660. https://doi.org/10.1177/1069072721998418

Kooij, D. T. A. M., Nijssen, H., Bal, P. M., & van der Kruijssen, D. T. F. (2020). Crafting an interesting job: Stimulating an active role of older workers in enhancing their daily work engagement and job performance. *Work Aging and Retirement. 6*(3), 165–174. https://doi.org/10.1093/workar/waaa001

Kozan, S., Işık, E., & Blustein, D. L. (2019). Decent work and well-being among low-income Turkish employees: Testing the psychology of working theory. *Journal of Counseling Psychology, 66*(3), 317–327. https://doi.org/10.1037/cou0000342

Lee, J. W., & Song, Y. (2019). Promoting employee job crafting at work: The roles of motivation and team context. *Personnel Review, 49*(3), 689–708. https://doi.org/10.1108/PR-07-2018-0261

Li, N., Liang, J., & Crant, J. M. (2010). The role of proactive personality in job satisfaction and organizational citizenship behavior: A relational perspective. *Journal of Applied Psychology, 95*(2), 395–404. https://doi.org/10.1037/a0018079

Moon, S. H., & Sandage, S. J. (2019). Cultural humility for people of color: Critique of current theory and practice. *Journal of Psychology and Theology, 47*(2), 76–86. https://doi.org/10.1177/0091647119842407

Nagy, N., Johnston, C. S., & Hirschi, A. (2019). Do we act as old as we feel? An examination of subjective age and job crafting behaviour of late career employees. *European Journal of Work and Organizational Psychology, 28*, 373–383. https://doi.org/10.1080/1359432X.2019.1584183

Nussbaum, M. C. (1990), Aristotelian social democracy. In B. Douglas, G. Mara, & H. Richardson (Eds.), *Liberalism and the good* (pp. 203–252). Routledge.

Petrou, P., Bakker, A. B., & van den Heuvel, M. (2017). Weekly job crafting and leisure crafting: Implications for meaning-making and work engagement. *Journal of Occupational and Organizational Psychology, 90*(2), 129–152. https://doi.org/10.1111/joop.12160

Richardson, M. S. (1993). Work in people's lives: A location for counseling psychologists. *Journal of Counseling Psychology, 40*(4), 425–433. https://doi.org/10.1037/0022-0167.40.4.425

Richardson, M. S. (2009). Another way to think about the work we do: Counselling for work and relationship. *International Journal for Educational and Vocational Guidance, 9*(2), 75–84. https://doi.org//10.1007/s10775-009-9154-3

Rottinghaus, P. J., Day, S. X., & Borgen, F. H. (2005). The career futures inventory: A measure of career-related adaptability and optimism. *Journal of Career Assessment, 13*(1), 3–24. https://doi.org/10.1177/1069072704270271

Rudolph, C. W., Katz, I. M., Lavigne, K. N., & Zacher, H. (2017). Job crafting: A meta-analysis of relationships with individual differences, job characteristics, and work outcomes. *Journal of Vocational Behavior, 102*, 112–138. https://doi.org/10.1016/j.jvb.2017.05.008

Savickas, M. L. (2002). Career construction: A developmental theory of vocational behavior. In D. Brown & Associates. (Eds.), *Career choice and development* (4th ed., pp. 149–205). Jossey-Bass.

Sen, A. K. (1993). Capability and well-being. In M. C. Nussbaum & A. K. Sen (Eds.), *The quality of life* (pp. 30–53). Clarendon Press.

Sen, A. K. (1999). *Development as freedom*. Oxford University Press.

Super, D. E. (1980). A life-span, life-space approach to career development. *Journal of Vocational Behavior, 16*(3), 282–298. https://doi.org/10.1016/0001-8791(80)90056-1

Svicher, A., & Di Fabio, A. (2021). Job crafting: A challenge to promote decent work for vulnerable workers. *Frontiers in Psychology. Organizational Psychology, 12*, Article 1827. https://doi.org/10.3389/fpsyg.2021.681022

Tims, M., Derks, D., & Bakker, A. B. (2016). Job crafting and its relationships with person-job fit and meaningfulness: A three-wave study. *Journal of Vocational Behavior, 92*, 44–53. https://doi.org/10.1016/j.jvb.2015.11.007

United Nations (2021). *Transforming our world: The 2030 agenda for sustainable development*. https://sdgs.un.org/2030agenda

Vogt, K., Hakanen, J. J., Brauchli, R., Jenny, G. J., & Bauer, G. F. (2016). The consequences of job crafting: A three-wave study. *European Journal of Work and Organizational Psychology, 25*(3), 353–362. https://doi.org/10.1080/1359432X.2015.1072170

Wang, D., Jia, Y., Hou, Z., Xu, H., Zhang, H., & Guo, X. (2019). A test of psychology of working theory among Chinese urban workers: Examining predictors and outcomes of decent work. *Journal of Vocational Behavior, 115*, 11. https://doi.org/10.1016/j.jvb.2019.103325

Watts, R. J., Diemer, M. A., & Voight, A. M. (2011). Critical consciousness: Current status and future directions. *New Directions for Child and Adolescent Development, 134*(Special issue), 43–57. https://doi.org/10.1002/cd.310

Woo, H. R. (2020). Perceived overqualification and job crafting: The curvilinear moderation of career adaptability. *Sustainability 12*(24), Article 10458. https://doi.org/10.3390/su122410458

Yao, C., Parker, J., Arrowsmith, J., & Carr, S. C. (2017). The living wage as an income range for decent work and life. *Employee Relations, 39*(6), 875–887. https://doi.org/10.1108/ER-03-2017-0071

Zacher, H., & Rudolph, C. W. (2019). Why do we act as old as we feel? The role of occupational future time perspective and core self-evaluations in the relationship between subjective age and job crafting behaviour. *European Journal of Work and Organizational Psychology, 28*(6), 831–844. https://doi.org/10.1080/1359432X.2019.1677609

Zhang, L., Lu, H., & Li, F. (2018). Proactive personality and mental health: The role of job crafting. *PsyCh Journal, 7*(3), 154–155. https://doi.org/10.1002/pchj.214

4

HUMANITARIAN WORK POLICY AND PRAXIS

Rosalind H. Searle and Ishbel McWha-Hermann

> No society can surely be flourishing and happy, of which the far greater part of the members are poor and miserable. It is but equity, besides, that they who feed, clothe, and lodge the whole body of the people, should have such a share of the produce of their own labour as to be themselves tolerably well fed, clothed and lodged.
>
> (Smith, 1776/1976, p. 33)

Introduction

Work serves an important function in people's lives; while it brings in economic resources, it has critical psychological benefits, including the means for self-determination, structure, and connection to others (Blustein, 2006). Work and organizational psychology (WOP),[1] however, has been accused of being a "servant to power" with its focus traditionally more aligned with the interests of corporations and their leaders and managers (Baritz, 1960; Carr, Hodgetts et al., Chapter 1). Yet, this perspective has been shifting as the areas of study in the field have broadened (Hakel, 2013; McWhirter & McWha-Hermann, 2021), and, more critically, in growing recognition of the need to include the perspectives of employees, communities, and societal consequences (Carr et al., 2012; Gloss et al., 2017). Weiss and Rupp's (2011) seminal article called for a rebalancing away from the dominance of the organization's perspective toward that of the worker, and to include their experiences of work and working. In the wake of the COVID-19 pandemic and clear evidence of its differential impacts for many workers (Blustein & Guarino, 2020), we take stock and consider afresh the merit of the current trajectory which provides unimagined wealth to

DOI: 10.4324/9781003440444-5

a tiny minority (Carr et al., Chapter 10; Lepore, 2021). The pandemic has made transparent the paradoxes of working lives, and more specifically their rewards. It has shown the dark side and dynamics of the disempowerment of a growing number of organizational actors—notably workers (Berti & Simpson, 2021). In response, we draw on a founder of the Enlightenment, Adam Smith (1776/1976), to foreground the workers' perspectives and in so doing provide a psychologically informed and more sustainable refocus on decent work and specifically living wages to respond to growing calls to address global racial inequality and injustice (McWha-Hermann, 2022; McWha-Hermann et al., 2021). Through challenging the current exploitative approach adopted toward the future of work and its all too human consequences (Burbano & Chiles, 2022; Connelly et al., 2020; Duggan et al., 2020), we contend that work can be productive and sustainable for both the organization and worker.

In this chapter, we consider the rich contributions of I/O psychology to our understanding of work: notably living wages (Meyer & Maleka, Chapter 7; Teng-Calleja et al., Chapter 8; Intraprasert et al., Chapter 9). We begin by briefly outlining the contrary evidence concerning work, before exploring the topic of wages and the additional perspectives I/O psychology provides. Then we explore three dynamic and interconnected multilevel activities where psychology has a contribution to make: *knowledge generation*, *dialog*, and *dissemination*. Under knowledge generation, we consider the production of new empirical evidence alongside the evaluation of existing practices pertinent to different stakeholders (Saner & Yiu, Chapter 5); dialog refers to the significance of dialogs to create and sustain an international multistakeholder community of interest regarding living wages; and finally dissemination concerns the development of new means and platforms to engage stakeholders and distribute this I/O psychology science, notably through the use of case studies, animations, and novel experiential immersive learning designed to raise awareness and change mindsets.

Good Work?

The pandemic accelerated existing changes that have been occurring in work: increasing the role of technology and its hidden governing algorithms, replacing set workplaces with mobile and remote working, and undermining work security and the employment relationship through the growing prevalence of gig work (de Vaujany et al., 2021; Kellogg et al., 2020; Kuhn, Chapter 12; Schmid & Dowling, 2020; Smids et al., 2020; Wood et al., 2019). Yet current and prior studies from workers' perspectives have provided important insights about work and what matters.

Challenging the prior orthodoxy about the benefits of work per se, medical studies have shown that it is the quality of the provision that provides its critical benefits (Chandola & Zhang, 2018). Critically, this study has revealed unemployment to be a preferable option to the reduced life expectancy and poor health that arise for workers and their communities from poor-quality work. There is, therefore, an increasing focus on understanding what makes work decent (Blustein et al., 2016), and on identifying its components and benefits for both an employing organization and the worker (Di Fabio et al., Chapter 3). For example, insecure work has been found to have deleterious consequences for organizations and for worker productivity (Seubert & Seubert, Chapter 14; Sverke et al., 2019). Similarly, the stringencies of gig work (Kuhn, Chapter 12) have been exposed and reveal rest and recovery to be integral components of sustainable work (Haar, Chapter 17; Sonnentag, 2018), while examination of work design shows the benefits of including task variety, feedback, and challenge (e.g., Parker & Jorritsma, 2021; Parker et al., 2017). Likewise, research has identified that work needs to be at the right level, rather than beneath the worker's capabilities (e.g., Erdogan & Bauer, 2021; McKee-Ryan et al., 2009; O'Shea et al., Chapter 15). Indeed, even the lives of the hard-to-place long-term unemployed can be transformed through training in careers search (Koen et al., 2010; van Hooft & van Hoye, Chapter 19), with job loss a benefit for those who are supported with career planning and exploration to understand the value of better job matches (Di Fabio et al., Chapter 3; van Hooft & van Hoye, Chapter 19; Zikic & Klehe, 2006).

Wages, Poverty, and the Living Wage

An important component of decent work, however, is the income derived from it. Study of wages has traditionally been the preserve of economists, yet there has been growing attention from management and I/O psychology scholars (e.g., Carr, 2023; Searle & McWha-Hermann, 2021; Yao et al., 2017). A common policy in many countries is the Minimum wage, which is designed to combat the unfair exploitation of workers through the provision of a floor for incomes (Jiang et al., Chapter 18; Lavelle et al., Chapter 16). While these wage floors may exist, evidence reveals that the actual value of wages has been perniciously undermined since the 1970s, initially through wage stagnation, and more recently with the concurrent and dramatic increases in other costs, including housing, fuel, and food (Burlinson et al., 2018; Liddell & Morris, 2010; Reeves et al., 2017; Saltzman et al., Chapter 2). An important psychological dimension to wages has also been disrupted, in that significant changes to work and working have disrupted previous notions of employment and job security (Griep et al., Chapter 13; Seubert & Seubert, Chapter 14). These changes have included the segmentation of work into its separate tasks, or gigs (Kuhn, Chapter 12); the divesting by organizations of employment benefits and protection (e.g., sickness and holiday pay); the replacement of employees by self-employed workers undertaking gig tasks and paid for their completion rather than the totality of the work and recovery from work (Kuhn, Chapter 12); the substitution of traditional career-structures with flexible working (Di Fabio et al., Chapter 3); and the removal of transparent employment relationships through secretive human resource (HR) algorithms (Duggan et al., 2021; Friedman, 2014; Kost et al., 2020; Taylor et al., 2017; Toaddy et al., Chapter 22; Watson et al., 2021). Together these changes have broken the previous panacea of work as a means to escape poverty (Carr et al., 2018).

Neoliberal economists have rallied against any effort to systematically raise minimal wage levels by arguing that this would distort the labor market and threaten employment (e.g., Frank, 1984; see Carr, et al., Chapter 10). Yet a founder of modern economics, Adam Smith, outlined in his 1796 *Wealth of Nations* the importance of *just* wages and of the moral responsibility of employers not only to recompense the worker's labor and effort with adequate reward as a means of sustaining them but also to offer wider benefits to society. In the wake of the French Revolution, his concern was that unjust income allocation would lead to worker revolt and destabilizing revolution in society. In response to the disparity between the minimum wage and the level required to enable a worker and their family to meet their basic material needs, the concept of a living wage was devised (Anker, 2006). It has no universally agreed rate; instead, it varies to reflect the different costs of living within each community or country (Stabile, 2008).

The conjunction between work and poverty and failure of wages to meet the actual needs of workers has fuelled attention for the living wage (Carr et al., 2016a). Experiences during the COVID-19 pandemic have demonstrated the very different consequences that arise from inequality and marginalization within societies (Allan & Blustein, 2022), which have been made even more salient by the significant health disparities for those in lower socioeconomic groups (Blustein & Guarino, 2020; Klug et al., Chapter 21). Indeed, it has graphically illuminated the increasing distance between the hours worked and their rewards, exacerbating existing fractures along lines of socioeconomic status, gender, age, ethnicity, and educational attainment (Blundell et al., 2020; Cassim, Chapter 20).

Building on Adam Smith's approach to fair wages and work, living wages and the notion of decent work on which they are premised are argued to be significant for three distinct reasons: sustainability, capability, and externality (for a more detailed review, see Searle & McWha-Hermann, 2020). Sustainability concerns the benefits of living wages to a worker and their family by providing the means for an often-contested level of basic provision (Stabile, 2008). Critically, sustainability recognizes that wages extend beyond the worker to enable their households to participate in society (Ciscel, 2000; Waltman, 2004). It includes personal sustainability, with such jobs offering the worker a level of provision that meets their economic needs and also includes provision for rest and recovery (Haar, Chapter 17). This level of reward is therefore diametrically opposite to that offered in the gig economy (Kuhn, Chapter 12) with its accompanying precarity and lack of recovery provision (Petriglieri et al., 2018; Wood et al., 2019).

Developing from this sustainability is the second benefit of living wages: the means to develop capability (Teng-Calleja et al., Chapter 8). This higher level of wage creates important psychological dimensions by offering the worker agency. It includes the means to make choices and afford freedoms in how to spend their time, liberating the worker not only from deprivation but also impoverishment (Sen, 1999). As a result, workers have choices about whether they spend time on self-improvement such as through further education and development, or with their family, or in benefiting their community (Haar, Chapter 17; Werner & Lim, 2016). The capacity for development is dynamic and can form part of a wider career plan (Stremersch et al., 2021; Taber & Blankemeyer, 2015; Verbruggen & De Vos, 2019). A further psychological component that is associated with capability concerns the effect on self-efficacy, leading individuals to feel more empowered, respected, and have greater self-pride (Folger, 1994; Spreitzer et al., 1997). This confidence can contribute to elevated life satisfaction (Arrowsmith & Parker, 2013). The benefits of capability extend beyond work into the family (Teng-Calleja et al., Chapter 8), creating positive spirals not only for the individual but also their household members that allows them to escape the poverty trap (Carr, et al., 2016b; Haar, Chapter 17; Haar et al., 2014).

A final benefit of the living wage occurs at the societal level in the form of reduced externalities, with positive consequences regarding health and social care costs, and the extension of life expectancy (Stabile, 2018). A key study demonstrated these health savings by examining operations at a Californian airport to reveal savings of $3.4 million per death prevented as a consequence of improved wage levels (Cole et al., 2005). Research from the Dominican Republic attests further to the improved self-reported health of living-wage recipients working in a garment factory compared to those in a nonliving-wage facility (Landefeld et al., 2014). A further comparative study outlined the improvements to cardiovascular health, as such workers were able to choose and buy better quality food (Rehkopf et al., 2018), while mental health benefits were found in the reduction in needed treatment for depression (Burmaster et al., 2015; see also, Klug et al., Chapter 21).

The effects of poverty on a household and the wider community are clearly multidimensional, with health studies showing not only an association between poverty and health declines but also lower provision of social support (Ahnquist et al., 2012; Sun et al., 2009). While prior studies outline the poorer health outcomes associated with poverty and lowered educational attainment (e.g., Braveman et al., 2010), these negative health outcomes are not universal with some individuals shown to have more resilient and adaptive coping responses (Chen & Miller, 2012). Yet, the long-term effects of elevated adverse childhood events and resultant stressors are clear with consequences related to insulin, blood pressure, and systemic inflammation (van der Kolk, 2014; Klug et al., Chapter 21).

Poverty is associated with negative spirals, as chronic ill-health leads to reduced short-term income followed by involuntary job loss, producing further reductions in the quality of subsequent employment opportunities and salary levels that necessitate additional disruptions to the individual and their family's housing provision, with implications for mental health and also their children's wellbeing and academic attainment as the resultant school changes disrupt education and the quality of social support (Rand, 2015; Wanberg, 2012). Studies during COVID-19 have revealed the heightened anxiety levels, and even terror that can arise from job losses (e.g., Blustein & Guarino, 2020). If we consider these household experiences replicated across entire communities, with diminished economic and social resources to respond, a picture emerges of the increased challenges and hurdles faced by those in lower socioeconomic groups. Psychologists are often involved in the delivery of a range of downstream interventions for communities associated with poverty, including mental health treatments, but also educational psychology behavioral interventions. The aforementioned chronic health problems leave these communities more exposed to experiences of loss and grief, and also to more frequent engagement with police, social services, and criminal justice. An inherent distrust of professionals can emerge with recipients critical of the type of support that is being provided reducing the acceptance of these provisions (Dudau et al., 2020).

Beyond Research: The Importance of Praxis

In this next section, we turn to three core areas of praxis through where psychology can contribute to efforts toward decent work and living wages: dialog, knowledge generation, and dissemination (see Figure 4.1). We specifically consider the role of I/O psychology in these three different areas and show the importance of integrated and recursive engagement across the areas. We start our discussion with knowledge generation.

Knowledge Generation

I/O research has offered significant new empirical evidence, to provide fresh perspectives and points of departure from those of economists (see Searle & McWha-Hermann, 2021 for a detailed review of the field and its development). Social psychology has provided important conceptual foundations that have been built on in this area, advancing insight into the mechanisms in operation in the context of poverty. Fiske (2007) has played a notable role through her

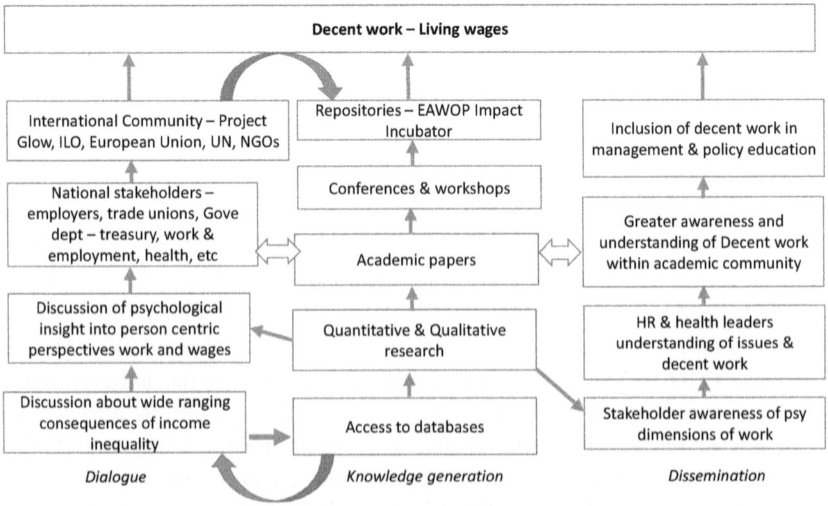

FIGURE 4.1 Dialog, Knowledge Generation, and Dissemination.

seminal work on prejudice to reveal the negative and exclusionary outcomes that arise from poverty because it triggers responses of disgust and withdrawal by others. Further exploration in the aftermath of the 2008 Global Financial Crisis has enabled important strides to be made in the understanding of interpersonal and intergroup processes and socioeconomic status to reveal questions about the deservingness of groups, and the roles of educational attainment, group behaviors, identity, stereotypes, and trust (Moya & Fiske, 2017). Critically, such work has revealed the fundamental role of social class in the life trajectories for individuals, as well as insight into individuals' and others' psychological reactions (Haar, Chapter 17).

Thought leaders in WOP have contributed by challenging the adequacy of prior studies, and providing an alternative, more humanitarian, perspective which challenges simplistic alignments with profit (Carr, 2013; Carr et al., 2012). Building on earlier research that considered the distinct motivational outcomes of wage inequality (Carr et al., 2005), further study has examined wages across multiple sectors within six countries (Carr et al., 2010). Synthesizing theories from development studies, management, and employment relations as well as psychology, these efforts have been utilized to empirically examine relationships between wages and capability (Carr, et al., 2016; Teng-Calleja et al., Chapter 8).

Psychological study of living wages has been important in opening-up the "black box" regarding worker perceptions of the quality of work life. The increase in scholarship aligns with growing awareness of the value of a quality-of-life agenda to more rigorously consider questions of workers' emancipation and wellbeing (Grote & Guest, 2016; Seubert & Seubert, Chapter 14). Part of this exploration of quality of life has been recognition of the impact of unemployment, particularly its psychological consequences, notably those concerning the fear of loss or diminished social status that arises, and the role of social class in employment (Ali et al., 2012). These efforts have been complemented by health studies that have identified the value of focusing on work quality as opposed to work per se (Chandola & Zhang, 2018); importantly, they have revealed that clear health benefits are derived from good-quality work.

Studies examining workers' perceptions have transformed prior abstract research on wages, to reveal insights from real workers in the contexts of families to better understand *how* workers experience "poverty traps" and the challenges faced in the transition from State-provided benefits into those derived from work (Carr, et al., 2016). Critically, they have identified the salary thresholds at which individuals notice improvements to their life satisfaction and work capability, revealing in these perceptions not a continuous, but rather a "spiked" relationship, with qualitatively differences between workers reporting having enough, versus insufficient to meet their basic needs. Such work has offered important granularity to the psychological measurement of quality of work life, to include life and job satisfactions, wage justice, workplace affective commitment, and mental wellbeing. From these more detailed studies of workers, important challenges are emerging to the diminishing marginal returns argument that has dominated the living-wage discourse, replacing it with more precise psychological tipping points. Subsequent research has extended the coverage of the psychological dimensions used to assess the quality of work life to include career satisfaction, and outcomes such as organizational citizenship behaviors and work-life balance (Carr et al., 2019). As a result, the tangible impact for employers of paying workers the living wage has been captured, alongside the productivity benefits that can be derived.

A second significant contribution from psychology has been to identify some of the psychological mechanisms that explain the inconsistent results concerning the effects of economic vulnerability. Research utilizing a panel of more than 700 employed German adults has shown the significant role of perceived financial strain in reducing the health and life satisfaction for those on low incomes (Klug et al., 2021; Chapter 21). This research has revealed the role of workers' perceptions of agency and control as important mediators in the relationship between economic vulnerability and mental health. Through such work, they have identified the significance of subjective insights as distinct from actual household financial situations, to reveal the pernicious consequences of perceived financial insecurity on mental wellbeing. These types of psychological strain can be formed in childhood and create salient affective, cognitive, and behavioral responses that arise from exposure to economic vulnerability.

A third contribution is the synthesis of psychological and sociological insights into decent work to delineate how individual capability (Teng-Calleja et al.,

Chapter 8) can be improved through the provision of a living wage (see Seubert et al., 2021, for a detailed review of the field and its development). This conceptual study drew out five aspects of decent work, including "reproductive material," which is concerned with living wages and job security; "social-communication," which focuses on its consequences for social integration, inclusion, cooperation, and concern; "legal-institutional," which considers the protection for workers through labor laws and their rights to participate in work; "status and recognition," which captures the significance of status and feeling appreciated; and finally, "meaningfulness," which includes the identification and meaning that are derived from work. Through this taxonomy, the distinct aspects of work can be examined to offer more comprehensive understanding of their distinct contribution and the consequences when only some elements are present. It provides a means to more systematically map the different relationships between living wages and an individual worker's quality of life as well as their specific needs.

A critique of prior wage studies that has advanced understanding is the recognition of the skewed nature of previous research (Haar, Chapter 17). Specifically, earlier studies have tended to focus on WEIRD (Western, educated, industrialized, rich and democratic) and POSH (higher socioeconomic) sample populations, hence examining the impact of wages in white-collar work (Haar, Chapter 17), and thus inherently more stable work contexts (Bergman & Jean, 2016; Gloss et al., 2017). These previous omissions are important and there is a re-doubling of attention on *who* is being studied, and what types of work are being included (McWha-Hermann et al., 2021; McWhirter & McWha-Hermann, 2021). Ensuring that studies examine actual precarious wage situations and their consequences for a wider range of workers has led to research into artisans and those undertaking informal street work (Groot & Hodgetts, 2015; Saxena, 2021; Jyoti & Arora, Chapter 6; Mahima & Tchangneno, Chapter 11). These developments are significant in the light of International Labor Organization (ILO; 2018) statistics showing that more than 61% of the world's population are working within the informal sector and therefore conspicuously removed from health and safety provisions enjoyed by other workers. In the United States, estimates suggest that 40% of the workforce receives low pay, which is insufficient to meet basic needs (Shook et al., 2020).

A further development is the extending of perspectives beyond the worker to understand the spillover consequences of low-paid work in the family and social spheres, especially their implications for health and wellbeing (e.g., Haar, Chapter 17; Shook et al., 2020). Such study has helped raise awareness and advanced knowledge for social workers, improving policy and practice interventions around low-income work, for example, by identifying the associated complications from food insecurity with adults either reducing or eliminating some meals altogether, and the health complications for their children. Further health challenges can arise from the discontinuous adherence to expensive medical treatments with more chronic issues emerging. While many clients are eligible for welfare and other benefits, instead they rely on more expensive payday loans. Unsurprisingly, such households are also more likely to have strained and conflict-laden interactions due to the additional financial pressures. Therefore, there are significant negative interactions for these families (Haar, Chapter 17).

Another important strand of research focuses on employers: specifically their choices to provide a living wage (Meyer & Maleka, Chapter 7). This type of study again provides important evidence to inform employer policy and interventions that can improve the uptake of national living-wage initiatives. Small- and medium-sized enterprises (SMEs) are significant employers for such study, with attention directed toward their decisions to voluntarily adopt these increased wage levels for their staff (Werner, 2017, 2021). Through this research, the drivers underlying decisions are identified, including the desire to care for employees, to support higher quality service delivery, as a component of social corporate responsibility concerns, and a means of deriving competitor advantage and accessing talent. However, these studies also reveal that there are significant challenges and barriers to be overcome, including through managing supply chains (e.g., Carr et al., 2021; Jyoti & Arora, Chapter 6; Mair et al., 2018).

Stakeholder Dialogs

Inherent to the development of knowledge concerning living wages and decent work is the significant role of dialogs between different stakeholders and researchers (see Figure 4.2). Dialogs are crucial in helping to guide research to address real-world issues and to informing and increasing adoption of research into policy (Saner & Yiu, Chapter 5). The relationships between knowledge generation and dialogs are recursive: each feeding into the other and stimulating further engagement and dissemination. There are examples of such dialogs in a number of studies such as those of Carr and colleagues, fostering significant and ongoing conversations that have shaped research evidence for policy makers and influenced the type of studies being undertaken to address previous areas of omission. The research agenda has been pushed forward and informed by these two-way dialogs between researchers and policy makers (Lavelle et al., Chapter 16; Saltzman et al., Chapter 2).

In this section, we consider the different stakeholders with whom engagement in dialog has occurred and remains important regarding the living wage and Decent Work Agenda. We begin with a person-centric focus to show the distinct levels at which attention is required with individual-, group-, organizational-, and institutional-level dialogs needing to be fostered. The significant effort devoted toward engagement is a central component to humanitarian work psychology research and involves two-way engagement between the different parties, with

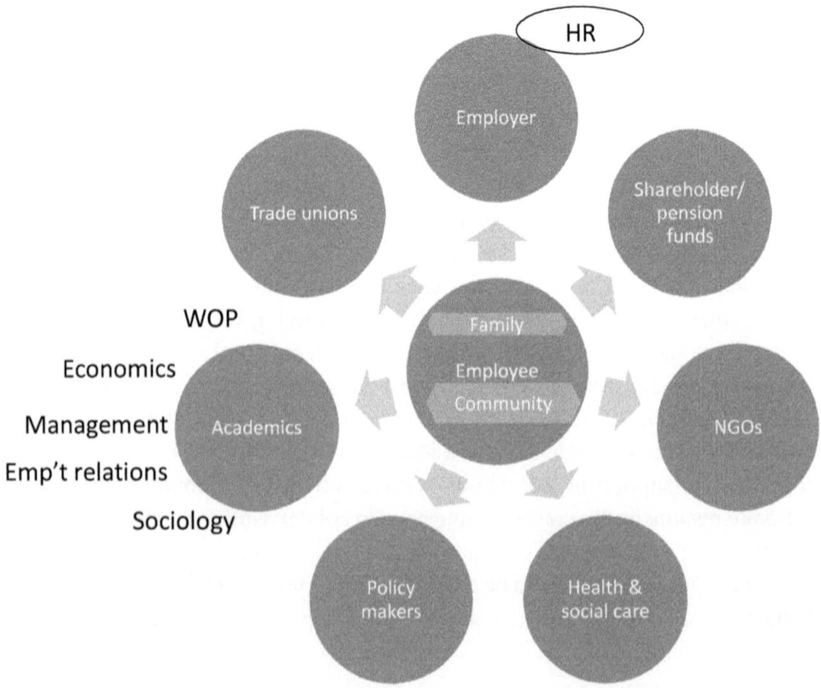

FIGURE 4.2 Stakeholder Dialogs that Advance Decent Work and Living Wages.

each gaining and developing their own insights. These processes should not be considered simple interactions between researcher and stakeholder but rather as dialogs that are vital to addressing the type and quality of questions researchers are engaged in answering. The dialogs can therefore be considered partnerships between different parties in an area of common interest (Jyoti & Arora, Chapter 6; Saner & Yiu, Chapter 5; Searle & Rice, 2021).

Workers and Their Families

An important stakeholder in living-wage research is the individual worker. The inclusion of this critical person-centric perspective distinguishes this research from other fields (Weiss & Rupp, 2011). Despite its focus on individuals, the voice of individual low-wage workers has largely been the purview of other disciplines, such as sociology and social work. The inclusion of this key stakeholder within growing WOP research reflects the increased interest in the study of the purpose and meaning of work (Blustein et al., 2016). Psychology has a considerable amount to offer in understanding worker perspectives, advocating for them, and bringing them together with employer perspectives to identify mutually beneficial solutions. Understanding of the link between living wages and worker wellbeing is a valuable contribution from I/O psychology. While this is important from a moral standpoint, there is also a vast body of psychological literature that informs the business case for enhanced worker wellbeing (Flint et al., 2014). Linking together bodies of research triangulates across the stakeholders and serves to sharpen research insight and impact. An example of this noted earlier is the attention to ensuring that pertinent work roles are included in research in order to offer more meaningful insight into the affect and effects of living wages for workers, such as workers in the garment and textiles industry (Saxena, 2022; Saxena & Tchagneno; Chapter 11; Jyoti & Arora, Chapter 6). Non-Government Organizations (NGOs) are an important group amplifying voices of workers, as we shall outline later, such as those involved in coffee production (Carr et al., 2021). Further, there has been care taken to include those in more precarious and informal work in research (Saxena, 2017). In addition, there is a growing awareness of the value of adding insight from families and communities to these conversations to capture the spillover impacts of low-paid work (Klug et al., Chapter 21; Shook et al., 2020).

Employers

Central stakeholders in any dialog pertaining to wages are employers (Yao et al., 2017). Attempts to engage and change their decisions on salary levels are critical not only to achieving change in the quality of life for workers (Carr et al., 2016b) but also for considering questions of organizational resilience and ongoing vitality. Aside from conversations about wage floors within organizations, there is growing attention on the lack of researcher engagement with those at the top of these same organizations (Searle & McWha-Hermann, 2021). Working conditions have been identified by international policy organizations as the number one challenge facing the world of work (ILO, 2019), however, tensions around wage levels post-pandemic remain an issue for employers, many of whom are trying to maintain previous low wage levels and enhance the flexibility that precarious work brings to their organizations. There remain many organizations that rely on business models that simply draw on State welfare support to subsidize the wage shortfall (Searle & McWha-Hermann, 2021). Dialog between employers, academic researchers, and policy makers can bring insight into these business models and State-level policies to achieve mutual benefits (Jyoti & Arora, Chapter 6; Saner & Yiu, Chapter 5). For example, incentivizing increased wage levels in organizations can free up State-level funds to be spent elsewhere.

Alongside dialogs about wage levels and decent work, there is also a growing impetus to change working hours to make them more accommodating of workers' lives, by offering greater reliability of income and hours (Griep et al., Chapter 13; Lavelle et al., Chapter 16). Through further I/O psychology interventions, notably in job design, real options can start to emerge for employers to enable them to offer decent work (Parker & Jorritsma, 2020). Yet stability in terms of income and hours of work remains critical to providing a sense of control for employees who need to access child- or elder-care (Lambert et al., 2019). Further, those in low-paid work may have complex health needs that necessitate time off for either their own or family member's medical care (Shook et al., 2020). Without employers' recognition of their roles in supporting these complex situations, workers will simply be unable to take unpaid leave without further exacerbating their financial circumstances, leading to ongoing decline in their health that ultimately leads to their forced exit from the organization.

An important group of employers where real strides have been made is SMEs in the UK, with Werner's (2017, 2021) studies showing the choices that are made and the drivers and challenges in the voluntary adoption of the living wage. Through researching owners and directors of SMEs, four distinct rationales have been identified, including drives to care for employees, to provide the basis for a high-quality service business model, as an indicator of their corporate social responsibility, and a means to challenge competitors and their practices. Through these insights, alongside policy interventions important levers for implementing the living wage and the means of achieving United Nations Sustainable Development Goal–8 (UN SDG-8; Decent Work and Economic Development) emerge. Working together in practice-informed partnerships will ensure further strides can be made into SDG-17 (Partnerships for Development).

HR Professionals

Professionals in human resource management (HRM) are a further stakeholder group to influence and engage in dialogs that complement the attention on employers (Teng-Calleja et al., Chapter 8). Professional bodies, such as the Chartered Institute of Personnel and Development (CIPD; n.d.) in the UK, have already identified living wages and decent work as an important strategy for organizations to adopt to improve workplace fairness. Researchers charting the employer experience regarding living wages (e.g., Heery et al., 2017; Werner, 2021) note the importance of HRM as the custodians of recognition and reward policy in organizations. In the United States and some other countries, an important component to workplace benefits is workers' medical insurance, yet there can be clear paradoxes in its actual use as workers perceive they cannot afford to draw on this cover (Shook et al., 2020). The combination of health care within an employment contract has long been recognized as a source of tension in the power inequity that arises in employment relationships, with the loss of health benefits leaving some workers more vulnerable to exploitation (Enthoven & Fuchs, 2006), especially if they perceive little or no alternative employment options. The loss of this workplace benefit to families can therefore be a means of coercive control (Lavelle & Smock, 2012).

Trade Unions

Trade Unions are a critical resource allowing those on low pay to access both voice and support (Shook et al., 2020). However, there is a clear paradox for such workers; while they can derive significant benefits from their union membership, they may not be able to afford to pay their dues. Research suggests that the decline of unionization has been an important contributing factor to escalating wage inequality (Western & Rosenfeld, 2011). Furthermore, in India, union membership has been identified as an important moderator for employee involvement and living-wage provision (Maleka et al., 2021). While there has been ongoing academic debate about the purpose of unions in the current work landscape, there is consensus on their significance in representing individual members and collective interests (Hodder & Edwards, 2015). These interests include improvement to the conditions of workers and transforming poor-quality work into that which sustains their members in a fair way. There can be a paradox in their position for many new sector employers who see them as a force to battle against, rather than a resource for improving the resilience of their workforce and thus their organization's viability. For example, there has been ongoing antiunion activity by Amazon in the United States (Fuchs et al., 2022), while in Germany and Italy their role in organizing and collective bargaining has been growing as working conditions of staff have declined (Cattero & D'Onofrio, 2018). Unions remain an important conduit to share evidence about living wages and their value to workers, offering additional support and amplification to workers' voices.

Pension Funds and Investors

An important and often-neglected stakeholder group in living-wage discussions are pension funds and their shareholders whose investments can make them powerful forces of influence over employers. Shareholder groups have repeatedly raised concerns about excessive executive pay (Franklin, 2022) and more recently called for urgent action on gender pay inequity (Rach, 2022). Financial investors are using information about companies' Environmental, Social & Governance practices to find insight into their management ethics (Van Duuren, et al., 2016). Studies using these insights show their value in identifying better performing stocks (Li et al., 2018). As the performance and health implications of low wages, long working hours, and poor-quality work become increasingly well documented, financial services and pension organizations could be an important source of pressure. Further, pension funds may start to see consequences for their funds with early drawdowns for early retirement due to ill-health. This is likely to be significant area for advocacy, as recognition of the unsustainability of these poor-quality work business models emerges, alongside the growing negative consequences for their own investment funds. Researchers and other groups should be bringing these concerns to the light.

Furthermore, beyond the potential cost to investors, pension funds are not immune from the social and moral costs of low wages. Sainsbury's, a large supermarket in the UK employing more than 189,000 people, has recently been identified as a target for a group of investors seeking the introduction of living wages (Jones, 2022), and questioning the morality of this employer's position on their lowest paid workers (Thomas, 2022). Providing evidence to investors may be a fruitful avenue for future dialog, and for influencing employers' quality of work decisions.

Non-Government Organizations (NGOs)

NGOs have been critical partners in maintaining and enhancing lobbying power on the issue of low pay. They continue to play a vital role in supporting dialogs, especially through amplifying the voices of those on low pay and in disseminating research. For example, in the UK, the Living Wage Foundation and those that focus on the different nations, such as Living Wage Scotland, have been important for helping to inform sample selection for studies, by identifying pertinent sectors and employers. Their role is especially critical for supporting longitudinal studies that will allow enable the capture of the psychological changes emerging in the transition onto a living wage from a minimum wage (Searle & McWha-Hermann, 2021).

Internationally, NGOs have also been important to these dialogs. IDH is an NGO involved in sustainable trade (see http://www.idhsustainabletrade.com). Their prior work demonstrates the significance of such organizations as critical conduits between researchers and multinationals in the food sector such as Unilever (see Meyer & Maleka, Chapter 7). Working with small-farm producers they have been active promoters of decent work and living wages, educating and informing those in all parts of the supply chain not only to create more resilient food supply but also improved working lives. As demands for corporate social responsibility grow, these organizations are at the forefront of both identifying issues of concern and identifying and celebrating success stories.

Health and Other Professionals

A further group of professionals who have growing interest in the consequences of low-paid work are those in health care (Shook et al., 2020). At the international level, the World Health Organization is an overarching institution with oversight of the positive effects of living wages for individuals, their families, and communities. Specific studies of the health consequences of living wages have identified their advantages for cardiovascular health (Rehkopf et al., 2018) and mental health (Burmaster et al., 2015). Medical health studies have also identified the value of unemployment over that of poor-quality work (Chandola & Zhang, 2018). Medical doctors are important professionals not only to draw into dialog to advance knowledge of the implications of low pay in reduced longevity or chronic ill-health but also to add weight to the arguments.

In addition, there are other professions who are working downstream dealing with the consequences of low-paid work, including social workers (Shook et al., 2020) and psychologists (Smith, 2015). Through creating collaborative conversations that draw together a variety of professionals who are responding to the consequences of low-paid work, more awareness can be developed of the clues and signals within households and communities, but also the means to devising responses to actually ameliorate the impacts and support societal and welfare needs.

Policy Makers

Policy makers include those at national and State/Federal levels responsible for devising the rules and standards within which employers have to operate. Their policy making regarding the regulation of workplaces and wage floors and ceilings are of particular importance for decent work. Their engagement in dialogs with academic researchers has increased as evidence of the State costs and consequences pertaining to unemployment have grown, highlighting the wider societal consequences of low-paid work (e.g., Paul & Moser, 2009; Stiglitz, 2015). Policy makers are concerned about wage discrimination and human rights (Blustein et al., 2016). Following previous scandals, such as the Bangladesh factory fires, there is growing awareness of the necessity to improve labor standards and working conditions, especially in sectors where foreign organizations are exploiting cheap wage options that place their citizens at risk of wage exploitation, and through unregulated, often-crowded, and vulnerable workplaces (e.g., Saxena, 2022).

Research by Carr and colleagues has demonstrated the dynamics of dialog with policy makers in New Zealand to the enrichment of both I/O psychology and policy (Carr et al., 2019; Carr, et al., 2016a; Carr, et al., 2016b; King, 2016; Parker et al., 2022; Yao et al., 2017). From exploratory work published in 2016 that unlocked the distinct tipping points for wages, their 2017 paper captured the development of fidelity around living wages extending beyond the worker and their family's wellbeing. They have tested and found support for Sen's (1999) capability arguments for living wages. The 2019 study provided important evidence for the economic value of living-wage levels, while their 2022 paper identified the key stakeholders impacted: the individual workers, organizations, sectors and industries, and national-level bodies. Through engagement in dialog, this work has educated policy makers about poverty cycles, and the multiple and ongoing negative consequences for the physical and economic health and wellbeing of workers, their families, and their communities (Meyer & Maleka, Chapter 7; Carr, 2023). Through these dialogs, awareness has shifted from wage floors to considering the value to society of going beyond mere economic subsistence into building quality of life through fairly remunerated work (Carr, et al, 2016a). The value of psychological understanding for policy makers has been demonstrated in the computing of the actual wage level at which the tipping points occur for individual workers, shifting them from surviving to thriving and being able to participate in society (Carr, 2023; Yao et al., 2017).

National policy institutions in many countries also provide researchers with important data tools, such as an annual socioeconomic panel surveys. These rich resources can be adapted by adding pertinent questions. These large-scale and nationally representative sample data collection tools have been used to advance awareness of the significant subjective dimensions of wages, notably their relationship with job satisfaction, wellbeing, fairness, and security (Klug et al., 2021; Chapter 21). These data have enabled researchers to elucidate the psychological consequences of individual economic vulnerabilities by distinguishing the components and consequences of actual and perceive financial strain.

Two critical partners that have been significant in propelling this topic upstream (Jiang et al., Chapter 18), and on to policy agendas are the United Nations and the International Labor Organization (ILO). The United Nations has given more emphasis to the living wage in its 2016–30 Agenda for Sustainable Development (United Nations, 2016) both explicitly and implicitly linking it to topics of fair remuneration and decent work within the Sustainable Development Goals. Likewise, the ILO's Decent Work Agenda has been a significant framework for dialog with many associated events and reports (ILO, 1999, 2008, 2019). These organizations have amplified the significance of living wage to other policy stakeholders as a means of providing more sustainable livelihoods and shared prosperity (Carr et al., 2020). Since the pandemic, however, there have been renewed efforts to pay attention to decent work and living wages as a means to enhance individual- and country-level resilience (ILO, 2021a, 2021b). Again pertinent studies have provided empirical evidence for these reports (e.g., Allan & Blustein, 2022; Blustein & Guarino, 2020). Furthermore, through gaining NGO consultative status at the United Nations (Saltzman et al., Chapter 2), numerous national and international professional psychology associations have fostered direct pathways for psychological research evidence to contribute to high-level policymaking (e.g., Society for Industrial and Organizational Psychology, n.d.). At a European level important partners in the reporting and awareness raising of issues related to decent work include organizations such as Eurofound, informing the European Union and its distinct nations' policies to support post-pandemic drives to build back better (Eurofound, 2020).

A further group with growing influence in public policy are commercial consultancy firms (Lahusen, 2002). These organizations are playing an increasing role in knowledge creation, as well as advising governments, and in their provision of technical, evaluation, and programming functions (Seabrooke & Sending, 2022). However, their for-profit position can be at odds with other policy influencers. Given their increasing utilization in this arena, they should not be overlooked as a partner in dialog.

Academics

A narrative review of this field over the last 20 years has charted the different academic disciplines with the interest and insights to advance dialogs (Searle & McWha-Hermann, 2021). While economists have been at the forefront of resistance to living wages, there is growing attention on the social costs of low pay. Contributions have come from a wide array of disciplines, including management, psychology, sociology, and labor relations. While there can be inherent turf disputes between these communities, working together they offer powerful contributions that add nuance to the inputs, processes, and outcomes of low-paid work. The prior review identified the diversity of their approaches to the operationalization and measurement of living wages and how these component elements could combine to create a powerful lobbying force for change. There is a paradox, however, as alongside teaching and research, many European universities vy with each other to show the impact of their academics' scholarship and research (Arnold et al., 2021). This is despite the fact that there is little, if any, formal workload allocated to academics for such endeavors. In addition, these efforts to achieve impacts can lead to perverse incentive structures for academia and increase the levels of competition between and within institutions, ultimately at the expense of its external stakeholders (Edwards & Roy, 2017).

Future Research Directions

There is an important drive to extend the topic of living wages into a more comprehensive agenda concerning decent work. There are obvious shortcomings in only addressing wages and salaries without considering other components of employee reward and recognition provisions. Research should focus on how aspects of decent work (such as opportunities for participation and employee voice) function to support or undermine organizational initiatives around living wages, and indeed the relative importance of different components of decent work on quality of life. Research is also needed to capture the wider benefits to the organization of altering wages, notably capturing their consequences for the balance sheet. Significant developments in this area are already challenging the prevailing view of wages as simply a cost rather than as the means of providing other benefits for the organization, such as reducing recruitment and selection costs, and building new capacity (Searle & McWha-Hermann, 2021). Moreover, research that positions employee experiences front and center in addressing societal challenges such as poverty and inequality is crucial. WOP research can be used to connect organizational policies and practices with broader issues, through understanding the multilevel and multilayered nature of decent work and its repercussions across families, communities, and society as a whole. For example, by understanding how living wages offer space for employees to spend more time with their families, and the resultant impact this has on child development and education, we can understand the pivotal role organizations play in broader issues of societal wellbeing.

In contrast to these countervailing competitive forces, within the context of decent work and living wages, there are already established networks of researchers, such as Project GLOW (Global Living Organizational Wage). This network has been examining the relationships between living wages and transformational changes in wellbeing and quality of life across a number of countries, including South Africa, The Philippines, the United States, Thailand, and New Zealand (Project GLOW, 2020). Recently, Project GLOW's study has extended to the People's Republic of China (Hu & Carr, 2020). Through the resultant dialogs across different countries, questions can be addressed about whether and how living-wage conceptualizations can transfer cross-culturally, and whether they could lead to a global theory of living wages (Project GLOW, 2020). Further interactions such as the European Association of WOP (EAWOP) small-group meeting on living wages in 2019 have sought to build links between research and practice (see http://www.eawop.org/reports). The emergence of the EAWOP impact incubator, with its remit to advance awareness and impact of WOP science, has made strides we outline in the section on dissemination.

An important further contribution from academics is in the development of content for education and training courses aimed at future managers and leaders to offer a more holistic perspective on living wages and decent work (e.g., Blustein, 2006; Landy & Conte, 2016). This topic can offer competitive advantage in the many education programs at undergraduate and master's levels for future managers alongside increasing provision of ethics education within business school syllabi through the inclusion of corporate social responsibility, notably in MBA provisions (e.g., Cornelius et al., 2007). However, there are new ways to start to engage and inform future managers as the next section will outline.

Dissemination

Academic papers are an important means to capture and disseminate research in any field. Within living-wage studies, these papers have been significant, but often siloed within disciplines that constrain the spread of arguments and conversations (Searle & McWha-Hermann, 2021). Attention from psychology on living wages has increased significantly in recent years (see Searle & McWha-Hermann, 2021 for a detailed historical review) and has been actively disseminated to other stakeholders, to raise awareness of the mechanisms of poverty, develop an employee-centric perspective, and draw out the distinct physical- and mental-health outcomes within households (e.g., Smith, 2015). Dissemination has promoted the benefits of living wages beyond subsistence, and their spillover consequences beyond the worker for households, and for societal participation (see, Haar, Chapter 17; Toaddy, Crawford et al., Chapter 22; Yao et al., 2017).

A further traditional method for dissemination that spans many stakeholders is through reports. These capture key evidence, advance knowledge transfer, often by including recommendations identifying the critical stakeholder groups within which important changes can occur. However, there can be tensions between authors and stakeholders where further action or change is required. Without preceding dialogs, these reports can fail to achieve the desired impacts. There can also be ideological divergence between different stakeholders which distorts the messaging or reduces its impact.

The density of text and the language used in academic papers and reports can create significant barriers to the sharing and uptake of new perspectives. In response to this concern, the EAWOP impact incubator (www.eawopimpact.org) has worked with NGO Living Wage Scotland to devised four briefing documents (see also, Saner & Yiu, Chapter 5). These documents were developed by WOP and other researchers who attended the EAWOP small-group meeting in June 2019 that included a day engaging with practitioners, employers, and NGOs to discuss the core challenges and barriers concerning the living wage. Through this active knowledge exchange and dialog process, greater clarity was achieved about what types of documents are needed to support organizational efforts. Four evidence-based documents were developed, including a definition of a living wage; the case for employers and workers; a checklist for HR professionals; and living wages in the supply chain.[2] They can be used as stand-alone items or combined into a pack to support engagement and inform different stakeholders. The language was designed to be accessible, and diagrams and pictures were added to convey the messages more clearly than through large bodies of text. These have been important resources for policy makers to engage with and consider the I/O psychology science within their local contexts and internationally.

In addition to this paper-based dissemination approach, efforts have been made to enhance understanding of the living wage without actively priming negative psychological associations such as disgust that can be inadvertently primed through discussion of poverty (Fiske, 2007). Working with animators, and deliberately including gender- and race-neutral characters, a simple picture-based animation was devised with voiceovers and subtitles in a variety of world languages. Lasting 2.5 minutes this was the first product launched by the EA-WOP impact incubator in May 2021. This webinar launch included not only the animation but also further subtitled I/O-science-based talks that are hosted on the associated YouTube channel. The animation has proven a popular resource for different stakeholders. In addition to being used to educate students, it has also been adopted by NGOs and activists through the Project GLOW community (e.g., Intrapraset et al., Chapter 9; Meyer & Maleka, Chapter 7; Teng-Calleja et al., Chapter 8).

Further examples of local change have also been achieved through collaboration between the authors, Living Wage Scotland, and local policy makers to support expansion of the concept beyond single living-wage employers into entire living-wage areas—in this case, the City of Edinburgh. The decision to become a living-wage place was taken by the City of Edinburgh Council as part of their ongoing poverty-reduction action plan (Edinburgh Poverty Commission, 2020). Through becoming a living-wage place, private-, public-, and third-sector employers work together to become beacon employers paying living wages to their employees and in their supply chains. As part of efforts to engage with employers, a series of four masterclasses were designed targeting SMEs to share knowledge about becoming a better place to work. Drawing on the science, the case for living wages and decent work was outlined and operationalized. This initiative is in its early stages but living wages are a central component to this local authority's decision to achieve social justice for their wider community.

Work that pays a living wage but does not provide decent working conditions has been demonstrated in studies to create downward spirals for individual workers (Carr et al., 2019). Drawing on the distinct interconnections, a novel approach to dissemination has included using immersive experiential education games technology to achieve social change (Klimmt, 2009) by exposing players to workplace decision-making and allow them to discern their impacts. Searle & McWha-Hermann's game is in the final stages of evaluation and has already received positive attention from the gaming community; at the time of writing, it is a finalist in the European Conference on Games Based Learning international educational games competition. Working with game makers and an artist, this approach has challenges. While incurring high production costs, it applies evidence-informed decision branches to underpin the play context and shape the players' experiences. Further supporting resources have also been produced, designed to provoke reflection on the experience and offer new learning about decent work and its value. This tool is designed to be used in an education and training context, without heavy use of text reducing the potential for engagement with those without good English. As a proof of concept, it represents an important and more immersive approach to dissemination and engaging diverse stakeholders.

Conclusion

Work is changing significantly, becoming increasingly precarious, with wage stagnation leaving workers even more vulnerable to rising living costs (Reeves et al., 2017). The combined impacts of reduced income and employment protection, and diminished job security, leave the working poor and their families trapped in a cycle of poverty, which ultimately impedes their development and that of their communities and wider society. The COVID-19 pandemic has provided salient evidence of the growing ineffectiveness of the previous panacea to poverty—work (Searle & McWha-Hermann, 2021; Smith, 2015). This increasing disconnect has consequences for societal harmony and cohesion. This chapter has outlined the three interconnected processes—knowledge generation, stakeholder dialogs, and novel approaches to dissemination—that are required to occur concurrently with developing compelling research to ensure the capture of empirical evidence and its translation to achieve societal change. There remains important further work to be done to better elaborate and understand the intersectionalities and pernicious combinations that act upon the work and rewards of low-paid workers (e.g., Allan et al., 2021; Blustein & Guarino, 2020). Drawing from Adam Smith's (1776/1976) seminal insights into the importance of transparent and fair wages beyond the worker, these developments seek to attend to past injustices to achieve a better and more sustainable quality of life for workers and their households. Through the three interlocked processes, we can make efforts to build from minimum rates of pay toward *decent* incomes and specifically living wages, and to considering work as a means of deriving a better quality of life and more sustainable workplaces (McWha-Hermann et al., 2021; Searle & McWha-Hermann, 2021). We chart the shifts in perspectives required by different stakeholders (Carr et al., 2018; Gloss et al., 2017). However, future research remains necessary to build and extend understanding of employee perceptions and experiences of living wages, including incorporating measurements of the individual, family, organizational, and societal consequences of living wages. Through these further developments, an understanding of the social embeddedness will be improved and the relationship between living wages and affective, cognitive, behavioral, and physiological indicators (such as self-efficacy and self-worth, wellbeing, job security, and work motivation) derived (McWha-Hermann et al., 2021).

Notes

1 Note that we use the term work and organizational psychology (WOP) here because this is the term commonly used within the UK and European context in which we work. We recognize that readers may be more familiar with other terms that are used interchangeably in practice, such as industrial-organizational (I/O) psychology, occupational psychology, or business psychology. Hereafter, therefore, we use the terms WOP and I/O psychology interchangeably.

2 Please visit www.eawopimpact.org/decent-work to find these.

References

Ahnquist, J., Wamala, S. P., & Lindstrom, M. (2012). Social determinants of health—A question of social or economic capital? Interaction effects of socioeconomic factors on health outcomes. *Social Science & Medicine, 74*(6), 930–939. https://doi.org/10.1016/j.socscimed.2011.11.026

Ali, S. R., Fall, K., & Hoffman, T. (2012). Life without work: Understanding social class changes and unemployment through theoretical integration. *Journal of Career Assessment, 21*(1), 111–126. https://doi.org/10.1177/1069072712454820

Allan, B. A., & Blustein, D. L. (2022). Precarious work and workplace dignity during COVID-19: A longitudinal study. *Journal of Vocational Behavior, 136*, Article 103739. https://doi.org/10.1016/j.jvb.2022.103739

Anker, R. (2006). Living wages around the world: A new methodology and internationally comparable estimates. *International Labour Review, 145*(4), 309–338. https://doi.org/10.1111/j.1564-913X.2006.tb00037.x

Arnold, J., Dries, N., & Gabriel, Y. (2021). Enhancing the social impact of research in work and organizational psychology—Beyond academia. *European Journal of Work and Organizational Psychology, 30*(3), 329–338. https://doi.org/10.1080/1359432X.2021.1915293

Arrowsmith, J., & Parker, J. (2013). The meaning of 'employee engagement' for the values and roles of the HRM function. *The International Journal of Human Resource Management, 24*(14), 2692–2712. https://doi.org/10.1080/09585192.2013.763842

Baritz, L. (1960). *The servants of power: A history of the use of social science in American industry*. Wesleyan University Press. https:/doi.org/10.1037/11283-000.

Bergman, M. E., & Jean, V. A. (2016). Where have all the "workers" gone? A critical analysis of the unrepresentativeness of our samples relative to the labor market in the industrial–organizational psychology literature. *Industrial and Organizational Psychology, 9*(1), 84–113. https://doi.org/10.1017/iop.2015.70

Berti, M., & Simpson, A. V. (2021). The dark side of organizational paradoxes: The dynamics of disempowerment. *Academy of Management Review, 46*(2), 252–274. https://doi.org/10.5465/amr.2017.0208

Blundell, R., Costa Dias, M., Joyce, R., & Xu, X. (2020). COVID-19 and Inequalities. *Fiscal Studies, 41*(2), 291–319. https://doi.org/10.1111/1475-5890.12232

Blustein, D. L. (2006). *The psychology of working: A new perspective for career development, counseling, and public policy*. https://doi.org/10.4324/9780203935477

Blustein, D. L., & Guarino, P. A. (2020). Work and unemployment in the time of COVID-19: The existential experience of loss and fear. *Journal of Humanistic Psychology, 60*(5), 702–709. https://doi.org/10.1177/0022167820934229

Blustein, D. L., Olle, C., Connors-Kellgren, A., & Diamonti, A. J. (2016). Decent work: A psychological perspective. *Frontiers in Psychology, 7*, 407–417. https://doi.org/10.3389/fpsyg.2016.00407

Braveman, P. A., Cubbin, C., Egerter, S., Williams, D. R., & Pamuk, E. (2010). Socioeconomic disparities in health in the United States: What the patterns tell us. *American Journal of Public Health, 100*(S1), S186–S196. https://doi.org/10.2105/AJPH.2009.166082

Burbano, V., & Chiles, B. (2022). Mitigating gig and remote worker misconduct: Evidence from a real effort experiment. *Organization Science, 33*(4), 1273–1299. https://doi.org/10.1287/orsc.2021.1488

Burlinson, A., Giulietti, M., & Battisti, G. (2018). The elephant in the energy room: Establishing the nexus between housing poverty and fuel poverty. *Energy Economics, 72*, 135–144. https://doi.org/10.1016/j.eneco.2018.03.036

Burmaster, K. B., Landefeld, J. C., Rehkopf, D. H., Lahiff, M., Sokal-Gutierrez, K., Adler-Milstein, S., & Fernald, L. C. (2015). Impact of a private sector living wage intervention on depressive symptoms among apparel workers in the Dominican Republic: A quasi-experimental study. *British Medical Journal Open, 5*(8), e007336. https://bmjopen.bmj.com/content/5/8/e007336

Carr, S. C. (2013). Poverty. In S. C. Carr & A. J. Marsella (Eds.) *Anti-poverty psychology*. Springer. https://doi.org/10.1007/978-1-4614-6303-0_1

Carr, S. C. (2023). *Wage and well-being: Toward sustainable livelihoods*. Springer.

Carr, S. C., Furnham, A., & MacLachlan, M. (2012). *Humanitarian work psychology*. Palgrave Macmillan.

Carr, S. C., Haar, J., Hodgetts, D., Arrowsmith, J., Parker, J., Young-Hauser, A., Alefaio-Tuglia, S., & Jones, H. (2019). An employee's living wage and their quality of work life: How important are household size and household income? *Journal of Sustainability Research, 1*(1), Article e190007. https://doi.org/10.20900/jsr20190007

Carr, S. C., Hodgetts, D. J., Potgieter, J., Meyer, I. (2021). Macropsychology for decent work. Sustainable livelihood. In M. MacLachlan & J. McVeigh (Eds.), *Macropsychology*. Springer. https://doi.org/10.1007/978-3-030-50176-1_9

Carr, S., C., Hodgson, M., R., Vent, D., H., & Purcell, I., P. (2005). Pay diversity across work teams: Doubly de-motivating influences? *Journal of Managerial Psychology, 20*(5), 417–439. https://doi.org/10.1108/02683940510602969

Carr, S. C., Maleka, M., Meyer, I., Barry, M.-L., Haar, J., Parker, J., Arrowsmith, J., Yao, C., Hodgetts, D., Jones, H., Young-Hausner, A., Afeaki-Mafile'o, E., Rasmussen, A.-H., Alefaio-Tugia, S., Falealili, B., Mafile'o, K., Pikula, T., Wolfgramm, N., 'Uhila, H.,…& Naithani, A. (2018). How can wages sustain a living? By getting ahead of the curve. *Sustainability Science, 13*(4), 901–917. https://doi.org/10.1007/s11625-018-0560-7

Carr, S. C., McWha, I., MacLachlan, M., & Furnham, A. (2010). International–local remuneration differences across six countries: Do they undermine poverty reduction work? *International Journal of Psychology, 45*(5), 321–340. https://doi.org/10.1080/00207594.2010.491990

Carr, S. C., Meyer, I., Saxena, M., Seubert, C., Hopfgartner, L., Arora, B., Jyoti, D., Rugimbana, R., Kempton, H., & Marai, L. (2021). "Our fair trade coffee tastes better": It might, but under what conditions? *Journal of Consumer Affairs, 56*(2). https:/doi.org/10.1111/joca.12416.

Carr, S. C., Parker, J., Arrowsmith, J., & Watters, P. A. (2016a). The living wage: Theoretical integration and an applied research agenda. *International Labour Review, 155*(1), 1–24. https://doi.org/10.1111/j.1564-913X.2015.00029.x

Carr, S. C., Parker, J., Arrowsmith, J., Watters, P., & Jones, H. (2016b). Can a 'living wage' springboard human capability? An exploratory study from New Zealand. *Labour & Industry, 26*(1), 24–39. https://doi.org/10.1080/10301763.2016.1152533

Cattero, B., & D'Onofrio, M. (2018). Organizing and collective bargaining in the digitized "tertiary factories" of Amazon: A comparison between Germany and Italy. In E. Ales, Y. Curzi, T. Fabbri, O. Rymkevich, I. Senatori, & G. Solinas (Eds.), *Working in digital and smart organizations* (pp. 141–164). Springer.

Chandola, T., & Zhang, N. (2018). Re-employment, job quality, health and allostatic load biomarkers: Prospective evidence from the UK Household Longitudinal Study. *International Journal of Epidemiology, 47*(1), 47–57. https://doi.org/10.1093/ije/dyx150

Chartered Institute of Personnel and Development. (n.d.). *Pay a fair and liveable wage*. https://www.cipd.co.uk/knowledge/culture/well-being/employee-financial-well-being/in-work-poverty/pay-fair-liveable-wage

Chen, E., & Miller, G. E. (2012). "Shift-and-persist" strategies: Why low socioeconomic status isn't always bad for health. *Perspectives on Psychological Science, 7*(2), 135–158. https://doi.org/10.1177/1745691612436694

Ciscel, D. H. (2000). The living wage movement: Building a political link from market wages to social institutions. *Journal of Economic Issues, 34*(2), 527–535. https://doi.org/10.1080/00213624.2000.11506292

Cole, B. L., Shimkhada, R., Morgenstern, H., Kominski, G., Fielding, J. E., & Wu, S. (2005). Projected health impact of the Los Angeles City living wage ordinance. *Journal of Epidemiology and Community Health, 59*(8), 645–650. https://doi.org/10.1136/jech.2004.028142

Connelly, C. E., Fieseler, C., Černe, M., Giessner, S. R., & Wong, S. I. (2020). Working in the digitized economy: HRM theory & practice. *Human Resource Management Review, 31*(1), Article 100762. https:/doi.org/10.1016/j.hrmr.2020.100762.

Cornelius, N., Wallace, J., & Tassabehji, R. (2007). An analysis of corporate social responsibility, corporate identity and ethics teaching in business schools. *Journal of Business Ethics, 76*(1), 117–135. https://doi.org/10.1007/s10551-006-9271-6

de Vaujany, F.-X., Leclercq-Vandelannoitte, A., Munro, I., Nama, Y., & Holt, R. (2021). Control and surveillance in work practice: Cultivating paradox in 'new' modes of organizing. *Organization Studies, 42*(5), 675–695. https://doi.org/10.1177/01708406211010988

Dudau, A. I., Favotto, A., Kominis, G., & Sicilia, M. (2020). Building trust in public sector networks: The role of rhetoric and persuasion. *Financial Accountability & Management, 36*(2), 134–150. https://doi.org/10.1111/faam.12229

Duggan, J., Sherman, U., Carbery, R., & McDonnell, A. (2020). Algorithmic management and app-work in the gig economy: A research agenda for employment relations and HRM. *Human Resource Management Journal, 30*(1), 114–132. https://doi.org/10.1111/1748-8583.12258

Duggan, J., Sherman, U., Carbery, R., & McDonnell, A. (2021). Boundaryless careers and algorithmic constraints in the gig economy. *The International Journal of Human Resource Management, 33*(22), 4468–4498. https://doi.org/10.1080/09585192.2021.1953565

Edinburgh Poverty Commission (2020) *A just capital: Actions to end poverty in Edinburgh*. https://edinburghpovertycommission.org.uk/wp-content/uploads/2020/09/20200930_EPC_FinalReport_AJustCapital.pdf.

Edwards, M. A., & Roy, S. (2017). Academic research in the 21st century: Maintaining scientific integrity in a climate of perverse incentives and hypercompetition. *Environmental Engineering Science, 34*(1), 51–61.

Enthoven, A. C., & Fuchs, V. R. (2006). Employment-based health insurance: Past, present, and future. *Health Affairs, 25*(6), 1538–1547.

Erdogan, B., & Bauer, T. N. (2021). Overqualification at work: A review and synthesis of the literature. *Annual Review of Organizational Psychology and Organizational Behavior, 8*(1), 259–283. https://doi.org/10.1146/annurev-orgpsych-012420-055831

Eurofound. (2020). *Living, working and COVID-19.* Publications Office of the European Union. https://www.eurofound.europa.eu/sites/default/files/ef_publication/field_ef_document/ef20059en.pdf
Fiske, S. T. (2007). On prejudice and the brain. *Daedalus, 136*(1), 156–159. https://doi.org/10.1162/daed.2007.136.1.156
Flint, E., Cummins, S. & Wills, J. (2014). Investigating the effect of the London living wage on the psychological wellbeing of low-wage service sector employees: A feasibility study, *Journal of Public Health, 36*(2), 187–193. https://doi.org/10.1093/pubmed/fdt093
Folger, R. (1994). Workplace justice and employee worth. *Social Justice Research, 7,* 225–241.
Frank, R. H. (1984). Are workers paid their marginal products? *The American Economic Review, 74*(4), 549–571. http://www.jstor.org/stable/1805123
Franklin, J. (2022, May 18) JPMorgan shareholders vote against Jamie Dimon's pay. *Financial Times.* https://www.ft.com/content/cd34c86b-1253-467a-aa83-23a78b81fcb4
Friedman, G. (2014). Workers without employers: Shadow corporations and the rise of the gig economy. *Review of Keynesian Economics, 2*(2), 171–188.
Fuchs, M., Dannenberg, P., & Wiedemann, C. (2022). Big tech and labour resistance at Amazon. *Science as Culture, 31*(1), 29–43.
Gloss, A., Carr, S. C., Reichman, W., Abdul-Nasiru, I., & Oestereich, W. T. (2017). From handmaidens to POSH humanitarians: The case for making human capabilities the business of I-O psychology. *Industrial and Organizational Psychology, 10*(3), 329–369. https://doi.org/10.1017/iop.2017.27
Groot, S., & Hodgetts, D. (2015). The infamy of begging: A case-based approach to street homelessness and radical commerce. *Qualitative Research in Psychology, 12*(4), 349–366. https://doi.org/10.1080/14780887.2014.960984
Grote, G., & Guest, D. (2016). The case for reinvigorating quality of working life research. *Human Relations, 70*(2), 149–167. https://doi.org/10.1177/0018726716654746
Haar, J. M., Russo, M., Suñe, A., & Ollier-Malaterre, A. (2014). Outcomes of work–life balance on job satisfaction, life satisfaction and mental health: A study across seven cultures. *Journal of Vocational Behavior, 85*(3), 361–373. https://doi.org/10.1016/j.jvb.2014.08.010
Hakel, M. (2013). Homo economicus, industrial psychology, and the greater good. In J. B. Olson-Buchanan, L. L. Koppes Bryan, & L. Foster Thompson (Eds.), *Using industrial-organizational psychology for the greater good: Helping those who help others* (pp. 559–566). Routledge.
Heery, E., Nash, D., & Hann, D. (2017). *The living wage employer experience.* Cardiff Business School, Cardiff University. https://www.cardiff.ac.uk/__data/assets/pdf_file/0015/2431050/Living_Wage_Employer_Experience.pdf
Hodder, A., & Edwards, P. (2015). The essence of trade unions: Understanding identity, ideology and purpose. *Work, Employment and Society, 29*(5), 843–854. https://doi.org/10.1177/0950017014568142
Hu, Y., & Carr, S. C. (2020). Living wages across the Pacific Rim: A localised replication study from China. *Journal of Pacific Rim Psychology, 14.* https://doi.org/10.1017/prp.2020.11
International Labour Organization. (1999). *Report of the director-general: Decent work.*
International Labour Organization. (2008). *World of work report 2008: Income inequalities in the age of financial globalization.*

International Labour Organization. (2018). The future of informal work, the future of statistics on informal work.

International Labour Organization. (2019). *World employment and social outlook—Trends 2019.*

International Labour Organization. (2021a). *Global wage report 2021.*

International Labour Organization. (2021b). *World employment and social outlook 2021.*

Jones, R. (2022, March 28). Investors call for Sainsbury's to pay workers 'real living wage'. *The Guardian.* https://www.theguardian.com/uk-news/2022/mar/28/investors-call-for-sainsburys-to-pay-workers-real-living-wage

Kellogg, K. C., Valentine, M. A., & Christin, A. (2020). Algorithms at work: The new contested terrain of control. *Academy of Management Annals, 14*(1), 366–410. https://doi.org/10.5465/annals.2018.0174

King, P. (2016). Setting the New Zealand living wage: complexities and practicalities. *Labour and Industry, 26*(1), 8–23. https://doi.org/10.1080/10301763.2015.1116054

Klimmt, C. (2009). Serious games and social change: Why they (should) work. In U. Ritterfeld, M. Cody, & P. Vorderer, P. (Eds.) *Serious games: Mechanisms and effects* (pp. 270–292). Routledge.

Klug, K., Selenko, E., & Gerlitz, J.-Y. (2021). Working, but not for a living: A longitudinal study on the psychological consequences of economic vulnerability among German employees. *European Journal of Work and Organizational Psychology, 30*(6), 790–807. https://doi.org/10.1080/1359432X.2020.1843533

Koen, J., Klehe, U.-C., Van Vianen, A. E. M., Zikic, J., & Nauta, A. (2010). Job-search strategies and re-employment quality: The impact of career adaptability. *Journal of Vocational Behavior, 77*(1), 126–139. https://doi.org/10.1016/j.jvb.2010.02.004

Kost, D., Fieseler, C., & Wong, S. I. (2020). Boundaryless careers in the gig economy: An oxymoron? *Human Resource Management Journal, 30*(1), 100–113. https://doi.org/10.1111/1748-8583.12265

Lahusen, C. (2002). Commercial consultancies in the European Union: The shape and structure of professional interest intermediation. *Journal of European Public Policy, 9*(5), 695–714.

Lambert, S. J., Henly, J. R., & Kim, J. (2019). Precarious work schedules as a source of economic insecurity and institutional distrust. *RSF: The Russell Sage Foundation Journal of the Social Sciences, 5*(4), 218–257. https://doi.org/10.7758/RSF.2019.5.4.08

Landefeld, J. C., Burmaster, K. B., Rehkopf, D. H., Syme, S. L., Lahiff, M., Adler-Milstein, S., & Fernald, L. C. H. (2014) The association between a living wage and subjective social status and self-rated health: A quasi-experimental study in the Dominican Republic. *Social Science & Medicine, 121,* 91–97. https://doi.org/10.1016/j.socscimed.2014.09.051

Landy, F. J., & Conte, J. M. (2016). *Work in the 21st century: An introduction to industrial and organizational psychology.* John Wiley & Sons.

Lavelle, B., & Smock, P. J. (2012). Divorce and women's risk of health insurance loss. *Journal of Health and Social Behavior, 53*(4), 413–431.

Lepore, J. (2021, November 4). Elon Musk is building a sci-fi world, and the rest of us are trapped in it. *The New York Times.* https://www.nytimes.com/2021/11/04/opinion/elon-musk-capitalism.html

Li, Y., Gong, M., Zhang, X. Y., & Koh, L. (2018). The impact of environmental, social, and governance disclosure on firm value: The role of CEO power. *The British Accounting Review, 50*(1), 60–75.

Liddell, C., & Morris, C. (2010). Fuel poverty and human health: A review of recent evidence. *Energy Policy, 38*(6), 2987–2997. https://doi.org/10.1016/j.enpol.2010.01.037

Mair, S., Druckman, A., & Jackson, T. (2018). Investigating fairness in global supply chains: Applying an extension of the living wage to the Western European clothing supply chain. *The International Journal of Life Cycle Assessment, 23*(9), 1862–1873. https://doi.org/10.1007/s11367-017-1390-z

Maleka, M. J., Schultz, C. M., van Hoek, L., Paul-Dachapalli, L., & Ragadu, S. C. (2021). Union membership as a moderator in the relationship between living wage, job satisfaction and employee engagement. *The Indian Journal of Labour Economics, 64*(3), 621–640. https://doi.org/10.1007/s41027-021-00322-0

McKee-Ryan, F. M., Virick, M., Prussia, G. E., Harvey, J., & Lilly, J. D. (2009). Life after the layoff: Getting a job worth keeping. *Journal of Organizational Behavior, 30*(4), 561–580. https://doi.org/10.1002/job.566

McWha-Hermann, I. (2022). Equal pay for work of equal value: Easier said than done. In D. L. Blustein & L. Y. Flores (Eds.), *Rethinking work: Essays on building a better workplace.* Routledge.

McWha-Hermann, I., Searle, R. H., & Carr, S. C. (2021). Striving for more: Work and organizational psychology (WOP) and living wages. *European Journal of Work and Organizational Psychology, 30*(6), 771–776. https://doi.org/10.1080/1359432X.2021.1972972

McWhirter, E. H., & McWha-Hermann, I. (2021). Social justice and career development: Progress, problems, and possibilities. *Journal of Vocational Behavior, 126*, 103–492. https://doi.org/10.1016/j.jvb.2020.103492

Moya, M., & Fiske, S. T. (2017). The social psychology of the Great Recession and social class divides. *Journal of Social Issues, 73*(1), 8–22. https://doi.org/10.1111/josi.12201

Parker, J., Arrowsmith, J., Young-Hauser, A., Hodgetts, D., Carr, S. C., Haar, J., & Alefaio-Tugia, S. (2022). Perceptions of living wage impacts in Aotearoa New Zealand: Towards a multi-level, contextualised conceptualisation. *Personnel Review.* Advance online publication. https://doi.org/10.1108/PR-01-2021-0037

Parker, S. K., & Jorritsma, K. (2021). Good work design for all: Multiple pathways to making a difference. *European Journal of Work and Organizational Psychology, 30*(3), 456–468. https://doi.org/10.1080/1359432X.2020.1860121

Parker, S. K., Morgeson, F. P., & Johns, G. (2017). One hundred years of work design research: Looking back and looking forward. *Journal of Applied Psychology, 102*(3), 403–420. https://doi.org/10.1037/apl0000106

Paul, K. I., & Moser, K. (2009). Unemployment impairs mental health: Meta-analyses. *Journal of Vocational Behavior, 74*(3), 264–282. https://doi.org/10.1016/j.jvb.2009.01.001

Petriglieri, G., Ashford, S. J., & Wrzesniewski, A. (2018). Agony and ecstasy in the gig economy: Cultivating holding environments for precarious and personalized work identities. *Administrative Science Quarterly, 64*(1), 124–170. https://doi.org/10.1177/0001839218759646

Project GLOW. (2020). International perspectives on living wages for sustainable livelihoods: Some lessons from Project GLOW (Global Living Organizational Wage). In W. L. Filho, A. M. Azul, L. Brandli, A. L. Salvia & T. Wall. (Eds.), *Decent work and economic growth* (pp. 620–629). Oxford University Press. https://doi.org/10.1007/978-3-319-95867-5_109

Rand, J. E. (2015). The far-reaching impact of job loss and unemployment. *Annual Review of Sociology, 41*, 359–375. https://doi.org/10.1146/annurev-soc-071913-043237

Rach, S. (2022, June 30). L&G calls for 'urgent action' as gender pension gap stays constant. *Financial Times.* https://www.ftadviser.com/pensions/2022/06/29/l-g-calls-for-urgent-action-as-gender-pension-gap-stays-constant/

Reeves, A., Loopstra, R., & Stuckler, D. (2017). The growing disconnect between food prices and wages in Europe: Cross-national analysis of food deprivation and welfare regimes in twenty-one EU countries, 2004–2012. *Public Health Nutrition, 20*(8), 1414–1422. https://doi.org/10.1017/S1368980017000167

Rehkopf, D. H., Burmaster, K., Landefeld, J. C., Adler-Milstein, S., Flynn, E. P., Acevedo, M. C., Jones-Smith, J. C., Adler, N., & Fernald, L. C. H. (2018). The impact of a private sector living wage intervention on consumption and cardiovascular disease risk factors in a middle income country. *BMC Public Health, 18*(1), 179. https://doi.org/10.1186/s12889-018-5052-2

Saxena, M. (2017). Workers in Poverty: An insight into informal workers around the world. *Industrial and Organizational Psychology, 10*(3), 376–379. https://doi.org/10.1017/iop.2017.29

Saxena, M. (2021). Cultural skills as drivers of decency in decent work: an investigation of skilled workers in the informal economy. *European Journal of Work and Organizational Psychology, 30*(6), 824–836. https://doi.org/10.1080/1359432X.2021.1918760

Saxena, S. B. (2022). Developing country responses to demands for improved labor standards: case studies from the garment and textiles industry in Asia. In K. A. Elliott (Ed.), *Handbook on globalisation and labour standards* (pp. 258–273). Edward Elgar Publishing.

Schmid, Y., & Dowling, M. (2020). New work: New motivation? A comprehensive literature review on the impact of workplace technologies. *Management Review Quarterly, 72,* 59–86. https://doi.org/10.1007/s11301-020-00204-7

Seabrooke, L., & Sending, O. J. (2022). Consultancies in public administration. *Public Administration, 100*(3), 457–471 https://doi.org/10.1111/padm.12844

Searle, R. H., & McWha-Hermann, I. (2020, November 12). Why living wages should be a priority during COVID-19. *The Conversation.* https://theconversation.com/why-living-wages-should-be-a-priority-during-covid-19-149559

Searle, R. H., & McWha-Hermann, I. (2021). "Money's too tight (to mention)": A review and psychological synthesis of living wage research. *European Journal of Work and Organizational Psychology, 30*(3), 428–443. https://doi.org/10.1080/1359432X.2020.1838604

Searle, R. H., & Rice, C. (2021). Making an impact in healthcare contexts: Insights from a mixed-methods study of professional misconduct. *European Journal of Work and Organizational Psychology, 30*(4), 470–481. https://doi.org/10.1080/1359432X.2020.1850520

Sen, A. (1999). *Development as freedom*. Oxford University Press.

Seubert, C., Hopfgartner, L., & Glaser, J. (2021). Living wages, decent work, and need satisfaction: An integrated perspective. *European Journal of Work and Organizational Psychology, 30*(6), 808–823. https://doi.org/10.1080/1359432X.2021.1966094

Shook, J., Goodkind, S., Engel, R. J., Wexler, S., & Ballentine, K. L. (2020). Moving beyond poverty: Effects of low-wage work on individual, social, and family well-being. *Families in Society, 101*(3), 249–259. https://doi.org/10.1177/1044389420923473

Smids, J., Nyholm, S., & Berkers, H. (2020). Robots in the workplace: A threat to—or opportunity for—meaningful work? *Philosophy & Technology, 33*(3), 503–522. https://doi.org/10.1007/s13347-019-00377-4

Smith, A. (1976). *An inquiry into the nature and causes of the wealth of nations*. Methuen. (Original work published 1776).

Smith, L. (2015). Reforming the minimum wage: Toward a psychological perspective. *American Psychologist, 70*(6), 557–565. https://doi.org/10.1037/a0039579

Society for Industrial and Organizational Psychology. (n.d.) *SIOP and the United Nations* https://www.siop.org/About-SIOP/Advocacy/SIOP-and-the-United-Nations

Sonnentag, S. (2018). The recovery paradox: Portraying the complex interplay between job stressors, lack of recovery, and poor well-being. *Research in Organizational Behavior, 38*, 169–185. https://doi.org/10.1016/j.riob.2018.11.002

Spreitzer, G. M., Kizilos, M. A., & Nason, S. W. (1997). A dimensional analysis of the relationship between psychological empowerment and effectiveness satisfaction, and strain. *Journal of Management, 23*(5), 679–704. https://doi.org/10.1177/014920639702300504

Stabile, D. (2008). *The living wage: Lessons from the history of economic thought.* Edward Elgar Publishing.

Stabile, D. R. (2018). Background of the Employment Act I: A living wage. In D. R. Stabile (Ed.), *Macroeconomic policy and a living wage: The Employment Act as redistributive economics, 1944–1969* (pp. 27–65). Springer International Publishing. https://doi.org/10.1007/978-3-030-01998-3_2

Stiglitz, J. (2015). *The great divide: Unequal societies and what we can do about them.* W. W. Norton. https://doi.org/10.1037/a0039579

Stremersch, J., Van Hoye, G., & van Hooft, E. (2021). How to successfully manage the school-to-work transition: Integrating job search quality in the social cognitive model of career self-management. *Journal of Vocational Behavior, 131,* Article 103643. https:/doi.org/10.1016/j.jvb.2021.103643

Sun, X., Rehnberg, C., & Meng, Q. (2009). How are individual-level social capital and poverty associated with health equity? A study from two Chinese cities. *International Journal for Equity in Health, 8*(1), 2. https://doi.org/10.1186/1475-9276-8-2

Sverke, M., Låstad, L., Hellgren, J., Richter, A., & Näswall, K. (2019). A meta-analysis of job insecurity and employee performance: Testing temporal aspects, rating source, welfare regime, and union density as moderators. *International Journal of Environmental Research and Public Health, 16*(14), Article 2536. https://doi.org/10.3390/ijerph16142536

Taber, B. J., & Blankemeyer, M. (2015). Future work self and career adaptability in the prediction of proactive career behaviors. *Journal of Vocational Behavior, 86*, 20–27. https://doi.org/10.1016/j.jvb.2014.10.005

Taylor, M., Marsh, G., Nicole, D., & Broadbent, P. (2017). *Good work: The Taylor review of modern working practices.* United Kingdom Government. https://assets.publishing.service.gov.uk/government/uploads/system/uploads/attachment_data/file/627671/good-work-taylor-review-modern-working-practices-rg.pdf

Thomas. H. (2022, July 6). Where the Sainsbury's pay defence doesn't add up. *Financial Times.* https://www.ft.com/content/6b1057bd-2bf1-46d7-9120-1e288fef0d3d

United Nations. (2016). *The sustainable development goals report.* https://unstats.un.org/sdgs/report/2016/the%20sustainable%20development%20goals%20report%202016.pdf

van der Kolk, B. (2014). *The body keeps the score: Mind, brain and body in the transformation of trauma.* Penguin.

van Duuren, E., Plantinga, A. & Scholtens, B. (2016). ESG integration and the investment management process: Fundamental investing reinvented. *Journal of Business Ethics 138,* 525–533 https://doi.org/10.1007/s10551-015-2610-8

Verbruggen, M., & De Vos, A. (2019). When people don't realize their career desires: Toward a theory of career inaction. *Academy of Management Review, 45*(2), 376–394. https://doi.org/10.5465/amr.2017.0196

Waltman, J. L. (2004). *The case for the living wage.* Algora Publishing.

Wanberg, C. R. (2012). The individual experience of unemployment. *Annual Review of Psychology, 63*(1), 369–396. https://doi.org/10.1146/annurev-psych-120710-100500

Watson, G. P., Kistler, L. D., Graham, B. A., & Sinclair, R. R. (2021). Looking at the gig picture: Defining gig work and explaining profile differences in gig workers' job demands and resources. *Group & Organization Management, 46*(2), 327–361. https://doi.org/10.1177/1059601121996548

Weiss, H., & Rupp, D. (2011). Experiencing work: An essay on a person-centric I/O psychology. *Industrial and Organizational Psychology, 4*(1), 83–97. https://doi.org/10.1111/j.1754-9434.2010.01302.x

Werner, A. (2017). A new living contract: Cases in the implementation of the living wage by British SME retailers. *Employee Relations, 39*(6), 850–862. https://doi.org/10.1108/ER-07-2017-0150

Werner, A. (2021). Why do managers of small and medium-sized businesses seek voluntary living wage accreditation? An exploration of choice rationales. *European Journal of Work and Organizational Psychology, 30*(6), 1–12. https://doi.org/10.1080/1359432X.2021.1908417

Werner, A., & Lim, M. (2016). The ethics of the living wage: A review and research agenda. *Journal of Business Ethics, 137*(3), 433–447. https://doi.org/10.1007/s10551-015-2562-z

Western, B., & Rosenfeld, J. (2011). Unions, norms, and the rise in U.S. wage inequality. *American Sociological Review, 76*(4), 513–537. https://doi.org/10.1177/0003122411414817

Wood, A. J., Graham, M., Lehdonvirta, V., & Hjorth, I. (2019). Good gig, bad gig: Autonomy and algorithmic control in the global gig economy. *Work, Employment and Society, 33*(1), 56–75. https://doi.org/10.1177/0950017018785616

Yao, C., Parker, J., Arrowsmith, J., & Carr, S. C. (2017). The living wage as an income range for decent work and life. *Employee Relations, 39*(6), 875–887. https://doi.org/10.1108/ER-03-2017-0071

Zikic, J., & Klehe, U.-C. (2006). Job loss as a blessing in disguise: The role of career exploration and career planning in predicting re-employment quality. *Journal of Vocational Behavior, 69*(3), 391–409. https://doi.org/10.1016/j.jvb.2006.05.007

5

NGO DIPLOMACY TO MONITOR AND INFLUENCE BUSINESS AND GOVERNMENT TO TACKLE WORK PRECARIOUSNESS

Raymond Saner and Lichia Yiu

This chapter focuses on the roles that Transnational Nongovernment Organizations (TNGOs) can perform, alongside psychologists whose jobs focus on work, labor relations, poverty reduction, development, and wellbeing, to help to tackle precarious work in all of these multifaceted forms (Saner & Yiu, 2012, 2014a). The chapter is based on the experience of the Centre for Socio-Eco-Nomic Development (CSEND), a United Nations (UN)-accredited non-government organization (NGO), and its work to promote social progress around the world. The chapter consists of five parts:

1 The first part introduces NGO diplomacy and contrasts it with traditional diplomacy, showing how societal actors can contribute to tackling precarious work.
2 The second part introduces the reader to a history of the application/or use of NGO diplomacy by the UN and its agencies to tackle precarity and traces how NGO diplomacy has been used by TNGOs and various national civil society organizations (CSOs), dating back to the founding of the UN in 1945. This historical analysis shows the growing participation of NGOs from both "developed" and "developing" countries, in tackling precarious work at different levels, from local to global.
3 Part 3 describes the main strategic tools and concepts articulated by CSEND. These tools can be used by I/O psychologists who may be seeking to work in roles as NGO diplomats to monitor and influence international organizations and international policy-making processes.
4 Part 4 narrates a case example of NGO diplomacy as it has been used in the deliberations on global public policy-making and standard-setting negotiations relating to work precariousness.

DOI: 10.4324/9781003440444-6

5 Finally, the chapter concludes with a summary of the main components of NGO diplomacy and how it is being used, and can be used, by I/O psychologists including researchers, in the context of interactions between state and nonstate actors to tackle precarious work and other issues of unequal treatment, discrimination, and lack of opportunity for development.

The overall objective of this chapter is to introduce the reader to the field of NGO diplomacy and its relevance for the study of work precariousness, such as working conditions in global supply chains (Jyoti & Arora, Chapter 6). Decent work deficits (DWDs), in the terminology of the International Labour Organization (ILO), are rampant in global supply chains and, in fact, one of the key attractors for foreign direct investment in developing countries. Work precariousness represents one of the manifestations of these DWDs in need of elimination. DWDs, according to the ILO, are "expressed in the absence of sufficient employment opportunities, inadequate social protection, the denial of rights at work and shortcomings in social dialogue" (ILO News, 2001).

During a colloquium on living wages organized by CSEND, Daniel Vaughan-Whitehead, ILO Senior Wage Analyst, stated that the "pay system" deficit is not sufficiently understood (CSEND, 2017), even though evidence collected so far shows use at the supplier level of practices including the keeping of double records, nonpayment of wages, nonpayment of overtime hours, and nonpayment of minimum wages. To attain sustainable livelihoods (Carr, Hodgetts et al., Chapter 1), organizations need to improve not only wage levels but also wage adjustments, wage bargaining, wage-fixing mechanisms, and pay systems. In other words, inclusive societies need a comprehensive "fair wage" policy rather than just a "living wage" policy. Tackling precarious work could be further facilitated by enabling freedoms of association and rights to collective bargaining, eliminating discrimination in respect of employment, abolishing child labor, and eliminating forced or compulsory labor in favor of safe and healthy work environments.

NGO Diplomacy

Traditionally, diplomacy has been about state-to-state interactions, be that on bilateral (two countries), plurilateral (several countries), or multilateral (many countries) bases. Diplomacy as defined by Satow (Satow et al., 1979, p. 3), for instance, was the exclusive domain of ministries of foreign affairs (MOFAs). For a more detailed overview of diplomacy's change of definition and practice, see Raymond Saner (2002). Today, however, globalization and democratization have rendered the professional boundaries of diplomacy more porous, and they have brought into question the territorial claims of traditional "diplomats." Alternative diplomatic actors have emerged both inside and outside the state and often act independently from MOFAs. For example, important line ministries, like the ministries of finance, agriculture, economics, industry, and health, often have their own small foreign affairs units staffed by diplomats on two- to three-year secondments from their country's MOFA. These smaller foreign affairs units assist their respective line ministries to prepare for meetings and negotiations in Washington (International Monetary Fund [IMF] and World Bank [WB]), Paris (Organization for Economic Co-operation and Development [OECD]), Geneva (World Health Organization [WHO], World Trade Organization [WTO], Nairobi (United Nations Environment Programme [UNEP]), and Vienna (International Atomic Energy Agency). The meetings of these line ministries not only at international organizations but also on bilateral and supra-national levels (e.g., at the European Union [EU], Association of Southeast Asian Nations, and the African Union) are coordinated by the MOFA and often include diplomats from the country's MOFA.

Alongside the proliferation of diplomats within state administrations, other nonstate actors have also emerged and become active in international affairs. These include business diplomats who represent transnational companies (TNCs) and business groups and NGO diplomats who represent transnational CSOs.

TNCs represented by business diplomats, and transnational NGOs represented by national and international NGO diplomats, are active globally and play stakeholder roles to influence international policies. They often have subsidiaries, i.e., NGO representative offices, in different parts of the world. Neither of these nonstate actor types (business and NGO diplomats) can sign international treaties, but they are often able to request consultation with their home state government on foreign-policy decisions. Sometimes too, they are invited to join national delegations attending international fora and conferences. In the context of the 2030 Agenda for Sustainable Development (UN, 2015), nonstate actors are organized into stakeholder groups to participate in the High-Level Political Fora, a UN General Assembly mechanism to monitor and review the implementation of the Sustainable Development Goals (SDGs) globally and within countries. Hence, they can make a difference to major policy decisions affecting, for instance, precarious work which is part of the SDG-8 on Decent Work and Economic Growth, and carry influence through their voices and representation.

Figure 5.1 illustrates the different diplomatic roles which have emerged over the last 30 years for state actors (diplomats from different government ministries) and nonstate actors, namely, TNC business diplomats and NGO diplomats from national and transnational NGOs. Initial work on relations between state and nonstate actors, such as the concept of the business diplomat, first introduced by the authors in 2000 (Saner et al., 2000), was first developed by members of CSEND. The concept of business diplomacy has received wide coverage from experts of the fields of international management and organizational sciences but less so in I/O psychology. The first applications of these new types of diplomacy

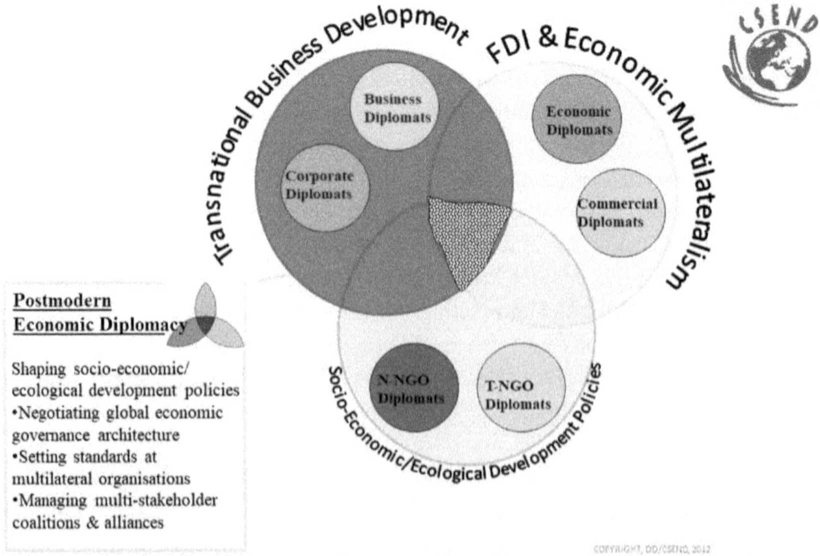

FIGURE 5.1 National and Nonstate Actors with Convergent and Divergent Interests.

Note: FDI = Foreign Direct Investment.

Source: Authors' Design Based on Previous Publications; Reproduced with Permission from CSEND.

(New Diplomacies [NDs]; see below) have been differentiated by sectorial context, for example, transnational NGO diplomacy (Saner & Yiu, 2012; Yiu & Saner, 2016), Humanitarian Diplomacy (Saner & Yiu, 2012), and development diplomacy (Saner & Yiu, 2006); all are facets of NGO diplomacy. Undoubtedly, however, more research needs to be done in this emerging, i.e., frontier, field. The goal of this chapter is to discuss how NGO diplomacy can be applied constructively, including by I/O psychologists, to help reduce poverty by alleviating work precarity and, to a broader extent, reduce resistance to the needed transformations called for by the 2030 Agenda for Sustainable Development. It is important to note, however, that NGO diplomacy focuses on civil society and NGO engagement with state and other nonstate actors in a broad sense, including on other topics that are important for civil society such as health, water, food, trade, education, human rights, and other socioeconomic policies, in addition to decent work and equity.

Role, Organization, and Function of NGO Diplomats

NGO diplomacy encompasses the interaction between state and nonstate actors such as businesses, civil societies, NGOs, and international organizations, through their various representatives. These can include applied professionals such as I/O psychologists who work in CSOs, which interact with the state and influence the state, yet are distinct from the state. CSOs could be charities, community groups, women's organizations, faith-based organizations, professional associations, trade unions, social movements, coalitions, advocacy groups, and other volunteer groups. NGOs may aim to implement civil society goals in CSOs such as the Red Cross; various centers for children's rights and care for migrants (Cassim, Chapter 20), older people, and minorities; and international organizations, including intergovernmental organizations with mandates to implement UN' charters such as the ILO (Fundamental Rights at Work), UN Office of the High Commissioner for Human Rights (OHCHR; Human Rights), WHO (UNEP), and others from other fields of human life (Pruthi, 2021).

I/O psychologists and other applied psychologists from the International Association of Applied Psychology and the Society for Industrial and Organizational Psychology (SIOP; which is an accredited NGO at the UN) have advised CSOs and NGOs worldwide. Psychologists also work in international organizations such as WHO, ILO, United Nations High Commissioner for Refugees (UNHCR), International Organization for Migration (IOM), and the United Nations Children's Fund. The disciplines of I/O, social psychology, psychology and societal development, environmental psychology, educational psychology, clinical and community psychology, health psychology, economic psychology, political psychology, psychology and law, and counseling psychology have particular competencies which help strengthen the mission and activities of CSOs, NGOs, and international organizations with regard to the reduction of precarity and to addressing violations of the principles of decent work (Saner & Yiu, 2019a). These competencies and experiential insights need to be leveraged to accelerate the eradication of work precarity: the root cause of intergenerational poverty, persistent deprivation, and other socioeconomic problems.

There are thus many areas and levels where NGO diplomats are active, and a distinction must be made between NGOs acting within national boundaries and those operating on an international level through their own foreign representation offices and/or through alliances with like-minded national and transnational NGOs. Distinctions can also be made with regard to domain expertise and activities. Economically oriented NGOs focus on economic policy, international economic development, and global business practice. NGO diplomacy thus may be viewed through the prism of the following taxonomy.

National NGO Diplomacy

National economic NGOs representing civil society are active in the labor and social spheres, within various constituencies. Their activities include advocating for the protection of universal human and labor rights and socioeconomic and cultural rights; consumer protections; anticorruption measures; environmental rights; rights to development; and protections and measures in other social and political spheres. The right to development is intimately connected to work on eradicating precariousness.

The number of national NGOs is growing fast, due in part to the fact that civil society now has greater access to information about, and a stronger influence on, corporate governance. Public voices and opinions can no longer be ignored by the holders of national political and economic power. National NGOs can also operate indirectly at international levels through TNGOs such as the Trade Union Advisory Committee, creating coalitions against the WTO, World Economic Forum, IMF, and other transnational enterprises. They can also be recognized by the UN through its accreditation and registration procedures to gain access to the international arena. The COVID-19 pandemic has also accelerated the online options for global participation.

Transnational NGO Diplomacy

TNGOs organize advocacy events and lobbying activities across borders; propose their own policy solutions in the international arena in areas such as child labor, living wages, human trafficking and slavery, and debt-rescheduling for "least developed countries" at the IMF; and block the negotiation of multilateral conventions on foreign investment at the OECD. TNGOs are also involved in implementing technical cooperation projects in developing and transitional economies, thereby complementing, and at times even substituting for, national governments in service delivery. In addition, they may offer cutting-edge research in critical areas for international cooperation, and in crisis management.

In contrast to national NGOs, therefore, TNGOs actively seek ways to influence the agendas of international governance bodies, by putting forward policy recommendations and lobbying in the corridors of international power. Dialog between major TNGOs and the WB during recent annual WB conferences is one example of this. Based on their domain expertise, these nonstate actors have taken the lead in many international fora, and they have narrowed the range of operational freedoms for traditional diplomats. TNGOs can be defined as follows (Figure 5.2).

Fundamentally, national and international NGO diplomats and their organizations create coalitions with other like-minded NGOs and stakeholders at national and international levels for joint campaigning at scale. The following examples illustrate how this is organized.

The growing participation of transnational NGOs in areas of international governance including human rights, economics, society and culture, health, education, the environment, and labor) takes place at multiple levels. These include local-national levels through national NGOs and at the international level through the monitoring and investigation of possible human rights violations, including

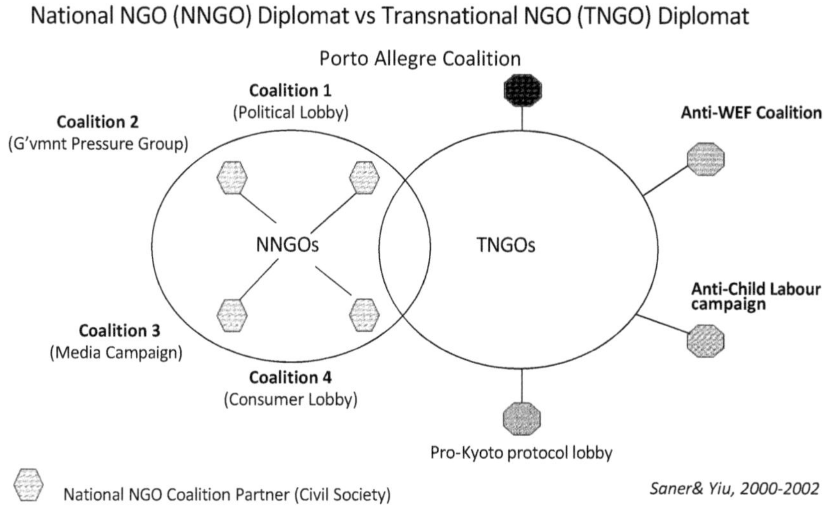

FIGURE 5.2 Territorial Spaces for the Advocacy of National and Transnational NGO Diplomats within the Porto Allegre Coalition.

by transnational global companies in the different countries where they operate and have supply and value chain subsidiaries (Jyoti & Tchangneno, Chapter 6). NGO diplomats regularly report on human rights conditions as part of investigations for regular UNHCR Universal Periodic Reviews (UPRs; OHCR, n.d.).

NGOs, both national and transnational, concerned with the negative impacts of industrial development on the environment and on disadvantaged groups of workers and their communities, can form alliances to jointly challenge States; on economic and business issues, through civil protests, campaigns, negative-ranking lists, and other means. Thus, NGOs can manage to stifle the ability of traditional sovereign actors to operate unimpeded, be this at a state-to-state level, or within the sphere of multinational standard-setting organizations, including those concerned with tackling precarious work. Two cases-in-point of standard-setting are the successful NGO campaign against smoking which resulted in the first binding agreement regulating the use of tobacco and in the continuing development of the OECD Guidelines for Multinational Enterprises (Saner & Yiu, 2017).

NGOs are challenging and exerting pressures on transnational enterprises at home and in foreign markets alike. One example can be seen in the work by INFACT (Multinational Monitor, 2001) to expose life-threatening labor abuses by TNCs through boycotts and organized grassroots campaigns to hold corporations accountable to consumers and to society at large (Intraprasert et al., Chapter 9; Searle & McWha Hermann, Chapter 4).

The internet has greatly changed the power relationship between state actors, transnational enterprises, and transnationally active NGOs (i.e., TNGOs).

More than 10.6 million entries for stakeholder-related websites can be found via Google alone. Global connectivity has added to the power and expertise of the NGO actors in global mobilization in ways which were unimaginable prior to the proliferation of the internet and mobile technologies. Applications of these new technologies have altered public and private relations and helped transform international relationships affecting the economic, social, and political spheres of societies and their citizens.

More specifically, the internet has become one of the most powerful and affordable tools for forming strategic alliances between NGOs and voluntary groups around the world. More importantly, they can now exert pressure on governments and on global companies for accountability by demanding more information, and more transparent government policies and business practices. For example, Information Technology tools are being used by NGOs to exert influence deep into the organizational structures of governments and global companies. Most significantly, NGO communities are promoting alternative development models, thereby directly challenging policy formulae such as the so-called Washington Consensus (Carr, Hodgetts et al., Chapter 1). Examples include CSEND's capacity-building strategy to help the ILO gain more influence within the IMF and the WB and a more recent campaign to support calls for a living wage (see below).

Internet-based virtual communities allow NGOs to pool resources and information on events happening on the ground. Making use of their information-gathering capacities and sophisticated policy analysis capabilities, transnational NGOs are increasingly active in the international policy arena, and in demanding their rights for supra-territorial representation, thereby challenging ministerial abilities to coordinate national economic policy at international fora. This includes or could include advocacy work for tackling precarious work.

This multiplicity of interactions between state actors and nonstate actors creates a space called the *NDs* (Saner & Yiu, 2003). For both groups, state and nonstate, it is important to recall that the goal of diplomacy is to build and sustain positive and constructive relations for mutual benefits. Therefore, NGO diplomacy remains fundamentally about influencing normative economic and social actors to seize new opportunities for civil society to influence public discourse and the writing of rules and regulations; for example, with regard to the reduction of poverty and protecting workers' rights. This work includes:

- Working with rule-making international bodies such as the ILO, WHO, and UNHCR, whose decisions affect international civic space and the role of NGOs.
- Forestalling potential conflicts with other state and nonstate actors to minimize political risks and potential conflicts.
- Testing novel solutions and pushing boundaries to allow for new solutions to emerge that contribute to inclusive and sustainable futures.

Using multiple international fora and media channels to support advocacy campaigns against work and other forms of human precariousness, NGO diplomats have to operate within the structures of globalization characterized by a complex set of interconnectivities and interdependencies with an increasing number of actors vying to influence the outcomes of these relationships. They lay competing claims to resources, markets, and legitimacy and are engaged in activities traditionally defined as belonging within the domain of diplomacy. This realignment of structural relationships has also affected the UN system itself. Much greater participation and influence by CSOs can be observed in deliberations on global policies and relations both within and beyond the confines of the UN system. Today, there is a dedicated liaison office within the UN which manages relations with NGOs and other CSOs. The same holds for all major UN agencies and international organizations. Most of these liaison offices were set up in the late 1990s or early 2000s. Indeed, SIOP and CSEND are among the NGOs accredited by the UN Economic and Social Council (ECOSOC), one of the six principal organs of the UN system (Whitt, 2017).

A History of NGO Participation in the UN and Related Agencies[1]

While most people today associate NGOs with the UN, it is important to recall that they have deeper historical roots beyond the advent of this organization. For more than 300 years, religious orders, missionary groups, merchant societies like the Hanse cities, and various scientific societies have existed on different continents. Some of these early NGOs were secret societies; others included Chinese benevolent societies in the United States and organizations for immigrant laborers.

Thomas Davis' book *NGOs: a New History of Transnational Civil Society* (2014) notes that some of these early NGOs such as the early socialist and Fabian societies also upheld outlawed political beliefs and operated in a clandestine fashion. Others had a strong morality-based advocacy orientation, for instance, those related to the antislavery movement and equal rights for women. Other examples include the antiwar movement which started before World War I and the Humanitarian International Federation of Red Cross Societies which later became the International Committee of the Red Cross.

The term "nongovernmental organization" was not in use before the UN was formed. When 132 international NGOs decided to cooperate with each other in 1910, they did so under the label "The Union of International Associations." The League of Nations officially referred to its "liaison with private organizations," while many of these bodies at that time called themselves international institutes, international unions, or simply international organizations (MBA Knowledge Base, n.d.). The first draft of the UN Charter did not make any mention of maintaining cooperation with private bodies. A variety of groups, mainly but not solely from the United States, lobbied to rectify this at the 1945 San Francisco conference, which established the UN. Not only did they succeed in introducing a provision for strengthening and formalizing the relations with private organizations that had previously been maintained by the League but they also greatly enhanced the UN's role in economic and social issues and upgraded the status of the ECOSOC to a "principal organ" of the UN. To clarify matters, new terminology was introduced to cover ECOSOC's relationship with two types of international organizations. Under Article 70 it stated that "specialized agencies, established by intergovernmental agreement" could "participate without a vote in its deliberations," while under Article 71 "non-governmental organizations" could have "suitable arrangements for consultation" (City University of London, n.d.). Thus, "specialised agencies" and "NGOs" became UN technical terms. Unlike much UN jargon, the term "NGO" passed into popular usage, particularly from the early 1970s onward.

Today, the term NGO is understood to mean an organization which is not part of any government and was not founded by a nation-state. NGOs are therefore seen as typically independent of governments. The term is generally restricted to social, cultural, legal, and environmental advocacy groups having goals that are primarily noncommercial. NGOs are usually nonprofit organizations that gain at least a portion of their funding from private sources. Current usage of the term is generally associated with the UN and authentic NGOs are those that are so designated by the UN. Because the label NGO is considered too broad by some as it can cover any nongovernmental organization many NGOs now prefer the term private voluntary organization.

NGOs are defined by the WB (Malena, 1995; WB, 2022) as "private organizations that pursue activities to relieve suffering, promote the interests of the poor, protect the environment, provide basic social services, or undertake community development" (Malena, 1995). Common usage varies between countries. For example, the term NGO is commonly used for domestic organizations in India, whereas these would be referred to as nonprofit organizations in the United States. Such organizations that operate at the international level are fairly consistently referred to as "nongovernmental organizations" in the United States and elsewhere.

There is a growing movement within the nonprofit/nongovernment sector to define itself in a more constructive and accurate way. The "nonprofit" designation is seen to be misleading for at least three reasons: (1) it says nothing about the purpose of the organization, only what it is not; (2) it focuses the mind on "profit" as being the opposite of the organization's purpose; and (3) it implies that the organization has few financial resources, which increases the likelihood of this being true. Instead of being defined by "non" words, organizations are suggesting new terminology to describe the sector. The term "social benefit organization" (SBO) is being adopted by some as the description which highlights their positive mission.

In this discourse, the term "CSO" is also being used by a growing number of organizations, such as the Center for the Study of Global Governance, and "citizen sector organization" (again abbreviated to the acronym CSO) has also been advocated to describe the sector as being both *of* citizens and *for* citizens. These labels define the sector as its own type of entity, without relying on the language of government and business; however, some have argued that the term CSO is not particularly helpful, given that most NGOs are, in fact, funded by governments. The term "SBO" seems to avoid that problem since it does not assume any particular structure, but rather focuses on the organization's mission.

Many diverse types of bodies are now described as being NGOs. There is no generally accepted definition of an NGO, and the term carries different connotations in different circumstances. Nevertheless, there are some fundamental features. Clearly, an NGO must be independent from the direct control of any government. In addition, there are four other generally accepted characteristics that exclude particular types of organizations. An NGO is not constituted as a political party; it will be nonprofit; it will not be a criminal group; and, in particular, it will be nonviolent. These characteristics apply in general usage because they match the conditions for recognition by the UN. The boundaries can sometimes be blurred, as some NGOs may in practice be closely identified with a political party; many NGOs generate income from commercial activities, notably consultancy contracts or sales of publications; and a small number of NGOs may be associated with violent political protests. Nevertheless, an NGO is never constituted as a governmental bureaucracy, a party, a company, a criminal organization, or a guerrilla group. Thus, for this chapter, an NGO is defined as an independent voluntary association of people acting together on a continuous basis, for some common purpose.

The involvement of NGOs in the UN has evolved since the founding of the UN in 1945 when it took the form of a consultative relationship with ECOSOC. As stated in the UN Charter, Article 71:

> The Economic and Social Council may make suitable arrangements for consultation with non-governmental organizations which are concerned with matters within its competence. Such arrangements may be made with international organizations and, where appropriate, with national organizations after consultation with the Member of the United Nations concerned.
>
> *(City University of London, n.d.)*

Ever since 1945, NGOs—mostly large international nongovernmental bodies—have interacted with the UN Secretariat and agencies, participated in UN agencies' programs, and consulted with UN member states. The 1970s and 1980s witnessed a significant increase in NGO participation in the activities of the UN organization. In this period, NGOs were recognized for their ability to shape the global agenda, as well as for their important role as operational actors delivering humanitarian and development assistance including aid to make work less precarious and enable livelihoods to become more sustainable.

A Turning Point for NGOs' Status and Role

The relationship between the UN and NGOs changed dramatically in the 1990s. This change was triggered by both a UN resolution recognizing the importance of CSOs as part of the global community and the angry outpouring of citizens across many countries expressing dissatisfaction with globalization, social hardships, and increasing inequality between the wealthy and poor segments of society in many countries.

The fall of the Berlin Wall in 1989 following the violent Tiananmen Square Incident resulted in a sea change in Eastern European countries. The dramatic political changes created a global consensus that democratization of the public space and greater engagement of the public in affairs that affect the public were "inevitable" and necessary in order to ensure governmental legitimacy and foster greater citizen satisfaction. In this climate, the UN decided to review the consultative status of NGOs with ECOSOC. Resolution 1296 of 1968 was replaced by Resolution 1996/31 adopted in 1996, which allows, among other things, subregional, regional, and national NGOs to be accredited by ECOSOC. Before that date, only international NGOs could apply for consultative status.

Today, the NGOs registered at CSO Net, the website of the NGO branch of the Department of Economic and Social Development (DESA); the UN DESA represents a vibrant community of civil societies of diverse nationalities and forms of organization and a wide range of interests. Even though not all registered NGOs enjoy consultative status, they all engage in UN conferences and summits in varying ways. Table 5.1 shows the number of organizations currently registered with DESA's CSO Net by region.

Today there is also a fairer representation of the regions across the world. Africa has the largest number of NGOs registered with DESA CSO Net (Table 5.1). Different types of NGOs have been registered with the United Nations Department of Economic and Social Affairs (UNDESA) and play important—and often complementary roles—during deliberations and negotiations at the High-Level Political Forum on Sustainable Development in New York, as well as during other important meetings called by ECOSOC. However, regarding the efforts to reduce precarity worldwide, one needs to take into account that workers are represented by only one of the nine official Major Groups of NGOs who take part in the UN deliberations led by ECOSOC. The opposing side to the workers is represented by the Business and Industry Major Group. This group

TABLE 5.1 Organizations by Region as Registered with DESA CSO Net (2022)

Organizations by region as registered on the DESA CSO Net (2022)

Diplomacy Dialogue

CSEND

Organisation by Region	Number	%
Africa	7196	49%
Asia	1552	11%
Europe	2266	15%
North America	2094	14%
Oceania	239	2%
Latin America & Caribean	736	5%
Not specified	581	4%
Total	14'664	100%

Source: UN DESA, NGO Branch, 07.2022.

Source: UN DESA (2022a); reproduced with permission from CSEND.

has a power advantage over the workers since businesses and employers are also represented by their ally the International Chamber of Commerce, which has permanent observer status at the UN General Assembly. There is no equivalent observer status at the UN General Assembly level for organizations which represent the interests of formal-sector employees or those of informal-sector workers. Hence, from a power-balance perspective, reducing precarity at (and through) the UN level requires functioning coalitions with other NGOs and Major Stakeholder Groups, Special Stakeholder Groups, and for governments to support the idea of reducing precarity and strengthening inclusive sustainable development in all UN member countries. This can be an achievable vision since reducing precarity will contribute to the attainment of different SDGs, such as SDG-1 (No Poverty), SDG-2 (Zero Hunger), SDG-3 (Good Health and Wellbeing), SDG-5 (Gender Equality), and SDG-10 (Reduced Inequalities).

Table 5.2 gives an overview of the types of nonstate actors that are registered on DESA CSO Net. NGOs are by far the largest group of nonstate actors accredited by the UN. Other types of nonstate actor organizations include CSOs (indigenous peoples' organizations, children and youth, disability, women, development and rights organizations, trade unions, and academics), NGOs (Working Group on Ageing—now called Stakeholder Group on Ageing, and volunteers), cooperatives, and the private sector. One exception in the list of stakeholder groups is local government. For NGOs and CSOs, the task of following all the deliberations and negotiations at the major UN agencies and leading large international NGOs is very demanding. Some of the activities happen at the UN headquarters in New York, while other activities might take place at Geneva-based UN agencies. Following and influencing complex negotiations at multiple sites requires a comprehensive understanding of what gets to be negotiated, where decisions are taken and in cooperation with whom, and of course financial and personnel resources which are often unavailable to NGOs, particularly those from the Global South.

Table 5.3 shows which NGOs focus on which UN agencies in Geneva, indicating a specialization of advocacy and targeting of UN agencies according to the NGOs' core advocacy interests.

TABLE 5.2 Organization Types of NGOs Registered with DESA CSO Net (2022)

Organisation Types of NGOs Registered on the UNDESA CSO Net (as of July 2022)

Types	Number
Association	763
Foundation	358
Institution	59
Inter-Governmental Organisation	50
Local Government	27
Non-Governmental Organisation	12301
Media	23
Private Sector	104
Trade Union	18
Others	139
Academics	192
Indigenous Peoples Organisations	273
Disability, Development and Rights Organisation	149
Open-ended Working Group on Ageing	72
Cooperative	21

Total: 14664

Source: UN DESA (2022b); reproduced with permission from CSEND.

TABLE 5.3 The United Nations Agencies and NGOs Based in Geneva (Non-Exhaustive List, Rows Not Aligned)

UN Agencies and International Organizations[a]	*NGOs with offices in Geneva*[b]
Conference on Disarmament	Amnesty International, UN Office
International Bureau of Education, UNESCO	Asian Forum for Human Rights and Development—FORUM-ASIA
International Labour Organization	Association for Inclusive Peace
International Trade Centre	Care International
International Telecommunication Union	Diplo Foundation

(*Continued*)

TABLE 5.3 (Continued)

UN Agencies and International Organizations[a]	*NGOs with offices in Geneva*[b]
Joint Inspection Unit	Geneva International Centre for Humanitarian Demining (GICHD)
Office of the United Nations High Commissioner for Human Rights[c]	Geneva Centre for the Democratic Control of Armed Force
United Nations Conference on Trade and Development	Global Fund to Fight AIDS, Tuberculosis and Malaria
United Nations Economic Commission for Europe	Geneva Centre for Security Policy
United Nations High Commissioner for Refugees	International Air Transport Association Office in Geneva (Headquartered in Montreal)
United Nations Human Rights Council	GICHD
United Nations Commission on Human Rights	International Committee of the Red Cross
United Nations Institute for Training and Research	International Federation of Red Cross and Red Crescent Societies
United Nations Office for the Coordination of Humanitarian Affairs	International Organization for Standardization
United Nations Research Institute for Social Development	International Union for Conservation of Nature
World Health Organization	Inter-Parliamentary Union
World Intellectual Property Organization	Médecins Sans Frontières
World Meteorological Organization	World Council of Churches
World Trade Organization	World Business Council for Sustainable Development
Intergovernmental Bodies	
European Organization for Nuclear Research (CERN)[d]	World Nature Organization
IOM[e]	Internet Governance Forum
Geneva Call	

Source: Saner and Yiu (2019a); reproduced with permission from CSEND.

[a] For a complete listing of international organizations in Geneva, please visit https://www.eda.admin.ch/missions/mission-onu-geneve/en/home/geneve-international/faits-et-chiffres.html.

[b] For a complete listing of the NGOs in Geneva, please visit https://www.ungeneva.org/en/engage/civil-society/ngo-list .

[c] The UN Commission on Human Rights was replaced in 2006 by the UN Human Rights Council of 47 elected members. The Office of the High Commissioner for Human Rights (OHCHR) was entrusted with the unique mandate to promote and protect the enjoyment and full realization, by all people, of all human rights (UN OHCHR, n.d.).

[d] CERN is an intergovernmental organization with 23 member states with a selected number of countries affiliated as Associate Member States and others with Observer status (CERN, n.d.).

[e] IOM was made a Related Organization to the UN through the adoption of a resolution by the Member States of the General Assembly on July 25, 2016 (IOM, 2016).

New Generations of NGO-UN Relations

The evolution of the roles and functions of NGOs within the UN environment has been both quantitative and qualitative (Ritchie & Rice, 1995). The evolution has happened gradually since the end of the Cold War in 1989. Large numbers of nongovernmental actors, such as national NGOs from "developing" countries; those from the Western hemisphere; and also those, albeit to a lesser extent, from Eastern and Central European post-communist societies, now appear at the major UN Conferences on the Environment and Development, Population and Development, Human Rights, Women's Rights, Social Development, Human Settlements and Food Security, and in their preparatory and follow-up processes.

Growing successes due to protests organized by the antiglobalization movement in the 1990s, and the advocacy and lobbying by debt-relief campaigners, were instrumental in ushering in and consolidating greater openness by the UN and its related institutions. The antiglobalization movement gate-crashed the WTO Ministerial Meeting in Seattle in 1997 and disrupted a series of other important international meetings such as the meetings of the WB and IMF (Washington D.C., 1998), G8 Summit (Genoa, 1999) and WTO Ministerial Meeting (Geneva, 1999). Meanwhile, debt-relief campaigners were able to kick-start debt-forgiveness processes for the poorest and most indebted countries and to replace the ineffectual structural adjustment programs at the IMF and WB with national poverty reduction strategy plans (PRSP). Since then (the late 1990s), eradication of poverty has become the sine qua non of NGO calls for change, coupled with calls for the redefinition of development. NGOs with their own policy-research capabilities and capacities have since been accepted as serious interlocutors in various policy forums and viewed as important partners in the democratic deliberations on global policy issues.

Ever since the end of the 1990s, NGOs have been allowed to be involved in the UN-organized world conferences, marking a turning point leading to the so-called second generation of UN-NGO relations, a term coined by Hill (2004). The necessity to strengthen relations between the UN and NGOs has subsequently been described in various documents, in particular the UN Millennium Declaration of September 2000 (UN, 2000). The commitment of UN member states to allow greater opportunity for NGOs to participate has subsequently been reaffirmed in the 2005 World Summit outcome document (UN, 2005, para. 172–174). This was reaffirmed again in the 2012 Rio+20 outcome document The Future We Want (UN, 2012), which arguably laid the foundations for the current UN SDGs (Chapter 1), including SDG-8 (Decent Work and Economic Growth).

The Strategic Tools of NGO Diplomacy

International relations have long since ceased to be the exclusive domain of nation-states. Instead, multiple actors participate in this space and actively seek ways to influence the negotiated outcomes. This trend has been particularly evident since the onset of the 21st century. Saner and Yiu (2003) call this enlargement of the operational sphere and changed nature of international relations the "post-modern variant" of diplomacy.

Although the participation of nonstate actors in foreign policy and international relations remains by and large a phenomenon that manifests mostly in industrialized countries, civil societies all over the world are learning fast and catching up due to the proliferation of information and communications technology (ICT) and the multiplicity of knowledge platforms now available online. Communications, information sharing and gathering, and mobilizing people and resources—all essential tasks of advocacy—are no longer impossible or prohibitively expensive. The costs of transportation have also been dropping steadily. The barriers to participation in national and international affairs are no longer insurmountable, and the resulting growth in participation by NGOs from non-Western parts of the world has brought forth a diversity of voices dissenting to the status quo and contributed to the evolution of the role of NGOs within the UN proper and global governance structures. The next logical evolution is for people to become self-organizing when their views and concerns are not included or considered in national and international debates. This phenomenon can be seen in the citizens' movements, with varying degrees of impact, emerging globally.

It is therefore more urgent than ever to understand the ways and means by which all actors and stakeholders can participate in global decision-making processes: especially in matters that concern us all, such as the reduction of precarity and promotion of decent work, climate change, the prevention of the proliferation of nuclear weapons, the right to information, sustainable development, water, and migration.

It is interesting to note that the boundaries between state and nonstate actors (including business organizations, philanthropic foundations, and NGOs) are increasingly blurred. Therefore, issue- or principle-based coalition and alliance building to tackle precarious work now cuts across the borders between governments, NGOs, foundations, and businesses, necessitating the skillful use of NGO diplomacy.

Seen from a systems point of view, the international policy arena can be subdivided into six processes with different combinations of stakeholder interactions. This contrasts with the traditional understanding of policy-making as being of a linear nature. The processes illustrated in Figure 5.3 below do not always follow the path shown as sometimes certain processes can be omitted, or processes can take place simultaneously, but the basic cycle as shown is observable in practice.

Before we describe each of the ND tools in Figure 5.3, we need to introduce two more significant developments: the PRSP; and the Decent Work Agenda (DWA; ILO, 2022). Both were high on the international development agenda and are now integrated into the 2030 Agenda for Sustainable Development as SDG-1 (No Poverty) and SDG-8 (Decent Work and Economic Growth).

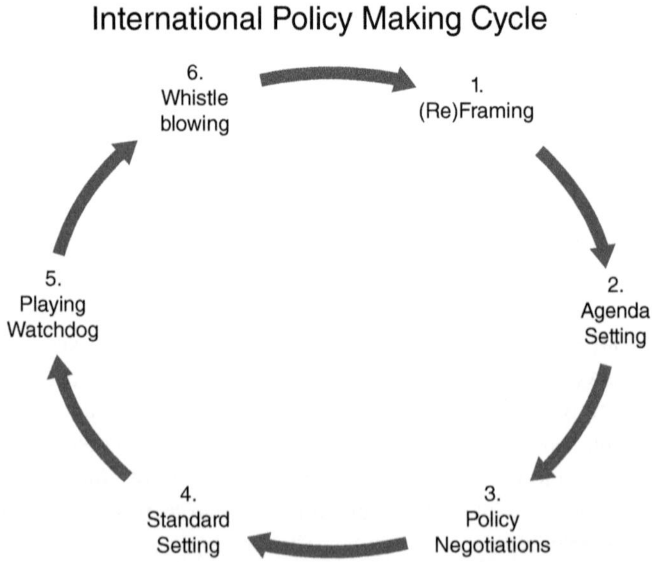

FIGURE 5.3 The International Policy-making Cycle and Space for Entry

Source: Saner and Michaelun (2009, p. 28); Reproduced with Permission from CSEND.

PRSPs

The SDGs were preceded by the Millennium Development Goals (MDGs, from 2000 to 2015; UN, 2000). Like the SDGs, their primary goal was to eradicate extreme poverty and hunger by halving the proportion of people living with less than US$1 per day. To achieve that goal, the international aid and development community (or industry) initiated the PRSPs in the 2000s: an effort that was spearheaded by the WB and the IMF. Launched in 1999 as an instrument to improve the situation of the poor in low-income, "developing" countries, the PRSPs represented different strategic intentions such as a policy device to achieve poverty reduction through social inclusion, a framework to coordinate bilateral and multilateral development assistance, and a driver to integrate low-income countries into the global financial and trade structures.

The PRSPs' key point of departure from other development instruments previously supported by the aid and development industry was a strong emphasis on the importance of national ownership along with extensive civil society participation. Recipient countries are—at least at the level of the stated principles—encouraged to take "the driver's seat in the PRSP process" and urged to give their citizens greater roles in both the policy planning and implementation processes (Global Policy Forum, 2004).

Although there has been much criticism of the legal foundation of the conditions imposed by the WB and the IMF (Saner & Guilherme, 2007, p. 931) and of the participation process itself, many countries opted to join the PRSP process, reckoning that the PRSPs presented genuine opportunities for like-minded organizations to come together and influence macroeconomic policies at the country level. Many NGOs, both national and transnational, felt that the PRSP process could provide an entry point for alternative policy advice, while the PRSP social dialog component could offer opportunities to exert influence in the policy debate and to take up significant roles in the implementation, monitoring, and assessment of the impacts of poverty reduction policies and strategies. PRSPs as policy intervention instruments have thus become primary policy tools for harnessing international support for the poorest countries of the world.

DWA

In an effort to reframe the poverty debate and reposition the place of work in society, the ILO devised a "powerful tool in selecting the path to the attainment of the interrelated goals and human development outcomes of the Millennium Declaration" (ILO, 2003, p. 7). This "powerful tool" was the DWA and was introduced at the 1999 International Labour Conference (ILO, 2008b, p. 1), the Decent Work framework is based on using work as a lever to promote inclusive economic growth and fair globalization. Decent Work involves:

> ...opportunities for work that are productive and deliver a fair income [emphasis added]; security in the workplace and social protection for families; better prospects for personal development and social integration; freedom for people to express their concerns, organize and participate in the decisions that affect their lives; and equality of opportunity and treatment for all women and men.
>
> *(ILO, n.d.)*

The international community has affirmed its commitment to the implementation of the principles contained in the DWA, for example:

- The consensus achieved at the Special Session on Social Development of the United Nations General Assembly in June 2000 recognized in its statement the need to "reassess, as appropriate, macroeconomic policies with the aims of greater employment generation and reduction in the poverty level while striving for and maintaining a low inflation rate" (UN, 2000).
- The 2005 United Nations World Summit resolved "to make the goals of full and productive employment and decent work for all, including for women and young people, a central objective of relevant national and international policies as well as of our national development strategies, including poverty reduction strategies, as part of our efforts to achieve the Millennium Development Goals" (UN, 2005, para. 47).

However, implementation of the DWA has required concerted effort and policy interventions on multiple levels, including those meant to cut across global economic structures, international and national institutional arrangements, societal norms, and gender relations. In addition, the focus on national strategies for decent work has had many policy implications and has required trade-offs that were likely to generate both structural and philosophical opposition and resistance. For example, an employment-friendly proposition did not fit well with the prevailing neoliberal Washington Consensus (Carr, Hodgetts, et al., Chapter 1), nor the hierarchy of ministries within most domestic power arrangements, with ministries of finance and economics generally leading, and labor ministries mostly at the bottom of the hierarchies).

Case Example: Negotiating for Inclusion of Decent Work in PRSPs[2]

Reframing

The first step toward influencing policy change to foster the inclusion of the DWA in national labor-related policies is to reframe the issue, as illustrated in Figure 5.3. The ILO has spotlighted the millions of working poor around the globe and their inability to escape from working-poverty traps (Meyer & Maleka, Chapter 7). This image of the "working poor" was powerful (Carr et al., Chapter 1). It confronted and disqualified the often-unspoken belief that the poor deserve to be poor because they are supposedly lazy and have only themselves to blame. This message of "working poor" was later connected to the policy narratives and images in the DWA.

Since 1999, the ILO has promoted a new paradigm, which states that poverty is the direct "consequence of social exclusion" and highlights the underlying structural causes which induce and perpetuate exclusion, including lack of access to democratic and legal systems, markets, state welfare provisions, and a lack of access to decent work. Rights, resources, and work relationships are all part of this poverty equation." After all, the poor do not cause poverty. Poverty is the result of structural failures and ineffective economic and social systems. It is the product of inadequate political responses, bankrupt imagination at the policy level, and insufficient international support (ILO, 2003, p. 1). This reframing was rooted in the work of Amartya Sen, Simon Maxwell, and others, and organizations like the Development Assistance Committee of the OECD and Overseas Development Institute (ODI). By launching the DWA, the ILO took on powerful international financial institutions and requested they pay more attention to the plight of the working poor and the collateral damage caused by their austerity policies.

After the first years of the PRSP experiment, many NGOs pointed out glaring omissions in employment creation and other key elements of the DWA were not included in the great majority of the actual PRSPs. Echoing these assessments, the ILO articulated three specific sets of concerns regarding the decent work content of the first generation of the PRSPs (ILO, 2005, para. 6; also ILO, 2002a, p. 7; ILO, 2002c, particularly para. 6 and para. 29) and proposed the following policy actions:

1 The PRSPs need to include a more thorough analysis of employment and other aspects of decent work.
2 Labor ministries and employers' and workers' organizations need to be more systematically integrated into the PRSP participatory processes.
3 More attention should be placed on equity in addition to growth in the PRSPs.

This review initiated the next phase of policy debate by highlighting that the right to participate in policy formulation was not sufficient for redirecting the development agenda. Active influencing and negotiations were needed concurrently at the international and country levels. As a result, capacity building was initiated for ILO staff and its constituents to strengthen the organization's advocacy capability. In this way, NGOs and NGO diplomacy have reframed the development agenda to include tackling precarious work.

Agenda-Setting

The strategic choice made by the ILO for the purpose of achieving progress on the above points was one of constructive engagement with national economic policy makers through its Decent Work Country Programmes (DWCPs) based on the conviction that the PRSP process constitutes a vehicle through which the voice of the ILO and its constituents can be heard at the level of national planning and budgeting. The DWCPs had two further basic objectives: to promote decent work as a key component of national development strategies and simultaneously organize ILO knowledge, instruments, advocacy, and cooperation for the purpose of putting this knowledge at the service of tripartite constituents in a results-based framework to advance the DWA in the field.

A DWCP was the expression of the ILO program and budget and was organized around a limited number of country program priorities and outcomes, which were further detailed in an implementation plan. Monitoring and evaluation (M&E) guidelines complemented this approach. The country program priorities and outcomes reflected the strategic results-oriented framework of the ILO, adapted to national situations and priorities. In turn, program and budget strategic outcomes and indicators were based on DWCP outcomes.

The DWA had four pillars (Somavia, 2002). They were and remain as follows:

- Employment—creating greater employment opportunities for women and men to secure a decent income
- Security and social protection—enhancing the coverage and effectiveness of social protection for all

- Rights at work—promoting and realizing fundamental workers' rights
- Representation and dialog—strengthening dialog on an inclusive and participatory basis

On the basis of these four pillars, a national strategy for *working out of poverty*, in the spirit of *decent work for all*, was proposed/supposed to include the following (ILO, 2003):

- *Skills development for sustainable livelihoods* (i.e., refocusing on vocational education and training and the skill needs of people living in poverty)
- *Investing in jobs and the community* (i.e., employment-intensive community-based programs)
- *Promoting entrepreneurship* (i.e., small- and medium-sized enterprise creation and supportive services from the government)
- *Making money work for poverty reduction* (i.e., microfinancing and microcredit-related law, regulations, and banks)
- *Building local development through cooperatives* (i.e., a new model for local participation, inclusion, and combating poverty)
- *Overcoming discrimination* (i.e., the right to equality of opportunity and treatment with respect to employment)
- *Working to end child labor* (i.e., an integrated gender-sensitive, family-centered strategy calling for adequate educational alternatives for children, access to income and security for their parents, and stronger laws and enforcement mechanisms)
- *Ensuring incomes and basic social security* (i.e., an adequate level of social protection as a basic right for all, and a people-to-people Global Social Trust).
- *Working safely out of poverty* (i.e., occupational health and safety)

Within this framework, an initiative was developed that first provided support to five pilot countries (Cambodia, Honduras, Mali, Tanzania, and Nepal), and then was expanded to several others. This initiative was based on preparing an analysis of the role of employment, and the various elements comprising decent work in poverty alleviation in collaboration with national authorities, and on organizing tripartite meetings in the countries to discuss the PRSPs. These country pilots demonstrated the economic gains from implementing the core conventions of the ILO as transmitted through its DWA by creating employment with minimum social protections through PRSP policy choices. ILO staff members armed with such evidence-based arguments were able to gain support from ministries of economics and finance to consider the employment benefits in the context of broader, more inclusive.

Policy Negotiation

Decent Work and Poverty Reduction Strategies—An ILO Advocacy Guidebook for Staff and Constituents (ILO, 2005) was developed by the authors for the ILO to help strengthen institutional capacity in policy negotiations with powerful domestic financial planning and management ministries and their international counterparts. As the Policy Integration Unit at the ILO was the focal point of the manual, staff members of the unit were asked to attend a workshop aimed at honing their negotiation skills and mastery of alliance building in the national policy-making arena of the PRSPs. Regional staff from countries where the DWA was being piloted were also engaged in a similar training process, together with their social partners in 2004–2006.

To the ILO's credit, wherever dedicated efforts were made, the inclusion of decent work in the PRSPs increased. The reviewable evidence (ILO, 2002a, 2005) indicated that the ILO's advocacy efforts produced various positive outcomes with direct relevance to previous concerns, as listed above. In all of the countries where the ILO was actively engaged with the PRSP process, the DWA—previously virtually absent in PRSP documents—was addressed. Furthermore, constituents' involvement in the preparation of the PRSPs sharply increased, and competence in linking decent work and poverty reduction was developed amongst key ILO counterparts, including those from within the NGO sector.

Policy negotiation worked.

Standard-Setting

However, one must ask to what extent the decent work perspective has really managed to become an *integral*, and thereby relatively sustainable, part of the PRSP policy matrix globally. Or, in other words, to what extent have efforts to promote the DWA been successful in bringing substantive change to the philosophy and practice of the PRSPs themselves? This question, which underpins the following sections of this case example, is felt to be particularly relevant, as experience shows that in the long-term, employment creation and protection of labor rights must be meaningfully included in all sector programs in order to ensure that poverty-reduction strategies generate significant and sustainable impact.

For several years, the ILO has been active in establishing the *ISO 26000: 2010: Guidance on Social Responsibility* (ISO, n.d.). This is a major engagement aimed at getting the international standard accepted by other actors using voluntary commercial mechanisms rather than resorting to binding international conventions, as has been tried before with less-than-satisfactory results. While the ILO continues to monitor the legal provisions concerning labor affairs in various countries, such monitoring has not achieved a significant impact. This change of tactics, evidenced by the ILO's joint work with the International Organization for Standardisation, demonstrated a new departure, setting new norms for the conduct of negotiations regarding working conditions. These new norms effectively create a diplomatic space for NGOs to contribute toward, and exercise ND in, the setting of standards (Figure 5.3).

A decade later, the newly published global Multidimensional Poverty Index (MPI) launched by the Oxford Poverty and Human Development Initiative (OPHI, n.d.) suggested a new and alternative international measure of poverty. The MPI gradually replaced the traditional income-based measures of poverty in subsequent UNDP *Human Development Reports*. This is a good example of *ND* at work. Additionally, this diplomacy work concluded the process of a paradigm shift, by reattributing the causes of poverty from individuals to work structures. This new standard setting strengthened the ILO's campaign for the inclusion of decent work and its related policy agenda into the PRSP.

Watchdog Functions

Monitoring and assessing progress toward decent work at the country level has been a long-standing concern for the ILO and its constituents. Against this background, the 2008 *ILO Declaration on Social Justice for a Fair Globalization* details that member states may consider "the establishment of appropriate indicators or statistics, if necessary, with the assistance of the ILO, to monitor and evaluate the progress made" (ILO, 2008a, para. II. B. ii.). In the past, countries repeatedly called for ILO technical cooperation inputs to support their efforts to monitor and assess progress toward decent work.

A watchdog project initiated in 2009 and financed by the EU (ILO, 2010), Monitoring and Assessing Progress on Decent Work worked with government agencies, including ministries of labor, and national statistics offices; workers' and employers' organizations; and research institutions to strengthen the capacity of developing and transitioning countries to self-monitor and self-assess progress toward decent work. The first set of 21 indicators developed by the project for the Asia-Pacific Region were put in a position to become operational.

In addition to defining statistical measures for monitoring and assessing decent work conditions in its member states, the ILO has continued to monitor the multidimensional factors that contributed to poverty and deprivation. Equally, if not *more*, effective are the NGOs acting as watchdogs to check whether the PRSPs include the DWA in the different sections of national development plans. What follows are a few examples of sector-focused watchdog functions which have been undertaken by CSOs.

Whistle Blowing

The theoretical framework underpinning the first generation of PRSPs was based largely on studies confirming the link between trade and growth, as well as on the notion that trade protection creates distortions by transferring income from the poor to the rich (Michalopoulos et al., 2002). The WB recognized the negative impact of trade liberalization on the (working) poor during the early phases of trade liberalization; however, it emphasized that the adjustment costs are typically short-term and that trade liberalization should favor labor in developing economies since their exports are typically labor-intensive. As a result, some of the corrective measures envisaged in the context of the DWA have been neglected.

This point was made by the United Nations Council for Trade and Development, in its *Least-Developed Countries Report* (UNCTAD, 2002), which criticized the first generation of PRSPs for emphasizing short-term stabilization over long-term development; and pointed out that trade issues are not treated seriously enough in the PRSPs as important aspects of long-term development strategies with the potential to build productive capacities and generate livelihoods.

Today, the accepted wisdom in the international development community is that "inclusive growth" is needed for job and employment creation. This is arguably a major development attributable, in part, to NGO diplomacy.

Back to the Beginning: Reframing

By many accounts, despite the ILO's significant efforts (and achievements), the full integration of the decent work perspective into the PRSP policy matrix was far from complete in the first generation of PRSPs. This matches overall assessments of the decent work content of first-generation PRSPs (ILO, 2002a; World Bank Independent Evaluation Group, 2002, 2006; World Bank Operations Evaluation Department, 2004). By and large, the first generation of PRSPs did not draw sufficiently on the DWA. They usually analyzed employment at length but gave limited consideration to social protections and often ignored rights at work and social dialog altogether. Employment creation and other decent work elements, such as education, health, environmental conservation, and rural development and governance issues, have been treated as add-ons without being thoroughly embedded in pro-poor growth strategies.

Nonetheless, thanks to the perseverance of NGOs acting as watchdogs and whistle-blowers, PRSPs have been revised and re-evaluated, and the new generation of PRSPs showed indications of more adequate inclusion of the DWA. Hence, another round of NDs was needed to help reverse the trend and strengthen the inclusion of decent work into future generations of PRSPs and other economic development instruments. Throughout this process, technical and subject matter experts spent more time and energy in fostering a conducive environment, which helped development actors and national governments realize that the ILO should be engaged in the PRSP process and have its DWA incorporated into the thinking of domestic and international policy makers for economic and human development, under SDG-8 (above).

Summary: Advice for Aspiring NGO Diplomats

Depending on available financial resource availability, research capacity, and organizational maturity, an NGO can determine its most effective sphere of operation and influence. For instance, the watchdog function can be an easy starting point for start-up NGOs that want to be engaged in the policy discourse. By monitoring the actual implementation of the policy commitments made publicly by the states, for example, a start-up NGO can accumulate the information and knowledge on specific issues required to become a serious dialog partner for other more established NGOs.

Issue Identification for Policy Advocacy by Work-Related NGOs

There are three different types of advocacy on which a work-related NGO could focus:

- *Positional advocacy*: Influencing the public and stakeholders to choose particular policies or to accept or reject particular values. In the above case, a rights-based approach to development was advocated.
- *Methodological advocacy*: Influencing the public to become active as problem-solvers and to use certain methods of problem-solving but remaining careful not to become an advocate for any particular position.
- *Standards-based advocacy*: Influencing the actors to adhere to and demand certain standards or codes of conduct by the public.

For example, in promoting better working conditions and fair pay, NGOs who advocate for the adoption of the DWA as part of the core of a PRSP development strategy might approach the campaign from the rights perspective (positional) or the accepted international norm perspective, such as the *OECD Guidelines for Multinational Enterprises* (OECD, 2011), or the *Guiding Principles on Business and Human Rights: Implementing the United Nations "Protect, Respect and Remedy" Framework* (UN OHCHR, 2011).

Three examples help clarify the suggested advocacy strategies. Regarding the inclusion of decent work in the PRSPs, from 2007 onward, actions by global civil society were organized as a large campaign coordinated by BetterAid, a coalition of major NGOs coordinated using a mechanism that grew out of successful experience in the global campaign against the OECD proposal for a Multilateral Agreement on Investment (1995–1998), which was ultimately defeated by the NGO coalition (Laxer, 2003).

Another well-documented example is the European Network on Debt and Development (Eurodad) advocacy in favor of debt-relief for the economically poorer and "least developed" countries (Bökkering & Van Hees, 1998). Prior to the campaigns by Eurodad, the IMF and the WB, faced with the staggering indebtedness of the highly indebted poor countries, thought that limited debt relief would make the debt of these countries "sustainable" and allow them "to grow out of" their debt through economic growth. In contrast, however, Eurodad emphasized that partial debt relief could not be used to manage the excessive debt of these countries and that they required more substantial debt forgiveness to fight poverty. The persistent and well-coordinated influence of Eurodad led international financial institutions to adopt poverty alleviation-based debt policies. The use of such tactics as monitoring of policies of international financial institutions, sharing relevant information with other NGOs, coordinating public pressure, promoting alternative policy frameworks, and negotiating text revisions with representatives of the financial institutions and national governments, all constitute excellent examples of development diplomacy (Saner, 2006).

M&E

A more current example is the effort by NGOs to advocate a bottom-up and inclusive approach to M&E of the implementation of the SDGs, including SDG-8, in the post-2015 era (Husch et al., 2014). Discussions and reviews of M&E research have been of key importance for the SDG accountability discussions. M & E are also considered fundamental governance mechanisms necessary to inform the policy makers and the public on the progress and impact of implementing the SDGs. Monitoring is an ongoing process that parallels, tracks, and traces day-to-day decisions and actions, while evaluation is an end-of-the-pipe activity seeking to assess and judge the validity of any decision or action against set criteria. With respect to the SDGs, an alliance of NGOs including CSEND proposed to use multiple data sources for both monitoring and evaluative processes, to integrate the use of new ICT methods and tools with the implementation of the SDGs and to augment "data analysis" through a reform of the statistical capacity of the global institutions as well as that of the national authorities. In view of the enormous volume of unstructured data produced by the citizens of the world, ways to incorporate data of varying quality and validity into the official monitoring of SDG implementation is also another important discussion. Through NGO diplomacy, it is expected that data use by the policy makers will increase. However, the capacity for data analytics-based advocacy is one of the shortcomings of many CSOs, especially in countries suffering most of the development deficits.

Globally civil society has come a long way in applying ND to participate in and steer development policy-making in the past decades. The existence of ICT infrastructures creates opportunities for CSOs to scale up their diplomacy and advocacy faster. Evidence-based diplomacy is of great value in the struggle against the injustices faced by the working poor and persistent precarity in many societies.

Future Research Directions

A few direct suggestions are offered here for how psychologists, in cooperation with other social scientists including economists, political scientists, anthropologists, and historians, could use their research capabilities to advance the struggle toward more inclusive and equitable development around the world, where gender equality in pay and wages remain desired and general precarity and DWDs reign.

There are several avenues for psychologists, especially I/O psychologists, to bring their skills to bear in the tradition of "research for impact" or "action research" to bring about the transformations needed to meet the SDGs and reduce systemic fragility and vulnerability and achieve sustainability of the planet. Without success in both these areas, precarious workers and other vulnerable groups will be the first to suffer due to natural and manmade catastrophes that scientists are signaling.

What are the transformations required to achieve the SDGs, assuming the principles of leaving no one behind, circularity, and economic de-couplings? In that respect, the SDGs can be grouped into six broad domains:

1 education, gender, and inequality (SDGs 1, 5, 7–10, 12–15, 17)
2 health, wellbeing, and demography (SDGs 1, 2, 3, 4, 5, 8, 10)
3 energy, decarbonization, and sustainable industry (SDGs 1–16)
4 sustainable food, land, water, and oceans (SDGs 1–3, 5, 6, 8, 10–15)
5 sustainable cities and communities (SDGs 1–16)
6 digital revolution for sustainable development (SDGs 1–4, 7–13, 17)

(Sachs et al., 2019)

Each of these six fundamental system transformations requires behavior change, system reconfiguration, design, realignment, and transition management. These transformations will only work if conditions are created in a semi-synchronized and cohesive manner from local to national, accumulated for global impact. The pathways to results are long and demand the collaboration of many actors and the consent of the bystanders. This is the ultimate platform for the engagement and participation by members of SIOP and other subdisciplines of psychology through research, consulting, monitoring, and teaching. *Diplomacy and various functions of advocacy (as expressed in the six-step cycle of Figure 5.3) require facts, evidence, and data at different levels of aggregation.* Without sufficient training, such competencies cannot be developed. Therefore, a comprehensive research agenda for data generation and knowledge creation can evolve around the 17 SDGs and their targets and indicators with a targeted focus on precarity.

The entry points for developing a related research agenda could be:

a To participate in the development of the so-called shadow reports alongside the voluntary national reports which countries present in New York during the UN-High-Level Policy Forum on the SDGs and the 2030 Agenda.

   A shadow report is a collective effort to research the factual implementation status of a country's official SDG implementation. It is understandable that governments tend to emphasize the achievements of their SDG implementation and to de-emphasize or even hide the gaps between expected target achievements versus realities on the ground. An excellent example is the shadow report titled *Four Years of SDGs in Bangladesh and the Way Forward: Looking through the Prism of Non-State Actors* by Citizen Platform for SDGs, Bangladesh (2019).

b To join any of the nine major groups and six stakeholder groups created in 1992 during the first United Nations Conference on Environment and Development.

   These are recognized formal representatives of nonstate actors accredited to the United Nations (High-Level Political Forum on Sustainable Development, n.d., https://sdgs.un.org/goals). The major groups include the Local Authorities Major Group, NGO Major Group, Scientific & Technological Community Major Group, Women's Major Group, Workers and Trade Unions Major Group, the Indigenous Peoples Major Group, and the Farmers Major Group. Also represented are Stakeholder Groups like the Sendai Group (Stakeholder Engagement Mechanism), the Civil Society Financing for Development Group, Stakeholder Group on Ageing, and the Stakeholder Group of Persons with Disabilities. All of these major and stakeholder groups have their own secretariats and focal points. What they often lack is social science research capabilities. Supporting any of these stakeholder groups will help them to address the more interconnected and interdependent issues, such as zero-carbon and nature-based economic growth and decent work conditions for all, more effectively.

c To engage in SDG data-related projects and activities around the world.

   A large number of the 193 UN member countries do not have adequate numbers of competent researchers who can help their respective governments gather sufficient quantities of the good-quality data needed in order for governments to be able to assess their SDG implementations and formulate more effective policies. The UNDESA and the UN Statistical Commission have now added qualitative methods of data collection, including transdisciplinary methods and citizen science (directly including citizens in their data collection) to the traditional quantitative data collection methods in their toolbox. Psychologists and social science researchers with competencies in novel citizen science approaches to data collection and analysis could offer help to their own national statistical authorities and collaborate with university-based research centers (Stockholm Environment Institute [SEI], 2019).

d To conduct research in the areas of partnerships and collaboration.

There are more than 6,000 partnerships registered with UNDESA, functioning at different levels. These partnerships are cross-sectoral, sometimes cross-border, multifaceted, and multistakeholder-oriented. Research is urgently needed to address the following questions which are commonplace at the micro level in the studies of organizations and related behavior but new at the sectoral, national, and global levels:

- What are the necessary conditions that facilitate high-performing partnerships?
- What are the typical partnership process and dynamics?
- What could be the behavioral patterns typical of a dysfunctional partnership?
- What are the requisite skillsets to lead or steer a complex partnership involving state authorities, businesses, and NGOs (international and local) in turbulent environments?

Diplomacy and negotiations are integral parts of this new research domain investigating how partnerships can work to promote and advance the SDGs. Different variants of the ND discussed in this chapter, e.g.., transnational NGO diplomacy (Saner & Yiu, 2012; Yiu & Saner, 2016), humanitarian diplomacy (Saner & Yiu, 2012), and development diplomacy (Saner & Yiu, 2006), which are all facets of NGO diplomacy and effective partnership formation. More research is needed in this emerging area for theory development and presents a new frontier for the interested I/O psychologist.

Resource

A very useful publication by the Conference of NGOs in Consultative Relationship with the United Nations (CoNGO, n.d.) provides guidance on the processes that need to be followed for accreditation by 13 different UN Agencies and could be of use for future NGO diplomats and NGOs who plan to influence policy-making, including through M & E research, at UN agencies.

Conclusion

A global-governance architecture is emerging where roles and rules of engagement for nonstate actors have been created and shaped in the process. Civil society has become a vital driver of democratization and of global decision-making, yet the attitudes and intentions of the other two stakeholder groups, i.e., governments and businesses, have been relatively unclear and mixed with regard to the proposal for an inclusive UN. Should the UN be just a talking shop where politicians meet to discuss issues without necessarily being obliged to follow through on their comments? Should the UN be just a pulpit where high-sounding principles and guidelines are being produced by political leaders without obligation for compliance by either the states or the businesses? According to Hill (2004):

> Civil society is drawn to the UN because it provides I based on the ethics, moral principles and aspirations of the Charter, in which governments exercise their power at the international level and in which even the smallest state has formal equality with the most powerful.
>
> *(Hill, 2004, p. 4)*

Analysis by the NGO CSEND conducted by the authors shows that NGO diplomats can deploy their social and network capitals and their "opinion" power to effect actual change. This transformation toward more inclusive decision-making might neither be immediate nor visible at first.

The engagement of civil society with the UN system and global governance processes has come a long way. The national NGOs and other grassroots organizations from the Global South have contributed to the constructive development of the UN system and the global governance system, but they have also triggered an evolution in the ways the established TNGOs perceive the world and understand our shared humanity and work/livelihood and development issues. Therefore, the authors hope that the example of the case analysis presented here will encourage broader participation in the global governance debate by citizens from "developing" countries through their own NGOs.

This chapter has focused on the roles that NGO diplomacy and NGO diplomats can play, the influence they can exert at national and international levels of business and government, and how applied psychologists who work in labor-related fields in I/O can use NGO diplomacy strategies and tactics to reduce precarious work and strengthen decent work and social justice by cultivating and practicing a number of the ND competencies explained in this chapter. These NDs include being both producers and consumers of ND research. In this way, new research regarding SDG implementation processes and governance can contribute greatly to the realization of an inclusive, just, and sustainable world.

Notes

1 This section draws on Saner and Yiu (2014b).
2 This section builds on a related section in Saner and Yiu (2014a).

References

Bökkering, S. and Van Hees, T. (1998). Eurodad's campaign on multilateral debt: The 1996 HIPC debt initiative and beyond. *Development and Practice, 8*(3), 7–85.

CERN. (n.d.). *Our member states.* https://www.home.cern/about/who-we-are/our-governance/member-states

Citizen Platform for SDGs, Bangladesh. (2019). *Four years of SDGs in Bangladesh and the way forward: Looking through the prism of non-state actors*. https://cpd.org.bd/wp-content/uploads/2019/07/Four-Years-of-SDGs-in-Bangladesh.pdf

City University of London. (n.d.). *Article 71 of the Charter of the United Nations*. http://www.staff.city.ac.uk/p.willetts/UN/CHT-A71.HTM

Conference of NGOs in Consultative Relationship with the United Nations. (n.d.). *The United Nations system.* http://ngocongo.org/the-un-system

CSEND. (2017, June 10). [Summary]. Colloquium: Is a living wage bad for the economy? Geneva. https://www.csend.org/images/articles/files/20170826-Summary_of_LW_seminar_at_U_GE_10_June_2017_RS.pdf

Davis, T. R. (2014), NGOs: A new history of transnational civil society. Oxford University Press.

Global Policy Forum. (2004). *Official IMF evaluation finds flaws in PRSP process*. https://archive.globalpolicy.org/component/content/article/209-bwi-wto/43077.html

High-Level Political Forum on Sustainable Development. (n.d.) *Stakeholders.* Retrieved February 4, 2023. https://hlpf.un.org/2022/stakeholders

Hill, T. (2004). *Three generations of UN-civil society relations.* https://archive.globalpolicy.org/component/content/article/177-un/31824-three-generations-of-un-civil-society-relations.html

Husch, J., Saner, R., Yiu, L., & Zeitz, P. (2014), *Monitoring of SGD implementation: Infrastructure and methodology—Proposal for action.* CSEND Policy Brief No. 14. https://www.csend.org/images/articles/files/Monitoring_SDG_Infrastructure__Methodology.pdf

ILO News (2001, June 1), *International Labour Conference to Explore "Decent Work Deficit"*. https://www.ilo.org/global/about-the-ilo/newsroom/news/WCMS_007843/lang–en/index.htm

International Labour Organization). (n.d.) *Decent work.* Retrieved December 18, 2022. https://www.ilo.org/global/topics/decent-work/lang–en/index.htm

International Labour Organization). (1999). *Report of the Director-General: Decent work.* https://www.ilo.org/public/english/standards/relm/ilc/ilc87/rep-i.htm

International Labour Organization). (2002a). ILO governing body report in 2002.

International Labour Organization). (2002b). *Poverty Reduction Strategy Papers (PRSPs): An assessment of the ILO experience.,* (Report No. GB283/ESP/3) https://www.ilo.org/wcmsp5/groups/public/—ed_norm/—relconf/—reloff/documents/meetingdocument/wcms_078846.pdf

International Labour Organization). (2002c). The Decent Work Agenda and poverty reduction, ILO contribution to the IMF/World Bank comprehensive review of the poverty reduction strategy process.

International Labour Organization). (2003). Time for equality at work: Global report under the follow-up to the ILO Declaration on Fundamental Principles and Rights at Work, International Labor Conference, 91st Session 2003 (Report I [B]). https://www.ilo.org/wcmsp5/groups/public/—dgreports/—dcomm/—publ/documents/publication/wcms_publ_9221128717_en.pdf

International Labour Organization). (2005). *Decent work and poverty reduction strategies (PRS): An ILO advocacy guidebook for staff and constituents.* https://www.ilo.org/wcmsp5/groups/public/—dgreports/—integration/documents/instructionalmaterial/wcms_079966.pdf

International Labour Organization). (2008a) *ILO declaration on social justice for a fair globalization.* https://www.ilo.org/wcmsp5/groups/public/—dgreports/—cabinet/documents/genericdocument/wcms_099766.pdf

International Labour Organization). (2008b). The Decent Work Agenda—Looking back, looking forward: A growing consensus. World of Work 64. https://www.ilo.org/global/publications/world-of-work-magazine/articles/WCMS_101697/lang–en/index.htm

International Labour Organization). (2010) *Monitoring and assessing progress on decent work (MAP).* Retrieved December 18, 2022, https://www.ilo.org/integration/themes/mdw/WCMS_123804/lang–en/index.htm

International Labour Organization). (2012). Decent work indicators: Guidelines for producers and users of statistical and legal framework indicators. In *ILO manual* (2nd ed.). https://www.ilo.org/wcmsp5/groups/public/—dgreports/—integration/documents/publication/wcms_229374.pdf

International Labour Organization). (2013). *Tripartite constituents.* https://www.ilo.org/global/about-the-ilo/who-we-are/tripartite-constituents/lang–en/index.htm

International Monetary Fund. (2002). Poverty Reduction Strategy Papers: A fact sheet.

International Organization for Migration. (2016). *IOM becomes a related organization to the UN.* https://www.iom.int/news/iom-becomes-related-organization-un

International Standards Association. (n.d.) ISO 26000: Social responsibility. https://www.iso.org/iso-26000-social-responsibility.html

Laxer, G. (2003). The Defeat of the Multilateral Agreement on Investment: National Movements Confront Globalism. In: Laxer, G., Halperin, S. (eds) *Global Civil Society and Its Limits.* International Political Economy Series. London: Palgrave Macmillan. https://doi.org/10.1057/9780230523715_9

Malena, C. (1995). *Working with NGOS: A practical guide to operational collaboration between the World Bank and non-governmental organizations.* https://documents1.worldbank.org/curated/en/814581468739240860/pdf/multi-page.pdf

MBA Knowledge Base. (n.d.). Non-governmental organization (NGO)—Definition, types and roles. https://www.mbaknol.com/general-business-articles/non-governmental-organization-ngo/

Michalopoulos, C., Schiff, M., & Tarr, D. G. (2002) Rules of thumb for trade policy. In B. M. Hoekman, A. Mattoo, & P. English (Eds.), *Development, trade and WTO: A handbook* (pp. 519–525). The International Bank for Reconstruction and Development/The World Bank. https://documents1.worldbank.org/curated/en/805981468763835259/pdf/297990018213149971x.pdf

Multinational Monitor. (2001). *GE can be beat*. https://www.multinationalmonitor.org/mm2001/072001/interview-mulvey.html

Organization for Economic Co-operation and Development. (2011). *OECD guidelines for multinational enterprises* (2011 ed.). https://www.oecd.org/daf/inv/mne/48004323.pdf

Oxford Poverty and Human Development Initiative. (n.d.) *Global Multidimensional Poverty Index*. https://ophi.org.uk/multidimensional-poverty-index/

Pruthi, S. (2021). *Difference between civil society and NGO: A critical analysis*. Enterslice. https://enterslice.com/learning/civil-society-and-ngo

Ritchie, C. & Rice, A. (1995). *Changing relationships between international nongovernmental organizations and the United Nations*. Union of International Organizations. http://www.uia.org/archive/TNGOs-un

Sachs, J., Schmidt-Traub, G., Mazzucato, M., Messner, D., Nakicenovic, N. & Rockstom, J., (2019) Six Transformations to Achieve the Sustainable Development Goals (SDGs). *Nature Sustainability2*: 805–814. https://doi.org/10.1038/s41893-019-0352-9

Saner, R. (2002). Zur Kultur eines Berufs: Was ist ein Diplomat? In E. Brandt & C. Buck (Eds.), *Auswärtiges Amt: Diplomatie als Beruf*. Leske & Budrich 333–339.

Saner, R. (2006). Development diplomacy by non-state actors: An emerging form of multistakeholder diplomacy. In J. Kurbalija, J. & V. Katrandjiev (Eds.), *Multistakeholder diplomacy: Challenges and opportunities*. Diplo. https://www.diplomacy.edu/wp-content/uploads/2021/06/MultistakeholderDiplomacy.pdf

Saner, R., & Guilherme, R. (2007). The International Monetary Fund's influence on trade policies of low-income countries: A valid undertaking? *Journal of World Trade 41*, 931–981.

Saner, R., & Michaelun, V. (Eds.). (2009). *State actor versus non-state actor negotiations*. Republic of Letters.

Saner, R., and Yiu, L. (2003). International economic diplomacy: Mutations in post modern times. In S. Mowby (Ed.) *Discussion papers in diplomacy*, Institute of International Relations (Clingendael).

Saner, R., & Yiu, L. (2012). The New Diplomacies and Humanitarian Work Psychology. In S. C. Carr, M. MacLachlan, & A. Furnham, A (Eds.), *Humanitarian work psychology* (pp. 129–166). Palgrave Macmillan.

Saner, R., & Yiu, L. (2014a). Designing learning systems for poverty reduction in least developed countries. In W. Reichman (Ed.), *Industrial and organizational psychology help the vulnerable* (pp. 164–185). Palgrave MacMillan. https://psycnet.apa.org/doi/10.1057/9781137327734_10

Saner, R., & Yiu, L. (2014b). Participation of civil society organizations in the United Nations and in the aid effectiveness discourse and related standard-setting negotiations. In K. Göymen & R. Lewis, (Eds.), *Public policy making in a globalized world* (pp. 149–183-YY). Istanbul Policy Center, Sabanci University. https://www.csend.org/images/articles/files/20150526_Participation_of_CSO_in_UN_in_Aid_Effectives.pdf

Saner, R., & Yiu, L. (2017). Negotiation and health diplomacy: The case of tobacco. In S. Matlin & I. Kickbusch (Eds.) *Pathways to global health: case studies in global health diplomacy* (Vol. 2, pp. 171–210). World Scientific Publishing.

Saner, R., & Yiu, L. (2019a) Activities and achievements of the IAAP team at the UN in Geneva. *Applied Psychology around the World, 1*(3), 95–101. https://iaapsy.org/site/assets/files/1082/apaw_vol1i3.pdf

Saner, R., & Yiu, L. (2019b, July 8–10) *Living wage and Sustainable Development Goal # 8* [Paper presentation]. 6th Conference of the Regulating for Decent Work Network, Geneva, Switzerland.

Saner, R., Yiu, L., & Sondergaard, M. (2000). Business diplomacy management: A core competency for global companies. *Academy of Management Executive*, *14*(1), 80–92.

Satow, E. M., Gore-Booth, P. H. (Ed.), Pakenham, D. (Ed.) (1979). *Satow's guide to diplomatic practice* (5th ed.) Longman.

SDG Knowledge Platform. (n.d.). *Major groups and other stakeholders (MGoS)*. Retrieved December 18, 2022, from https://sustainabledevelopment.un.org/mgos

Somavia, J. (2002, September 18). Address by Juan Somavia, Director-General of the International Labour Office on decent work and social viability to the Diplomatic Club of Geneva. https://www.ilo.org/public/english/bureau/dgo/speeches/somavia/2002/clubdiplomatic.htm

Stockholm Environment Institute. (2019). *Citizen science and the United Nations Sustainable Development Goals.* https://www.sei.org/publications/citizen-science-and-the-united-nations-sustainable-development-goals/

United Nations. (2000). *Twenty-fourth special session of the General Assembly entitled "World Summit for Social Development and beyond: Achieving social development for all in a globalizing world": Report of the Secretary-General* (A/55/344). https://digitallibrary.un.org/record/424837?ln=en

United Nations. (2000). *United Nations Millennium Declaration: Resolution adopted by the General Assembly* (A/RES/55/2). https://digitallibrary.un.org/record/422015?ln=en

United Nations. (2005). 2005 World Summit outcome: Resolution adopted by the General Assembly (A/RES/60/1). https://digitallibrary.un.org/record/556636?ln=en

United Nations. (2012). *The future we want: Resolution as adopted by the General Assembly* (A/RES/66/288). https://digitallibrary.un.org/record/734344?ln=en

United Nations. (2015). *Transforming our world: The 2030 Agenda for Sustainable Development: Resolution adopted by the General Assembly* (A/RES/70/1). https://digitallibrary.un.org/record/3923923?ln=en

United Nations Conference on Trade and Development. (2002) *The least developed countries report, 2002: Escaping the poverty trap.* https://unctad.org/webflyer/least-developed-countries-report-2002

United Nations Department of Economic and Social Affairs NGO Branch. (2022a) *Organizations by region as registered on the DESA CSO Net (2022).* Retrieved December 18, 2022, from Integrated Civil Society Organizations System.

United Nations Department of Economic and Social Affairs NGO Branch. (2022b) *Organizations by type as registered on the DESA CSO Net (2022).* Retrieved December 18, 2022, from Integrated Civil Society Organizations System.

United Nations Human Rights Council. (n.d.). *Universal periodic review.* https://www.ohchr.org/en/hr-bodies/upr/upr-main

United Nations Office of the High Commissioner for Human Rights. (n.d.) *Mandate of UN human rights.* https://www.ohchr.org/EN/ABOUTUS/Pages/Mandate.aspx

United Nations Office of the High Commissioner for Human Rights. (2011). *Guiding principles on business and human rights: Implementing the United Nations "Protect, Respect and Remedy" Framework.* https://www.ohchr.org/sites/default/files/documents/publications/guidingprinciplesbusinesshr_en.pdf

Whitt, J. E. (2017, January 3). *United Nations 101: The six primary organs of the UN.* AMUN. https://www.amun.org/united-nations-primary-organs/

World Bank. (2022). Defining civil society.

World Bank Independent Evaluation Group. (2002). *IMF/World Bank comprehensive review of the Poverty Reduction Strategy Papers (PRSP) Approach.* https://www.imf.org/external/np/prspgen/review/2001/index.htm

World Bank Independent Evaluation Group. (2006). *Annual review of development effectiveness 2006: Getting results.* https://documents1.worldbank.org/curated/en/700621468137398728/pdf/Annual-Review-of-Development-Effectiveness-2006-getting-results.pdf

World Bank Operations Evaluation Department. (2004). *Operations Evaluation Department (OED) review of the Poverty Reduction Strategy (PRS) Process: Mauritania case study.* https://documents1.worldbank.org/curated/en/266031468051532811/pdf/821290WP0prsp000Box379840B00PUBLIC0.pdf

Yiu, L., & Saner, R. (2016). Humanitarian work psychology: Unique contributions and theoretical development in the context of the global development agenda. In I. McWha-Hermann, D. Maynard, & M. O'Neill Berry (Eds.), *Humanitarian work psychology and the global development agenda* (pp. 192–200). Routledge.

6

"LET'S JUST TALK ABOUT IT!"

Combating Precarious Work in Global Supply Chains

Divya Jyoti and Bimal Arora

Introduction

Despite growing recognition and many local and global initiatives developed by governments, civil societies, and the private sector, millions of workers engaged in producing goods and services as part of global supply chains continue to suffer in situations of modern slavery and working poverty. One key reason for the limited success of initiatives to address workplace precarity is the wide gaps between those with lived experience, those who design the solutions, and those expected to implement these solutions. Top-down approaches are developed and followed with the best intentions, but they can often be experienced as moral imperialism and may even end up generating adverse consequences instead of the desired positive ones. Might it be possible then, to combat precarious work by bridging the gaps between the diverse range of actors in supply chains? How might the gaps be narrowed? It was this quest to bridge the gaps in order to foster improved understandings of precarious workplaces and nurture empathetic collaborative approaches that led to the first India and Sustainability Standards International Dialogues and Conference in 2015 (India and Sustainability Standards [ISS], n.d.). Drawing on the authors' experiences[1] of conceptualizing, designing, organizing, and establishing this forum for international dialog, this chapter presents and reflects upon an inclusive all-of-supply chain, interorganizational, and cross-sectoral approach to combating precarious work.

Centre for Responsible Business (CRB): A Brief Background

The CRB (n.d.) was incubated through a three-year public-private partnership between Deutsche Gesellschaft für Internationale Zusammenarbeit (GIZ); Social Accountability International (SAI); and Business Social Compliance Initiative

DOI: 10.4324/9781003440444-7

(BSCI), now known as Amfori. The initial guiding premise for CRB was that the precarity generated and persisting in the supply-chain operations of international companies can be tackled if the technical, procedural, and knowledge capacities of all businesses involved in the supply chains were strengthened. From this departure point, CRB engaged in mapping the landscape of supports available to suppliers and developed content, pedagogy, and facilitation and training capabilities and designed advisory interventions. In doing so, the CRB team engaged with a range of actors involved in international trade, from workers to governments, and through this engagement soon became conscious of the conundrum they were facing.

Tackling Precarious Work: The Conundrum

Although primarily guided by economics, the opening up of global trade and the formation of global production networks has inevitably forged connections between people; places; products; organizational processes; and cultural beliefs, norms, and practices. While working with governments; multinational corporations; and not-for-profit institutions in India, and the EU, US, and UK, it gradually became evident to the team at CRB that although terms like "social compliance," "worker protection," "worker safety," and "ethical trade" were used by all, defined in specific ways, the associated interpretations, meanings, and emotions that accompanied them varied widely. Even if there was some consensus on how the terms were understood, the ways to realize the envisioned objectives were diverse and often guided by conflicting sets of values. It was no surprise then that we sometimes found ourselves caught in the middle of disagreements and misunderstandings. The most frustrating aspect was that while everyone had a genuine intention, nothing really moved forward. An illustrative example would be useful here to elaborate both the conceptual conundrum and roadblocks that we have faced in our collective efforts to tackle precarious work along global supply chains (see also, Saxena & Tchagneno, Chapter 11).

A Case of "Ethical" Fashion Production

The issue of working conditions in manufacturing facilities, particularly those making fashion garments and accessories, has been widely discussed and debated globally, particularly in India. While some have argued that the issue here is the intent of the owners of the garment-manufacturing factories, and the governments where these factories are located, GIZ, BSCI, and SAI started with the premise that it was not about intent but instead about skills and capabilities. That is, the companies running the factories often lacked the infrastructure and technical and human capabilities to create ethical workplaces, and if their capabilities and skills were enhanced, they would be more able to follow the established international norms, standards, and codes of conduct and would be able to offer improved working conditions to their workers. With the support of GIZ, BSCI, and SAI, CRB developed content and identified personnel with experience in offering training and advice in ethical manufacturing and then designed a range of programs, with the brands and the Indian government, to address this "capability" challenge[2] (Arora, 2011).

Over the span of a couple of years, it became evident through the persistence of the challenges that they cannot be answered by capability enhancement alone. No amount of expert training, tools, or training resources can help with navigating the intra/interorganizational and intra/intergovernmental and regional politics, which often underpin misunderstandings and confusions, and limits the outcomes of efforts to create ethical trade.

For instance, when we asked certain activists based in Europe why they only targeted big-brand's suppliers located in India, and why other brands with manufacturing facilities in Europe offering equally or more precarious working conditions were not questioned, we failed to get an adequate response. The response was similar when we questioned certain standard-setting and certification bodies about why the emphasis in their work was only on export markets. How is it possible to work with production facilities in silos and not even think about the domestic market in manufacturing countries? We noticed events discussing working conditions and due diligence were often organized at pan-European and pan-US levels, with hardly any voices of manufacturers included in the conversation.[3] In some cases, raising uncomfortable questions resulted in CRB team members being labeled as too academic, losing favor with some of the event organizers, and sometimes even being subtly and diplomatically ousted from committees and forums. Thankfully, such instances were few and the vast majority of organizations were very open when we asked uncomfortable questions and shared our analyses, concerns, and limitations.

A brief research project CRB undertook highlighted how hundreds of thousands of dollars were being invested in projects in the textile and garment industries in India in locations and on issues that seemed to be attracting media attention but were achieving little toward creating lasting sustainable change (Solidaridad, 2014[4]). In our analysis, a primary reason that limited the prospects of various efforts was that neither the workers for whom change was desired, nor the suppliers who had to implement the proposed changes, were involved in the design and development of these interventions, and their views and experiences remained largely hidden and overlooked. Instead, the standards for ethical production and associated programs were all designed by "experts" located in 'other' sociocultural and geographic contexts, but factories were expected to follow and implement them. As we met more and more factory owners, managers, and workers, it became evident that the everyday struggles of the people working in the factories were not always visible and consequently not understood by 'others'. These challenges included receiving contradicting messages from personnel in different departments (often the sustainability and production departments) of the same brand companies, difficulties with auditing agencies and their personnel, infrastructural challenges, and production planning issues (Jyoti, 2020[5]). Furthermore, the country-based local staff of brands and auditing agencies also often felt unheard and powerless. Factories experienced codes and standards as an imposition, governments thought they were an "export requirement," brands were being repeatedly questioned and kept looking for responses, and civil society actors felt lost in this conundrum.

Talking about Precarity: Conceptualizing ISS (India Sustainability Standards)

Surrounded by such chaos and fragmentation as described above, the CRB faced something of an existential crisis. What could a handful of passionate individuals, who could relate to all the actors and who were able to see the world from each actor's point of view, do? How could we share what we witnessed, and why would we be heard? Would we get a seat at the table? As a young and small organization, what was the most effective way to live up to our guiding value of *enabling change for impact*? Who should define the impact, and who would the impact be for and why?

It was in response to these questions that Bimal first proposed the idea of *manak manch*, "platform for standards," which was ultimately branded as ISS. The choice to frame the narrative around voluntary sustainability standards (VSS) was deliberate. Since its initial consultative meetings in mid-2010 during its formative stages as an organization, CRB had been forging partnerships and engaging in relationships of varying depth, ranging from conversations to joint interventions, with a number of societal actors, including governments, quasi-government departments and agencies, charities, businesses of varying sizes, academic institutions, research organizations, and media, among others.

In this work in the politically fraught spaces of sustainable-development negotiations, the roadblocks revealed themselves time and time again. It became evident that the need for VSS (United Nations Council for Trade and Development [UNCTAD], n.d.; United Nations Forum on Sustainability Standards [UNFSS], n.d.) had come to be accepted by all actors in varying degrees, despite their differences and disagreements, and that VSS also resonated with the founding premise of CRB. The proposal was to offer a platform for dialog where the motivations for, and value, limitations, content, design, development, challenges, outcomes, benefits, and achievements of VSS could be discussed alongside the experiences of the different actors along the supply chains who are involved with them in various ways.[6] We wanted to encourage people who would otherwise perhaps not have met into the same room to have a facilitated dialog and exchange (KNN India Knowledge and News Network, 2018[7]). This is not an easy goal to achieve, and although it was, perhaps, not the first attempt in this direction, CRB had established itself as offering a unique approach. We wanted to offer the credibility and trust we had earned, as well as the ability we had demonstrated to understand the multifaceted challenges, without blame, in order to facilitate progressive decisions and actions; that is, to provide "a safe space for difficult conversations," as Bimal described it. It is also pertinent to note here that while CRB provided the idea for these meetings, these safe spaces are co-constructed. CRB offers the platform, but the conversations and deliberations are designed and led by the various actors themselves.

While Bimal was convinced about the need for the discussions, even he was surprised with the response and support ISS received in its early days. In 2014, the meeting was organized as an experimental, day-long event, but the encouraging response and overwhelming support led us to expand the scope and remit in 2015 to become a three-day event spanning multiple industries, issues, and challenges. It had seemed almost impossible when Bimal first proposed it. How could a small team pull off an event of the nature and scale he had in mind? But he made it happen. He inspired the team and the overwhelmingly positive responses from hundreds of people ensured that there would be no looking back. Bimal believed in people's energy and the potential in collaboration, and the success of ISS reaffirmed this belief.

Today, ISS is established as a globally recognized and sought-after platform where issues of national and international relevance are raised, analyzed, and debated, and actions pledged. These issues range from child labor in mining industries to living wages in the tea sector, and reflecting on jewelry supply chains to understanding what circularity may mean for fashion production, as a few examples (ISS, n.d.). Just as Bimal imagined it and proposed to his young and inexperienced team in 2015, ISS has gained a life of its own.

The beauty of ISS is not only that it has conceived and provided a platform for annual all-of-supply-chain, interorganizational, and cross-sectoral dialogs, but there is also critical and powerful work happening all year round on the various issues and themes, and around the different networks that are conceptualized and established at the annual conference. The India Water Stewardship Network (2017), VSS Collaboration India (Centre for Responsible Business, n.d.), and the India Sustainability Palm Oil Coalition (I-SPOC, n.d.) are a few examples of these networks. Other meetings result in partnerships, and joint working groups, and some remain ongoing conversations. Irrespective of the specific form or mode adopted, it has become increasingly evident that co-constructing safe spaces for dialog and deliberation offers a productive approach to tackling workplace precariousness that is situated at the intersection of psychological, geopolitical, cultural, and economic practices (CRB, 2019).

Toward Ending Precarity—Concluding Reflections

ISS's dialogic approach to combating precarity in society, and in workplaces, is a potent approach. It has enabled an improved understanding of intersectionality and the various forces and dynamics at play, and it offers possibilities and opens pathways where none seemed to exist. This is, perhaps, one reason why the number of people and organizations joining the movement only continues to grow. However, dialog is no panacea: just a beginning, and a rather humble one. Despite the scale ISS has achieved, the attention and participation it attracts, and the conversations it has initiated, much more remains to be done, and what has been achieved has not been without challenges. As Bimal and I reflected on ISS in one of our recent conversations (before his demise),[8] we wondered how many lives have been impacted by this work? Have we meaningfully affected even one? How many people's lives are better because of these safe-space conversations? How far are we from ensuring that the perpetual cycle of persistent precarity is ended? What is the distance that needs to be travelled between actors having an open conversation, making a commitment, taking action, and ultimately making a difference to people's lives and circumstances? How can we talk about the impact of this work? Can it be measured? How? We have heard many times that this is valuable work, but what is the "value"? Who is defining it? Who is measuring it? What difference has ISS really made, and for who? There are no readily available answers; maybe if Bimal was still around, he and I would have progressed further in our discoveries, but for now all I have to offer in conclusion is an invitation. ISS is an interesting, much celebrated, well-accepted, and unique initiative, but it requires examination, questioning, and analysis. I invite readers to join us in conceptualizing, participating in, and facilitating our efforts to address the issues of sustainable work.[9] The underlying ideas of ISS are conversation and collaboration and, as researchers we cannot understand the issues without ourselves putting these ideas into practice.

Future Research Directions

The work at CRB and ISS, and my own ongoing ethnographic research and practice with factory workers in India and Leicester in the UK, shows that there are a number of issues that require further reflection, exploration, and consideration by scholars interested in combating precarity in global supply chains through dialogic approaches and indeed more broadly addressing the following questions for I/O psychology and Humanitarian work psychologists:

- To what extent are those who are intended as beneficiaries of interventions to combat precarious work—the marginalized, underrepresented actors, often factory and farm workers—included in defining the structures and spaces within which the "dialog" and "practices" are intended to influence change? What can be done to broaden and deepen the inclusion of people in precarious work in such structures and spaces?

- What defines "precarity" and *who* is defining it? How representative and inclusive are the definitions and to what extent are "precarious workers" themselves involved in articulating the issues and challenges?
- Who is designing, defining, and implementing interventions and setting the terms of reference for the "dialog" and approaches to tackle precarity? Where does the power lie? And how is the power enacted, strengthened, challenged, and reinforced? To what extent do questions and considerations of colonialism have a role (or not) in the development and deployment of various approaches intended to tackle precarious work in global supply chains?
- What are the unintended consequences and possible dark sides of the interventions?
- How are we defining and measuring "effectiveness" and "impact"?
- What methodological approaches are we using and to what extent is our methodological toolkit suitable for bringing in the voices of various and multiple actors?
- As alternatives to the popular and dominant research methods employing questionnaires, surveys, and interviews; how might we draw on ethnographic studies and research methods underpinned by phenomenological perspectives for examining some of these issues?

Through ongoing critical analysis and reflection on the various interventions and efforts to 'tackle' precarity, we may be able to illuminate that which often gets taken-for-granted. This may help to minimize the unintended and often even adverse consequences for those living in precarity, in whose name various interventions are designed, promoted, and implemented. As a research respondent, a factory worker in north India once put it to me, "If you look at the lives of people like us and try to understand…really try to understand, only then can you begin to get or do anything for us."

Notes

1 Bimal was the Founding Chief Executive Officer of CRB and was serving as the Chairperson of the Governing Body alongside his role at Manchester Metropolitan University at the time of his passing. Divya was a key member of the foundational team involved with CRB from when it was an idea on paper in 2010, and she continues to be an advisor with the organization. Both authors worked together in setting up CRB, ideating, conceptualizing, developing, and executing projects, reflecting on their individual and combined experiences, and building the institution in its formative years.

2 For a fuller description of this work, see a presentation by Bimal on the textile sector (Okhla Garment and Textile Cluster [OGTC], 2011). The author is grateful to OGTC for making this recording publicly available.

3 This was the case between 2010 and 2013. It is heartening to note that since then there have been progressive and deliberate efforts to make the various forums more inclusive, but there is indeed, still a long way to go.

4 The study undertaken in 2012 with support from Solidaridad India was a part of an internal strategic exercise at CRB, and therefore, unfortunately, the results are not publicly available.

5 These issues have been highlighted and raised by different scholars and researchers over the years. For a review and further discussion, see Jyoti (2020).
6 At the time when we were working on ISS, we did not see it in as an example of deliberative democracy but in recent years, Bimal could see strong resonances and possibilities for rich theoretical insights; this was something he was working on before his death.
7 See KNN India Knowledge and News Network (2018) for an excerpt from an interview with Bimal discussing some of the challenges faced by small- and medium-sized enterprises, CRB's work, and the conference theme for 2018. The author expresses gratitude to KNN India Knowledge and News Network and its founding organizations for this interview and making them publicly available.
8 Despite moving away from actively working together day to day on CRB, Bimal and I maintained our reflective discussions as ISS had become like a child that we were seeing grow up, and we often reflected on the organization's intellectual trajectory. CRB's impact was, and is, a constant inspiration.
9 The author can be contacted at d.jyoti@lancaster.ac.uk

References

Arora, B. (2011, September). *Responsible fashion: Theory and practice* [Conference session]. 7th International Conference on Apparel and Home Textiles, New Delhi, OGTC.

Centre for Responsible Business. (n.d.). *About us.* https://c4rb.org/about-crb/

Centre for Responsible Business. (n.d.). *VSS Collaboration India.* https://c4rb.org/vss-collaboration-india/

Centre for Responsible Business. (2019). *CRB film full 081019hd.* https://youtu.be/P8Wxm9rGPEw

India Sustainable Palm Oil Coalition. (n.d.) *I-SPOC.* https://www.indiaspoc.org/index

India and Sustainability Standards. (n.d.). About 'India and sustainability standards'. https://www.sustainabilitystandards.in/

India Water Stewardship Network. (2017). Draft terms of reference (ToR). https://a4ws.org/wp-content/uploads/2017/05/IWSN_ToR_June16.pdf

Jyoti, D. (2020) *Living international corporate social responsibility: Experiences of workers in an internationalised factory in India* [Unpublished PhD thesis], Aston University.

KNN India Knowledge & News Network. (2018). *MSMEs are growing and Indian policies are supporting them to grow globally: Expert* [Video]. YouTube. https://youtu.be/rvSx_c3I5l0

KNN India Knowledge & News Network. (2019). *Buyer & supplier entities as well as other stakeholders should come together & contribute to SDGs* [Video]. YouTube. https://youtu.be/mtiLn182yDM

Okhla Garment and Textile Cluster. (2011). Responsible fashion: Theory and practice [Video]. YouTube. https://youtu.be/ViyZ6cnrklA

United Nations Council for Trade and Development. (n.d.). *Voluntary sustainability standards.* Retrieved February 7, 2023, from https://unctad.org/topic/trade-analysis/voluntary-sustainability-standards

United Nations Forum for Sustainability Standards. (n.d.). *What are voluntary sustainability standards (VSS)?* Retrieved February 7, 2023, from https://unfss.org/home/about-unfss/

PART II

Fair Incomes

7

THE LIVING WAGE IN SOUTH AFRICA

A Psychological Approach from Cape Town and Tshwane

Ines Meyer and Molefe Maleka

> The fetishism of the wage may well be the source of capitalist ideologies of freedom and equality, but the employment contract is not the founding moment. For capitalism begins not with the offer of work, but with the imperative to earn a living.
>
> (Denning, 2010, p. 80)

Introduction

One indicator of precarious work is a wage that is too low to cover even basic needs. "Living-wage" movements thus advocate that income through work should always exceed failing minimum wages. Instead, wages should be high enough to enable individuals not just to survive, but to live a more decent life, and allow for savings as a protection against unforeseen expenses. Though different methods of determining such living-wage levels exist, these tend to take an econometric approach based on the cost of goods or median wage levels. In this chapter, we outline why—and how—considering living wages through the lens of industrial and organizational (I/O) psychology can produce relevant new insights. We do so in relation to three key points:

- It is possible and desirable to determine living-wage amounts based on individuals' subjective experiences of freedom from precariousness rather than econometrically.
- Rather than leading to job losses, as frequently argued, living wages are beneficial to individuals, employers, and society.
- Psychological science provides tangible ways in which the implementation of living wages could be advanced.

DOI: 10.4324/9781003440444-9

As living wages are particularly relevant in contexts in which the state does not provide a social safety net to protect individuals from poverty or where this safety net is inadequate, we substantiate each point through empirical evidence derived from South Africa, as one such context.

Since the beginning of the 21st century, living-wage movements have advocated for employers to offer wage levels that enable employees to live a decent life and also accumulate savings as protection against unforeseen expenses. Prominent movements exist in the United Kingdom (Living Wage Foundation, https://www.livingwage.org.uk; and Living Wage Scotland, https://scottishlivingwage.org), New Zealand (Living Wage Aotearoa New Zealand, https://www.livingwage.org.nz), parts of the United States of America (US; Living Wage For US, https://livingwageforus.org), and in the textile industry in Asia in the form of the Asia Floor Wage Alliance (AFWA; https://asia.floorwage.org), for example. The International Labor Organization (ILO), a United Nations agency representing 187 national governments, employers, and workers, adopted the Declaration on Social Justice for a Fair Globalization at its annual conference in 2008. The declaration reiterates and outlines the four pillars of decent work (see Saner & Yiu, Chapter 5): (1) employment creation, (2) social protection, (3) rights at work, and (4) social dialog, and member organizations' commitment to realize these. A minimum living wage is included as a requirement (ILO, 2008). Through the lobbying of the ILO, decent work, and by implication living wages (though not directly mentioned), is also included as Goal 8 of the United Nations Sustainable Development Goals (UN SDG-8: Decent Work and Economic Development; UN, 2015). UN member states have committed to realizing these goals by 2030 (Carr, Hodgetts et al., Chapter 1).

Despite living wages regaining prominence in the 21st century, the concept itself emerged much earlier; adequate living wages were included in the preamble to the ILO's founding constitution in 1919 as a necessary means to improve labor conditions (ILO, 2015b). The context to this was rising worker exploitation since the first industrial revolution. Post-World War I, this led to the understanding that a socially just world would be required for sustainable and universal peace to stand a chance. This view remained prominent between the two World Wars. In 1933, U.S President F.D. Roosevelt emphasized the importance of living wages in his statement on the National Industrial Recovery Act. He proclaimed: "No business which depends for existence on paying less than living wages to its workers has any right to continue in this country" (Roosevelt, 1933, para 4). In 1948, the need for just and fair remuneration was reemphasized when it was included as a human right in the United Nations Universal Declaration of Human Rights (UN, 1948; see Satlzman et al., Chapter 2). Specifically, Article 23(3) states that income for work should afford everyone who works, and their family, a life worthy of human dignity. If required, this income should be supplemented through social security measures. Thus, it makes employers and the state together responsible to enable individuals' financial wellbeing.

This right was realized in several countries post-World War II, including in the social democracies of Central and Northern Europe, and in socialist states where substantive government-funded social security measures were implemented (ILO, 2016). In the following decades, conversations about employers' responsibility to provide just and fair remuneration which would allow for a dignified life became less frequent. Living-wage debates were replaced by debates about minimum wages which were based less on worker needs and more on ensuring a competitive economy while also benefitting low-income workers (Hurley et al., 2018).

Today, in most of the world, wages for a large part of the working population remain low. The ILO (2019) reported that in 2018, more than half of the 3.3 billion people employed globally were unable to experience economic wellbeing and security and that worldwide, 21% of workers qualified as "working poor," as their income was below the poverty line (Carr, Hodgetts et al., Chapter 1).

The need for adequate wage floors as a safeguard against precarity is thus at least as urgent today as it was when it was first introduced in the late 1800s and early 1900s (Carr, Hodgetts et al., Chapter 1). For the last century, discussion of the topic has been largely confined to the field of economics (Carr et al., 2016b). In their review of 115 academic, peer-reviewed papers on the subject of the living wage published between 2000 and 2020, Searle and McWha-Herman (2021) found that only since 2014 has the subject been considered in a wider range of disciplines, including behavioral sciences, business, geography, law, management, medicine and health, philosophy and ethics, urban planning, and applied psychology (Searle & McWha-Hermann, Chapter 4).

It is understandable that, historically, living wages have not been a topic of interest in psychology. As a discipline, psychology has focused on individual- and group-level analyses. I/O psychology, specifically, has restricted its vision to focus on individual behavior at work at one end of the field and organizational-level constructs at the other. Within I/O psychology, the topic of "pay" thus fits exclusively within this realm. We have gained a sound understanding of the relevance of pay fairness and its consequences for employee attitudes (e.g., organizational commitment, motivation, and job satisfaction) and behavior (organizational citizenship behavior, counterproductive work behavior, absenteeism, and turnover; see, for example, Cohen-Charash & Spector, 2001; Colquitt et al., 2001; Judge et al., 2010). We know about ideal reward structures (e.g., Kahnemann & Deaton, 2010; Martocchio, 2015; Shaw & Zhou, 2021) and how to determine pay at different job levels scientifically, through the use of job analysis (e.g., Harvey, 1991). Only recently have calls surfaced advocating for psychology (MacLachlan & McVeigh, 2021) and I/O psychology (Bal & Dóci, 2018; Dóci & Bal, 2018) to consider and inform macrolevel issues and debates.

Psychology's absence from living-wage discussions meant that a person-centric stance has been missing in living-wage research (Di Fabio et al., Chapter 3; Searle & McWha-Herman, 2021, Chapter 4; Seubert & Seubert, Chapter 14; Teng-Calleja et al., Chapter 8). In this chapter, we: (1) outline how psychology can enrich the living-wage debate through discussion of novel, human-centric ways in which living wages are determined; (2) highlight the benefits of living wages for individuals, organizations, and societies; and (3) outline tangible ways in which the adoption of living wages by employers can be advanced. After a brief definition of the concept of the living wage, we discuss each of these three points in turn.

Bar a few exceptions, most research on living wages to date has been conducted in the world's wealthier nations. For an overview, see Searle and McWha-Herman (2021, Chapter 4). As living wages are particularly relevant in contexts in which state-provided social protections are absent or inadequate to protect individuals from living in poverty (World Bank [WB], 2018), we highlight empirical evidence collected in psychological research in one such context: South Africa.

According to the WB, South Africa is the world's most unequal society (WB, 2022a). The wealthiest 10% of the population own 71% of the country's wealth, while the bottom 60% own 7% (WB, 2022b). It is estimated that 33.9% of people of working age are unemployed (Stats SA, 2022). In part, this results from centuries of colonization and apartheid; in part from ineffective policy implemented after apartheid had ended. Prior to the 1990s, apartheid legislation excluded Black employees in South Africa from managerial, technical, and professional jobs; and Black workers from collective bargaining through the Industrial Conciliation Acts of 1921 and 1956 (Act no. 28 of 1956). As a result, Black workers were employed in insecure jobs that paid low wages. As in many societies in the world since the 1990s, South Africa's chosen path to inclusive prosperity has been economic growth. Greater participation in the labor market is seen as key to socioeconomic uplift. Implicitly, what seems to count primarily is that employment is *created*, not as much what this employment *looks like*. To date, this strategy has shown limited success; poverty in South Africa increased between 2011 and 2016 (Stats SA, 2017). Roughly, half the adult population lives below the upper bounds of the poverty line (Stats SA, 2019).

As reported earlier, poverty is not restricted to the unemployed. Low-income earners also get trapped in poverty cycles; for example, when they have to rely on loans to cover basic needs or unexpected expenses. This can happen when expenses increase once an individual secures employment. Additional transport cost to get to and from work and clothing needs can mean expenses exceed the income received. This was highlighted by digital labor platform workers who were interviewed for South Africa's 2022 Fairwork report (Fairwork, 2022). In such a context, work creates a poverty trap in which individuals become poorer when they work than they were previously, as outlined in poverty trap theories (e.g., Ghatak, 2015). Although the state in South Africa does provide social security measures, these are funded by a small taxpayer base and are insufficient. An increase in labor participation rates without at least equal focus on what the created employment looks like can thus result in more precarious livelihoods.

Living Wages: A (Non-) Definition

As Reynaud (2017) pointed out in his review of the history of the living wage and the ILO, there is, to date, no one accepted way of defining a living wage. The six example definitions provided by Hurley et al. (2018) and listed in Table 7.1 use different measures. Some suggest that wage levels need to enable self-respect and allow for a life of dignity; others do not. Equally so, only some definitions state explicitly that income through work needs to allow employees to participate in civic and social life (see also Carr et al., 2016a, 2016b, 2018; Yao et al., 2017). Another difference is whether a living wage fulfills only the employee's needs, or also those of their family. Provisions for unexpected expenses are referred to in one definition, but not in others. Lastly, not all definitions refer to the need for a living wage to allow for a minimally acceptable, socially acceptable, or decent standard of living.

Searle and McWha-Herman (2021) add that a living wage needs to be high enough to allow for a life independent of welfare and other public subsidies (see also Ciscel, 2000), an aspect not mentioned in any of the definitions provided in Table 7.1.

TABLE 7.1 Examples of Living-Wage Definitions

The income necessary to provide workers and their families with the basic necessities of life. A living wage will enable workers to live with dignity and to participate as active citizens in society (Living Wage Aotearoa New Zealand webpage)
A wage level that offers workers the ability to support families, to maintain self-respect, and to have both the means and the leisure to participate in the civic life of the nation (Glickman, cited in Anker & Anker, 2017)
Remuneration received for a standard work week by a worker in a particular place sufficient to afford a decent standard of living for the worker and her or his family. Elements of a decent standard of living include food, water, housing, education, healthcare, transport, clothing, and other essential needs, including provision for unexpected events (Anker & Anker, 2017)
A wage that has been accepted in a particular place and context, as a consistent means of maintaining an agreed standard related to living costs for the lowest paid workers (Hirsch & Valadez-Martinez, 2017, p. 106)
A wage that makes possible a minimum acceptable standard of living (Living Wage Ireland, 2017)
A measure of income that allows an employee a basic but socially acceptable standard of living (UK Living Wage Commission)

Source: Hurley et al. (2018, p. 14).

As a result of the various living-wage definitions and operationalizations, it is not surprising that estimated living-wage levels vary widely (Searle & McWha-Herman, 2021). In the following section, we briefly outline the main approaches to determining living wages and then present why we believe a psychological approach to determining living-wage levels is preferable.

Toward a Psychological Approach to Determining Living-Wage Levels

Protect People Not Jobs

(WB, 2019)

Without an authoritative definition, it is impossible to determine one gold standard method for calculating living-wage amounts, thresholds, or ranges. Consequently, several methods have been proposed. Most of these are based on one of two broad approaches: they calculate a living wage statistically, either as a percentage of an existing wage or as an amount that exceeds the poverty line (the main approach in living-wage campaigns in the Unites States); or econometrically, by considering the cost of goods (Hurley et al., 2018).

One of the most widely used and accepted econometric approaches was developed by Anker (2011). Proponents of the Anker methodology include the UK's Living Wage Foundation and the Netherlands-based IDH Sustainable Trade Initiative (https://www.idhsustainabletrade.com/living-wage-platform/). Anker believed that living-wage calculations should be based on the cost of a nutritious diet, housing costs, family size, education, and health-care expenses and consider the number of working individuals in the household. He also advocated for different living wages for rural and urban areas. In addition, employees who earn a living wage should be able to save for the future (Anker & Anker, 2013). Lastly, the living wage needs to be earned during regular working hours and exclude benefits, as benefits may reduce the cash component available to employees.

The credibility of Anker's methodology lies in its transparency and use of detailed secondary data. Living-wage calculations based on the Anker approach are available for many countries. In South Africa, Anker and Anker (2013) determined a living wage for rural areas by drawing on data from individuals employed in the wine industry in one of South Africa's nine provinces. The authors derived a cash living wage for permanent workers who received free housing and transportation to town each week, as well as one month's salary as a bonus. Household costs were determined based on normative standards for decent housing, and other costs were determined based on observed household expenditure from a household income and expenditure survey.

A fundamental flaw of econometric approaches like the Anker methodology lies in how the items to be included in living calculations are determined; in other words, who gets to decide what is required for a decent life? At best, this question is answered through focus-group data or interviews with low-income workers, or through household surveys. In other cases, groups of "experts" agree on the items to be included in the basket of goods. Once identified, the income amount required to secure this basket is determined (Hurley et al., 2018). In South Africa, the amount is summarized in the consumer price index (CPI) and includes transport costs, medical expenditure, and food (Mohr et al., 2016). These items are similar to those Anker (2006, 2011) has suggested for inclusion in living-wage calculations.

The CPI is used as a baseline during salary negotiations in collective bargaining to determine wage increments for low- and middle-income employees (Bendix, 2019). Trade unions typically negotiate for a salary increment linked to the CPI, plus a certain percentage. The challenge with CPI-related increases highlights the difficulty with using externally determined basket of goods to determine a living wage; for employees who are earning low wages, the increment is too low to assist them to move out of poverty. Additionally, some of the items in the CPI basket do not apply to the working poor. Low-income workers typically do not qualify for mortgages to purchase homes, but the cost of housing is included in the CPI calculation. As the cost of housing increases at a lower rate than food or transport, the CPI tends to underestimate the actual percentage increase in expenses for low-income workers.

The absence of an authoritative living-wage amount for South Africa means that employers who want to pay living wages do not have a benchmark on which to base the lowest wages offered. At times, this has meant that living wages have been estimated without an explicit formula. For example, the Association of Mineworkers and Construction Union won their demand for a monthly living wage of 12,500 South African Rand for miners (ILO, 2015a). Prior to this, miners had earned around R5,000. They believed that if they earned double this amount, their salaries would be sufficient. They requested an additional R2,500 in the hope that the mine's management would grant them an additional "sympathy" payment (Sinwell, 2013).

In their *Non-Executive Directors Report 2022*, PricewaterhouseCoopers South Africa (PwC SA, 2022) adopted a pragmatic approach to determining a living wage for South Africa. They collected the living-wage data from 26 European countries and conducted a cost-of-living and exchange-rate adjustment to determine a living wage for South Africa. At its core, this approach still relies on econometrics, as it is based on baskets of goods determined by individuals who are not low-wage earners and whose realities thus differ from the individuals whom the living wage is meant to serve (see, Teng-Calleja et al., Chapter 8).

Another challenge with an econometric approach to living wages is that it is based on a set number of individuals per household, and a specific number of dependents. Working with averages in this regard does not account for the variability in household sizes and thus means that the living wage does not fulfill the intended purpose for many. The same applies to the assumed number of working individuals per household. This is understandable, as accounting for such differences increases the complexity of information and calculations required (Hurley et al., 2018). PwC SA addressed this by providing living-wage amounts for individuals who are the only household member; for a four-person household; and as collective monetary amounts for families with four, five, and six members (PwC SA, 2022).

Given the challenges with econometric approaches, Searle and McWha-Herman's (2021) review of living-wage research presents encouraging findings. Since 2016, alternative ways of determining living wages have started emerging in the literature, e.g., a 2019 special issue of *Transfer: European Review of Labour and Research* (Müller & Schulten, 2019; Yoelao et al., 2019). This is encouraging as research from different disciplines might contribute to building a more comprehensive perspective, for example, by highlighting local contextual- and individual-level factors, such as different costs of living in rural versus urban areas, and living standard norms, for which a number of living-wage proponents have been advocating (e.g., Anker, 2006; Anker & Anker, 2017; Hurley et al., 2018).

The flaws with the econometric approach outlined so far broadly relate to a mismatch between the conceptualizations and operationalizations of living wages. The same applies to statistic approaches that derive living-wage levels from median salaries or poverty lines. As outlined in this chapter's first section, living-wage definitions generally include terms such as adequate, fair, just, decent, dignity, and quality of life. Veit-Wilson (1998) has pointed out that these are difficult to quantify. It might explain why the econometric approach has resorted to external agents to define and assign a monetary amount to concepts such as decency and dignity.

The problem here, though, is that what an adequate standard of living, or a life with dignity, mean is inherently subjective (Hurley et al., 2018). It could be argued that removing subjective assessments from determining living wages renders the living-wage amounts thus obtained as invalid. Rather than removing subjectivity, a psychological lens could be used to determine living wages. Since its inception as a discipline, psychology has been concerned with how best to quantify subjective experiences. A human-centered psychological approach to determining living wages based on psychological science would be to collect subjective assessments from low-income workers, quantify these and compare them against each worker's income. This makes it possible to identify the income level workers themselves quantify as one where they can live a life with dignity and acquire a decent standard of living. This renders the questions of household size and geographic environment less relevant, as individuals' experiences are informed by their specific circumstances. When making a subjective assessment about how adequate and decent they perceive their lives to be, these circumstances are implicitly included. This raises the possibility that there is, in fact, one determinable global living-wage rate or range, instead of localized living-wage amounts.

In what follows, we detail the research which has arisen from this argument, initiated in 2015 in New Zealand by Stuart C. Carr. Since 2016, it has been pursued by researchers under the umbrella of Project GLOW (Global Living Organization Wage). At the time of writing, Project GLOW is a network of researchers in almost 30 countries who are seeking to answer the question of whether there is one global living-wage amount that enables people, organizations, and communities to prosper and thrive. Project GLOW's approach takes the view that living wages are not only subjective and relative but also far-reaching. They not only relate to wage amounts but also consider the ability to adequately participate in organizational and social life. The approach aligns with public policy and employment rights enshrined in the ILO's concept of "decent work," including job satisfaction and voice, justice, identity, and empowerment (ILO, 2008). In that way, the work conducted by Project GLOW aligns with the UN SDGs: specifically SDG-1 (Poverty Eradication) and SDG-8 (Economic Growth & Decent Work), and thus with international development imperatives.

Unlike statistical and econometric living-wage methodologies, this approach to living wages is theoretically grounded. It is based on Amartya Sen's (1999) capability approach. Sen has described poverty as not just caused by a lack of financial means—an implicit assumption of statistical and econometric approaches—but by the deprivation of capabilities which individuals require to live a good life (Allmark & Machaczek, 2015; Meyer, 2014; Sen, 1985; Yao et al., 2017). Capabilities (see also Teng-Calleja et al., Chapter 8) are the freedoms available to individuals to make choices that achieve specific "functionings." Functionings, in turn, are the "beings" (what an individual can be, for example, healthy) and "doings" (what an individual can do, for example, choose a career) which a person reasonably values (Elliott, 2021; Sen, 1985). Financial means, such as an individual's income, fall under what Sen (1999) called "endowments": the resources that enable individuals' capabilities, and thus ultimately their functionings. Income is also closely linked with what Sen termed conversion factors: that is, the individual, social, and environmental contextual factors that influence how individuals use their endowments. Income matters, as it enables functionings through enhancing capabilities, and thus the capabilities framework is a comprehensive approach to the wellbeing of individuals. It considers which of the opportunities that people value are available to them (functionings), an individual's ability to choose the opportunities they value (capabilities), the availability of resources (resources/endowments), and the contextual characteristics to achieve desirable outcomes in life (conversion factors), as well as the ability to be an active member in society (agency) (Chiappero-Martineti &

Ventkatapuram, 2014). Subjectivity is a central element of the approach as it explicitly considers that individuals value different capabilities and functionings.

In Sen's framework, income is not an end-product but a means that contributes to individuals realizing their capabilities. Capabilities, in Sen's (1999) view, provide individuals with choice over those aspects of their lives which reasonably matter to them, and thus with freedom. In work contexts, this means that wages need to be high enough to allow employees freedom and thus empower them to live dignified lives (Maleka et al., 2021; Sen, 1999). Working conditions can directly and indirectly contribute to individuals' freedom; fair treatment at work contributes not only to greater productivity but also to employees' self-esteem, and mental and physical health (Mani et al., 2013), and higher wages provide employees with greater choice, for example, through broadening educational opportunities for themselves and their families, or the diet options available.

We thus see prosperity as not solely grounded in financial means, but in the light of Sen's (1999) proposition that prosperity is the degree to which individuals perceive they have a choice about different aspects of their lives. This has led us to base our psychological approach to living wages on the assumptions that it is insufficient to determine wage levels based on economic factors alone without considering psychological variables, that a wage level allowing for a decent life (i.e., a living wage), can be empirically determined via these psychological variables, and that paying such living wages benefits individuals, organizations, and communities.

By now, several survey studies using the psychological approach to living wages have been conducted under the ambit of Project GLOW. In each of these, individuals' income through work was plotted against their self-assessed quality of life. Different studies have employed variations of Sen's quality of life operationalization. The initial data collected outside shopping malls in New Zealand (Carr et al., 2018; Yao et al., 2017) included a number of psychological indicators of quality of work-life (empowerment at work, job security, job satisfaction, pay satisfaction and fairness, pride in work) and quality of life (stress levels, physical wellbeing, general life satisfaction). The same measure was subsequently used to collect data in shopping centers frequented by low-income individuals in two urban areas in South Africa in 2016 (Carr et al., 2018) and 2019 (Maleka et al., 2021). Additionally, Nthulenyane (2019) assessed the relationship between income and quality of work-life as indicated through job satisfaction, organizational commitment, quality of work-life, and fairness and income among low-income employees in the South African banking sector.

In the Philippines, Teng-Calleja et al. (2021, Chapter 8) measured capabilities more directly. They employed Sycip et al.'s 2008 (as cited in Teng-Calleja et al., 2021, Chapter 8) capabilities measure. Participants indicated the degree to which they valued each of 11 life domains (or capabilities) followed by the degree to which they were able to achieve each of them. The domains included material and nonmaterial aspects, such as access to information, political participation, housing, and the quality of neighborhood. The same measure was employed in a household study conducted in South Africa's Cape Town municipality in 2019 (Botha, 2021).

Lastly, to take advantage of data from a large, nationally representative sample, Gaya (2021) identified indicators of wellbeing, as per Sen's capabilities' approach, in the National Income Dynamics Study (NIDS). The NIDS is income panel research started in 2008 which collects follow-up data from approximately 28,000 individuals every 2 years, with the intention of tracking South Africans' wellbeing (Leibbrandt et al., 2009). Unfortunately, the wellbeing measure in the NIDS consisted of a single question: "How do you feel about your life as a whole right now?" answered on a ten-point scale ranging from "very dissatisfied" to "very satisfied."

Measuring overall life satisfaction through a single item requires individuals to make a cognitive judgment of their general perception of, and feeling about life (Myers & Diener, 1995; Prasoon & Chaturvedi, 2016). Such cognitive judgments are prone to biases and are thus unreliable. For example, the assessment is likely to be unduly influenced by recent positive or negative events. Carr et al.'s (2018) measure, however, assesses individuals' quality of life more holistically by focusing on cognitive, emotional, and physical aspects. To account for the problems associated with single-item measures, Gaya et al. (2018) plotted income collected in the NIDS against the data collected using the Centre for Epidemiologic Studies' Short Depression Scale (CES-D 10; Anderson et al., 1994). They considered this a measure of *non*wellbeing.

Plotting income against the holistic measures of quality of life and work-life which Carr et al. (2018) had employed in samples in New Zealand and South Africa, an S-shaped curve emerged. It followed a rise-pause-rise pattern for the relationships between both income and quality of life, and income and quality-of-work-life, as schematically depicted with the solid curved line in Figure 7.1 (Carr et al., 2018; Maleka et al., 2021; Nthulenyane, 2019; Yao et al., 2017). Up to a certain income range, wages do not enable individuals' capabilities, that is, choice over the life domains which they value. In Carr et al.'s (2018) research, this amount was approximately 2,000 when applying purchasing power parity in both the South African and New Zealand data. This provided initial evidence that there might indeed be a global living-wage amount or range. At wages below this amount, individuals remained trapped in poverty as they were unable to obtain freedom over life choices which mattered to them. Similar to research depicting the relationship between income and happiness (e.g., Kahneman & Deaton, 2010), at higher income levels wage increases were no longer associated with increased capabilities. Maleka et al. (2021) also found that the relationship between income and job satisfaction and employee engagement was stronger for unionized employees. As Carr et al. (2018) and Yao et al. (2017) have pointed

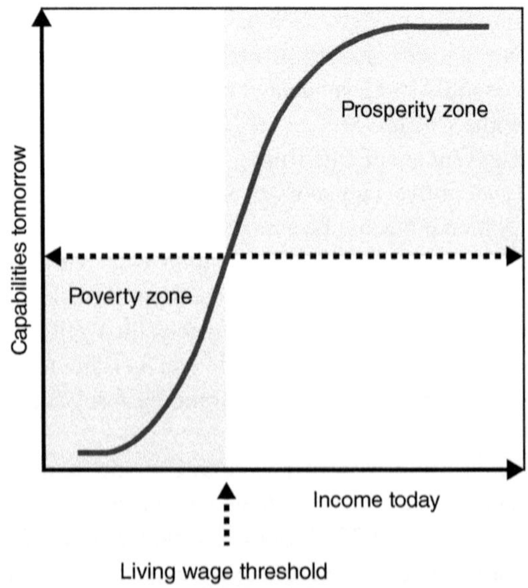

FIGURE 7.1 Rise-Pause-Rise Curve Indicating the Relationship between Income and Sen's Conceptualization of Quality of (Work-)Life.

Note: Adapted from Carr et al. (2018).

out, the results support both poverty-trap theories and theories of diminishing returns, albeit at different points on the curve; at low-income levels, an increase in income does not enable individuals to realize their capabilities; they remain trapped in poverty instead. This speaks against the assumption that any job is better than no job, as at the bottom end of the wage-spectrum income does not enable wellbeing. At higher income levels, diminishing returns are observed as the relationship between valued life domains and income tapers off when income increases further.

The typical *S*-curve-shape did not emerge in Gaya's (2021) research in which she considered a singular life-satisfaction measure. As outlined earlier, this might be due to problems with single-item measures. Her research did show, however, what drives the relationship between income and life satisfaction; at all income levels, there were individuals who were highly satisfied with their lives. The higher the income, the lower the number of individuals became who were dissatisfied with their lives. This indicates that income might not, in fact, increase wellbeing or quality of life but rather decreases *un*wellbeing, or a lack of quality of life. Using the same sample, but plotting depression against individuals' income, Gaya et al. (2018) found that the CES-D 10 items captured two distinct dimensions: depression, and a factor that they termed "optimism."

For the depression measure, the pattern of results corresponded to Gaya's findings; there was only a slight overall trend for depression scores to be lower when income increased. This trend was driven by there being fewer, and eventually no individuals with strong depressive symptoms as income increased. That is, with increasing income severe negative depressive symptoms fell away. When considering the optimism dimension, the results resembled those depicted in Figure 7.1; optimism, i.e., positive feelings, increased with higher income in a rise, pause, rise pattern. The same pattern emerged in Botha's (2021) South African data in which she considered individuals' self-perceived possibility to realize valued capabilities as indicator of quality of life. As in Gaya (2021) and Gaya et al.'s (2018) studies, her data also showed that the relationship between capability fulfillment and income was such that at higher levels of income, there were fewer individuals who experienced an *absence* of choice over the life domains they valued. At a monthly income of R10,000, nobody reported a lack of capability. This led Botha to define a living wage as a monthly income of at least R10,000. When using job attitudes as indicator of quality of work-life, Nthulenyane (2019) had identified a living-wage amount of R15,000. These results lend support to the assumption that insights of psychological science are valuable when determining living-wage amounts, and that these tend to be higher than living wages that are determined econometrically and statistically.

The Benefits of Living Wages to Individuals, Employers, and Society

Better business makes the greater good.

(Mayer, 2018)

So far, we have outlined the benefits of psychologically determined living wages for the individual employee, and possibly their immediate household. However, by improving people's wellbeing, living wages can also have spill-over effects into society-at-large (ILO, 2016; see Haar, Chapter 17; Klug et al., Chapter 21). For example, data from the Dominican Republic has shown that employees working at factories that paid living wages had lower rates of depression than employees at factories without living-wage incomes (Burmaster et al., 2015). Higher income among these employees was not related to greater obesity (Rehkopf et al., 2018) and employees reported higher social status and better health (Landefeld et al., 2014). These results resemble those of Bindman's (2015) research in the United States in which obesity even decreased after living wages had been introduced, as did smoking, chronic diseases, and psychological disorders, such as depression. Such results suggest that living wages can reduce the burden on health systems (Klug et al., Chapter 21).

A common argument raised against the increase of wages at the lower end of the wage spectrum is that it will lead to jobs losses, or at least slow down job creation, and lower profits and investments while driving up prices (Carr et al., 2016b; Patel et al., 2020). Evidence of the effect of living wages on the broader economy are still scarce. To date, possible negative economic effects can only be deduced from minimum-wage research. In this regard, the European Foundation for the Improvement of Living and Working Conditions found that "The evidence from research increasingly suggests that when prudently set, they do so with little or no negative effects on employment outcomes" (Hurley et al., 2018, p. 57).

Minimum wages, however, tend to be set at a level low enough to minimize most possible negative effects they could have. Living-wage amounts thus tend to be substantially higher. In the examples referred to by Hurley et al. (2018) they exceeded the applicable minimum wages by between 15% and over 80%. Research on the broader economic effects of living wages themselves is difficult, because unlike minimum wages, living wages are usually not a legislative requirement and are implemented by individual employers rather than being rolled out widely. Empirical evidence suggests that for organizations who implement living wages, the effects are positive rather than negative. Data collected from over 800 living-wage-accredited organizations in the UK (Heery et al., 2017a) showed that the main reported challenges all related to labor costs, such as a higher spend on wages, lower wage differentials, and higher costs for subcontracted services (as accredited organizations are obligated to contract services from living-wage-accredited employers). Only 15% of the surveyed employers saw these to be of major significance; however, 42% saw them as being of limited significance. Almost all employers (93%) felt that they had benefited from becoming living-wage accredited. However, there is research which suggests that consumers might choose to buy products from employers who they know to be paying employees a living wage, treating employees well, and trading fairly (Lappeman et al., 2019). The fear of negative economic impacts thus remains a theoretical argument for now.

Theoretical arguments also exist for positive economic impacts from living wages. Living wages can help increase economic growth due to a greater income share among employees; stimulate domestic consumption; and, in turn, generate rather than reduce jobs. Job creation is a possible consequence, as the greater wage cost may be offset by greater employee productivity, and lower absenteeism and turnover (Carr et al., 2016b). This reduces costs associated with recruitment, and with induction periods during which new employees are not yet working to their full potential (Maleka et al., 2019).

In Fairris and Reich's (2005) study, greater efficiency and better use of organizational resources by employees after the introduction of living wages has been found to partially offset the increase in organizational costs. Additionally, the income tax generated by employees who are earning a living wage assists governments in offering public services (King, 2016).

While living wages arguably divert responsibility of care for citizens from the state toward employers, there is by now substantial empirical evidence that offering living wages is not simply a good deed by employers but benefits organizations too. For example, the Living Wage Foundation in the UK has been able to show that a living wage not only empowered employees to live a decent life but also that organizations who paid it reaped positive benefits (Living Wage Foundation, n.d.). In Scotland, organizations' profit margins increased after the introduction of living wages and attrition rates reduced (Searle & McWha-Hermann, 2021, Chapter 4; see also Carr et al., 2011).

From an economic perspective, the underlying mechanism might be that higher wages make it more costly for employees to lose their jobs, thus making it likely for them to increase their efforts in response to the introduction of living wages (Shapiro & Stiglitz, 1984; also Brenner, 2004). Further behavioral changes in response to the implementation of living wages in the US and UK included better quality of work and lower levels of absenteeism among employees receiving living wages (Gregg, 2000).

Such behavioral changes can also be explained through a psychological lens: the implementation of living wages can trigger changes in employee attitudes. Beyond the monetary benefits, living wages also communicate to employees that they are valued. This is likely to increase job and career satisfaction, motivation, work engagement, feelings of empowerment, affective commitment, various organizational citizenship behaviors, and work-life balance, as well as lower turnover intention (Carr et al., 2011, 2016b, 2018, 2019; Searle & McWha-Herman, 2021, Chapter 4; Zeng & Honig, 2017). An additional benefit of living wages for the individual has been raised by Smith (2015); as living-wage employment takes employees out of poverty, it also removes such employees from the stigma associated with being poor: a stigma experienced in the form of continuous micro-aggressions such as rudeness, being treated as incompetent, or literally not being seen.

Advancing the Implementation of Living Wages through Psychological Science

> Psychology is an important aspect of both how we speak and about what we say regarding the great issues of our times.
>
> *(O'Shea et al., 2021, p. 97)*

Statutory minimum wages are a popular policy tool to boost wages among the lowest paid employees (Hurley et al., 2018). As outlined introduction in the to this chapter, minimum wages are typically insufficient to elevate individuals out of poverty; this helps explain why minimum-wage labor contributes to more than half of the working population living precarious lives (ILO, 2019). This highlights the urgency with which minimum-wage incomes need to be raised to living-wage levels. It is possible that in "developing" nations, high rates of poverty and unemployment together with the strongly held yet flawed belief that "any job is better than no job" restrict the wage debate to statutory minimum wages rather than centering it on living wages.

This is the case in South Africa. Here, a National Minimum Wage Act that prescribes minimum earnings in employment sectors not governed by collective bargaining agreements was only introduced in 2018 (National Minimum Wage Act, 2018). It followed a lengthy tripartite consultation process between government, trade unions, and the business sector led by the National Wage Commission. To date, the living-wage concept is largely unknown to the South African public and conversations are often limited to trade union circles and the nonprofit sector.

There are, however, multinational organizations with operations in South Africa who have committed to paying living wages along their supply chains (e.g., Unilever). Several South African businesses have also implemented some form of living wage (e.g., BeanThere Coffee) or are considering it (e.g., We Are Food, The Smollan Group). Woolworths, a large national retail chain, announced in 2021 that it is working toward providing at least living wages to all its almost 30,000 shopfloor employees.

In addition, the National Minimum Wage Commission has been tasked with ensuring that the minimum wage increases to a living-wage amount in the midterm. This gives hope that the concept is gaining recognition. Yet another supporting legal instrument, if passed, is the Companies Amendment Bill 2021 (cl 3.7) that will require for-profit organizations to report the pay ratio between the highest and lowest 5% of earners in their employ. Currently, this is proposed as a reporting requirement only, but it would open the door for penalties in cases in which the pay disparity is considered too large. Next, we describe the collaborative approach adopted by the Living Wage South Africa Network to create greater awareness and buy-in for living wages. We focus on how we have drawn on psychological science to advocate for commitment to working toward living wages.

In March 2021, we hosted the first meeting of what became the Living Wage South Africa Network (see also, Jyoti & Arora, Chapter 6). We had invited individuals and organizations from across South Africa who had been identified as working on the topic of living wages to explore whether there was value in forming a network to coordinate the disparate living-wage work taking place in the country. We loosely aligned the process with the actualizing social and personal identity resources (ASPIRe) model (Haslam et al., 2003). It assumes that the effectiveness of a group of diverse stakeholders is grounded in creating a shared social identity which allows members to identify with an over-arching higher order identity. At the start of the process, it is thus important to work toward a shared sense of "us."

We were thus deliberate about the way in which to approach the initial meeting to shape group and power dynamics from the start. With individuals from a wide range of backgrounds and interests (e.g., remuneration consultants at large consulting firms, microbusinesses, researchers, and activists representing civil society organizations), it was important to ensure that everyone's voice was heard. This increased the likelihood of a living-wage network being able to leverage social capital: that is, the resources inherent in a network which is held together through alliance and relationships between its members which, in turn, shape the network's reputation and contribute to network members feeling proud to belong to the network and a sense of loyalty and commitment (Haslam et al., 2003).

To achieve this, we adopted a facilitative style and collective decision-making approach in the initial and subsequent network meetings. Through facilitated discussion between members at network meetings, we were able to reach decisions without taking a traditional leadership role (Bose et al., 2017). This was of particular importance because we had initiated the meeting and were the link between all parties present so could easily have been perceived as decision-makers.

With a clear—and limited—agenda (to explore the need for, and interest in, a South African living-wage network and develop an overview of the existing work and initiatives to advance the living-wage concept in South Africa), we scheduled the meeting for two hours to allow for sufficient time to share ideas. Through this, we sought to surface different social identities among those present (e.g., community advocates, business representatives, and academics) and to recognize, respect, and make use of the values, norms, and skills associated with these identities to inform the network's future work.

In the ASPIRe model, a shared identity is created through respect for others; fairness in interactions; trust in others (and demonstrating that trust); and allowing equal opportunities by respecting, harnessing, and fostering members' different personal and social identities. We considered this to have been a success when members proposed and agreed to the Chatham House rule being applied in meetings. The rule states that any individual is allowed to share and use information received in the meeting without revealing the identity or affiliation of the information provider or any other meeting participant (Chatham House, n.d.).

We also achieved a second aim articulated in the ASPIRe model: to allow for meaningful goals that are acceptable to all (Cvitanovic et al., 2020). Shared goals contribute toward creating a shared vision, especially in groups of stakeholders with different interests. The outcomes of the initial meeting were that a living-wage network would be valuable and would need to explore particular aspects of research, the available resources, and engage in advocacy.

Research Questions

Develop data-driven-answers to the following questions:

- What constitutes a just wage in the South African context and how should it be calculated?
- Is any work better than no work?
- How might living-wage employment be balanced with a possible rise in unemployment?
- What is the role of trust in the successful implementation of living wages (e.g., trust between labor and management)?
- What other preconditions are required to implement a living wage?
- What types of incentives to implement living wages could be provided (e.g., tax incentives)?

These questions are relevant not just in the South African context. They present research-initiating questions for individuals interested in living-wage research. What such research could look like is elaborated at the end of this chapter.

Resource Provision via Network Website

- Case studies of leading examples (to convince organizational leadership of benefits of paying living wages through real-world examples)

Advocacy

- Launch living-wage campaign

We also agreed to meet quarterly. In all subsequent meetings in 2020, we continued with the discussion-based approach instituted at the initial meeting, in alignment with Monteiro and Keating's (2009) guidelines of manifesting a shared social identity and shared goals through repeated meetings. Through these meetings, we established specific operating principles which aligned with the way in which the network would operate.

Rather than work toward enforcement of living wages, we focus on supporting employers who seek to implement living wages voluntarily. We understand living wages as an approach rather than an amount. For reasons outlined by Root (2019), legal prescriptions regularly trigger compliance failures. Instead, for living wages to have the best possible effects for individuals, organizations, and society, they need to be incorporated into a broader value-based approach. The key motivation for living-wage employers in the UK, for example, where living-wage accreditation is also voluntary, was that the payment of living wages was value- or mission-led. Owners and senior managers particularly desire to be perceived as socially responsible or good employers (Heery et al., 2017b).

Recent evidence from South Africa has shown that paying living wages alone, without them being integrated into a broader initiative, is not enough. For example, university employees who earned within what the Living Wage Network would consider a living wage embarked on strike action because they were aggrieved about excessive working hours (Tlhabye, 2022).

We also agreed to focus on highlighting success cases that could make the introduction of living wages desirable to other industry players and possibly create healthy competition among employers to implement socially sustainable labor practices.

At the end of the first year, it was obvious that enthusiasm among members was waning. While the Living Wage Network had grown in numbers, members did not often return to meetings after their initial engagement, though they did continue to receive written updates and information. This indicated that it was important to shift focus toward setting shared, clear, and measurable goals: another step in the ASPIRe model (Haslam et al., 2003). We thus chose a small number of achievable goals from the list generated in the initial meetings, resulting in network members co-creating a position paper for the corporate sector in which we highlighted the business and moral imperatives of living wages. We accompanied this with a media campaign to raise public awareness.

Through the Network meetings, it became evident that beyond raising interest in living wages, we needed to be able to provide practical advice on what an appropriate living-wage amount for South Africa was, as well as how to determine and implement it. We are currently conducting a national living-wage study based on Teng-Calleja et al.'s (2021, Chapter 8) living-wage approach to determine a benchmark living-wage amount, which we hope to update annually.

After two years of operating informally, we require a formal structure. This is important as the Living Wage Network provides an avenue for individuals who would like to advocate for living wages, but whose voices are constrained by having to represent their own employer when engaging in living-wage debates. The network allows them to express their views publicly without being identified as an individual or as an employee of a particular employer. By setting up a living-wage coordinating network in South Africa deliberately based on psychological principles, we hope to increase the number of employers who buy into the importance of paying individuals living wages.

Future Research Directions

We have described a psychological approach as a more humanistic method to determining living wages. It accounts for the fact that individuals' quality of life is subjective. In this way, it gives those who stand to benefit from a living wage greater agency than is possible with econometric and statistical approaches. A second advantage of this approach is that it is firmly grounded in theory, such as Sen's (1999) capabilities approach. It has also guided the way in which Project GLOW members measure living-wage levels.

Since 2015, we have been continuously refining the measures for use in different countries (e.g., New Zealand, the Philippines, and South Africa). This has allowed us to develop a quantitatively sound way of measuring what monetary amount constitutes a living wage. It has also enabled us to demonstrate that it is, indeed, possible to determine living-wage amounts and ranges based on subjective, psychological, and theory-based measures. Lastly, we even have initial evidence that there might be one global living wage by showing parity when cost-of-living differentials in two highly different contexts (e.g., New Zealand and South Africa) are included. We require data from additional societies. This would allow us to determine with greater confidence not only if there is indeed a global organizational living wage, but also which factors beyond wages might influence living-wage ranges (e.g., the availability of legislated employment benefits, such as medical insurance or transport subsidies). We invite interested researchers to replicate the studies conducted in New Zealand and South Africa in their local contexts and to join Project GLOW.

The approach we outlined also takes into consideration the idea that wages stand for more than "just" money. Living wages, by definition, afford individuals quality of life and work life, not merely economic subsistence. We believe that it is fundamental to consider these aspects when debating issues of human development and sustainability, instead of focusing exclusively on economic indicators. What arises from this is the question if any work is really better than no work: an assumption implicit in the use of unemployment figures as the sole indicator of societal health. Our thinking suggests that it might be preferable not to work if the available work provides an income below living-wage levels. We require data from a wide variety of contexts to substantiate—or refute—this thesis. If our hypothesis is supported empirically, it means that popular narratives such as "we need to create jobs (at all costs)" and "rising unemployment levels are necessarily a cause for concern" need to change. The relevant data would contribute to informing a *humanomic* way of thinking about the link between work and stable livelihoods. Morson and Schapiro (2017) have advocated for humanomics, with strong links between the humanities and economics, as it would contribute to more applicable economic models that would result in more effective and just economic policy. With its thorough understanding of human behavior at work, I/O psychology is ideally positioned to provide the humanistic angle to topics which have historically been considered belonging to the domain of economics.

So far, our research has mainly focused on how best to determine a living-wage amount or range and on employees' reactions to living wages, but upcoming research needs to consider employers' perspectives. Here, research should explore which factors support employers accepting the importance of paying living wages. One possibly crucial variable is trust. Research could explore whether greater levels of trust between employees and management means employers are more likely to support living wages and, in turn, reduce the chances for wage disputes. Additionally, we require evaluation studies that track the impact of living wages on employees and organizational outcomes, such as changes in employee wellbeing, job satisfaction and commitment, absenteeism rates, turnover intentions, attrition and retention rates, individual productivity, and organizations' financial performance. Here, longitudinal research would be of particular value as we currently do not know about the long-term impact of living wages on organizational level outcomes and on employees' quality of life, for example. Equally so, in-depth qualitative research that explores the experiences of living-wage employers, employees earning below the living-wages threshold, and employees earning at least living wages is scarce. Qualitative accounts would assist in interpreting the quantitative results. Through the type of living-wage research described in this chapter I/O psychology has the chance to counter work precarity—and in that way contribute toward greater prosperity at individual, organizational, and societal level.

References

Allmark, P., & Machaczek, K. (2015). Financial capability, health and disability. *BMC Public Health, 15*(1), 1–5. https://doi.org/10.1186/s12889-015-1589-5

Anderson, E. M., Malmgren, J. A., Carter, W. B., & Patrick, D. L. (1994). Screening for depression in well older adults: Evaluation of a short form of the CES-D. *American Journal of Preventive Medicine, 10*(2), 77–84.

Anker, R. (2006). Living wages around the world: A new methodology and internationally comparable estimates. *International Labour Review, 145*(4), 309–338. https://doi.org/10.1111/j.1564-913X.2006.tb00037.x

Anker, R. (2011). *Estimating a living wage: A methodological review* (Conditions of Work and Employment Series No 29). International Labour Office. http://www.ilo.int/wcmsp5/groups/public/—ed_protect/—protrav/—travail/documents/publication/wcms_162117.pdf

Anker, R. & Anker, M. (2013). *A shared approach to estimating living wages: Short description of the agreed methodology*. Global Living Wage Coalition. https://files.fairtrade.net/standards/GLWC_Anker_Methodology.pdf

Anker, R., & Anker, M. (2017). *Living wages around the world: Manual for measurement*. Edward Elgar Publishing.

Bal, P. M., & Dóci, E. (2018). Neoliberal ideology in work and organizational psychology. *European Journal of Work and Organizational Psychology, 27*(5), 536–548. https://doi.org/10.1080/1359432X.2018.1449108

Bendix, S. (2019). *Labour relations: A Southern African perspective* (3rd ed.). Juta.

Bindman, A. (2015). A healthy living wage. *Journal of the American Medical Association, 314*(21), 2224–2225. https://doi.org/10.1001/jama.2015.16105

Bose, T., Reina, A., & Marshall, J. A. R. (2017). Collective decision-making. *Current Opinion in Behavioral Sciences, 16*, 30–34. https://doi.org/10.1016/j.cobeha.2017.03.004

Botha, M. (2021). *Shifting from survival to decent living: Evaluating individuals' capabilities to live the life they value in relation to their income*. [Unpublished master's dissertation, University of Cape Town]. http://hdl.handle.net/11427/35649

Brenner, M. D. (2004). The economic impact of living wage ordinances. In D. M. Figart (Ed.), *Living wage movements* (pp. 208–229). Routledge.

Burmaster, K. B., Landefeld, J. C., Rehkopf, D. H., Lahiff, M., Sokal-Gutierrez, K., Adler-Milstein, S., & Fernald, L. C. (2015). Impact of a private sector living wage intervention on depressive symptoms among apparel workers in the Dominican Republic: A quasi-experimental study. *BMJ Open, 5*(8), e007336. https://bmjopen.bmj.com/content/5/8/e007336

Carr, S. C., Leggatt-Cook, C., Clarke, M., MacLachlan, M., Papola, T. S., Pais, J., Thomas, S., McAuliffe, E., & Normand, C. (2011). *What is the evidence of the impact of increasing salaries on improving the performance of public servants, including teachers, doctors/nurses, and mid-level occupations, in low- and middle-income countries: Is it time to give pay a chance*. EPPI Centre, University of London. https://assets.publishing.service.gov.uk/media/57a08ab9e5274a31e000073a/Increasing_salaries_2011Carr.pdf

Carr, S. C., Maleka, M., Meyer, I., Barry, M. L., Harr, J., Parker, J., Arrowsmith, J., Yao, C., Hodgetts, D., Jones, H., Young-Hausner, A., Afeaki-Mafile'o, E., Rasmussen, A.-H. Alefaio-Tugia, S., Falealili, B., Mafile'o, K., Pikula, T., Wolfgram, N., 'Uhila, H., …, Naithani, A. (2018). How can wages sustain a living? By getting ahead of the curve. *Sustainability Science*, https://doi.org/10.1007/s11625-018-0560-7.

Carr, S. C., Parker, J., Arrowsmith, J., Watters, P., & Jones, H. (2016a). Can a 'living wage' springboard human capability? An exploratory study from New Zealand. *Labour & Industry: A Journal of the Social and Economic Relations of Work, 26*(1), 24–39. https://doi.org/10.1080/10301763.2016.1152533

Carr, S.C., Parker, J., Arrowsmith, J., & Watters, P.A. (2016b). The living wage: Theoretical integration and an applied research agenda. *International Labour Review, 155*(1), 1–24. https://doi.org/10.1111/j.1564-913X.2015.00029.x

Chatham House. (n.d.). *Chatham house rule*. https://www.chathamhouse.org/about-us/chatham-house-rule

Chiappero-Martinetii, E., & Ventkatapuram, S. (2014). The capability approach: A framework for population studies. *African Population Studies, 28*(2), 708–720. https://doi.org/10.11564/28-2-604

Ciscel, D. H. (2000). The living wage movement: Building a political link from market wages to social institutions. *Journal of Economic Issues, 34*(2), 527–535. https://doi.org/10.1080/00213624.2000.11506292

Cohen-Charash, Y., & Spector, P. E. (2001). The role of justice in organizations: A meta-analysis. *Organizational Behavior and Human Decision Processes, 86*(2), 278–321. https://doi.org/10.1006/obhd.2001.2958

Colquitt, J. A., Conlon, D. E., Wesson, M. J., Porter, C. O. L. H., & Ng, K. Y. (2001). Justice at the millennium: A meta-analytic review of 25 years of organizational justice research. *Journal of Applied Psychology, 86*(3), 425–445. https://doi.org/10.1037/0021-9010.86.3.425

Companies Amendment Bill. (2021). https://www.gov.za/sites/default/files/gcis_document/202110/45250gen586.pdf

Cvitanovic, C., Colvin, R. M., Reynolds, K. J., & Platow, M. J. (2020). Applying an organizational psychology model for developing shared goals in interdisciplinary research teams. *One Earth, 2*(1), 75–83. https://doi.org/10.1016/j.oneear.2019.12.010

Denning, M. (2010). Wageless life. *Global Histories of Work, 66*, 79–97. https://doi.org10.1515/9783110437201-011

Diener, E., & Diener, C. (2011). Monitoring psychosocial prosperity for social change. In R. Bieswas-Diener (Ed.), *Positive psychology as social change* (pp. 53–71). Springer.

Dóci, E., & Bal, P. M. (2018). Ideology in work and organizational psychology: The responsibility of the researcher. *European Journal of Work and Organizational Psychology, 27*(5), 558–560. https://doi.org/10.1080/1359432X.2018.1515201

Elliott, A. (2021). *Money and sustainability: Examining the potential moderating role of financial capability and decent work on the relationship between income and quality of life.* [Unpublished master's dissertation. University of Cape Town]. http://hdl.handle.net/11427/35723

Fairris, D., & Reich, M. (2005). The impacts of living wage policies: Introduction to the special issue. *Industrial Relations, 44*(1), 1–13. https://doi.org/10.1111/j.0019-8676.2004.00370.x

Fairwork. (2022). *Platform work amidst the cost of living crisis.* https://fair.work/wp-content/uploads/sites/17/2022/09/Fairwork-SA-Ratings-2022-EN.pdf

Gaya, L. (2021). *Money does not buy happiness... or does it: An investigation of the relationship between individual income and life satisfaction in the National Income Dynamics Study* [Unpublished master's thesis, University of Cape Town]. http://hdl.handle.net/11427/33785

Gaya, L., Meyer, I., & Maleka, M. (2018, August 31). *National income dynamics & sustainable livelihoods in South Africa* [Paper presentation]. 2nd International Conference: Healthier Societies Fostering Healthy Organizations: A Cross-Cultural Perspective, Florence.

Ghatak, M. (2015). Theories of poverty traps and anti-poverty policies. *The World Bank Economic Review, 29*(Suppl. 1), S77–S105. https://doi.org/10.1093/wber/lhv021

Gregg, P. (2000). The use of wage floors as policy tools. *OECD Economic Studies, 31*(2), 133–146.

Harvey, R. J. (1991). Job analysis. In M. D. Dunnette & L. M. Hough (Eds.), *Handbook of industrial and organizational psychology* (pp. 71–163). Consulting Psychologists Press.

Haslam, S. A., Eggins, R. A., & Reynolds, K. J. (2003). The ASPIRe model: Actualizing social and personal identity resources to enhance organizational outcomes. *Journal of Occupational and Organizational Psychology, 76*(1), 83–113. https://doi.org/10.1348/096317903321208907

Heery, E., Hann, D., & Nash, D. (2017a). The Living Wage campaign in the UK. *Employee Relations, 39*(6), 800–814. https://doi.org/10.1108/ER-04-2017-0083

Heery, E., Hann, D., & Nash, D. (2017b). *The living wage employer experience*. Cardiff Business School. https://www.cardiff.ac.uk/__data/assets/pdf_file/0015/2431050/Living_Wage_Employer_Experience.pdf

Hirsch, D., & Valadez-Martinez, L. (2017). *The living wage*. Agenda Publishing. https://doi.org/10.2307/j.ctv5cg8j7

Hurley, J., Vacas-Soriano, C. Muraille, M., & Lantto, E. (2018). *Concept and practice of a living wage.*European Foundation for the Improvement of Living and Working Conditions. http://eurofound.link/ef18064

International Labour Organization. (2008). *Declaration on social justice for a fair globalization.* https://www.ilo.org/wcmsp5/groups/public/—dgreports/—cabinet/documents/genericdocument/wcms_099766.pdf

International Labour Organization. (2015a). *Towards a South African national minimum wage*. https://www.lrs.org.za/wp-content/uploads/2021/01/Towards-a-South-African-National-Minumum-Wage.pdf

International Labour Organization. (2015b). *World employment and social outlook: Trends 2015*. https://www.voced.edu.au/content/ngv:67477

International Labour Organization. (2016). *The right to social security in the constitutions of the world: Broadening the moral and legal space for social justice*. https://www.ilo.org/wcmsp5/groups/public/—ed_norm/—normes/documents/publication/wcms_518153.pdf

International Labour Organization. (2019). *The working poor or how a job is no guarantee of decent living conditions: A study based on ILO's global estimates of employment by economic class (ILOSTAT Spotlight on Work Statistics No. 6)*. https://ilo.org/wcmsp5/groups/public/—dgreports/—stat/documents/publication/wcms_696387.pdf

Judge, T. A., Piccolo, R. F., Podsakoff, N. P., Shaw, J. C., & Rich, B. L. (2010). The relationship between pay and job satisfaction: A meta-analysis of the literature. *Journal of Vocational Behavior*, *77*, 157–167. https://doi.org/10.1016/j.jvb.2010.04.002

Kahneman, D., & Deaton, A. (2010). High income improves evaluation of life but not emotional well-being. *Proceedings of the National Academy of Sciences*, *107*(38), 16489–16493. https://doi.org/10.1073/pnas.1011492107

King, P. (2016). Setting the New Zealand living wage: Complexities and practicalities. *Labour & Industry: A Journal* of the *Social* and *Economic Relations* of *Work*, *26*(1), 8–23. http://doi.org/10.1080/10301763.2015.1116054

Landefeld, J. C., Burmaster, K. B., Rehkopf, D. H., Syme, S. L., Lahiff, M., Adler-Milstein, S., & Fernald, L. C. H. (2014). The association between a living wage and subjective social status and self-rated health: A quasi-experimental study in the Dominican Republic. *Social Science & Medicine, 121*, 91–97. https://doi.org/10.1016/j.socscimed.2014.09.051

Lappeman, J., Orpwood, T., Russell, M., Zeller, T., & Jansson, J. (2019). Personal values and willingness to pay for fair trade coffee in Cape Town, South Africa. *Journal of Cleaner Production, 239,* 118012. https://doi.org/10.1016/j.jclepro.2019.118012

Leibbrandt, M., Woolard, I., & de Villiers, L. (2009). *Methodology: Report on NIDS wave 1.* N.i.D.S. Technical Paper No.1. http://www.nids.uct.ac.za/publications/technical-papers/108-nids-technical-paper-no1/file

Living Wage Foundation (n.d.). *What is the real living wage?* https://www.livingwage.org.uk/media-key-information-and-statistics#:~:text=The%20real%20Living%20Wage%20is%20an%20hourly%20rate%20of%20pay,Wage%20on%20a%20voluntary%20basis

MacLachlan, M., & McVeigh, J. (Eds.). (2021). *Macropsychology: A population science for sustainable development goals*. Springer.

Maleka, M. J. (2021). *The effects of macroeconomic indicators on organization psychology factors: Evidence from Namibia, South Africa, and Zimbabwe*. Sage Publishers. https://doi.org/10.4135/9781529761412

Maleka, M. J., Mpofu, M., Hlatywayo, N. Meyer, I., Carr, S., & Parker, J. (2019). Employee engagement, organizational commitment and job satisfaction in Namibia,

South Africa, and Zimbabwe: An exploratory study. *Journal of Psychology in Africa, 29*(4), 393–400. https://doi.org/10.1080/14330237.2019.1647964

Maleka, M. J., Schultz, C. M., Van Hoek, L., Dachapalli, L., & Ragadu, S. C. (2021). Union membership as a moderator in the relationship between living wage, job satisfaction and employee engagement. *The Indian Journal of Labour Economics, 64,* 621–640. https://doi.org/10.1007/s41027-021-00322-0

Mani, A., Mullainathan, S., Shafir, E., & Zhao, J. (2013). Poverty impedes cognitive function. *Science, 976.* https://doi.org/10.1126/science.1238041

Martocchio, J. J. (2015). *Strategic compensation: A human resource management approach* (8th ed.). Pearson.

Mayer, C. (2018). *Prosperity: Better business makes the greater good.* Oxford University Press.

Meyer, M. F. (2014). *The relationship between quality of life, education, and poverty & inequality in South Africa: The capability approach as an alternative analytical framework* [Unpublished PhD thesis, University of the Western Cape]. http://etd.uwc.ac.za/xmlui/handle/11394/4104

Monteiro, M., & Keating, E. (2009). Managing misunderstandings: The role of language in interdisciplinary scientific collaboration. *Science Communication, 31*(1), 6–28. https://doi.org/10.1177/1075547008330922

Mohr, P., Yu, D., & Mollentze, S. (2016). *Economic indicators* (5th ed.). Van Schaik.

Morson, G., & Schapiro, M. (2017). *Cents and sensibility: What economics can learn from the humanities*. Princeton University Press.

Müller, T., & Schulten, T. (2019). Editorial. *Transfer: European Review of Labour and Research, 25*(3), 255–257. https://doi.org/10.1177/1024258919874710

Myers, D. G., & Diener, E. (1995). Who is happy? *Psychological Science, 6*(1), 10–19.

National Minimum Wage Act 9 of 2018 (SA). Government of South Africa. https://www.gov.za/sites/default/files/gcis_document/202112/45649gon1616.pdf

Nthulenyane, T. (2019). *Employees' perceptions about how a living wage relates to human resources management outcomes at an engineering company* [Unpublished master's dissertation]. Tshwane University].

O'Shea, M., McVeigh, J., & MacLachlan, M. (2021). Macropsychology and Public Persuasion. In J. McVeigh and M. MacLachlan (Eds.), *Macropsychology* (pp. 87–155). Springer.

Patel, L., Mthembu, S., & Graham, L. (2020). The national minimum wage in the agriculture and domestic work sectors report of a qualitative study of stakeholder responses to the national minimum wage. https://www.labour.gov.za/DocumentCenter/Publications/Basic%20Conditions%20of%20Employment/The%20National%20Minimum%20Wage%20in%20the%20Agriculture%20and%20Domestic%20Work%20Sectors.pdf

Prasoon, R., & Chaturvedi, K. R. (2016). Life satisfaction: A literature review. *The Researcher-International Journal of Management Humanities and Social Sciences, 1*(2), 25–32. http://theresearcherjournal.org/pdfs/01021220163.pdf.

PricewaterhouseCoopers South Africa (PwC SA). (2022). *Non-executive directors: Practices and fees trends report* (5th ed.). https://www.pwc.co.za/en/assets/pdf/ned-report-2022.pdf

Rehkopf, D. H., Burmaster, K., Landefeld, J. C., Adler-Milstein, S., Flynn, E. P., Acevedo, M. C., Jones-Smith, J. C., Adler, N., & Fernald, L. C. (2018). The impact of a private sector living wage intervention on consumption and cardiovascular disease risk factors in a middle income country. *BMC Public Health, 18*(1), 1–8. https://doi.org/10.1186/s12889-018-5052-2

Reynaud, E. (2017). *The International Labour Organization and the living wage: A historical perspective* (Conditions of Work and Employment Series No. 90). International Labour Office, Inclusive Labour Markets, Labour Relations and Working Conditions Branch. https://www.ilo.org/wcmsp5/groups/public/—ed_protect/—protrav/—travail/documents/publication/wcms_557250.pdf

Roosevelt, F. D. (1933). *Statement on N.I.R.A.* https://www.presidency.ucsb.edu/documents/statement-nira

Root, V. (2019). The compliance process. *Indiana Law Journal, 94*, 203–251. https://scholarship.law.nd.edu/law_faculty_scholarship/1364

Searle, R., & McWha-Herman, I. (2021). "Money's too tight (to mention)": A review and psychological synthesis of living wage research. *European Journal of Work and Organizational Psychology, 30*(3), 428–443. https://doi.org/10.1080/1359432X.2020.1838604

Sen, A. (1985). Wellbeing, agency and freedom: The Dewey lectures 1984. *The Journal of Philosophy, 82*(4), 169–221. https://doi.org/10.2307/2026184

Sen, A. (1999). *Development as freedom*. Oxford University Press.

Shapiro, C., & Stiglitz, J. E. (1984). Equilibrium unemployment as a worker discipline device. *The American Economic Review, 74*(3), 433–444. https://www.jstor.org/stable/1804018

Shaw, J. D., & Zhou, X. (2021). Explained pay disperson: A 20-year review of human resource management research and beyond. In M. R. Buckley, A. R. Wheeler, J. E. Baur, & J. R. B. Halbesleben (Eds.), *Research in personnel and human resources management* (Vol. 39, 47–69). Emerald Publishing. https://doi.org/10.1108/S0742-730120210000039002

Sinwell, L. (2013). The Marikana strike: The origins of a living wage demand and changing forms of worker struggles in Lonmin Platinum Mine, South Africa. *Labour, Capital and Society/Travail, Capital et Société, 46*(1/2), 92–115. http://www.jstor.org/stable/44706422

Smith, L. (2015). Reforming the minimum wage: Towards a psychological perspective. *American Psychologist*, 70(6), 557–565. https://doi.org/10.1037/a0039579

Stats, S. A. (2017). *Poverty trends in South Africa: An examination of absolute poverty between 2006 and 2015.* https://www.statssa.gov.za/publications/Report-03-10-06/Report-03-10-062015.pdf

Stats SA (2019). *Five facts about poverty in South Africa.* https://www.statssa.gov.za/?p=12075

Stats, S. A. (2022). *Quarterly labour force survey (QLFS): Quarter 2: 2022.* https://www.statssa.gov.za/publications/P0211/P02112ndQuarter2022.pdf

Teng-Calleja, M. R., Clemente, J. A., Menguito, M. L., & Bertulfo, D. J. (2021). Toward the pursuit of what people value: Determining a living wage based on capability gaps. *International Perspectives in Psychology: Research, Practice, Consultation, 10*(2), 59–73. https://doi.org/10.1027/2157-3891/a000007

Tlhabye, G. (2022, February 9). University of Pretoria's insourced security, food services staff continue protest against working conditions. *IOL.* https://www.iol.co.za/pretoria-news/news/university-of-pretorias-insourced-security-food-services-staff-protest-against-working-conditions-5094538b-9939-4678-b0d6-b6c8ea3fce30

United Nations. (1948). *Universal declaration of human rights*. https://www.un.org/sites/un2.un.org/files/2021/03/udhr.pdf

United Nations. (2015). *Transforming our world: The 2030 Agenda for Sustainable Development*. https://sustainabledevelopment.un.org/content/documents/21252030%20Agenda%20for%20Sustainable%20Development%20web.pdf

Veit-Wilson, J. (1998). *Setting adequacy standards: How governments define minimum incomes*. Policy Press.

World Bank. (2018). *Poverty and shared prosperity: Piecing together the poverty puzzle*. https://openknowledge.worldbank.org/bitstream/handle/10986/30418/9781464813306.pdf

World Bank. (2019). *World development report 2019: The changing nature of work*. https://thedocs.worldbank.org/en/doc/508871547017407762-0080022019/render/ENG1stsessionCemMeteWDR2019.pdf

World Bank. (2022a). *In Southern Africa, leveling the playing field at birth critical to reducing inequality, intergenerational poverty*. https://www.worldbank.org/en/region/afr/publication/in-southern-africa-leveling-the-playing-field-at-birth-critical-to-reducing-inequality-intergenerational-poverty

World Bank. (2022b). *Inequality in Southern Africa: Assessment of the Southern African Customs Union*. https://documents1.worldbank.org/curated/en/099125303072236903/pdf/P1649270c02a1f06b0a3ae02e57eadd7a82.pdf

Yao, C., Parker, J., Arrowsmith, J., & Carr, S. C. (2017). The living wage as an income range for decent work and life. *Employee Relations, 39*(6), 875–887. https://doi.org/10.1108/ER-03-2017-0071

Yoelao, D., Mohan, K. P., & Sombatwattana, P. (2019). A qualitative construction of sufficiency living wage in Thailand based on the sufficiency economy philosophy. *International Perspectives in Psychology: Research, Practice, Consultation, 8*(4), 227–239. https://doi.org/10.1037/ipp0000117

Zeng, Z., & Honig, B. (2017). A study of living wage effects on employees' performance-related attitudes and behaviour. *Canadian Journal of Administrative Sciences/Revue Canadienne des Sciences de l'Administration, 34*(1), 19–32. https://doi.org/10.1002/CJAS.1375

8

CLOSING THE CAPABILITY GAP IN TACKLING PRECARIOUS WORK

Mendiola Teng-Calleja, Donald Jay Bertulfo, and Jose Antonio R. Clemente

Two-thirds of the global working population are engaged in precarious work (International Labour Organization [ILO], 2021c). This means that they are working in conditions that do not provide security or social protection, deny them labor rights, and pay irregular and low wages (ILO, 2011). Experiences of income loss, reduced work hours, and job insecurity became more widespread across sectors and countries amid the COVID-19 pandemic (ILO, 2021a), and it is those in precarious employment who have been most affected by the crisis (Matilla-Santander et al., 2021).

More often than not, precarious workers receive lower wages than those engaged in more formal employment (ILO, 2019c), and being employed does not necessarily equate to material wellbeing or a decent living for workers and their families (ILO, 2019b). Thus, determining the *difference* between wages that promote a decent life and the income currently received by most workers can orient us to ways of tackling precarious work conditions.

As Sen states, "Inadequate income is a strong predisposing condition for an impoverished life" (1999, p. 87). A low income not only means living in financial hardship but also being deprived of one's ability to achieve aspirations of intrinsic value. To further understand precarity, it is important to capture the experience of precariousness from the perspective of fair income and the human need to attain valued functioning. More specifically, this means measuring how precarious employment expands the gap between aspirations and workers' capacity and the freedom to achieve these valued functionings.

Measuring the experience of precarity and linking it to an economic solution, such as provision of a fair income, is not straightforward. For instance, precarious work, on the one hand, can be described in terms of objective

DOI: 10.4324/9781003440444-10

work characteristics, such as type of work contract, work hours, access to health insurance, and availability of retirement benefits (e.g., Allan et al., 2021; Kalleberg et al., 2000; Seubert & Seubert, Chapter 14). On the other hand, determining an income level that will lift workers out of poverty has been fraught with challenges, such as difficulty in finding a global consensus on how much income is "enough," the ethics of determining a precise value for labor, and a focus on what employers can provide instead of what employees need to thrive (Searle & McWha-Hermann, 2021, Chapter 4; see also, Intraprasert et al., Chapter 9; Meyer & Maleka, Chapter 7). It is from this current context that we ask how can psychology contribute further to global efforts to reduce work precarity.

In this chapter, we present both the process and results from a study conducted in the Philippines of one of the first weighted psychometric approaches that can be utilized in enriching our understanding of fair income in the context of precarity. Our aims are two-fold. First, we propose a psycho-economic gauge of precarity, which links individual assessments of what constitutes a decent life (i.e., the psychological perspective) and the wage level that may enable the attainment of such life (i.e., the economic perspective). We argue that this alternative approach is important in refocusing attention on the issue of precarity to a more person- or worker-centric perspective. Second, we also discuss how "human resource management" (HRM) practitioners in particular, and employers or organizations in general, can contribute greatly to minimizing precarity by ensuring provision of decent work through living wages. We are cognizant of the reality that employers are not always welcoming of the idea of increasing wages at the expense of profit and the overall sustainability of organizations. However, we propose some strategies to consider, as ways to provide fair income to workers based on what may work for them in their context. Above all, this chapter aligns with the social justice ethos that underlies the very idea of decent work (Blustein et al., 2016; Di Fabio et al., Chapter 3).

With this social justice foundation in mind, we propose the concept of a capability gap, which we describe as the difference between what one values (and therefore aspires to) and what one perceives as achievable (Teng-Calleja, Menguito, et al., 2021). Our research used a set of valued domains, culled from a nationwide survey on wellbeing conducted by Sycip et al. (2008), that described what constitutes a good or decent life in our context. These valued domains include housing and quality of neighborhood; employment and quality of working life; savings, wealth, and assets; social relationships; leisure and spare-time activities; physical health; psychological/mental health and emotional wellbeing; religion and spiritual life; information and knowledge; government performance; and political participation. A weighted capability measure with weightings determined by the perceived importance of the 11 domains of a good life was used to estimate a wage rate at which workers' valued *functionings* are, on average (and based on idiosyncratic sample characteristics), well-covered, and determine the capability gap.

The following sections describe the core issues of employment and a decent living as they relate to precarious work. The discussion focuses on the situation of workers in the Philippines and provides the backdrop for the development of our proposed measure of precarity in the context of wages (see also, Seubert & Seubert, Chapter 14). This is followed by a presentation of the proposed weighted psychometric approach that may be used as a means to gauge human thriving in the workplace. We argue that this kind of measurement and assessment process can help to build the case against precarious work conditions. The recommended way of determining wages takes a worker-centered approach for determining a fair income (Meyer & Maleka, Chapter 7). The chapter ends with propositions on how I/O psychologists can help close these gaps through their roles in HRM and/or as leaders in organizations.

Employment and Decent Living

The high incidence of poverty in developing countries such as the Philippines heightens the urgency and importance of advocating for a decent life for workers and their families (Gavilan, 2018; National Anti-Poverty Commission, 2015). In fact, poverty is not only a problem of the unemployed but of the employed as well. Living conditions for minimum-wage earners are made even more precarious, because of insufficient government spending on social services (Rey, 2020), leaving low-income workers without an economic safety net to buffer unforeseen life shocks. Currently, the daily minimum wage for the country's 43.7 million workers (Gavilan, 2018) ranges from roughly US $5.64/day to US $10.74/day, depending on the location of one's workplace. IBON Foundation, a nonprofit development organization, recommends that a family of five residing in the National Capital Region needs US $20.08/day to cover their basic expenses (IBON Foundation, 2019): a far cry from government-mandated minimum wage rates.

Herein lies one of the central issues when it comes to employment and decent living. As the ILO (2019a) asserts, employment is not a guaranteed route out of poverty. In other words, people may be employed but their lives are far from decent because they live in households with income below the accepted poverty line. Thus, they are referred to as the working poor. In the Philippines, 3% of employed individuals are extremely poor, 18% are moderately poor, and 32% are near poor (ILO, 2021b). Although it is challenging to pinpoint exactly which factors cause employed individuals to remain as working poor, the working-poverty rate "is a valuable indication of *quality of employment* and the state of the labour market's health [emphasis added]" (ILO, 2019a). The working-poverty rate in the Philippines reinforces the idea that it is not enough to have a job. For individuals to lead decent lives, they need to have decent work. Decent work is the antithesis of precarious work, which is most likely unstable, unsafe, and unfair (Allan et al., 2021). Jobs need to be of high quality, and earnings should be sufficient for a decent living.

We focus our attention on the living wage because some scholars suggest that decent work offers such a wage (e.g., Seubert et al., 2021, Seubert & Seubert, Chapter 14). However, the dominant conversations on wages in Philippine society are still focused on the idea of a "minimum," which centers on meeting basic needs, as opposed to ascertaining a liveable income that enables workers' wellbeing. Carr et al. (2013) and Carr, Parker, Arrowsmith, and Watters (2016) suggest that formal workplaces are important contexts where barriers and enablers that inhibit or permit achievement of a high quality of life can be identified. Specifically, they point to the consequential role that wages or income play in moving people out of poverty. The assumption is that mesosystems (e.g., organizations and their reward contingencies) and macrosystems (e.g., government and its policies) contribute to the attainment of individual goals associated with a decent life through the provision of decent and sustainable wages.

If poverty is restricted opportunity then decent income can potentially not only reduce this by allowing people to not just meet their basic needs but also attain more freedoms and opportunities to make choices (Carr, 2013) and function in ways that they intrinsically value (Carr et al., 2017). Thus, income potentially plays a role in shaping employees' quality of work-life and overall wellbeing. For example, if workers value having a comfortable home, savings, or nurturing social relationships, the wage that they receive must facilitate the achievement of these outcomes.

A decent wage is also consistent with global efforts to achieve particular Sustainable Development Goals (SDGs), which include reducing inequality within and among countries (SDG-10), promoting healthy lives and wellbeing (SDG-3), and promoting decent work for all (SDG-8; United Nations Development Programme, 2015). In relatively less economically developed countries like the Philippines, a living wage would offer a substantial wage increase that might free the working poor from the poverty trap (SDG-1) and allow them to meet basic physiological needs such as food (SDG-2). Although the number of SDGs that can be met by providing living wages is arguable, a report by the Living Wage Foundation (n.d.-b) suggests that decent income is relevant to the attainment of eight out of the 17 goals. This is because a living wage provides a sense of security that allows workers to spend a modest amount on enhancing their wellbeing, pay debts, and save money for the education of their children, as well as participate in society overall.

In addition to a decent wage, reward contingencies in organizations including total rewards compensation packages have been shown to drive some indicators of work performance (Cerasoli et al., 2014). Better performance arguably leads to better organizational outcomes, including higher productivity and profit. Previous research on the antecedents of organizational citizenship behaviors (OCBs) likewise points to the importance of rewards (e.g., wages) that are within the control of organization leaders (e.g., Podsakoff et al., 2000). OCBs are discretionary behaviors beyond the workers' formal job requirements that enable organizational effectiveness (Organ, 1988; Podsakoff et al., 2000). It should be noted, however, that extant psychological research linking wages and OCBs seems to focus more on pay cognitions, as opposed to the potential direct effects of actual wages on employee behaviors. Pay cognitions are appraisals or assessments of rewards, recognition, and pay as outcomes of one's job (Lee & Allen, 2002; Organ & Konovsky, 1989). These perceptions have been operationalized in various ways: fairness in rewards allocation or distributive justice (Netemeyer et al., 1997); satisfaction with compensation (Danish & Usman, 2010); perceptions of how an organization rewards and recognizes employee's performance (Danish & Usman, 2010; Lomoya et al., 2015, Red & Teng-Calleja, 2021); and extrinsic job satisfaction (Mohammad et al., 2011). Although actual wages received by individuals are usually not measured, findings from these studies hint at the possibility of OCBs as likely outcomes of workers having the freedom and opportunities to pursue and enjoy what they value in life, especially as a consequence of receiving adequate wages.

In this regard, the provision of decent wages is one of the many necessary structural conditions of decent work that potentially benefit the overall health and success of organizations. We emphasize that other structural conditions, such as promoting and institutionalizing organizational fairness (e.g., Whitman et al., 2012), workplace safety (e.g., Beus et al., 2016), freedom from harassment and discrimination (e.g., Ozeren, 2014), and communication and cooperation opportunities (e.g., Seubert et al., 2021) are important dimensions of decent work and also lead to favorable workplace outcomes but are beyond the scope of this chapter. What we aim to highlight at this point is that it is within the control of organizations to institutionalize support for workers' optimal functioning through just policies and mechanisms related to financial incentives that minimize, if not eradicate, precarity. There is some evidence that organizations are incentivized to provide this support through reduced turnover, absenteeism, overtime, training needs, and overall organizational costs that partially mitigate increased wage costs (Searle & McWha-Hermann, 2021, Chapter 4).

More importantly, we argue that there needs to be a shift in focus from the firms and businesses that set the compensation rates just high enough to motivate the employees to act in accordance with the interest of their employers to the employees themselves. Not only is it ethical, humane, and socially just to move poor wage earners out of the poverty trap, reduce income inequality, and ensure a decent and dignified life for the workers and their families, but this argument also foregrounds quality of life as an important end goal in itself beyond mere survival.

Individuals enjoying a decent life are not simply subsisting but thriving as well. Because employees are not mere cogs in a machine, they need to be viewed as agentive and capable of achieving a high quality of life. Thus, a broader and more holistic perspective on fair income that accounts for this agency needs to be adopted to ensure that workers are provided opportunities to thrive. A holistic approach to minimizing precarity attempts to increase a sense of security in several aspects of wellbeing including material (e.g., money and basic goods), systemic (e.g., structures that promote social relationships and freedom to exercise religion), and subjective aspects (e.g., opportunities to feel empowered in the workplace). It also takes into consideration both micro (e.g., individual needs) and macro (e.g., community and workplace) levels of analysis (see Binder, 2014).

For instance, being in a healthy physical condition enables a person to engage in many activities that are enjoyable and worthwhile. It also avoids incurring extra cost when one's health fails. Indeed, long-term illness in the Philippines is an important cause of poverty, as evidenced in health-compromised groups wherein sufferers not only experience the pain of sickness but also the eventual suffering of their families due to the depletion of their savings to pay for healthcare (Racelis, 2016). Results of a study by Teng-Calleja et al. (2021a) in which a sample of low- and middle-income employees rated physical health as very important for them to be able to say that they have a good life support such a premium given to good health (Teng-Calleja et al., 2021a).

Decent employment that provides a regular source of income is instrumental in securing the basic necessities in life, such as providing food for the family, permanent housing in safe neighborhoods, and education. As previously mentioned, provision of a decent wage is a structural enabler of one's capability to do, acquire, or pursue what is deemed an important activity, commodity, freedom, or entitlement (Anand & Sen, 2000), such as saving and accumulating assets that will ensure a stable and comfortable life. With earnings from gainful employment covering one's basic requirements, an employee may feel more confident to pursue other activities that have the potential to contribute to their wellbeing (Seubert et al., 2021; see also, Haar, Chapter 17; Klug et al., Chapter 21).

In a study in New Zealand, based on theory developed by Carr, Parker, Arrowsmith, Watters, and Jones (2016), Carr et al. (2017) showed that income was not linearly related to job satisfaction, empowerment at work, occupational pride, community participation, physical wellbeing, or mental stress. Instead, there seems to exist a critical income level, threshold, or pivot point where capabilities significantly improve. They refer to this critical income level or threshold as the living wage (Carr et al., 2017; Meyer & Maleka, Chapter 7). One implication of this study is that any type of income raise might not necessarily minimize the precarity experienced by low-wage earners. A specific threshold has to be identified and met before the benefits to the workers manifest themselves.

Consistent with a worker-centered and agentive formulation of employee wellbeing, the aforementioned outcomes predicted by living wages were collectively referred to as perceived capabilities. Thus, employees' subjective assessments of freedoms enjoyed at work (e.g., freedom to voice one's concerns in the workplace) and freedoms enjoyed in everyday life (e.g., capability to participate in community life) need to be ascertained and consequently supported. A holistic perspective also incorporates such subjective indicators of quality of life.

Furthermore, other work-related factors such as the quality of the work environment, and the relationships they cultivate with their coworkers, are motivating factors for Filipino workers (Ilagan et al., 2014). This is perhaps not surprising given that coworkers provide individuals with various kinds of psychosocial supports (e.g., camaraderie and emotional support) and material resources (Jimmieson et al., 2010). In general, the relationships that people enjoy with their nuclear family and relatives provide the social, emotional, and financial capital that are necessary for the pursuit of a good life in the Philippine context (Jocano, 2001; Sycip et al., 2008). As posited by the spillover theory of work-family conflict (Eby et al., 2005), employees who have more positive experiences at home are likely to demonstrate desirable behaviors in the workplace (Haar, Chapter 17). This implies that a decent life may involve building meaningful relationships within and outside one's family, nurturing them, and enjoying them.

Aside from what Sycip et al. (2000) refer to as horizontal relationships with family and friends, a secure vertical relationship with a supreme being may also be important in the attainment of a good life for Filipino employees. In the Philippines, it is normative to place a high degree of importance on spirituality from birth (Ocampo et al., 2013). Thus, if practicing one's religion and spirituality are valued, employees might need to be given the space and opportunity to engage in them as well through attendance at worship services, observance of religious rituals, seeking God's guidance through prayer and devotion, and helping others, etc. Interestingly, a sample of Filipino migrant workers highly endorsed faith in God as a cause of one's socioeconomic mobility, which was then associated with engagement and persistence in work-related tasks (Bernardo et al., 2018).

The discussion thus far underscores that fair income enables commodity acquisition and fulfillment of material desires. In sum, we argue that any assessment of quality of life that meets our goals of a holistic understanding of employee wellbeing and workplace performance should include the perceived opportunities, freedoms, and entitlements that people have and can have. The experience of precarity is exacerbated by the inability to function in ways that are valued and the lack of societal structures that provide opportunities for an individual to exercise the freedom to choose to do and be whatever one values. Unrestricted opportunities may lead to the achievement of basic and complex life goals (e.g., enjoying good health, living decently, and having an education; Carr, Parker, Arrowsmith, & Watters, 2016; Clark, 2005; Nussbaum, 2011; Sen, 1993).

Weighted Capability as a Gauge of Precarity

The central question of this chapter relates to how employee precarity can be minimized and thus how high quality of life can be enabled. To frame precarity for this purpose, we drew inspiration from Sen's (1993) capability approach to human development because of its aspirational qualities and focus on the agency of the person. The aim is not to simply describe what people consider important in their lives but to also assess the enabling factors in their environment that can serve as impetus for action. To elaborate on this, we present an approach to measuring worker capabilities that considers individual valued-life domains. We claim that this approach can potentially be used as a psycho-economic gauge of precarity, allowing us to explore its relationship with living wages. In this section, we present the results of a study which applied this measure in a specific socioeconomic context and investigated its alignment with existing theory on living wages.

When individuals are restricted in their choices and become incapable of achieving what they value, they are potentially in a state of constant insecurity. Precarity then, we propose, is also an experience of a widened capability gap. A capability gap is an individual's inability to do, acquire, or pursue what one deems as an important activity, commodity, freedom, or entitlement. It is the difference or discrepancy between what one values and what one perceives as attainable. We suggest an index of capability gaps that takes into consideration individual preferences and goal pursuits by asking individuals to report how much they value various domains of a good life (e.g., savings and religion) and whether they feel free to pursue or achieve what they rate as important given their current income, creating what we referred to previously as a psycho-economic gauge of precarity.

Sen (1993) initially based the concept of one's capability on the idea of functionings, which are achievements or various ways of being that can range from basic goals of living (e.g., being adequately nourished) to more complex, abstract, and valued goals (e.g., being happy). Beyond these, being capable means having the freedom to achieve valued resources or goals (Sen, 1993) or having the "freedoms or opportunities created by a combination of personal abilities and the political, social, and economic environment" (Nussbaum, 2011, p. 20). Capable individuals can choose the kind of life they would like to lead because they perceive such desired ways of being as attainable.

In other words, Sen's conceptualization of "capabilities" proposes the assessment of quality of life in terms of the activities one values and one's freedom and capacity to engage in these valued activities. Taking this as an inspiration, we constructed a singular measure of perceived capability made up of the participants' ratings of the relative importance of specific domains of a good life and their perception of the extent to which they are able to attain quality of life in each domain. A weighted capability score was then calculated for each individual worker by multiplying and summing the freedom and importance scores across all 11 items or domains (see Table 8.1) and dividing by the sum of importance ratings for that individual. Hence, by design, our weighted capability measure can be interpreted as the mean of perceived freedom across all valued-life domains considered, weighted by the perceived importance of each

TABLE 8.1 Description of the Eleven (11) Domains of Magandang Buhay (A Good Life)

Domains of Life	*Description*
Housing and Quality of Neighborhood	Having a safe place to live that is near your place of work, school, etc.; safe from fire and flood; clean and well built, with electricity, water, and toilet facilities, and where you have good relations with your neighbors
Employment & Quality of Working Life	Having a regular, permanent, and legal employment; a safe place to work that is near your home and gives you a gainful employment; that is suitable to your education; and where you enjoy good relations with your boss and peers
Savings, Wealth, and Assets	Having your own house and land, appliances, savings, and being free from debt
Social Relationships	Being with your spouse, child/children, and friends, and enjoying the love of your friends and relatives
Leisure and Spare Time Activities	Having time for yourself, being able to rest, relax, and have fun with your loved ones
Physical Health	Being free from sickness and disability; able to exercise regularly; having regular and nutritious food, enough sleep, and a long life
Psychological/Mental Health & Emotional Wellbeing	Valuing oneself, having an alert mind, being calm and at peace, having the ability to make personal decisions, feeling respected by your family and other people; having the ability to handle your problems and face changes
Religion and Spiritual Life	Having the opportunity to worship, pray, give alms to the church, and do good to others
Information and Knowledge	Having the ability to read and write, finish college, learn through different means aside from school (e.g., watching TV or reading the newspaper), having access to education, and being able to use your education
Government Performance	Having a country that is peaceful, crime-free, has good public services and stable economy, where citizens are united, and where there are equal justice and opportunities for everyone
Political Participation	Knowing what is happening in the country, being free to vote in elections, join community organizations, and to express political opinions

of those domains. Higher scores in the weighted capability measure mean lower capability gaps and greater perceived freedom to attain quality of life in the valued domains. Inversely, lower score equates to greater capability gap and more experiences of precarity.

In the aforementioned survey on living wages that we conducted with over 500 respondents (selected via systematic random sampling) from low- and middle-class communities in the Philippines, we used the proposed weighted capability measure discussed above to derive a living wage estimate that captured eleven domains of a "good life," as identified by Sycip et al. (2008). These eleven domains reflect what Filipinos value as comprising a "good life" (see Table 8.1 for a more detailed description of each valued domain). We point out that other cultures and communities may have different sets of valued domains. Thus, while we take this empirical exercise as an attempt to apply a more holistic method to the estimation of living wages, careful consideration and customization may be needed to adapt this for use in other cultures. What we describe here is the process used to calculate a weighted capability measure.

This way of measuring capability has several strengths. First, it is multidimensional in that it considers the multiple material and non-material factors that comprise quality of life. Second, having a singular capability measure bypasses the difficulty associated with examining each domain of quality of life in isolation from other related, but not necessarily similar, domains. Third, our measure acknowledges the heterogeneity in individual valuations of different domains of quality of life. By construction, weights may vary from respondent to respondent and depend primarily on self-reported value assignments. This allowed us to construct a weighted capability measure based on respondents' own subjective value assignments. Lastly, aggregating across domains of quality of life enabled us to transform discrete measures of valued-life outcomes into one continuous measure of perceived capability. The importance of this variable transformation would become apparent in the next process where we take the weighted capability measure and plot it against the self-reported income of respondents.

In the next stage of our analysis, we tested different functional form approximations to identify the curve that best characterizes the relationship between weighted capability and self-reported monthly income using the data we obtained from the survey. This approach allowed us to link current income with individual assessments of the components of a decent life. When applied to precarity, this psycho-economic approach has the potential to refocus the debate on wage levels toward a more person- or worker-specific perspective. As a quick technical note, we did not control for other variables that may influence the relationship between the two variables mentioned. Here, our goal was to discover the shape of the curve and not the determinants of the relationship between capability and income as commonly done in more sophisticated econometric or statistical work.

For this empirical part of the process, we considered general functional forms such as linear, quadratic, exponential, logistic, and Gompertz. There are many other functional forms that could be added to this initial set, but we chose the fundamental ones for brevity and ease of demonstration. A more detailed discussion of the methodology, as well as the results described here, can be found in Teng-Calleja, Clemente, et al. (2021). Our simulations and goodness-of-fit tests indicated some consistency with the theoretical conceptualization of incomes and capabilities posed by Carr, Parker, Arrowsmith, and Watters (2016) who visualized the relationship between current incomes and future capabilities as following a sigmoidal curve. Our results using actual survey-collected data show that a sigmoidal curve seems to best represent the relationship between income and capabilities, although strictly speaking our data inputs represented current income and current (rather than future) perceived capabilities.

The results of the approximation procedure we describe above provided us with some confidence in the alignment between current theorizing on living wages and data collected on the ground. Extending the analysis further, we took the best fitting curve from the previous exercise to estimate a ballpark figure that would give us a living wage estimate using a theoretically informed approach.

Carr, Parker, Arrowsmith, Watters, and Jones (2016) conceptualized the living wage as the "point of inflection" above which wages become theoretically sufficient to adequately meet valued functionings. We identified the income level at which capability crossed the mid-point of 3/5, from capability gap to surplus, at the inflection point of the best fitting curve. Data from our sample indicate that about PhP 23,000 (US $440) per month was needed by workers in our sample to feel capable of achieving quality of life in valued-life domains. Through consultation, we found this estimate converged with estimates by other worker groups (Meyer & Maleka, Chapter 7) and was close to what was being lobbied for at the time of the study (2016–2017, pre-COVID-19) as the benchmark monthly minimum wage for workers in Manila. Again, we raise the caveat that the amount may very well vary from our estimate, depending on where and when (e.g., post-COVID) measurements are made and also the demographic characteristics of respondents. Understanding variation in estimates is outside the scope of this exercise; it does however provide an initial basis for future measurement-based studies on living wages.

Implications for I/O Psychology: Rethinking Remuneration and Rewards

Building a case against precarious work conditions means championing workers' wellbeing. As can be gleaned from the previous sections, measuring gaps in wellbeing or human thriving in the workplace will enable organizations, particularly I/O psychologists practicing HRM, to make a case for a worker-centered approach to determining incomes and benefits. The first steps are to integrate ways of measuring these gaps and determining fair incomes through a capability approach and to find ways to rethink and recalibrate how the organization determines work remuneration and rewards. The following section discusses recommended ways of moving forward.

Recalibrating the Baseline

In many countries, including the Philippines, the minimum wage is considered the baseline or "minimum amount of remuneration that an employer is required to pay wage earners for the work performed during a given period, which cannot be reduced by collective agreement or an individual contract" (ILO, 2015, p. 1). Nonetheless, data that point to more than 700 million workers not earning enough to bring themselves and their families out of poverty (United Nations, 2019) imply that the minimum wage usually falls short of the living wage. Given this, advocating for a good life for workers and families means shifting the prevailing mindset in organizations on what is considered baseline pay from a minimum wage to a decent wage.

Following the earlier proposition for measuring gaps in the provision of fair incomes, HRM practitioners can either collaborate to conduct a living-wage study to collectively estimate the income that will help close the capability gap in their context (e.g., country, region, and industry) or work to identify specific capability gaps in their own workplaces. The dimensions of a good life presented in Table 8.1 may be broad enough to transcend contextual nuances, but tailoring the domains to findings of localized wellbeing studies is an alternative. In countries like the United Kingdom and New Zealand, there are national organizations (e.g., Living Wage Foundation, n.d.-a; Living Wage Movement Aotearoa New Zealand, n.d.) that help determine and monitor living wages. Secondary data from these organizations, or primary data gathered using a weighted psychometric approach to determining a local living wage as outlined here, can help inform and provide estimates for any new, in-context, wage baseline.

Differentiations above the Baseline

Setting the living wage as the baseline does not mean throwing away everything that we know about job evaluation and compensation and benefits incentivization and administration. Theories that relate motivation to worker attraction, performance, engagement, and retention still hold true in most instances. The value of a job versus other jobs in the organization and a worker's level of performance can remain as bases for differentiations in income above the proposed baseline. Note that this baseline now reflects not just the minimum wage that workers and families can live by but what is a fair income that will promote capabilities and ensure attainment of valued outcomes. Doing so will ensure contribution to organizational success through alignment of individual and teamwork outcomes with organizational goals and strategies, maintaining desired levels of productivity, and continuous innovation and work process improvements.

There is recent evidence of the feasibility of establishing a win-win scenario for employers and workers on income and benefits. The story of Quest Diagnostics (Quest), for example, shows how the provision of a living wage and an environment that enables human thriving improves organizational performance and the lives of workers (Good Jobs Institute, 2017b; Ton, 2017). Quest is a health diagnostics company based in the United States and has operations in India, Ireland, and Mexico. Their products and services are utilized by clients from over 130 countries (Quest Diagnostics, n.d.). In 2017, Quest was featured in a case study by the Good Jobs Institute, a start-up, nonprofit social enterprise with a mission to "help companies thrive by creating good jobs" (Good Jobs Institute, 2017a). The case study was about Quest's transformation efforts in its call centers that began in 2015. The case noted how Quest was experiencing a high turnover rate (60% per annum) that was costing the company $10.5 million in direct replacement costs each year. To address the issue, Quest raised wages, created clearer career paths with incremental pay increases, and improved employee training. Concurrently, expectations for attendance and overall performance by employees were raised. The efforts to provide fair income and growth opportunities reaped benefits not just for the employees but for the organization as well. In 1.5 years, turnover was cut in half and absenteeism dropped from 12.4% to 4.2%. The improvements in employee performance were also experienced by the clients with Quest employees' faster answer and transfer rates. The transformation efforts also resulted in cost savings of up to $1.3 million. The savings came from newly implemented process improvements: many of which were driven by their call-center representatives (Good Jobs Institute, 2017; as cited by Mahoney, 2021). The experience of Quest Diagnostics is an example of how respecting and advocating for workers' right to a good life may result not only in desirable work attitudes and behaviors (Red & Teng-Calleja, 2021) but may also improve services and financial health (Jayachandran, 2020).

A Complementary Approach

It is very likely that some organizations, especially given the challenges that arose due to the COVID-19 pandemic, will argue that it is simply not realistic for them to use the living wage as a baseline salary for all employees. Even if this proposition is disputable, a complementary approach can add to ways of supporting workers' attainment of a good life through HR policies and programs. Specifically, organizations may adopt a total rewards strategy and provide not only financial rewards to workers but also integrate *benefits* that are tailored to employee needs (Milkovich et al., 2014). Popularly known as the flexible-benefits program, this strategy of customizing benefits gives workers the freedom to choose rewards from their benefits allocation (Martires, 1988). Flexible benefits can be provided in addition to salaries or as a way to complement (not replace, see Belser & Sobeck, 2012) the provision of the living wage.

Using the capability approach based on the dimensions of a good life presented earlier, the following table presents additional or complementary ways of closing the gaps in fair income. Note that the differences between current paradigms and the propositions in this chapter mean that the recommendation to provide these benefits and programs comes from the standpoint that these will help to ensure a decent life for workers and their families. This can be done through the provision of a living wage, and/or other complementary ways to compensate for an organization's proven lack of capacity to increase wages of all organization members. In instances where employers are able to provide a living wage for all, the programs for a good life can serve as a framework for additional ways of closing capability gaps. The examples in Table 8.2 are mostly from organizations in the Philippines, where the authors are situated. Practices and programs were chosen based on their alignment with the 11 dimensions of a good life presented earlier in the chapter. The examples come from existing or recent practices in organizations of varying sizes and industries and illustrate that HR and organizational initiatives that promote human thriving are feasible.

When working with limited resources, organizations may be able to identify domains of a good life to focus on, based on the capability gaps and thresholds for reversing them that have been identified among their workers. Enhanced capability can be one of the organization's success indicators and can be capitalized on as part of its brand. Constantly monitoring and evaluating achievements in this area, as well as continuously strengthening programs that promote a good life, will allow the workers and their organization to thrive together.

Conclusions and Future Research Directions

I/O psychologists who endeavor to minimize precarity can promote human thriving by initiating assessments of quality of life in their workplaces. They can do this in a manner that captures employees' perceived capabilities—opportunities, freedoms, and entitlements that they have and can have—provided that structures such as decent wage thresholds, which allow the expression of valued functionings, are enabled and met. A study among Filipino employees illustrates (1) the importance of enabling capabilities through decent wages that afford wellbeing and a good life and (2) a process for doing so, in accordance with SDG-8 and with local values and world views. If employees are paid a living wage and are provided with benefits and programs that help not only to close gaps in fair income but also open opportunities for capabilities to grow, their potential for thriving (not just subsistence) will increase.

TABLE 8.2 Complementary/Additional Ways of Closing the Gaps in Fair Income

Programs for a Good Life	*Examples of Organizational Programs and Practices*
Physical Health • Access to nutritious food in the workplace • Programs to encourage healthy eating • Access to wellness and healthcare services	• TaskUs, a global outsourcing company created the Food Forward program where employees are given access to nutritious food through their "integrity store" for a five-peso donation (equivalent to US $1 cent) (Gonzales, 2018). • Google provides nutritious meals to its employees in their campus cafes and microkitchens and has onsite massage services and chiropractic treatment as well as physicians and physical therapists. They also have on-site fitness centers and classes (Google Careers, n.d.). • Some organizations in developing countries where there is limited national health insurance coverage provide healthcare access for workers through health maintenance organizations (see Martires, 1988, for an example in the Philippines).
Psychological/Mental Health and Emotional Wellbeing • Space where people can relax, be at peace, and practice mindfulness • Promotion of mental health	• Toyota Motors Philippines has a reflection room where workers can unwind and an expression room where they can use a punching bag to express strong emotions (Menguito, 2013). • TaskUs has a holistic wellness program that includes private consultations with mental health professionals and in-house and outsourced life coaches as well as online Zumba, yoga, and meditation sessions (TaskUs, 2021). • Some organizations in the Philippines also provide psychological first aid and counseling to employees whenever disaster strikes, as well as creating mechanisms for colleagues to provide the emotional support needed to cope with disasters (Teng-Calleja et al., 2020).
Savings, Wealth, and Assets • Programs that allow workers to have a home and to build savings	• Google provides retirement savings plans and access to financial advisors/planning services to help workers manage their finances (Google Careers, n.d.). • Petron provides a Savings and Land Home Ownership Plan as well as a Group Life Insurance Plan to their employees (Ilac, 2013).

Leisure and Spare Time Activities • Programs that allow workers to have time for themselves, to rest, and have fun with loved ones	• Jollibee Foods Corporation holds Family Fun Days to allow employees to engage in leisure activities with their family and colleagues (Jollibee Foods Corporation, n.d.). • Petron subsidizes employee clubs (e.g., Photography Club, Painting Club, Racquet Club for those interested in badminton, Tenpinner Club for bowling enthusiasts, and Ikebana for those who are into Japanese arts) (Ilac, 2013). • Most organizations provide vacation leave to employees and some include tour packages in flexible benefits programs.
Information and Knowledge • Provision of scholarship grants to workers • Training and development opportunities	• Meralco, a power distribution company, offers a Master of Engineering in Electrical Engineering Program in partnership with a state university, as well as leadership and professional development programs and an internal coaching program (Hechanova, 2013). • GlaxoSmithKline has a management training and leadership development program. They also have a learning center where over 500 books, periodicals, and electronic learning materials are accessible to workers (Inocentes-Lombos, 2013).
Religion and Spiritual Life • Programs that allow workers to express their spirituality in the workplace with coworkers that share the same beliefs	• Meralco supports employee clubs such as CFC Family Ministries, Singles for Christ, and Meralco Christian Fellowship (Meralco, n.d.). • Some organizations build spirituality-related wellness facilities such as rooms for prayer or meditation and provide opportunities and allocate finances for spiritual recollections or retreats (Hechanova, 2018).
Social Relationships • Flexible work arrangements to help workers manage/harmonize professional and personal lives • Paid leave so workers can spend quality time with their loved ones • Programs that promote inclusivity	• Accenture provides a range of flexible work options such as telecommuting, flexible schedules (e.g., compressed work weeks or extended weekends), and client-site flexibility (Accenture, n.d.). • UnionBank and San Miguel Corporation offer paid leave so that employees can go on a vacation with their loved ones (San Miguel Corporation, 2022; Union Bank of the Philippines, 2022). • Mondelez Philippines allows its employees to work from home one to four days per month, depending on the nature of their job and subject to their manager's approval. They also grant female employees 120-day paid maternity leave and cover pre- and postnatal consultations, providing discounts for pre-natal milk, loans, and cash assistance (Human Resources Online, 2018).

(Continued)

Programs for a Good Life	*Examples of Organizational Programs and Practices*
	• Accenture and Sofitel provide breastfeeding facilities for working mothers (MetroCebu News, 2019; Sofitel Manila, 2019). • Shell (a petroleum company) promotes inclusivity in the workplace through leadership and employee awareness trainings on sexual orientation. They also have initiatives such as flying the Pride flag outside of their offices during Pride month and celebrating International Coming Out Day (Shell, n.d.).
Housing and Quality of Neighborhood • Housing loans • Safe housing and accommodation for employees who volunteered to work onsite during the pandemic and assistance in relocating to preferred homes in the provinces during COVID-19.	• The Bank of the Philippine Islands offers low interest rates to their workers for housing loans (BPI, n.d.) so they can invest in a home of their choice that is aligned with their investment capacity. • Synchrony Global Services, a call center and back-office support business, on the one hand, housed close to a thousand employees in nearby world-class hotels to ensure their safety as they worked onsite amid COVID-19. Canva Philippines, on the other hand, helped transport employees who wanted to relocate back to their family homes or nearby provinces as they worked remotely during the pandemic (Great Place to Work Philippines, 2021).
Employment and Quality of Working Life • Safety and protection in the workplace • Opportunities for personal development • Recognition for work • Programs that promote healthy working relationships between peers	• Cemex, an international cement manufacturing company, uses safety protocols, including protocols on workplace cleaning and commuting to and from work, based on the World Health Organization guidelines, in all its global offices (BusinessMirror, 2020). • Manila Water's cadetship program provides an opportunity for new hires to be mentored by experienced professionals in the field so they can be prepared for management positions. They also have a Lunch with the President program where the company president eats lunch with selected employees from different departments. In this informal gathering, workers hear firsthand about the career journey of their President and the hurdles he overcame to be successful. They also get to know the other members of the management team and learn about their plans and are able to ask for their support on issues and concerns and issues (Cementina-Olpoc, 2013).

	• The Philippine Long Distance Company (PLDT, a telecommunications company) gives the Best Employees in Transformation or PLDT B.E.S.T award for workers that help in the organization's transformation efforts. The award comes with perks such as opportunities to travel (Sanchez, 2013).
Political Participation • Active promotion of awareness and participation in political events within and outside the immediate confines of the organization	• The drug company GlaxoSmithKline also has HR Rounds. These are meetings, learning sessions, and fellowships aimed at discussing and addressing employee concerns (Inocentes-Lombos, 2013). • United Laboratories (Unilab) has an Employees Council that serves as a platform to voice workers' concerns to management. This council has representation from the different divisions and regularly discusses with management the needs of all employees (Presbitero, 2008).
Contributing to Government Performance • Programs that allow workers to meaningfully contribute to society	• DHL (a logistics company) holds a yearly Employee Opinion Survey where workers have an opportunity to potentially influence organizational strategies (DHL Philippines, 2022). • Shell promotes LGBT inclusion across all of its international offices regardless of the host country's legislation on sexual orientation and gender identity expression (Shell, n.d.). • Several organizations also have Corporate Social Responsibility programs that allow workers to contribute to environmental protection and sustainability, promote education across sectors, and protect marginalized groups, among others (see for example the initiatives of the Alcantara Group in Mindanao, Philippines through the Conrado and Ladislawa Alcantara Foundation (n.d.))

The recommendations noted above are shared with the knowledge that conversations on wages and benefits can be contentious (Teng-Calleja, et al., 2015) and may invoke articulations of conflicting economic interests between company management and employees. I/O psychologists, especially those in HRM, may find themselves at the center of these disagreements as they navigate through their roles as employee champions and strategic business partners (Ulrich, 1996). Building a case for a worker-centered approach in determining income and benefits will require data and insights from empirical studies.

Given this, I/O psychologists who seek to champion decent wages and advocate against precarious work, either as an HRM professional or an academic, may consider embarking on research that:

- Documents experiences using single (company-level) or multiple (industry-level) case studies of organizations that assess the quality of life of employees using a capability approach as well as interventions employed to address identified capability gaps and their outcomes;
- Explores differences in living wages across societies using a quality of life/wellbeing framework as opposed to a purely econometric approach; and
- Relates the provision of decent wages and utilization of complementary/additional ways of closing gaps in fair income to employees (e.g., employee satisfaction, engagement, commitment, performance, and productivity) and organizational outcomes (e.g., revenue, return on assets, customer satisfaction, and shareholder value).

Because the arguments presented in this chapter on minimizing work precarity hinge on the ability to identify a living wage that may work in the Philippine context, we reiterate that the psycho-economic approach we employed in the estimation of such a wage is preliminary and may require further refinement. In a previous paper, we suggested that the response scale we used to measure capability gaps needs to be validated such that a step-change in workers' capabilities occurs in an intersubjectively reproducible way (Teng-Calleja, Clemente et al., 2021). Additionally, the subjective measures of capability gaps may be validated by relating perceptions of gaps with available objective measures related to the proposed dimensions of wellbeing, such as measures of physical health, existence of policies related to job security and occupational safety standards, access to spaces for leisure, number of trainings provided, and personal savings of employees. The goal of these future studies is to ensure that the basis for the computation of the living wage has adequate and sound support.

Finally, research on work precarity and provision of living wages rarely involves the perceptions and experiences of decision-makers in the workplace. The feasibility and sustainability of any major changes in the workplace, including but not limited to ascertaining a decent income for all, require the support of all stakeholders of an organization. It is also important for I/O psychologists to determine possible roots of resistance, especially among key decision-makers in the workplace that may come with shifting toward a socially just and worker-centered workplace. Future researchers may wish to explore the factors that will increase support for changes in the wage structures of employees experiencing precarity and the institutionalization of programs and activities that will complement policies on fair income. These studies may help to identify strategies and interventions that may allay the anxieties of top management about trading off costs of closing the capability gap against the benefits of fair income and less precarity for the organization but most especially for the employees.

Avenues to communicate research findings must be sought and optimized, not just to bridge research with practice but to influence policies across pay grades, industries, sectors, and societies. Building cases through rigorous research will strengthen I/O psychologists' credibility and hopefully muster support for their advocacies to promote decent work and resist precarity among organizational stakeholders.

References

Accenture. (n.d.). *Accenture work environment.* Retrieved February 20, 2023, from https://www.accenture.com/us-en/careers/life-at-accenture/work-environment

Allan, B. A., Autin, K. L., & Wilkins-Yel, K. G. (2021). Precarious work in the 21st century: A psychological perspective. *Journal of Vocational Behavior, 126*. https://doi.org/10.1016/j.jvb.2020.103491

Anand, S., & Sen, A. (2000). Human development and economic sustainability. *World Development, 28*, 2029–2049. https://doi.org/10.1016/S0305-750X(00)00071-1

Belser, P., & Sobeck, K. (2012). At what level should countries set their minimum wages? *International Journal of Labour Research, 4*, 105–127. https://labordoc.ilo.org/discovery/delivery/41ILO_INST:41ILO_V1/1269099580002676

Bernardo, A. B., Clemente, J. A. R., & Wang, T. Y. (2018). Working for a better future: Social mobility beliefs and expectations of Filipino migrant workers in Macau. *Australian Journal of Psychology, 70*(4), 350–360. https://doi.org/10.1111/ajpy.12209

Beus, J. M., McCord, M. A., & Zohar, D. (2016). Workplace safety: A review and research synthesis. *Organizational Psychology Review, 6*(4), 352–381. https://doi.org./10.1177/2041386615626243

Binder, M. (2014). Subjective well-being capabilities: Bridging the gap between the capability approach and subjective well-being research. *Journal of Happiness Studies, 15*(5), 1197–1217. https://doi.org/10.1007/s10902-013-9471-6

Blustein, D. L., Olle, C., Connors-Kellgren, A., & Diamonti, A. J. (2016). Decent work: A psychological perspective. *Frontiers in Psychology, 7*, 407. https://doi.org/10.3389/fpsyg.2016.00407

BPI. (n.d.). *Employees.* Retrieved February 20, 2023. https://www.bpi.com.ph/governance/stakeholder/employees

BusinessMirror. (2020, June 2). *CEMEX implements 50 new hygiene and safety protocols*. https://businessmirror.com.ph/2020/06/02/cemex-implements-50-new-hygiene-and-safety-protocols/

Carr, S. C. (2013). *Anti-poverty psychology*. Springer.

Carr, S. C., Parker, J., Arrowsmith, J., Haar, J., & Jones, H. (2017). Humanistic management and living wages: A case of compelling connections? *Humanistic Management Journal, 1*(2), 215–236. http:/doi.org/10.1007/s41463-016-0018-y

Carr, S. C., Parker, J., Arrowsmith, J., & Watters, P. A. (2016). The living wage: Theoretical integration and an applied research agenda. *International Labour Review, 155*(1), 1–24. https://doi.org/10.1111/j.1564-913X.2015.00029.x

Carr, S. C., Parker, J., Arrowsmith, J., Watters, P. A., & Jones, H. (2016). Can a 'living wage' springboard human capability? An exploratory study from New Zealand. *Labour & Industry, 26*(1), 24–39. http://doi.org/10.1080/10301763.2016.1152533

Cementina-Olpoc, M. (2013). People management: The Manila Water way. In A. L. P. Florentin, M. R. M. Hechanova, & M. Teng-Calleja (Eds.), *Strategic human resource management in the Philippines: Learning from the best* (pp. 16–38). People Management Association of the Philippines Center for Research and Publications.

Cerasoli, C. P., Nicklin, J. M., & Ford, M. T. (2014). Intrinsic motivation and extrinsic incentives jointly predict performance: A 40-year meta-analysis. *Psychological Bulletin, 140*(4), 980–1008. http://doi.org/10.1037/a0035661

Clark, D. A. (2005). Sen's capability approach and the many spaces of human well-being. *The Journal of Development Studies, 41*(8), 1339–1368. https://doi.org/10.1080/00220380500186853

Conrado and Ladislawa Alcantara Foundation. (n.d.). *About*. https://alcantarafoundation.wordpress.com/about/

Danish, R. Q., & Usman, A. (2010). Impact of reward and recognition on job satisfaction and motivation: An empirical study from Pakistan. *International Journal of Business and Management, 5*(2), 159–167. http://doi.org/10.5539/ijbm.v5n2p159

DHL (2022). *No matter what you do your contribution makes a difference*. https://www.dhl.com/ph-en/home/careers/working-here.html

Eby, L. T., Casper, W. J., Lockwood, A., Bordeaux, C., & Brinley, A. (2005). Work and family research in IO/OB: Content analysis and review of the literature (1980–2002). *Journal of Vocational Behavior, 66*(1), 124–197. https://doi.org/10.1016/j.jvb.2003.11.003

Gavilan, J. (2018). In numbers: What you need to know about the Philippine labor sector. *Rappler*. https://www.rappler.com/newsbreak/iq/201448-facts-labor-sector-philippines

Gonzales, J. (2018, April 16). *Introducing Food Forward: Challenging the virtue of 'free food' as an employee benefit*. https://www.sunstar.com.ph/article/428667

Good Jobs Institute. (2017a). *About the Good Jobs Institute*. http://goodjobsinstitute.org/about-us/

Good Jobs Institute. (2017b). *Good jobs transformation at Quest Diagnostics*. https://goodjobsinstitute.org/portfolio/good-job-strategy-at-quest-diagnostics/

Google Careers. (n.d.). *Benefits at Google*. Retrieved February 20, 2023. https://careers.google.com/how-we-care-for-googlers/

Great Place to Work Philippines. (2021). *Philippines best workplaces 2021: Honoring the heroism of Filipino workers and employees*. https://www.greatplacetowork.com.ph/philippines-best-workplaces-2021/

Hechanova, M. (2013). One Meralco: People powering up for a brighter Philippines. In A. L. P. Florentin, M. R. M. Hechanova, & M. Teng-Calleja (Eds.), *Strategic human resource management in the Philippines: Learning from the best* (pp. 179–201). People Management Association of the Philippines Center for Research and Publications.

Hechanova, M. R. M., & Go, J. M. C. (2018). Building a culture of workplace wellness: Perspectives from Philippine organizations. *International Journal of Research Studies in Psychology*, *7*(2), 71–83. https://doi.org/10.5861/ijrsp.2018.3010

Human Resources Online. (2018, June 28). *Mondelez Philippines on pioneering open and inclusive programs*. https://www.humanresourcesonline.net/mondelez-philippines-on-pioneering-open-and-inclusive-programs

IBON Foundation. (2019, April 14). *Family living wage for a family of five members in NCR*. https://www.ibon.org/family-living-wage-for-a-family-of-five-members-in-ncr/

Ilac, E. J. (2013). Putting people first in Petron. In A. L. P. Florentin, M. R. M. Hechanova, & M. Teng-Calleja (Eds.), *Strategic human resource management in the Philippines: Learning from the best* (pp. 61–83). People Management Association of the Philippines Center for Research and Publications.

Ilagan, J. R. A., Hechanova, M. R. M., Co, T. A. C., & Pleyto, V. J. Z. (2014). Bakit ka kumakayod? Developing a Filipino needs theory of motivation. *Philippine Journal of Psychology, 47*(1), 117–143.

Inocentes-Lombos, E. A. L. (2013). GlaxoSmithKline's prescription for organizational success. In A. L. P. Florentin, M. R. M. Hechanova, & M. Teng-Calleja (Eds.), *Strategic human resource management in the Philippines: Learning from the best* (pp. 100–121). People Management Association of the Philippines Center for Research and Publications.

International Labour Organization (ILO). (2011). *From precarious work to decent work. Policies and regulations to combat precarious.* https://www.ilo.org/wcmsp5/groups/public/—ed_dialogue/—actrav/documents/meetingdocument/wcms_164286.pdf

International Labour Organization (ILO). (2015). *How to define a minimum wage?* https://www.ilo.org/global/topics /wages/minimum-wages/definition/lang--en/index.htm

International Labour Organization (ILO). (2019a). *The working poor or how a job is no guarantee of decent living conditions.* https://ilo.org/wcmsp5/groups/public/—dgreports/—stat/documents/publication/wcms_696387.pdf

International Labour Organization (ILO). (2019b). *World employment and social outlook – Trends 2019.* https://www.ilo.org/wcmsp5/groups/public/—dgreports/—dcomm/—publ/documents/publication/wcms_670542.pdf

International Labour Organization (ILO). (2021a, January 25). ILO Monitor: COVID-19 and the world of work. (7th ed.). https://www.ilo.org/global/topics/coronavirus/impacts-and-responses/WCMS_767028/lang--en/index.htm

International Labour Organization (ILO). (2021b). *ILOSTAT database* [database]. https://ilostat.ilo.org/topics/working-poor/

International Labour Organization (ILO). (2021c). *The 2030 development agenda: Goal #8: Decent work and economic growth.* https://www.ilo.org/global/topics/sdg-2030/goal-8/lang--en/index.htm.

Jayachandran, S. (2020, June 18). How a raise for workers can be a win for everybody. *The New York Times*. https://www.nytimes.com/2020/06/18/business/coronavirus-minimum-wage-increase.html

Jimmieson, N. L., McKimmie, B. M., Hannm, R. L., & Gallagher, J. (2010). An investigation of the stress-buffering effects of social support in the occupational stress process as a function of team identification. *Group Dynamics: Theory, Research and Practice, 14*(4), 350–367. https://doi.org/10.1037/a0018631

Jocano, F. L. (2001). *Filipino worldview: Ethnography of local knowledge*. Punlad Research House.

Jollibee Foods Corporation. (n.d.). *Here in Jollibee, you beelong.* Retrieved February 20, 2023. https://www.jollibee.com.ph/Careers/

Kalleberg, A. L., Reskin, B. F., & Hudson, K. (2000). Bad jobs in America: Standard and nonstandard employment relations and job quality in the United States. *American Sociological Review, 65*(2), 256–278. https://doi.org/10.2307/2657440

Lee, K., & Allen, N. J. (2002). Organizational citizenship behavior and workplace deviance: The role of affect and cognitions. *Journal of Applied Psychology*, *87*(1), 131–142.

Living Wage Foundation. (n.d.-a). *About us*. https://www.livingwage.org.uk/living-wage-foundation

Living Wage Foundation. (n.d.-b). *The sustainable development goals and the living wage.* https://www.livingwage.org.uk/sites/default/files/19_09_24_LW_SDG_Report%20FINAL.pdf

Living Wage Movement Aotearoa New Zealand. (n.d.). *The living wage movement.* https://www.livingwage.org.nz/the_living_wage_movement

Lomoya, M. G., Pingol, M. B., & Teng-Calleja, M. (2015). Antecedents of job satisfaction and organizational citizenship behaviors among agency-hired blue-collar contractual workers in the Philippines. *Philippine Journal of Psychology*, *48*(1), 1–27.

Mahoney, C. (2021, February 11). Companies that have the most workers earning a living wage have higher returns on assets. *Just Capital.* https://justcapital.com/news/companies-that-have-the-most-workers-earning-a-living-wage-have-higher-returns-on-assets/

Martires, C. R. (1988). *Human resource management: Principles and practices*. National Bookstore.

Matilla-Santander, N., Ahonen, E., Albin, M., Baron, S., Bolíbar, M., Bosmans, K., Burström, B., Cuervo, I., Davis, L., Gunn, V., Håkansta, C., Hemmingsson, T., Hogstedt, C., Jonsson, J., Julià, M., Kjellberg, K., Kreshpaj, B., Lewchuk, W., Muntaner, C., … & Bodin, T. (2021). COVID-19 and precarious employment: Consequences of the evolving crisis. *International Journal of Health Services, 51*(2), 226–228. https://doi.org/10.1177/0020731420986694

Menguito, M. L. M. (2013). Strengthening human resources: The Toyota way. In A. L. P. Florentin, M. R. M. Hechanova, & M. Teng-Calleja (Eds.), *Strategic human resource management in the Philippines: Learning from the best* (pp. 144–178). People Management Association of the Philippines Center for Research and Publications.

Meralco. (n.d.). *Employee development and engagement.* Retrieved February 20, 2023. https://company.meralco.com.ph/corporate-governance/employee-development-and-engagement

MetroCebu News. (2019, September 26). *Accenture recognized as 'breastfeeding-friendly workplace' by the Philippine Pediatric Society.* https://metrocebu.news/accenture-recognized-as-breastfeeding-friendly-workplace-by-the-philippine-pediatric-society/

Milkovich, G., Newman, J., & Gerhart, B., (2014) *Compensation* (11th ed.). McGraw Hill.

Mohammad, J., Habib, F. Q., & Alias, M. A. (2011). Job satisfaction and organisational citizenship behaviour: An empirical study at higher learning institutions. *Asian Academy of Management Journal, 16*(2), 149–165.

National Anti-Poverty Commission. (2015). *Poverty count.* http://www.napc.gov.ph/?q=articles/poverty-count

Netemeyer, R. G., Boles, J. S., McKee, D. O., & McMurrian, R. (1997). An investigation into the antecedents of organizational citizenship behaviors in a personal selling context. The *Journal of Marketing, 61*(3), 85–98.

Nussbaum, M. C. (2011). *Creating capabilities: The human development approach.* Belknap Press.

Ocampo, A. C., Mansukhani, R., Mangrobang, B., & Juan, A. M. (2013). Influences and perceived impact of spirituality on Filipino adolescents. *Philippine Journal of Psychology, 46* (1), 89–113.

Organ, D. W. (1988). *Organizational citizenship behavior: The good soldier syndrome.* Lexington Books.

Organ, D. W., & Konovsky, M. A. (1989). Cognitive versus affective determinants of organizational citizenship behavior. *Journal of Applied Psychology, 74*(1), 157–164.

Ozeren, E. (2014). Sexual orientation discrimination in the workplace: A systematic review of literature. *Procedia-Social and Behavioral Sciences, 109*, 1203–1215. https://doi.org/10.1016/j.sbspro.2013.12.613

Podsakoff, P. M., MacKenzie, S. B., Paine, J. B., & Bachrach, D. G. (2000). Organizational citizenship behaviors: A critical review of the theoretical and empirical literature and suggestions for future research. *Journal of Management, 26*(3), 513–563.

Presbitero, A. A. (2008). Building organizational culture: The Unilab experience. In M. R. M. Hechanova, & E. P. Franco (Eds.), *Leading Philippine organizations in a changing world: Research and best practices* (pp. 127–138). Ateneo de Manila University Press.

Quest Diagnostics (n.d.). *What we do.* Accessed February 20, 2023. https://www.questdiagnostics.com/our-company/what-we-do

Racelis, M. (2016). Kahit dukha'y dakila! Socio-cultural perspectives on poverty and well-being. In C. D. Ortigas, & M. Racelis (Eds.), *Overcoming poverty: Multidisciplinary perspectives principles and practices* (pp. 131–162). C&E Publishing.

Red, C. L., & Teng-Calleja, M. (2021). Examining the relationship between labor law compliance and employee perceptions, attitudes and behaviors. *Employee Responsibilities and Rights Journal, 33*, 337–357. https://doi.org/10.1007/s10672-021-09369-z

Rey, A. (2020, September 29). In Duterte's 2021 budget, Filipinos are on their own. *Rappler.* https://www.rappler.com/newsbreak/in-depth/filipinos-welfare-employment-education-duterte-2021-national-budget/

San Miguel Corporation. (2022). *San Miguel Corporation Human Resources.* https://www.sanmiguel.com.ph/page/human-resources. No longer accessible.

Sanchez, J (2013). Pushing for lasting and deep transformation: The PLDT story. In A. L. P. Florentin, M. R. M. Hechanova, & M. Teng-Calleja (Eds.), *Strategic human resource management in the Philippines: Learning from the best* (pp. 84–99). People Management Association of the Philippines Center for Research and Publications.

Searle, R. H., & McWha-Hermann, I. (2021). "Money's too tight (to mention)": A review and psychological synthesis of living wage research. *European Journal of Work and Organizational Psychology, 30*(3), 428–443. https://doi.org/10.1080/1359432X.2020.1838604

Sen, A. (1993). Capability and well-being. In M. C. Nussbaum & A. Sen (Eds.), *The quality of life* (pp. 30–53). Oxford University Press.

Sen, A. (1999). *Development as freedom*. Random House.

Seubert, C., Hopfgartner, L., & Glaser, J. (2021). Living wages, decent work, and need satisfaction: An integrated perspective. *European Journal of Work and Organizational Psychology, 30*(6), 808–823. https://doi.org/10.1080/1359432X.2021.1966094

Shell. (n.d.). *Supporting our LGBT talent at Shell.* https://www.shell.com.ph/careers/diversity-inclusion/lgbt-talent-at-shell.html

Sofitel Manila. (2019, May). *Sofitel Philippine Plaza Manila is the first accredited Mother-Baby Friendly Hotel Workplace in Metro Manila.* https://www.sofitelmanila.com/news/sofitel-philippine-plaza-manila-is-the-first-accredited-mother-baby-friendly-hotel-workplace-in-metro-manila/ No longer accessible.

Sycip, L., Asis, M. M., & Luna, E. (2000). *The measurement of Filipino well-being: Technical report.* University of The Philippines Center for Integrative and Development Studies.

Sycip, L., Asis, M. M., & Luna, E. (2008). The measurement of Filipino well-being: Findings from the field. In C. J. Paz (Ed.), *Ginhawa, kapalaran, dalamhati: Essays on well-being, opportunity/destiny and anguish* (pp. 13–29). University of the Philippines Press.

TaskUs. (2021, June 4). *TaskUs's Wellness and Resiliency initiatives featured on PH's Radyo5 program for Mental Health Awareness Month.* https://www.taskus.com/news-feature/taskuss-wellness-and-resiliency-initiatives-featured-on-phs-radyo5-program-for-mental-health-awareness-month/

Teng-Calleja, M., Baquiano, M., & Montiel, C. (2015). From "Good day" to "Sign here": Norms shaping negotiations within a face culture. *Negotiation and Conflict Management Research, 8*(4), 228–242. https://doi.org/10.1111/ncmr.12060

Teng-Calleja, M., Clemente, J. A., Menguito, M. L., & Bertulfo, D. J. (2021). Toward the pursuit of what people value: Determining a living wage based on capability gaps, *International Perspectives in Psychology, 10*(2), 59–73. https://doi.org/10.1027/2157-3891/a000007

Teng-Calleja, M., Hechanova, M. R. M., Sabile, P. R., & Villasanta, A. P. V. O. (2020). Building organization and employee resilience in disaster contexts. *International Journal of Workplace Health Management, 13*(4), 393–411. https://doi.org/10.1108/IJWHM-09-2019-0122

Teng-Calleja, M., Menguito, M. L., & Clemente, J. A. R. (2021). *Capability gaps: What it is and why it matters in the workplace*. Institute of Philippine Culture.

Ton, Z. (2017, December 1). How to build a business on good jobs. *HBR.* https://hbr.org/2017/12/how-to-build-a-business-on-good-jobs

Ulrich, D. (1996). *Human resource champions: The next agenda for adding value and delivering results*. Harvard Business School Press.

Union Bank of the Philippines. (n.d.). *Careers.* Retrieved February 20, 2023. https://www.unionbankph.com/ubcareers

United Nations. (2019). *Sustainable Development Goals: Promote inclusive and sustainable economic growth, employment and decent work for all.* https://www.un.org/sustainabledevelopment/economic-growth/

United Nations Development Programme. (2015). *Human development report 2015: Work for human development.* https://www.undp.org/publications/human-development-report-2015

Whitman, D. S., Caleo, S., Carpenter, N. C., Horner, M. T., & Bernerth, J. B. (2012). Fairness at the collective level: A meta-analytic examination of the consequences and boundary conditions of organizational justice climate. *Journal of Applied Psychology, 97*(4), 776–791. https://doi.org/10.1037/a0028021

9

SUFFICIENCY LIVING WAGE IN THAILAND

Exploring Buddhist Influences on Sustainable Livelihoods and Happiness

Dusadee Yoelao Intraprasert, Kanu Priya Mohan, and Piyada Sombatwattana

Introduction

All members of the United Nations have adopted the 17 Sustainable Development Goals (SDGs) as drivers of development across the world and are striving to varying degrees to achieve these goals by 2030 (Carr, Hodgetts et al., Chapter 1; Saltzman et al., Chapter 2). However, progress is being impacted negatively by critical concerns, including the impacts of climate change and the COVID-19 pandemic: both of which are affecting lives and livelihoods. This chapter introduces the concept of a *sufficiency living wage* (SLW) and we discuss how this could contribute toward sustainable livelihoods in these challenging times. Furthermore, we explore linkages between living wages (LW) and sustainable development in the context of Thailand.

Once these initial foundations for the chapter are established, our attention turns to the influence of Buddhist teachings on Thai ways of living and understandings of a sustainable LW. Such a wage is positioned as a means of promoting not only basic material standards of living but as also facilitating worker pathways to happiness. This broader cultural perspective is contrasted with the more instrumentalist perspective that is hegemonic within market economies. Next, the SLW is considered in relation to fostering human capabilities and efforts to realize the SDGs. Included are details on the specific meaning of SLW and how it can be measured. This chapter concludes with a discussion of the policy implications of such a wage for Thailand and other countries as well as considerations for an implementation strategy.

DOI: 10.4324/9781003440444-11

LW and Its Contribution toward Sustainable Living

Minimum wages (MWs) have been set in many countries in recognition of important links between work and income and poverty and wellbeing, and as a basic social safety net. Originally, such MWs were intended to be set at LW levels and as a means of lifting people out of poverty and reducing state dependency (Levin-Waldman, 2000). However, even in countries where the original MW was set at LW levels, the value of the MW has been eroded over time and this has contributed to growing in-work poverty in many jurisdictions (Schulten & Luebker, 2019). Recent promotion of the LW is a response to such situations and an effort to ensure that if people engage in gainful employment, they should in all fairness be able to support themselves and their families and to participate in civic life.

Most countries have incorporated MW policies to ensure a minimum level of payment for work and to ensure "a just and equitable share of the fruits of progress to all" (ILO, 2017, p. 1). As noted by the International Labor Organization, MWs have been set by 90% of the member states, but compliance still needs careful monitoring (ILO, 2017). Whether MW policies are changed or not, the concept of the LW seems more beneficial in terms of leading sustainable positive changes for the world. Our concern in this chapter is with the LW and its potential benefit for workers, communities, organizations, and society in Thailand.

The agenda for LW has gained impetus over the last few decades. This development is linked to issues of sustainability and positive and inclusive outcomes at multiple levels, including enhancing the wellbeing of individual workers and communities and providing productivity gains for organizations. For many scholars, the LW offers one mechanism to springboard capabilities and improve the quality of life of workers and also their families (Carr et al., 2017, 2018, 2019). As noted, the LW is becoming more of a necessity since it seeks to provide more than a basic income for workers and also enable civic participation and the ability to save against unforeseen shocks in the future (Carr, Hodgetts et al., Chapter 1). Thus, the LW, which is more than the MW, has been noted as a monetary threshold that can also promote worker empowerment, pride, and job satisfaction, as well as addressing issues of wage fairness, and thereby overall life satisfaction (Carr et al., 2018, 2019; Hu & Carr, 2020). These outcomes have also been noted to have positive impact on classic organizational concerns regarding job commitment, retention, and productivity (Carr et al., 2019).

Furthermore, the LW has been positioned as a key mechanism for promoting at least three of the UN's SDGs: SDG-1 (reducing poverty), SDG-8 (decent work and economic growth), and SDG-10 (reducing inequalities; The Living Income n.d.). Thus, as noted by researchers (Carr et al., 2018, 2019; Meyer & Maleka, Chapter 7), the LW aligns well with the tenets of psychology regarding sustainability and could contribute toward the achievement of the SDGs, through decent work and sustainable economic development. According to a report by the Living Wage Foundation UK (2019), the LW has a wider impact on other SDGs as well since the extra money can be used by workers for children's education (SDG-4, quality education), taking care of their health and wellbeing (SDG-3, good health, and wellbeing), and saving for future, which in turn could reduce inequalities, and so on.

The Context of Thailand

In this chapter, we showcase a discussion regarding the LW in Thailand, a fast-emerging Southeast Asian economy that "aspires to become a high-income economy by 2037" (Organisation for Economic Co-operation and Development [OECD], 2019). According to the World Bank (2022), the success of Thailand's economic development has been noted along with impressive recent reductions in poverty. Economic growth increased at "an average annual rate of 7.5% in the boom years of 1960–1996 and 5% during 1999–2005 following the Asian Financial Crisis" (World Bank, 2022). However, since 2015 there has been stagnation in economic development: a situation exacerbated by the COVID-19 pandemic (World Bank, 2022).

Thailand adopted MW policy in1972 and there have been successive hikes in the amount over subsequent years; the last being in 2020 (Ministry of Labor, 2020). Currently there is a debate going on nationally regarding an increase to the MW to ensure that low-income and precarious workers are better supported (Bangkok Post, 2022). However, as noted by several researchers, the MW policy has had mixed results in reducing economic inequalities and uplifting the well-being of workers (Attakrit, 2015; Kunadilokkamon et al., 2014; Lathapipat & Poggi, 2016), mostly because the effectiveness of law enforcement has been questionable and not the same across all sectors such as SMEs (Attakrit, 2015). Relatedly, this chapter examines the rising need for not only increases in the MW but also the introduction of an LW in Thailand. In recommending such an initiative, it is important to consider the meaning and value of an LW from the perspective of Buddhist teachings and practices, which influence the country's economic development strategy and inform common understandings of work and happiness among Thai people.

Buddhist Economy and Happiness

Given the prominence of Buddhist teaching in Thailand, it should be not a surprise that discussions around the economy also include happiness and personal growth. In this section, we aim to explore the links between Buddhist beliefs, a Buddhist economy, and happiness in the context of Thailand. More specifically, we attend to links between Buddhist teachings and the Thai way of living, contrast Buddhist and market economies, and link this discussion to the promotion of an economic approach for Thailand that includes an LW.

The Influence of Buddhist Teachings on the Thai Way of Living

A vast majority of Thai people practice the Buddhist religion: 94.6% as reported recently (Thailand Board of Investment, 2022). Correspondingly, Buddhist teachings and practices have had a deep impact on Thai society, at personal (psychological), sociocultural, and national policy levels, including the direction and character of our economic development (Winzer et al., 2018; Winzer & Gray, 2019). Further, research by Winzer et al. (2018) showed that the observance of the five precepts of Buddhism, practices such as meditation, and commitment to humanistic values were associated with greater levels of happiness among Thai people. It has been noted by researchers that unlike the Western concept of happiness that is linked to material possession, Buddhism focuses on inner happiness that comes from wisdom and harmonious relations with others (Kittiprapas, 2018).

Happiness is a very important concept because it is a core Buddhist goal for human life. The meaning of happiness has been studied by philosophers and psychologists within the Western cannon. For example, Aristotle viewed happiness as living in a manner that actively expresses excellence of character or virtue. It has been argued from within this tradition that happiness is not simply a psychological phenomenon but is also a phenomenon that invokes issues of ethics (Haybron, 2000). Psychologists have defined happiness in terms of three different components: psychological happiness, prudential happiness, and perfectionist happiness (Sirgy, 2012, 2021). Buddhism presents a richer and more nuanced understanding of happiness as a phenomenon.

The word *sukha* is used in Buddhist teachings with reference to the concept of happiness. The generic meaning of sukha is a fulfillment of a person's needs or desires toward flourishing and living a good life. From the teachings of Buddha, "all things are rooted in desire"; this means that all human engagements have their origin in desire (Payutto, 2019, p. 856). Desires are divided into two kinds: firstly, the negative kind, such as desire to obtain, to seize, to become, to possess, or to destroy; and secondly, the positive kind, as the wish to act, to engage, to improve, to do good, and to reach a state of virtue or completion. From the perspective of desires, people with positive desires will experience happiness in creating the causes for prosperity for individuals and relating with others, while those with negative desires will experience happiness in consuming the fruits of prosperity. *Sukha* has three levels; the lowest level is the satisfaction of acquiring what one needs or desires; the next level is the happiness that comes from being a better self, giving to others, and contributing to society; and the highest level of happiness is derived from being emancipated or liberated from all impurities of mind or defilements, including *lobha* (greed), *ahirikaṃ* (shame), and *dosa* (hate). These three levels of happiness were known in Pali as *samissukha* (related to sensory happiness), *niramissukha* (linked to positive state of mind), and *niramistarasukha* or *nippansukha* (linked to the state of bliss from meditation) accordingly. The first two levels of *Sukha* can be achieved by ordinary persons, but the last one can only be achieved by a Buddhist saint or monk (Payutto, 2006). The highest level is also described as enlightenment; "[in] enlightenment as a resultant state, we are primarily referring to the enlightened quality of purity—the perfected state where all negativities and limitations have been purified" (Dalai Lama, 2002). The level of *sukha* a person seeks will influence their behavior, and action toward others and environments.

To develop *sukha* from a lower to higher level requires education of the spirit, *lamrim* (stages of the path texts) teaching and training one's mind (Dalai Lama, 2002; Payutto, 2016). Many examples of Buddhist education have been proposed. First, the threefold training: training of moral discipline, mental concentration, and wisdom. The main purpose of such training is to achieve wisdom or *paññа*: the ability to understand everything in its own nature. If the mind has been trained to a point to be able to understand that there is no such a thing as the "self," it is at the point wher*e* paññа has been cultivated and misunderstanding will gradually disappear. The mind will gradually be freed from all defilements and realize a higher state of happiness. Relatedly, the true sukha in Buddhadhamma (Buddhist way) is more associated with mental development than with any form of acquisition (Puntasen, 2007). Another key proposition here relates to the practices of the four noble truths and the noble eightfold path. The first noble truth is that suffering exists; the second is to look deeply and find the causes of suffering; the third is the cessation of behaviors that cause suffering; and the fourth points to the pathways that lead to this cessation and toward well-being. From the perspective of the four noble truths, Magnuson (2007) suggests an analysis of and reorientating of the US free market or neoliberal economic system to create a new human community and ecology of economic wellbeing. He proposed creating a *mindful economy* by restructuring key economic institutions and redefining the structures of ownership, the relationships between workers and managers, how consumers and producers interact, the nature and functions of financial systems and financial instruments, public policy, ideas of what "fairness" and "justice" mean, as well as ecology and people's relationships to their natural environment. He also suggested using the four truths to analyze economic systems, including (1) there are system conditions that give rise to pathology embedded in the economy of the United States; (2) these conditions are largely, but not exclusively, rooted in the logic and culture of capitalism itself; (3) there is much people have done, and can do, to change the conditions of the system by building alternative institutions; and (4) there is a pathway for changing system conditions. In addition, there will be three principles of *rightness*, including (1) social justice, equity, and democracy; (2) ecological sustainability; and (3) rights to enough stability to guide economic activities. Such a reorientation would place the needs of human beings and their flourishing as a foundational concern over and above that of profit generation and wealth extraction by elites, which is the primary function of neoliberal economies. Such economies can be characterized as involving minimal government regulation in a system of exchange that is designed to generate increased material wealth for the wealthy and is associated with increased inequities in the distribution of resources.

Relatedly, evaluating development after practicing Buddhist teachings involves four dimensions of outcome, also called *bhavana* in Pali, which include physical relations, human relations, ethics and morals, and development of wisdom. A lay person who practices Buddhist ways to achieve happiness should demonstrate an awareness of their needs and desire at the right level; caring for other people, their community, and their environment; and the ability to evaluate the good and bad aspects of their activities (Payutto, 2001, 2019). It is also important that the economic and work foundations are in place to enable opportunities for such flourishing and the cultivation of happiness.

Comparison between Buddhist and Market Economies

While the hegemony of the market or neoliberal economy shapes the activities of the modern world, we can observe many dangers and difficulties such as increased income disparities, environmental deterioration, poverty, and conflicts. Thus, we are looking for alternative economic arrangements that bring peace and sustainability to our world. A Buddhist economy may offer a better option for humanity (Ng, 2020; Payutto, 2019; Schumacher, 1973, 2011). Table 9.1 displays some of the key differences in terms of the four dimensions between the Buddhist and free market economies. In applying the concepts of the Buddhist economy to the processes of production, consumption, and investment, we may be able to help the future generations and society.

Buddhist Economy for the "Right" Economy, Work, and Consumption

Learning and practices in the first three levels of happiness/sukha will enable a person to transcend to true happiness. The steps to achieve this happiness through the Buddhist teachings are often referred to as the eightfold path. This path comprises three aggregates: firstly, the wisdom factor comprising right view and thought; secondly, the morality factor comprising right speech, action, livelihood; and lastly, the concentration factor comprising right effort,

TABLE 9.1 Elements of Buddhist vs. Market Economies

Elements	*Buddhist Economy*	*Market Economy*
Principles of reasoning and motivation	• Right consumption (consuming with awareness of others' needs and of nature) • Freedom from self-harm and from oppression of others • Economy as a support to human development and quality of life • Harmony with human nature • Four noble truths, noble eightfold path • Less is more • Small is beautiful • Adequate/appropriate technology	• Rationality • Maximizing profits • Minimizing expenses • Optimizing economic results • More is more • Bigger is better • Endless technological race
Variables	• Moral discipline • Mindfulness, perseverance, patience • Wisdom • Noble eightfold path (e.g., right livelihood) • Compassion, generosity, nonviolence, genuine care, no-harm, equity • Price is not sufficient information for responsible decision-making • Tangible things as well as intangible qualities and values	• Utility, profits, expenses, consumption • Work/employment • investment • Marginal rate of change, utility, productivity, efficiency • Bias toward measurable quantities • Price contains sufficient information to disengage moral responsibilities • "Market" size and share
Behavioral forces	• Cessation of suffering • Compassion and wisdom • Mind-driven by each individual's choices • Spiritual advancement as the ends • Overall wellbeing	• Greed/desire, fear, ignorance • Self-interest • Market-driven by the invisible hand • Economic welfare as the ends • Material wellbeing
Relationships	• Collaboration, cooperation, win-win relationships as ends in themselves	Competition, zero-sum game, win-lose • Instrumental use relationships as means

Note: Adapted from Ng (2020) and Payutto (2016).

mindfulness, and concentration. Each of these is described as "right," but not in the typical English sense of the word "right" as being "good" or "correct." In the Buddhist sense, "right" refers to whole, complete, or perfect (Ng, 2020), and truly beneficial, healthy, or wholesome as through our awareness we come to see what is beneficial to the community, the environment, and ourselves (Magnuson, 2007, p. 277). Correspondingly, "right livelihood" is a crucial element within Buddhist economics. This concept is central to notions of the acquisition and expenditure of wealth. Right livelihood involves relinquishing wrong livelihood and earning one's living righteously and persevering in maintaining an upright livelihood and not harming others. Acquisition of wealth is in righteous ways, without abusing or harming others. Moreover, the expenditure of wealth is for one's happiness and the happiness of those for whom one is responsible, for charity, and for meritorious purposes (Payutto, 2019, p. 1255).

This concept of right livelihood is central to notions of the meaning of work as a kind of utility that enables human beings who engage in it to develop their personal faculties, to overcome their ego centeredness by joining in shared endeavors and tasks with others, and bringing goods and services needed to contribute to the common good and become enlightened (Schumacher, 1973). The morality factor of the eightfold path is important as it establishes a stable and disciplined environment for the worker's activities and provides focus and commitment. It is important for each nation state to establish proper policies to support and promote morality in society and promote economic policies for reducing poverty. Similarly at the organizational level, managers and employers should practice moral and virtuous conduct in their roles, which may include organizing work according to their employees' capabilities, providing wages and bonuses appropriate to their work and living situations, providing welfare and security, sharing profits, and providing days off and holidays (Payutto, 2019, pp. 1277–1281).

Working is an important activity for economic production, but what work constitutes and how it is understood differs between free market and Buddhist economics. These differences in understandings of work relate to the two kinds of desire that are central to the Buddhist tradition: the desires for the lower and higher levels of sukha or happiness. In the case of the desire for higher happiness (which includes the desire for self-development and the development of human potentialities), the results of the work itself provide satisfaction. If, however, the work is done with the lower level desire for material things, then the results of the work itself are merely the conditions needed to acquire the things that one desires. The difference between the two desires as related to work lies in that in the first case work is perceived as a potentially satisfying activity, and in the second as a necessary chore.

For work to become right work from this perspective, we must have a love for the job and a thirst for the knowledge and development that it provides. These orientations are important for people to commit themselves to the work with dedication and determination and, rather than as seeing it as simply a means of providing for lower level material desires and distractions. It is important that through work, people are afforded and gain opportunities for personal growth. This perspective on right work does not ignore material issues such as money and the provision of adequate resources so that workers and their families can participate in the social and cultural life of Thailand. When the pay and conditions of the work are right, the worker, the organization they work for, and the broader community and economy can also benefit through the worker's positive perception of the job and their increased commitment.

So far we have considered the concept of right work and begun to use this concept to extend and broaden contemporary understandings of the LW and the benefits of decent work. Relatedly, Buddhism is full of teachings referring to *the middle way*, *the right amount*, and *knowing moderation*; all these terms may be considered synonyms for the idea of balance and equilibrium (Payutto, 2006) in decent work. According to free market economics, the term consumption refers to the use of goods and services to answer wants and needs, and to provide higher levels of satisfaction. However, in the Buddhist view, when consumption leads to the enhancement of higher sukha (by being a better self and giving for others and society), then that consumption is said to be *right consumption.* The key point here is that an LW and decent work involves not only being able to buy and consume goods and services. Decent work is a task that not only consumes one's time but also enables one to consume that time agentively to cultivate in oneself a better being who contributes positively to those around them and to society in general. LW from decent work can enable Buddhist consumption practices such as moderation and mutual care. Knowing moderation in this way also means knowing the optimum amount: how much is "just right." Knowing the right amount of consumption refers to an awareness of that optimum point where the enhancement of higher happiness coincides with the experience of satisfaction in contributing to self and others. The reasons and purposes of consumption must be reflected on wisely before something is consumed. For example, the purpose of eating is to sustain our lives, for the health of the body, to eradicate painful feelings of hunger that have arisen, and to prevent new ailments arising (e.g., from overeating). We eat in moderation to be able to carry on our lives with ease. We eat so that the energy we derive from the food can support a noble and happy life. Whenever we consume anything, we should understand the meaning of what we are doing in this way and consume in such a way as to experience results that conform to that purpose, taking just the right amount, or the "middle way." The same imperatives apply to work.

To become a person practicing right consumption, one should be aware of what one consumes, the triggers for the consumption, and the state of mind when consuming, along with the consequences to oneself, others, and the environment of our consumption. Thus, economic systems need to contribute to the development of human potentialities and enabling humanity to lead noble lives and enjoy increasingly higher and sustainable levels of happiness.

SLW and Human Capabilities

We now present some foundations from our previous research for a new perspective on the LW from Thailand. To explore the LW from psychosocial and religiocultural perspectives, we designed mixed methods research to develop a new construct of an *SLW*. The aim was to find out how workers in Thailand integrate their need for an LW within the framework of the Buddhist sufficiency economy philosophy (SEP) (Yoelao et al., 2019, 2021). Let us first share an overview of the SEP.

The SEP, Linkages with Buddhist Teachings, and the SDGs

As shared in the previous section, Buddhist teachings have a profound influence on the Thai ethos. In fact, these teachings have been the underpinnings of economic development since the adoption of the SEP in Thailand in 1997 (Puntasen, 2017). The SEP was first presented by the late King Rama IX of Thailand, as interconnected guiding principles for the Thai people to follow in order to emerge from the financial crisis at that time (Mongsawad and Thongpakde, 2016). There are three interlocking principles of SEP (Barua & Tejativaddhana, 2019). *Moderation* involves avoiding extremes and overindulgence. *Reasonableness* involves making rational decisions and being able to understand the causal connection between actions and consequences. *Self-immunity* involves the ability to cope with the likely impacts arising from future change. To practice these three principles and strive toward sufficiency, two conditions are necessary. These are *knowledge* and *morality/virtue*, where knowledge is simply "what is known" and can be developed; while virtues are the "positive values of a person" that could be inherited, learned, or emerge through discernment (Barua & Tejativaddhana, 2019). The term "sufficiency" means that when a situation arises, moderation, reasonableness, and self-immunity can be applied while practicing the virtues (such as persevering, and being tolerant and trustworthy) and applying knowledge (using proper understanding about the situation to make informed choices). These practices can enable one to develop resilience and provide protection from the impacts of internal and external changes (Office of the National Economic and Social Development Board, 2007, as cited in Mongsawad & Thongpakde, 2016).

Through subsequent strategic planning and development policies (Puntasen, 2017), the SEP has been seen to influence Thai people's ways of living at the personal, communal, and national levels (Kittiprapas, 2018, 2020). Studies have validated the positive influences of SEP, such as enhanced social capital and welfare among community-based organizations (Amornsiriphong & Piemyat, 2012), and enhanced self-immunity among students who practice SEP (Choochom, 2015), to name a couple. In their metaanalysis of research done on SEP in Thailand, Barua and Tejativaddhana (2019) synthesized the research and reported several areas of impact from practicing SEP, including economics, society, the environment, health, education, and the wellbeing of the Thai people.

Mongsawad and Thongpakde (2016) noted that the SEP has provided an alternative path to development that is different from the free-market economic focus. The authors noted that SEP recognizes the importance of trade and globalization, whilst also acknowledging the risks of "free" trade. These risks are taken into consideration in the strategic planning for SEP and mitigated through application of the three principles of moderation, reasonableness, and self-immunity. Furthermore, SEP encourages people to avoid greed and overindulgence whilst still pursuing economic development in the current epoch of globalization (Barua & Tejativaddhana, 2019). In this regard, Puntasen (2017) has noted that SEP is like a "bridge" for understanding the application of Buddhist teachings, especially a "middle path," to economic development.

SEP philosophy provides a sustainable approach to economic development that is centered on human wellbeing. This is important, especially when there is growing concern for economic crises and monetary fluctuations, natural resource depletion, environmental degradation, endemic poverty, and drastic income inequalities (Barua & Tejativaddhana, 2019; Mongsawad & Thongpakde, 2016). In recent research, Jitsuchon (2019) has highlighted how SEP provides an alternative way to achieve sustainable development since it provides a holistic perspective that includes consideration for both physical (material) and spiritual wellbeing, with development as a multidimensional endeavor that includes communities and voluntary participation as vital factors on the path to sustainable development for all.

The Meaning of SLW

Keeping in view the value of SEP in the Thai context, our mixed methods research was developed to explore how the indigenous SEP approach relates to efforts to achieve an LW for workers. First, qualitative research was conducted to develop the definition of the SLW (Yoelao et al., 2019). The participants in this research component were 12 blue-collar workers who worked at a riverside resort in Thailand: specially selected since it had won an award for implementing the SEP guidelines within the tourism industry. These workers were invited to participate in interviews because they were identified by the research team as "workers who had absorbed the concept of SEP in their work," but who were not yet paid an LW. The workers shared how, if they were to earn an LW, they could fulfill additional needs in their current and future lives and better provide for themselves and their families, for example, by buying a vehicle for a part-time occupation, caring for children and parents, repaying loans, and engaging in charitable endeavors that speak to personal growth through service to others.

Next, we asked participants to think about SEP in relation to an LW and how they would use it. Participants responded in a manner reflective of key Buddhist principles relating to service toward self and others whilst considering issues of sustainability in terms of preparedness for shocks. As one participant stated:

> [People] should think deeply about how to allocate their income to serve themselves and their families' basic daily needs, for investment, and saving for uncertainty or…be happy with whatever you have. Not spending on unnecessary things…know how to save money…[I] hoped for a happy family and that was not something that came from getting more wage or the things that could be bought from the higher wages.
>
> *(Yoelao et al., 2019)*

This extract also reflects the mindfulness of participants regarding their consumption and its relationship to a possible LW.

From the interview accounts, we concluded that the SLW could be understood as a psychological construct with two main dimensions: *sufficiency of wages* (measured in terms of cognitive and behavioral components), and *psychological utility* (measured in terms of cognitive and affective components). The cognitive dimension of the SLW concerns beliefs about spending wages according to the three tenets of SEP. As one participant expressed: "I believe in not spending extravagantly," which relates to the moderation aspect of SEP. The behavioral dimension is linked to the actions taken by the participants based on SEP. One participant stated, "I wouldn't spend the money more than what I have…Need to be economical so I can keep on living," representing moderation in action. Psychological utility (measured in terms of cognitive and affective components) concerns the positive feelings about the utility of LW comprising two dimensions: the tangible and the intangible. The tangible is measurable; as one of the participants said, "I'm willing to tell anyone how much money I earn," while the intangible shows the affective dimension; for instance, a participant expressed, "I am happy to have money to support my parents every month." In the next phase of our research, quantitative items were generated from the qualitative survey to develop a measure for an SLW and to test the extent to which these two main dimensions were evident in a broader sample of workers.

The Measurement of SLW

In this phase of our research, we developed the SLW scale, which is a 22-item, self-report scale, with items measured on a 5-point Likert scale, ranging from 1 (*strongly disagree)* to 5 (*strongly agree)* (Yoelao et al., 2021). To test the psychometric properties of the SLW scale, data was collected from 428 workers (both white- and blue-collar) from various organizations in Thailand. The results showed that the scale had good psychometric quality.

Furthermore, exploratory factor analysis of the SLW scale was conducted, and three distinct factors were identified. Additional analyses showed high internal reliability (using Cronbach's coefficient Alpha) for all the three factors of the SLW scale: Perceived Psychological Utility (PPU) (α = .87), Moderate Consumption (MC) (α = .78), and Living with Self-Immunity (LSI) (α = .76). Each factor of the SLW scale is further described:

- LSI: shows linkages to the SEP principle of self-immunity. This is clear from some of the items, e.g., "I believe that I have enough money for the security of my family and children."
- PPU: shows the cognitive and affective dimensions of the construct in terms of the perception of the utility of the increased wages, e.g., "I am glad that I have money to support my parents every month," and "The wages I earn make me feel proud of myself."
- MC: links to the SEP principle of moderation, e.g., "I spend only as much as I have," and "I save some money every month."

We conducted additional research to evaluate the role of an SLW as a predictor of work and life capabilities (WLC). The sample was 391 white- and blue-collar workers in Thailand. The findings from this research confirmed the positive significant effects of all three dimensions of an SLW on WLC (Mohan et al., 2023). Furthermore, this research verified the hypothesized role of an SLW as a mediator of the relationship between pay fairness (wage justice) and WLC. Results showed that an SLW could enhance the perceived value of pay fairness in both WLC. The concept of an SLW is linked to Buddhist practices that are commonly engaged in by the research participants. We concluded that workers could achieve not only material happiness from their jobs and increased wages, but a deeper inner happiness grounded in the enhanced capabilities resulting from being able to live a meaningful life, such as the ability to help others.

Recommendations for SLW in Thailand

LW Policy Implications in Thailand

Leveraging off decent work to realize human potential within the SEP system requires us to consider issues such as rates of pay and the setting of minimum and LW. Official wage determinations made through tripartite wage setting processed started in Thailand in 1973 and have been regularly reviewed since. The concept of the MW is applied according with International Labor Organization agreements that are foundational to many Thai policies such as The Minimum Wage-Fixing Machinery Convention No. 26, The Minimum Wage Fixing Machinery (Agriculture) Convention No. 99, and Minimum Wage Fixing Convention No. 131. Following The Announcement of the Revolutionary Council No. 103 (dated March 16, 1972), the National Wage Committee, comprising representative of three parties—government agencies, employees, and employers—has the duty of considering and proposing the amount of the MW (Labor Economy Division, 2021). This is applied using the same methods for wage setting as used in other countries (Kristensen & Cunningham, 2006; Thompson, 2016). The wage that is set is based on the principle of providing assurance of a basic level of remuneration for unskilled laborers who have little-to-no chance of bargaining effectively with their employers for fair wages (Ministry of Labor, 2022).

The first set rate of 12 Thai Baht (US$0.035) per day, for 4 provinces: Bangkok, Samutprakarn, Nonthaburi, and Pathumthani, was announced in 1973. On October 1, 1977, enforcement of the new rate was expanded to every province. Rate adjustments have mostly been announced annually but are not compulsory. Adjustments also depend on current economic conditions, with some adjustments being made once a year, in some years, and no change in other years (Thailand Development Research Institute, 2014). The Labor Protection Act 1998 further adjusted the minimum-wage determination process and moved it from a centralized to a decentralized process for establishing official provincial MWs (Thailand Development Research Institute, 2014). Each regional subcommittee uses local economic and social data to calculate the MW for each province. They propose the rate to the National Wage Committee, Ministry of Labor, and the House of Parliament consecutively for approvals (Labor Economy Division, 2022). At present, MWs around the country are set between 313 and 336 Thai Baht per day (about $9.13–9.80; Ministry of Labor, 2020).

The Labor Commission of the House of Parliament has studied and provided data that support the necessity of changing the wage determination method outlined above from a focus on an MW to an LW (Theeraksoponphong, 2022). This shift was recommended because our study surfaced problems in current pay determination processes. For example, the method to calculate the MW is based on macroeconomic data like the rate of inflation, cost of living index, and so forth. These sources of data do not really represent individuals' cost of living. Therefore, reliance on macroeconomic data should be replaced with actual household data that better reflects costs in real life. In addition, the setting of MWs has not considered additional costs associated with nurturing dependents. The implementation of employee representation in provincial subcommittees is also in doubt with some employee representatives agreeing to MW levels that are realistically too low. The data showed that less than half of the 77 provinces have provincial labor unions and less than 1% of these have been active in MW-setting processes. This demonstrates that the tripartite wage setting system is not working as it should. These issues have been submitted to the Thai Parliament's agenda by the Labor Commission for further consideration.

To find an appropriate LW rate in Thailand and to consider a process for implementation, we collected data from six representatives from diverse areas, including employers, an economist, a human resource expert, a political scientist, and behavioral scientists. Interviews were conducted during May 2022. The thematic analyses of these interviews revealed insights about implementing the LW in Thailand. The participants said that they supported the concept that wages should be adjusted in congruence with workers' costs of living. However, employers' ability to pay should also be considered. The government should also be responsible for controlling or subsidizing public utility prices because most of these operate as state enterprises. Workers should also consider their consumption behaviors.

Implementation of the SLW in Thai Organizations and Other Countries

As mentioned above, the SEP concept was promoted all around Thailand, not only for individuals but also for organizations (Taolanon, 2012). The SLW has only recently been developed through our research and is currently in the phase of being introduced in Thai organizations. SEP has been implemented in Thai organizations in various forms; for instance, moderation is interpreted as focusing more on long-term benefits than short-term; reasonableness is understanding customers, markets, competitors, and even, themselves, and making decisions based on these data rather than emotions; and self-immunity involves responding properly to any changes related to the businesses using contingency plans (Kasikorn Bank, 2017; Office of the National Economic and Social Development Council, 2006; Thairath, 2021). As a consequence of the COVID-19 pandemic, the employment situation and many jobs are in jeopardy. Workers in many sectors are needing to learn not only to adjust their tasks but also their spending in terms of disposable income and psychological management. The SLW is proposed as a crucial psychological technique to deal with this difficult situation (Mohan et al. 2023).

Exploring processes for adopting the SLW in organizations, we landed on the framing of this initiative in terms of human resource (HR) development to foster organizational socialization and human capital development. Researchers in I/O psychology emphasize the significance of organizational socialization for both organizational and employee wellbeing (Chao, 2012; Ellis et al., 2015). As noted, the concept of the SLW is fit for purpose in Thailand due to its foundations in Buddhist teachings, including the four noble truths and the noble eightfold path, which expound the practice of the middle path. The SLW concept has emerged from in-depth interviews and quantitative surveys of the experiences and needs of Thai blue-collar workers. These workers were employed in organizations that also follow the core values of the SEP that was established during the time of King Rama IX of Thailand, and at a time when there was a strong impetus toward sufficiency-economy practices. We believe that the SLW concept reflects the integration of SEP principles with practices of equitable or fair wage-setting. Applied to workers in Thailand, the SLW concept can benefit society by mediating perceptions of wage justice and demonstrate commitment toward the cultivation of human capabilities (Teng-Calleja et al., Chapter 8) through wage-setting practices.

As a psychological concept, an SLW is suitable for exploration in organizational settings in non-Buddhist countries. The promotion of an SLW in the non-Buddhist countries could begin by translating the Buddhist threefold teaching and the practice of the four noble truths into daily working life and HR training. Examples of applied psychological research based on successful implementations of Buddhist philosophy can be seen in various areas, including the treatment of addictive behaviors and depression, and the concept of emotional intelligence. Starting from the time of recruitment and selection, HR professionals should consider supporting the practice of an SLW through coaching and mentoring techniques; both of which are focused on supporting the wellbeing of individual employees (Al Hilali et al., 2020; Jarosz, 2021). Raising awareness about the SLW could be meaningful for the enhanced wellbeing of workers. If organizations set HR strategies to practice an SLW, it could be impactful, since researchers have reported positive impacts from organizational support, leadership, and communication to achieve work socialization (Cooper-Thomas & Anderson, 2006; Ellis et al., 2015).

Conclusion and Future Research Directions

Further research in Thailand is necessary to extend present understandings of the impacts of the SLW on work-related outcomes for workers, organizations, and societal development. This is necessary as previous studies have shown that sufficiency thinking as in SEP has diverse cognitive aspects and can result in various of behavioral outcomes, including self-reliance, resilience, and self-immunity (Barua & Tejativaddhana, 2019).

From the LW perspective, Yao et al. (2017) have noted that an LW allows individuals to "choose and achieve" what they desire to do with their wages. Confirming this, SLW research has shown that the people can use the principles of moderation, reasonableness, and self-immunity to evaluate the value and utility of an increase in wages.

Integrated with the Buddhist teachings, the SLW implies MC and an alternative approach to looking at economic development. More important is that this can include inner happiness for workers that is not related to material possessions

(Kittiprapas, 2018). In a metaanalysis of SEP-related research, Barua and Tejativaddhana (2019) concluded that sufficiency thinking is reflective of a balance between various human dimensions, including physical needs, psychological functioning, and socioenvironmental influences. Thus, the SLW could be explored in terms of providing a mechanism for enhancing wellbeing in a sustainable way for workers and their organizations, as well as the environment and communities they live in.

References

Al Hilali, K. S., Al Mughairi, B. M., Kian, M. W., & Karim, A. M. (2020). Coaching and mentoring concepts and practices in development of competencies: A theoretical perspective. *International Journal of Academic Research in Accounting, Finance and Management Sciences, 10*(1), 41–54. https://doi.org/10.6007/IJARAFMS/v10-i1/6991

Amornsiriphong, S., & Piemyat, S. (2012). Social capital: Means of social safety net and social protection in Thai communities. *Procedia Engineering, 32*, 1152–1156. https://doi.org/10.1016/j.proeng.2012.02.070

Attakrit, L. (2015). Does the minimum wage reduce wage inequality? Evidence from Thailand. *IZA Journal of Labor & Development, 4*(21), 1–23. https://doi.org/10.1186/s40175-015-0041-7

Bangkok Post. (2022, May 4). *Explainer: Inside the case for a minimum wage hike.* https://www.bangkokpost.com/business/2304394/explainer-inside-the-case-for-a-minimum-wage-hike

Barua, P., & Tejativaddhana, P. (2019). Impact of application of sufficiency economy philosophy on the well-being of Thai population: A systematic review and meta-analysis of relevant studies. *Journal of Population and Social Studies, 27*(3), 195–219. https://so03.tci-thaijo.org/index.php/jpss/article/view/139845

Carr, S. C., Haar, J., Hodgetts, D., Arrowsmith, J., Parker, J., Young-Hauser, A., Alefaio-Tuglia, S., & Jones, H. (2019). An employee's living wage and their quality of work life: How important are household size and income? *Journal of Sustainability Research, 1*, 1–19. https://doi.org/10.20900/jsr20190007

Carr, S. C., Maleka, M., Meyer, I., Barry, M. L., Haar, J., Parker, J., Arrowsmith, J., Yao, C., Hodgetts, D., Jones, H., Young-Hauser, A., Afeaki-Mafil'o, E., Rasmussen, A.-H., Alefaio-Tugia, S., Falealili, B., Mafile'o, K., Pikula, T., Wolfgramm, N., 'Uhila, H., … & Naithani A. (2018). How can wages sustain a living? By getting ahead of the curve. *Sustainability Science, 13*, 901–917. https://doi.org/10.1007/s11625-018-0560-7

Carr, S., Parker, J., Arrowsmith, J., Harr, J., & Jones, H. (2017). Humanistic management and living wages: a case of compelling connections? *Humanistic Management Journal, 2*(1), 215–236. https://doi.org/10.1007/s41463-016-0018-y

Chao, G. T. (2012). Organizational socialization: Background, basics, and a blueprint for adjustment at work. In S. W. J. Kozlowski (Ed.), *The Oxford handbook of organizational psychology* (Vol. 1, pp. 579–614). Oxford University Press.

Choochom, O. (2015). A causal relationship of living behavior based on sufficiency economy philosophy for Thai university students. *Procedia – Social and Behavioral Sciences, 177*, 260–264. https://doi.org/10.1016/j.sbspro.2015.02.329

Cooper-Thomas, H. D., & Anderson, N. (2006). Organizational socialization: A new theoretical model and recommendations for future research and HRM practices in organizations. *Journal of Managerial Psychology, 21*, 492–516. https://doi.org/10.1108/02683940610673997

Dalai Lama. (2002). *The essence of the heart sutra.* Wisdom Publications.

Ellis, A. M., Bauer, T. N., & Erdogan, B. (2015). New-employee organizational socialization: Adjusting to new roles, colleagues, and organizations. In J. E. Grusec & P. D. Hastings (Eds.), *Handbook of socialization: Theory and research* (pp. 301–322). The Guilford Press.

Haybron, D. M. (2000). Two philosophical problems in the study of happiness. *Journal of Happiness Studies, 1*, 207–225. https://doi.org/10.1023/A:1010075527517

Hu, Y., & Carr, S. C. (2020). Living wages across the Pacific Rim: A localised replication study from China. *Journal of Pacific Rim Psychology, 14*, e18. https://doi.org/10.1017/prp.2020.11

International Labour Organization. (2016). Who should set minimum wages? In *Minimum Wage Policy Guide* (pp. 24–31). https://www.ilo.org/wcmsp5/groups/public/—ed_protect/—protrav/—travail/documents/publication/wcms_508566.pdf

International Labour Organization. (2017). *Minimum wage policy guide: An introduction.* ILO.

Jarosz, J. (2021). The impact of coaching on well-being and performance of managers and their teams during pandemic. *International Journal of Evidence Based Coaching and Mentoring, 19*(1), 4–27. https://doi.org/10.24384/n5ht-2722

Jitsuchon, S. (2019). Thailand's sufficiency economy philosophy as an alternative path to sustainable development. *European Journal of Sustainable Development, 8*(2), 191. https://doi.org/10.14207/ejsd.2019.v8n2p191

Kasikorn Bank. (2017). Sām khō̜ phō̜phīang yāngrai thurakit tōyang yūn [Three items: How to do sufficient to bring business for sustainable growth]. Published to be effective on October 5, 2017. Retrieved August 1, 2022, from https://www.kasikornbank.com/th/business/sme/KSMEKnowledge/article/SMETips/Pages/3-ways-business-sufficiency-economy-application.aspx

Kittiprapas, S. (2018). *Buddhist sustainable development: A new approach in happiness and development*. Thammasat University Press.

Kittiprapas, S. (2020). Happiness determinants in a Buddhist community: Where inner happiness matters. *Thammasat Review of Economic and Social Policy, 6*(1), 84–134. https://www.happysociety.org/uploads/HsoDownload/9508/download_file.pdf

Kristensen, N., & Cunningham, W. (2006). *Do Minimum Wages in Latin America and the Caribbean Matter? Evidence from 19 Countries*. (World Bank Policy Research Working Paper 3870). https://doi.org/10.1596/1813-9450-3870

Kunadilokkamon, V., Buarod, B., Simavara, K., Doonlayathaveesit, N., Choonhahlai, S., & Teerathiti, N. S. (2014). Phonkrathop khō̜ng nayōbāi khāčhāng rǣngngān sāmrō̜i bāt nai dān khunnaphāp chīwit lǣ sawatdikān khō̜ng rǣngngān sathānprakō̜pkān khanāt klāng lǣ khanāt yō̜m ‘m m ̄ lam lūk kā čhangwat Pathum Thānī [The Effect of the 300 Baht minimum wage policy towards quality of life and welfare of the smes workers in Lam Luk Ka District, Pathum Thani Province]. *Academic Journal Phranakhon Rajabhat University*, *5*(1), 118–128.

Labor Economy Division. (2021). Khūmū kān patibat ngān khō̜ng samnakngān khana kammakān khāčhāng [Operations manual of Office of Wage Committee]. Office of

Permanent Secretary, Ministry of Labor. Published to be effective on March 2021. Retrieved on May 31, 2022, from https://www.mol.go.th/wp-content/uploads/sites/2/2021/03/1.คู่มือของสำนักงานคณะกรรมการค่าจ้าง.pdf

Labor Economy Division. (2022). Khūmū̄ kān patibat ngān khō̜ng samnakngān khana kammakān khāčhāng [Operations Manual of Office of Wage Committee]. Office of Permanent Secretary, Ministry of Labor. Published to be effective on March 2, 2022. Retrieved May 31, 2022, from https://www.mol.go.th/wp-content/uploads/sites/2/2022/03/Manual-minimumwage-for2Mar2565-1.pdf

Lathapipat, D., & Poggi, C. (2016). *From many to one: Minimum wage effects in Thailand*. Puey Ungphakorn Institute for Economic Research. https://www.pier.or.th/dp/041/

Levin-Waldman, O. M. (2000). The rhetorical evolution of the minimum wage. *Rhetoric & Public Affairs 3*(2), 131–153. https://doi.org/10.1353/rap.2010.0153.

Living Wage Foundation UK. (2019). *The sustainable development goals and the living wage*. https://www.livingwage.org.uk/sites/default/files/19_09_24_LW_SDG_Report%20FINAL.pdf

Magnuson, J. C. (2007). Pathways to a mindful economy. *Society and Economy, 29*(2), 253–284. http://www.jstor.org/stable/41472084

Mohan, K. P., Yoelao, D., & Sombatwattana, P. (2023). Mediating effects of sufficiency living wage between pay fairness and work/life capabilities among workers in Thailand. *Kasetsart Journal of Social Sciences 44* (1), 51–60. https://doi.org/10.34044/j.kjss.2023.44.1.06

Ministry of Labor. (2020). Minimum wage. New minimum wage rate table, under the national wage committee's notification on minimum wage rate (No. 10), published to be effective on January 1, 2020. https://www.mol.go.th/en/minimum-wage

Ministry of Labor. (2022). Rūang kānkamnot khāčhāng khantam [Minimum Wages Determination]. Retrieved May 30, 2022, from https://www.mol.go.th/wp-content/uploads/sites/2/2019/07/minimumwages_2.pdf

Mongsawad, P., & Thongpakde, N. (2016). Sufficiency economy philosophy: A holistic approach to economic development and mainstream economic thought. *Asian Social Science, 12*(7), 136–142. https://doi.org/10.5539/ass.v12n7p136

Ng, C. H. E. (2020). *Introduction to Buddhist economics: The relevance of Buddhist values in contemporary economy and society*. Palgrave Macmillan.

OECD. (2019). *Multi-dimensional review of Thailand: Volume 3: From analysis to action*. https://doi.org/10.1787/7ef9363b-en

Office of the National Economic and Social Development Council. (2006). Sētthakit phō̜phīang kap thurakit ʻēkkachon [Sufficiency economy and private sector]. Published to be effective on April 26, 2006. Retrieved August 1, 2022, from https://www.ryt9.com/s/nesd/84180

Payutto, P. A. (2001). *Buddhadhamma*. Thammasapa.

Payutto, P. A. (2006). *Buddhist teaching* (11th ed.). Sahathammmika.

Payutto, P. A. (2016). *Buddhist economics*. Wat Nyanavesakavan.

Payutto, P. A. (2019). *Buddhadhamma: The laws of nature and their benefits to life*. Buddhadhamma Foundation.

Puntasen, A. (2007). Buddhist economics as a new paradigm towards happiness. *Society and Economy, 29*(2), 181–200.

Puntasen, A. (2017). From wealth to well-being and finally nibbana: A bridge from traditional to Buddhist economics. *Prajñā Vihāra, 18*(1), 98–140. http://www.assumptionjournal.au.edu/index.php/PrajnaVihara/article/view/2921

Sirgy, M. J. (2012). *The psychology of quality of life: Hedonic well-being, and eudaimonia.* (2nd ed.) Springer.

Sirgy, M. J. (2021). *The psychology of quality of life: Wellbeing and positive mental health.* (3rd ed.). Springer.

Schulten, T., & Luebker, M. (2019). *WSI Minimum Wage Report 2019: Time for substantial minimum wage rises and a European minimum wage policy.*(Report No. 46e). Institute of Economic and Social Research. https://www.boeckler.de/pdf/p_wsi_report_46e_2019.pdf

Schumacher, D. (2011). *Small is beautiful in the 21st century: The legacy of E. F Schumacher*. Green Books.

Schumacher, E.F. (1973). *Small is beautiful: A study of economics as if people mattered.* HarperCollins.

Taolanon, A. (2012). Kānprayukchai pratyā khọ̄ng sētthakit phọ̄phīang khọ̄ng phāk thurakit ʻēkkachon [Sufficiency economy philosophy application in private sector]. Office of the National Economic and Social Development Council.

Thailand Board of Investment. (2022). *Thailand in brief: Social and culture*. Retrieved May 11, 2022, from https://www.boi.go.th/index.php?page=social_and_culture

Thailand Development Research Institute. (2014). Phonkrathop thāng sētthakit čhāk nayōbāi khāčhāng rǣngngān khon sāmrọ̄i bāt tọ̄ wan læ ngœ̄ndư̄an parinyā trī 15,000 bāt [Economic effect from minimum wage policy 300 Baht per day and 15,000 baht for bachelor degree]. TDRI Report (No. 101, March 2014). To be effective on April, 2014. Retrieved May 30, 2022, from https://tdri.or.th/wp-content/uploads/2014/04/wb101.pdf

Thairath. (2021). Nam lak pratyā khọ̄ng sētthakit phọ̄phīang sū krabūankān phatthanā thurakit yāng mī khunnatham [Adopt philosophy of sufficiency economy for business development process with morality]. Published to be effective on April 28, 2021. Retrieved August 1, 2022, from https://www.thairath.co.th/lifestyle/life/2078726

Theerakosonphong, K. (2022). Kānsamrūat khākhrọ̄ngchīp khọ̄ng rǣngngān: khọ̄sanœ̄ kān yok radap khāčhāng khantam læ māttrathān kān damrong chīwit thī mī khunkhā [Survey of labors' cost of living: Proposal for levelling minimum wage and decent standard of living]. (Final Report, No. 25) Working Group for Guidelines for Solving Labor Wage Problems to be in Accordance with the Current Situation, Labor Commission, House of Parliament.

The Living Income. (n.d.). *Living Income and the Sustainable Development Goals (SDG's)*. Retrieved February 20, 2023, from https://www.living-income.com/sdg-s-and-living-income

Winzer, L., & Gray, R. S. (2019). The role of Buddhist practices in happiness and health in Thailand: A structural equation model. *Journal of Happiness Studies, 20*, 411–425. https://doi.org/10.1007/s10902-017-9953-z

Winzer, L., Samutachak, B., & Gray, R. S. (2018). Religiosity, spirituality, and happiness in Thailand from the perspective of Buddhism. *Journal of Population and Social Studies, 26*(4), 332–343. https://so03.tci-thaijo.org/index.php/jpss/article/view/127099

World Bank. (2022). *The World Bank in Thailand.* Retrieved May 11, 2022, from, https://www.worldbank.org/en/country/thailand/overview#1

Yao, C., Parker, J., Arrowsmith, J., & Carr, S. C. (2017). The living wage as an income range for decent work and life. *Employee Relations*, *39*(6), 875–887. https://doi.org/10.1108/ER-03-2017-0071

Yoelao, D., Mohan, K. P., & Sombatwattana, P. (2019). A qualitative construction of sufficiency living wage in Thailand based on the sufficiency economy philosophy. *International Perspectives in Psychology: Research, Practice, Consultation, 8*(4), 227–239. https://doi.org/10.1037/ipp0000117

Yoelao, D., Sombatwattana, P., & Mohan, K. P. (2021). Development and validation of the sufficiency living wage scale for workers in Thailand. *Thailand and the World Economy*, *39*(1), 23–38. https://so05.tci-thaijo.org/index.php/TER/article/view/242467

10

TACKLING WAGE INEQUALITY

The Maximum Wage[1]

Stuart C. Carr, Veronica Hopner, Darrin J. Hodgetts, and Megan Young

> What improves the circumstances of the greater part can never be regarded as an inconveniency to the whole. No society can surely be flourishing and happy, of which the far greater part of the members are poor and miserable [while a far smaller minority at the very top are extremely wealthy].
>
> (Smith, 1776, p. 96, parenthesis added)

Inequality has been described as out of control (Oxfam, 2020). Wage inequality is a part of that process which affects a vast number of workers globally (McWha-Hermann, 2023). In the United States (US) prior to the pandemic, for instance,

> The gap between executive compensation and average worker pay [had already] been growing for decades... In 1989, that ratio was 61:1. From 1978 to 2019, compensation grew 14% for typical workers and a staggering 1,167% for CEOs...The COVID-19 pandemic only compounded these disparities, as hundreds of companies awarded their leaders [with] pay packages worth significantly more than most Americans will make in their entire lives.
>
> *(Gelles, 2021, p. 2)*

There are ways to slow down the wage inequality train, however. The people *who* must matter most in the application and benefit from that braking process are—of course—the workers themselves: not researchers, politicians, or shareholders. But so too, do those few whose wages are usually far higher— namely, the Chief Executive Officers (CEOs). *How* industrial and organizational (I/O)

DOI: 10.4324/9781003440444-12

psychology can start to help tackle wage inequality is by developing reliable, valid, and inclusive measures of the ratios between the top (CEO) and bottom wage rungs in any organization, sector, or supply chain. *Where* the ratio is set depends on context. The living wage—higher than a bare minimum wage (Smith, 2015)—is the lowest ethical denominator in that ratio (as argued in other chapters). A sustainable numerator however will be determined by whatever objective ratio results in a reduction of subjective precariousness and an increase in felt fairness among employees themselves. *Why* this is important is that wage inequality is an anathema to sustainable livelihoods and human security, since relative pay is often the most salient determinant of felt pay fairness (Furnham, 2019; McWha-Hermann, 2023). The next frontier in I/O psychology theory today is developing a model of wage equity, meaning fair wages that reflect what people bring to the work, and which contribute to tackling global inequality, sustainably (Carr, 2023). "Sustainability" is a core feature in the United Nations (UN) Sustainable Development Goals (SDGs), and this chapter examines two of them in particular: SDG-8 (Decent Work and Economic Growth) which includes fair incomes and SDG-10 (Reduced Inequalities; United Nations Department of Economic and Social Affairs n.d.).

For some time now, wage packages at the ceiling of many organizations have been growing far more than those at the bottom. Wages at the ceiling have been a major drain on organizational resources that could be used to achieve greater pay equity and to address the risks to the health of precariat workers on the wage floor (International Labour Organization [ILO], 2013, pp. 88–89). Left unchecked and unbridled (ILO, 2013), high pay for executives deprives the greater part of the workforce of a fair income and security (ILO, 2022). This chapter shines a spotlight on the very top rung of the organizational pay scale, at the level of the CEO. Setting a maximum wage for the CEO may be one way to achieve wage incomes that are fairer and thus more sustainable for the greater part. The maximum wage can be considered as a human handbrake[2] that any socially responsible organization may apply to limit runaway wage inequality and work precariousness.

Focusing on the concept of a maximum wage actually marks out a new trilateral frontier for I/O psychology. In the past, I/O has overlooked (1) the foot of the wage ladder, (2) the very top rung (above the upper-middle wage classes in "talent management"), and (3) relativities between these two positions on the wage spectrum (Carr, 2022). These oversights, and in particular (3), have arguably cut I/O psychology adrift from wage policies at the UN. For example, the ILO (2013) has proposed that a suitable measure of wage inequality is the relationship between both ends of the wage spectrum. It is proposed that CEO wages should be tethered to the wage floor: in this case via some maximum wage *ratio* between these two poles. A ratio means, in effect, that CEO wages can only go higher (in absolute terms) if the shop-floor wage lifts too (albeit still by a lesser amount in absolute terms[21]). There is a thus potential here for the introduction of a relative maximum wage to slow the inequality train down to help keep wage inequality within acceptable limits by offering an incentive for CEOs to raise wages at the bottom of the spectrum, in order to increase theirs at the top.

For I/O psychology, the idea of a maximum wage invites a discussion that the profession has never really had, but which is today long overdue, about class at work (Kallschmidt & Eaton, 2019). Class structures key aspects of everyday relations at work (DiTomaso & Parks-Yancy, 2014). These relations include, for example, social and socioeconomic wage comparisons, such as those between CEOs and the shop floor (Schein, 1996). People *class*-ify themselves (Netuveli & Bartley, 2012) and often experience microclass-ifications by others at work (see, Kallschmidt & Eaton, 2019) and in ways that centralize inequalities in pay (Baron & Pfeffer, 1994) and wellbeing (Marmot et al., 1991). People in work look up and down the wage hierarchies to understand their own place and value in organizations and society more generally (Furnham, 2019). Below, we outline a process model of partnership in relative wage-setting between key stakeholders, which can help set ratios that embody fairer remuneration and more sustainable livelihoods within organizations. We explore how ratio-capping wages at the very top of that ladder, far from restricting anyone, may actually benefit the whole.

Conceptual Distinctions

Media and research discussions of wage inequality often entangle at least three entangled, but conceptually distinct, threads: wealth inequality, income inequality, and wage inequality. Echoing Adam Smith (1776), such inequalities of wealth, income, and wages are bad for all of society. From the late 2000s (Easterly, 2007), a swathe of high-profile research has highlighted wealth, income, and wage inequalities as rapidly growing and warranting global concern for economic stability, sustainability, equity, efficiency, and growth (Berg et al., 2012; Doyle & Stiglitz, 2014; International Monetary Fund [IMF], 2011; Ostry, et al., 2014). As noted by the Dabla-Norris et al. (2015, p. 4):

> Complementarities between growth and income equality objectives suggest that policies aimed at raising average living standards can also influence the distribution of income and ensure a more inclusive prosperity…Equality…is an important value in most societies.

To get to our focus on wage inequality, it is important to first disentangle it from wealth and income inequalities (Carr, 2022).

1 Wealth inequality refers to the uneven distribution of existing assets or wealth within and across societies. For example, some people become wealthy by birth

or inheritance, by lottery, opportune investments, or high-status businesses; well-timed entrepreneurial start-ups especially can create near-monopolies and extreme wealth. Excessive wealth inequalities are increasingly being challenged, however, as unfair. For example, the "Occupy Movement" started in the U against a rapid rise in wealth inequality between the top 1% and the remaining, less wealthy 99% since the Great Recession in 2007/2008 (Stiglitz, 2011).

2 Income inequality can overlap with and increase wealth inequalities but is not the same phenomenon. Income inequality is about the uneven distribution across society of income that is "earned" from salary and wages. The relationship between wealth and income inequalities gets complicated, particularly when existing wealth or income is then mobilized to extract further resources from other persons and groups. For example, so-called mum and dad investors may inherit wealth from family and then combine this with income from wages to invest in multiple domestic dwellings as a means of extracting unearned rent from occupants. Here we can see a classic distinction between money that is made through investment and money that is earned through wages ("Who Exactly are the 1%?", 2012).

3 Wage inequality can be conceptualized as a form of income disparity that relates more specifically to the uneven distribution of salary or wage income within and across societies. Central are issues of wage differentials between employees within an organization and between sectors, nation-states, and regions. Such inequalities in wages are often shaped by intersectional issues of class, gender, ethnicity, ableism, place, and so forth. For example, a CEO of an FTSE 100 clothing conglomerate might earn as much in one year as 10,000 people working in garment factories in Bangladesh (Oxfam, 2017). In general, the distribution of global labor income (from wages) is lopsided, with a worker in the top 10% earning the equivalent in purchasing power parity (PPP) of $7,445 per month and a worker in the bottom 10% just PPP$22: a ratio of 338.4:1 (ILO, 2019). It is impossible to see how any human being could ever be 338 times more productive or valuable than any other, whatever the level of their education, training, experience, or motivation (Hills, 2014).

4 Having conceptualized wage inequality, one more differentiation is necessary: wage inequality compared to whom? In this case, a fundamental distinction can be drawn between comparing wages within an organization, from the floor to the CEO ceiling, versus comparing them between organizations, from general shop-floor wages compared to wages in general for CEOs. One comparison is more proximal; the other is much more distal. The level of subjective wage inequality may thereby differ depending on whether an employee compares differences within their own organization (intra) or in relation to how other organizations (inter) operate wage structures (Song et al., 2015). Social psychological theories of reference groups (Sherif, 1936), and social

comparison (Festinger, 1950, 1954) imply that the more salient comparison is likely to be the one that is more proximal (Festinger et al., 1950), i.e., within the same organization (Carr, 2010). Consistent with that indication, in a more contemporary policy context, the ILO (2013) argued that wage ratios should be set at organizational level within the organization. Tackling wage inequality thus becomes as much (if not more) a function of human resources and I/O psychology, rather than just a distal obligation on governments (Lavelle et al, Chapter 16; Searle & McWha-Hermann, Chapter 4).

Historical Context

Maximizing wages is not a new idea; it started as far back as Ancient Greece. Plato reportedly told his student Aristotle that no citizen[3] should earn more than five times what the least-compensated citizen worker earned (Crystal, 1991; Desai et al., 2010). Fast-forward to World War II, when in 1942 US President F. D. Roosevelt suggested that the marginal tax rate should be increased to 100% for any gross annual income over US$25k at the time to discourage wartime profiteering (Pizzigati, 2018). These responses effectively offer a starting point to consider caps on any wage above a particular level. In the case of Roosevelt, anyone who earned above $25k as a gross wage would effectively receive no further income above this level. As it happened, Roosevelt's proposal was eventually rejected by the US Congress. However, it reminds us today that in times of crisis, and with the right political will, governments might use progressive taxes and other policies as tools for tackling inequalities by regulating wages (Saner & Yiu, Chapter 5; Searle & McWha-Hermann, Chapter 4).

Governments have on occasion intervened more successfully in setting maximum wages, at least on a sector-wide basis. For example, a centralized, cross-sectoral-level lever was enacted by the Dutch government in 2010, when it refused to fund any NGO organization that paid its own CEO leader above 160,000 Euros per annum. Nor are sector-wide levers confined to regulating civil-society organizations that rely partly on government funding. During the recession of the 1980s for instance, as part of its own governance, Spain's Mondragon Cooperative adopted a maximum differential ratio between the highest and lowest paid employees: in this case of 3:1 (Jones, 2013). After the recession, as the demand for skilled managers increased, the ratio was increased, first to 4.5:1 (in 1987) and then to 8.9:1 (in 2002). Consistent with its own ethos of cooperation, this ratio was still narrower than for corporations in the rest of Spain but not totally out-of-kilter with these either.

In 2012, the newly elected French President Francois Hollande suggested capping the top salaries of company executives at a ratio of 20 times the wage of their own lowest paid workers. This idea of a ratio within organizations was not new; for instance, in the 1970s, the management guru Peter Drucker had suggested the same kind of idea and ratio (Kennedy et al., 2019). In 2013, the government of Switzerland went a step further than ideation. It held a national referendum on whether or not to limit monthly earnings for the highest paid employee of any given Swiss firm to the yearly earnings of its lowest paid employee in the same year. This proposal was concertedly opposed by employer lobby groups, and it did not pass into law. However, it did garner more than a third of the national vote, indicating that the idea of moving to a maximum wage *ratio* was gaining traction. Moreover, the location of responsibility for that wage ratio was now clearly not just governmental but also organizational.

An influential trope at the time of the Swiss referendum was that capping CEO wages would make Swiss organizations less competitive. This is misleading. The ILO's *World of Work* report for that same year had focused precisely on repairing the social and economic fabric after the previous recession (ILO, 2013). The ILO advised in the report that ratio wage caps neither hobble CEO wages nor do they make them any less competitive as organizations. For example, a CEO's remuneration can still go up provided the CEO brings lower wage rungs with them. In other words, if a CEO wants to raise their own wage, they must also raise the pay of Adam Smith's (1776) "greater part," employed within the same organization (ILO, 2013).

Unfortunately for Smith's "greater part" of humanity, efforts to stop executive boards from benchmarking CEOs against lavishly paid members of peer-group companies have failed (Schumpeter 2021: 4). The whole world of work though is now firmly in what Kurt Lewin (1947) might have dubbed a great "unfreezing moment" (Burnes, 2020). According to the Society for Human Resource Management (SHRM), in any post-COVID-19 world, "The CEO pay *ratio* may see renewed scrutiny and discussion…" (Sammer, 2021).

Stakeholder Groups

Assuming SHRM is right, the next question is, scrutiny by and for whom? Although we prioritize labor (worker) groups, union or not, in this chapter (and volume), the discussion below includes other groups because they too are impacted by the wage inequalities experienced between shop-floor and CEO wage classes. All are relevant stakeholders (Freeman, 1984). They are all part of the greater good (Smith, 1776), and they are interlinked (Sustainable Livelihoods, Section 1). Wage inequalities affect labor groups (as occupations and/or as members of labor unions), executive boards, shareholders, and the general public.

In terms of workers who make up labor groups, a comparatively rare type of study conducted in the Netherlands involved wage scrutiny by workers (Gallego, 2016). About 1,500 respondents were asked to indicate their own income level on two different versions of the survey form using two different cut-offs for the top bracket: either EUR 82K and above or EUR 32K and above. When the top bracket on the form was higher (82K and above), the participants whose own income was lower (EUR 24K or less) reported moderately lower levels of social trust (in people generally) alongside moderately higher support for social cooperation (over self-interest) compared to when the bar was lower (EUR 32K). Hence, when made to feel comparatively worse off, workers trusted others less and craved cooperation more.

Such findings are important because they remind us that feelings of inequality and inequality intensity among workers are sensitive to social context. Feelings of unfairness about wage differentials are fluid and dynamic, as well as being steady state. One implication of these twin aspects of feelings about wage inequality is that paying inordinately high CEO wages during a pandemic may leave workers who are tightening their own wage belts feeling even more unfairly wage-deprived than usual—and less trusting of upper management. Without amelioration, this may end up lowering staff morale for the majority and thereby lower performance (Jacquart & Armstrong, 2013; Kennedy et al., 2019).

A key stakeholder group responsible for addressing such organizational concerns are the members of executive boards. To specifically tackle the deleterious amplification of wage differentials, the ILO has proposed there should be some practical and moral "relative limits" set on CEO pay: "An ambitious option would be to impose limits on total executive compensation relative to other wages in the firm. This would provide an incentive for executives to strive towards improving the salaries of their [own] employees" (ILO, 2013, p. 89). The report went further, adding suggestions about *who* should be involved in the process of setting such capped differentials. Organizations should introduce a "say on pay [for] employee representatives on company boards" (ILO, 2013, p. 90). More worker say-on-pay results in less excessive levels of executive compensation (ILO, 2013, p. 90). This say could also help to incorporate wage differentials into the wage-setting processes at other places of work, e.g., through sector-wide pay agreements (Meyer & Maleka, Chapter 7). By this potential pathway, some of the *inter*firm wage inequalities highlighted by Song et al. (2015) might also be redressed (Carr, 2022).

As well as their responsibilities toward employees, organizations are also accountable to shareholder groups (Friedman, 1962). Evidence suggests that companies who pay their CEOs more sometimes have lower returns on their stocks and shares (Jacquart & Armstrong, 2013; Malmandier & Tate, 2009). Of course, this linkage is not always negative. In the literature on executive pay and stock performance, wage inequality goes by different names, ranging from pay "variation" (Conroy et al., 2014) and "dispersion" (Bloom, 1999; Messersmith et al., 2011) to wage "disparity" (Siegel & Hambrick, 2005). At some point, perhaps, wage inequality is deemed to cross some kind of qualitative *threshold*. These seem to be more and more morally critical. The implication of a threshold is that the gap itself starts to be counter-productive for the whole organization and for the people who depend on it for their own living and wellbeing.

Beyond the factory gates, in wider society across the US, Desai et al. (2010) have gauged the relationship between the total compensation paid to an organization's CEO and the company's/firm's adherence to human rights. Across a total of 85 such firms controlled for organization size, CEO wages (for 2005) were significantly, but alas *negatively*, predictive of the company's ratings on human rights (in 2006). According to Desai et al., "This finding suggests that the higher the level of CEO compensation, the *less* that human rights were upheld by the organization," (2010, p. 325, emphasis added). These human rights of course begin with the employees who are working inside the organization itself (Erdogan et al., 2015). This includes the shop floor (Reichman & Carr, 2022). Thus, we arrive back at worker groups, emphasizing once more the interconnectedness and the inherent social relationality of people's (1) wage and (2) wellbeing (Carr, 2023).

Worker Perceptions of Wage Inequality and the Gini Coefficient

The only ultimate arbiter of whether a wage is unfair is the worker themselves, whether as occupational groups in labor unions or as individuals. On this assumption, a UK survey gathered workers' perceptions of the size of the gap between their own wages and the wages paid to others in the same organization (Petrescu & Simmons, 2008). The survey asked workers directly for their assessment of workplace pay gaps, alongside questions about job attitudes and satisfaction. Petrescu and Simmons (2008) found that UK workers who reported the gap was "too big" were also more likely to be relatively dissatisfied with their jobs. These data were cross-sectional, meaning that it is hard to know which was driving which: wage gaps leading to dissatisfaction, dissatisfaction leading to negative perceptions of wage gaps, or some third factor and combination.

A cleaner way of fathoming links between wage inequality and how workers feel about it might be to take an independent measure of the inequality and then see how it covaries with levels of wellbeing. Easily the best known approach for gauging material wage-related *income* inequality, which might therefore work for wage inequality, is the Gini coefficient. Conceived by Italian statistician, demographer, and sociologist Corrado Gini (Carr & Gini, 2011), Gini coefficients range from 0 (total equality, all members of the society or group have the same income) to 1 (maximal inequality, where 1 member of the society or group receives the entire group's income). The bigger the Gini, the more wealth is held in fewer hands. The 0–1 interval is derived from the Lorenz curve, represented by the arc in Figure 10.1. Lorenz curves portray visually the proportion of income that is already earned by an increasingly cumulative percentage of the wider population, in any general or particular economy of interest.

In Figure 10.1, the Lorenz curve is topped by a diagonal line. This line represents a line of perfect equality, in which 10% of the income would already be held by 10% of the population, 90% by 90%, and so on. The size of the area

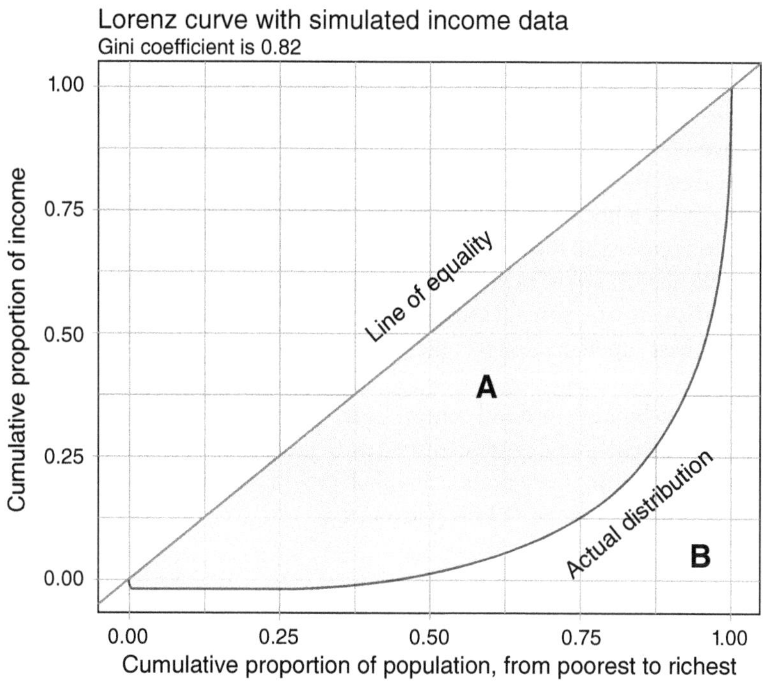

FIGURE 10.1 A Hypothetical Lorenz Curve and Gini Coefficient.

Source: Ellis (2017).

between the line and the Lorenz curve (indicated by zone A) reflects the amount of total income reserved for the elite few. Thus, the bigger the ratio becomes, between zone A and the actual distribution, zone B, the more inequality is present in the social system. In Figure 10.1, for instance, we can see that the larger proportion is contained in zone A; whilst the smaller proportion is contained in zone B. Here a hypothetical Gini is reported by Ellis (2017) as .82 (Figure 10.1).

In principle, the Gini coefficient can be applied to any size of economic grouping, and it can also be calibrated using any personal or household/family income. In practice, macroeconomists, for example, will often use the Gini coefficient to capture income diversity for whole countries, for example, the US has a coefficient of .41 (family income) and New Zealand .36, as well as across whole regions like the EU (.30, averaged across the 27 member countries), and even for the world as a whole (the estimates vary but appear to hover between .61 and .68). Generally, the Gini coefficient has been used to calculate income inequality for countries and, occasionally, for sectors.

These country-level Gini's have already been widely linked empirically to individual wellbeing, health, and happiness (Wilkinson & Pickett, 2009). That is, the lower the Gini coefficient, the greater the health and wellbeing. It is important to note however that a low country Gini on its own does not represent national prosperity. Income from wages is not necessarily all milk-and-honey; countries and workplaces with lower Gini coefficients (theoretically good) may still have other barriers to upward mobility and wellbeing (e.g., endemic poverty, or a complete lack of infrastructure, and everyone dirt poor). Meanwhile, countries with a higher Gini (theoretically bad) may still have good options for people to prosper and thrive; for example, countries that humanely and progressively take in millions of skilled refugees whose wages are temporarily (but only temporarily) nil. The point of these provisos is that any such coefficient, or ratio, is always best supplemented by other indicators of [in]equality:

> It helps to build theoretical schemes that must not be confused with reality, but may be compared with reality, so as to judge if, in what way and to what extent, they differ from reality, and thus provide an opportunity for a deeper analysis of the structure of the phenomena.
>
> *(Gini, 1965, p. 106)*

Although the example in Figure 10.1 concerns inequality of income, the same coefficient could equally well be applied to capture the inequality of wages in any given organization. The "organizational Gini coefficient" (OGC) might be a useful, midlevel way of capturing wage inequality (Carr & Gini, 2011). Perhaps the single main limitation of the Gini coefficient, though, is that it remains highly abstracted. An OGC is unlikely to be the kind of ratio that people would readily employ in their own workplaces. In most everyday settings, highest-to-lowest wage ratios might be a simpler, and more intuitive and relatable, measure of wage inequality levels.

There are already such ratios in use in economics, for example, the Palma ratio conceived by Cobham and Sumner (2013) based on earlier empirical observations that incomes generally consistently fell within a discernible middle 50% of the population (Palma, 2011). This in turn was straddled by a visibly higher top 10% and a visibly lower bottom 40%. Looking at these two markedly differentiated clusters, the categories of an upper wage class and a lower working wage class appear to be a relatively intuitive fit with the way incomes are distributed in any given population:

> A Gini Coefficient of.5 implies serious inequality but yields no intuitive statement for a non-technical audience. In contrast, the equivalent Palma of 5.0 can be directly translated into the top-bottom focused statement that the richest 10 percent earn Plato's *five times* the income of the poorest 40 percent of the nation.
>
> *(Cobham & Sumner, 2013, p. 31, emphasis added)*

Nonetheless, any Palma ratio also depends for its basis (and utility) on whether there is actually a clear middle 50%, a clear top 10%, and a clear bottom 40%. This is increasingly less the case as organizations move onto digital platforms (ILO, 2021). A similar point applies to a range of other, arguably less intuitively obvious, ratio measures, which also make distributional assumptions that may not subtend in any actual income distribution (Organization for Economic Co-operation and Development [OECD], 2016).

In the final analysis, when the concern, like ours in this chapter, is with everyday wage inequality, at work, in a particular organization; the most basic, and also obvious form of ratio to consider, is the ratio between the wage paid to the CEO and the wage paid to workers on the shop or factory floor. Given that the wage paid at the floor should be at least a living wage (Carr et al., 2018; Meyer & Maleka, Chapter 7), the wage paid to the CEO for that organization will then be determined by the wage already being paid to the lowest paid work group, on the wage floor, in the same organization. However, even though we know the numerator, the value of the ratio *itself* first needs to be decided. Only after it is decided can the CEO wage be set in such a way as to respect that ratio and thereafter preserve it. This is because the CEO has to raise the wage of the greater part before lifting their own.

Where and on What Basis to Set the Wage Ceiling?

To recap, introducing a ratio between the wage ceiling and floor in an organization's pay scale is a strategy for I/O psychologists and HRMs to consider for addressing indecent or precarious work conditions, in conjunction with the issues around productivity covered in previous sections. The problem we have now is that nobody has so far estimated systematically what ratio, if any, may be acceptable to Adam Smith's (1776) "greater part" of any given organization. What is currently lacking are studies of how different ratios map to people's senses of fairness, wellbeing, and thriving in organizations.

Ideally, we would have a wide range of studies in which preexisting wage ratios were plotted against perceived fairness among workers their wellbeing, and the security of decent work. Just as wellbeing is often a curvilinear function of wage level in the absolute, with a clear cusp at the level of the living wage where wellbeing ticks upward (Carr et al., 2022), the same might be true of relative wages in the form of a wage ratio. An inflection point, at which wellbeing peaked for the greater part of workers, would help to set any maximum wage ratio in-context, for more sustainable livelihoods.

An illustration of how this might work can be found in a societal study of links between income inequality as measured by the Gini coefficient and happiness (which is often taken as a measure of one key facet of wellbeing) by Yu and Wang (2017). These researchers analyzed the links between national Gini coefficients at the time and happiness scores in wellbeing surveys, for the US and countries of Western Europe (excluding Scandinavia). Income was measured across households and happiness was measured as personal feeling.

In each region, a non-linear, inverted-U relationship was found between income inequality at a societal level and personal happiness at the individual level. There appeared to be clear inflection points (Yu & Wang, 2017, p. 4) across the tops of each curve. Beyond that upper limit, happiness and wellbeing generally falls, possibly to socially unsustainable levels, for poor and rich alike (Cornia & Court, 2001). Thus, this study showed not only how but also where a ratio value might actually be set, including, in principle, within organizations. Being Gini-based, this study reflects perhaps quite an equity-related approach and did not necessarily address directly the possibilities that people may find "equality" (not the same as equity) and/or "need" to be salient considerations (McWha-Hermann, in press). However, one would also expect that these considerations, if salient, would still likely permeate through to, and thus be reflected in, personal levels of satisfaction and happiness (i.e., they would be captured indirectly).

A study linking pay dispersion to actual workplace productivity was conducted by Mahy et al. (2011). Pay dispersion was predictive of productivity at the level of firms. Specifically, the relationship found between pay dispersion and productivity was another inverted U. The amount of pure pay dispersion at first related positively to productivity (more space for effort = more productivity); however, at moderate levels of dispersion, a productivity apex was reached after which the dispersion was again seen to be linked to productivity but now *negatively* (possibly via perceived unfairness).

The points of inflection in these studies, one focused on wellbeing and the other on productivity, both ranged approximately on either side of a Gini coefficient of .30—implying at least a possibility of some recurring optimal range for wage ratios for the greater good. But what would a Gini of, say, circa .30 actually mean? Here the relative abstractedness of a Gini coefficient itself, as noted above, starts to become an issue; specifically, how is .30 converted back into any usable, specific maximum wage *value*, either at the top and/or bottom, in the form of a ratio?

A more viable starting point, and a future direction, is to ask researchers to start conducting many more such studies of how wage ratios, between naturally/actually occurring top and bottom wage rungs in organizations, relate to individual and organizational wellbeing. In concert with setting decent wages, a process for setting relative wages could then build a more grounded sense of what ratios people feel are decent, possibly by involving not only workers but also consumers more broadly (Mohan et al., 2018). Such studies might also find, for example, that points of inflection drop when unexpected crises hit everyone (see above).

If so, HRMs would then have a better idea of where to set it, or at least advise where it be set for the greater good, across the organization as a whole.

In the interim, there is a more direct approach which is more localized and pragmatic; ask employees themselves, from all wage levels, to give their say on what kind of ratio *they* find acceptable, subjectively. Such a request might escape social desirability effects, insofar as a ratio does not set the baseline or the ceiling. It merely asks how many times higher than the floor the ceiling can, sustainably, go. For example, one international team of I/O researchers have already asked a sample of professional expatriate and host country national workers (HCNs) how much more an expatriate could earn, compared to their HCN homolog. Across six very different countries and economies, both wage groups converged on a modal ratio interval; any ratio between 2:1 and 3:1 was generally considered as being reasonable, by both groups, HCN and expatriate workers, given added costs, for relocation etc., for the expatriates (for details in each country studied, see Carr et al., 2010).

In principle, this kind of process would help to set a maximum wage ratio at the organizational and perhaps even supply chain level. In practice, while "advising" HRMs to codesign nonprecarious wage thresholds is one thing, *persuading* them is likely another. Evidence on the vagaries of wage inequality has been gathering for some time, as we can see from the review above, In short, we already know many of the answers about *how* to manage wage equality. Paying people fairly is the focus of a massive literature that demonstrates the upsides, for both organizations and employees, of preserving organizational justice (e.g., Colquitt et al., 2001; MacLachlan et al., 2010; Wiseman et al., 2022). In organizational politics however, evidence might be ignored, or dismissed as fake news. In the final analysis, decisions about *if* and *where* an organization sets its maximum and minimum wage levels come down to an organization's governance and moral compass.

The issue then becomes one of improving and, if necessary, leveraging improvements in governance. This is more a question of new diplomacies than research or theory (Saner & Yiu, 2012, 2014). Such new diplomacies are designed to address complex issues relating to poverty reduction and other SDGs through the use of dialog and innovations in problem-solving, policy, and practice. When such diplomatic strategies fail to gain traction, resolving the inequality issue may come down (or rather, up) to activists and/or governments to address at a more macro level (McVeigh & MacLachlan, 2021; Song et al., 2015). At the multilateral level, such as the UN, some of the most persuasive recommendations for managing wage inequality within organizations can be found in the landmark, pre-pandemic, post-Great Recession (2007–2009) ILO inter-governmental *World of Work Report 2013* (ILO, 2013). Much of the attention in that landmark report was focused on the notion of a maximum wage, at the CEO's end of the wage spectrum, with total wage amounts to include the three main wage elements (base salary, bonus, and shares). This unusual document synthesized the following main recommendations for "good governance."

Rein in CEO: shop-floor wage ratios. The first recommendation was to rein in CEO to shop-floor ratios to under three figures (i.e., a max of 99:1, which is arguably still way too high). This was based on addressing "concerns about equity" (ILO, 2013, p. 89), which I/O psychology often defines as outcomes-for-inputs relative to other employees. Case illustrations included Solar World, which has limited its CEO's wage to a ratio of 20:1 against the average wage in the organization, and the US-based Whole Foods Market, in which the cash component of the CEO wage was set at 19 times their average employee's wage.

Link CEO Wages (Compensation Packages) More Clearly to Firm Performance

According to the ILO (2013), maximum wage ratios would "provide an incentive for executives to strive towards improving the salaries of their employees. Such policies could be imposed by shareholders or could be considered as broader guidelines by governments" (ILO, 2013, p. 89). The possibility exists for governmental as well as organizational policies in our view. We would further contend that these ratios could still be too high, in the eyes of at least some employees. Accordingly, the issue of *where* to set a maximum ratio should ultimately be anchored in the judgment of the greater part.

Make Horizons Longer—Rather Than Shorter Term

A third recommendation was to link CEO pay to performance, as short-term bonuses were accounting for more than one-third of CEO pay, and more than two-thirds when combined with share-based compensation (ILO, 2013, p. 82). Such short horizons may create incentives for executives to raise stock values short-term and disincentivize longer term goals. The perverse effect is motivationally important because of a negative correlation between short-term–focused CEO compensation and corporate *social* performance, for example, on employee relations, protection of the environment, and wider income inequality (ILO, 2013, pp. 83–84; see also above, on human rights). Instead of setting performance goals over two years, the report suggested they could be staggered over a five-year period (ILO, 2013, p. 88). Such goals could then be widened to include social benefits, e.g., improving workplace safety and reducing carbon emissions (ILO, 2013, p.89). In addition to such measures, countries like Denmark and India have placed limits on the proportion of CEO wages that can be variable, as opposed to fixed, in an effort to stem short-term gains at the expense of longer term societal wellbeing (ILO, 2013, p. 84).

Provide a Say-on-Pay for Shareholders (in the Private Sector)

A further recommendation was introducing more inclusive say-on-pay. Referring largely to the private sector, company shareholders could be given more opportunity to decide by voting on the constituent elements of the CEO wage (across shares, bonuses, and base pay) as well as, presumably, the ratio itself. In some cases, only a "qualified minority" would be required in order to block an excessive proposed pay deal. For example, in Switzerland in March 2013, a "citizens' initiative on executive compensation" (ILO, 2013, p. 90) was approved for Swiss public companies listed either on the Swiss or overseas stock exchanges. The new requirements included a mandatory vote by shareholders on an aggregate wage for the directors and senior managers, a prohibition on silk parachutes and signing-on bonuses (short-short–term incentives) for members of corporate governing bodies, annual elections by shareholders for board chairperson and board members, and sanctions under criminal law for breaking any of the above regulations.

Improve the Management Function of Boards of Directors

This recommendation to improve the management function, for example, by keeping board and executive functions separated, was formulated in defense of employee stakeholders who had to bear the brunt of the 2007–2009 financial crisis and later "adjustment costs" (ILO, 2013, p. 90). This is important because it signals a clear link to work precariousness. The ILO (2013) recommended that there should be:

> …a more stakeholder-oriented corporate governance framework—one which continues to include shareholder interests but attempts to limit failed management policies and attends to the valid interests of other stakeholders, particularly those who bear the cost of externalities…To that end, consideration might be given to (1) disconnecting the roles of CEO and chairman of the board, (2) ensuring that independent directors and experts are an important component of the board, and (3) encouraging corporations to include social partners and employee representatives on their boards of directors, as is already the case in some countries."
>
> *(ILO, 2013, p. 90)*

Separations like this, between the executive board and management, alongside employee ownership (Jones, 2013), have been found not only to predict lower CEO wages, relatively speaking, but also to boost CEO wage transparency (Ben-Amar & Zeghal, 2011). Thus, a *structuring* of wage-determining groups and processes can contribute to bettering organizational wage governance. Indeed, improving organizational structures is the overarching theme in these key ILO recommendations.

Applying Theory for Managing Tensions and Conflict around Wage Caps

As Kurt Lewin wrote in 1951, "There is nothing more practical than a good theory," (Lewin, 1951, p. 169). Lewin's point is often interpreted as a call-to-arms for theorists to provide new ideas and pathways for tackling a particular challenge (in this case precarious work). In this final section, we start to develop an applied theory of wage inequality. We can start from an assumption that higher waged groups and individuals will not economically disempower themselves readily. Initiatives to set wage ceilings or caps are likely to provoke resistance: just like efforts to raise the wage floor (Intraprasert et al, Chapter 9; Meyer & Maleka, Chapter 7). These resistances in turn can create social and economic tensions and potentially escalate into conflict (Senge, 1992). In what follows, we utilize a primarily equity-based perspective to predict what may happen next.

The rise of wage inequality has the potential to be destructive, in a social and occupational sense (Carr, 2023). From an applied psychological perspective, privilege may initially motivate the privileged to work harder to justify the relative gap they enjoy. Meanwhile, workers who are relatively more deprived (paid much less, relatively speaking) may feel that some relative advantage is merited. We saw this, for example, with respect to expatriate: HCN wages (Carr et al., 2010; Marai et al., 2010; McWha et al., 2017, 2021), in which there was a recognition, on both sides of the wage fence, that at least some gap was probably warranted. However, when the gap becomes too large, the relatively privileged employees begin to internalize their relative status into negative stereotypes of the low-waged group, helping to justify the gap to themselves. Workers on the lower waged side, meanwhile, started to resent the way they are class-ified and waged and slowly began to disengage. Over time, productivity may start to fall, with demotivation at *both* ends of the wage spectrum—a process termed *double demotivation* (MacLachlan, Carr, & McAuliffe, 2010). Some forms of double motivations may be in train today as countries around the world continue to import cheap labor and make exceptions to minimum wage statutes on the dubious grounds that they come from lower wage labor markets.

One of the first casualties of any excessive wage inequality at work is wellbeing, either directly through lowered purchasing power for items like food (McLellan, 2017), or more indirectly, through emotionally corrosive wage injustice (D'Ambrosio et al., 2018). The result is likely to be an escalating dynamic of mutually reinforcing disengagement, with *illbeing* at the lower end of the wage-wellbeing spectrum, and either burnout or rent-seeking at the top. To be clear, these are predictions, not certainties. No doubt there will be circumstances, like a pandemic, when even having a job is felt to be a privilege, and having the responsibility for safeguarding them will motivate CEOs to work extra hard on everyone's collective behalf. On average though, and in the long run, excessive wage inequality, we contend, is probably bad for business and bad for wellbeing (Reichman & Carr, 2020). As such, new diplomacies are invaluable for framing such initiatives as mutually beneficial to workers, organizations, and CEOs, whose ability to increase productivity and to work in harmony should be enhanced. These diplomacies have applications not only within organizations but also across them in global, regional, and local supply chains. The distances that subtend across these gaps are often massive and out of sight but not necessarily out of mind, for workers and consumers alike.

Future Research Directions

A maximum wage implies a minimum wage, and in particular, the striking of a sustainable *balance* between the two. In that sense, tackling precarious work is inherently linked to tackling both maximum AND minimum wages, as a gestalt (see above; ILO, 2013). The question of a maximum wage thus becomes linked—through the concept of balance—to fairness. Fair(er) incomes (see this section) enable more sustainable livelihoods (Section 1, Chapters 1–6). They can be a handbrake on runaway inequality. In this chapter, we drew on interdisciplinary research on maximum wages and wage inequality. We found that I/O research has overlooked not only the lower end of the wage-wellbeing spectrum but also its very upper reaches. Future I/O research must, therefore, induct new ways to help (1) link wage ceilings to wage floors, (2) enhance fair incomes, and (3) sustain livelihoods. These new ways may include *exnovative*, *exonomic*, or *sociogramic* approaches.

Exnovation

Exnovation is the opposite of innovation. It entails eliminating the unsustainable from workplace practices in order to replace them with more just and sustainable alternatives (Carr, 2022). In this case, according to the ILO (2013), the "unsustainable" is CEO wages (when they become excessive). "Excessive" though needs to be defined and replaced with more accountable, inclusive, and fair wage differentials compared to other wage rungs and especially to the wage floor (ILO, 2013). A first step for exnovating unsustainable CEO wages might thus be to ask all affected employees what kind of relative measure and standard would work for them, against these criteria. What forms of measure, absolute or relative, and, if relative, type(s) of ratio, would be fair(est) to those same employee/er groups? This question—namely of acceptability, operationalized as fair incomes—needs to be asked not only within but also across organizational contexts, including supply chains and sectors. From that initial step, research may then begin to ask what *level* of ratio, e.g., between occupational groups, would be considered fair(est) by most groups (Carr et al., 2010). We have suggested a living wage as a basic denominator, but is that psychologically acceptable? Research should of course also explore the roles of socioeconomic, sociopolitical, and sociocultural diversity, in *how* people frame the idea of a maximum wage, and what specific measures they consider to be accountable, inclusive, and fair.

Exonomics

This means addressing factors that impact daily life but which remain unmeasured and uncounted in economic models (Weiner & Brown, 1990). Overlooked factors may include environmental, health, and moral considerations, for instance. Wage inequality in general and maximum wages (in relation to minimum ones) in particular arguably embody all three. In terms of a research direction, we have argued in this chapter that humanitarian work psychology needs to take a more serious note of the implications for wellbeing through, for example, (un) fairness at work, that wage (in)equalities have. Future research can and should, therefore, explore the potential and actual benefits for justice and ultimately justice-related wellbeing, of lower rather than higher levels of wage inequality, and lowered maximum wages. At what point, if any for instance, do wage ratios become inflection points, for the wellbeing of diverse groups at work? Are there any upper and lower thresholds for maximum living-wage ratios that impact the sustainability of the organization itself and thus on livelihoods for all? What is the role of public perception in the impact of wage ratios, when disclosed or exposed, on everyday consumer behavior?

Sociograms

Sociograms help to capture links between groups, and the import of those linkages, in everyday lives (Moreno, 1934). Work and life are not separate, and I/O psychology has arguably attempted to isolate one (work) from the other (life). Work-life balance is a point on the road, but what the research on maximum wages tells us is that I/O needs to take much wider strides within its ambit and ethos. These include researching the often-uncharted consequences of setting unfair maximum wages, on all work groups, including the supply chains of those groups, within and across communities; for example, the effects on public health and safety, ecosystem destruction, and human security in general (Hodgetts et al., 2022). Future research on the maximum wage, and its role in tackling precarious work, needs to be more interdisciplinary and include all 17 of the UN SDGs (UN, 2021). In particular, levels of maximum wage, as defined above, need to be mapped to their consequences for a shared ecosystem.

Notes

1 This chapter has been partly abridged, extracted, and adapted from Carr (2023).
2 We prefer the metaphor of a handbrake rather than entire braking system, since eliminating wage inequality will require additional forms of braking mechanisms. Other chapters in the handbook illustrate some of them.
3 It is not clear whether slaves would have been counted as citizens in the scope and ambit of this remark.

References

Baron, J. N., & Pfeffer, J. (1994). The social psychology of organizations and inequality. *Social Psychology Quarterly, 57*, 190–209.

Ben-Amar, W., & Zeghal, D. (2011). Board of directors' independence and executive compensation disclosure transparency. *Journal of Applied Accounting Research, 12*, 43–60.

Berg, A., Ostry, J. D., & Zettelmeyer, J. (2012). What makes growth sustained? *Journal of Development Economics, 98*, 149–66.

Bloom, M. (1999). The performance effects of pay dispersion on individuals and organizations. *Academy of Management Journal, 42*, 25–40.

Burnes, B. (2020). The origins of Lewin's three-stage model of change. *The Journal of Applied Behavioural Science, 56*, 32–59.

Carr, S. C. (2010). Global mobility and local economy: It's work psychology, stupid. In S. C. Carr (Ed.), *The psychology of global mobility* (pp. 125–150). Springer.

Carr, S. C. (2023). *Wage and wellbeing: Towards sustainable livelihood.* Springer.

Carr, S. C., & Gini, C. (2011). Project organizational Gini coefficient. *The Industrial and Organizational Psychologist, 49*, 102–104.

Carr, S. C., Haar, J., Hodgetts, D., Jones, H., Arrowsmith, J., Parker, J., Young-Hauser, A., & Alefaio, S. (2022). Pandemic or not, worker subjective wellbeing pivots about the living wage point: A replication, extension, and policy challenge in Aotearoa New Zealand. *Frontiers in Psychology, 13*, 828081. https://doi.org/10.3389/fpsyg.2022.828081

Carr, S. C., Maleka, M., Meyer, I., Barry, M. L., Harr, J., Parker, J., Arrowsmith, J., Yao, C., Hodgetts, D., Jones, H., Young-Hausner, A., Afeaki-Mafile'o, E., Rasmussen, A.-H. Alefaio-Tugia, S., Falealili, B., Mafile'o, K., Pikula, T., Wolfgram, N., 'Uhila, H., … & Naithani, A. (2018). How can wages sustain a living? By getting ahead of the curve. *Sustainability Science, 13*, 901–917. https://doi.org/10.1007/s11625-018-0560-7

Carr, S. C., McWha, I., MacLachlan, M., & Furnham, A. (Eds.). (2010). Remuneration discrepancies and poverty reduction: Elephant salaries in the international development parlour. The *International Journal of Psychology, 45*(5), 321–380.

Cobham, A., & Sumner, A. (2013). *Is it all about the tails? The Palma measure of income inequality.* Centre for Global Development.

Colquitt, J. A., Conlon, D. E., Wesson, M. J., Porter, C.O. L. H., & Ng, K. Y. (2001). Justice at the millennium: A meta-review of 25 years of organizational justice research. *Journal of Applied Psychology, 86*, 425–445.

Conroy, S. A., Gutpa, N., Shaw, J. D., & Park, T. Y. (2014). A multilevel approach to the effects of pay variation. *Research in Personnel and Human Resources Management, 32*, 1–64.

Cornia, E. A., & Court, J. (2001). *Inequality, growth and poverty in the era of liberalisation and globalization.* United Nations University.

Crystal, G. S. (1991). *In search of excess: The overcompensation of American executives.* W. W. Norton.

Dabla-Norris, E., Kochhar, K., Suphphiphat, N., Ricka, F., & Tsounta, E. (2015). *Causes and consequence of income inequality: A global perspective* (IMF Staff Discussion Note SDN/15/13). International Monetary Fund. https://www.imf.org/external/pubs/ft/sdn/2015/sdn1513.pdf

D'Ambrosio, C., Clark, A. E., & Barazzetta, M. (2018). Unfairness at work: Wellbeing and quits. *Labour Economics, 51*, 307–316.

Desai, S. D., Brief, A. P., & George, J. M. (2010). Meaner managers: A consequence of income inequality. In R. M. Kramer, A. E. Tenbrunsel, M. H. Bazerman, & D. M. Messick (Eds.), *Social decision making: Social dilemmas, social values, and ethical judgements* (pp. 315–332). Routledge.

DiTomaso, N., & Parks-Yancy, R. (2014). The social psychology of inequality at work: Individual, group, and organizational dimensions. In J. McLeod, E. Lawler, & M. Schwalke (Eds.), *Handbook of the social psychology of inequality* (pp. 437–58). Springer.

Doyle, M. W., & Stiglitz, J. E. (2014). Eliminating extreme inequality: A sustainable development goal, 2015–2030. *Ethics & International Affairs, 28*, 5–13.

Easterly, W. (2007). Inequality does cause underdevelopment: Insights from a new instrument. *Journal of Development Economics, 84*, 755–76.

Ellis, P. (2017). Sampling distribution of weighted Gini coefficient. *Free Range Statistics.* Retrieved 2021, July 6, from http://freerangestats.info/blog/2017/08/05/weighted-gini

Erdogan, B., Bauer, T. N., & Taylor, S. (2015). Management commitment to the ecological environment and employees: Implications for employee attitudes and citizenship behaviours. *Human Relations, 68*, 1669–1691.

Festinger, L. (1950). Informal social communication. *Psychological Review, 57*, 271–282.

Festinger, L. (1954). A theory of social comparison processes. *Human Relations, 7*, 117–140.

Festinger, L., Schachter, S., & Back, K. (1950). *Social pressures in informal groups: A study of human factors in housing.* Harper.

Freeman, R. E. (1984). *Strategic management: A stakeholder approach.* Pitman.

Friedman, M. (1962). *Capitalism and freedom.* University of Chicago Press.

Furnham, A. (2019). Pay secrecy. *European Business Review, Nov/Dec*, 69–72.

Gallego, A. (2016). Inequality and the erosion of trust among the poor: Experimental evidence. *Socio-Economic Review, 14*, 443–460.

Gelles, D. (2021, April 24). CEO pay remains stratospheric, even at companies battered by pandemic. *The New York Times.*

Gini, C. (1965). On the characteristics of Italian statistics. *Journal of the Royal Statistical Society, 128*, 89–109.

Hills, T. (2014, February 24). Are top executives paid enough? Should there be a maximum wage, or not? *Psychology Today.* https://www.psychologytoday.com/ca/blog/statistical-life/201402/are-top-executives-paid-enough

Hodgetts, D. J., Hopner, V., Carr, S. C., Bar-Tal, D., Liu, J., Saner, R., Yiu, L., Horgan, J., Searle, R., Massola, G., Hakim, M., Marai, L., King, P., & Moghaddam, F. M. (2022). Human security psychology: A linking construct for an eclectic discipline.

Review of General Psychology. Advance online publication. https://doi.org/10.1177/10892680221109124

International Labour Organization. (2013). *World of work report 2013: Repairing the economic and social fabric.*

International Labour Organization. (2019). *The global labour income share and distribution: Key findings*. https://www.ilo.org/wcmsp5/groups/public/—dgreports/—stat/documents/publication/wcms_712232.pdf

International Labour Organization. (2021). *The role of digital labour platforms in transforming the world of work.*

International Labour Organization. (2022). *Decent work.* https://www.ilo.org/global/topics/decent-work/lang--en/index.htm

International Monetary Fund. (2011). All for one: Why inequality throws us off balance. *Finance & Development, 48*, 1–39.

Jacquart, P., & Armstrong, J. S. (2013). The ombudsman: Are top executives paid enough? An evidence-based review. *Interfaces, 43*, 1–27.

Jones, D. C. (2013). Employee ownership as a mechanism to enhance corporate governance and moderate executive pay levels. *Interfaces, 43*, 599–601.

Kallschmidt, A. M., & Eaton, A. A. (2019). Are lower social class origins stigmatized at work? A qualitative study of social class concealment and disclosure among white men employees who experienced upward mobility. *Journal of Vocational Behaviour, 113,* 115–128.

Kennedy, L., Murphy, R., Anderson, S., & Hildyard, L. (2019). *The fat cat diet: A progressive plan for wage fairness*. Centre for Labour and Social Studies.

Lewin, K. (1947). Group decision and social change. In T. Newcomb, & E. Hartley (Eds.), *Readings in social psychology* (pp. 330–344). Henry Holt.

Lewin, K. (1951). *Field theory in social science.* Harper & Row.

MacLachlan, M., Carr, S. C., & McAuliffe, E. (2010). *The aid triangle: Recognizing the dynamics of dominance, justice and identity*. Zed Books.

Mahy, B., Rycx, F., & Volral, M. (2011). Does wage dispersion make all firms productive? *Scottish Journal of Political Economy, 58*, 455–489.

Malmandier, U., & Tate, G. (2009). Superstar CEOs. *Quarterly Journal of Economics, 124*, 1593–1561.

Marai, L., Kewibu, V., Kinkin, E., Peniop, P., Salini, C., & Kofana, G. (2010). Remuneration disparities in Oceania: Papua New Guinea and Solomon Islands. *International Journal of Psychology, 45*, 350–359.

McWha-Hermann, I., Jandric, J., Wakefield, S., Carr, S. C., Grund, C., & Moutou, M. (2017). *Project FAIR: Exploring practical pathways for reward fairness in international NGOs*. University of Edinburgh.

McWha-Hermann, I., Marai, L., MacLachlan, M., & Carr, S. C. (2021). Developing evidence-based alternatives to dual salary systems. *International Perspectives in Psychology: Research, Practice, Consultation, 10*(4), 243–246. https://doi.org/10.1027/2157-3891/a000023

Marmot, M. G., Stansfeld, S., Patel, C., North, F., Head, J., White, I., Brunner, E., Feeney, A., & Davey Smith, G. (1991). Health inequalities among British civil servants: The Whitehall II study. *The Lancet, 337*, 1387–1393.

McLellan, R. K. (2017). Work, health, and worker wellbeing: Roles and opportunities for employers. *Health Affairs, 36*, 206–213.

McVeigh, J., & MacLachlan, M. (2021). The macropsychology of COVID-19: Psychological governance as pandemic response. *American Psychologist.* https://doi.org/10.1037/amp0000909

McWha-Hermann, I. (2023). Equal pay for work of equal value: Easier said than done. In D. L. Blustein & L. Y. Flores (Eds), *Rethinking work: Essays on building better workers*. Routledge.

Messersmith, J. G., Guthrie, J. P., Ji, Y.-Y., & Lee, J.-Y. (2011). Executive turnover: The influence of dispersion and other pay system characteristics. *Journal of Applied Psychology, 96*, 457–469.

Mohan, B., Schlager, T., Deshpandé, R., & Norton, M. I. (2018). Consumers avoid buying from firms with higher CEO-to-worker pay ratios. *Journal of Consumer Psychology, 28*(2), 344–352.

Moreno, J. L. (1934). *Who shall survive?* Beacon House.

Netuveli, G., & Bartley, M. (2012). Perception is reality: Effect of subjective versus objective socio-economic position on quality of life. *Sociology, 46,* 1208–1215.

Organization for Economic Cooperation and Development. (2016). *Household income and wealth: Income inequality and poverty.* Organization for Economic Cooperation and Development.

Ostry, J. D., Berg, A., & Tsangarides, C. G. (2014). *Redistribution, inequality, and growth.* (IMF Staff Discussion Note 14/02). International Monetary Fund. https://www.imf.org/external/pubs/ft/sdn/2014/sdn1402.pdf

Oxfam. (2017). *An economy for the 99%.* https://www-cdn.oxfam.org/s3fs-public/file_attachments/bp-economy-for-99-percent-160117-en.pdf

Oxfam. (2020). *Time to care: Unpaid and underpaid care work and the global inequality crisis.* https://policy-practice.oxfam.org/resources/time-to-care-unpaid-and-underpaid-care-work-and-the-global-inequality-crisis-620928/

Palma, J. G. (2011). Homogenous middle vs. heterogeneous tails, and the end of the inverted U: The share of the rich is what it's all about. *Development and Change, 42*, 87–153.

Petrescu, A. I., & Simmons, R. (2008). Human resource management practices and workers' job satisfaction. *International Journal of Manpower, 29,* 651–7.

Pizzigati, S. (2018). *The case for a maximum wage.* Wiley.

Reichman, W., & Carr, S. C. (2020). Human rights is the business of business. In N. Rubin (Ed.), *Cambridge handbook of psychology and human rights* (pp. 428–442). Cambridge University Press.

Sammer, J. (2021, June 4). *Executive pay growth during the pandemic faces scrutiny.* Society for Human Resource Management. https://www.shrm.org/resourcesandtools/hr-topics/compensation/pages/executive-pay-growth-during-the-pandemic-faces-scrutiny.aspx

Saner, R., & Yiu, L (2012). The new diplomacies and humanitarian work psychology. In S. C. Carr, M. MacLachlan, & A. Furnham (Eds.), *Humanitarian work psychology* (pp. 129–165). Palgrave-Macmillan.

Saner, R., & Yiu, L. (2014). Business diplomacy competence: A requirement for implementing the OECD Guidelines for Multinational Enterprises. *The Hague Journal of Diplomacy, 9*, 311–33.

Schein, E. H. (1996). Three cultures of management: The key to organizational learning. *Sloan Management Review, 38*, 9–20.

Schumpeter. (2021, May 13). Will shareholders halt the inexorable rise of CEO pay? *The Economist*. https://www.economist.com/business/2021/05/13/will-shareholders-halt-the-inexorable-rise-of-ceo-pay

Senge, P. (1992). *The fifth discipline*. Random House.

Shaw, J. D. (2014). Pay dispersion. *Annual Review of Organizational Psychology, 1*, 521–544.

Sherif, M. (1936). *The psychology of social norms*. Harper & Row.

Siegel, P. A., & Hambrick, D. C. (2005). Pay disparities within top management groups: Evidence of harmful effects on performance of high-technology firms. *Organization Science, 16*, 259–274.

Smith, A. (2015). *The wealth of nations*. W. Strahan & T. Cadell (Original work published 1776).

Smith, L. (2015). Reforming the minimum wage: Towards a psychological perspective. *American Psychologist, 70*, 557–65.

Song, J., Price, D. J., Guvenen, F., Bloom, N., & von Wachter, T. (2015). *Firming up inequality*. (Working Paper 21199). National Bureau of Economic Research.

Stiglitz, J. E. (2011, May 24). Of the 1%, by the 1%, for the 1%. *Vanity Fair.* https://www.vanityfair.com/news/2011/05/top-one-percent-201105

United Nations Department of Economic and Social Affairs. (n.d.). *Sustainable development.* https://sdgs.un.org/

Weiner, E., & Brown, A. (1990). Exonomics: What economics fails to explain. *The Futurist, 24*, 36–9.

Who exactly are the 1%? (2012, January 21). *The Economist.* https://www.economist.com/united-states/2012/01/21/who-exactly-are-the-1

Wilkinson, R., & Pickett, K. (2009). *The spirit level: Why equality is better for everyone*. Penguin.

Wiseman, J., & Stillwell, A. (2022). Organizational justice: Typology, antecedents and consequences. *Encyclopedia, 2*, 1287–1295

Yu, Z., & Wang, F. (2017). Income inequality and happiness: An inverted U-shaped curve. *Frontiers in Psychology, 8*. https://doi.org/10.3389/fpsyg.2017.02052

PART III

Work Security

11

INFORMAL WORK AS SUSTAINABLE WORK

Pathways to Sustainable Livelihoods

Mahima Saxena and Charles L. Tchagneno

According to estimates by the World Bank (Ohnsorge & Shu, 2021) and the International Labour Organization (ILO, 2021), over two-thirds of the world's workforce now lives and works in the informal economy (Jyoti & Arora, Chapter 6). This equates to more than 2 billion individuals globally who work in the informal sector (ILO, 2021). In middle- and low-income countries, before the COVID-19 crisis, the informal sector was considered a job sponge for absorbing those who lost their jobs in the formal economy (ILO, 2022). According to the *World Employment and Social Outlook: Trends 2022*, at the very beginning of the pandemic, informal workers were three times more likely than formal ones to lose their jobs (ILO, 2022). As the crisis continued, informal employment remained "stubbornly below its pre-crisis level" (ILO, 2022, p. 29).

Despite the colossal scale of the informal economy, the path to human welfare is persistently viewed as being via the much smaller formal economy and associated systems, which are themselves under threat from precarious work conditions (ILO, 2022; International Trade Union Confederation, 2018). The continuing blind faith in formal work is most evident perhaps in the myriad of "skills-creation" programs that attempt to either (a) transition informal workers *from* informal work *into* formal work or (b) provide skills through training programs for workers to get jobs that are often at the base of the pyramid (for instance, see Adams et al., 2013; Development Asia, 2014; ILO, 2014; Ohnsorge & Yu, 2021; Saxena, 2021; Walther, 2012). Two immediate implications of (a) and (b) are that (c) the informal sector is largely unskilled and inferior to its smaller formal counterpart and (d) that people who work in the informal sector aspire to graduate into formal sector jobs.

DOI: 10.4324/9781003440444-14

From a humanitarian work psychology perspective (Carr et al., 2012), which is inherently salutogenic, this chapter challenges all four implications, and with them, the premise that the path to growth and development is by transitioning workers from the vast informal sector into a much smaller—and itself increasingly precarious—formal one. We show that the scale of skills and work in the informal economy is colossal, grossly underrated, and just as importantly, not ready or willing to formalize itself (Saxena, 2021; Tchagneno, 2018).

The informal sector is largely *assumed* to be unskilled (Saxena, 2017) and is laden with negative stereotypes. As such, it becomes evident that informal-sector perspectives are not taken seriously either in academic discourse or in policy-making. First, we challenge existing notions surrounding informal work and work in the informal economy, noting that various stereotypes contribute to a misleading and misinformed understanding of informal sector skills and related livelihood goals. Next, working upward from the premise that the informal economy encompasses myriad forms of skills and skilled work, we present two country case studies that offer solutions for leveraging the skills and motivations that are already present in abundance in the informal sector to enable relatively sustainable livelihoods. Our central premise is that the *economic* viability of work (i.e., "jobs") is at the forefront and tends to dominate current scholarly and policy discourse; and that the *psychological* viability of work is ignored, which leads to blanket notions of "transitioning from informal- to formal-sector work" being considered the gold standard of developmental aspirations.

We do not deny the many aspects of precarity in informal-sector work. Informal-sector work is undoubtedly often dangerous, insecure, unprotected, own account, and, in general, "vulnerable" (ILO, 2019). However, we argue that this same precariousness does not automatically mean that informal work is necessarily "inferior" or "unsustainable." We illustrate this via our cross-continent industrial and organizational (I/O) psychology research investigations in India and Cameroon.

In India, we find that informal work is precarious but far from unskilled. Instead, we *discover* (Spector, 2017) highly skilled work in India which is embedded in the lived psychological realities of informal workers, appropriately referred to as *cultural skills* leading to *sustainable work*. To institute a change in this form of work (for instance, via informal to formal transition programs) would be to rip the workers from their own experiential realities. In Cameroon, we show that such transition programs do not take into account the perspectives of the informal workers themselves. We question the need to "impose" transition programs and describe the perspectives of Cameroonian informal workers.

Ultimately, both studies question the presumptions that informal-sector work is bad, unskilled, and useless and that workers need to transition *away* from practicing their indigenous cultural skills. Furthermore, we suggest that the reason why most informal-to-formal restructuring programs fail is because they do not take informal-sector perspectives seriously. We argue that such programs can strip communities of their cultural heritage and even cause psychological trauma. Put together, we contend that grassroots perspectives are key to fostering and supporting inclusive development via sustainable livelihoods. Finally, based on these country case studies, one from India and one from Cameroon, we present a five-point plan for *future research directions and policy development* that we hope will contribute to forging a path from informal skills to more sustainable work, and livelihoods, for millions of workers around the world (Jyoti & Arora, Chapter 6).

Overview of the Informal Sector

Multidisciplinary Foci of the Informal Sector

The informal sector has been studied and researched in numerous disciplines. In effect, the conceptualization of informality has become more complex with the porosity of boundaries in the social sciences (Lautier, 2013). Since work in the informal sector is not a part of mainstream I/O psychology (see below), we provide some definitions to fully describe how diverse disciplines understand this domain. Next, we illustrate the stereotypes that tend to dominate this discourse and argue that it is these stereotypes that have led to the evident neglect of informal-sector perspectives in both academia and in policy-making.

Definitions

According to the ILO (2014), the informal sector is characterized by (a) ease of entry into its activities, for instance, with few or no formal qualification requirements, such as domestic help in China (Dong, 2020); (b) reliance on local resources since production is often artisanal, for example, woodworking in Peru (Holley, 1995), or based on local means of production, for example, sand mining in Cameroon (Weng & Margules, 2022); (c) family ownership of microenterprises, for example, a woman who sets up a tailoring business out of her home in Indonesia using a microcredit loan (Tipple, 2005); (d) small scale of activities, for example, a potter who produces and sells his wares at the local bazaar in northern India (Saxena, 2021); (e) labor-intensive and adapted technology, for example, a daily wage manual laborer in agricultural work in India (Saxena, 2015) or in construction in the US (Bohn & Owens, 2012); (f) skills acquired outside the formal school system, for example, intergenerational occupations such as weaving in Nepal (Saxena, 2023); and (g) unregulated and competitive markets, for example, vegetable sellers at the local farmer's market who compete for walk-up customers in Egypt (Radchenko, 2014).

The above-mentioned characteristics of the informal sector make it apparent that in many ways, informal-sector work is fundamentally different, even orthogonal, to formal-sector work. The formal sector is regulated and taxed and is mostly tied to organizations or organization-like entities, and thus caters to the concept of a "job" as opposed to "work." If we remove the elements of regulation and taxation from the formal sector, the formal quite readily becomes *in*formal. With informality, come issues related to precariousness and its consequences—such as lack of benefits, social protections, medical provisions, and so on. *We surmise that these issues are glaring and often so conspicuous that the academic and policy-focused on-lookers do not see beyond the obvious ills of informal work.*

Global Perspectives on the Informal Sector

Multidisciplinary literature from different parts of the world presents a different, albeit mostly negative, view of the informal sector. Much of the academic and policy-making interest in the informal sector has come from sub-Saharan Africa since the early 1990s. Mougoué (2010) used the term informal sector to refer to, at least in the context of sub-Saharan Africa, economic activities that take place within the context of criminal, social, and fiscal legislation or which escape national accounting systems, representing all nonagricultural production units that do not have a taxpayer number and/or do not keep formal written accounts. It is therefore the set of activities that escape economic and social policies and therefore possible regulation by the state (Mougoué, 2010).

Similarly, Kélodjoué (2006), another African scholar, defines the informal sector as one where the set of activities produce goods and services from which individuals derive employment and income. The broader purpose of such activities is the creation of income and jobs for the local communities and people, rather than maximizing profit or return on investment—as is generally the case in the formal sector. Kélodjoué (2006) notes that these activities are "informal" in the sense that most of them are not recorded or registered in official statistics and that they operate on a very small scale and with a low level of organization. With Kélodjoué (2006), we begin to see, as well, a more *people-centric* understanding of the informal sector with a sharper and more humanitarian focus on people, communities, and work, rather than on organizations and financial bottom lines.

In the sociological realm, the informal sector is associated with peri-urban neighborhoods as economic spaces associated with no fixed type of work or activities. It is based on the premise that those who work in the informal sector keep moving from one income-generating activity to another: essentially, having no fixed job but rather moving to whatever allows income generation (Lautier, 2013).

Over time, in the discipline of sociology, the informal sector has come to be understood as a social group with a marginal culture, having all the characteristics of marginality (Lautier, 2013). Gradually, therefore, the terms "informal," "excluded," and "marginal" came to be used interchangeably across sociological studies on the informal sector, particularly in the literature from Latin America (Lautier, 2013). In general, in the context of informality in Africa and South and Central America, the informal sector refers to the realm that does not contribute to its nation's economic growth. As in sociology, in the field of economics, the informal sector is considered a sector that includes a homogenous set of activities that do not contribute to the national economy (Medina & Schneider, 2018).

Such was the state of confusion that in economics, the informal sector began to be likened to various animals, which we argue presents a dehumanized view of those who live and work in this realm. For instance, within the economic literature, the informal sector has been described as being like a giraffe: difficult to define by conventional standards but easy to recognize upon meeting (Lubell, 1991; Singer, 1970). The giraffe morphed into an elephant for Mead and Morrison (1996) who contended that the informal sector is too large to go unnoticed *and* for the state to "deal with" by simple measures. For Charmes and Adair (2014), the informal sector can also be compared to a chameleon in its ability to become invisible and slip through the cracks of regulation: "But, for sure, it is not a dinosaur, it is hardly in danger of extinction!" (p. 7).

Critiques of the Current Literature

As we have attempted to show in the brief review above, it is evident that there is much terminological confusion and overlap in defining and understanding the informal sector. We are not the first to call out the terminological confusion and the limitations of the different concepts and definitions surrounding informal-sector work; other scholars have also disagreed with the historical and modern conceptualizations of the informal sector.

For instance, Lautier (1990) noted that there are many different definitions of the informal sector, but it is difficult to identify in practice. Similarly, the idea of a *homogenous* informal sector was criticized by Tokman (1987). According to Tokman's (1987) historical critique, this sector is heterogenous and cannot have a single criterion for identification.

Several sociological studies (see Lautier, 2013) refute the "ease of entry" for workers—often considered a criterion for identifying the informal sector, by groups such as the ILO (ILO, 2014; see above). According to critics of the idea that the informal sector facilitates easy entry and presents few barriers to entry (Lautier, 2013), this does a disservice to the colossal scale of the informal economy by associating it with underemployment and poor contribution to the national GDP: thereby legitimizing policies that justify formalization of the economy.

We argue that the history of research and policy attention to the informal sector is also a function of broader colonial prejudices (Haynes, 2012) that dominate academic literature in the sciences, humanities, and social sciences (Singh et al., 2018). Historically, informal work has been a feature of countries around the world that underwent colonization by European powers in the last five centuries. What was labeled "informal work" (essentially, nonindustrialized work) has been, in fact, a highly effective way of organizing societies and guaranteeing livelihoods and occupational success to the people of a region (Saxena, 2017). Colonial prejudices have perpetrated serious and adverse racial injustice (Bonds & Inwood, 2016; Saito, 2020) and permeate society and academia alike (Saxena, 2023). We also see this in the literature on informal work as a continuation of the racial injustice perpetrated against those who work in nonindustrialized, informal settings.

To sum up, in this section, we showed that academic and policy work on the informal sector is laden with definitional fuzziness, terminological confusion, and prejudice. Meanwhile, it can be argued that psychology, in terms of research and policy action on the informal sector, is conspicuous by its absence (see, Jyoti & Arora, Chapter 6).

Psychology's Role in the Informal Sector

What stands out based on the review in the current section is that there is limited understanding of the informal sector from a psychological perspective. Informality and the informal sector have not been well recognized, researched, and engaged within the discipline of psychology. We contend that our field, specifically I/O psychology, can significantly contribute to the understanding of informality and ultimately have a positive impact on the lives of those who live and work in this sector. By using the science of the mind and behavior to understand the experiences of those in the informal economy, I/O psychology will expand its body of knowledge and, importantly, make meaningful contributions to the world of work of millions of those who stand to benefit the most from it. In particular, humanitarian work psychology could contribute to the creation of a zeitgeist in which our research can actively strive to be free from colonial biases, prejudiced attitudes, and racial injustice. We take a step in this direction in the following subsection. Specifically, we argue that the prejudices about the informal sector that dominate academic literature have led to stereotyped notions of the informal sector.

Stereotypes about the Informal Sector

Overall, several themes tend to dominate the current state of the *nonpsychology* literature on the informal sector. These are the ideas that informal sector work (a) is not carried out in accordance with legal or established procedures (for example, see ILO, 2014); (b) is disorganized and unproductive and does not contribute to the national GDP and related indices of economic growth and development (see Kélodjoué, 2006); (c) is part of a "primitive" (Rosaldo, 2021), hidden, underground, or shadow economy (for example, see Medina & Schneider, 2018); and (d) that these unregulated economic activities of the poor are carried out by hiding from the official authorities for reasons including tax evasion and noncompliance with the law (for example, see Mutukwa & Tanyanyiwa, 2021).

We argue that these (colonially) prejudiced views of the informal sector do not represent the complete truth regarding those who live and work in the informal economy (Saxena, 2017). We further argue that the above-mentioned prejudices have led to *stereotyped* ideas of informal-sector work as being unskilled, low-skilled, and of individuals who operate in the informal sector as being incompetent (Saxena, 2021). Such a stigmatized, negative view of the informal sector therefore lends credibility to the idea that the informal sector is inherently problematic and needs to be reformulated or restructured. This also undermines informal workers' capacity for growth and development. Formalization, therefore, emerges as the solution (Rosaldo, 2021). This solution is then implemented, for example, via various work-restructuring programs or reskilling or upskilling interventions (Saxena, 2017, 2021).

Understanding work in the informal sector in the sociocultural contexts of countries with high rates of informality requires a de-stereotyping of the traditional definitions of this concept. Globally, the informal sector is heterogenous, highly differentiated, and consists of economic activities and work arrangements that are diverse and disparate (Saxena, 2017). Sweeping stereotyping of the informal sector has done a disservice to the over 2 billion people who live and work in this sector.

We are not disputing that the informal sector and those who work within its bounds are marginalized, often associated with poverty, and suffer from the absence of benefits, protections, and occupational health and safety standards. However, we contend that sweeping labels that notate informal-sector work as unskilled or semiskilled, illegal, shadow, dark, criminal, and so on are invalid and do not correspond with the complex and nuanced realities on the ground. Such labels tend to whitewash the realities and unique work and life experiences of billions of people around the world.

In terms of the outcomes of these stereotypes, we go a step further to argue that individuals who work in the informal economy are suffering due to the prevailing stereotypes. Since development is largely seen as arising through professional, office-based jobs that are safe from harassment (POSH jobs; Gloss et al., 2017), there is a state of neglect that tends to dominate even well-intentioned research and policy initiatives that inadvertently fail to truly capture the context of informal-sector skills and the nature of work in the informal economy. Since the vast majority of those who work in the informal sector often battle poverty (Williams, 2014), this state of neglect leads to work that is unsafe and vulnerable to exploitation and precarious income, and occupational hazards. *We contend that there cannot be complete development until informal-sector skills are actively and meaningfully incorporated into policy programs and provided support.*

We propose a new approach to this. Instead of trying to *formalize* informal skills, we believe that we need to navigate from informal skills to sustainable work (Saxena, 2021). In the sections that follow, we propose a new way of understanding work in the informal sector by taking a grassroots perspective in order to leverage the skills that are already present to achieve sustainable work and inclusive growth aligned with United Nations Sustainable Development Goals (UN SDGs; UN, 2022). We will present a five-point plan that we hope will spur research activities by I/O psychologists in this area and simultaneously contribute meaningful insights to policy initiatives that are designed to better the lives of those in poverty.

From Informal Skills to Sustainable Work

A Ray of Hope

We define informal skills as those learned and practiced behaviors (Lowe et al., 2010) that enable individuals in the informal sector to work and earn a livelihood, for example, handloom weaving skills (Kar, 2012) used as part of the informal cottage industry in India or indigenous regalia-making skills in Native American communities (Harrison, 2008; Native Languages of the Americas, n.d.). Based on our work, we found *sustainable work* existing as skilled work in the informal sector that was reliant on traditional knowledge and cultural skills and was found to be *psychologically* sustainable (Saxena, 2021). This form of work is inherently meaningful to the workers and ignites a sense of purpose; feelings of dignity, identity, and self-esteem; aligns with local cultural values; and fosters contentment and hope (Saxena, 2021). Such psychological sustainability is core to intergenerational thriving and flourishing. These values also lead to policy outcomes that are aligned with the capability perspective (Carr & MacLachlan, 1998). The capability perspective provides a context in which people can be seen as striving to achieve their natural, innate capabilities (Sen, 1999; Teng-Calleja et al, Chapter 8).

In this section, we present two complementary grassroots case studies that unpack the lived psychological perspectives of those who possess informal skills and work in the informal sector. These research projects in Asia and Africa were aimed at expanding our understanding of skills in the informal economy by capturing the voices of those who engage in informal work in India and the attitudes surrounding informal-to-formal transition programs in Cameroon (Hill, 2001;

Williams & Nadin, 2012a). Both elevate the perspectives of informal-sector workers. By bringing the voice and perspectives of informal-sector workers to the fore, our I/O psychology studies demonstrate grassroots-level inclusion in academic literature and show how these can inform inclusive policy efforts.

India

A series of investigations were conducted in India to understand the nature and experience of work in the informal economy. Through the voices of the workers, captured in situ (Schein, 2012) while they were working using advanced I/O research methods (Spector, 2017), this research presents the first-person perspectives of informal workers in rural India in their own words. Supported and facilitated by the Society for Industrial and Organizational Psychology (Saxena et al., 2015), this was the first psychological investigation to capture the *work experiences* (Weiss & Rupp, 2011) of highly skilled workers in the informal economy (Saxena, 2017).

While I/O psychology has largely focused on work *within* organizations, this project focused on work *outside* organizational boundaries, by artisans in India. This broader project broke many prevailing stereotypes that regard informal-sector work as lowly (Williams & Bezeredi, 2018), unskilled (Amaral & Quintin, 2006; Hatton, 2017), disempowering (Meagher, 2014), and a last resort for workers (Williams & Bezeredi, 2018). As discussed in the previous sections, many of these stereotypes have roots in academic disciplines that have a longer history of engaging with and researching the informal sector than the field of I/O psychology (for instance, economics; Godfrey, 2011; Williams & Nadin, 2012b) and often inadvertently propagate prejudiced notions (Saxena, 2017) regarding the informal sector. The project compels us to reconsider and reevaluate how we approach work in the informal economy.

Pottery is a common occupation in many parts of the world. In India, as in many other parts of Asia, it is practiced as a source of income and livelihood in both rural and urban areas (Chen & Doane, 2008). Nested within the informal economy, these informal workers are not taken seriously as skilled workers and tend to get clumped along with unskilled or low-skilled forms of informal work (such as street vending or agricultural labor).

Neglect by governments, heavy taxation by colonizing powers, inadequate infrastructural support, and absence of appropriate supply chains are some of the reasons why, despite engaging in skillful and highly engaging work, the work of these communities is under threat. For example, potters were largely able to make a decent living until recently. However, due to the influx of inexpensive plastic products (for example, cheap plastic cups at throwaway prices that are produced in large-scale commercial manufacturing units) backed by more "developed" organizations, commercialized supply chains, in economically "modern" sectors, their work and, by extension, their livelihoods are currently under threat and require urgent attention. Psychology can play a very important role in this area. In our investigation (Saxena, 2021), we found incredibly robust psychological indicators of pride in workmanship, psychological resilience, and sustainability that can be overlooked and misunderstood if viewed through a purely economic lens. Below, we describe some of these robust findings from our work:

Cultural Skills and Intergenerational Occupations

It was found that this informal-sector work was reliant on knowledge and skills that likely originated thousands of years ago (Hazarika, 2006) and were passed on to each successive generation in a continuous, unbroken chain of cultural skill transfer (Saxena, 2021). Amazingly, these skills are still present in local communities and have required nothing in terms of infrastructure (financial or otherwise) to be communicated cross-generationally. Thus, first and foremost, this investigation revealed that, contrary to popular perceptions, this informal-sector work was labor intensive, highly skilled, and represented heritage knowledge. Importantly, the research revealed that the informal sector includes highly skilled work. Thus, it is meaningful in reshaping our understanding of informal-sector work as far more complex and nuanced than previously understood.

Generational Knowledge

These skills are a core part of the cultural heritage that informs the fundamental worldview of the potters. The manifestation of these cultural learnings, as they translate into work (Weiss & Rupp, 2011) and products (beautiful and functional pottery items), leads to feelings of wellbeing, a positive sense of duty toward broader society, and pride. Potters consider themselves a critical part of society and integral to the continuation of traditional knowledge, occupations, and ways of life. Thus, as both envoys and users of cultural knowledge, they are part of a complex chain of work-related skills, expertise, and learnings that we know little about. This investigation has opened a gate to a path far beyond merely *recognizing* informal-sector skills to fostering a holistic and valid psychological *understanding* of the skills and giving them their rightful place in scholarly and policy dialogs.

Beyond "Me"—A Sense of Duty Toward All

In the potter community, we found an internalized sense of duty toward the environment, society, and the planet (Saxena, 2021). This was an eye-opening finding, especially against the contrasting backdrop of the stereotypes of informal workers being illiterate and uneducated (Agarwala, 2006), unproductive (La Porta & Shleifer, 2014), and incompetent (Webb et al., 2013). The informal workers embodied "dharma"—a sense of righteous duty (Bhawuk, 2019). This is a complex, multidimensional, and nuanced way of perceiving the world and perceiving life itself. It emphasizes *giving* (for instance, *to* society) more than *taking* (for instance, *from* the environment). It represents "doing for others" and wellbeing—not for the individual potter but for "mother earth," nature (a loose translation for the Sanskrit word "prakriti"), and all of humankind. Many pottery items are integral to rituals and ceremonies surrounding life's milestones (the birth of a child, death and cremation, marriage, and festivals).

The most revealing aspect of these interactions appeared when the informal artisans were asked *why* they continued to work in this sector, recognizing that it came with abject poverty and related ills. Their response was in the form of two questions; if they stopped, (a) how would society be able to continue to mark the milestones on the journey of life? and (b) how would cultural skills be passed on to posterity? Thus, they embodied much more than merely the identity of a worker; they were teachers, cultural messengers, and carriers of a body of intergenerational knowledge that is considered sacred and has continued for time immemorial. Potters continued to work in this domain by choice, not due to lack of options in the formal economy, which is what most informal-to-formal restructuring programs are premised on. Thus, pottery facilitated flourishing beyond jobs in the here-and-now. The informal work carried a profound personal and intergenerational meaning that was associated with thriving across past and future generations.

Well-being and Positive Affect

It was this sense of "something bigger than me" that gave potters a heightened sense of meaningfulness, a sense of purpose, and identity alignment with local cultural values. This social embeddedness fostered increased positive affect and feelings of wellbeing overall and whenever they worked in their traditional occupation. This operated as a protective factor against the effects of the poor income and provided intrinsic psychological resources (Baumeister, 2007; Hobfoll, 1989) to persevere in the face of adversity.

Psychologically Sustainable Work

This work came to be defined as psychologically sustainable (Saxena, 2021) in that it was intrinsically replenishing (Kaplan, 1995), meaningful, and instilled hope and contentment. The internal resources amassed through personal meaning and dignity protected against the resource-depleting aspects of working (Sonnentag, 2001) such as mental weariness, physical fatigue, and exhaustion (Shirom et al., 2006). This work fostered thriving and increased wellbeing which made it sustainable. By virtue of being deeply intertwined with the workers' sense of identity, dignity, and social embeddedness, the form and format of the work enables thriving and is decent, positive, and personally meaningful to the local community and the informal workers—the potters themselves.

Takeaways and Recommendations

We were struck by the findings of this investigation, which contrasted with the dominant themes that govern current dialog on informal-sector work (e.g., Godfrey, 2011; Williams & Bezeredi, 2018). What is regarded as an unskilled, meaningless, and noncontributing type of work and economy was fostering deep meaning, flourishing, and psychological resilience in potters who were otherwise facing adversity, particularly economic.

This work gave more than it took: to the community, environment, and nature. In doing so, and informed by culturally salient worldviews, it was free from the depleting aspects of work that lead to negative occupational health outcomes, such as burnout, mental exhaustion, and cognitive weariness. The form of work revealed in this investigation was deeply psychologically engaging (Saxena, 2021). So, the natural next question is, what are the implications of this investigation in terms of the relationship between informal-sector skills and safe and secure livelihoods? We answer this question below.

The findings and observations from this study in India corroborate our premise that due to a limited and often-stereotyped understanding of informal-sector work and informal skills, emphasis is put upon "formalizing" these skills and work without an appreciation for the lived experience of the worker in informal work. It is clear that we can no longer conceive of the vast variety of forms and formats of informal work as a single broad category, nor can we assume that all those in the informal sector are engaged in "indecent" work due to a lack of choice or opportunities in the formal employment space.

We contend that economic formalization (i.e., informal-to-formal economy transition) programs are a simplistic, often mechanistic approach to "change" things that appear bad on the surface. In other words, as we've discussed, the informal sector *appears* to be suffering from adversities such as poverty, occupational hazards, apparent disorganization, and so on. This apparent and more *visible* state of affairs, combined with the prejudiced approach by academic literature on the topic (La Porta & Shleifer, 2014), lead to policy programs that are large-scale and sweeping (Saxena, 2021), even over entire geographic regions, such as a nation-wide program to formalize informal workers as we will see in the next case study on Cameroon, and spatially blind. By the latter, we mean that such sweeping transition programs do not consider the nuances of informal work in the local communities in question and therefore are oblivious to the psychological realities of the workers who inhabit the informal space.

Such spatially blind, large-scale, sweeping transition programs assume informal work to be low-skilled and attempt to reskill individuals so they can find work in a different occupation such as computer repair (Williams & Nazarov, 2018) or upskill workers by changing the existing informal skillset through different means, for example, through greater technological input or reliance on machinery. Such programs often end up in failure (ILO, 2018). As it was found, potters passionately wanted to continue to work in their deeply meaningful and satisfactory intergenerational legacy occupation (Saxena, 2021). One can only imagine the unhappiness and discontent that would emerge from being pulled from their occupation (*assumed* unskilled due to its existence in the informal economy) and being forced to work in a different, "skilled" occupation (where skills-training has taken place) where one's cognitive frame of reference would shift from "doing good for the world" to simply "earning a paycheck." Therefore, we argue that the psychological sustainability of work ought to be a core component of decent work and living wages (Saxena, 2021).

A different approach is needed: one that legitimizes, accepts, and actively promotes informal-sector skills as critical vehicles for inclusive development strategies. To do this, based on the Indian investigation, our first recommendation is that skilled and unskilled work in the informal sector must be treated separately in policy and scholarly activities. Skilled and unskilled work are fundamentally different, and grave injustice is done to the lived experience of millions of workers when academic discourse and even well-intentioned policy efforts fail to disentangle the two (Saxena, 2021). Within the context of skilled informal work, transitioning *away* from intergenerational skills and cultural work, particularly those that have evolved locally over millennia of human history, may not be warranted or needed and is perhaps the reason why most "transition to formal economy" (ILO, 2014) programs fail.

Following the series of investigations in India, we briefly describe a multilayered framework of responses that were and could be undertaken to provide a voice and support for skilled informal workers and protect intergenerational livelihoods. Instead of *changing* the skills already present, a needs analysis of the local economy should be conducted to understand how supportive infrastructure around the informal skilled work can sustain and strengthen skills that are already present. For instance, in the investigation with intergenerational potters, we found threats to the occupation as a consequence of the "modern" economy (Saxena, 2021). These include, for example, the pervasive availability and indiscriminate use of cheaper plastic cups and dishes in place of ecofriendly pottery products, meaning potters can't make enough sales to survive.

This income precarity threatens the UN SDGs (UN, 2022) on ending poverty (SDG-1), inequality SDG-10), and hunger (SDG-2), and providing decent work and fostering economic growth (SDG-8). Furthermore, SDG-12 focuses on sustainable consumption. Pottery items produced by the informal artisans in

India are ecofriendly; produced in an environmentally conscious manner without the use of artificial colors, dyes, or harmful chemicals; and were naturally biodegradable. Unlike plastics, which threaten both life on land (SDG-15) and life on water (SDG#-4) (Jambeck et al., 2015), pottery dishes and cups facilitate responsible and sustainable consumption. Pottery cups, if they were to replace throwaway paper or plastic cups for tea and coffee worldwide, could ultimately positively impact SDG-12 by decreasing our climate-change footprint and biodiversity loss through cutting fewer trees, minimizing factories and the fuel that is consumed for production, and consequently reducing pollution (UN, 2022). Fair-trade supply circles that facilitate the movement of products from the producer (the potter) to the consumer globally would lead to increased positive affect for all parties involved (Carr et al., 2021). Ultimately, the zero toxicity of pottery cups, and reduction of the burden on the world's landfills (King et al., 2006), would be a win-win for multiple SDGs beyond work and employment.

Needs analyses to uncover the threats to informal-sector skills should be specific to regions, occupations, and cultures. They may lead to important insights for supporting and protecting livelihoods that rely on informal skilled work. An immediate response could be the creation of a fair supply circle where individuals with access, networks, and resources could personally connect poor, highly skilled workers in low-income rural areas (e.g., the Indian potters) with boutique stores in a high-income urban areas (for instance, downtown Chicago) to sell their wares to consumers at fair prices, enabling them to make decent livings (Carr et al., 2021).

Relatedly, wider supporting infrastructure such as raw material procurement and supply lines are often not readily available for informal-sector workers. To enhance and facilitate informal-sector work and, by extension, informal-sector livelihoods, an economically viable ecosystem within which informal skills are embedded should be created and, if present, improved. In other words, we don't recommend changing the workers (which is usually what most transition programs do), instead, we recommend changing the wider infrastructure, i.e., the systems to support informal work and government and policymaker attitudes surrounding informal-sector work (Lewin, 1948).

Governmental initiatives such as provision of fair-trade supply lines for cottage industries (Bacon, 2005) and corporate social responsibility efforts (CSR; Lindgreen & Swaen, 2010) could be prime vehicles for driving ecosystem support for boosting microentrepreneurial informal activities. For instance, organizations could use their resources and existing supply networks to help local governments create supply lines that provide living wages to the producer by connecting them to consumers. Similarly, multilateral organizations can be involved by allocating effort and resources toward creating supportive networks in place of transition programs. In other words, instead of creating informal-to-formal transitions, we recommend that multilateral bodies change their focus to providing supportive infrastructure to protect and facilitate locally valued, culturally important livelihoods—like the one uncovered in India. In so doing, we would be leveraging UN SDG-17 (Partnership for the Goals) to achieve sustainable development via supporting SDG-1 to end poverty, SDG-2 to end hunger, SDG-8 for providing decent work, and SDG-10 for reducing inequality.

Cameroon

Informal skills in Cameroon generally involve small-scale activities such as trade, catering, processing, sewing, mechanics, welding, and masonry. Those working in the informal sector are generally employed in production units that qualify as "informal," for instance, in shoeshine workshops, street vending stalls, small-scale craft manufacturing, food processing, car and household appliance repair shops, passenger or freight transportation, artisanal housing construction and renovation, microcredit, and small currency exchange (Kélodjoué, 2006).

Informal workers in Cameroon represent roughly 90% of the workforce, yet they contribute 20% of the Gross National Product (GNP; Republic of Cameroon National Institute of Statistics, 2005, 2011; see also Kouete, 2020). Furthermore, 75% of them are underemployed (Republic of Cameroon National Institute of Statistics, 2011; see O'Shea et al, Chapter 15). Cameroonian authorities have recognized the importance of the informal sector, its weak contribution to the GNP, and the international pressure to uphold the Decent Work mandate. They view informal-work restructuring programs as being the only path to foster informal worker wellbeing (Peter-Cookey & Janyam, 2017). Given these, the nation has engaged in several programs and public policies to transfer informal-sector work to the formal sphere via informal-work restructuring programs. However, many of these programs and policies fail (Kouete, 2020).

Little effort has been directed to understanding the perspectives of informal workers in terms of what they think and how they think about transitioning to the formal economy via work-restructuring programs. We realized that it is critically important to understand the perspectives of Cameroonian informal workers (Tchagneno, 2018). This would not only reveal if transitioning from the informal sector to the formal sphere is a worthy pursuit but also how these programs should be designed to allow workers to fully utilize their skills and increase their contribution to the national economy while ensuring decent work. Indeed, the experiences of the Student Training Entrepreneurial Promotion program (Gielnik et al., 2016) or the Entrepreneurial Finance Lab (EFL; Klinger et al., 2013) illustrate how the consideration of specific informal workers and informal-enterprises factors could be fundamental in their development and success. For example, the EFL is a tool developed to facilitate access to finance for small- and medium-sized enterprises. Yet, despite the failure of many of the below-mentioned public programs and policies to transfer informal work to the formal sector via informal-work restructuring programs, little research has focused on how informal actors perceive this drive toward formalization, what they think about it, and how they process information about it. Understanding these factors would allow us to see not only the relevance of bringing them into the mold of the formal sector as the sole path to wellbeing (Peter-Cookey & Janyam, 2017) but also how to design programs that allow them to develop their skills and make the informal sector perform well for the national economy while ensuring decent work and allowing that sector to keep its specificities.

A pioneering study was conducted with a small sample of informal production unit owners to investigate sociocognitive determinants (knowledge, perceived credibility, and perception of information) of intention to engage in programs to restructure informal work. The choice to focus the investigation on sociocognitive variables was justified by the fact that many programs and initiatives to formalize informal enterprises and workers were previously based on socioeconomic and fiscal variables and resulted in structural interventions (ILO, 2018). And while these initiatives generally included strong incentives, holistic approaches, and consultation with other common denominators (ILO, 2018), they tended to neglect the individual informal worker or informal enterprise promoter, what he or she thinks and feels, and their motivations and perceptions: all things which could explain the failure of formalization initiatives or resistance to their implementation on the ground.

Following this investigation, a larger study with promoters and owners of small- and medium-sized businesses in the city of Yaoundé, Cameroon who were offering informal employment in the tertiary, processing, and primary sectors responded to questionnaires that collected worker and business owner views on informal work restructuring programs. The informal agricultural sector was not a part of this data-collection effort. This study was not publicly funded, which distanced us from the public institutions whose relationship with the informal sector is often one of mistrust and suspicion (Tchagneno, 2018).

For the measurement of knowledge about informal work restructuring programs (Alba & Hutchinson, 2000) and perceptions of the information about informal restructuring programs, participants responded to two questions concerning the existing formalization programs. These involved respondents' evaluations of the information and communications about these programs and the perceived credibility of the informal work formalization programs and the actors in charge of implementing them, assessed via items related to perceived quality, efficiency, feasibility, and trust in the programs (Hovland et al., 1953); perceived credibility of actors (Hill, 2001; Tchagneno et al., 2019); the desire to enlist in informal work restructuring programs (de Mel et al., 2013); and intention to engage in an informal work restructuring program based on the planned behavior model of Ajzen (1991) within the next one-year period (Knabe, 2012).

This research found that knowledge about and the perceived credibility of informal work restructuring programs and the perception of information about the programs predicted behavioral intentions among informal production unit promoters. Furthermore, in terms of the perceived credibility of the actors, it was found that both positive and negative perceptions about the qualities of the agents in charge of informing and mobilizing informal work actors determined the intention of these informal workers and work promoters to engage in programs. These qualities of the agents explained a significant ~8% variance in intention to engage, with positive qualities of the information-giver (such as kindness, seriousness, and competence) emerging as stronger influences on intention than negative qualities (such as dishonesty, corruption, and jealousy). Additionally, desire to engage in the program was found to be a significant *mediator* between predictors (knowledge about the informal restructuring programs, their perceived credibility, and the perception of information) and outcome variables (the intention to engage in informal restructuring programs).

These results which highlight socio-cognitive determinants of the intention to engage in informal work restructuring programs are in line with other recent studies which have shown that variables from the theory of planned behavior contributed to explaining the intention to engage in informal work restructuring programs by both informal workers and informal production unit promoters (Tchagneno & Doutre, 2021). Indeed, this previous research showed that the intention to engage in the above-mentioned programs varied both with attitudes and subjective norms. Furthermore, it has shown that both workers and owners of informal enterprises were skeptical about engaging in restructuring programs because of the normative and practical beliefs that surrounded these programs of corruption and nepotism, among others. Workers and owners tend to believe that they could only benefit from the programs if they had well-placed connections capable of influencing decision-making within the administrations that manage these programs, or if they bribed the agents of the administrations. They were more willing to engage in the programs if they thought people important to them (well-placed connections, family, friends, etc.) would appreciate or support their involvement.

Connecting the Two Case Studies

We would now like to reflect on the questions posed in the summary of the I/O investigation with informal workers in India and the new perspective based on the findings of the Cameroonian project. The broader contributions of the Indian and Cameroonian projects are that we should be seeing the perspectives of informal workers as central to academic research and policy-making. Informal-sector perspectives should *drive* the academic discourse and any policy interventions (if needed). We propose that to give informal work its rightful place implies joint actions on part of individuals, groups, and organizations. Specifically, we make a case for the following key points.

First, de-stereotyping informal work is about stripping it of the negative and often subjective attributes that contribute to prejudice about informal work and informal workers. This stereotyping sees informal work as temporary and transient and limits the possibilities for the informal worker to find meaning and sustainability in their current work and thus limits their ability to be ready to develop and reach their full potential. As discussed above, research and policy activity that is driven by stereotypes can create further hurdles for informal workers. This requires widespread awareness and an open mindset on part of policymakers and academics.

Second, based on our work (Saxena, 2021; Tchagneno, 2018), we recommend that I/O psychologists serve as key change-makers by engaging in grassroots needs analysis to understand, first of all, *if* the informal working population desires or wants to transition to the formal economy. This should be done *before* multilateral agencies, policy-making bodies, and local governments deploy work-restructuring programs. By conducting needs analysis *before* any informal-to-formal work programs are implemented, we could include the *perspectives* of informal workers in the creation and deployment of interventions, *if* the interventions are needed, so that they correspond to the workers' expectations and take into account their visions of the world, and of work, in particular. Due to the prevalent stereotype-driven understanding of informal work, workers are often neglected. As has been argued before (ILO, 2020), we advocate strongly for renewed attention by local governments and state agencies on creating conditions for decent work (with fair working conditions, health and social insurance, etc.). As seen in Saxena (2021), I/O psychologists can play a prominent role in educating governments about the psychological impacts of the lack of decent work and advocacy for greater attention on the psychological and health needs of informal workers.

Additionally, it is also clear from this investigation that more engagement with the informal economy from a psychological perspective is warranted to fully understand the landscape and psychological realities of the informal work ecosystem around the world and protect livelihoods that depend on sustainable work.

Future Research Directions

In this section, we present a five-point integrated research and policy plan for taking informal work more seriously and thereby tackling precarious work. Our central premise is the notion that the informal economy houses myriad complex and meaningful skills that support livelihoods that have to date been largely neglected in work science and policy-making. We suggest that researchers and policymakers take the following approach *prior* to the creation of any informal-to-formal work restructuring or transition programs (which are at the core of many development programs). Particularly, we propose trying to answer the following five questions *before* implementing any such transition programs, with the objective of (a) due diligence at a bare minimum and the objective of (b) including and empowering skilled informal workers to achieve sustainable growth and development via sustainable work as the ultimate goal.

To answer the questions that we propose below, we hope that grassroots efforts will yield rewards for (a) expanding the I/O research base and (b) bringing about a meaningful change in the lives of those who have been historically marginalized through research-informed policy practice. To apply I/O psychology to the informal sector, we propose researching the following six questions in a stepwise manner (see Table 11.1). Below, we elaborate on how this research could yield interesting insights and policy directions.

Research Question 1. Are Skills Present?

This approach investigates whether skills are already present in the local community that works in the informal sector. This question has a yes or no answer but is an important one if one is to forge a way forward that leverages skills that may be present in local populations. As we saw in the Indian investigation, informal workers were labeled "unemployed" due to their lack of formal jobs, but their work and skills led to productive and meaningful work experiences that were central to their identity and could pave the way to solving important development problems, including the provision of decent, sustainable work.

We propose answering this question through on-the-ground, grassroots-level psychological research and analysis (Aguinis, 2019a, 2019b; Campbell, 2013), in situ, of those who work in the informal sector. The methodology should be rigorous and in cases where previous explanatory frameworks are lacking, qualitative as well as inductive and abductive approaches to research may be fruitful. For instance, an economic perspective might see no skills in an Indian community of rural, informal workers (Saxena, 2021) but a psychological perspective revealed culturally embedded skills, indigenous knowledge, and frameworks that have opened to understanding a millennium-old, resilient occupation that is highly skilled.

Such research would need to be sensitive to local culture, geography, language, and traditions. For example, in the Indian example, sensitivity to local customs and traditions was maintained and respected through several interpersonal communication strategies: specifically, by dressing as the locals do while spending time with them and maintaining cultural norms such as different modes and ways of communication with those who were older versus those who were younger. It is not possible to list every cultural nuance, but these are some examples of how respect can be communicated to the local communities through behavior. These respectful behaviors should be contextualized to rural versus urban environments and any other pertinent grassroots reality. For example, dressing like the local community would not hold as much meaning in an urban community due to the effects of globalization and changes to customary dress as it does in the rural set-up. These aspects need to be carefully assessed in relation to the location.

Relatedly, in some cases, as seen in the Indian example, such an effort may require an outright rejection of organizationally informed understandings of work. Due to limited theoretical and empirical I/O frameworks that explain skilled informal work in rural settings, we had to start from the ground-up by taking a non-deductive approach. We therefore suggest a firm commitment to understanding work in the target sector will have an increased probability of revealing the skills that are present underneath, often hidden behind the mirage of stereotypes and negative labels.

Taking a Deep Dive into Skills

If skills are present, we recommend trying to understand the nature of the informal-sector skills in the local community. The research should strive to answer questions regarding how long these skills have been practiced by asking questions such as: Are these skills inter-generational? Are they traditional or modern skills? To what extent are the skills part of existing occupations and livelihoods? By this last question, we mean: To what extent do these skills contribute to current occupations? In the case of India, for example, while newer technology, techniques, and factory-made ceramic goods are widely available, the workers in Saxena's (2021) study were practicing intergenerational skilled occupations that were still reliant on traditional knowledge and indigenous worldviews.

If the skills concern product-creation, then uncovering the process surrounding what is done, what form of raw materials are needed, and so forth, would also be meaningful information to glean. Unique findings may thus be revealed. For example, the researcher may discover that perhaps skills were procured through urban training or apprenticeship programs and yield work for those who have now returned to rural areas due to unemployment in urban settings. This was the case during the COVID-19 pandemic in 2020 and 2021 when reverse migration occurred in India (Irudaya Rajan et al., 2020) when many daily-wage workers traveled back from their urban places of work to return to their home-villages. Similarly, many migrant populations bring skills with them that can boost local economies, but the overall contribution is not large enough and therefore may slip under the radar of national surveys.

In the same vein, rural-to-urban migration can lead to loss of intergenerational skills when poor workers go to urban areas in search of employment and work in the formal economy. For instance, a traditionally skilled goldsmith from a rural part of India moving to an urban setting might undertake employment in construction or some other type of manual labor due to a lack of opportunities in their traditional type of work. In this case, their set of skills honed over the generations will be left unused. We see this also in migration to "developed" countries. Afghan refugees in the US between 2021 and 2022 after the US pull-out from Afghanistan brought with them indigenous skills related to agriculture, languages, ethnic cooking, arts and crafts, machinery, and so on (International Rescue Committee, 2022). They have often ended up engaging in precarious, informal, freelance work that might tap into their skills but isn't enough to generate a living income.

Research Question 2. Economically, How Can Informal Skills Sustain Local Communities and Provide Comfortable and Viable Livelihoods?

Aligned with the UN SDG-17, partnerships between I/O psychologists and economists; local government agencies; and those who understand regional supply-lines, the fiscal and labor ecosystems, supply and demand, etc. could yield fruitful avenues for research and policy development. Such I/O partnerships could reveal the earning potential of utilizing informal skills in an ecosystem that is supportive and facilitates trade, production, and informal work. It could also reveal if informal work is part-time or full-time, if the work is skilled (versus unskilled), and the potential for informal work to create sustainable livelihoods. Throughout it is also important to consider whether the informal workers themselves think that the work they do is viable.

Answers to the questions above can determine if a transition to the formal economy, training in new skills (also known as upskilling or reskilling), or changes in the surrounding ecosystem are needed. The research questions are premised on the separation of *skills* from the (informal) *sector*. For example, in the Indian investigation, using research methods illustrated in Saxena (2021), it was found that while the work itself was highly skilled, the surrounding market ecosystem failed to provide adequate support to lead to viable financial outcomes. Instead of intervening through informal-to-formal restructuring, potentially useful interventions include raising awareness amongst district *tehsildars* (local government and municipality), writing policy briefs, and spreading awareness amongst policymakers (Saxena, 2021) about the lack of supportive infrastructure for informal artisans. Thus, a "research-informed intervention" would focus on the supporting infrastructure around artisanal work rather than changing the nature of work or reskilling the target population). We caution against stopping here. We believe that answering all five questions in our five-point research and policy agenda will yield holistic answers to create meaningful and inclusive interventions on the pathway toward sustainable work.

Research Question 3. What Is the Psychological Viability of Using Informal-Sector Skills to Sustain Communities and Provide Comfortable Livelihoods?

As discussed in earlier sections of this chapter, we believe there is often confusion between the two objectives of psychological and economic viability for informal-sector skills that leads to forced conversion and transition programs that do not meet the needs of the local population and often end in resistance or failure.

Thus, we suggest trying to understand if the local community finds their skilled work meaningful and important (beyond and separate from financial outcomes). Capturing the lived experience of skilled work in the informal sector embedded within the workers' realities, spaces, places, ecology, and culture is key to understanding their perspectives. Such an approach is the most useful for adding to the body of knowledge about work and working across different contexts and formats (Bergman & Jean, 2016; Weiss & Rupp, 2011). From a policy standpoint, research that reveals the personal psychological meanings of the skills in the hearts and minds of the local workers (e.g., the case study with Indian potters) might prevent imposed informal-to-formal transitions. Thus, it would be serving the important purpose of including psychological as well as financial viability in the achievement of SDG-8 (Decent Work and Economic Growth) as a win-win for all.

Methodologically, we recommend keeping our minds open mind to alternative methods that may not be mainstream in research toolkit. For example, in both India and Cameroon, we have relied heavily on qualitative tools such as interview techniques, focus-group discussions between multiple stakeholders, and non-deductive (including inductive and abductive) research methods for asking questions, collecting and analyzing data, and interpreting the results. These approaches can yield useful outcomes. For example, in India, the implication is that a reskilling or upskilling program is not needed and would likely end in failure due to the deep personal meanings of, and attachment to, the skilled work in the target population's experiential realities. In effect, trying to bring about a change in the skills that are already present in the rural ecosystem will likely contribute to cultural erosion and skill eradication—a counterproductive effort that is destructive for local populations. Similarly in Cameroon, we see the importance of psychological variables in determining the success or failure of informal-to-formal work restructuring programs for informal workers.

To better understand the perspective of informal workers, future studies could rely on qualitative tools such as activity analysis. This could make it possible to identify (and find solutions) to inner conflicts which can arise from confrontations between the informal activity itself, the experiences of the workers, and the stereotypes that surround informal work in general.

Other points to note here concern the *nature* of skilled work. If it is intergenerational, it may be highly relevant personally and tied to workers' sense of identity and work ethic. On the one hand, such intergenerational sustainable work is a core component of sustainable livelihoods (Carr, 2019), which are intergenerational and interdependent, prosocial, and not individualized and lonely. On the other hand, it may be that the skills are meaningful but the work itself lends to possible abuse and exploitation. Again, in this case, it may not be the work itself that would need to be modified but the ecosystem which allows the possible exploitation of the workers. Questions such as whether the work is decent, and what vulnerabilities may be present in the context of the surrounding environment of this work, can inform the researcher and policymaker on how best to help and support vulnerable workers. *Again, it is important to be mindful of the needs and desires of the local communities, particularly in cases where previous informal-to-formal restructuring programs have seen failure.*

Research Question 4. What Kind of Organizational Partnerships Might Help to Uncover Existing Skills and Decide Whether Formalization is the Right Approach for Bringing about Sustainable Livelihoods?

Based on information collected with respect to Question 3, we recommend codesigning a holistic plan with community stakeholders for aiding skilled workers in the informal sector.

SDG-17 focuses on diverse partnerships to do good for the world. To answer the previous questions in our five-point approach, we seek to apply I/O psychology to bring about positive change in the lives of skilled informal-sector workers. This could involve leveraging the resources and pre-existing networks of businesses (local, national, and multinational), organizations, and multilateral bodies in the developmental space. Organizations may engage in these initiatives as part of CSR. National businesses may purchase directly from local producers at a fair and living wage. In the Indian example, building supply chains may help boost the producer-to-consumer linkages from the artisans to the end users. These supply chains can be made fair and viable (Carr et al., 2021). Such knowledge- and expertise-sharing multistakeholder-inclusive partnerships would facilitate UN SDG-17 by incorporating global, national, and local entities that share the vision and goal of placing informal-sector work at the center of sustainable development.

We see this in the Cameroonian example, where a restructuring program based on a partnership approach that understands the psyche of the informal worker and works with the needs and visions of the people is more likely to flourish and be successful. We learned why informal workers in Cameroon have resisted change, and we delved into their attitudes and emotional concerns about transitioning. Ultimately, we recommend interventions only if absolutely needed based on the desires of the local community and minimizing the intrusion and interference in the lives of the people involved when implementing economically driven informal-to-formal transition programs. A good approach may be to think about changing the systems around the informal worker (e.g., creating fair and decent supply chains) to facilitate work and growth as opposed to changing the person (e.g., through skill-training in a different occupation).

Research Question 5. What Kinds of Government Interventions Might Help to Boost Indigenous Skills and Livelihoods in Alignment with Local Aspirations?

Local and national governments may have a key role to play in boosting informal-sector skills by using indigenous methods to promote local work. In some respects, not-for-profit governmental entities can play a more important role than multilateral and non-governmental bodies in promoting work, employment, and living wages for local communities (Saner & Yiu, Chapter 5). In the Indian example, creating formal craft bazaars and seasonal festival markets, connections and pathways from artisans to consumers, programs for direct purchase by cottage emporiums at fair trade prices, advertising to raise awareness in local rural communities and urban areas, and providing marketing help are all areas where the local tehsil and zila (district) administration can work directly with informal workers using state aid.

In the Cameroonian example also, from Table 11.1, local government entities may be more successful in creating credible messages that are aligned with indigenous needs and aspirations. By using local officials who share information early-on, one-on-one, and espousing the positive attributes of the informational agent, the government can aid efforts that lead to successful outcomes for restructuring programs.

Finally, for the perspectives of informal workers to be taken seriously, we recommend including informal work in national and state-level census surveys. Informal work is often omitted from economic census surveys, which can further the perceptions and stereotypes of informal work being unproductive and not contributing to national GDPs (Yah et al., 2018). This might also be an area where humanitarian work psychologists can partner with economists to work toward more inclusive census surveys.

TABLE 11.1 Future Research Directions Based on the Five-Point Research and Action Plan

Main Research Questions	*Additional Research Queries Based on the Main Research Questions*
Does the local community in the informal sector currently possess skills that serve a livelihood purpose?	Are the skills intergenerational?
Are they traditional?	
Are they modern skills?	
To what extent are the skills part of existing occupations and livelihoods?	
To what extent do these skills contribute to current occupations?	
How do/can the informal skills sustain the local communities and provide comfortable and viable livelihoods?	Are supply lines in place?
What is the economic structure of the activity or production that is engaged in by the local community?	
What is the psychological viability of informal-sector skills to sustain communities and provide comfortable livelihoods?	Are these skills meaningful to the local community beyond a source of earning?
Do they carry intergenerational or indigenous meaning?	
Are families involved in this work?	
What kind of organizational partnerships might help with recognition of existing skills and to investigate whether formalization is the right approach for bringing about sustainable livelihoods?	Do communities want to enter the formal sector?
Do they want training to learn new skills?	
What kind of government interventions might help to boost indigenous skills and livelihoods that are aligned with local aspirations?	How can these combine with local and non-government agencies and NGOs?

Conclusion

In this chapter, we have adopted a salutogenic rather than a deficit approach to skills and aspirations in the informal economy to make a broader case for taking the perspectives of informal workers seriously and treating them respectfully and inclusively. We premised our chapter on the notion that many of the skills and goals that are already present in the informal economy are fundamental to and critical for sustainable livelihoods and therefore sustainable global development. We made a case that the vast majority of the literature on the topic of informal-sector skills treats workers in the informal economy as largely unskilled, low-skilled, or poorly skilled and eager to join the formal sector when they may not be so inclined at all.

Taking a multidisciplinary approach, we presented some of the stereotypes that tend to dominate scholarly and policy narratives in fields such as economics and sociology concerning informal-sector work and skills. We then presented evidence that there are indeed skills present in the informal economic system, contrary to common notions that those who live and work in the informal economy are "unskilled" and a burden on society.

This is a space that is ripe for humanitarian work psychology to provide meaningful insights for broader human wellbeing by focusing on the structures that may prevent livelihoods from being sustainable. We illustrated the role of psychology in leveraging informal-sector skills using investigations in two continents. In India, we demonstrated the importance of these skills for creating psychologically sustainable work that has co-evolved with local communities and may be able to solve the problems of youth unemployment, hunger, and poverty and provide inclusive and sustainable development in a way that is respectful of local cultures and traditional livelihoods (Saxena, 2021). The problem was shown to be located outside of informal work itself, in the wider market(s) and surrounding ecosystems. In Cameroon, where government has initiated informal-to-formal transition programs, we showcased how psychological factors may enhance our understanding of how to create successful and meaningful transitions that are free from prejudice and bias (Tchagneno, 2018). Overall, we showed how and why it is important to take informal-worker perspectives seriously and how these perspectives, if fully supported, can lead to capabilities that are aligned with local aspirations and expectations.

Based on these field investigations, we have provided a five-point framework for future humanitarian work psychology research efforts and translational (applied) work in the area of informal-sector skills in an inclusive, sustainable, and, most importantly, respectful manner. Our recommendations follow a stepwise approach, beginning with scholarly outcomes that can be translated into suggestions for policy-making. We reiterated that while aspects of the informal economy are challenging, skills that are present therein hold the potential to drive inclusive sustainable development. There is an urgent and critical need to understand the informal economy for what it is, without preset assumptions and stereotypes. Forcing people out of the informal workspace will not work in the long term. We consider informal work as an important tool for achieving sustainable development and poverty eradication. Greater attention needs to be paid to supporting these skills and psychology can lead this initiative.

Fundamentally, the voice of the worker and a shift in mindset are needed to create infrastructural support around the work within the informal space. Facilitating and supporting informal-sector skills can contribute to eradicating poverty by promoting sustained economic growth, enhancing social inclusion, improving human welfare, and creating opportunities for employment and decent work for all, while maintaining the healthy functioning of the Earth's ecosystems.

References

Adams, A. V., de Silva, S. J., & Razmara, S. (2013). *Improving skills development in the informal sector: Strategies for Sub-Saharan Africa*. https://elibrary.worldbank.org/doi/abs/10.1596/978-0-8213-9968-2

Agarwala, R. (2006). From work to welfare: A new class movement in India. *Critical Asian Studies, 38*(4), 419–444. https://doi.org/10.1080/14672710601072996

Aguinis, H. (2019a). Defining performance and choosing a measurement approach. In H. Aguinis (Ed.), *Performance management* (4th ed., pp. 99–122). Chicago Business Press.

Aguinis, H. (2019b). Measures results and behaviors. In Aguinis, H. (Eds.), *Performance management* (4th ed., pp. 123–152). Chicago Business Press.

Ajzen, I. (1991). The theory of planned behavior. *Organizational Behavior and Human Decision Processes, 50*(2), 179–211. https://doi.org/10.1016/0749-5978(91)90020-T

Alba, J. W., & Hutchinson, J. W. (2000). Knowledge calibration: What consumers know and what they think they know. *Journal of Consumer Research, 27*(2), 123–156. https://doi.org/10.1086/314317

Amaral, P. S., & Quintin, E. (2006). A competitive model of the informal sector. *Journal of Monetary Economics, 53*(7), 1541–1553. https://doi.org/10.1016/j.jmoneco.2005.07.016

Bacon, C. (2005). Confronting the coffee crisis: Can fair trade, organic, and specialty coffees reduce small-scale farmer vulnerability in northern Nicaragua? *World Development, 33*(3), 497–511. https://doi.org/10.1016/j.worlddev.2004.10.002

Baumeister, R. F., Vohs, K. D., & Tice, D. M. (2007). The strength model of self-control. *Current Directions in Psychological Science, 16*(6), 351–355. https://doi.org/10.1111/j.1467-8721.2007.00534.x

Bergman, M. E., & Jean, V. A. (2016). Where have all the "workers" gone? A critical analysis of the unrepresentativeness of our samples relative to the labor market in the Industrial–organizational psychology literature. *Industrial and Organizational Psychology, 9*(1), 84–113. https://doi.org/10.1017/iop.2015.70

Bhawuk, D. P. S. (2019). LokasaMgraha: An indigenous construct of leadership and its measure. In S. Dhiman & A. D. Amar (Eds.), *Managing by the Bhagavad Gītā: Timeless lessons for today's managers* (pp. 273–297). Springer. https://doi.org/10.1007/978-3-319-99611-0_14

Bohn, S., & Owens, E. G. (2012). Immigration and informal labor. *Industrial Relations: A Journal of Economy and Society, 51*(4), 845–873. https://doi.org/10.1111/j.1468-232X.2012.00707.x

Bonds, A., & Inwood, J. (2016). Beyond white privilege: Geographies of white supremacy and settler colonialism. *Progress in Human Geography, 40*(6), 715–733. https://doi.org/10.1177/0309132515613166

Campbell, J. (2013). Assessment in industrial organizational psychology: An overview. In K. F. Geisinger (Ed.), *APA handbook of testing and assessment in psychology* (pp. 355–396). American Psychological Association.

Carr, S. C. (2019). Standing up for sustainable livelihoods: From poverty to prosperity. In K. C. O'Doherty & D. Hodgetts (Eds.), *The Sage handbook of applied social psychology*. https://doi.org/10.4135/9781526417091

Carr, S. C., De Guzman, J. M., Eltyeb, S. M., Furnham, A., MacLachlan, M., Marai, L., & McAuliffe, E. (2012). An introduction to humanitarian work psychology. In S. C. Carr, M. MacLachlan, & A. Furnham (Eds.), *Humanitarian work psychology* (pp. 3–33). Palgrave Macmillan. https://doi.org/10.1057/9781137015228_1

Carr, S. C., & MacLachlan, M. (1998). Actors, observers, and attributions for third world poverty: Contrasting perspectives from Malawi and Australia. *The Journal of Social Psychology, 138*(2), 189–202. https://doi.org/10.1080/00224549809600370

Carr, S. C., Meyer, I., Saxena, M., Seubert, C., Hopfgartner, L., Arora, B., Jyoti, D., Rugimbana, R. O., & Kempton, H. (2021). "Our fair-trade coffee tastes better": It might, but under what conditions? *Journal of Consumer Affairs,* Sept., 1–16.

Charmes, J., & Adair, P. (2014). L'inconstant caméléon, ou comment appréhender l'informel? [The fickle chameleon, or how to apprehend the informal?], *Mondes en développement, 166*(2), 7–16. https://doi.org/10.3917/med.166.0007

Chen, M., & Doane, D. (2008). *Informality in South Asia: A review.* WIEGO.

de Mel, S., McKenzie, D., & Woodruff, C. (2013). The demand for, and consequences of, formalization among informal firms in Sri Lanka. *American Economic Journal: Applied Economics, 5*(2), 122–150. https://doi.org/10.1257/app.5.2.122

Development Asia (2014, May 11). *Policy brief: Strategies for transforming businesses from informal to formal.* https://development.asia/policy-brief/strategies-transforming-businesses-informal-formal

Dong, Y. (2020). Spinners or sitters? Regimes of social reproduction and urban Chinese workers' employment choices. *International Journal of Comparative Sociology, 61*(2–3), 200–216. https://doi.org/10.1177/0020715220946074

Gielnik, M. M., Frese, M., Bischoff, K. M., Muhangi, G., & Omoo, F. (2016). Positive impact of entrepreneurship training on entrepreneurial behavior in a vocational training setting. *Africa Journal of Management, 2*(3), 330–348.

Gloss, A., Carr, S. C., Reichman, W., Abdul-Nasiru, I., & Oestereich, W. T. (2017). From handmaidens to POSH humanitarians: The case for making human capabilities the business of I-O psychology. *Industrial and Organizational Psychology, 10*(3), 329–369. https://doi.org/10.1017/iop.2017.27

Godfrey, P. C. (2011). Toward a theory of the informal economy. *Academy of Management Annals, 5*(1), 231–277. https://doi.org/10.5465/19416520.2011.585818

Harrison, S. J. (2008). *The maintenance of traditional methods and symbolism in southwestern Native American art* [Unpublished PhD dissertation]. The University of Georgia. https://getd.libs.uga.edu/pdfs/harrison_steven_j_200812_phd.pdf

Hatton, E. (2017). Mechanisms of invisibility: Rethinking the concept of invisible work. *Work, Employment and Society, 31*(2), 336–351. https://doi.org/10.1177/0950017016674894

Haynes, D. E. (2012). The historical and global contexts of artisan production. In D. E. Haynes, *Small town capitalism in Western India: Artisans, merchants, and the making of the informal economy* (pp. 1870–1960). Cambridge University Press.

Hazarika, M. (2006). Neolithic culture of Northeast India: A recent perspective on the origins of pottery and agriculture. *Ancient Asia, 1*, 25–44. https://doi.org/10.5334/aa.06104

Hill, E. (2001). Women in the Indian informal economy: collective strategies for work life improvement and development. *Work, Employment and Society, 15*(3), 443–464. https://doi.org/10.1177/09500170122119101

Hobfoll, S. E. (1989). Conservation of resources: A new attempt at conceptualizing stress. *American Psychologist, 44*, 513–524. https://doi.org/10.1037/0003-066X.44.3.513

Holley, H. (1995). Limits to and development strategies for the informal sector. A case study about informal woodworking entrepreneurs in Trujillo/Peru. *International Journal of Sociology and Social Policy, 15*(10), 283–294. https://doi.org/10.1108/eb013233

Hovland, C. I., Janis, I. L., & Kelley, H. H. (1953*). Communication and persuasion.* Yale University Press.

International Labour Organization (ILO). (2014). *Transitioning from the informal to the formal economy.* https://www.ilo.org/wcmsp5/groups/public/—ed_norm/—relconf/documents/meetingdocument/wcms_218128.pdf

International Labour Organization (ILO). (2018). *World employment and social outlook: Trends 2018.* https://www.ilo.org/global/research/global-reports/weso/2018/lang–en/index.htm

International Labour Organization (ILO). (2019). Tackling vulnerability in the informal economy. https://www.ilo.org/wcmsp5/groups/public/—ed_protect/—protrav/—travail/documents/publication/wcms_711804.pdf

International Labour Organization (ILO). (2020). *World employment and social outlook: Trends 2020.* https://www.oitcinterfor.org/en/node/7708

International Labour Organization (ILO). (2021). *World employment and social outlook: Trends 2021.* http://www.ilo.org/global/research/global-reports/weso/trends2021/WCMS_795453/lang–en/index.htm.

International Labour Organization (ILO). (2022). *World employment and social outlook: Trends 2022.* https://www.ilo.org/wcmsp5/groups/public/—dgreports/—dcomm/—publ/documents/publication/wcms_834081.pdf

International Rescue Committee. (2022, February 16). *What is next for Afghans who fled to the United States?* https://www.rescue.org/article/what-next-afghans-who-fled-united-states

International Trade Union Confederation. (2018). *ITUC global rights index: The world's worst countries for workers.* https://www.ituc-csi.org/IMG/pdf/ituc-global-rights-index-2018-en-final-2.pdf

Irudaya Rajan, S., Sivakumar, P., & Srinivasan, A. (2020). The COVID-19 pandemic and internal labour migration in India: A 'crisis of mobility.' *The Indian Journal of Labour Economics, 63*(4), 1021–1039. https://doi.org/10.1007/s41027-020-00293-8

Jambeck, J. R., Geyer, R., Wilcox, C., Siegler, T. R., Perryman, M., Andrady, A., Narayan, R., & Law, K. L. (2015). Plastic waste inputs from land into the ocean. *Science, 347*(6223), 768–771. https://doi.org/10.1126/science.1260352

Kaplan, S. (1995). The restorative benefits of nature: Toward an integrative framework. *Journal of Environmental Psychology, 15*(3), 169–182. https://doi.org/10.1016/0272-4944(95)90001-2

Kar, S. K. (2012). Knowledge process of rural handloom community enterprise. *Society and Business Review, 7*(2), 114–133. https://doi.org/10.1108/17465681211237592

Kélodjoué, S. (2006). Comment mesurer les activités productives des populations dans les pays sous ajustement structurel économique: l'exemple du Cameroun [How to measure the productive activities of populations in countries under economic structural adjustment: The example of Cameroon]. *Actes du colloque international de Aveiro.* https://www.erudit.org/fr/livres/actes-des-colloques-de-lassociation-internationale-des-demographes-de-langue-francaise/population-travail-actes-colloque-aveiro-2006/001400co/

King, A. M., Burgess, S. C., Ijomah, W., & McMahon, C. A. (2006). Reducing waste: Repair, recondition, remanufacture or recycle? *Sustainable Development, 14*(4), 257–267. https://doi.org/10.1002/sd.271

Klinger, B., Castro, L., Szenkman, P., & Khwaja, A. (2013). *Unlocking SME finance in Argentina with psychometrics* (Technical Note No. IDB-TN-532) Inter-American Development Bank. https://publications.iadb.org/publications/english/viewer/Unlocking-SME-Finance-in-Argentina-with-Psychometrics.pdf

Knabe, A. P. (2012). *Applying Ajzen's theory of planned behavior to a study of online course adoption in public relations education [Unpublished PhD dissertation].* Marquette University.

Kouete, V. (2020). *Cameroon: 90% of the labor force trapped in the informal sector.* Private Sector & Development. https://blog.private-sector-and-development.com/2020/01/23/cameroon-90-of-the-labor-force-trapped-in-the-informal-sector/

La Porta, R., & Shleifer, A. (2014). Informality and development. *Journal of Economic Perspectives, 28*(3), 109–126. https://doi.org/10.1257/jep.28.3.109

Lautier, B. (1990). Wage relationship, informal sector and employment policy in South America. *The Journal of Development Studies, 26*(2), 278–298. https://doi.org/10.1080/00220389008422152

Lautier, B. (2013). Sociologie de l'emploi, informalité des relations de travail et stratégies familiales en Amérique latine [Sociology of employment, informality of labor relations and family strategies in Latin America]. *Cahiers de Genre, 2*(55), 199–217. https://doi.org/10.3917/cdge.055.0199

Lewin, K. (1948). *Resolving social conflicts: Selected papers on group dynamics*. Harper.

Lindgreen, A., & Swaen, V. (2010). Corporate social responsibility. *International Journal of Management Reviews, 12*(1), 1–7. https://doi.org/10.1111/j.1468-2370.2009.00277.x

Lowe, N., Hagan, J., & Iskander, N. (2010). Revealing talent: Informal skills intermediation as an emergent pathway to immigrant labor market incorporation. *Environment and Planning A: Economy and Space, 42*(1), 205–222. https://doi.org/10.1068/a4238

Lubell, H. (1991). *The informal sector in the 1980s and 1990s.* Development Centre of the Organisation for Economic Co-operation and Development.

Mead, D., & Morrisson, C. (1996). The informal sector elephant. *World Development, 24*(10), 1611–1619.

Meagher, K. (2014). Disempowerment from below: Informal enterprise networks and the limits of political voice in Nigeria. *Oxford Development Studies, 42*(3), 419–438. https://doi.org/10.1080/13600818.2014.900005

Medina, L., & Schneider, F. (2018). *Shadow economies around the world: What did we learn over the last 20 years?* (IMF Working Paper No. 2018/017) International Monetary Fund. https://www.imf.org/en/Publications/WP/Issues/2018/01/25/Shadow-Economies-Around-the-World-What-Did-We-Learn-Over-the-Last-20-Years-45583

Mougoué, B. (2010). http://cipre-cmr.org/fr/index.php?

Mutukwa, M. T., & Tanyanyiwa, S. (2021). De-stereotyping informal sector gendered division of work-a case study of Magaba home industry, Harare, Zimbabwe. *African Journal of Public Affairs, 12*(1), 188–206.

Native Languages of the Americas. (n.d.) *Southwest Native American art*. http://www.native-languages.org/southwestern.htm

Ohnsorge, F., & Yu, S. (Eds.). (2021). *The long shadow of informality: Challenges and policies*. https://thedocs.worldbank.org/en/doc/37511318c092e6fd4ca3c60f0af0bea3-0350012021/related/Informal-economy-full-report.pdf

Peter-Cookey, M. A., & Janyam, K. (2017). Reaping just what is sown: Low-skills and low-productivity of informal economy workers and the skill acquisition process in developing countries. *International Journal of Educational Development, 56*, 11–27. https://doi.org/10.1016/j.ijedudev.2017.07.005

Radchenko, N. (2014). Heterogeneity in informal salaried employment: Evidence from the Egyptian Labor Market Survey. *World Development, 62*, 169–188. https://doi.org/10.1016/j.worlddev.2014.05.007.

Republic of Cameroon National Institute of Statistics. (2005). *Enquête sur l'emploi et le secteur informel au Cameroun en 2005 Phase 1, Enquête sur l'emploi: Rapport principal.*

Republic of Cameroon National Institute of Statistics. (2011). *Deuxième enquête sur l'emploi et le secteur informel au Cameroun (EESI 2) Phase 1, Enquête sur l'emploi: rapport principal.*

Rosaldo, M. (2021). Problematizing the "informal sector": 50 years of critique, clarification, qualification, and more critique. *Sociology Compass, 12*, 9–14.

Saito, N. T. (2020). *Settler colonialism, race, and the law: Why structural racism persists*. NYU Press.

Saxena, M. (2015). Communicable disease control in South Asia. In I. McWha-Hermann, D. C. Maynard, & M. Berry (Eds.), *Humanitarian work psychology and the global development agenda* (pp. 69–83). Routledge. https://doi.org/10.4324/9781315682419-6

Saxena, M. (2017). Workers in poverty: An insight into informal workers around the world. *Industrial and Organizational Psychology, 10*(3), 376–379. https://doi.org/10.1017/iop.2017.29

Saxena, M. (2021). Cultural skills as drivers of decency in decent work: An investigation of skilled workers in the informal economy. *European Journal of Work and Organizational Psychology, 30*(6), 824–836. https://doi.org/10.1080/1359432X.2021.1918760

Saxena, M. (2023). *Intergenerational occupations: A typology and research agenda* (Manuscript under review).

Saxena, M., Sall, E., Scott, J., Rupp, D., Saari, L. Foster Thompson, L., Osicki, M., & Mallory, D. (2015). News from the SIOP-United Nations team: Exploring work experiences of informal workers and promoting decent work for all. *The Industrial-Organizational Psychologist, 53*(1), 172–175.

Schein, V. E. (2012). Women, work and poverty: Reflections on research for social change. In S. C. Carr, M. MacLachlan, & A. Furnham (Eds.), *Humanitarian work psychology* (pp. 249–265). Palgrave Macmillan. https://doi.org/10.1057/9781137015228_11

Sen, A. (1999). *Commodities and capabilities*. Oxford University Press.

Shirom, A., Nirel, N., & Vinokur, A. D. (2006). Overload, autonomy, and burnout as predictors of physicians' quality of care. *Journal of Occupational Health Psychology, 11*, 328–342. https://doi.org/10.1037/1076-8998.11.4.328

Singer, H. W. (1970). Dualism revisited: A new approach to the problems of the dual society in developing countries. *The Journal of Development Studies, 7*(1), 60–75. https://doi.org/10.1080/00220387008421348

Singh, S., Granski, M., Victoria, M. d. P., & Javdani, S. (2018). The praxis of decoloniality in researcher training and community-based data collection. *American Journal of Community Psychology, 62*(3–4), 385–395. https://doi.org/10.1002/ajcp.12294

Sonnentag, S. (2001). Work, recovery activities, and individual well-being: A diary study. *Journal of Occupational Health Psychology, 6,* 196–210. https://doi.org/10.1037/1076-8998.6.3.196

Spector, P. E. (2017). The lost art of discovery: The case for inductive methods in occupational health science and the broader organizational sciences. *Occupational Health Science, 1*(1), 11–27. https://doi.org/10.1007/s41542-017-0001-5

Tchagneno Tene, C. L. (2018). *Analysis of the socio-cognitive determinants of the intention to engage in informal work restructuring programs in Cameroon* [Unpublished PhD thesis]. Grenoble Alpes University.

Tchagneno, C. L., & Doutre, É. (2021). Explaining the intention to engage in informal work restructuring programs using the Theory of Planned Behavior. *Bulletin de Psychologie, 574*(4), 297–316. https://doi.org/10.3917/bupsy.574.0297

Tchagneno, C. L., Wassouo, E., Minkoue Pira, L., & Doutre, E. (2019). Construction et validation d'une échelle de mesure des représentations sociales du travail informel [Construction and validation of a scale for the measurement informal work social representations]. *Pratiques Psychologiques, 25*(4), 399–417. https://doi.org/10.1016/j.prps.2018.07.001

Tipple, G. (2005). The place of home-based enterprises in the informal sector: Evidence from Cochabamba, New Delhi, Surabaya and Pretoria. *Urban Studies, 42*(4), 611–632. https://doi.org/10.1080/00420980500060178

Tokman, V. E. (1987). El sector informal: Quince años después. *El Trimestre Económico, 54*(3), 513–536.

United Nations. (2022). *The sustainable development goals report.* https://unstats.un.org/sdgs/report/2022/The-Sustainable-Development-Goals-Report-2022.pdf

Walther, R. (2012). *Building skills in the informal sector* (UNESCO document 2012/ED/EFA/MRT/PI/08). UNESCO. https://unesdoc.unesco.org/ark:/48223/pf0000217864

Webb, J. W., Bruton, G. D., Tihanyi, L., & Ireland, R. D. (2013). Research on entrepreneurship in the informal economy: Framing a research agenda. *Journal of Business Venturing, 28*(5), 598–614. https://doi.org/10.1016/j.jbusvent.2012.05.003

Weiss, H. M., & Rupp, D. E. (2011). Experiencing work: An essay on a person-centric work psychology. *Industrial and Organizational Psychology: Perspectives on Science and Practice, 4*, 83–97. https://doi.org/10.1111/j.1754-9434.2010.01302.x

Weng, L., & Margules, C. (2022). Challenges with formalizing artisanal and small-scale mining in Cameroon: Understanding the role of Chinese actors. *The Extractive Industries and Society, 9*, 101046. https://doi.org/10.1016/j.exis.2022.101046

Williams, C. (2014). *The informal economy and poverty: Evidence and policy review* (SSRN Scholarly Paper No. 2404259). SSRN. https://papers.ssrn.com/abstract=2404259

Williams, C. C., & Bezeredi, S. (2018). Explaining and tackling the informal economy: A dual informal labour market approach. *Employee Relations, 40*(5), 889–902. https://doi.org/10.1108/ER-04-2017-0085

Williams, C. C., & Nadin, S. (2012a). Tackling the hidden enterprise culture: Government policies to support the formalization of informal entrepreneurship. *Entrepreneurship & Regional Development, 24*(9–10), 895–915. https://doi.org/10.1080/08985626.2012.742325

Williams, C. C., & Nadin, S. (2012b). Work beyond employment: Representations of informal economic activities. *Work, Employment and Society, 26*(2), 1–10. https://doi.org/10.1177/0950017012437006

Williams, C., & Nazarov, I. (2018). *Supporting the transition from the informal to formal economy in Azerbaijan.* https://www.researchgate.net/publication/361287628_Supporting_the_transition_from_the_informal_to_formal_economy_in_Azerbaijan

Yah, N. C., Tingum, N. E., & Kum, F. V. (2018). Determinants of informal sector employment in urban labor markets in Cameroon. *Jurnal Ekonomi dan Studi Pembangunan, 10*(2), 140–152.

12

MAKING A GO OF IT IN THE GIG ECONOMY

Understanding Risk in Platform-Based Work

Kristine M. Kuhn

Millions of people worldwide find work via digital platforms that match clients and consumers with independent workers for tasks and short-term projects. The advent of platform-based employment was heralded as offering workers opportunities for greater flexibility and autonomy but has also sparked criticism from those who view the gig economy as exemplifying the worst aspects of precarious work, most notably in terms of shifting greater risk from companies to individuals. Although the empirical research base on gig workers has increased dramatically in recent years, the literature to date has been characterized by a static perspective and fragmentation across various academic disciplines. This chapter presents a framework for examining the risks to individuals performing platform-based gig work. We compare platform-based employment to other forms of contingent work as well as to traditional employment and highlight defining features of gig work that are increasingly common in traditional employment. A selective, cross-disciplinary review of recent research findings helps to clarify key issues and identify knowledge gaps where empirical research is most needed.

Risk is most often defined as the probability of loss or harm but can also be thought of as the uncertainty associated with the likelihoods of various outcomes and the scope of those outcomes. Here the risks of gig work are conceptualized broadly. Specifically, this chapter examines multiple aspects of pay risk, such as the likelihood of receiving promised payment and income volatility, risks to workers' subjective wellbeing, and risks to their physical safety. In addition, this chapter considers a career dynamics perspective, addressing risks and rewards to individuals over time (Klug et al., Chapter 21). While understudied to date,

DOI: 10.4324/9781003440444-15

examining how choices about engaging in gig work affect individuals' future career opportunities and wellbeing will be crucial to evaluating the true impact of platform-based employment.

Scope and Background

Although some writers continue to define gig work as any sort of freelancing or independent contracting arrangement (e.g., Caza et al., 2022; Mas & Pallais, 2020), the term is now commonly understood to refer to labor facilitated by intermediary platform companies that connect self-directed workers with client organizations or consumers via apps or web sites. This includes virtual freelancing and crowdwork provided entirely online (such as Amazon's Mechanical Turk or Upwork) as well as location-based tasks and services (such as Uber or DoorDash). Although recent years have seen the launch of specialized platforms that facilitate professional services such as remote access to independent licensed therapists, and some large corporations operate their own in-house platforms for vetted freelance professionals (Kuhn et al., 2021), here we limit our focus to the prototypical large labor platforms that are essentially open and do not require professional-level credentials or university degrees (which does not necessarily imply that such gig labor is unskilled; see, Saxena & Tchagneno, Chapter 11).

Electronically mediated labor markets represent a novel type of employment arrangement (Kuhn & Maleki, 2017). As a governance mechanism, they present unique challenges for regulators, policy makers, and traditional companies (Kuhn et al., 2021; Vallas & Schor, 2020). In contrast to other nonstandard work arrangements such as temping through agencies and part-time employment, gig workers on these platforms are (nominally) independent. Therefore, they have not been afforded the same labor protections often offered to employees in wealthy countries, such as minimum-wage guarantees and paid leave. In contrast to conventional self-employment and freelancing, gig workers are more often subject to constraints imposed by platform companies, many of which determine wage rates and/or implement policies that shape working conditions. Some evidence suggests the platform-based, nonprofessional gig work may pose special challenges in comparison to traditional freelancing and independent contracting (Caza et al., 2022).

Gig-labor platforms can offer individuals either a substitute for more stable employment or a quick way to earn supplemental income. Because many people perform gig labor sporadically or as a side hustle and may or may not consider such work a job, precise assessments of the size of the gig-labor[1] workforce are lacking. Household survey and economic data indicate that the gig economy grew rapidly over the past decade and was estimated to be between 1% and 3% of overall employment in 2019 (Schwellnus et al., 2019). In the United States (US), 16% of adults have earned money from an online labor platform at some point, and 9% did so in the past year (Anderson et al., 2021). Surveys in Australia (McDonald et al., 2019) and European countries (Huws et al., 2017) have similarly estimated that between 10% and 20% of adults have done at least occasional paid platform-based work. Millions of people worldwide have registered accounts on virtual freelance and crowdwork labor platforms, and these numbers have continued to rise in recent years (Kässi et al., 2021). While the onset of the COVID-19 pandemic saw rapid shifts in the type of gig labor performed—fewer ride-shares and more food delivery—the overall number of people performing gig work continued to grow (Tiku, 2020).

Research on the demographic characteristics of the platform labor force suggests those who depend heavily on this form of income are disproportionately likely to be from vulnerable or disadvantaged populations. A 2021 US survey found that those who had earned money from gig labor platforms in the past year were more likely to be younger, from lower income households, and Hispanic or Black in comparison to the overall population (Anderson et al., 2021). Similarly, platform workers in Canada tend to be younger and of visible minority status (Glavin et al., 2021). Platform-based workers in Europe also skew younger, although it is noteworthy that over 15% are estimated to be older than 55 (Huws et al., 2017). Approximately equal numbers of men and women perform gig work, although there are gender disparities in the type performed (Churchill & Craig, 2019). For example, women are much less likely to be ride-share drivers (Cook et al., 2021). In many urban contexts, location-based platform work is dominated by migrants (Van Doorn et al., 2020). Gig work, which can potentially allow workers more control over when and how much to work, is also likely to attract workers with disabilities or caregiving responsibilities (Harpur & Blanck, 2020).

Pay and Risk for Platform-Based Workers

In a standard traditional employment arrangement, employees know how much money they will earn each hour or week and are confident of receiving it. While variable pay is a component of many compensation plans, for most lower- and middle-class employees this is generally framed positively as a potential gain (e.g., some probability of receiving a bonus on top of a guaranteed hourly wage or salary). When performance-based pay is a relatively small proportion of pay, such plans are not typically perceived as risky (Kuhn, 2013; Kuhn & Yockey, 2003). Entrepreneurship research takes as a given that self-employment includes greater acceptance of risk, including the possibility of business failure after a substantial investment of time and money. The status of gig workers is somewhat betwixt and between that of employees and microentrepreneurs (Kuhn & Maleki, 2017), and the pay risk of this form of labor can be considered from a number of perspectives.

Comparative Earnings

Platform-based work can be viewed as risky if it tends to make workers worse off financially than if they pursued other ways of making money. To date, most research on pay in the gig economy has focused on how much workers earn, with the underlying goals of assessing whether platform-based labor provides a living wage and whether it exposes workers to hidden costs that may not be properly factored into their calculations.

For example, ride-hailing platforms advertise that drivers in the US can make well over $30 an hour, but their true earnings have been an ongoing subject of controversy. Earnings are affected by city, tips, nature of service (UberX, Comfort, etc.), and incentives offered by platforms, as well as driver behavior. In Uber-sponsored research conducted in 2014, 71% of US drivers reported ride-hailing had increased their overall income and 11% reported a decrease; analyses of administrative data indicated that platform earnings were similar or better in comparison to taxi and limousine driving (Hall & Krueger, 2018). Berg and Johnston (2019), however, argued that this analysis did not appropriately adjust for the full range of job-related expenses and relied on outdated data.

More recently Cook et al. (2021) used Uber records to calculate that the average driver in the US grosses over $21 per hour, but the debate over how to assess real earnings of platform-based ride-hailing continues. Some independent analyses concluded that, after accounting for various expenses including gas and vehicle depreciation, many drivers were actually losing money with each mile, although these analyses were revised after criticism (see Henao & Marshall, 2019, for a review). Focusing on the Denver area, Henao and Marshall (2019) used three common expense scenarios to estimate net average hourly wages between $5.72 and $10.46 per hour before taxes and show how driver strategies (e.g., cruising vs. waiting) affect real earnings. On the one hand, discovering that real earnings are lower than advertised may be one reason that driver turnover on platforms is high. On the other hand, depreciation costs are not realized until cars are sold, and the ability to earn money quickly may help prevent individuals from falling prey to high-interest short-term loans, leaving them better off financially even if their true post-expense earnings are low.

Hara et al. (2018) found the vast majority of Mechanical Turk workers earned only a few dollars an hour, with only 4% earning above $7.25 (the US federal minimum wage). Moreover, workers on Mechanical Turk and other crowdwork platforms also spend uncompensated time managing payments and searching for work. Toxtli et al. (2021) estimated an average of 33% of worker time on Mechanical Turk to be uncompensated, although their analyses also suggested this figure was lower for more experienced workers and those who used the tools to find better work opportunities. From a comparative perspective, it could be argued that commuting to a traditional job (a cost not incurred by workers on these types of virtual labor platforms) also constitutes uncompensated time, and many hourly waged employees also experience wage theft, including being required to work off the clock (Hallett, 2018).

In order to examine how platform-based work changes income profiles over time relative to traditional forms of freelancing, Garin et al. (2020) analyzed US tax filings, comparing the earnings trajectories of those who entered into each type of precarious work. Although reductions in income were likely to precede entry into both types of work, for younger workers, platform-based work was associated with an upward trend in earnings over time, which was not true for other freelance work (Garin et al., 2020).

Most research on gig workers is based on Western nations, but the global nature of platforms like Uber, as well as the burgeoning number of local platform start-ups, implies that national context must be considered when evaluating the financial risks of platform-based work. In contrast to the US, where platform earnings are often supplemental, the majority of gig workers in emerging economies are heavily dependent on platform-derived income (Guest & Zhou, 2021). In a survey of over 4,000 location-based platform workers in 15 countries (primarily delivery, driving, and domestic work), most respondents were satisfied with financial returns from this work, but this ranged from almost 70% of respondents in India, which has very low per capita income, to only 32% in Ukraine (Guest & Zhou, 2021).

The fact that crowdwork and freelance platforms allow workers in emerging economies to work remotely for overseas employers seems likely to provide them a net income benefit. Lehdonvirta et al. (2019) found that workers in sub-Saharan Africa and Southeast Asia reported better financial returns for their skills and labor, as well as other benefits, from working via digital platforms compared to working for local business-processing outsourcing companies.

Likelihood of Overt Financial Loss

While time spent searching for tasks and car depreciation can be classified as losses, from a psychological perspective, they are not as salient as more overt losses such as from nonpayment for completed tasks or increased debt. More than seven decades ago, humorist Robert Benchley wrote that "a freelance is one who gets paid by the word, per piece, or perhaps." Even in the current century, a common challenge facing freelancers is the risk of being paid late or not at all for completed work (Kuhn, 2016). In one survey, 71% of freelancers reported having struggled to collect payment for completed work (Freelancers Union, 2015). Digital labor platforms that process payments can mitigate nonpayment risk for independent workers. While Uber drivers may not know precisely how much they will earn on a given day, they can be confident of being paid for completed trips. On the one hand, the Upwork freelancing platform balances transaction risk between clients and workers by providing escrow and dispute resolution services and will guarantee pay for workers on hourly contracts who agree to electronic surveillance.

On the other hand, Amazon's Mechanical Turk notoriously allows clients to reject any submission and not pay a worker for a completed task; unfair rejections due to poor task design, unscrupulous clients, or technical problems have been viewed as a major risk to workers on this platform (McInnis et al., 2016). Moreover, having a submission rejected makes it more difficult for workers to secure future tasks on the platform because their rejection rate functions as a reputational measure clients use to screen out potential hires. Hara et al. (2018) found that outright rejections on the platform were rare (<0.1% of submissions), but over 12% of tasks were returned (i.e., a worker accepted a task but did not submit it). This level of returns represents a significant time loss to workers, and most likely reflects workers attempting to avoid the reputational cost associated with client rejection (Hara et al., 2018).

Compared to starting a new business, the size of potential loss incurred from gig work is typically limited. Launching even a small new business often requires borrowing substantial sums of money, and most fail within a few years. Conversely, barriers to entry for most types of platform-based labor are quite low.[2] Creating a profile on Upwork or registering on Mechanical Turk are relatively quick processes, and for those individuals who already have access to appropriate technology, no additional capital investment is necessary. Although some ride-hailing drivers rent or finance a vehicle privately or through a platform, most people who dip their toes in the gig economy by driving already possess a vehicle. While a significant proportion of platform-based drivers become inactive (i.e., quit) after a short period of time (Hall & Krueger, 2018), they have not usually incurred additional debt as a result of having done so.

Another way to evaluate the comparative risk of gig work versus traditional self-employment is presented by Burtch et al. (2018), who tracked the entry of UberX into local areas in conjunction with rates of Kickstarter (a crowdfunding platform for new ventures) campaign launches and survey measures of self-employment. They found a significant negative relationship between the ridesharing platform's entry into an area with these measures of entrepreneurial activity, but they further conclude that gig economy platforms primarily reduce "lower quality entrepreneurial activity" by providing feasible income-earning opportunities for the unemployed and underemployed (Burtch et al., 2018; O'Shea et al., Chapter 15).

It is also useful to consider the typical experience of people who attempt to earn money via participation in multilevel marketing (MLM) schemes or direct sales. In this business model, people sell physical products (such as clothing, jewelry, or essential oils) and also earn commissions on sales from people they directly or indirectly recruit to be part of their "downline." As with platform-based work, people are often attracted to MLMs by the opportunity to "be their own boss." Because the demographics and motivations of people who join these organizations overlap significantly with those of platform workers, MLMs are sometimes included in discussions of the gig economy (DeLiema et al., 2021). Not only do the vast majority of MLM sellers fail to earn any profit, but also an estimated half lose money because MLMs typically require sellers to purchase substantial inventory and heavily market costly training seminars; many people who join MLMs in hopes of getting out of debt end up deeper in debt (DeLiema et al., 2021; Taylor, 2011). The likely greater probability of significant financial loss constitutes an important distinction between MLMs and labor platforms.

Variation in Pay Rates

Beyond average hourly earnings, uncertainty regarding expected pay is a characteristic feature of platform-based work and thus also an important component of workers' experiences of risk. On some freelance platforms workers can bid for projects or negotiate compensation with clients, similar to traditional freelancing, but the platforms may still make changes to fees or policies that suddenly alter earnings (Blaising et al., 2021). On crowdwork platforms such as Mechanical Turk, workers choose from available postings, attempting to balance the nature of the task and payment offered by the client. Unfortunately, it appears to be difficult for these workers to accurately predict the hourly wages of advertised microtasks (Saito et al., 2019). On most location-based platforms the task rates, fees, and pay structure are controlled by the platform and are often subject to seemingly arbitrary changes. Tipping is nominally under the control of customers, but the design decisions platform companies make (such as whether to have a default tip amount) can also affect workers' experiences of pay uncertainty. Uncertainty regarding how much one is likely to earn in a given hour, how that pay will be determined, and how often pay policies change may well be factors that distinguish platform-based work from other forms of employment.

Ride-hailing companies use surge pricing to balance the supply of drivers with market demand: a complex, multi-layered, and efficiency problem (Besbes et al., 2021). Uber-sponsored research has reported that this dynamic pricing increases drivers' earnings and reduces waiting times (Lu et al., 2018). Other researchers have argued that surge pricing is not a reliable way for drivers to boost earnings and that its "very dynamism is characteristically fickle and opaque" (Rosenblat & Stark, 2016, p. 3767). A recent quasi-experimental study conducted in China found the introduction of surge pricing benefited part-time drivers more so than full-time drivers (Miao et al., 2021).

The Instacart food delivery platform provides another example of worker frustration arising from changes in pay structures, resulting in two class-action lawsuits to date (Oladipo, 2021). Previously shoppers were paid by the order, but then the platform began using algorithms to bundle orders into batches, requiring shoppers to visit multiple addresses. The platform also discontinued a commission system which paid workers extra for heavy items and large orders. Instacart workers select from batches described by total earnings including tips, but customers were allowed to alter tip amounts after delivery; some customers engaged in "tip-baiting" by offering a high tip to secure a slot and then clawed it back later (Tiku, 2020).

Income volatility. Income volatility makes it difficult to budget, plan for the future, and make good financial decisions, particularly for vulnerable households that lack savings to weather drops in income. For low- and moderate-income American households, significant month-to-month income volatility is common. In an analysis of 1 million Chase Bank customers, 55% experienced more than a 30% average month-to-month change in total income, most of which was due to changes in labor income (Farrell & Grieg, 2016). While some volatility in labor income was due to job loss or transition, most was attributable to fluctuations within a distinct job (e.g., changes in hours worked, commissions, or bonuses). But, as argued by Morduch and Schneider (2017, p. 41), "if companies are passing on volatility to their employees, they pass it on even more to contingent workers." Platform-based workers' pay per hour can fluctuate significantly, along with the number of hours they choose or are able to source work, and so monthly income from platform-based work is likely to be especially volatile.

If labor-platform income is used to compensate for a shortfall in nonplatform income, however, then overall household income volatility can be reduced. This appears to be a very common motivation for choosing to engage in platform-based work (Farrell & Grieg, 2016) and has long been touted as a benefit of the gig economy. If income from traditional waged jobs is unpredictable, labor platforms should allow individuals to quickly and easily smooth income flows and thereby avoid taking on high-interest debt or falling delinquent (Farrell & Grieg, 2016). Based on analyses of a large data set of Americans' personal finances, Koustas (2018) found that most people who began working via on-demand labor platforms did so after significant declines in income and assets. In other words, while cross-sectional data would show an association between gig work and financial precarity, financial distress is likely to have preceded entry into gig work. The gig economy is not an option available to everyone, however, as its viability will depend on geographic location and technical skills; at the societal level, platform-based work can be viewed more as a symptom of instability rather than a solution to it (Morduch & Schneider, 2017).

Two studies have used difference-in-differences designs based on the temporal and geographic rollout of Uber services in the US to examine associations with platform-work availability and household financial outcomes. Nian et al. (2021) found Uber's entry to be associated with a lower rate of personal bankruptcy filings and further that this apparent reduction was most marked in counties with high poverty and unemployment rates. Conversely, Daniels and Grinstein-Weiss (2019) analyzed the trajectories of low-income families and found that, while UberX availability was associated with a reduction in income volatility, it actually increased financial hardship among this population by reducing overall take-home pay. They proposed that low-wage employees are less likely to benefit from supplemental gig work because their non-gig jobs are less flexible (Daniels & Grinstein-Weiss, 2019).

In wealthy nations, safety net programs such as unemployment and retirement benefits help cushion households from income shocks and job loss. In the US, independent contractors have not ordinarily been eligible for unemployment benefits, and one-way platform companies such as Uber have profited from drivers' classification as self-employed by the avoidance of payroll taxes normally charged to employers to fund this benefit. At the outset of the COVID pandemic in 2020, however, special legislation temporarily extended unemployment benefits to gig workers and other independent contractors; thousands of Uber and Lyft drivers were also able to take advantage of disaster-assistance programs targeted toward small businesses (Siddiqui & Van Dam, 2021). A number of proposals have been advanced to extend some measure of social insurance benefits to gig workers, with European Union legislation at an advanced stage at the time of this writing (Chan, 2021).

Risks to Subjective Wellbeing

Is platform-based work risky to individuals' psychological and emotional wellbeing? Financial precarity in and of itself is detrimental to mental health, and so isolating any effects specific to platform-based working compared to plausible alternatives in a given context is challenging (see Apouey et al., 2020). In addition, psychological effects are likely to be nuanced and contingent on what measures of subjective wellbeing are used, platform type, and individual differences (Saltzman et al., Chapter 2). Most research on this question to date can be summarized as a debate over whether the greater autonomy and control advertised by labor platforms have significant welfare-enhancing benefits (Chen et al., 2019), analogous to those observed for self-employment (Binder & Blankenberg, 2021), or whether the algorithmic management and technological structure inherent in platform-based work not only nullify this supposed autonomy but also pose risks to psychological wellbeing. Another research stream, which also crosses disciplinary boundaries, is centered on possible negative effects arising from the lack of interpersonal relationships with coworkers and other social factors.

Autonomy and control. How decision-making authority is divided among workers, customers, and the platform company varies a great deal across platforms, but all platform-based workers, by definition, have some ability to decide when and how long they work (Kuhn & Maleki, 2017). In London, one study found Uber drivers, mainly immigrants with relatively low earnings from the app, had higher levels of happiness and life satisfaction than employees comparable to those of the self-employed, although drivers also reported more anxiety compared to both groups; the authors provide suggestive evidence that these gig workers' greater satisfaction is attributable to the value they placed on autonomy and flexibility (Berger et al., 2020).

Many scholars, however, view the purported autonomy of gig work as something of a mirage. Rosenblat and Stark (2016) detail how Uber exercises significant indirect control over drivers. Based on their study of food-delivery platforms and interviews with workers in Australia, Veen et al. (2020) conclude that these workers have markedly little agency, even if some have adopted the entrepreneurial framing touted by the platforms. They argue that platforms' ability to monitor workers in real time (described as "the panoptic disposition of the technological infrastructure"), large information asymmetries that constrain workers' choices, and the obfuscated black-box nature of the platform's performance management systems all operate as strong control levers on workers (Veen et al., 2020). If gig workers objectively have little autonomy over their work, but subjectively consider it to be an advantage of platform-based employment (Goods et al., 2019), then it is especially critical that researchers are clear and thoughtful when defining and measuring autonomy in this context.

Other research presents a more optimistic take on gig workers' autonomy. In their interviews with workers located in emerging economies who do tasks such as data entry and translation for foreign clients via freelance platforms, on the one hand, Wood et al. (2019) found substantial evidence for worker discretion over which tasks to do, how to do them, and in what order; even those workers who performed lower skilled tasks tended to describe their work as involving complexity and problem-solving. On the other hand, Wood et al. (2019) also highlight a disconnect between the value workers placed on the autonomy afforded by platform-based labor and their lived experiences. For example, these workers often had to work at night in order to be in sync with clients located in other time zones, even while many reported appreciating the temporal flexibility platform-based work offered (Wood et al., 2019).

The psychological effects of income volatility are likely to be deeply intertwined with control. Based on a survey of Americans registered on Mechanical Turk who self-reported the volatility of their income (from all sources), Peetz et al. (2021) found that those with more volatile incomes also had greater trouble making ends meet, as would be expected; this was not the case, however, for those who perceived themselves as having control over the month-to-month swings in their income. In a recent survey of platform workers in the US, most respondents rated their pay as somewhat or very fair, but fewer than half said they understood how platform companies determine how much they get paid (Anderson et al., 2021). While this survey did not specifically address perceived control over pay, understanding is a logical precursor to control. This survey is also noteworthy because it was based on a large representative sample and therefore included a variety of types of platform-based work (Anderson et al., 2021).

Even on freelance platforms like Upwork, where workers can bid for projects, advertise their own pay rates, or negotiate with clients, some workers may still view the platform as ultimately in control. As described by one anonymous worker (quoted in de la Vega et al., 2021), "Upwork isn't a freelancing platform. It's a gig economy platform. That means they set all of the rules and guidelines, control supply and demand, and ensure that their customers are happy."

Algorithmic management. In the gig economy, the issue of worker control is intertwined with the debate over algorithmic management. Platforms use technology to automate many decision-making processes that affect workers, from surge pricing to task scheduling to deactivating (i.e., firing) workers whose average customer satisfaction rating falls below a cut-off. Algorithmic management is increasingly a common feature of organizational life, however, and thus shapes the experiences of many corporate employees as well as those of gig workers (Kellogg et al., 2020). For example, personnel management at Amazon warehouses is almost fully automated, with almost all aspects driven by software (Dzieza, 2020).

Most behaviorally oriented organizational scholars appear to take a dim view of algorithmic management, and its shortcomings form a central argument underlying many academic and popular critiques of the gig economy business model. Rahman (2021) describes the evaluative algorithms used by a freelance labor platform as an "invisible cage," in which the criteria for success are unpredictable and the opaqueness undermines workers' ability to understand and respond. At the time of this writing, the European Union is evaluating proposed regulations that would require gig labor platforms to be more transparent about algorithms and to adopt human oversight and appeal processes (Chan, 2021).

It is not necessarily obvious, however, that algorithmic management is more opaque or psychologically aversive than more traditional forms of managerial control exercised over employees. Langer and Landers' (2021) review of algorithmic management research characterized the "tension between being under constant control but at the same time feeling autonomy because of having no human boss" as an underlying theme. In fact, algorithmic management systems can be viewed as fairer than human managers in the sense that they are not seen as having discriminatory motives or as driven by personal agendas (Langer & Landers, 2021). Myhill et al. (2021) found gig workers evinced little apparent concern over technological control, although this varied across platforms and with workers' degree of financial dependence.

In attempting to determine whether algorithmic management is uniquely stressful for platform workers, research by Norlander et al. (2021) is of particular interest. The two studies they present are rare examples of testing differences between platform-based and traditional employment models while holding the nature of the work performed constant. In a between-persons comparison, Uber drivers perceived greater control and autonomy in their work than did taxi drivers, although this could be partially due to selection effects (Norlander et al., 2021). Their second study used a within-persons experimental design and a sample of full-time, licensed limousine chauffeurs who also sourced work via the Uber Black platform; counterintuitively, they find platform management appears to increase perceptions of control and task enjoyment compared to the presumably human-centered management of limousine companies, even when the limousine drivers owned their own company (Norlander et al., 2021).

Based on nationally representative samples of Canadian workers, Glavin and Schieman (2022) reported a positive association between mental distress and primary reliance on platform-based gig work. But they find no support for algorithmic control as a contributing factor; rather, most of the association was explained by financial uncertainty, as platform-dependent workers were more distressed than employees with comparable financial troubles (Glavin & Schieman, 2022).

Both gig workers and employees, however, often do resist algorithmic control, both individually and collectively (Kellogg et al., 2020), indicating that some aspects of algorithmic management and its implementation can be stressful or aversive. Meijerink and Bondarouk (2023) propose that algorithmic management should be conceptualized as simultaneously restraining and enabling worker autonomy. In addition to detailing ways in which algorithmic management tools can benefit both gig workers and platforms, they provide examples of how some gig workers have been able to leverage algorithms for their own advantage by exploiting bugs in the system (Meijerink & Bondarouk, 2023).

Social Factors

An extensive literature has demonstrated the impact social relationships with coworkers and supervisors have on the satisfaction and emotional wellbeing of traditional employees. Although interpersonal conflict at work can be draining, workplace friendships and social supports can mitigate effects of work-related stresses and help individuals thrive (e.g., Chiaburu & Harrison, 2008; House, 1981). Because gig work is not conducive to forging ongoing interpersonal relationships, increased social isolation may prove risky to mental health over time.

In Wood et al.'s (2019) qualitative research with virtual gig workers, the loneliness of working at home without face-to-face contact was a common theme, although one quantitative study (Caza et al., 2021) has reported no significant difference in perceived social isolation between platform and non-platform precarious workers. Using a large, nationally representative sample, however, Glavin et al. (2021) found that platform-based workers were lonelier than permanent-waged employees, temporary employees, and the self-employed. Moreover, this difference remains significant, although weakened, when financial strain was included in the model. Somewhat surprisingly, ride-hailing drivers were lonelier than online crowdworkers (Glavin et al., 2021). Several studies have examined how gig workers, despite the isolating and fragmented nature of their work, can still form bonds with their fellow workers via virtual communities (e.g., Panteli et al., 2020).

Another social factor relevant to gig work is status; the extent to which other people view your work with respect has implications for subjective wellbeing even after accounting for associations with power and income (Magee & Galinsky, 2008). On the one hand, much on-demand gig work could be viewed as low status, consistent with low barriers to entry and low earnings. On the other hand, Phung et al. (2021) found that Uber drivers in Toronto avoided the moral and social stigma associated with taxi drivers, who were perceived as not being able to get any other type of work, whereas even full-time Uber drivers avoided this taint.

Sessions et al. (2022) studied status effects for people with a full-time waged job and a side hustle, including both platform-based (Uber, TaskRabbit) and nonplatform-based hustles. Status inconsistency between the two roles was associated with greater stress and emotional exhaustion; contrary to their expectations, it did not matter whether the side-hustle or regular job had higher status (Sessions et al., 2022).

Safety Risks

There is no question that many location-based gig workers face risks to their personal safety. A recent survey of US platform workers found 35% had felt unsafe while working and 19% had been sexually harassed. Globally, workers on delivery and ride-hailing platforms are especially likely to report safety concerns (Guest & Zhou, 2021). While it is not necessarily established that risks to gig workers are greater compared to risks to similar nonplatform workers, there are legitimate reasons to speculate this may be the case. The platform-based business model, which negates responsibilities and regulations generally associated with an employer-employee relationship, may increase the likelihood of adverse events and/or amplify their negative consequences. In countries such as the US, low-wage workers in many occupations face significant risks of physical injury or sexual harassment, but employers have financial incentives to reduce these risks to their employees. In the face of public pressure, some prominent platforms have adopted policies intended to address safety risks, but they do not have the same legal obligations or incentives that traditional employers do.

Contingent workers such as temporary and seasonal employees are at higher risk of work-related disease and injury (Quinlan et al., 2001), but the basic regulatory framework provides some level of protection to those classified as employees. Although companies may be able to game workers' compensation policies by outsourcing risky jobs to temporary agencies (Ellen et al., 2012), temporary employees injured at work are still eligible for benefits whereas platform workers classified as independent contractors are not. In a particularly stark example, observers noted that the families of employees and a police officer killed in a mass shooting at a grocery store were eligible for death benefits, whereas the family of another victim, an Instacart shopper, had to solicit donations (Oladipo, 2021).

Although in general driving is risky work, the platform-based business model may pose heightened dangers. Because many gig workers who provide ride-hailing and delivery services often do so as a side hustle, they may work very long hours overall, increasing the risk of accidents caused by fatigue. Surge pricing may also encourage them to drive when weather conditions are dangerous, and faster speeds are linked to higher earnings (Cook et al., 2021). Drivers also receive negligible health and safety training. In all, the emergence of the gig economy driver has been termed "a perfect storm of risk factors" to health and safety (Christie & Ward, 2019, p. 115).

While delivery and driving platforms receive the most attention in this context, risks attending gig workers who do domestic and caring work also merit attention. Macdonald (2021) interviewed Australian workers who provide support services to adults with disabilities, either as independent workers facilitated by a specialized gig-labor platform and/or as employees of a service-provider organization. These care workers face "personalized risks" from aggressive and inappropriate clients. Workers did not expect, and did not receive, much support from platforms, but they also had minimal support or even contact from service provider organizations when officially employed by them. Macdonald (2021) not only suggests that platforms may worsen risks for this occupation, especially by heightening the need to maintain high client ratings, but also notes that traditional employers in this market seem to be abrogating their responsibilities as employers.

Career Risks

One particularly understudied topic in the gig economy is the effect of platform work on individual career dynamics over time. Advocates hold that gig labor platforms can be a godsend for people with limited employment opportunities, such as recent immigrants. Yet even gig workers who report fairly high levels of work satisfaction do not typically wish to continue working via platforms for long (Guest & Zhou, 2021). While most Americans view gig work as a good way to make extra money, it is not perceived as a good way to build a career

(Anderson et al., 2021). For the increasing number of people who earn income primarily or solely via gig platforms, it is therefore critical to know whether this work helps them develop skills that may transfer to more stable employment, and what gig work experience signals to traditional employers who evaluate job applicants.

Working via online freelance platforms may help develop transferable skills and support career development. Blaising et al. (2021) found that some freelancers are able to leverage platforms to engage in career exploration and gain new skills and work experiences, some of which may be transferable. For example, one of their interviewees experimented with ways to manipulate platform algorithms to uncover visibility hacks and was able to expand this to nonplatform contexts (Blaising et al., 2021). Freelance platforms can foster the development of entrepreneurial skills and identity (Bellesia et al., 2019). Workers with high reputation scores on a freelancing platform may be able to subcontract work to lower paid peers (Wood et al., 2019), but the fact that internal platform reputation information (reviews and ratings) seems to have little signaling value when workers attempt to transfer their experience to a different platform or to a traditional employer remains a significant barrier (Blaising et al., 2021).

While entry-level employment at an organization may potentially provide training or mentorship that allows high-performing employees to advance to roles with greater responsibility, this is not a possibility for on-demand, location-based gig workers. So a key question is how gig-economy experience helps or hinders them if they seek more stable employment. Pedulla (2020) has shown that hiring managers often interpret a history of part-time or temporary agency work experience negatively, although observed bias interacts with the race and gender of the applicant. Professional recruiters evaluate former self-employed entrepreneurs more negatively than comparable job applicants with traditional employment experience (Waddingham et al., 2021).

To date, one experiment has specifically tested the effects of platform-based work experience on subsequent career outcomes. Adermon and Hensivk (2022) conducted an audit study in Sweden using profiles of fictitious recent high-school graduates who had either been unemployed, had gig-work experience via a food-delivery platform, or had traditional work experience delivering mail. Both types of work experience involved an independent service job requiring traveling around a city by bicycle, but callback rates were higher for applicants with traditional job experience. Gig experience may be viewed as a signal of lower worker quality, taken as an indicator the applicant was rejected by other companies and unable to get more stable employment. Having gig work experience did, however, slightly increase callback rates in comparison to unemployment (Adermon & Hensivk, 2022).

The fact that the availability of gig work can allow people to avoid prolonged spells of unemployment, and perhaps to mask how few hours they worked during periods of challenging life circumstances, may be beneficial for their future job prospects. On the one hand, even in a time of low unemployment, almost half of large US organizations use software to automatically filter out all entry-level jobseekers with an employment history gap of more than six months (Fuller et al., 2021). On the other hand, many organizations have hiring policies requiring references from current or recent managers, which would put platform-based workers at a marked disadvantage.

Future Research Directions

While the research reviewed here provides many reasons to be concerned about the various risks faced by gig workers, few studies to date have examined how gig workers themselves conceptualize and perceive risks related to their work. Moreover, it can be challenging to attribute effects to the platform-labor model as separate from other precarious work or to selection effects for those who elect to do gig work. Future research grounded in psychological theory that compares working via a gig platform to working as an employee (either through a temporary agency or in standard employment) while holding work tasks constant offers significant opportunity for improved understanding of how employment arrangements affect risk. Longitudinal individual-level research that incorporates assessments of risks associated with gig work compared to other feasible ways to earn income, and their effects on behaviors and choices, is also needed.

Much of the research to date on gig workers has understandably been based on single surveys or qualitative interviews. Future studies that incorporate methods such as daily diaries and experience sampling could address important questions regarding the issues identified here. For example, how do gig workers' day-to-day experiences of income volatility affect their well-being? How does individual-level variation in social interactions with clients and other gig workers influence stress and other outcomes?

Research on career risks associated with on-demand gig work is particularly needed and should be informed by organizational psychology theory and practice. In addition to examining the interplay between side hustles and regular employment, it would be useful to understand when and how platform-dependent workers can best leverage their gig experiences when seeking more stable employment, as well as the practical and psychological effects of gig work experiences on developing an entrepreneurial career.

Conclusion

Gig labor platforms can provide vital opportunities for some vulnerable workers to better their individual circumstances, yet this business model may contribute to riskier working conditions. In wealthy countries, the regulatory status of gig workers as independent contractors has been the subject of controversy and legal action for many years. At the time of this writing, most Americans believe ride-hailing drivers should continue to be classified as independent contractors (Anderson et al., 2021) but significant legislative changes intended to make gig work less precarious and risky may soon be enacted in several countries (Chan, 2021). In some countries, policies to address health and safety risks to gig workers were introduced in response to the COVID pandemic, either due to government requirements or initiated by platforms, although many platform companies arguably leveraged the crisis to further entrench their business strategy at the expense of worker rights (Howson et al., 2022).

On a final positive note, platform cooperatives represent a new business model that combines collective ownership and governance with digital platform infrastructure to offer better protection and rewards to gig workers. For example, a French computer programmer makes delivery-app software available to worker-owned cooperatives with the goal of empowering couriers (Atkinson, 2021). Whether such initiatives will be able to compete with established platforms backed by venture capital such as Deliveroo is an open question, but legislative changes that require platform companies to accept more responsibility for workers may render the playing field more level. In a recent feasibility analysis, Bunders et al. (2022) conclude this model may be unlikely to succeed in some segments of the gig economy, such as remote microtasking, but for ride-hailing and professional work, platform cooperatives may have competitive advantages over capitalistic platforms.

Notes

1 These estimates distinguish labor from other ways of earning money via online platforms such as selling items on Ebay or renting rooms via Airbnb, which are even more common.
2 One exception is the Arise platform, which facilitates home-based customer service work for corporate clients and requires its "independent" contractors to pay upfront training costs (Armstrong et al. 2020).

References

Adermon, A., & Hensvik, L. (2022). Gig-jobs: Stepping stones or dead ends? *Labour Economics, 76*, 102–171.

Anderson, M., McClain, C., Faverio, M., & Gelles-Watnick, R. (2021). *The state of gig work in 2021*. Pew Research Center. https://www.pewresearch.org/internet/2021/12/08/the-state-of-gig-work-in-2021/

Apouey, B., Roulet, A., Solal, I., & Stabile, M. (2020). Gig workers during the COVID-19 crisis in France: Financial precarity and mental well-being. *Journal of Urban Health, 97*(6), 776–795.

Armstrong, K., Elliott, J., & Tobin, A. (2020, October 2). Meet the customer service reps for Disney and Airbnb who have to pay to talk to you. *ProPublica.* Retrieved February 27, 2023, from, https://www.propublica.org/article/meet-the-customer-service-reps-for-disney-and-airbnb-who-have-to-pay-to-talk-to-you

Atkinson, A. (2021, May 11). More than a job: The meal delivery co-ops putting fairness into the gig economy. *Guardian.* https://www.theguardian.com/world/2021/may/11/more-than-a-job-the-meal-delivery-co-ops-making-the-gig-economy-fairer

Bellesia, F., Mattarelli, E., Bertolotti, F., & Sobrero, M. (2019). Platforms as entrepreneurial incubators? How online labor markets shape work identity. *Journal of Managerial Psychology, 34*(4), 246–268.

Berg, J., & Johnston, H. (2019). Too good to be true? A comment on Hall and Krueger's analysis of the labor market for Uber's driver-partners. *ILR Review, 72*(1), 39–68.

Berger, T., Frey, C. B., Levin, G., & Danda, S. R. (2019). Uber happy? Work and well-being in the 'gig economy'. *Economic Policy, 34*(99), 429–477.

Besbes, O., Castro, F., & Lobel, I. (2021). Surge pricing and its spatial supply response. *Management Science, 67*(3), 1350–1367.

Binder, M., & Blankenberg, A. K. (2021). Self-employment and subjective well-being. In K. F. Zimmermann (Ed.), *Handbook of labor, human resources and population economics*. Springer-Verlag

Blaising, A., Kotturi, Y., Kulkarni, C., & Dabbish, L. (2021). Making it work, or not: A longitudinal study of career trajectories among online freelancers. *Proceedings of the ACM on Human-Computer Interaction, 4*(CSCW3), 1–29.

Bunders, D. J., Arets, M., Frenken, K., & De Moor, T. (2022). The feasibility of platform cooperatives in the gig economy. *Journal of Co-operative Organization and Management, 10*(1), 100167.

Burtch, G., Carnahan, S., & Greenwood, B. N. (2018). Can you gig it? An empirical examination of the gig economy and entrepreneurial activity. *Management Science, 64*(12), 5497–5520.

Caza, B. B., Reid, E. M., Ashford, S., & Granger, S. (2022). Working on my own: Measuring the challenges of gig work. *Human Relations, 75*(11), 2122–2159.

Chan, K. (2021, December 10). *EU plan to boost gig economy workers is latest blow to apps*. Associated Press. https://apnews.com/article/technology-business-europe-economy-european-union-8e88b69ca6085b99e34e385e4cac1942

Chen, M. K., Rossi, P. E., Chevalier, J. A., & Oehlsen, E. (2019). The value of flexible work: Evidence from Uber drivers. *Journal of Political Economy, 127*(6), 2735–2794.

Chiaburu, D. S., & Harrison, D. A. (2008). Do peers make the place? Conceptual synthesis and meta-analysis of coworker effects on perceptions, attitudes, OCBs, and performance. *Journal of Applied Psychology, 93*(5), 1082–1103.

Christie, N., & Ward, H. (2019). The health and safety risks for people who drive for work in the gig economy. *Journal of Transport & Health, 13,* 115–127.

Churchill, B., & Craig, L. (2019). Gender in the gig economy: Men and women using digital platforms to secure work in Australia. *Journal of Sociology, 55*(4), 741–761.

Cook, C., Diamond, R., Hall, J. V., List, J. A., & Oyer, P. (2021). The gender earnings gap in the gig economy: Evidence from over a million rideshare drivers. *The Review of Economic Studies, 88*(5), 2210–2238.

Daniels, K., & Grinstein-Weiss, M. (2019). *The impact of the gig-economy on financial hardship among low-income families*. SSRN 3293988.

Dzieza, J. (2020). How hard will the robots make us work? *The Verge*. https://www.theverge.com/authors/josh-dzieza/archives/2

de la Vega, J. C. A., E. Cecchinato, M., & Rooksby, J. (2021, May). "Why lose control?" A study of freelancers' experiences with gig economy platforms. In *Proceedings of the 2021 CHI Conference on Human Factors in Computing Systems* (pp. 1–14).

DeLiema, M., Bosley, S., & Shadel, D. (2021). Multi-level marketing as "gig" work: Worker motivations, characteristics, and outcomes in the US. *Journal of Labor and Society, 25*(1), 83–121. https://doi.org/10.1163/24714607-bja10029

Ellen, M., Lippel, K., Ron, S., Agnieszka, K., Liz, M., Carrasco, C., & Pugliese, D. (2012). Workers' compensation experience-rating rules and the danger to workers' safety in the temporary work agency sector. *Policy and Practice in Health and Safety, 10*(1), 77–95.

Farrell, D., & Greig, F. (2016). *Paychecks, paydays, and the online platform economy: Big data on income volatility*. JP Morgan Chase Institute.

Freelancers Union. (2015). *The costs of nonpayment*. https://blog.freelancersunion.org/2015/12/10/costs-nonpayment/

Fuller, J. B., Raman, M., Sage-Gavin, E., & Hines, K. (2021). *Hidden workers: Untapped talent*. Harvard Business School. https://www.hbs.edu/managing-the-future-of-work/Documents/research/hiddenworkers09032021.pdf

Garin, A., Jackson, E., Koustas, D. K., & McPherson, C. (2020, May). Is new platform work different from other freelancing? In *AEA Papers and Proceedings* (Vol. 110, pp. 157–61). American Economic Association.

Glavin, P., Bierman, A., & Schieman, S. (2021). Über-alienated: Powerless and alone in the gig economy. *Work and Occupations, 48*, 399–431.

Glavin, P., & Schieman, S. (2022). Dependency and hardship in the gig economy: The mental health consequences of platform work. *Socius, 8* (2022), Article 23780231221082414.

Goods, C., Veen, A., & Barratt, T. (2019). "Is your gig any good?" Analysing job quality in the Australian platform-based food-delivery sector. *Journal of Industrial Relations, 61*(4), 502–527.

Guest, P., & Zhou, Y. (2021). *The global gig workers*. Rest of World. https://restofworld.org/2021/the-global-gig-workers/

Hall, J. V., & Krueger, A. B. (2018). An analysis of the labor market for Uber's driver-partners in the United States. *ILR Review, 71*(3), 705–732.

Hallett, N. (2018). The problem of wage theft. *Yale Law and Policy Review, 37*, 93–152.

Hara, K., Adams, A., Milland, K., Savage, S., Callison-Burch, C., & Bigham, J. P. (2018, April). A data-driven analysis of workers' earnings on Amazon Mechanical Turk. In *Proceedings of the 2018 CHI conference on human factors in computing systems* (pp. 1–14). Association for Computing Machinery.

Harpur, P., & Blanck, P. (2020). Gig workers with disabilities: opportunities, challenges, and regulatory response. *Journal of Occupational Rehabilitation, 30*(4), 511–520.

Henao, A., & Marshall, W. E. (2019). An analysis of the individual economics of ride-hailing drivers. *Transportation Research Part A: Policy and Practice, 130*, 440–451.

House, J. S. (1981). *Work, stress, and social support*. Addison Wesley.

Howson, K., Ustek-spilda, F. U., Bertolini, A., Heeks, R., Ferrari, F., Katta, S., Cole, M., Reneses, P. A., Salem, N., Sutcliffe, D., Steward, S., & Graham, M. (2022). Stripping back the mask: Working conditions on digital labour platforms during the COVID-19 pandemic. *International Labour Review, 161*(3), 413–440. https://doi.org/10.1111/ilr.12222

Huws, U., Spencer, N., Syrdal, D. S., & Holts, K. (2017). *Work in the European gig economy: Research results from the UK, Sweden, Germany, Austria, the Netherlands, Switzerland and Italy.* FEPS, UNI Europa, University of Hertfordshire. https://uhra.herts.ac.uk/bitstream/handle/2299/19922/Huws_U._Spencer_N.H._Syrdal_D.S._Holt_K._2017_.pdf

Kässi, O., Lehdonvirta, V., & Stephany, F. (2021). *How many online workers are there in the world? A data-driven assessment.* SSRN 3810843.

Kellogg, K. C., Valentine, M. A., & Christin, A. (2020). Algorithms at work: The new contested terrain of control. *Academy of Management Annals, 14*(1), 366–410.

Koustas, D. K. (2019, May). What do big data tell us about why people take gig economy jobs? In *AEA Papers and Proceedings* (Vol. 109, pp. 367–371). American Economic Association.

Kuhn, K. M. (2013). Judgments about pay. In S. Highhouse, R. S. Dalal, & E. Salas (Eds.), *Judgment and decision making at work* (pp. 179–197). Routledge.

Kuhn, K. M. (2016). The rise of the "gig economy" and implications for understanding work and workers. *Industrial and Organizational Psychology, 9*(1), 157–162.

Kuhn, K. M., & Maleki, A. (2017). Micro-entrepreneurs, dependent contractors, and instaserfs: Understanding online labor platform workforces. *Academy of Management Perspectives, 31*(3), 183–200.

Kuhn, K. M., Meijerink, J., & Keegan, A. (2021). Human resource management and the gig economy: Challenges and opportunities at the intersection between organizational HR decision-makers and digital labor platforms. In M. R. Buckley, A. R. Wheeler, J. E. Bauer, & J. R. B. Halbesleben (Eds.), *Research in Personnel and Human Resources Management* (pp. 1–46). Emerald Publishing.

Kuhn, K. M., & Yockey, M. D. (2003). Variable pay as a risky choice: Determinants of the relative attractiveness of incentive plans. *Organizational Behavior and Human Decision Processes, 90*(2), 323–341.

Langer, M., & Landers, R. N. (2021). The future of artificial intelligence at work: A review on effects of decision automation and augmentation on workers targeted by algorithms and third-party observers. *Computers in Human Behavior,* Article 106878.

Lehdonvirta, V., Kässi, O., Hjorth, I., Barnard, H., & Graham, M. (2019). The global platform economy: A new offshoring institution enabling emerging-economy microproviders. *Journal of Management, 45*(2), 567–599.

Lu, A., Frazier, P., & Kislev, O. (2018). *Surge pricing moves Uber's driver partners.* SSRN 3810246.

Macdonald, F. (2021). 'Personalised risk' in paid care work and the impacts of 'gig economy' care platforms and other market-based organisations. *International Journal of Care and Caring, 5*(1), 9–25.

Magee, J. C., & Galinsky, A. D. (2008). Social hierarchy: The self-reinforcing nature of power and status. *Academy of Management Annals, 2*(1), 351–398.

Mas, A., & Pallais, A. (2020). Alternative work arrangements. *Annual Review of Economics, 12*, 631–658.

McDonald, P., Williams, P., Stewart, A., Mayes, R., & Oliver, D. (2019). *Digital Platform Work in Australia: Prevalence, Nature and Impact.* https://eprints.qut.edu.au/203119/1/65060881.pdf

McInnis, B., Cosley, D., Nam, C., & Leshed, G. (2016, May). Taking a HIT: Designing around rejection, mistrust, risk, and workers' experiences in Amazon Mechanical Turk. In *Proceedings of the 2016 CHI conference on human factors in computing systems* (pp. 2271–2282). Association for Computing Machinery.

Meijerink, J., & Bondarouk, T. (2023). The duality of algorithmic management: Toward a research agenda on HRM algorithms, autonomy and value creation. *Human Resource Management Review, 33*(1), Article 100876.

Miao, W., Liu, Y., Wang, W., Deng, Y., & Tang, C. S. (2021). The effects of surge pricing on driver behavior in the ride-sharing market: Evidence from a quasi-Experiment. *Journal of Operations Management.* Advance online publication. https://doi.org/10.2139/ssrn.3909409/

Morduch, J., & Schneider, R. (2017). *The financial diaries.* Princeton University Press.

Myhill, K., Richards, J., & Sang, K. (2021). Job quality, fair work and gig work: The lived experience of gig workers. *The International Journal of Human Resource Management, 32*(19), 4110–4135.

Nian, T., Zhu, A., & Gurbaxani, V. (2021). The impact of the sharing economy on household bankruptcy. *Management Information Systems Quarterly, 45*(3), 1213–1248.

Norlander, P., Jukic, N., Varma, A., & Nestorov, S. (2021). The effects of technological supervision on gig workers: organizational control and motivation of Uber, taxi, and limousine drivers. *The International Journal of Human Resource Management, 32*(19), 4053–4077.

Oladipo, G. (2021, October 5). Tired of being stepped on: Instacart workers urge customers to delete the app. *Guardian.* https://www.theguardian.com/us-news/2021/oct/05/instacart-shoppers-working-conditions-customers-delete-app

Panteli, N., Rapti, A., & Scholarios, D. (2020). 'If he just knew who we were': Microworkers' emerging bonds of attachment in a fragmented employment relationship. *Work, Employment and Society, 34*(3), 476–494.

Pedulla, D. (2020). *Making the cut: Hiring decisions, bias, and the consequences of non-standard, mismatched, and precarious employment.* Princeton University Press.

Peetz, J., Robson, J., & Xuereb, S. (2021). The role of income volatility and perceived locus of control in financial planning decisions. *Frontiers in Psychology, 12*, Article 648043. https://doi.org/10.3389/fpsyg.2021.638043

Phung, K., Buchanan, S., Toubiana, M., Ruebottom, T., & Turchick-Hakak, L. (2021). When stigma doesn't transfer: Stigma deflection and occupational stratification in the sharing economy. *Journal of Management Studies, 58*(4), 1107–1139.

Quinlan, M., Mayhew, C., & Bohle, P. (2001). The global expansion of precarious employment, work disorganization, and consequences for occupational health: A review of recent research. *International Journal of Health Services, 31*(2), 335–414.

Rahman, H. A. (2021). The invisible cage: Workers' reactivity to opaque algorithmic evaluations. *Administrative Science Quarterly, 66* (4), 945–988.

Rosenblat, A., & Stark, L. (2016). Algorithmic labor and information asymmetries: A case study of Uber's drivers. *International Journal of Communication, 10*, 3758–3784.

Saito, S., Chiang, C. W., Savage, S., Nakano, T., Kobayashi, T., & Bigham, J. P. (2019). Turkscanner: Predicting the hourly wage of microtasks. In *The web Conference: Proceedings of The World Wide Web Conference 2019* (pp. 3187–3193). Association for Computing Machinery. https://doi.org/10.1145/3308558.3313716

Schwellnus, C., Geva, A., Pak, M., & Veiel, R. (2019). *Gig economy platforms: Boon or bane?* OECD Economics Department Working Paper No. 1550 https://doi.org/10.1787/18151973

Sessions, H., Nahrgang, J. D., Baer, M. D., & Welsh, D. T. (2022). From zero to hero and back to zero: The consequences of status inconsistency between the work roles of multiple jobholders. *Journal of Applied Psychology, 107*(8), 1369–1384.

Siddiqui, F., & Van Dam, A. (2021, March 16). As Uber avoided paying into unemployment, the federal government helped thousands of its drivers weather the pandemic. *Washington Post.* https://www.washingtonpost.com/technology/2021/03/16/uber-lyft-unemployment-benefits/

Taylor, J. M. (2011). *The Case (for and) against multi-level marketing.* Consumer Awareness Institute.

Tiku, N. (2020, May 23). Desperate workers rush to delivery app jobs to find low pay and punishing rules. *Washington Post.* https://www.washingtonpost.com/technology/2020/05/23/gig-work-instacart-shipt-amazon-flex-doordash/

Toxtli, C., Suri, S., & Savage, S. (2021). Quantifying the invisible labor in crowd work. *Proceedings of the ACM on Human-Computer Interaction, 5*(CSCW2), 1–26.

Vallas, S., & Schor, J. B. (2020). What do platforms do? Understanding the gig economy. *Annual Review of Sociology, 46*, 273–294.

Van Doorn, N., Ferrari, F., & Graham, M. (2020). *Migration and migrant labour in the gig economy: An intervention.* SSRN.

Veen, A., Barratt, T., & Goods, C. (2020). Platform-capital's 'app-etite' for control: A labour process analysis of food-delivery work in Australia. *Work, Employment and Society, 34*(3), 388–406.

Waddingham, J., Zachary, M. A., & Walker, H. J. (2021). Screened out: Recruiter evaluations of job applicants with prior entrepreneurial experience. In *Academy of Management Proceedings* (Vol. 2021, No. 1, p. 11971). Academy of Management.

Wood, A. J., Graham, M., Lehdonvirta, V., & Hjorth, I. (2019). Good gig, bad gig: Autonomy and algorithmic control in the global gig economy. *Work, Employment and Society, 33*(1), 56–75.

13

SUSTAINABLE PSYCHOLOGICAL CONTRACTS

A Pathway for Addressing Precarious Employment

Yannick Griep, Sarah Bankins, Johannes M. Kraak, Ultan Sherman, and Samantha D. Hansen

Introduction

The nature of work has changed significantly over the last several decades. Employment in the traditional sense has moved from office buildings to a gig economy characterized by an increasing number of forms of precarious employment, such as self-employment, algorithmic management, platform work, and insecure temporary employment (Kuhn, Chapter 12). Although these changes have brought about numerous benefits in terms of increased work flexibility for both employees and employers, they have also made work more insecure, isolating, and demanding: essentially changing the nature of the traditional employee-employer relationship. In this chapter, we first outline how work has become more precarious and how this impacts employee wellbeing. We then discuss the notion of sustainable human resource management (HRM) and how its key principles can help mitigate and minimize the negative effects of precarious work. Next, we suggest how these principles can be embedded into a new type of psychological contract, namely, a sustainable and high-quality psychological contract, and discuss how organizations and employees can create, maintain, and repair said psychological contracts. Building on this, we introduce some guiding principles that organizations can use to implement sustainable and high-quality psychological contracts as a way to alleviate or prevent precarious employment conditions.

The nature of work has changed drastically in the past five decades. The 1950s organizational research was mainly concerned with the study of male blue-collar factory workers who had to go to a physical location to do a physically demanding job day-in-day-out at the same factory from the start to the

DOI: 10.4324/9781003440444-16

end of their careers. Today, organizational research has shifted to the study of knowledge workers who can work anywhere and anytime and who are able to switch jobs whenever they want. Such changes to the nature of work and the context in which companies operate have brought along numerous advantages such as better paying jobs, more flexibility, and less dangerous work. However, they have also had serious implications for the type of employment relationship one holds with one's employer. That is, employment has shifted from a standard employment relationship (SER; International Labour Organization [ILO], 2011) based on ideas of mutual loyalty, permanency of employment, and job security to forms of employment that are characterized by precarity, a lack of security or guarantees of future work, and a focus on neoliberal principles (see Bankins et al., 2020; Cooper, 2002; Guest, 2004).

This focus on the new employment deal has gained significant momentum over the past decade through changes in work design and digital platforms that have created new paths to precarious employment. Such changes include the increasing use of gig work, where workers may work simultaneously for multiple employers, or wherein employees are situated in triadic employee-agency-employer relationships (Bankins et al., 2020; Duggan et al., 2020). Such changes also include the adoption of digital platforms that facilitate on-demand connections between workers and employers, but that also creates isolating and distanced forms of work where the actual "employer" may be unclear. Given the obvious, often employer-oriented, benefits of these changes, such as short-term performance indicators (Marchington, 2015), stakeholder interests, and profit (Dundon & Rafferty, 2018), an important question arises: Are these changes to the employee-employer relationship just as beneficial to the employees experiencing them?

In response to this question, much research demonstrates that precarious work can create significant and negative effects on worker wellbeing and other critical outcomes (Allan et al., 2021; Kalleberg, 2021; Klug et al., Chapter 21; Patulny et al., 2020). These widespread issues have driven the development of international agencies such as the ILO, which is charged with promoting labor standards and developing policies and programs aimed at ensuring *decent* work for all people. The Decent Work Agenda calls for the provision of quality jobs that are characterized by the provision of fair incomes generated in safe working environments and that afford dignity and equality in work. Consistent with this, research findings indicate that organizations require more sustainable approaches to HRM. Such approaches require organizations to place more value on human capabilities (Teng-Calleja et al., Chapter 8) and adopt more holistic and integrated strategies for people management (Wilkinson, 2005). Although many types of organizational practices can support the enactment of sustainable HRM, we present a novel employee-focused approach that identifies ways that employers can leverage features of the *psychological contract* to strengthen both the sustainability and quality of the employment relationship.

The psychological contract refers to a mental model of the perceived obligations between an employee and their employer (Rousseau, 1989, 1995). For example, an employee may believe that the organization is obligated to provide a caring and safe environment for employees in exchange for that employee's hard work. As such, the psychological contract acts as a guide for employees to navigate the employee-employer exchange relationship. The psychological contract offers an important framework to study the employment relationship (Freese & Schalk, 2008), and as employment affords critical rights and generates important benefits for workers (ILO, 2021), the psychological contract represents a meaningful starting point to work toward sustainable HRM and, ultimately, toward positive outcomes such as employee wellbeing and retention.

Following from the ILO's Decent Work Agenda and the United Nations' Sustainable Development Goals (SDGs) more generally, we first discuss the nature, drivers, and consequences of precarious employment. Next, we discuss the use of sustainability and sustainable HRM as stepping-stones to the development of a high-quality employment relationship and sustainable psychological contract. Finally, we discuss how organizations can implement and maintain sustainable psychological contracts for all, including precarious, employees.

Increasingly Precarious Employment: Its Nature, Drivers, and Consequences

Across much of the 20th century, the SER broadly, though neither exhaustively nor equitably (Benach et al., 2014), characterized the nature of employment exchanges across many industrialized countries (Grimshaw et al., 2016; ILO, 2011). The SER reflected employment that was stable and certain. Characterized by full-time hours, permanent contracts, adequate wages, and long-term employment, the SER was supported by regulatory protections that provided clear and enforceable minimum standards of employment and collective employee representation (Grimshaw et al., 2016; ILO, 2011). However, since the 1970s, the emergence of more flexible and precarious forms of employment has eroded the SER (Benach et al., 2014).

Known by various terms such as nonstandard, atypical, gig, flexible, and contingent work (Benach et al., 2014), precarious work is "performed in the formal and informal economy and is characterized by variable levels and degrees of objective (legal status) and subjective (feeling) characteristics of uncertainty and insecurity" (ILO, 2011, p. 5). The *uncertainty* that characterizes precarious work reflects several dimensions. Employees may have sustained uncertainty regarding *employment duration*, with an increasing proliferation of nonstandard employment contracts or arrangements such as short-term, casual, seasonal, and zero-hours (Avram, 2020; ILO, 2011). The nature of the employment relationship itself may be uncertain, whereby a worker may not be considered as an "employee" and it may be unclear who or what constitutes the "employer." For example, changes to employment regulations, among other factors, mean workers can be characterized in a range of ways such as contractors, subcontractors, and self-employed, which leaves them without the standard employment protections of "employees" (Cappelli & Keller, 2013). Triadic (agency-employee-employer) and potentially tetradic (supplier-employee-employer-customer) employment relationships (Sherman & Morley, 2020) result in having multiple employers simultaneously, further driving uncertainty and ambiguity by blurring the psychological contract obligations and obscuring who is accountable for meeting them (ILO, 2011). These aspects of uncertainty then lead to various forms of *insecurity*. An overriding issue is that precarious employment often means workers have little or no access to legislative, regulatory, and other social protections that once underpinned the SER (Gunn et al., 2021), leading to a lack of control over the conditions in which they work (Campbell & Price, 2016). This generates insecurity and inadequacy regarding income, benefits, access to collective representation, and the ability to express one's voice at work (Gunn et al., 2021; ILO, 2011). In this chapter, precarious work includes those forms of work marked by varying degrees of uncertainty and insecurity that affect both formal and informal workers (Gunn et al., 2021; Jyoti & Arora, Chapter 6; Saxena & Tchagneno, Chapter 11).

These precarious work characteristics are not new (ILO, 2011), as various forms of uncertainty and insecurity have historically shaped the nature of employment. However, over many decades, several converging forces have contributed to increasing levels and forms of precarious employment that have resulted in a recommodification of labor (Benach et al., 2014). Shifts to neoliberal economic agendas in many countries have seen the deregulation of labor markets, the relaxing of employment-related protections, and a greater focus on strategies for efficiency and profit maximization such as outsourcing and offshoring work (Benach et al., 2014). Economic and other shocks, including the 2018 Global Financial Crisis and 2020 onset of the COVID-19 pandemic, have tended to exacerbate these trends and heighten worker insecurity through increased use of restructuring, downsizing, and more precarious and flexible forms of employment: all meant to reduce organizational costs (Matilla-Santander, Ahonen et al., 2021; Han & Hart, 2021).

The use of digital labor platforms also intensifies uncertainty and insecurity in employment (Kuhn, Chapter 12). Such platforms create different employment relationships "where the relationship between the worker and a consumer is established via a digital intermediary acting as a shadow employer" (Kahancová et al., 2020). Such platforms may crowdsource workers to undertake microwork (wherein tasks are available to a "geographically dispersed crowd"; ILO, 2021) or enlist workers to undertake various on-demand service tasks such as manual labor, deliveries, or cleaning (Kahancová et al., 2020; Sherman & Morley, 2020).

In such digital contexts, there is often uncertainty regarding who the employer is. Further, the use of "contractor" or "self-employed" work arrangements reduces coverage by regulatory safeguards, leading to insecurity in income, working hours and opportunities for collective representation, (Kahancová et al., 2020; Kuhn et al., 2021). The rapid rise of digital platform and app work has called attention to the role of algorithmic management in both more precarious and more traditional forms of labor. When deployed in the context of the employment relationship, algorithms can make decisions about many aspects of the work arrangement that would typically be made by managers and HR professionals, such as recruitment, performance management, reward management, and talent management (McDonnell et al., 2021). While algorithmic management is one of the distinguishing features of app work, there is increasing evidence of it diffusing into more traditional forms of employment (e.g., automated shortlisting as part of the hiring process). Replacing tasks previously done by human managers with algorithms is another example of the erosion of the SER and the increasing pervasiveness of uncertainty and insecurity in contemporary working relationships. Indeed, the last decade of research on gig working consistently spotlights the negative experience of gig workers being subjected to the tyranny of the app (Lehdonvirta, 2018).

Not all workers will experience precarious employment negatively (Lewchuk & Clarke, 2011); the effects of precarious work are contingent upon multiple factors such as alternative income sources and career opportunities (Campbell & Price, 2016). However, there is consistent evidence that sporadic and long-term precarious employment is associated with adverse consequences at the individual and population levels. For example, evidence indicates that precarious work leads to degraded health (Benach et al., 2014; Gunn et al., 2021; Lewchuk & Clarke, 2011; Matilla-Santander, Martínez-Sánchezet al., 2021): both physical (e.g., occupational injury, exhaustion, and fatigue;) and mental (e.g., anxiety and symptoms of depression), as well as to higher levels of employment strain (e.g., high uncertainty and lack of support; Clarke et al., 2007). Moreover, as a result of workplace uncertainty and insecurity, precarious workers are also confronted with heightened deprivations beyond the workplace associated with poverty (Benach et al., 2014; Carr, Hodgetts, et al., Chapter 1).

Taken together, the prevalence of precarious employment does not bode well for meeting the ILO's Decent Work Agenda and UN SDG-8, nor for heeding calls for organizations to adopt more sustainable, dignity-oriented approaches to people management (e.g., Bal & de Jong, 2017). Given the generally poor outcomes precarious employment generates for workers, the sustainability of these forms of work has been questioned (e.g., Clarke et al., 2007; Kuhn et al., 2021). We next discuss issues of sustainability and the use of sustainable HRM to generate and maintain high-quality psychological contracts as a means of curbing the uncertainty and insecurity associated with precarious employment.

Countering Precarious Work: Sustainable HRM

Broadly, the notion of sustainability refers to using resources in ways that ensure those resources can be renewed, remain available for future use, and do not become exhausted (Pfeffer, 2010). Thus, sustainability encompasses a range of goals including renewal and recycling, conservation of natural resources and minimization of waste, and preservation of natural ecosystems and cultural resources for future generations (Pfeffer, 2010). Notions of sustainability can then extend to the adoption of sustainable organizational practices relating to ecological, social, and/or economic concerns (Linnenluecke & Griffiths, 2010). Historically, management research on sustainability has focused more on the physical rather than the social aspects of the environment (Pfeffer, 2010). However, there is an increasing emphasis on ensuring that "the needs, potential and aspirations of individuals…take centre stage in the workplace," (Wilkinson et al., 2001, p. 1497) through the sustainable management of people. Specifically, *sustainable HRM* "requires the organization to recognize and place value on human capabilities that take a more holistic and integrated approach to people management" (Wilkinson, 2005, p. 1079), with a focus on the sustained application of practices that are participative (Gollan, 2005). Although sustainable HRM can include organizational strategies to encourage employees to conserve natural resources, e.g., "green HRM" (see Stahl et al., 2020), given our focus on precarious employment, we explore how organizations can sustainably manage their *people* (Teng-Calleja et al., Chapter 8).

Discussions around the nature of sustainable HRM continue to grow and evolve. Here we draw from Gollan's (2000) model to highlight five critical principles of sustainable HRM. First, sustainable HRM adopts a *long-term perspective* (Stankevičiūtė & Savanevičienė, 2018) which eschews a narrow focus upon short-term financial gains (Wilkinson et al., 2001). Such a perspective entails designing work in ways that foster, rather than exploit, workers and encourage workers to be employed and remain so in the future (Van Dam et al., 2017), and that does away with the traditional "hire and fire" approach (Stankevičiūtė & Savanevičienė, 2018). Second, sustainable HRM uses *employee consultation and participation* in decisions that affect them at work. This helps to create a meaningful social dialog, opportunities for a voice, and at least some sense of empowerment, and may ultimately require employers to surpass the employee benefits afforded by law (Gollan, 2000; Stankevičiūtė & Savanevičienė, 2018). Third, sustainable HRM values *employee development* of proximal skills and competencies (Gollan, 2000) as well as more distal skills and competencies that will enable potential future needs to be met (Macke & Genari, 2019). Fourth, *employee care* supports the health and wellbeing of workers, critical to the precarious work context (Stankevičiūtė & Savanevičienė, 2018). Employee care involves providing appropriate workplace health and safety measures and supporting workers to achieve work-life balance, enabling workers to fulfill their obligations both within and outside of work (Gollan, 2000; Gollan & Xu, 2014). The final dimension of sustainable HRM identified by Gollan (2000) concerns *organizational systems and structures*. Promotion and disciplinary processes, reporting structures, policies, and the like are designed to reflect, support, and facilitate the application of the aforementioned characteristics of HRM sustainability.

The enactment of sustainable HRM principles should help alleviate and even counter unsustainable increases in precarious employment and its associated negative effects on workers. In particular, adopting these principles could help reduce the employment strain and related physical and mental consequences that many precarious workers face (Clarke et al., 2007). Employment strain comprises many of the key aspects of uncertainty and insecurity that underpin precarious employment, as discussed earlier. Specifically, employment strain entails employment relationship uncertainty, i.e., uncertainty over the nature, type, and extent of future work; employment relationship effort, i.e., efforts to find and sustain employment across potentially multiple employers; and employment relationship support, i.e., support through formal collectives like unions and personal, social, and familial networks (Clarke et al., 2007). For example, organizational adoption of a longer term orientation toward their employees, offering meaningful forms of dialog and participation in workplace decisions, and providing developmental opportunities could lessen the uncertainty and effort forms of strain while enhancing employment relationship support, respectively. Relatedly, as proposed by Cross and Swart (2021), given the rise of precarious work in the form of independent contractors across most industries, HRM now ought to take on more responsibility for these workers traditionally viewed as outside the boundaries of the organization and beyond the obligations of the HR function. That is, HRM needs to extend its remit to cater to the human needs of the growing population of precarious workers (Jyoti & Arora, Chapter 6).

While a range of external factors influence how, and to what extent, organizations implement sustainable HRM practices (Gollan & Xu, 2014; Macke & Genari, 2019; Stahl et al., 2020), we argue that one important way such practices can be embedded within the employment relationship is by making them key features of the psychological contract.

Sustainable Psychological Contracts: A Route to Sustainable HRM

The psychological contract refers to "a cognitive schema, or system of beliefs, representing an individual's perceptions of his or her own and another's obligations, defined as the duties or responsibilities one feels bound to perform" (Rousseau et al., 2018, p. 1081). Precarious forms of employment have generally been linked to a degraded psychological contract, with its characteristic uncertainty and insecurity creating weakened mutual ties between an employer and their employees (Grimshaw et al., 2016), feelings of unjust treatment leading to increased perceptions of psychological contract breach (Benach et al., 2014), and erosion of trust (Sharkie, 2005). We propose that a sustainable psychological contract would address such difficulties and facilitate the ILO's Decent Work Agenda for precarious workers. Traditionally, the study of psychological contracts has taken three distinct approaches: evaluation-oriented, content-oriented, and feature-oriented Rousseau & Tijoriwala, 1998. Below we discuss how each of these approaches may contribute to informing a more sustainable psychological contract among precarious workers.

Evaluation-oriented approaches to the study of psychological contracts examine how the degree of fulfillment or breach of the contract affects employee and employer outcomes such as job satisfaction and performance, respectively. Like typical employees, at certain points in the employment relationship, precarious workers evaluate how well the organization is fulfilling their psychological contracts, and they display similar reactions to psychological contract breach when it occurs (McLean Parks et al., 1998; Saltzman et al., Chapter 2). Consistent with social exchange theory and the norm of reciprocity (Blau, 1964; Gouldner, 1960), research shows that when an employee perceives that the employer is fulfilling its obligations, the employee is motivated to reciprocate by fulfilling their obligations to the employer, e.g., by engaging in high levels of in-role and extra-role performance (e.g., Conway et al., 2011; Cropanzano & Mitchell, 2005; Hansen & Griep, 2016; Maia & Bastos, 2015; Turnley et al., 2003). However, when employees believe that the employer has not fulfilled its obligations, e.g., by breaching its psychological contract obligations (Morrison & Robinson, 1997), they can demonstrate a host of negative attitudes, e.g., decreased satisfaction, and negative behaviors, e.g., counterproductive work behaviors, toward the organization (for meta-analyses see Bal et al., 2008; Zhao et al., 2007; see also Griep & Vantilborgh, 2018a, 2018b). Therefore, as with typical employees, employers should strive to fulfill their obligations to employees in a timely manner to facilitate positive outcomes. However, fulfillment in and of itself does not guarantee the establishment of decent work for precarious workers because it does not guarantee the delivery of high-quality contract terms, which we propose are critical to the sustainable psychological contract.

Content-oriented approaches examine differences between sets of transactional, i.e., economically focused contract terms such as regular pay raises and attractive health benefits, versus relational, i.e., socioemotionally focused contract terms such as supportive supervision and developmental opportunities, contract terms, and associated outcomes. Historically, the content of the psychological contracts of precarious workers focuses strongly on economic terms, with little content devoted to socioemotional terms. Moreover, the quality of the economic terms is typically lacking due to limited social benefits and statutory entitlements and low wages (Vosko, 2010). This is inconsistent with what the ILO deems to be decent work. As such, psychological contracts of precarious workers can be strengthened to provide higher quality terms including fair treatment, equality, fair pay, and safe working conditions, thereby leading to a more sustainable employment relationship.

Content- and evaluation-oriented approaches have contributed greatly to understanding psychological contract processes. However, a feature-oriented approach offers a unique opportunity to help with the development and maintenance of sustainable psychological contracts for precarious employees. Feature-oriented approaches to the study of psychological contracts examine employee and employer outcomes as a function of distinct collections of characteristics or attributes, e.g., scope, duration, and tangibility, that distinguish different types of contracts, most notably transactional and relational contracts (Rousseau & Tijoriwala, 1998). Transactional contracts are focused on explicit and tangible obligations that are often short term and require little emotional engagement between the parties. Conversely, relational contracts are focused on more socio-emotional attributes that are less tangible, more subjective, long lasting, and commitment oriented. To date though, few studies (e.g., McInnis et al., 2009; McLean Parks et al., 1998; Rousseau & McLean Parks, 1993) have adopted a feature-oriented approach. To facilitate this approach, and building on the seminal work of Rousseau and Tijoriwala (1998), Sels et al. (2004) proposed a useful framework containing six key psychological contract features. In the current chapter, we now use this framework to introduce a new type of psychological contract, which we label the *sustainable psychological contract*.

According to Sels et al. (2004), *tangibility* is one useful feature to distinguish among different types of psychological contracts. Tangibility is the degree to which employees perceive the terms of their psychological contract as clear, explicit, and identifiable by others (Rousseau & McLean Parks, 1993; McLean Parks et al., 1998). High tangibility—as opposed to intangibility which is characterized by high trust (Lee et al., 2000) and broad role definitions (Ang et al., 2000)—is positioned as a key characteristic of the sustainable psychological contract as it is associated with more positive outcomes. Tangibility is facilitated by comprehensive labor laws and regulations and, within organizations, explicit job descriptions and performance requirements (Sels et al., 2004). This feature then helps generate secure and stable employment conditions. For instance, in app-work arrangements, workers often complain about the inconsistent and ever-shifting remuneration on offer (Kuhn & Maleki, 2017) and this is often a primary reason why individuals rarely stay working in this domain for a prolonged period of time.

Second, psychological contracts can be distinguished in *scope*, ranging from narrow to broad. This feature refers to the extent to which one's work-life boundaries are flexible (McLean Parks et al., 1998). Psychological contracts that are *narrow in scope* generally reflect employees setting clear divisions between their work and home lives, an economically-focused exchange relationship, and little exhibition of extra role or citizenship behaviors by employees (Peel & Inkson, 2000; Sels et al., 2004). Such characteristics are strongly associated with precarious employment. In contrast, psychological contracts that are *broad in scope* reflect reciprocal care between employer and employee, employer recognition of employees' non-work commitments, and employees engaging in extra role behaviors (Ang et al., 2000; Diaz-Saenz & Witherspoon, 2000; Krausz, 2000; Sels et al., 2004; Shah et al., 2000). Given the lasting benefits to both employees and employers, psychological contracts that are broader in scope pair better with calls by the ILO for "decent work." Therefore, the psychological contracts of precarious workers can be made more sustainable by broadening the scope. In light of the consequences of the COVID-19 pandemic for driving more hybrid and remote employment arrangements and its impacts on work-life balance, for instance, adopting a broader scope for the psychological contract between both parties is more likely to facilitate a more effective working relationship.

Third, Sels et al., (2004) suggest that *stability* reflects the extent to which the psychological contract is static or dynamic over time (see also McLean Parks et al., 1998). Psychological contracts that are stable or static contain fixed terms that are often rules-based and are ultimately largely inflexible (Kabanoff et al., 2000; McInnis et al., 2009; Rousseau & McLean Parks, 1993; Sels et al., 2004). In other words, such contracts promote maintenance of the status quo, including the maintenance of precarious employment. In contrast, psychological contracts that are more dynamic evolve over time, with their terms often reinterpreted and remaining flexible (Morishima, 2000; Rousseau, 2000; Sels et al., 2004). This flexibility enables organizations and employees alike to make changes to an undesirable situation, such as precarious employment. As such, enhanced dynamism and flexibility should be a key feature of the sustainable psychological contract. Again, as an example of a rigid, precarious working arrangement, in the gig working domain, workers are increasingly looking for a more codetermined working relationship as a means to counteract the strict application of the algorithm (Duggan et al., 2020). Consequently, there are a host of ongoing legal cases around the globe and collective industrial action by gig workers seeking to gain more control over the terms of employment.

Fourth, psychological contracts can also be distinguished by *time frame*, which reflects the expected length of employment (MacNeil, 1985; Rousseau & McLean Parks, 1993; Sels et al., 2004). Consistent with precarious employment, psychological contracts with a *short-term orientation* are often characterized by insecure and unstable employment, high job mobility and employability, and time-limited contracts (Ang et al., 2000; Rousseau, 2000).

In contrast, psychological contracts with a *long-term orientation* are associated with job security, closed internal labor markets—including opportunities for internal promotion—and little external mobility and turnover (Cadin, 2000; Sels et al., 2004). The erosion of the SER and the advent of increasing forms of precarious work reflects a short-term psychological contract. Consistent with the long-term perspective of sustainable HRM, the sustainable psychological contract must reflect a longer-term orientation. While the temporal structure of work may be changing in many employment contexts (Lehdonvirta, 2018), it is still important for organizations to view working relationships as a potentially long-term endeavor: especially with those precarious workers who may be disconnected and marginalized from a typical SER. Such a long-term orientation could be achieved by investing in employees through training and development of their skills and competencies, for example.

Fifth, psychological contracts can also be distinguished by their *exchange symmetry*, or the degree to which the employee and employer are equal partners in the relationship. Given that unequal psychological contracts tend to favor the employer, exchange symmetry can also be understood as the degree to which employees accept or tolerate an unequal employment relationship (Sels et al., 2004). *Unequal* psychological contracts are characterized by a strong organizational hierarchy, employee feelings of inequality, limited employee privileges, and a conformist attitude toward the established hierarchy (Sels et al., 2004). In contrast, *equal* psychological contracts are based on principles of reciprocal respect, informality, low power distance between parties, open interactions, flat organizational structures, and respect for achievement and merit rather than a focus on status or hierarchy (Sels et al., 2004). Thus, we propose that the sustainable psychological contract is characterized by an equal symmetry in the exchange relationship, as it considers the needs of both employee and employer in an effort to promote decent work (i.e., equality, fairness, respect) for precarious workers. Drawing on Cross and Swart's (2021) argument that HRM needs to adopt a more inclusive approach to managing precarious workers such as independent contractors, organizations seeking more equality in working relationships not only hold the prospect of developing more sustainable psychological contracts but also of creating a more just society founded on the principles of decent work (Dundon & Rafferty, 2018). In other words, equal psychological contracts could be achieved by meaningfully including workers' voices when making decisions that concern the conditions of their work.

Finally, the *contract level* refers to employees' perceptions of whether their employment relationship is underpinned by collective agreements or reflects more individualized arrangements (Sels et al., 2004). *Individually regulated* psychological contracts, despite the numerous benefits of idiosyncratic deals found in the literature (Liao et al., 2018), are often characterized by the presence of few laws to guarantee employment conditions, minimal labor protections, and place significant emphasis on the individual employee as the driver for their success. Indeed, for some employees with individually regulated psychological contracts, the situation is bleak. For example, it has been argued that in the absence of proper legal protections to ensure decent working conditions, employers increase the use of contingent contracts that place the burdens of fluctuating workloads upon workers (Brenner et al., 2014). In contrast, *collectively regulated* psychological contracts allow participation by both the employee and employer to establish mutual obligations. These agreements are reinforced through generally applicable rules, group consensus, consistent and equitable treatment of all employees, and a more prominent role for collective bargaining entities to protect employment conditions and facilitate job security (Sels et al., 2004). Drawing on related characteristics of sustainable HRM, e.g., employee consultation and participation, the sustainable psychological contract is established and regulated collectively, providing voice and agency to precarious workers. As work arrangements across the globe increasingly move away from the SER model, there are growing calls for increased collective action amongst workers in this domain to negotiate a more codetermined working relationship (Searle & McWha-Hermann, Chapter 4). It is likely that creating more sustainable psychological contracts, that are collectively designed and regulated, can help achieve this aim.

Taken together, we propose that the sustainable psychological contract is characterized by (1) high tangibility, (2) broad scope, (3) high flexibility, (4) long-term orientation, (5) equal exchange symmetry, and (6) collective regulation. In what follows, we present recommendations for the implementation and management of sustainable psychological contracts for all, including precarious, employees.

Implementing Sustainable Psychological Contracts

In the previous sections, we discussed the increase in precarious employment against the backdrop of emerging sustainable HRM practices, as well as how organizations can contribute to sustainable HRM through implementation of high-quality sustainable psychological contracts. We conclude this chapter by presenting three concrete guidelines that organizations and HR practitioners can use when implementing a sustainable psychological contract to alleviate or prevent precarious employment conditions.

The psychological contract literature has only focused implicitly on sustainability. Two critical issues in the literature have prevented a coordinated effort to chart a sustainable psychological contract. First, the psychological contract literature has focused almost exclusively on non-precarious working groups such as professional and white-collar employees (O'Leary-Kelly et al., 2014). Second, the sustainable HRM literature lacks a single and unambiguous definition of what constitutes sustainable HRM practices (Järlström et al., 2018). The first attempts to integrate the psychological contract and sustainable HRM literature positioned the psychological contract as an outcome of HR processes. For instance, Susomrith (2020) proposed that the psychological contract would be an outcome (with job satisfaction and engagement being other outcomes) of Kramar's (2014) sustainable HRM model. We believe that a sustainable psychological contract should be holistic and should give direction to how organizations shape their sustainable HRM practices for all employees. In what follows, we present three guidelines to assist organizations in their implementation of sustainable psychological contracts as the starting point when creating high-quality relationships with their employees. At this point, it is worthwhile noting that the three guidelines we are proposing will require a shift in mindsets among internal and external organizational stakeholders, e.g., policy makers, HR management systems, and managers, and a shift from employer-oriented monetary benefits to a much stronger focus on and central positioning of employee rights and benefits such as quality jobs, dignity in work, decent wages, equality, and safe conditions for all employees. When discussing and presenting our three guidelines, we put managers at center stage as role models who are able to promote and advocate adherence to sustainable psychological contracts.

The first guideline refers to creating a sustainable psychological contract that adheres to the principles set out in the UN SDGs. In particular, SDG-8 calls for the promotion of *sustained, inclusive, and sustainable economic growth, full and productive employment and decent work*. SDG-1 calls for an *end to poverty*, SDG-10 calls for the *reduction of inequality*, and SDG-17 for *strengthening the means of implementation and revitalization of the global partnership for sustainable development*. Although a sustainable psychological contract could include broader values associated with corporate social responsibility (CSR), it should at the very least include and protect access to full and productive employment and decent work for all, provide a livable wage, and reduce inequality (Carr, Hopner et al., Chapter 10; Meyer & Maleka, Chapter 7). In doing so, the sustainable psychological contract would ensure that all employees, especially those in precarious employment, have a stronger chance of meeting the SDG objectives.

The ILO (2015) report on the future of work emphasized a floor of minimum protection for everyone. This concept is noteworthy because it calls on employers to provide decent work and wages rather than providing the minimum legal requirements. In support of this, we refer to the Glasgow Living Wage Initiative, which was first introduced for Glasgow City Council employees in 2009 but has since grown with adoption by 400 employers, representing 89,000 employees. Employers who adhere to the principles of the Glasgow Living Wage Initiative agree to pay their employees above legal minimum requirements so employees better meet their basic needs. Having said that, creating a sustainable psychological contract is not simply about providing decent pay. Combining the principle of a "floor of minimum protection" with the SDG objectives allows employers to determine other basic elements that any sustainable psychological contract should entail. For instance, another ILO (2019) report mentioned elements such as better workplace health and safety, universal social protection for employees, respect for workers' rights, improved integration of differently abled people and minorities, workers having some control over their working hours, and opportunities for ongoing learning. Decent work and living wages are topics that are getting increased traction in both academic and professional circles. An example is the European Association of Work and Organizational Psychology research incubator held in May 2021. Another example is the Global Living Organizational Wage project started in 2016 which currently has interdisciplinary hubs, composed of academics and organizations, in 25 countries (Meyer & Maleka, Chapter 7).

The second guideline is to determine which groups of precarious employees will be included when developing a sustainable psychological contract. Currently, many individuals are working as freelancers or independent contractors, and although they are dependent on the organization for their income, they do not benefit from the same advantages, such as bonuses, retirement benefits, or social protection, that regular "inhouse employees" benefit from (e.g., Lemsom, 2021; Malingre, 2021). In addition to the numerous organizational benefits that one can expect from providing employees, and especially precarious employees, with a sustainable psychological contract, e.g., increased performance and extrarole behavior (Turnley et al., 2003), organizations also face numerous external pressures that are likely to accelerate this process in the near future. That is, there are currently many national and supranational initiatives to reclassify gig workers in precarious employment (Satariano & Peltier, 2021), with the most visible one being the European Union initiative that could see over 5 million Europeans working for online labor platforms being requalified as "inhouse" employees rather than precarious gig workers (Malingre, 2021). While some organizations have responded negatively to this initiative, several large players have welcomed the EU policy proposals (Satariano & Peltier, 2021). Thus, organizations face an important choice; should they include all individuals who could be considered employees, thereby anticipating possible future requirements as well as changes in public opinion; or do they try to resist this potential change until it becomes inevitable? Our advice would be to include all individuals and offer them access to a sustainable psychological contract, including access to the same benefits as inhouse employees, to secure the future of these precarious employees and ultimately secure the success of their organization and favorable public opinion.

The third guideline for organizations is to ensure that their HR professionals and managers 'walk the talk'. Specifically, this implies that when organizations create sustainable psychological contracts for all individuals working for them, they are shaping a framework with a set of expectations and exchange terms to which they themselves will have to adhere. It is important, as with any type of contract, to ensure fulfillment of the sustainable psychological contracts. This benefits the organization by strengthening its reputation and encouraging people to buy its products or apply for jobs (Puncheva-Michelotti et al., 2018) and by strengthening employee retention (Dögl & Holtbrügge, 2014). On the flipside, if an organization fails to fulfill their part of the sustainable psychological contract, the organization might be seen as falsely trying to present itself as being socially responsible, leading to perceptions of CSR-washing (Ginder et al., 2021) among potential customers and employees. Hence, it is crucial for organizations to include HR professionals and managers in the process of creating and implementing sustainable psychological contracts for all of their employees. More specifically, HR professionals and managers should understand the necessity of implementing said sustainable psychological contracts, understand what a sustainable psychological contract entails, and what an organization expects from them in terms of creating, implementing, and monitoring sustainable psychological contracts. For example, HR professionals and managers should be vigilant for potential shortfalls regarding the minimum floor of protection and agreed-upon SDG goals. This represents a cultural shift for HR professionals and managers who currently supervise precarious employees through narrow exchange relationships characterized by compliance. Moving to a sustainable psychological contract implies a shift from a narrow and specific set of exchange terms to a more open-ended approach characterized by the creation of high-quality relationships with all employees, including precarious employees. As an important party in creating, maintaining, and repairing psychological contracts (e.g., Rousseau et al., 2018), HR professionals and managers should thus receive training in managing expectations regarding exchange terms as well as how to support employees when specific sustainable exchange terms cannot be fulfilled.

Future Research Directions

Our work also promotes some interesting avenues for future research. First, as previously argued by Griep et al. (2022), future research could explore ways to design work that supports – rather than diminishes - employees and provides access to better and more stable income (e.g., via retirement safety nets; collective protection schemes against income loss: in line with SDG-8) and improved collective voice and representation (e.g., strengthening of workers' voice and unionization: in line with SDG-10) could create sustainable psychological contracts and ultimately protect employees from exploitation commonly found in a more narrowly focused psychological contract mainly premised upon financial gains (see also Sels et al., 2004; Wilkinson et al., 2001). Related to this point, scholars should investigate if investing in continuous education, the development of skills and competencies, and the broader development of employee employability (in line with SDG-4) would enable employees to meet their current and future needs while boosting their internal and external employability (see also Forrier et al., 2018). Some interesting avenues to explore with regard to investing in the attraction, retention, and sustainable employability of employees include the following: providing paid internships for new talent, investing in training on the job, and providing personal development budgets to give employees some autonomy in choosing educational opportunities that suit them (De Grip & Sauermann, 2013). It would be worthwhile to investigate if these actions foster the creation of sustainable psychological contracts and hence increased performance and satisfaction in the workplace.

Second, we advocate for more research into the role of creating social dialog, providing opportunities for employee participation, reinstating a sense of ownership and pride, and surpassing the minimum requirements imposed by laws to create a sustainable psychological contract, and ultimately a workforce that can sustain itself over time. In this regard, it would be worthwhile to explore the role of psychological contract inducements such as mutual respect, lower power distance between employment parties, more informal interactions and open communication, and respect for merit and achievement over power or status (Sels et al., 2004) in the creation and maintenance of a fulfilled and sustainable psychological contract.

Conclusion

The value of psychological contract theory as an analytical lens in organizational psychology is that it provides useful insights into the nature and dynamics of working relationships. Given the rise of precarious employment relationships across most domains of work in the last decade, coupled with a general move away from the SER model, it is surprising then that very few researchers have drawn upon psychological contract theory to help explain and understand the experience of precarious work. To help address this issue, the chapter makes the case for a sustainable psychological contract as a means through which the challenges of precarious employment can be addressed. Against the backdrop of the rapid emergence of new forms of precarious employment such as gig-working, we advance the idea that focusing on the underlying properties of the psychological contract, known as psychological contract *features* in the literature, holds the prospect of helping employers to create more effective and sustainable working agreements. We argue that future exchange relationships built upon key psychological contract foundations can help to reduce precariousness in employment and can help all contributing parties to create more durable and meaningful work.

References

Allan, B. A., Autin, K. L., & Wilkins-Yel, K. G. (2021). Precarious work in the 21st century: A psychological perspective. *Journal of Vocational Behavior, 126*, Article 103491. https://doi.org/10.1016/j.jvb.2020.103491

Ang, S., Tan, M. L., & Ng, K. Y. (2000). Psychological contracts in Singapore. In D. M. Rousseau & R. Schalk (Eds.), *Psychological contracts in employment: Cross-national perspectives* (pp. 213–230). Sage.

Avram, S. (2020). *Zero-hours contracts: Flexibility or insecurity? Experimental evidence from a low income population.* Institute for Social and Economic Research, University of Essex. http://hdl.handle.net/10419/248577

Bal, P. M., & de Jong, S. B. (2017). From human resource management to human dignity development: A dignity perspective on HRM and the role of workplace democracy. In M. Kostera & M. Pirson (Eds.), *Dignity and the organization* (pp. 173–195). Palgrave Macmillan.

Bal, P. M., De Lange, A. H., Jansen, P. G., & Van Der Velde, M. E. (2008). Psychological contract breach and job attitudes: A meta-analysis of age as a moderator. *Journal of Vocational Behavior, 72*(1), 143–158. https://doi.org/10.1016/j.jvb.2007.10.005

Bankins, S., Griep, Y., & Hansen, S. D. (2020). Charting directions for a new research era: Addressing gaps and advancing scholarship in the study of psychological contracts. *European Journal of Work and Organizational Psychology, 29*(2), 159–163. https://doi.org/10.1080/1359432X.2020.1737219

Benach, J., Vives, A., Amable, M., Vanroelen, C., Tarafa, G., & Muntaner, C. (2014). Precarious employment: Understanding an emerging social determinant of health. *Annual Review of Public Health, 35*, 229–253. https://doi.org/10.1146/annurev-publhealth-032013-182500

Blau, P. M. (1964). *Exchange and power in social life.* Wiley & Sons.

Brenner, N., Peck, J., & Theodore, N. (2014). New constitutionalism and variegated neo-liberalization. In S. Gill & A. C. Cutler (Eds.), *New constitutionalism and world order* (pp. 126–142). Cambridge University Press.

Cadin, L. (2000). Does psychological contract theory work in France? In D. M. Rousseau & R. Schalk (Eds.), *Psychological contracts in employment: Cross-national perspectives* (pp. 67–86). Sage.

Campbell, I., & Price, R. (2016). Precarious work and precarious workers: Towards an improved conceptualisation. *The Economic and Labour Relations Review, 27*(3), 314–332. https://doi.org/10.1177/1035304616652074

Cappelli, P., & Keller, J. R. (2013). Classifying work in the new economy. *Academy of Management Review, 38*(4), 575–596. https://doi.org/10.5465/amr.2011.0302

Clarke, M., Lewchuk, W., de Wolff, A., & King, A. (2007). 'This just isn't sustainable': Precarious employment, stress and workers' health. *International Journal of Law and Psychiatry, 30*(4–5), 311–326. https://doi.org/10.1016/j.ijlp.2007.06.005

Conway, N., Guest, D., & Trenberth, L. (2011). Testing the differential effects of changes in psychological contract breach and fulfillment. *Journal of Vocational Behavior, 79*(1), 267–276. https://doi.org/10.1016/j.jvb.2011.01.003

Cooper, C. L. (2002). The changing psychological contract at work. *Occupational Environment Medicine, 59*(6), 355. https://doi.org/10.1136/oem.59.6.355

Cropanzano, R., & Mitchell, M. S. (2005). Social exchange theory: An interdisciplinary review. *Journal of Management, 31*(6), 874–900. https://doi.org/10.1177/0149206305279602

Cross, D., & Swart, J. (2021). In a flash of time: knowledge resources that enable professional cross-boundary work. *Journal of Professions and Organization, 8*(1), 1–18. https://doi.org/10.1093/jpo/joaa025

De Grip, A., & Sauermann, J. (2013). The effect of training on productivity: The transfer of on-the-job training from the perspective of economics. *Educational Research Review, 8*, 28–36. https://doi.org/10.1016/j.edurev.2012.05.005

Diaz-Saenz, H. R., & Witherspoon, P. D. (2000). Psychological contracts in Mexico. In D. M. Rousseau & R. Schalk (Eds), *Psychological contracts in employment: Cross-national perspectives* (pp. 158–175). Sage.

Dögl, C., & Holtbrügge, D. (2014). Corporate environmental responsibility, employer reputation and employee commitment: an empirical study in developed and emerging economies. *The International Journal of Human Resource Management, 25*(12), 1739–1762. https://doi.org/10.1080/09585192.2013.859164

Duggan, J., Sherman, U., Carbery, R., & McDonnell, A. (2020). Algorithmic management and app-work in the gig economy: A research agenda for employment relations and HRM. *Human Resource Management Journal, 30*(1), 114–132. https://doi.org/10.1111/1748-8583.12258

Dundon, T., & Rafferty, A. (2018). The (potential) demise of HRM? *Human Resource Management Journal, 28*(3), 377–391. https://doi.org/10.1111/1748-8583.12195

Forrier, A., De Cuyper, N., & Akkermans, J. (2018). The winner takes it all, the loser has to fall: Provoking the agency perspective in employability research. *Human Resource Management Journal, 28*(4), 511–523. https://doi.org/10.1111/1748-8583.12206

Freese, C., & Schalk, R. (2000). Psychological contracts in the Netherlands. Dualism: Flexibility and security. In D. M. Rousseau & R. Schalk (Eds.), *Psychological contracts in employment: Cross-national perspectives* (pp. 176–194). Sage.

Freese, C., & Schalk, R. (2008). How to measure the psychological contract? A critical criteria-based review of measures. *South African Journal of Psychology, 38*(2), 269–286. https://doi.org/10.1177/008124630803800202

Ginder, W., Kwon, W.-S., & Byun, S.-E. (2021). Effects of internal–external congruence-based CSR positioning: An attribution theory approach. *Journal of Business Ethics, 169*, 355–369. https://doi.org/10.1007/s10551-019-04282-w

Gollan, P. J. (2000). Human resources, capabilities and sustainability. In D. Dunphy, J. Benveniste, A. Griffiths, P. Sutton (Eds.), *Sustainability—The corporate challenge of the 21st century* (pp. 55–77). Allen and Unwin.

Gollan, P. J. (2005). High involvement management and human resource sustainability: The challenges and opportunities. *Asia Pacific Journal of Human Resources, 43*(1), 18–33. https://doi.org/10.1177/1038411105050305

Gollan, P. J. & Xu, Y. (2014). Fostering corporate sustainability: Integrative and dynamic approaches to sustainable HRM. In I. Ehnert, W. Harry, & K. J. Zink (Eds.), *Sustainability and human resource management: Developing sustainable business organizations* (pp. 225–245). Springer.

Gouldner, A. W. (1960). The norm of reciprocity: A preliminary statement. *American Sociological Review, 25*(2), 161–178. https://doi.org/10.2307/2092623

Griep, Y., Kraak, J. M., & Beekman, E. M. (2022). Sustainability is dead, long live sustainability! Paving the way to include the people in sustainability. *Group & Organization Management*. Advance online publication. https://doi.org/10.1177/10596011221127107

Griep, Y., & Vantilborgh, T. (2018a). Let's get cynical about this! Recursive relationships between psychological contract breach and counterproductive work behaviour. *Journal of Occupational and Organizational Psychology, 91*(2), 421–429. https://doi.org/10.1111/joop.12201

Griep, Y., & Vantilborgh, T. (2018b). Reciprocal effects of psychological contract breach on counterproductive and organizational citizenship behaviors: The role of time. *Journal of Vocational Behavior, 104,* 141–153. https://doi.org/10.1016/j.jvb.2017.10.013

Grimshaw, D., Johnson, M., Rubery, J., & Keizer, A. (2016). *"Reducing precarious work" Protective gaps and the role of social dialogue in Europe* [PowerPoint slides]. European Public Service Union. https://www.epsu.org/sites/default/files/article/files/Precarious%20work%20and%20social%20dialogue.pdf

Guest, D. E. (2004). The psychology of the employment relationship: An analysis based on the psychological contract. *Applied Psychology: An International Review, 53*(4), 541–555. https://doi.org/10.1111/j.1464-0597.2004.00187.x

Gunn, V., Håkansta, C., Vignola, E., Matilla-Santander, N., Kreshpaj, B., Wegman, D. H., Hogstedt, C., Ahonen, E. Q., Muntaner, C., Baron, S., Bodin, T., & The Precarious Work Research Group. (2021). Initiatives addressing precarious employment and its effects on workers' health and well-being: A protocol for a systematic review. *Systematic Reviews, 10,* Article 195.https://doi.org/10.1186/s13643-021-01728-z

Han, W. J., & Hart, J. (2021). Job precarity and economic prospects during the COVID-19 public health crisis. *Social Science Quarterly, 102*(5), 2394–2411. https://doi.org/10.1111/ssqu.13031

Hansen, S. D., & Griep, Y. (2016). Psychological contracts. In J. Meyer (Ed.), *Handbook of employee commitment* (pp. 119–135). Edward Elgar Publishers.

International Labour Organization (ILO). (2011). *From precarious work to decent work: Policies and regulations to combat precarious employment.* https://www.ilo.org/wcmsp5/groups/public/@ed_dialogue/@actrav/documents/meetingdocument/wcms_164286.pdf

International Labour Organization (ILO). (2015). The future of work centenary initiative (Report of the Director General, International Labour Conference ILC.104/DG/1). https://www.ilo.org/wcmsp5/groups/public/—ed_norm/—relconf/documents/meetingdocument/wcms_369026.pdf

International Labour Organization (ILO). (2019) *Expert group meeting on Sustainable Development Goal 8: Promote sustained, inclusive and sustainable economic growth, full and productive employment and decent work for all—Review of progress and prospects.* https://sustainabledevelopment.un.org/content/documents/25385Meeting_report_SDG8_final.pdf

International Labour Organization (ILO). (2021). *The role of digital labour platforms in transforming the world of work.* ILO.

Järlström, M., Saru, E., & Vanhala, S. (2018). Sustainable human resource management with salience of stakeholders: A top management perspective. *Journal of Business Ethics, 152*, 703–724. https://doi.org/10.1007/s10551-016-3310-8

Kabanoff, B., Jimmieson, N., & Lewis, M. (2000). Psychological contracts in Australia: A fair go" or a "not-so-happy transition"? In D. M. Rousseau & R. Schalk (Eds.), *Psychological contracts in employment: Cross-national perspectives* (pp. 29–46). Sage.

Kahancová, M., Meszmann, T. T., & Sedláková, M. (2020). Precarization via digitalization? Work arrangements in the on-demand platform economy in Hungary and Slovakia. *Frontiers in Sociology, 5*, 3. https://doi.org/10.3389/fsoc.2020.00003

Kalleberg, A. L. (2021). Precarious lives: Filling the gaps. *Contemporary Sociology: A Journal of Reviews, 50*(2), 114–118. https://doi.org/10.1177/0094306121991073d

Kramar, R. (2014). Beyond strategic human resource management: Is sustainable human resource management the next approach? *The International Journal of Human Resource Management, 25*(8), 1069–1089. https://doi.org/10.1080/09585192.2013.816863

Krausz, M. (2000). Effects of short- and long-term preference for temporary work upon psychological outcomes. *International Journal of Manpower, 21*(8), 635–647. https://doi.org/10.1108/01437720010379529

Kuhn, K. M., & Maleki, A. (2017). Micro-entrepreneurs, dependent contractors, and instaserfs: Understanding online labor platform workforces. *Academy of Management Perspectives, 31*(3), 183–200. https://doi.org/10.5465/amp.2015.0111

Kuhn, K. M., Meijerink, J., & Keegan, A. (2021). Human resource management and the gig economy: Challenges and opportunities at the intersection between organizational HR decision-makers and digital labor platforms. In M. R. Buckley, A. R. Wheeler, J. E. Baur, & J. R. B. Halbesleben (Eds.), *Research in personnel and human resources management* (Vol. 39, pp. 1–46). Emerald Publishing.

Lee, C., Tinsley, C. H., & Chen, G. Z. X. (2000). Psychological and normative contracts of work group members in the United States and Hong Kong. In D. M. Rousseau, & R. Schalk (Eds.), *Psychological contracts in employment: Cross-national perspectives* (pp. 87–103). Sage.

Lehdonvirta, V. (2018). Flexibility in the gig economy: managing time on three online piecework platforms. *New Technology, Work and Employment, 33*(1), 13–29. https://doi.org/10.1111/ntwe.12102

Lemsom, M. (2021, June 2). Werkgevers en vakbonden willen onzeker werk inperken en hopen op steun van nieuw kabinet *EenVandaag*. https://eenvandaag.avrotros.nl/item/werkgevers-en-vakbonden-willen-onzeker-werk-inperken-en-hopen-op-steun-van-nieuw-kabinet/

Lewchuk, W., & Clarke, M. (2011). *Working without commitments: The health effects of precarious employment*. McGill-Queen's University Press.

Liao, C., Wayne, S. J., & Rousseau, D. M. (2016). Idiosyncratic deals in contemporary organizations: A qualitative and meta-analytical review. *Journal of Organizational Behavior, 37*(S1), 9–29. https://doi.org/10.1002/job.1959

Linnenluecke, M. K., & Griffiths, A. (2010). Corporate sustainability and organizational culture. *Journal of World Business, 45*(4), 357–366. https://doi.org/10.1016/j.jwb.2009.08.006.

Macke, J., & Genari, D. (2019). Systematic literature review on sustainable human resource management. *Journal of Cleaner Production, 208*, 806–815. https://doi.org/10.1016/j.jclepro.2018.10.091

MacNeil, I. R. (1985). Relational contract: what we do and do not know. *Wisconsin Law Review, 3*, 483–525.

Maia, L. G., & Bastos, A. V. B. (2015). Organizational commitment, psychological contract fulfillment and job performance: A longitudinal quanti-qualitative study. *BAR-Brazilian Administration Review, 12*(3), 250–267. https://doi.org/10.1590/1807-7692bar2015140061

Malingre, V. (2021, December 9). La Commission européenne veut faire des livreurs de Deliveroo et des chauffeurs d'Uber des salariés. [English translation] *Le Monde.* https://www.lemonde.fr/economie/article/2021/12/09/la-commission-europeenne-veut-faire-des-livreurs-de-deliveroo-et-des-chauffeurs-d-uber-des-salaries_6105315_3234.html

Marchington, M. (2015). Human resource management (HRM): Too busy looking up to see where it is going longer term? *Human Resource Management Review, 25*(2), 176–187. https://doi.org/10.1016/j.hrmr.2015.01.007

Matilla-Santander, N., Ahonen, E., Albin, M., Baron, S., Bolíbar, M., Bosmans, K., Burström, B., Cuervo, I., Davis, L., Gunn, V., Håkansta, C., Hemmingsson, T., Hogstedt, C., Jonsson, J., Julià, M., Kjellberg, K., Kreshpaj, B., Lewchuk, W., Muntaner, C., … & Bodin, T. (2021). COVID-19 and precarious employment: Consequences of the evolving crisis. *International Journal of Health Services, 51*(2), 226–228. https://doi.org/10.1177/0020731420986694

Matilla-Santander, N., Martín-Sánchez, J. C., González-Marrón, A., Cartanyà-Hueso, A., Lidón-Moyano, C., & Martínez-Sánchez, J.M. (2021). Precarious employment, unemployment and their association with health-related outcomes in 35 European countries: A cross-sectional study. *Critical Public Health, 31*(4), 404–415. https://doi.org/10.1080/09581596.2019.1701183

McDonnell, A., Carbery, R., Burgess, J., & Sherman, U. (2021). Technologically mediated human resource management in the gig economy. *The International Journal of Human Resource Management, 32*(19), 3995–4015. https://doi.org/10.1080/09585192.2021.1986109

McInnis, K. J., Meyer, J. P., & Feldman, S. (2009). Psychological contracts and their implications for commitment: A feature-based approach. *Journal of Vocational Behavior, 74*, 165–180. https://doi.org/10.1016/j.jvb.2008.12.007

McLean Parks, J., Kidder, D. L., & Gallagher, D. G. (1998). Fitting square pegs into round holes: Mapping the domain of contingent work arrangements onto the psychological contract. *Journal of Organizational Behavior, 19*(S1), 697–730. https://doi.org/10.1002/(SICI)1099-1379(1998)19:1+<697::AID-JOB974>3.0.CO;2-I

Morishima, M. (2000). *Japan at a deadlock.* Springer.

Morrison, E. W., & Robinson, S. L. (1997). When employees feel betrayed: A model of how psychological contract violation develops. *Academy of Management Review, 22*(1), 226–256. https://doi.org/10.5465/amr.1997.9707180265

O'Leary-Kelly, A. M., Henderson, K. E., Anand, V., & Ashforth, B. E. (2014). Psychological contracts in a nontraditional industry: Exploring the implications for psychological contract development. *Group & Organization Management, 39*(3), 326–360. https://doi.org/10.1177/1059601114525851

Patulny, R., Mills, K. A., Olson, R. E., Bellocchi, A., & McKenzie, J. (2020). The emotional trade-off between meaningful and precarious work in new economies. *Journal of Sociology, 56*(3), 333–355. https://doi.org/10.1177/1440783320934156

Peel, S., & Inkson, K. (2000). Economic deregulation and psychological contracts. In D. M. Rousseau & R. Schalk (Eds.), *Psychological contracts in employment: Cross-national perspectives* (pp. 195–212). Sage.

Pfeffer, J. (2010). Building sustainable organizations: The human factor. *Academy of Management Perspectives, 24*(1), 34–45. https://doi.org/10.5465/amp.24.1.34

Puncheva-Michelottia, P., Hudson, S., & Jin, G. (2018). Employer branding and CSR communication in online recruitment advertising. *Business Horizons, 61*(4), 643–651. https://doi.org/10.1016/j.bushor.2018.04.003

Rousseau, D. M. (1989). Psychological and implied contracts in organizations. *Employee Responsibilities and Rights Journal, 2*(2), 121–139. https://doi.org/10.1007/BF01384942

Rousseau, D. M. (1995). *Psychological contracts in organizations: Understanding written and unwritten agreements.* Sage.

Rousseau, D. M. (2000). *Psychological contract inventory: Technical report version 2.* https://www.andrew.cmu.edu/user/rousseau/0_reports/PCI.pdf

Rousseau, D. M., Hansen, S. D., & Tomprou, M. (2018). A dynamic phase model of psychological contract processes. *Journal of Organizational Behavior, 39*(9), 1081–1098. https://doi.org/10.1002/job.2284

Rousseau, D. M., & McLean Parks, J. (1993). The contracts of individuals and organizations. In L. L. Cummings & B. M. Staw (Eds.), *Research in organizational behavior* (pp. 1–47). JAI Press.

Rousseau, D. M., & Tijoriwala, S. A. (1998). Assessing psychological contracts: Issues, alternatives and measures. *Journal of Organizational Behavior, 19*(S1), 679–695. https://doi.org/10.1002/(SICI)1099-1379(1998)19:1+<679::AID-JOB971>3.0.CO;2-N

Satariano, A., & Peltier, E. (2021, December 9). Europe pushes new rules turning gig workers into employees. *The New York Times.* https://www.nytimes.com/2021/12/09/technology/european-commission-gig-workers-uber.html

Sels, L., Janssens, M., & Van Den Brande, I. (2004). Assessing the nature of psychological contracts: A validation of six dimensions. *Journal of Organizational Behavior, 25*(4), 461–488. https://doi.org/10.1002/job.250

Shah, S., Rousseau, D., & Schalk, R. (2000). Caste, commitments, and change. In D. M. Rousseau & R. Schalk (Eds.), *Psychological contracts in employment: Cross-national perspectives* (pp. 104–124). Sage.

Sharkie, R. (2005). Precariousness under the new psychological contract: The effect on trust and the willingness to converse and share knowledge. *Knowledge Management Research & Practice, 3*(1), 37–44. https://doi.org/10.1057/palgrave.kmrp.8500051

Sherman, U. P., & Morley, M. J. (2020). What do we measure and how do we elicit it? The case for the use of repertory grid technique in multi-party psychological contract research. *European Journal of Work and Organizational Psychology, 29*(2), 230–242. https://doi.org/10.1080/1359432X.2019.1668844

Stahl, G. K., Brewster, C. J., Collings, D. G., & Hajro, A. (2020). Enhancing the role of human resource management in corporate sustainability and social responsibility: A multi-stakeholder, multidimensional approach to HRM. *Human Resource Management Review, 30*(3), 1–16. https://doi.org/10.1016/j.hrmr.2019.100708.

Stankevičiūtė Ž. & Savanevičienė A. (2018) Designing sustainable HRM: The core characteristics of an emerging field. *Sustainability, 10*(12), 4798. https://doi.org/10.3390/su10124798

Susomrith, P. (2020). Incorporating psychological contract into the sustainable HRM Model. In S. Vanka, M. B. Rao, S. Singh, & M. Rao Pulaparthi (Eds.), *Sustainable human resource management* (pp. 57–69). Springer Nature.

Turnley, W. H., Bolino, M. C., Lester, S. W., & Bloodgood, J. M. (2003). The impact of psychological contract fulfillment on the performance of in-role and organizational citizenship behaviors. *Journal of Management, 29*(2), 187–206. https://doi.org/10.1177/014920630302900204

Van Dam, K., Van Vuuren, T., & Kemps, S. (2017). Sustainable employment: the importance of intrinsically valuable work and an age-supportive climate. *The International Journal of Human Resource Management, 28*(17), 2449–2472. https://doi.org/10.1080/09585192.2015.1137607

Vosko, L. (2010). *Managing the margins: Gender, citizenship and the international regulation of precarious employment.* Oxford University Press.

Wilkinson, A. (2005). Downsizing, rightsizing or dumbsizing? Quality, human resources and the management of sustainability. *Total Quality Management and Business Excellence, 16*(8–9), 1079–1088. https://doi.org/10.1080/14783360500163326

Wilkinson, A., Hill, M., & Gollan, P. (2001). The sustainability debate. *International Journal of Operations & Production Management, 21*(12), 1492–1502. https://doi.org/10.1108/01443570110410865

Zhao, H. A. O., Wayne, S. J., Glibkowski, B. C., & Bravo, J. (2007). The impact of psychological contract breach on work-related outcomes: A meta-analysis. *Personnel Psychology, 60*(3), 647–680. https://doi.org/10.1111/j.1744-6570.2007.00087.x

14

DEFINING WORK-RELATED PRECARIOUSNESS AND HOW TO MEASURE IT TO SECURE HEALTH AND WELLBEING

Christian Seubert and Lisa Seubert (née Hopfgartner)

Introduction

In recent decades, labor market changes have given rise to insecure and unstructured forms of employment, increasing the risk for precarization of workers' lives (Kalleberg, 2011). Although awareness of the problems associated with such forms of employment has increased (Carr, Hodgetts et al., Chapter 1), it is by no means clear what is meant by "precarious employment" (Bodin et al., 2020). Various authors have proposed different sets of dimensions to define precarious employment, focusing either on objective characteristics of the employment relationship and/or subjective experiences associated with holding such employment. In this chapter, we discuss and integrate interdisciplinary approaches to conceptualize and measure precarious employment, contributing to establishing a comprehensive, multidimensional definition of the phenomenon.

After situating the concept of precarious employment in its historical and socioeconomic background, we present the results of a narrative review of prominent, predominantly sociological, conceptions of precarious employment, identifying common themes among them. Our findings converge with the results of a systematic review on definitions of precarious employment used in (mostly empirical) research studies (not necessarily referring to or encompassing all conceptions included in the narrative review), yielding three core objective dimensions of the precarious employment relationship (Kreshpaj et al., 2020). To represent a comprehensive perspective on subjective experiences of precarious employment, we relied on a five-dimensional framework rooted in sociological research (Brinkmann et al., 2006). Synthesizing objective and subjective factors, we extend a multidimensional framework of precarious employment (Bodin et al., 2020) that

DOI: 10.4324/9781003440444-17

distinguishes three dimensions of objective characteristics of the precarious employment relationship (insecure employment, inadequate income, lack of rights, and protection) by differentiating five dimensions of subjective experiences of precarious employment (reproductive—material, social—communicative, legal—institutional, status and recognition, and meaningful—subject-related). Considering conditions of precarious employment together with subjective experiences of precariousness, acting as early warning indicators of impaired wellbeing and health provides a framework for a more complete investigation and thus understanding of the phenomenon.

Second, we discuss how precarious employment can be measured comprehensively based on the multidimensional framework presented. After briefly summarizing existing measurement approaches, we extract recommendations for objective features of the employment relationship to focus on. Regarding subjective experiences of precarious employment, we summarize findings on the development and validation of a scale to measure subjective experiences of work-related precariousness.

Third, we offer a criticism of precarious employment as a concept by reflecting on problems that may occur due to a "Global North" perspective on this topic. By removing the standard employment relationship (SER) as a reference point, the pervasiveness of precarious employment across the globe, particularly in the Global South, can be fully grasped and given a stronger research focus. We suggest ways in which research on precarious employment could be given greater relevance by considering different contexts across countries with specific historical, economic, and political backgrounds, cultures, organizations, and individual characteristics.

We conclude the chapter by providing recommendations to further strengthen research on precarious employment, highlighting the potential of both qualitative and quantitative research. We hope that our contribution encourages more researchers in industrial and organizational (I/O) psychology and other fields to dedicate their research efforts to advancing this important topic in order to promote more decent work for all workers, whether holding formal or informal, standard or atypical employment relationships.

Contextualizing Research on Precariousness Employment

Following the second Industrial Revolution in Western capitalism at the beginning of the 20th century, the world of work has been subject to several waves of transformation. Before the 1970s, the "breadwinner model" had been socially established in Western European and North American society, with men earning the livelihood for the family and women being responsible for domestic work and children (Betti, 2018). This traditional division between gainful employment and domestic work resulted in the classic (male) standard or "normal" employment relationship, defined as permanent full-time work with full integration into social systems (Kalleberg, 2000; Mückenberger, 1985), as the dominant and desirable form of employment. Since the 1970s, however, the SER has been continuously eroded, accompanied by a simultaneous increase of nonstandard (atypical) employment (e.g., Kalleberg, 2011; Keller & Seifert, 2013; Mückenberger, 1989). Atypical employment differs from SER by at least one criterion and therefore covers a wide range of employment relationships, such as part-time work, marginal employment, temporary work, fixed-term employment, or (solo-) self-employment (Keller & Seifert, 2013). While atypical employment need not always be precarious and, conversely, even a stable employment relationship is not necessarily exempt from precarity (Benach et al., 2016; Julià, Vives, et al., 2017), atypical employment implies higher risk for precariousness (Keller & Seifert, 2013; Tompa et al., 2007). Therefore, the increase in atypical employment is associated with an increase in precarious employment because atypical employment conditions tend to offer less security, less integration, as well as more social deprivation (Benach & Muntaner, 2007; Gallie, 2013; Kalleberg & Hewison, 2013). The International Labour Organization (ILO, 2016) specified that nonstandard (or atypical) employment is about the contractual form of an employment relationship, whereas precariousness refers to the attributes of the job (e.g., low pay, insecure employment, low levels of control, and no social security coverage).

According to Kalleberg and Vallas (2018), there are at least four different but highly interrelated drivers for the growth of precarious employment: deunionization, financialization, globalization, and the digital revolution. Deunionization weakened organizational protections for employees, which gave rise to flexible or atypical work arrangements and deregulated wage determination (e.g., Western & Rosenfeld, 2011). Financialization refers to stock market investments, which diminish the value of stakeholders (first and foremost workers but also managers) in relation to shareholders' expectations, thus confronting employees with outsourcing and downsizing on a regular basis (Kalleberg & Vallas, 2018). Globalization is associated with political deregulation and processes of restructuring in order to react more quickly to market changes and global competition, which results in passing market risks down to employees and global competition among workers (Bronfenbrenner & Luce, 2004). The digital revolution boosted the drivers mentioned before by reducing capital requirements and by expediting the mobility of capital and the management of global commodity and value chains (Kalleberg & Vallas, 2018). The consequences of these drivers of precarious employment are not limited to work and the workplace; they also affect individual health, wellbeing, family formation, and social life in general (Kalleberg & Vallas, 2018).

From this perspective on precarious employment as emerging from within rich, affluent societies in the Global North, the phenomenon is preliminarily delineated as the loss of vital features of a job (such as job stability, adequate wages, and social protections) that enable upward social mobility (Han, 2018). Having set the stage for understanding the embeddedness of research on precarious employment in its historical and socioeconomic context, we will now review influential conceptions of the subject (Hopfgartner, 2019).

Precarious Employment: Definition and Concepts

The term *precarious* derives lexically from the French word *précaire* and means "dependent on chance; uncertain" (Oxford University Press, n.d.). Barbier (2011) traces the origin of the word back to the Latin *precor* (pray) or *precarius* (obtained by praying), signifying something that is uncertain or is only be obtained by praying. The origin of the word also goes back to Roman law, in which the *precarium* was:

> a gratuitous of grant of enjoyment of land or goods, revocable at will, even though a contrary agreement had been made…Common applications were permissions by a creditor… to hold the property…It was a liberality, not a mutual benefit, differing from gift only in the right to resume it at any time.
>
> *(Buckland & Stein, 1963, p. 524)*

In the context of work, the term precarious already appears in Marxian philosophy, albeit it is used nonspecifically (e.g., Marx, 1867/1962). The debate on precarity was significantly influenced by French sociologists Pierre Bourdieu and Robert Castel as well as former ILO economist Gerry Rodgers. Bourdieu (1998) describes precarity as a societal tendency toward generalized social insecurity that is driven by economic and employment systems. Hence, precarity not only has a disciplining effect on those directly affected but also unsettles those not (yet) precariously employed (Dörre et al., 2006). Precarity as suggested by Bourdieu (1998) refers to a broad understanding of the term intended to serve as a discursive weapon but too vague for scientific analysis (Brinkmann et al., 2006). Castel (1995/2003) describes precarity as a pervasive transformation of working society, driven by the recurrence of employment forms previously deemed to be overcome. He explains the transformation as a process of social disintegration, leading to a working society divided into (1) a *zone of integration*, (2) a *zone of precariousness*, and (3) a *zone of disaffiliation*. It is important to note that Castel (1995/2003) primarily dealt with the social question in the 21st century and with the effects of insecure employment relationships, but he did not present a differentiated conception of precarious employment. Congruent with Castel, Jahoda (1981) pointed out very early the importance of "latent benefits of work" and conducted empirical investigations of disintegration effects due to job loss at the societal and individual levels.

Another line of research on precarious employment was established by Rodgers (1989), who defined the phenomenon on the basis of four dimensions: (1) *degree of certainty of continuing work*, (2) *control over work* (e.g., wage, working conditions, and pace of work), (3) *legal and social protections* (e.g., against unfair working conditions, discrimination and unemployment, and health and pension insurance), and (4) *adequacy of income*. "The concept of precariousness involves instability, lack of protection, insecurity, and social or economic vulnerability" (Rodgers, 1989, p. 3). This conception stimulated research on precarious employment by a number of researchers (e.g., Amable et al., 2001; Cano Cano, 1998; Keller & Seifert, 2007; Tompa et al., 2007; Tucker, 2002). According to Betti (2018), Rodgers's conception is the most influential and persistent and, for the first time, introduced an Anglophone audience to the discourse. Whereas the main focus of Rodgers (1989) is objective or structural aspects of the employment relationship (e.g., duration of employment contract), Castel's (1995/2003) definition centers more on subjective aspects of social integration through work. More recent conceptions tend to combine objective and subjective aspects (e.g., Brinkmann et al., 2006; Tompa et al., 2007; Vives et al., 2010). Figure 14.1 highlights the conceptions and their relations that will be elaborated in this work. Other authors, such as Barbier (2011), Benach et al. (2014), Betti (2018), and Kreshpaj et al. (2020), discuss and summarize the scientific and societal discourse on precarious employment with different foci.

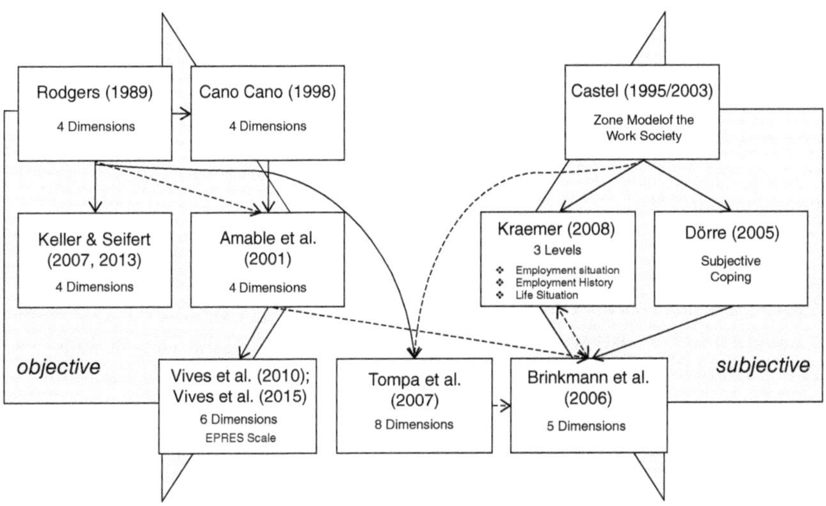

FIGURE 14.1 Conceptions of Precarious Employment.

Source: Hopfgartner (2019). Solid Lines Indicate Direct References to Earlier Work in Later Work, Whereas Dashed Lines Indicate Conceptual Congruencies; With Permission.

Work by Keller and Seifert (2007, 2013) related to the four dimensions described by Rodgers (1989) and defined an employment relationship as precarious if at least one of the following four criteria is missing: (1) *wage* above two-thirds of the median hourly wage, (2) *employment stability* defined as the opportunity for continuous employment (rather than holding a specific job), (3) *employability* (i.e., the ability of an individual to find and maintain employment in working life), and (4) *social security* (i.e., health, unemployment, and particularly pension insurance).

The conception of precarious employment by Amable et al. (2001) is also based on theoretical considerations of Rodgers (1989) and Cano Cano (1998), who translated Rodgers's conception into Spanish. On the basis of a literature analysis, expert interviews, and focus-groups, Amable et al. (2001) confirmed Rodgers's dimensions, with slightly varying labels and a different order: (1) *temporality*, (2) *vulnerability*, (3) *income level*, and (4) *social security*.

Tompa et al. (2007) developed an eight-dimensional conception of precarious employment, including and breaking down Rodgers's (1989) four dimensions: (1) *degree of certainty of continuing work* (i.e., employment and employability security), (2) *control over work processes* (e.g., tasks, time schedule, workflow, and access to adequate resources), (3) *legal and institutional protection* (e.g., against unfair dismissal and unhealthy working conditions, labor legislation, collective bargaining, and labor unions), and (4) *income and benefits adequacy* (e.g., sufficiency of labor-market earnings, financial benefits, and social security benefits). In addition, they added the following four new aspects: (5) *work-role status* (status, recognition, and social position within an organization and in society), (6) *sociocultural environment* (quality and quantity of available social support at work by colleagues), (7) *risk of exposure to physical hazards* (physical, biological, chemical, radioactive, and other hazards that can endanger health), and (8) *opportunities for vocational training and career promotion* (training opportunities both within organizations and for better opportunities on the labor market).

On the basis of Castel's (1995/2003) tripartite zone model of the work society (integration, precariousness, and disaffiliation) and an extensive qualitative study, Dörre (2005) developed a typology of subjective coping with precarious employment. He distinguishes between nine different types of employment-related (dis)integration (Dörre et al., 2006): within the zone of integration: (1) *secure integration* ("the safe ones"), (2) *atypical integration* (the "unconventionals" or "self-managers"), (3) *insecure integration* ("the destabilized"), (4) *endangered integration* ("those in fear of social falling") within the zone of precariousness, (5) *precarious employment as a chance/temporary integration* ("the hopeful ones"), (6) *precarious employment as an involuntary arrangement* ("the realistic ones"), (7) *bearable precariousness* ("the content ones") within the zone of disaffiliation, (8) *surmountable exclusion* ("those trying hard"), and (9) *controlled exclusion/pseudo-integration* (the "quasi-excluded"). In addition to this typology, Dörre (2005) provided a comprehensive definition of precarious employment:

> An employment relationship can be described as precarious if the employees' levels of income, protection and integration clearly fall below a standard defined and agreed upon by the current society. Job insecurity and wages below the subsistence level are…central indicators of precarity. Loss of meaning, social isolation, status insecurity, lack of recognition and planning deficits represent precarization tendencies that primarily reflect a perspective of [impeded] self-fulfillment in specific work activities.
>
> *(p. 252)*[1]

On the basis of this definition and extensive interview data, Brinkmann et al. (2006) investigated specific coping mechanisms within the zone of precariousness, identifying the following five dimensions of subjective experiences associated with precarious employment: (1) *reproductive-material*, (2) *social-communicative*, (3) *legal-institutional (participation)*, (4) *status and recognition*, and (5) *meaningful-subject–related*.[2] Finally, Kraemer (2008) adds a multilevel perspective to research on work-related precariousness. In addition to focusing on the current employment situation, he suggests additional temporal (individual employment history) and contextual (whole life situation) factors be taken into account in the analysis.

Synthesis: Toward a Comprehensive Framework of Precarious Employment

Table 14.1 compares the criteria occurring in the various conceptions discussed above. All conceptions share the criteria of *job security*, *wages above the subsistence level*, and *integration in social security systems*, which could therefore be described as core characteristics that are not fulfilled in precarious employment relationships. Although *job insecurity* is included in all conceptions, it is defined and measured in different ways, either through fixed-term employment (objective) or through perceived fear of losing one's job (subjective). Keller and Seifert (2007, 2013) consider job (in)security only indirectly in the form of employment stability as a proxy. The criteria *aspects of control and influence* mainly refer to working conditions already addressed by Rodgers (1989), albeit in an unspecific manner. Amable et al. (2001) and Vives et al. (2010), respectively, included working conditions regulated by employment contracts as objective criterion and the powerlessness to practice and exercise rights as subjective criterion in this respect. Tompa et al. (2007) included aspects of control and influence in the dimension control over work processes, whereas Brinkmann et al. (2006) captured worker participation with the legal-institutional (participation) dimension. The criterion *integration in activities offered by employer* encompasses

TABLE 14.1 Comparison of Concepts and Their Criteria for Precarious Employment

Criteria	*Rodgers (1989)*	*Cano Cano (1998)*	*Castel (1995/ 2003)*	*Keller & Seifert (2007, 2013)*	*Amable et al. (2001)*	*Dörre (2005)*	*Vives et al. (2010)*	*Tompa et al. (2007)*	*Brinkmann et al. (2006)*
Job security	✓	✓	✓	✓	✓	✓	✓	✓	✓
Wages above subsistence level	✓	✓	✓	✓	✓	✓	✓	✓	✓
Integration in social security systems	✓	✓	✓	✓	✓	✓	✓	✓	✓
Aspects of control and influence	✓	✓			✓		✓	✓	✓
Integration in activities offered by employer				✓				✓	✓
Social relationships			✓		✓	✓	✓	✓	✓
Status and recognition						✓		✓	✓
Meaning in and identification with work						✓			✓

Source: Hopfgartner (2019). We have summarized the criteria included in all the conceptions into positively worded generic terms, such that precarious employment is characterized by nonfulfillment of these criteria; with permission.

employability addressed by Keller and Seifert (2007, 2013), opportunities for on-the-job training and protection against hazards (Tompa et al., 2007), as well as participation opportunities (Brinkmann et al., 2006). Although the criterion *social relationships* is included in many conceptions, its definitions vary. Some conceptions focus on social deprivation (Castel, 1995/2003, social exclusion; Dörre, 2005, social isolation; Brinkmann et al. 2006, unequal integration into social networks at the workplace). Amable et al. (2001) and Vives et al. (2010) include defenselessness against workplace authoritarianism, while Tompa et al. (2007) focused on social support in the workplace. The criterion *status and recognition* is discussed by Tompa et al. (2007) as encompassing status, recognition, and social position within the organization and in society and by Dörre

(2005) and Brinkmann et al. (2006) as status and recognition in society. *Meaning in and identification with work* are extremely important for subjective coping with precarious employment, thus permanent loss of meaning in work reflects tendencies of precarization (Brinkmann et al., 2006; Dörre, 2005).

In summary, the predominantly sociological conceptions discussed here mainly differ in their incorporation of objective indicators of and/or subjective experiences associated with precarious employment. Across all the conceptions discussed here, we found Brinkmann et al.'s (2006) work to be the most comprehensive as it is the only one that encompasses all the criteria included in any of the other conceptions. Furthermore, while the conceptions propose unique sets of criteria as defining precarious employment, all of them share a set of three criteria: *job security*, *wages above subsistence level*, and *integration with social security systems*. This is in line with a systematic review of definitions and operationalizations of precarious employment in 63 mostly empirical studies by Kreshpaj et al. (2020), who found *employment insecurity*, *income adequacy*, and *lack of rights and protection* as overarching criteria of precarious employment.

Objective Indicators of Precarious Employment

In an effort to find a uniformly recognized definition of the term, the Network on the Coordination and Harmonisation of European Occupational Cohorts (OMEGA-NET) recently proposed a broad theoretical framework for precarious employment (Bodin et al., 2020) and defined objective indicators of precarious employment in terms of the three dimensions that were found by Kreshpaj et al. (2020) and in our narrative review (Figure 14.2).

According to Kreshpaj et al. (2020), *employment insecurity* thus comprises (1) contractual relationship insecurity, (2) contractual temporariness, (3) contractual underemployment, and (4) multiple employment relationships, possibly in different sectors. *Inadequate income* should distinguish between (1) labor income and (2) income from other sources and should also take into account (3) income volatility. *Lack of rights and protection* is defined by (1) lack of unionization, (2) lack of social security, (3) lack of regulatory support, and (4) lack of workplace rights. This meso-level definition of the precarious employment relationship is the core of the framework model, which includes additional upstream and downstream elements at other levels (Bodin et al., 2020). At the macro level, the precarious employment relationship is preceded by global economic, social, or political trends that influence the prevalence and design of different employment relationships. Current processes of globalization, technological development, and the declining prevalence of unionization are relevant here (Arnold & Bongiovi, 2013; Kalleberg & Vallas, 2018; Keune & Pedaci, 2019). The micro level encompasses the potential consequences for the individual of engaging in precarious employment. Precarious employment may trigger three

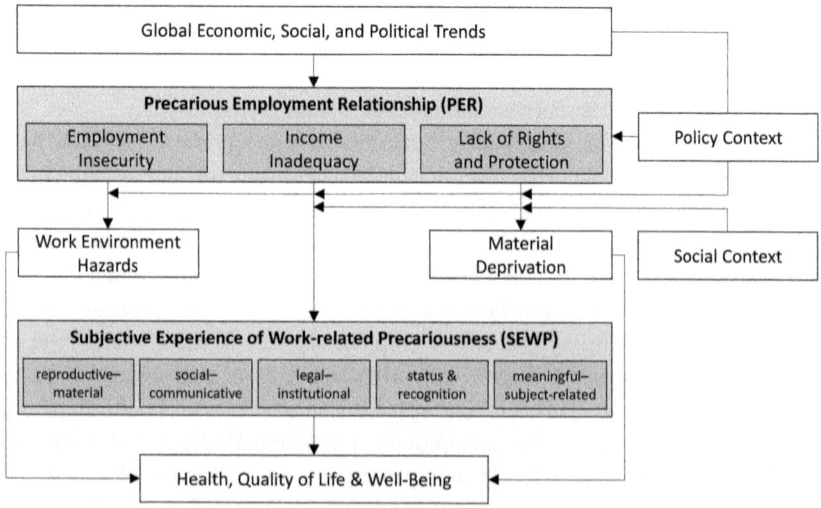

FIGURE 14.2 Theoretical Framework for Precarious Employment.

Sources: Bodin et al. (2020) and Brinkmann et al. (2006). Adapted from "Precarious Employment in Occupational Health—an OMEGA-NET Working Group Position Paper," by T. Bodin et al., *Scandinavian Journal of Work, Environment & Health, 46*(3), 321–329. https://doi.org/10.5271/sjweh.3860. CC BY 4.0.

possible pathways, which in turn are associated with impairments in wellbeing and health (Julià, Vanroelen, et al., 2017). These include (1) *work-related experiences of precarity* (cognitive-affective perceptions of insecurity and deprivation), (2) *work environment hazards* (harmful physical and psychosocial working conditions), and (3) *material deprivation* (a low standard of living due to low income). These mediating processes are in turn moderated by embeddedness in different political and social contexts, such as national occupational health and safety laws and social security systems; material, personal, or social resources available to an individual; and membership in disadvantaged or privileged groups (e.g., in terms of gender, ethnicity, age, disability, education, and sexual orientation). Regarding the effects of precarious employment on health and wellbeing, a systematic review based on 16 longitudinal studies found detrimental effects of job insecurity (moderate-quality evidence) and temporary employment (very low-quality evidence) on indicators of mental health (Rönnblad et al., 2019). No effects were found for unpredictable working hours as a possible additional aspect of precarious employment, with a very small evidence base. Studies that used multidimensional measures of precarious employment found larger effect sizes.

The three-dimensional core model follows recurring calls (e.g., Benach et al., 2016; Rönnblad et al., 2019) for a uniformly defined basis for objectively measuring precarious employment conditions in order to provide conceptual clarity and improve cross-study comparability (Bodin et al., 2020; Kreshpaj et al., 2020).

What about the Individual?

At this point, it's important to focus on the distinction between the objective criteria associated with precarious employment relationships and the subjective experiences of work-related precariousness. None of the three objective dimensions is sufficient in itself to account for subjective perceptions of precariousness by an individual; rather, the different factors accumulate to foster precarious employment conditions that are more likely to have negative consequences (Ervasti & Virtanen, 2019).

However, even the presence of a combination of objective features does not necessarily make a situation precarious for the individual in their subjective experience. For example, a person may hold a temporary part-time job with low pay but because they are the second wage earner in their household and their partner shares their wages equally, they do not perceive themselves to be in a precarious situation, even though they are dependent on their partner (i.e., it is "bearable precariousness" according to Dörre et al., 2006). This simple example hints at the difficult task of identifying all the relevant bits of information from an individual's current employment situation, employment history, and whole life situation (Kraemer, 2008) when focusing on objective conditions alone. Bringing in a psychological perspective, transactional stress theory proposes that coping with a situation results from both objective conditions and the subjective appraisal of these conditions which together determine whether a threat (i.e., precariousness) is perceived (Lazarus & Folkman, 1984). Furthermore, even if such an appraisal does not lead a person to perceive a threat (i.e., precariousness in the example above), a process of social comparison may be at work (Mai et al., 2019): spinning the example further, the person may compare themselves with colleagues who hold the same job but have a permanent full-time contract, receive higher pay, and are well-integrated in the social networks at the workplace (i.e., social comparisons by workers in the peripheral labor market with peers in the core labor market; Beard & Edwards, 1995), triggering feelings of relative deprivation and inequity. This shows that the subjective perception of the situation, rather than the objective situation per se, is the main factor that determines the effects on the individual (Mai et al., 2019): subjective experiences of work-related precariousness are the proximal medium that transmutes the effects of unfavorable conditions into medium- and long-term health impairments and reduced quality of life (Klug et al., Chapter 21).

Subjective Experiences of Work-Related Precariousness

In addition to the objective factors that constitute precarious employment, at the meso level of the contractual relationship, subjective experiences of work-related precariousness at the micro level of the individual codetermine the effects on the individual and should be of particular interest as well. While the subjective experience of precariousness is already included in the theoretical framework by Bodin et al. (2020) as one of three pathways, it was not given deeper consideration. Empirically, a number of qualitative studies examined different elements of this experience, such as insecurity, unfairness, powerlessness, stigmatization, discrimination, and stress (Bosmans et al., 2015; Bosmans, Hardonk, et al., 2016; Bosmans, Mousaid, et al., 2016), but without attempting to systematize it. Drawing on the findings of our narrative review of precarious employment conceptions, we assume clusters of subjective experiences that are specific to work-related precariousness. We have therefore expanded Bodin et al.'s (2020) framework to include the most comprehensive conception of subjective experiences of work-related precariousness (Brinkmann et al., 2006), grounded in 88 semistructured and 30 expert interviews. Next, we give an overview of the five dimensions of subjective experiences of work-related precariousness (more details can be found in Hopfgartner, 2019; Seubert et al., 2019, 2021).

The reproductive-material dimension primarily covers perceptions of inadequate wages and job insecurity. Accordingly, long-term life planning may be hampered due to unstable financial situations and job insecurity. Hence, a wage level that does not maintain one's livelihood (Meyer & Maleka, Chapter 7) and falls below a cultural minimum (Intrapsert et al., Chapter 9; Teng-Calleja et al., Chapter 8) carries a risk of precarization. Regarding subjective job insecurity, Rönnblad et al. (2019) found highly consistent adverse effects of job insecurity on mental health in their meta-analysis.

The *social-communicative dimension* covers integration into social networks at work and aspects of work-related communication. Accordingly, an employment relationship carries a risk of precarization if equal social integration at work is hindered and important work-related information is withheld. Supervisor and collegial social supports are well-established social resources (Kurtessis et al., 2017), and social inclusion is strongly connected to health (Lewchuk et al., 2008).

The *legal-institutional (participation) dimension* includes protection by labor law, integration into social security systems (e.g., health and pension insurance, company agreements), health and safety regulations at work, and opportunities for employee participation and codetermination as well as further training and career advancement. Accordingly, an employment relationship carries a risk of precarization if it does not grant full integration into labor law and social security provisions, thus excluding the individual from protection and possibilities for participation. Social security systems (characterized by the availability of unemployment insurance and access to vocational training) can buffer the negative relationship between job insecurity and both job satisfaction and commitment (Debus et al., 2012). Meta-analytic evidence suggests that lacking opportunities for organizational participation negatively impacts work behavior (Weber et al., 2020).

The *status and recognition dimension* covers recognition and appreciation received through work. Accordingly, an employment relationship carries a risk of precarization if one's work is less recognized and valued by personally relevant people and groups. Because employment allows social relationships to form with colleagues and clients, it is also a valuable source of status and recognition (Jahoda, 1981). Precarious work is generally seen as an undesirable and unfavorable form of employment and hence is associated with less recognition and appreciation by others. High-status jobs also correlate with higher wellbeing (e.g., Batinic et al., 2010), whereas lower social class (measured as a composite of employment grade, job title, and education) appears to be associated with poorer health (e.g., Borg & Kristensen, 2000; Carr, Hopner et al., Chapter 10).

The *meaningful-subject–related dimension* relates to the experience of meaningfulness and fulfillment at and through work and the degree to which employees identify with their work. Accordingly, an employment relationship carries a risk of precaritization if it is accompanied by consistent perceptions of loss of meaning and lack of identification with one's work. In their meta-analysis, Allan et al. (2019) confirmed the positive effects of meaning on work engagement, commitment, and job satisfaction, which in turn predicted self-rated performance, organizational citizenship behavior, and withdrawal intentions.

The five dimensions are representative of the other conceptions of precarious employment discussed above. Central to the reproductive-material dimension is the topic of (in-)sufficient wages, which was first mentioned by Rodgers (1989) and is included in all other conceptions mentioned here. The social-communicative dimension encompasses integration into social networks at the workplace. This dimension includes social aspects of vulnerability addressed by Amable et al. (2001) and Vives et al. (2010), as well as the sociocultural environment mentioned by Tompa et al. (2007). The legal-institutional (participation) dimension deals with institutional and social rights as well as participation opportunities and is comparable to Rodgers's (1989) legal and social protection dimension as well as including the risks of exposure to physical hazards and opportunities for vocational training and career advancement discussed by Tompa et al. (2007). The status and recognition dimension largely aligns with work-role status by Tompa et al. (2007).

Measuring Precarious Employment

As can be expected given the different conceptualizations of the subject, precarious employment has been measured quite heterogeneously in previous studies, with measures often being generated in an ad hoc manner and varying depending on the referenced theory, self-developed constructs, the available data, and the number of dimensions (Kreshpaj et al., 2020). A notable exception is the employment precariousness scale (EPRES; Vives et al., 2010, 2015), which is based on a conception of precarious employment by Amable et al. (2001), which itself can be traced back to Rodgers, (1989) and Cano Cano (1998, cp. Figure 1). The EPRES scale consists of six subscales: (1) *temporariness* (contract duration), (2) *disempowerment* (ability to negotiate employment conditions), (3) *vulnerability* (against authoritarian treatment), (4) *wages* (sufficiency; possibility of economic deprivation), (5) *rights* (entitlement to workplace rights and social security benefits), and (6) [ability to] *exercise rights* (power to exercise workplace rights). Developed as a tool for epidemiological studies, the EPRES was used in the 2010 and 2015 national Spanish Psychosocial Work Environment Survey (Vives et al., 2015) and was recently adapted to be used with information available from the 2015 European Working Conditions Survey (EWCS; Padrosa et al., 2021). A validated version in Swedish is also available (Jonsson et al., 2019). In the results from the EPRES adaptation for the 2015 EWCS data, difficulties with the ability to exercise rights and with wage levels showed the highest prevalence across Europe (Padrosa et al., 2021), with greater prevalence of overall precariousness and poorer health among women, particularly in Central and Eastern European welfare states (Padrosa et al., 2022). In Spain, comparisons between workers with permanent versus temporary employment contracts showed consistently higher ratings of precariousness for temporary workers in all dimensions, with temporariness, wages, and ability to exercise rights exhibiting the largest differences (Vives et al., 2015).

While objective criteria such as those measured in the EPRES constitute an important part of work-related precariousness, scholars have called for the development of complementary scales of precarious work from a subjective standpoint (Allan et al., 2021). As laid out above, neither objective conditions nor subjective experiences alone determine precariousness; rather, it's the interactions between the objective situation and the subjective perception of the situation that constitutes the precariousness of a particular employment situation (Mai et al., 2019). This brings the framework presented here back into focus and integrates the current evidence about objective factors and subjective experiences (Bodin et al., 2020; Brinkmann et al., 2006), which informs the following recommendations for measuring precarious employment. Regarding objective indicators of precarious employment, we refer to the converging evidence for three broad dimensions (Hopfgartner, 2019; Kreshpaj et al., 2020) and propose measures related to the themes and subthemes of each of the dimensions identified by Kreshpaj et al. (2020). Thus, *employment insecurity* could be measured by (1) contractual relationship insecurity (unstable employment, such as indirect employment via agency work or self-employment), (2) contractual temporariness (any type of fixed-term employment), (3) contractual underemployment (part-time, marginal employment), and (4) multiple employment relationships, possibly in different sectors (number of employment contracts and sectors). *Inadequate income* could be measured by (1) labor income, (2) income from other sources, and (3) income volatility. *Lack of rights and protection* could be measured by (1) lack of unionization (existence of and membership in a union or other forms of employee representation), (2) lack of social security (integration into organizational or statutory social security systems), (3) lack of regulatory support (effectiveness of labor law and occupational health and safety measures), and (4) lack of opportunities to exercise workers' rights (e.g., protection against dismissal, discrimination, and harassment).

Regarding the subjective side of work-related precariousness, we refer to the work by Brinkmann et al. (2006), grounded in conceptions developed by Castel (1995/2003) and Dörre et al. (2006). Based on this approach, Seubert et al. (2019, 2020) developed the SEWP (Subjective Experience of Work Precariousness) scale: a self-report instrument measuring the five dimensions of subjective experience of work-related precariousness. The SEWP scale is intended to capture universal perceptions of precarious employment contingent on the objective facts of the employment situation. This is achieved by the use of the cognitive anchor, "Due to my employment situation,…" at the beginning of each item, followed by experiences representative for each dimension, for example, "…I usually don't have any wages left by the end of the month" (*reproductive-material* dimension), "…I am not integrated well into the social circles at work" (*social-communicative* dimension), "…my voice is not represented in workplace matters" (*legal-institutional (participation)* dimension), "…I am less respected for my work by society" (*status and recognition* dimension), and "…I often see no meaning in my work" (*meaningful-subject–related* dimension).

To date, the five subscales have been validated in German (Seubert et al., 2020), confirming them as simple, reliable, and valid measurements. Regarding incremental validity in particular, the SEWP instrument has not only predicted additional variance over and above well-established proxies for each of the five dimensions but it was also the strongest (or second-strongest in one case) predictor for each of the outcomes of emotional exhaustion, depression, and disengagement with work.

An overall test of the framework presented here, including all three objective and five subjective dimensions, as well as psychosomatic and psychological complaints and ability to work as outcomes, was carried out by Czilczer et al. (2022). Similar to studies by Padrosa et al. (2021, 2022) who applied the EPRES to existing items in the EWCS, Czilczer et al. (2022) applied the framework to existing items from the national 2015 and 2017 Working Time Surveys of the German Federal Institute of Occupational Safety and Health. Structural equation modeling confirmed a strong mediating role of subjective experiences of work-related precariousness, substantiating their presumed role as vital pathways for translating negative effects of precarious employment to health outcomes. We therefore particularly recommend measuring subjective experiences of precarious employment as sensible early-warning indicators of impending health impairment as a result of precarious employment conditions. An English-language version is currently being validated. The instrument is available at request by the authors.

Importantly, both objective attributes of the precarious employment relationship as well as subjective experiences of work-related precariousness jointly determine the precarious employment phenomenon (Mai et al., 2019) and should therefore not be measured in isolation. Focusing on (combinations of) objective conditions alone cannot demonstrate their adversity, while a one-sided focus on subjective experiences runs the risk of individualizing a structural problem and thus abstracting from power relations (Shanahan & Smith, 2021). Precarious employment is, by definition, an issue grounded in unfavorable attributes of the contractual relationship with negative effects on the individual (Dörre, 2005; ILO, 2016). Therefore, both objective and subjective aspects should be considered collectively and related to one another to allow for a complete picture as possible of a complex, multidimensional phenomenon in which multiple conditions accumulate and exert negative effects on the individual to be justly labeled precarious (Kreshpaj et al., 2020; Seubert et al., 2019). However, the aspiration to draw an unbiased picture of precarious employment requires not only clarifying what to include in conceptions but also what may be implicitly excluded by such conceptions as a result of a particular Northern-centric perspective.

Precarious Employment Is Pervasive and Not Exclusive to the Global North

The debate on precarious employment developed in the context of Western capitalism, where SER was regarded as the norm and precarious employment was defined as a deviation from this gold standard (Breman & van der Linden, 2014). This perspective, however, mainly holds only for Western Europe and North America, and even within this sphere, SER was a historical exception associated with the affluence of Western society from the 1950s until the 1970s (Betti, 2018). In contrast, informal employment shares many features with precarious employment and has long been the norm and is still the standard for 60% of the global working population (ILO, 2018). Therefore, by defining precarious employment as "nonstandard" employment, Northern-centric conceptions tend to neglect informally employed workers around the globe, thereby reproducing geographical hierarchies of development (Han, 2018). Furthermore, contemporary research in I/O psychology in general has been characterized as being biased toward formally employed workers in secure jobs in affluent countries (Gloss et al., 2017; the majority of studies cited in this chapter also suffer from this shortcoming), thus underrepresenting the legitimate interests of precariously employed workers all over the world.

A more comprehensive approach to conceptualizing precarious employment requires abandoning the notion of "a paradise lost" (the SER) and instead recognizing the pervasiveness of precarious employment in the world and explicitly considering contextual (e.g., sociocultural, economic-political, historical, and personal) conditions when investigating precarious employment in a given place and time (Seubert et al., 2022). More recent approaches to the study of precarity have broadened their research foci to explicitly consider the Global South, post-colonial, and feminist perspectives (Arnold & Bongiovi, 2013; Betti, 2018). For example, Seubert et al. (2021) have proposed how the salience of different facets of decent work (defined as the absence of aspects of precarious employment) may be influenced by personal, organizational, and country-level contextual factors, thereby opening an avenue for future research on precarious employment in different organizational, economic, political, and cultural contexts: and incidentally, contextualization also.

Rigorous scrutiny of the relevance and applicability of conceptions of precarious employment in non-Western contexts could lead not only to better, more context-sensitive conceptions but also draw attention to the ubiquitous requirement to promote decent work across the globe, no matter how its absence is labeled. A broadened approach to the investigation of precarious employment also has the potential to spotlight the political and economic stakeholders that benefit from and thus promote precarious employment: especially in the Global South (Lee & Kofman, 2012). In doing so, scholars can contribute to addressing humanitarian concerns through their research (Gloss et al., 2017).

Recommendations for Expanding Research and Increasing Practical Impact

Given the substantive prevalence of precariously employed workers across the globe (ILO, 2018), high-quality quantitative and qualitative research that advances our understanding of unfavorable work and employment conditions that contribute to the precarization of workers' lives is clearly needed. Large-scale quantitative studies, such as the EWCS in Europe (Eurofound, 2017), could contribute reliable information about the prevalence of precarious employment and the burden for workers. Observational, possibly longitudinal studies could inform a growing evidence base on associations between objective features of precarious employment (or configurations thereof, as are typically found in specific jobs, such as gig-, click-, or crowdwork; Eurofound, 2018) and subjective perceptions of precariousness, as well as impaired wellbeing and health. Qualitative studies could explore the far-reaching consequences of workers' experiences with precarious jobs which force them to lead precarious lives (Hopfgartner et al., 2022). Building awareness of the extent of precarious employment and its negative consequences is key to making this a salient topic in the public and political discourse (Searle & McWha-Hermann, Chapter 4; Saner & Yiu, Chapter 5).

We also urge researchers to engage in more contextualized research; work-related precariousness is a multifaceted phenomenon, varying with people's historical, economic-political, sociocultural, and personal backgrounds (Seubert et al., 2022). Apart from establishing general associations, it's vital to identify how objective conditions interact with subjective perceptions in specific contexts. For instance, such contextualization could prompt cross-cultural studies comparing the salience of dimensions of precarious employment (Seubert et al., 2021) or gender studies of structural exploitation (Hopfgartner et al., 2022).

Such research could also help uncover who really benefits from and who pays for the problems caused by precarious employment (Meyer & Malake, Chapter 7). At the organizational level, precarious jobs may initially provide more flexibility for the employer—however, motivated, committed, and engaged workers are a competitive advantage in the long run. Therefore, employers, and HR managers, should be aware of the hidden costs resulting from the negative consequences of precarious employment (e.g., less commitment, performance, and productivity and more deviance and turnover) that may outweigh the purported benefits of direct monetary cost savings (Searle & McWha-Hermann, 2021). Furthermore, cost reductions at the expense of safe, health-promoting, and dignified jobs can be seen as externalities that are shifted from the organization to their workers who have to cope with illness, insecure lives, and poverty, as well as society which has to fund, for example, medical treatment, unemployment benefits, and social welfare. Unions are called upon to stand up against precarious employment in general even though precariously employed workers are often not unionized, because rising precarious employment will only further erode the collective influence that unions can exert due to a large member base. It follows naturally from this vicious circle that it should be in the best interest of policy makers to apply preventive measures (e.g., labor laws, regulations, and other obligations) to prevent externalities from occurring and promote decent work instead. The agendas of international organizations such as the ILO's Decent Work Agenda (Eurofound & ILO, 2019) and the United Nations' Sustainable Development Goals (SDGs; UN, 2015) may provide regulatory guidance.

Finally, we recommend that researchers interested in precarious employment explore related but hitherto separated fields and join forces with scholars working on similar issues. As an example, Seubert et al. (2021) have proposed the integration of research on precarious employment with research on living wages (Carr et al., 2016; Searle & McWha-Hermann, 2021) and decent work (Eurofound & ILO, 2019) on the grounds that they share similar values and aims—namely, to contribute to the fulfillment of a number of SDGs (UN, 2015), most prominently SDG-1 (No Poverty), SDG-8 (Decent Work and Economic Growth), and SDG-10 (reducing inequalities).

Notes

1 Translation by the authors.
2 While Brinkmann et al. (2006) refer to the fifth dimension as "work content-related," other publications use the more tangible label "meaningful-subject–related" (Dörre et al., 2004; Kraemer, 2008). We opted to use the latter term.

References

Allan, B. A., Autin, Kelsey, L., & Wilkins-Yel, K. G. (2021). Precarious work in the 21st century: A psychological perspective. *Journal of Vocational Behavior, 126,* Article 103491.

Allan, B. A., Batz-Barbarich, C., Sterling H. M., & Tay, L. (2019). Outcomes of meaningful work: A meta-analysis. *Journal of Management Studies, 53*(3), 500–528.

Amable, M., Benach, J., & González, S. (2001). La precariedad laboral y su repercusión sobre la salud: Conceptos y resultados preliminares de un estudio multimétodos [Precarious employment and its health-related impact: Concepts and preliminary results of a multi-methods study]. *Archivos de Prevención de Riesgos Laborales, 4*(4), 169–184.

Arnold, D., & Bongiovi, J. R. (2013). Precarious, informalizing, and flexible work: Transforming concepts and understandings. *American Behavioral Scientist, 57*(3), 289–308.

Barbier, J.-C. (2011). *"Employment Precariousness" in a European cross-national perspective. A sociological review of thirty years of research* (CES Working Paper). HAL Archive. https://halshs.archives-ouvertes.fr/halshs-00654370/document

Batinic, B., Selenko, E., Stiglbauer, B., & Paul, K. I. (2010) Are workers in high-status jobs healthier than others? Assessing Jahoda's latent benefits of employment in two working populations. *Work & Stress, 24*(1), 73–87.

Beard, K. M., & Edwards, J. R. (1995). Employees at risk: Contingent work and the psychological experience of contingent workers. In C. L. Cooper & D. M. Rousseau (Eds.), *Trends in organizational behavior* (Vol. 2, pp. 109–126). Wiley.

Benach, J., & Muntaner, C. (2007). Precarious employment and health: Developing a research agenda. *Journal of Epidemiology & Community Health, 61*(4), 276–277.

Benach, J., Vives, A., Amable, M., Vanroelen, C., Tarafa, G., & Muntaner, C. (2014). Precarious employment: Understanding an emerging social determinant of health. *Annual Review of Public Health, 35*(1), 229–253.

Benach, J., Vives, A., Tarafa, G., Delclos, C., & Muntaner, C. (2016). What should we know about precarious employment and health in 2025? Framing the agenda for the next decade of research. *International Journal of Epidemiology, 45*(1), 232–238.

Betti, E. (2018). Historicizing precarious work: Forty years of research in the social sciences and humanities. *International Review of Social History, 63*(2), 273–319.

Bodin, T., Çağlayan, Ç., Garde, A. H., Gnesi, M., Jonsson, J., Kiran, S., Kreshpaj, B., Leinonen, T., Mehlum, I. S., Nena, E., Orellana, C., Peckham, T., Seixas, N.,

Vanroelen, C., & Julià, M. (2020). Precarious employment in occupational health—An OMEGA-NET working group position paper. *Scandinavian Journal of Work, Environment & Health, 46*(3), 321–329.

Borg, V., & Kristensen, T. S. (2000). Social class and self-rated health: Can the gradient be explained by differences in life style or work environment? *Social Science and Medicine, 51*(7), 1019–1030.

Bosmans, K., De Cuyper, N., Hardonk, S., & Vanroelen, C. (2015). Temporary agency workers as outsiders: An application of the established-outsider theory on the social relations between temporary agency and permanent workers. *Society, Health & Vulnerability, 6*(1), Article 27848.

Bosmans, K., Hardonk, S., De Cuyper, N., & Vanroelen, C. (2016). Explaining the relation between precarious employment and mental well-being. A qualitative study among temporary agency workers. *Work, 53(*2), 249–264.

Bosmans, K., Mousaid, S., De Cuyper, N., Hardonk, S., Louckx, F. & Vanroelen, C. (2016). Dirty work, dirty worker? Stigmatisation and coping strategies among domestic workers. *Journal of Vocational Behavior, 92*, 54–67.

Bourdieu, P. (1998). *Acts of resistance: Against the new myths of our time*. Polity Press.

Breman, J., & van der Linden, M. (2014). Informalizing the economy: The return of the social question at a global level. *Development and Change, 45*(5), 920–940.

Brinkmann, U., Dörre, K., Röbenack, S., Kraemer K., & Speidel, F. (2006). *Prekäre Arbeit. Ursachen, Ausmaß, soziale Folgen und subjektive Verarbeitungsformen unsicherer Beschäftigungsverhältnisse* [Precarious work. Causes, extent, social consequences and subjective coping with insecure employment relationships]. Friedrich-Ebert-Stiftung.

Bronfenbrenner, K., & Luce, S. (2004). *The changing nature of corporate global restructuring: The impact of production shifts on jobs in the US, China, and around the globe.* US–China Economic and Security Review Commission.

Buckland, W. W., & Stein, P. (1963). *A textbook of Roman law from Augustus to Justinian* (3rd ed.). Cambridge University Press.

Cano Cano, E. (1998). *Precarización laboral, flexibilidad y desregulación* [Precarization of work, flexibility and deregulation]. Mimeo.

Carr, S. C., Parker, J., Arrowsmith, J., & Watters, P.A. (2016). The living wage: Theoretical integration and an applied research agenda. *International Labour Review, 155*(1), 1–24.

Castel, R. (1995/2003). *From manual workers to wage laborers: Transformation of the social question* (R. Boyd, Ed. & Trans.). Transaction Publishers (Original work published 1995).

Czilczer, C., Seubert, C., Hopfgartner, L., & Glaser, J. (2022, July 11–13). *What makes work precarious? Identifying indicators for precarious employment* [Paper presentation]. International Conference on Critical and Radical Humanist Work and Organizational Psychology, Innsbruck, Austria.

Debus, M. E., Probst, T. M., König, C. J., & Kleinmann, M. (2012). Catch me if I fall! Enacted uncertainty avoidance and the social safety net as country-level moderators in the job insecurity-job attitudes link. *Journal of Applied Psychology, 97*(3), 690–698.

Dörre, K. (2005). Prekarität – Eine arbeitspolitische Herausforderung [Precariousness – A labour policy challenge]. *WSI-Mitteilungen, 58*(5), 250–258.

Dörre, K., Kraemer, K., & Speidel, F. (2004). Marktsteuerung und Prekarisierung von Arbeit—Nährboden für rechtspopulistische Orientierungen? Hypothesen und empirische Befunde [Market regulation and precarization of labour—A breeding ground for right-wing populist orientations? Hypotheses and empirical findings]. In J. Bischoff, K. Dörre, & E. Gauthier (Eds.), *Moderner Rechtspopulismus. Ursachen, Wirkungen, Gegenstrategien* [Modern right-wing populism: Causes, effects, counter-strategies] (pp. 77–118). VSA-Verlag.

Dörre, K., Kraemer, K., & Speidel, F. (2006). The increasing precariousness of the employment society. *International Journal of Action Research, 2*(1), 98–128.

Ervasti, J., & Virtanen, M. (2019). Research strategies for precarious employment. *Scandinavian Journal of Work, Environment & Health, 45*(5), 425–427.

Eurofound. (2017). *Sixth European working conditions survey—Overview report (2017 update).* Publications Office of the European Union.

Eurofound. (2018). *Non-standard forms of employment: Recent trends and future prospects*. Publications Office of the European Union.

Eurofound, & International Labour Organization. (2019). *Working conditions in a global perspective.* International Labour Organization and Publications Office of the European Union.

Gallie, D. (2013). *Economic crisis, quality of work and social integration: The European experience.* Oxford University Press.

Gloss, A., Carr, S. C., Reichman, W., Abdul-Nasiru, I., & Oestereich, W. T. (2017). From handmaidens to POSH humanitarians: The case for making human capabilities the business of I-O psychology. *Industrial and Organizational Psychology, 10*(3), 329–369.

Han, C. (2018). Precarity, precariousness, and vulnerability. *Annual Review of Anthropology, 47*, 331–343.

Hopfgartner, L. (2019). *Ist Prävention für die Arbeit 4.0 noch zeitgemäß? Arbeitssschutz und die derzeitige Praxis betrieblicher Prävention in Österreich im Kontext von Arbeit 4.0* [Is prevention still up to date for the 'new work'? Occupational safety and health and the current practice of workplace prevention in Austria in the context of new work]. Pabst Science Publishers.

Hopfgartner, L., Seubert, C., Sprenger, F., & Glaser, J. (2022). Experiences of precariousness and exploitation of Romanian transnational live-in care workers in Austria. *Journal of Industrial Relations, 64*(2), 298–320. https://doi.org/10.1177/00221856211063923

International Labour Organization (ILO). (2016). *Non-standard employment around the world. Understanding challenges, shaping prospects.* International Labour Office.

International Labour Organization (ILO). (2018). *Women and men in the informal economy: A statistical picture* (3rd ed.). International Labour Office.

Jahoda, M. (1981). Work, employment, and unemployment. Values, theories, and approaches in social research. *American Psychologist, 36*(2), 184–191.

Jonsson, J., Vives, A., Benach, J., Kjellberg, K., Selander, J., Johansson, G., & Bodin, T. (2019). Measuring precarious employment in Sweden: Translation, adaptation and psychometric properties of the Employment Precariousness Scale (EPRES). *BMJ Open, 9,* Article e029577.

Julià, M., Vanroelen, C., Bosmans, K., Van Aerden, K., & Benach, J. (2017). Precarious employment and quality of employment in relation to health and well-being in Europe. *International Journal of Health Services, 47*(3), 389–409.

Julià, M., Vives, A., Tarafa, G., & Benach, J. (2017). Changing the way we understand precarious employment and health: Precarisation affects the entire salaried population. *Safety Science, 100(*A), 66–73.

Kalleberg, A. L. (2000). Nonstandard employment relations: Part-time, temporary and contract work. *Annual Review of Sociology, 26*, 341–365.

Kalleberg, A. L. (2011). *Good jobs, bad jobs. The rise of polarized and precarious employment systems in the United States, 1970s to 2000s*. Russell Sage Foundation.

Kalleberg, A. L., & Hewison, K. (2013). Precarious work and the challenge for Asia. *American Behavioral Scientist, 57*(3), 271–288.

Kalleberg, A. L., & Vallas, S. P. (2018). Probing precarious work: Theory, research and politics. In A. L. Kalleberg & S. P. Vallas (Eds.), *Precarious work: Causes, characteristics, and consequences* (pp. 307–334). Emerald.

Keller, B., & Seifert, H. (Eds.). (2007). *Atypische Beschäftigung. Flexibilisierung und soziale Risiken* [Atypical employment. Flexibilization and social risks]. Friedrich-Ebert-Stiftung.

Keller, B., & Seifert, H. (2013). Atypical employment in Germany. Forms, development, patterns. *Transfer: European Review of Labour and Research, 19(*4), 457–474.

Keune, M., & Pedaci, M. (2019). Trade union strategies against precarious work: Common trends and sectoral divergence in the EU. *European Journal of Industrial Relations, 26*(2), 139–155.

Kraemer, K. (2008). Prekarität—Was ist das? [Precarity—What is it?]. *Arbeit, 17*(1), 77–90.

Kreshpaj, B., Orellana, C., Burström, B., Davis, L., Hemmingsson, T., Johansson, G., Kjellberg, K., Jonsson, J., Wegman, D. H., & Bodin, T. (2020). What is precarious employment? A systematic review of definitions and operationalizations from quantitative and qualitative studies. *Scandinavian Journal of Work, Environment & Health, 46*(3), 235–247.

Kurtessis, J. N., Eisenberger, R., Ford, M. T., Buffardi, L. C., Stewart, K. A., & Adis, C. S. (2017). Perceived organizational support: A meta-analytic evaluation of organizational support theory. *Journal of Management, 43*(6), 1854–1884.

Lazarus, R. S., & Folkman, S. (1984). *Stress, appraisal, and coping.* Springer.

Lee, C. K., & Kofman, Y. (2012). The politics of precarity: Views beyond the United States. *Work and Occupations, 39*, 388–408.

Lewchuk, W., Clarke, M., & de Wolff, A. (2008). Working without commitments: Precarious employment and health. *Work, Employment & Society, 22*(3), 387–406.

Mai, Q. D., Jacobs, A. W., & Schieman, S. (2019). Precarious sleep? Nonstandard work, gender, and sleep disturbance in 31 European countries. *Social Science & Medicine, 237*, Article 112424.

Marx, K. (1867/1962). *Das Kapital. Kritik der politischen Ökonomie. Erster Band. Buch I: Der Produktionsprozeß des Kapitals* [Capital. A critique of political economy. Volume I. Book One: The process of production of capital]. Dietz (Original work published 1867).

Mückenberger, U. (1985). Die Krise des Normalarbeitsverhältnisses—Hat das Arbeitsrecht noch Zukunft? [The crisis of the standard employment relationship—Does labour law still have a future?]. *Zeitschrift für Sozialreform, 31*(7 & 8), 415–434; 457–475.

Mückenberger, U. (1989). Non-standard forms of employment in the Federal Republic of Germany: The role and effectiveness of the state. In G. Rodgers & J. Rodgers (Eds.),

Precarious jobs in market regulation: The growth of atypical employment in Western Europe (pp. 267–285). International Institute for Labour Studies.

Oxford University Press. (n.d.). Precarious. *Lexico.com UK dictionary*. Retrieved February 01, 2022, from https://www.lexico.com/definition/precarious

Padrosa, E., Bolíbar, M., Julià, M., & Benach, J. (2021). Comparing precarious employment across countries: Measurement invariance of the Employment Precariousness Scale for Europe (EPRES-E). *Social Indicators Research, 154,* 893–915.

Padrosa, E., Vanroelen, C., Muntaner, C., Benach, J., & Julià, M. (2022). Precarious employment and mental health across European welfare states: A gender perspective. *International Archives of Occupational and Environmental Health, 95,* 1463–1480. https://doi.org/10.1007/s00420-022-01839-7

Rodgers, G. (1989). Precarious work in Western Europe: The state of the debate. In G. Rodgers & J. Rodgers (Eds.), *Precarious jobs in market regulation: The growth of atypical employment in Western Europe* (pp. 1–16). International Institute for Labour Studies.

Rönnblad, T., Grönholm, E. Jonsson, J., Koranyi, I., Orellana, C., Kreshpaj, B., Chen, L., Stockfelt, L., & Bodin, T. (2019). Precarious employment and mental health: A systematic review and meta-analysis of longitudinal studies. *Scandinavian Journal of Work, Environment & Health, 45*(5), 429–443.

Searle, R. H., & McWha-Hermann, I. (2021). "Money's too tight (to mention)": A review and psychological synthesis of living wage research. *European Journal of Work and Organizational Psychology, 30*(3), 428–443.

Seubert, C., Hopfgartner, L., & Glaser, J. (2019). Beyond job insecurity: Concept, dimensions, and measurement of precarious employment. *Psychologie des Alltagshandelns, 12*(2), 33–45.

Seubert, C., Hopfgartner, L., & Glaser, J. (2020, June 16–22). *Beyond job insecurity: Measuring subjective experiences of precarious employment.* [Paper presentation]. 2020 Annual Conference of the Society for Industrial and Organizational Psychology (SIOP), Online. https://www.siop.org/Annual-Conference/Registration-and-Resources/Past-Conference-Programs/ProgramSearch-20

Seubert, C., Hopfgartner, L., & Glaser, J. (2021). Living wages, decent work, and need satisfaction: An integrated perspective. *European Journal of Work and Organizational Psychology, 30*(6), 808–823.

Seubert, L., McWha-Hermann, I., & Seubert, C. (2022). *Critical reflection and critical reflexivity as core processes for critical WOP: Precarious employment as an example* [Manuscript submitted for publication]. Department of Psychology, University of Innsbruck, Austria.

Shanahan, G., & Smith, M. (2021). Fair's fair: Psychological contracts and power in platform work. *The International Journal of Human Resource Management, 32*(19), 4078–4109.

Tompa, E., Scott-Marshall, H., Dolinschi, R., Trevithick, S., & Bhattacharyya, S. (2007). Precarious employment experiences and their health consequences: Towards a theoretical framework. *Work, 28*(3), 209–224.

Tucker, D. (2002). *'Precarious' non-standard employment—A review of literature.* (New Zealand Department of Labour Occasional Paper Series 2002/2). Labour Market Policy Group, Department of Labour.

United Nations (UN). (2015). *Transforming our world: The 2030 agenda for sustainable development.* United Nations.

Vives, A., Amable, M., Ferrer, M., Moncada, S., Llorens, C., Muntaner, C., Benavides, F. G., & Benach, J. (2010). The Employment Precariousness Scale (EPRES): Psychometric properties of a new tool for epidemiological studies among waged and salaried workers. *Occupational and Environment Medicine, 67*(8), 548–555.

Vives, A., Gonzàlez, F., Moncada, S., Llorens, C., & Benach, J. (2015). Measuring precarious employment in times of crisis: The revised Employment Precariousness Scale (EPRES) in Spain. *Gaceta Sanitaria, 29*(5), 379–382.

Weber, W. G., Unterrainer, C., & Höge, T. (2020). Psychological research on organisational democracy: A meta-analysis of individual, organisational, and societal outcomes. *Applied Psychology: An International Review, 69*(3), 1009–1071.

Western, B., & Rosenfeld, J. (2011). Unions, norms, and the rise in US wage inequality. *American Sociological Review, 76*(4), 513–537.

15

CONCEPTUALIZING UNDEREMPLOYMENT AS A TYPE OF PRECARIOUS WORK

Identifying Career-Stage Antecedents of Underemployment in Order to Address It

Deirdre O'Shea, José Maria Peiró, and Donald M. Truxillo

This chapter aims to develop a deeper understanding of underemployment as a form of precarious work. We first review definitions, forms, and degrees of underemployment, including various antecedents of underemployment. We consider the ways in which underemployment can manifest at different career stages, as well as its antecedents and outcomes across these stages. We advance understanding of how different forms of underemployment may differentially manifest and impact specific societal groups (e.g., younger generations, older workers, and women), who have often experienced significant levels of precarious employment, underemployment, insecurity, and dislocation. These intersections require a nuanced approach to addressing underemployment, sensitive not only to the different types of underemployment but also to people at different career stages and as members of subgroups by sex and immigration status, employment sector, location, country, and community. We finish with a discussion of various interventions that target these factors which contribute to underemployment and conclude with recommendations for future research and policy formation.

Underemployment is one way in which precarious employment can manifest, although underemployment itself may not always be precarious in nature. Underemployment (especially involuntary underemployment) as a form of precarious employment has become increasingly prevalent over the last few years and as such, deserves consideration in its various forms. For example, the Organization for Economic Co-operation and Development (OECD) *Employment Outlook 2021* states that "underemployment saw a swift increase since the start of the

DOI: 10.4324/9781003440444-18

pandemic doubling from 5.4% to 11% of the labor force in just a quarter." More recently, it has decreased in some countries with the pandemic recovery, although unemployment has grown (OECD, 2021, p. 32). The increase in underemployment is not just circumstantial due to the pandemic. A 2019 OECD report on the future of work pointed out that workers across OECD countries were finding underemployment to be on the rise; "many, and in particular low-wage, workers cannot find full-time employment; or they would like more hours than their employers are willing or able to provide" (OECD, 2019, cited in OECD, 2021, p. 239). For example, several broader work and societal trends such as zero-hours contracts, the gig economy, and the increasing lack of retirement security are contributing to precarious forms of underemployment. There is also a need to understand the factors that impact underemployment for specific groups (e.g., for people at different career stages) in order to address the specific needs of people of different ages and career stages and in different cultures, economies, and contexts. As a case in point, COVID-19 underlined that certain subgroups (e.g., women, racial and ethnic minorities, and migrants) are employed in "essential jobs" that tend to have characteristics of precarious underemployment (e.g., underpaid, with precarious hours of work) with few opportunities for remote work (Kuhn, Chapter 12).

This chapter highlights how issues such as current social justice crises are linked to underemployment as a specific form of precarious work. To redress precarious underemployment, a multilevel, multidimensional, and multistakeholder approach is required, which takes into account the unique needs of different societal groups and encompasses national policies and laws, societal changes, and labor unions. We consider a range of approaches that have been (or should be) adopted within each of these categories and conclude with recommendations for future research and policy.

Definition: Underemployment as a Form of Precarious Work

To better understand *underemployment*, it is useful to contrast it with the concept of *full-time, regular employment*, which has been defined by Kalleberg et al. (2000) as "jobs where work is performed on a fixed schedule, at the firm's place of business under the firm's control and with mutual expectation of continued employment" (p. 257). Over the last two decades, changes in technology, work organization, labor markets, and organizational forms have promoted several forms of underemployment that Ashford et al. (2007) have called *nonstandard work*. A decade later, Spreitzer, Cameron, and Garrett (2017) revisited the issue, describing these fast-growing phenomena as *alternative work arrangements*. Under some circumstances, these work forms and employment types are precarious.

We acknowledge that the definition of precarious work remains vague and multifaceted (International Labour Organization [ILO], 2012). However, efforts have been made to characterize it by the experience of one or more of the following features: (a) insecurity regarding the continuity of the contract, especially when the end of the contract involves loss of income and difficulty finding another job; (b) insufficient pay for maintain a minimum standard of living (with sufficient pay being termed a living wage); (c) degradation and vulnerability related to the working conditions; and (d) nonexistent or limited social protections for workers (Cano Cano, 2000, p. 62). Insecurity can manifest as insufficient pay, lack of stable employment, short-term contracts, lack of integration into social security systems, lack of workplace rights, and statutory entitlements (Barnard, 2014; Keller & Seifert, 2006; Vosko, 2010), being at high risk of poverty (Olsthoorn, 2014), or uncertain, unpredictable, and unsafe employment (Kalleberg, 2009). A key commonality between all these experiences is a lack of control or power over one's work (Spreitzer et al., 2017), which is also what distinguishes underemployment that is precarious in nature, in comparison to underemployment that is not precarious, and which is the choice of the individual. Given the need to make these distinctions clearer, we refer to the definition by Cano Cano (2000) which identifies the features that make a flexible, nonstandard type of job a precarious one, distinguishing it from other flexible nonstandard work that may not be considered precarious.

The lack of control is also a reason why precarious work is not just an individual experience. The so-called precariat is a social category or collective identity described by Standing (2018, p. 5) as a "class-in-the-making," characterized by different levels of *relative deprivation* and *consciousness.* The precariat "can be characterized by three dimensions: distinctive relations of production (patterns of labor and work), distinctive relations of distribution (sources of social income), and distinctive relations to the state (loss of citizenship rights)" (Standing, 2018; see also Standing, 2017).

Thus, this chapter focuses on a set of phenomena characterized as underemployment, which often is tainted with precarious features. Coined more than a century ago (Evans, 1915), underemployment refers to work that is lesser or inferior compared to some standard (Feldman, 1996). Underemployment is a multidimensional construct (McKee-Ryan & Harvey, 2011) and describes a type of work that does not fully benefit from the human capital of the people performing it, quantitatively or qualitatively. It also suggests that people's real or potential contributions are insufficiently recognized or repaid.

Feldman (1996) described five forms of underemployment, through overeducation, overqualification, working outside one's field of expertise (skills misfit), time-related shortage (e.g., part-time, temporary), and undercompensation for one's work. However, additional issues need to be considered to properly appraise these five types of underemployment. First, each component needs to be further specified and operationalized (e.g., time-related shortage may refer to part-time, temporary, intermittent, or even zero-hours employment). Second, underemployment is relative to what is considered "normal" employment. Third, whether a person chooses part-time employment is relevant for a person to be considered underemployed. An underemployed person is a part-time employee who works involuntarily in such a type of job. However, not every underemployed worker can be considered to be working in a precarious job. As we stated earlier in the chapter, following Cano Cano (2000), a number of conditions need to exist for a job to be considered precarious, and we have also pointed out that the lack of control or power over one's work is a key feature of precariousness. Fourth, underemployment must be perceived negatively by the person and include insecurity. Fifth, these phenomena are dynamic, occur over time, and may change in nature or meaning to the person (see the implications of a person-centric approach of unemployment in Peiró et al., 2015). Sixth, several underemployment features cluster together, representing different employment patterns that are more or less precarious, that may be legal or illegal. Seventh, it is important to consider both objective and subjective approaches to underemployment in operationalizing and measuring it (Feldman, 1996; Seubert & Seubert, Chapter 14).

Labor market research (e.g., annual labor market outlooks; see OECD, 2021) suggests that we need to describe underemployment carefully to be able to accurately compare it across countries. The OECD glossary of statistical terms[1] states that underemployment occurs when a person's employment is inadequate in relation to specified norms, taking into account his or her occupational skill. It also notes that underemployment may be *visible* (when an employee is involuntarily working less than they want and would work more if they could) or *invisible* (when employee skills are not adequately utilized).

A complementary approach is to consider subjective perceptions of underemployment (García-Castro, et al., 2018; McKee-Ryan and Harvey, 2011); Allan et al. (2017) have pointed out that researchers often focus on overqualification (Erdogan & Bauer, 2021) or overeducation, which encompasses a person having more education, experience, and skills than is required for a job (e.g., Erdogan et al., 2011a, 2011b; Maynard et al., 2006). These authors have developed subjective, continuous measures for six additional underemployment dimensions: *pay* (underpaid compared with a previous job or others performing similar job), *status* (lower status than in a previous job), *hours* (working fewer hours per week than desired), *temporary work* (being involuntarily employed in time-limited, temporary, contingent, precarious, or intermittent work), field (people working outside of their area of education, training, or expertise), and *poverty wage employment* (people in the labor force who still live in poverty).

Underemployment can have negative effects on wellbeing and health. Underemployed workers report lower levels of health and wellbeing than adequately employed workers, but the specific effects vary by the type of underemployment (Friedland & Price, 2003). Friedland and Price (2003) found that employees who were underemployed reported more chronic disease, lower functional health, and lower positive self-concept, while those who are income-underemployed reported lower functional health, higher depressive symptoms, and lower positive self-concept compared to adequately employed workers. Research has also found that the negative effects of underemployment on mental health and wellbeing are similar in nature to the effects of losing one's job or being unemployed. For example, Dooley et al. (2000) found that underemployment was associated with similar (higher) levels of depression as unemployment, when compared to those in adequate employment (Dooley et al., 2000). More recently, using nationally representative British surveys, Mousteri et al. (2020) found that underemployment predicted distress in a matched sample of workers and that the underemployment effect was comparable to increases in distress after job loss. In a US-based study during the COVID-19 pandemic, Lee et al. (2021) demonstrated that being unemployed or underemployed was associated with higher depression and anxiety, and some evidence that these effects were exacerbated in segments of society who disproportionately experience employment insecurity (e.g., Hispanic and black Americans, women, young adults, those without a college degree).

Antecedents of Underemployment

Contextual Antecedents

Atypical forms of employment, including underemployment, have been growing in recent decades as a result of technological innovations, globalization, recessions, and demographic changes (Benach et al., 2014; Kalleberg, 2009). Thus, the occurrence of underemployment is unevenly distributed across the world, populations, and territories. In fact, there is significant evidence showing that a number of contextual factors clearly influence these rates, especially when the analysis considers these phenomena in an integrated way with other labor market situations, such as activity, unemployment, different types of precarious jobs, and informal employment. Aiming to contextualize the underemployment phenomenon, we briefly outline some of the main contextual antecedents of underemployment. More specifically, we will focus on national economies and labor markets, crises, and shocks (e.g., recessions and pandemics), sector and industry differences, and the urban/rural divide (see Figure 15.1).

Global and national economies influence the types, rates, and nature of employment available in a particular country and/or region and also drive

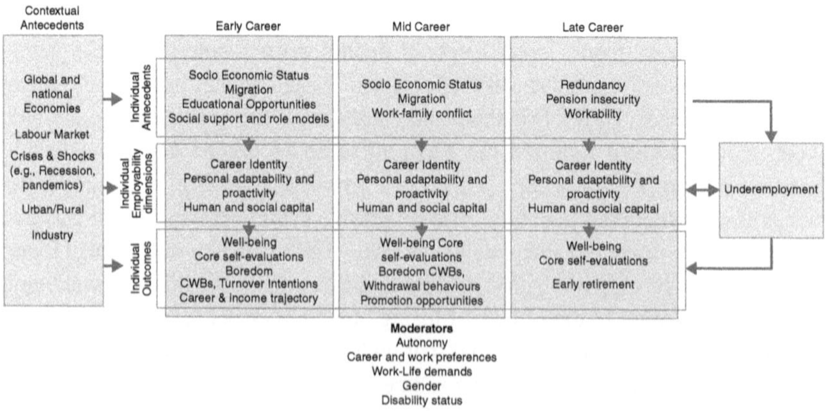

FIGURE 15.1 A Dynamic, Career-Stage Perspective on the Spectrum of Degrees of Employment.

immigration. Geography can play a part in the type of industries in a particular region or country, in turn influencing labor market demands for different types of skills. For example, the demand for low-cost goods has led to so-called factory towns in regions of the world with cheaper labor costs. These factories received attention when reports of worker suicides because of the poor working conditions began to hit the media over the last two decades (Hille, 2010; Johnson, 2011; Pomfret & Siu, 2010). Workers in such regions may have little choice in their employment type, and regardless of their education and skills, may end up working in jobs that do not fit their skills, and being unable to reach their potential. These factory towns illustrate the lack of opportunities for workers in such industries and regions to develop valuable skills and experience which would provide them with employment choices and opportunities.

It is unsurprising that we also see differences in underemployment across countries, and that underemployment has grown at different rates in different countries during the last decade. The Great Recession (2007–2009) played a role in this increase, in the case of countries such as Ireland, Italy, Greece, and Spain (Jagannathan et al., 2013; Russell & McGinnity, 2014). However, in some countries its growth has been due to structural reasons such as the prevalence of low-skilled occupations in the labor market because of the production system structure. Thus, national economies, particularly during times of recession, can limit the opportunities for full-time employment and for employment that matches one's skill levels. For example, underemployment rose sharply in many countries after the economic crisis of 2007–2009 and has been slow to return to precrisis levels. In 2014, the OECD published a report aimed at preventing unemployment and underemployment from becoming a structural issue, suggesting several structural reforms to improve the situation. Analysis of underemployment changes in OECD countries suggested a trend that has grown in recent times:

> The main structural change contributing to the positive trend adjusted for the economic cycle is the slow but steady growth of the service sector…For example, in 2017 'Accommodation and food services' had a share of underemployed workers of around 12.2%, against only 1.8% in manufacturing.
>
> *(OECD, 2019, p. 101)*

Issues of underemployment came to the fore once again during the COVID pandemic, which began at the start of 2020. In the *OECD Employment Outlook* (2021), during the COVID-19 pandemic it was noted:

> Underemployment saw a swift increase since the start of the pandemic, doubling from 5.4% to 11% of the labor force in just one-quarter…In the third and fourth quarters of 2020, labor underutilization fell back sharply—by 4 percentage points—with falling underemployment driving the bulk of the decline. It is worth noting, however, that in many countries where underemployment contracted the most, unemployment increased.
>
> *(OECD, 2021, p. 32)*

Differences in urbanization across regions can also play a part in underemployment. Disparities between the rates of underemployment are clear between rural and urban areas in many countries. The sectoral composition and characteristics of business firms differ as more knowledge-intensive companies are located in urban areas, while in rural areas routine-intensive work and mature industries prevail. Regional differences within countries may produce dissatisfaction and discontent in important segments of the population, especially those living in rural areas because megatrends such as globalization, technological innovation, and demographic changes may produce stronger disadvantages in these areas compared to urbanized regions (OECD, 2018).

The Proliferation of the Gig Economy and Underemployment

The gig economy is an example of a macroeconomic trend that is having a substantial influence in driving underemployment (Kuhn, Chapter 12). Automation and digitalization are introducing big changes in the labor market, employment, and jobs (Carr, Hodgetts et al., Chapter 1). These technological changes promote underemployment as they increase bifurcation in the labor market. For instance, this bifurcation reduces the number of jobs requiring middle-level skills and creates a fall in wages for workers without third-level education (Autor, 2019). Although shrinking the number of middle-skilled jobs may cause some lucky employees to move up toward more complex jobs, more often they move to low-skilled jobs and underemployment in terms of skills and wages.

Not all platform work is precarious, and some offers advantages for workers, such as autonomy and flexibility. However, in many of its forms, it produces underemployment and precarious work. Gallup (2018) describes,

> …a tale of two gig economies. Independent gig workers (freelancers and online platform workers) often enjoy the advantages of non-traditional arrangements while contingent gig workers (on-call, contract, and temp workers) are treated more like employees without the benefits, pay, and stability that come with traditional employment.
>
> *(p. 2)*

Watson et al. (2021) have conceptualized different forms of gig work, identifying *primary characteristics* (common to all types of gig work) and *secondary characteristics* (specific to some types) of gig work. Primary characteristics include project-based compensation, temporariness, and some flexibility in when/how/where the work is performed. Secondary characteristics, i.e., that do not apply to all/gig work, include technology-enabled networks, crowd work, remote work, and agency-based work. The authors distinguish five profiles of gig workers based on these primary and secondary characteristics: gig service providers, gig goods providers, gig data providers, agency gig work, and traditional gig work. The authors suggest that service and data providers are likely to be the most overqualified in terms of education and job field, and that goods providers, agency gig workers, and traditional gig workers are likely to experience hours underemployment (Watson et al., 2021).

Although the gig economy and digital platforms may offer good job opportunities and be a better fit for some workers, they can be associated with numerous underemployment characteristics for others. They can also have negative implications for workers' wellbeing for other reasons (Todoli Signes et al., 2020). First is the technological connection to the platform, which typically requires the worker to show availability in order to get assigned "hits" or "projects," and the fact that these assignments are regulated by an algorithm. Second, the increased process and performance monitoring by customers and employers through the digital platform reduces worker control. Third is the social isolation of workers in some gig jobs (e.g., limited contact with other workers, supervisors, and customers) and that those relations are mediated by the platform. Fourth, gig work often implies high levels of uncertainty and insecurity, and given the competition, it is usually associated with low wages. In addition, workers are often not considered employees but freelancers, and thus social benefits and employee protections are very limited or nonexistent. This type of gig work is often considered a complementary source of income instead of a full-time, primary job, but in fact it is the main or the only source of income for many gig workers, and the amount of compensation is often uncertain for the worker. Fifth, platform work is designed and implemented through algorithms that regulate many of the important processes that influence work characteristics, which in turn influence compensation and working conditions. Human resource management practices are mostly regulated by the algorithms, with huge amounts of data obtained about the workers and their performance, and workers cannot discuss the different situations they encounter with any human supervisor. In short, these algorithms lead to increased monitoring, loss of control, work intensification, decreased autonomy, biases and discrimination produced by the algorithms, lack of transparency in decisions, misfunctioning and sabotage, and lack of human interaction.

In addition, digitalization has an impact on work arrangements and employer-employee relations by blurring concepts such as "employee" and the "employment contract." Among the nonstandard forms of work, gig work is gaining momentum as a type of short-term contract work, often mediated by a virtual platform between the gig worker and an employer or a consumer (Keith et al., 2020). The contractual relations may vary widely and include app work, crowd work, and capital platform work: all based upon technological features (Duggan et al., 2020). Thus, gig work is often precarious. In many ways, it can lead to underemployment because the work arrangements bypass many of the regular responsibilities of an employer with legal ambiguities about whether workers should be considered employees.

Moderators

Career Stages and Age Groups

The causes and effects of underemployment likely vary at different stages of an individual's career, with some factors having a more significant impact at early- versus mid- and late-career. We map these differential causes and outcomes in Figure 15.1 and discuss potential boundary conditions in the remainder of this chapter. Today's world of work is characterized by career interruptions, opt-outs, and temporary work assignments, so that contemporary career models are more fluid and flexible than in the past (Mainiero & Gibson, 2018). This makes it challenging to definitively identify underemployment in contrast to personal employment choices of individuals at different points in their career. Thus, our model is likely a simplification but serves to identify some key differences across one's working life (Di Fabio et al., Chapter 3).

Broad global changes have wide-ranging and sometimes long-lasting effects on the employment market and thus are likely to impact rates of underemployment. Macro contextual antecedents, such as those we described in the preceding two sections—the economy, the labor market, global crises, and shocks (e.g., recessions and pandemics), geography (whether one lives in an urban or rural location), and the industry one works in—differentially impact the likelihood of underemployment for any age group or career stage. However, these antecedents may have greater effects at some career stages than others. While it is difficult to precisely define a career stage, we broadly consider early career to be the first 10–15 years of ones working life, midcareer to be 15–25 plus years after beginning work, and late career to be within 5–10 years of projected retirement date (e.g., Mainiero & Gibson, 2018). We acknowledge that, as some argue, life stages may be more appropriate than career stages, and that with modern careers, it is more commonplace to change careers at some stage during one's life (e.g., someone in midlife may change careers and could be in the early stage of a new one; e.g., Mainiero & Gibson, 2018). Thus, we draw some generalizations to analyze underemployment at different life/career stages but do not claim that these distinctions are hard and fast rules.

Events such as recessions, crises, and shocks can lead to underemployment for specific cohorts of the population more than others. For example, the recession of 2007–2009 led to high rates of unemployment particularly in the young adult population, and underemployment for those who were able to find work. These were associated with negative wellbeing and worker dissatisfaction (Heyes et al., 2017). More recently, public health measures adopted to curb the spread of COVID-19 resulted in many businesses having to close for varying periods of time. These businesses tended to be in the entertainment and food industries (e.g., theaters and restaurants) and in "nonessential" services (e.g., clothing stores). These closures resulted in large numbers of workers becoming unemployed or being put on reduced working hours for unspecified periods of time. Many of the jobs in these industries tend to be filled by young people (e.g., part-time jobs during university years). As a result, when this industry was curtailed as a result of the recession, younger age groups tended to be disproportionately affected in terms of their employment. This also had a negative impact on older people, who were more at risk of severe illness from COVID but have less access to paid sick leave than younger workers and are also more likely to be engaged in unpaid care, for example, of spouses (Ghilarducci & Farmand, 2020). Thus, for many older workers, and particularly those in frontline work, their work became more precarious, they were more likely to experience absences from work (as a result of their own health, or that of a vulnerable person in their care), and many had to leave the workplace, evidenced by the fact that employment rates for older workers dropped more substantially for those over 50 (and even more so for those 61–70) during the pandemic (Goda et al., 2021).

The labor market at the inception of one's career influences the types of job that are available, and the knock-on effects of underemployment particularly at early career stages may also impact the trajectory of one's career. Such workers may miss out on important work experiences and opportunities that enable them to climb the career ladder. For example, Burgess et al. (2003) found that for those with fewer skills, unemployment at school-leaving age had enduring adverse effects, but not for those with more skills. Similarly, research using cluster analysis of the 2012 Catalan Youth Survey (Verd et al., 2019) demonstrated that those aged 20–29 when the recession hit were more likely to have a trajectory of precarious employment. Furthermore, lower educational attainment made it more likely that a young person would have experienced a trajectory of more unstable employment.

Underemployment and unemployment in these early years also result in greater inequality and disadvantage in terms of income (Crystal, 2021). These effects are not only restricted to income and career trajectories; they also change a person's approach to managing and leading later in their career. Research by Schoar and Zuo (2017) demonstrated that managers who began their careers during a recession became CEOs more quickly, but typically at smaller firms. There were also likely to adopt a more conservative approach, such as lower investment in capital expenditures and more cost cutting. Thus, underemployment as a result of recessions can affect managerial careers via distortions.

Underemployment in midcareer—typically one of the most productive periods of one's working life—can impact the trajectory of one's employment, re-employment, and future promotion opportunities. It may come about because of downsizing and organizational restructuring and have somewhat different impacts than in either early- or late-career stages. For example, executives who lost their job as a result of downsizing tended to be re-employed in jobs that paid less, were at lower organizational levels, and did not fully utilize their skills (Feldman et al., 2002). The resulting experience of underemployment was associated with poorer wellbeing and associated with the experience of relative deprivation. Miller and Cepuran (2019) investigated the impact of the Great Recession (2007–2009) on those born in the 1960s and 1970s (who would have been roughly midcareer). Using the Longitudinal Study of American Life, they showed that although most participants did not experience negative economic consequences, there were negative effects for a significant subset. Educational attainment was the strongest predictor of economic impact by the recession on individuals in this cohort (i.e., higher education was associated with fewer negative impacts). Impacts were unrelated to gender but were exacerbated by being African American (Miller & Cepuran, 2019).

However, gendered differences in rates and experiences of underemployment may be particularly prevalent to consider in midcareer. Midcareer females are more likely to experience work interruptions (e.g., to have a family) which can not only slow their career progression but also have longer lasting effects, even influencing their pensions at retirement age (Betti et al., 2015; Bonnet et al., 2006; Vara, 2013). Women's careers tend to be more discontinuous and include multiple employers compared to men's careers, which have traditionally followed linear patterns (Mainiero & Gibson, 2018). Indeed, changes in employment status may be partially explained by changing priorities for men and women during midcareer. Drawing on the Kaleidoscope career model, Mainiero and Gibson (2018) demonstrated that balance, defined as individuals' desire to have quality experiences in both work and family domains, takes on more importance for women midcareer compared to men. Strategies to rebalance work and family priorities include taking part-time employment, opting out of the workforce temporarily, arranging work in accordance with one's family situation, or trying to meet the demands of both work and family demands simultaneously (Mainiero & Sullivan, 2006).

Emerging research suggests that congruent temporal focus (the extent to which individuals orient their attention to the past, present, or future; Shipp et al., 2009) between a mother returning from maternity leave and her manager may have an impact on her future career. Freeney et al. (2021) demonstrated that a congruent and broader temporal focus is associated with more positive relational and career outcomes, compared to an incongruent focus where one dyadic partner holds a narrow temporal focus (e.g., a present focus on the maternity leave only). A congruent, broader temporal focus allows those returning from maternity leave and their line managers to reduce their reliance on typical motherhood biases and instead consider a lifespan perspective on potential future contributions over the course of her career (Freeney et al., 2021).

Indeed, relational and interpersonal processes appear to influence whether overqualification, a particular form of underemployment, has positive or negative effects on the individual. Deng et al. (2018) demonstrated in two studies that an individual's ability to influence interpersonally moderated the relationship between perceived overqualification and social acceptance, and this in turn influenced in-role job performance, interpersonal altruism, and team-member proactivity. Thus, interpersonal aspects of underemployment appear to be important as they can influence whether an employee feels valued and whether their manager values them. Those who are overqualified may serve as mentors to others and have many positive benefits for an organization, but only if there are positive social relations with coworkers (Deng et al., 2018).

Finally, career stability and mobility in older workers is a function of the motivation to change careers, the ability to change careers (Feldman, 2007), and attitudes toward older workers (Potočnik et al., 2009, 2010, 2013; Tordera et al., 2020), which may limit their ability to change careers due to limited opportunities (McCarthy et al., 2014). Underemployment in later career stages may be associated with experiencing redundancy or with older workers not receiving a pension once retirement age has been reached, which could result from either personal circumstances or policy-related issues. This is also influenced by historical context, social heterogeneity, and biological paces that influence the timing of retirement (Han & Moen, 1999). Research has shown that there is negative relationship between age and re-employment status and speed, particularly for those over the age of 50 (Wanberg et al., 2016). Even when older workers regain employment, they may be underemployed, only finding employment in roles that do not align with their skills or qualifications (representing overeducation, overqualification, and skills misfit as forms of underemployment) or in temporary and part-time employment (time-related shortage) and lower paying roles. Perceived overqualification affects the relationship between perceived age discrimination (e.g., from a supervisor), withdrawal behaviors, and somatic symptoms (Triana et al., 2017).

Those who have passed retirement age but must work for financial reasons are more likely to be employed in part-time and lower paying roles (e.g., Munnell et al., 2012; Whoriskey, 2017). Although the trajectory of one's career will not be impacted in the same way as for someone experiencing underemployment in the early-career stage, other negative outcomes are evident. For example, working in an occupation characterized by higher levels of mental demands (rather than lower demands) has been associated with higher levels of cognitive functioning before retirement and a slower rate of cognitive decline after retirement (Fisher et al., 2014).

Gender

As noted throughout this chapter, different groups have different experiences of underemployment. Some studies have shown that women face more precarious work than men, and this is an even greater issue for women with children (Albelda et al., 2020). This issue may be partly due to the work sectors in which women are employed. This is because underemployment is most common in jobs that women are likely to perform (Kamerāde & Richardson, 2017).

Employment Sector

Increasing numbers of alternative work arrangements in the industrialized workforce and their flexibility in terms of location, scheduling, and the type of employment relationship involved (e.g., direct employment; agency work; gig work) can all lead to sectoral differences (e.g., between ride-share drivers, temporary technology employees with a chance to gain a permanent position, and agricultural workers) in the degree of control and power people have over their work (Spreitzer et al., 2017); as noted throughout this chapter, these are key factors that can affect the experience of underemployment. For instance, some gig workers may enjoy the freedom of controlling when they work and for whom, whereas the experience would be quite different for someone who only works gigs because they may need to cope with insufficient gigs and a lack of benefits. As noted earlier, the issue of choice and autonomy appears to affect the experience of underemployment.

Immigrant Status

Immigrant workers are particularly vulnerable in terms of instability of work, lack of power, and vulnerability to underpayment or wage theft (Cassim, Chapter 20). A common example is in the agricultural sector (e.g., workers involved in harvesting or in meat-packing plants). While the degree of protection for these workers varies by country, their actual protections are often unclear. Some immigrant workers may be willing to put up with poor pay or working conditions because they see taking a temporary job as a choice to get by financially, whereas the experience could be quite different for others who fear speaking up (Campbell et al., 2019; Cassim, Chapter 20).

Disability Status

The experience of underemployment is particularly relevant for people with disabilities, who are more likely to be underemployed and more likely to be negatively impacted by the experience (e.g., in their mental health); in fact, the effects of disability and underemployment in combination have more negative effects than the sum of the independent effects of each (Milner et al., 2017). On the positive side, providing accommodations seems to significantly mitigate the effects of underemployment for workers with disabilities (Konrad et al., 2013).

Realities and Dynamics of Underemployment Uncovered During the Recent Pandemic

The recent COVID pandemic uncovered several vulnerabilities for those who are underemployed or in precarious work. For example, some who were in the most unstable and underpaid positions (e.g., gig workers working for ride-sharing services) found themselves out of work. In the US, many who were underpaid or vulnerable (e.g., immigrant workers working in the meat industry) often continued to work under close-contact conditions that made them particularly susceptible to the virus (Krebs, 2021); in fact, these workers were considered the most "essential," given the least work flexibility, and were relatively powerless to address these issues—a key factor that affects the experience of underemployment. These issues were exacerbated when the precarious job required work outside of the home while balancing parenting needs (e.g., children out of school and learning at home). The limited empirical research on how the pandemic affected underemployed workers is still unfolding. Research from the US early in the pandemic (Lee et al., 2021) showed that those who were underemployed were more likely to suffer from depression and anxiety, and that employment insecurity was more likely to affect Hispanics, Blacks, women, those without a college degree, and young adults. However, recent economic discussions suggest that the worst underemployment due to the pandemic may be improving due to a tight labor market (Dean Avila & Lunsford, 2022). Clearly, the experience of the pandemic suggests that the value of policies (Lavelle et al., Chapter 16; Searle & McWha-Hermann, Chapter 4) focused on labor protections and financial supports that were provided in many countries during the pandemic.

Other Possible Moderators: When Is Underemployment Less Onerous?

Underemployment may not always be experienced as onerous or undesirable; that is, there are times when underemployment may have fewer negative outcomes or have positive outcomes as well. First, a worker may choose underemployment given their current life circumstances; for example, the underemployment may be experienced positively when it is seen as a temporary situation (e.g., as a bridge while looking for other work) or when the person needs the flexibility of gig work to control their time (e.g., when involved in caregiving). Second, a person may choose underemployment when it benefits them personally; for example, underemployment may be perceived positively when the job addresses a meaningful vocation or calling, when it allows people to spend more time with family, or when someone early in their career chooses a job that provides important opportunities and skills. These findings of worker choice may be consistent with the finding that employee empowerment can reduce the negative outcomes of overqualification (Erdogan & Bauer, 2009). Although reviews of the overqualification literature (e.g., Erdogan & Bauer, 2021; Liu & Wang, 2012) identify these and other potential moderators of the negative effects of perceived overqualification, the empirical evidence for their effects is still unclear (Harari et al., 2017).

Although these moderators may reduce the negative experience of underemployment, they also suggest which groups may fall into underemployment for longer than they wish, or against their will. For example, older people who have lost their job may be glad to have underpaid or unstable work in the short term as a bridge, but this might also become a long-term situation from which they cannot emerge, with consequences for their financial health and retirement. Those who are pursuing societally valuable work may get satisfaction from doing so, but over the long-term it may still be stressful and financially unviable. And someone who takes a job for caregiving reasons may be glad of the flexibility but may also face the negative outcomes of underemployment such as stress, exhaustion, and financial challenges. In short, underemployment may provide a number of advantages to particular people in particular contexts, but this does not necessarily remove its negative consequences.

Mediators: Underemployment and Employability Dimensions

Underemployment is inherently linked with the idea of employability because employability enhances an individual's likelihood of gaining employment (Fugate et al., 2004). Thus, we map employability dimensions between antecedents and outcomes of underemployment in Figure 15.1. Employability is a form of work-specific proactive adaptability that enables workers to identify and realize career opportunities (Fugate et al., 2004). It represents a form of work adaptability that consists of three dimensions: career identity, personal adaptability and proactivity, and human and social capital (Fugate et al., 2004). These employability dimensions are important in the context of underemployment as they facilitate movement between jobs and within and between organizations. For example, they help individuals to navigate and negotiate environmental demands.

Career identity refers to one's self-definition within the career context (e.g., who I am, or who I want to be; Fugate et al., 2004) and acts as a cognitive compass that motivates an individual to actively adapt to, realize, or create opportunities according to their aspirations (Fugate et al., 2004). Career identities are often articulated as narratives, which are shaped by one's possible selves (Fugate et al., 2004), demonstrating the importance of this career dimension in underemployment. For example, those who experience underemployment at young ages may not develop career identities and narratives associated with success and may not be able to clearly see their future work self, and thus engage in less proactive career behaviors (e.g., Strauss et al., 2012). Personal adaptability and proactivity are particularly important elements of work performance and careers with the rising globalization and rapidly changing organizational contexts (Griffin et al., 2007). Fugate et al. (2004) argue that optimism, propensity to learn, openness, internal locus of control, and general self-efficacy are the specific personal constructs that are particularly important for employment adaptability. Finally, human and social capital influences one's ability to identify and realize career opportunities as they can aid in job search activities. Human capital, referring to relevant education and experience, is strongly associated with career progression (e.g., Judge et al., 1995), and social networks can extend an individual's ability to identify opportunities across organizations and industries and over time (Fugate et al., 2004).

These employability dimensions appear to be promising as starting points for developing strategies to address unemployment and indeed, quite a few studies have subsequently demonstrated links between these and positive employment outcomes. In a study conducted during the recession, protean career attitudes (individual's motives to follow a particular career path, and the development of their own definition of what constitutes a successful career; Gubler et al., 2014) were found to be significantly associated with increased self-esteem and job search activity and predicted re-employment in a group of unemployed individuals (Waters et al., 2014).

Strategies for Addressing Underemployment: A Multilevel, Multidimensional, Multistakeholder Approach

As we have demonstrated throughout this chapter, there are many and varied antecedents that contribute to the experience of underemployment and tackling them requires consideration of their multilevel nature and the multiple stakeholders involved. In the first instance, identifying an appropriate strategy or strategies for addressing the issue of underemployment requires a diagnosis of where in this multilevel system the problem lies for a particular individual or group of underemployed workers. In this regard, the preceding sections of this chapter will be useful.

Quite often there are multiple, interacting causes, and so in this section we consider what strategies have been effective to date or may be effective but require further research and investigation. We organize these strategies into government policy, organizational and individual levels. Government policy is needed to reduce or remove underemployment, although this does not negate the responsibility of organizations. Individual-level strategies help individuals to either cope with the effects of underemployment or to develop knowledge and skills to move out of underemployment and gain working conditions that meet their desires and needs regarding employment.

Policy and Government Interventions

National policy can play a role in ensuring that workers are able to avail themselves of decent work and fair working conditions (Jiang et al., Chapter 18; Lavelle et al., Chapter 16). It could be argued that underemployment exists in part because it can benefit employers, so they may not be motivated to address underemployment. Government policies and interventions may serve as incentives to discourage employers from offering precarious forms of underemployment. Changes in job quality has been a recurring theme over the last decades (Kalleberg, 2011, 2016), which have contributed to experiences of underemployment and precarious working condition (Ryan et al., 2019). In particular, the terms and conditions of employment have led to many workers experiencing precarious work associated with unstable contracts and wages (Meyer & Maleka, Chapter 7), uncertainty regarding working hours, no access to social rights or a collective voice, and overall vulnerability in their conditions of employment (Vanroelen et al., 2021). Governments can play a role in ensuring that employment contracts are fair (Lavelle et al., Chapter 16). For example, O'Sullivan et al. (2020) demonstrated how government actions can result in a weak regulatory environment that can facilitate the emergence of zero-hours contracts (work where there are no guaranteed hours offered by the employer). In particular, labor laws and social protection are avenues for protecting people with significant working time uncertainty (O'Sullivan, 2019). Indeed, the OECD (2021) has identified a need to tighten up legislation at national and EU levels regarding the outsourcing of employees (termed domestic outsourcing): a trend that has been associated with substantial increases in underemployment over the past few decades. While there is an EU directive that establishes a legal requirement to maintain pay, working conditions, and collective agreements during a transfer, merger, or divestiture which is applicable also when a worker shifts from one firm to another, in practice outsourced workers do not tend to remain at their previous levels of pay and terms of work (OECD, 2021). These are issues that can and should be addressed through changes in legislation (Lavelle et al., Chapter 16).

Relatedly, the advent of the gig economy (Kuhn, Chapter 12) has resulted in a need to tighten up labor law which determines who is an employer and what their responsibilities are toward workers (OECD, 2021). In certain circumstances, gig workers are forced into a situation of self-employment, which takes the onus off the employer to provide appropriate terms and conditions for such workers. Thus, changes in labor and employment law are necessary to protect workers from such contingent contracts and associated underemployment (Lavelle et al., Chapter 16). While this will help, by itself it may not be enough (van Doorn et al., 2020). Social policy changes are also required to support workers on contingent contracts. Most social security or social insurance systems are built on an assumption of secure employment in traditional jobs (Friedman, 2014) and thus do not always provide security in the face of under- or unemployment for workers in gig or contingent forms of employment (Kuhn, Chapter 12).

Moreover, contingent labor is often provided by migrant workers, which adds further precarity (van Doorn et al., 2020). To address these intersecting issues, van Doorn et al. (2020) suggest that transnational regulatory arrangements for the governance of gig platforms are needed, which extend beyond labor law and include consumer protection and competition legislation, and stricter regulation of financial markets and data rights of workers. In brief, they suggest a need for political and policy efforts to strive to secure universal labor protections, living wage standards, and access to public welfare systems to address the multiple layers of vulnerability (van Doorn et al., 2020) that can contribute to precarious work and underemployment.

More broadly, governments need to consider specific strategies to address issues of underemployment for migrant workers. Past research has demonstrated that immigrant workers' rights are often systematically violated, and the problems are rooted in how jobs are designed and managed (de Castro et al., 2006). In turn, work organization factors are associated with occupational injury and illness and job loss, yet employer responses included indifference and various forms of retaliation (de Castro et al., 2006). In such instances where organizations and employers are not engaging in responsible and ethical work practices, national and government policy must and should protect workers. Unfortunately, even in countries with strong legislation regarding employment rights, immigrants either do not possess the means or feel too vulnerable to insist that their rights be upheld. Overqualification is a further common type of underemployment experienced by migrants and negatively associated with job satisfaction: especially for migrants who identify strongly with their host society (Wasserman et al., 2017). Wassermann and Hoppe (2019) demonstrated that perceived overqualification in immigrants was associated with higher levels of depressive symptoms and lower levels of life satisfaction, but the relationship with life satisfaction is attenuated with increasing optimism. Optimism can be developed through micro-interventions and so interventions that enhance optimism may help immigrants to cope with perceived overqualification (Wasserman & Hoppe, 2019).

Particular government policies may also be needed to reduce the negative effects of career shock events (e.g., recessions and pandemics), particularly on the career trajectories of younger workers. Taking a macrolevel perspective, Schoon and Bynner (2019) reviewed evidence on young people in Europe and the US making the transition from school to work before and after the 2008 Great Recession. They argued that although the 2008 financial crisis brought with it reduced employment opportunities for young people and accelerated existing trends toward prolonging education and precarious employment, there were considerable variations across countries. This emphasizes the importance of social institutions in supporting young people during this transition, particularly during times of crisis. Transition systems that created bridges between education and employment were associated with lower youth unemployment but importantly, more protective transition regimes were also protective against temporary employment (Schoon & Bynner, 2019).

The experience and impact of underemployment is wide and varied, and it should not come as a surprise that these effects may be subject to cultural differences. For example, across two studies, Luksyte et al. (2022) demonstrated that person-environment (P-E) fit but not relative deprivation explained why collectivism values assuaged the negative effect of perceived overqualification on outcomes such as organizational citizenship behaviors, personal initiative, work engagement, and life satisfaction. Thus, although we have offered several strategies at policy and government levels, we need to be aware that further research is required to understand the nuances of different cultures and government policies in terms of their applicability beyond the context in which they are implemented.

Interventions at the Organizational Level

Organizations and employers have an important role to play in addressing underemployment as they are important agents in creating jobs. Maynard (2011) proposed a three-pronged classification for organizational responses to underemployment. The first approach is to curb *objective* underemployment by increasing the match between the employee and the kind of work they are suited for and would like. The second approach focuses on managing or improving work-related perceptions of employees who feel underemployed, and finally, when it is not possible or practical to reduce objective or perceived underemployment, organizations can try to prevent or alleviate the negative outcomes that are associated with it (Maynard, 2011).

Curbing objective underemployment tends to be difficult to achieve in reality because of the financial implications for organizations if they are to reduce the number of workers who are employed on a low-wage, part-time, or temporary basis (Maynard, 2011), and indeed this trend is on the rise. However, there are some things that can be done. For example, overqualification can be tackled through in-house promotions and looking for opportunities to better utilize the skills and experience of overqualified employees (Maynard, 2011).

Managing or improving work-related perceptions of underemployment is the second category identified by Maynard (2011). Alfes et al. (2016) investigated the role of interpersonal relationships at work in reducing the perceptions of overqualification. They found that the quality of the relationships that employees held with their leader and with their team reduced perceptions of overqualification. Moreover, leader-member exchange and team cohesiveness also weakened the negative relationship between perceived overqualification and job satisfaction. Thus, interpersonal relationships again appear to be a key aspect in the perception of overqualification and mitigating its negative effects.

Empowerment is a strategy that attempts to alleviate the negative outcomes of underemployment (the third strategy identified by Maynard, 2011), which is also related to the roles of autonomy and choice noted throughout this chapter. In particular, it may be an effective strategy to mitigate the negative effects of *overqualification* such as lower job attitudes and greater withdrawal. Drawing on relative deprivation theory, Erdogan and Bauer (2009) demonstrated that empowerment ameliorated the negative effects of perceived overqualification on job satisfaction, intentions to remain, and voluntary turnover in a sample of young workers (average age 22 years) in a major retail clothing chain in Turkey.

Empowerment was conceptualized as meaning, self-determination, competence, and impact (Spreitzer, 1995). Interestingly, in this study, overqualification was associated with high objective performance (Erdogan & Bauer, 2009), and this effect remained whether employees felt empowered or not. However, empowerment needs to be used cautiously. In some instances, the perception of receiving more responsibilities (i.e., empowerment) combined with certain forms of underemployment (e.g., underpayment) may be onerous to workers and exacerbate feelings of relative deprivation and perceived injustice (Saltzman et al., Chapter 2).

Relatedly, the provision of task idiosyncratic deals (i-deals) has been found to buffer the negative relationship between perceived overqualification and demands-abilities misfit and boredom (Howard et al., 2022). However, even such seemingly positive interventions can have some negative consequences; the provision of i-deals also intensified overqualified employees' perceptions of being envied by coworkers and reports of experienced incivility, thereby heightening interpersonal stressors (Howard et al., 2022).

Andrei and Parker (2022) advocate for three organizational meta-strategies to better manage an *older and diverse workforce*. The "3i" framework—include, individualize, and integrate—is proposed as three broad sets of approaches that can guide organizational actions and practices. The "include" strategies focus on creating an inclusive climate for older workers. The "individualize" strategies aim to adapt work to specific challenges, needs, and preferences of employees at different ages, and the "integrate" strategies focus on facilitating effective collaboration and knowledge-sharing processes across the diverse age groups in the workplace (Andrei & Parker, 2022). A systematic review by Pak et al. (2019) suggested that offering job resources to older workers has a positive effect on their ability, motivation, and opportunity to continue working. They also concluded that work ability was most negatively related to job demands, whereas employability was positively associated with developmental practices in organizations. Practically, this suggests that HR practices should make sure that there is a balance between job demands and resources to maintain or improve work ability (Pak et al., 2019; see also Brady et al., 2020). In addition, accommodation practices could be used to lower job demands that are decreasing ability, motivation, and opportunity to continue working, and developmental opportunities should be offered regardless of age (Pak et al., 2019).

Older workers may be motivated to change jobs and careers because of changing skill requirements, changing work contexts, or the decline in the demand for labor in their occupation (Feldman, 2007). However, their opportunities to do so may be limited. Thus, organizational and government policies are necessary to increase the ability of older workers to change careers by reducing age stereotypes and creating opportunities for older workers to share their knowledge and skills, perhaps through mentoring others, for example. Older workers may have substantial career embeddedness (Feldman, 2007), with a lot of tacit knowledge and social networks that are very beneficial within an organization. Indeed, high-quality interpersonal relationships at work can mitigate the negative relationship between perceived overqualification and job satisfaction (Alfes et al., 2016).

Some research has demonstrated that poor-quality connections and interpersonal networks exacerbate the impact of underemployment in its various forms (e.g., Alfes et al., 2016; Deng et al., 2018). This can also factor into lower quality leader-member exchange relationships and further disadvantage those experiencing underemployment in terms of relative deprivation (Bolino & Turnley, 2009). Thus, focusing on interpersonal relationships and social capital within and across organizations should be a useful strategy to increase employability (e.g., Fugate et al., 2004) and counter underemployment.

Organizations that adhere to values regarding corporate social responsibility may be more likely to focus on providing quality work for employees. Business schools have a role to play in teaching students from early in their career (as potential future organizational leaders and managers) the importance of such ethical conduct and social responsibility. In this regard, the United Nations (UN) Principles for Responsible Management Education[2] initiative has a vision to create a global movement and drive thought leadership on responsible management education, and develop future leaders who make responsible decisions to advance sustainable development and decent work. They provide many resources to support business schools in promoting and enacting this vision, including programs for incorporating the UN Sustainable Development Goals into leadership education, of which decent work is one. Thus, business schools can be a driving force for early intervention in teaching values regarding corporate social responsibility and ethical treatment of workers.

Interventions at the Individual Level

Career attitudes, career adaptability, and proactive career behaviors and self-management appear to be important skills and approaches at the individual level that are associated with re-employment and addressing underemployment. Career self-management qualities, including adaptability and proactivity, appear to be effective in reducing unemployment and underemployment. For example, Waters et al. (2014) demonstrated that career-development programs that foster positive capacities such as the adoption of a protean career orientation are beneficial for individuals to become re-employed, even during periods of high unemployment such as during the Great Recession. This is consistent with research by Sylva et al. (2019) who demonstrated that career initiative was related to increases in demands-abilities fit over time, suggesting that it may be useful in the skills misfit form of underemployment.

Career adaptability, referring to the ability to change to fit new career-related consequences, can facilitate job search and job changes to a qualitatively better job, which has been proposed to help when individuals are experiencing economic stress or underemployment (Klehe et al., 2012). It has been associated with high career performance, career satisfaction (Zacher, 2015) and negatively related to career entrenchment (Zacher et al., 2015). Career adaptability is a component of career self-management, and career self-management interventions have been effective for increasing organizational responsiveness, pay increases, and faster job transitions (Raabe et al., 2007). However, more research is needed on such interventions in terms of their effectiveness in contexts of underemployment specifically. We also need to examine their potential at different career stages and different ages.

Such relationships are also influenced by HR practices and organizational support, which may be particularly pertinent for underemployment (Teng-Calleja et al., Chapter 8). Jung and Takeuchi (2018) demonstrated a positive relationship between career self-management and satisfaction for younger employees, which was stronger when developmental HR practices and organizational support were high. However, for middle-aged employees, the positive relationship was stronger when these factors were low; middle-aged employees who perceived a lack of developmental practices or support showed marked improvements in career satisfaction by engaging in career self-management behaviors (Jung & Takeuchi, 2018). Relatedly, Tordera et al. (2020) found that certain HR practices (specifically, performance appraisal, recruitment and selection, security, and exit management) were more beneficial for younger employees, whereas contingent pay and a competitive salary were more beneficial for older employees in terms of career sustainability. Although these findings do not pertain to underemployment specifically, they point to the relevance of career adaptability in combination with organizational development and support practices for employees across age categories.

Kooij (2020) has suggested that self-regulation may help to restore P-E fit when workers experience career shocks, like those experienced as a result of the COVID-19 pandemic. In particular, she suggests that older adults may have responded more effectively to measures to counter COVID-19 (e.g., Losada-Balter et al., 2020) because they have an effective range of self-regulation strategies that help them maintain or restore P-E fit. Although this has yet to be tested, it presents an interesting possibility that the development of four types of self-regulation strategies that maintain or restore P-E fit may serve as protective factors against certain types of underemployment (e.g., skills misfit). These strategies and examples as outlined by Kooij (2020) are: *proactive goal engagement* (e.g., upgrading skills and competencies), *proactive goal disengagement* (e.g., using the current situation or career shock to reflect on past career experiences), *adaptive goal engagement* (e.g., asking a colleague for help with new technology), and *adaptive goal disengagement* (e.g., downgrading the importance of using new technology or work systems). Training workers, and particularly older workers, in proactive and adaptive self-regulation may help maintain P-E fit and potentially reduce the likelihood of underemployment. Indeed, there is existing evidence in research with older workers that career management interventions hold promise; Vuori et al. (2012) demonstrated that a resource-building group intervention led to reduced intentions to retire early seven months after the intervention.

Self-regulation during job search has also been identified as a useful strategy for migrants. Zikic and Klehe (2021) identified mechanisms through which migrants may proactively self-regulate toward better employment quality. Looking at a group of migrants in Canada, they found that barriers such as a perceived lack of language proficiency and credential recognition weakened migrants' self-regulation efforts in the form of career-related exploration (goal establishment) and planning (goal planning), but proactivity and social support fostered self-regulation. Importantly, career planning predicted migrants' quality of employment nine months later (Zikic & Klehe, 2021).

Thus, self-regulation interventions focused on proactive and adaptive goal regulation could hold particular promise across age groups and for disadvantaged minority groups in helping them to reduce underemployment, improve their P-E fit, and improve their career opportunities. Relatedly, job crafting interventions can be useful, particularly as they can improve the person-job fit. Research by Debus et al. (2020) demonstrated that overqualified employees were more likely to withdraw from their work and intended to exit when they engaged in low levels of job crafting, whereas when individuals engaged in high levels of crafting, the relationship was reversed or nonsignificant. Kooij et al. (2017) demonstrated that a job crafting intervention focused on crafting one's strengths and weaknesses (via an intervention) was associated with demands-abilities and need-supplies fit in older workers specifically (but not for younger workers). More recently, Zhang et al. (2021) found with the use of two-wave and dual-source data that perceived overqualification is positively related to job crafting strengths and job crafting interests, and that the former was related to supervisor-rated task performance.

In various forms, several countries have introduced supports and pathways to aid individuals to enter the workplace or gain employment that fits their skills. In the context of long-term unemployment, Whelan (2018) examined the effectiveness of a high-support intervention compared to services-as-usual, finding that the intervention led to improvements over time in wellbeing and employability, albeit with several more positive effects observed amongst the men who took part in the intervention. The intervention, enhancing employability through positive interventions for improving career potential (EEPIC) , comprised an individualized job-seeking support intervention, consisted of four stages over 8–12 weeks and aimed to support a job seeker in developing skills necessary for the labor market while building self-efficacy and esteem. In the first stage, the individual's needs were assessed, which led to the development of a tailored career guidance process (Stage 2) which aimed to build career clarity, career identity, and improve self-esteem and career efficacy. Stage 3 entailed developing career plans, and Stage 4 involved the implementation of the career plan, supported by a guidance practitioner. The study showed that both groups experienced increases in hope, agency, perceptions of improved employability, and career efficacy and the intervention participants were more likely to be engaged in training or supported employment and less likely to be job seeking. The process evaluation revealed three important themes with regard to implementation aspects of the intervention, including the important roles of (1) the practitioner-client relationship, (2) the service setting, and (3) the skill sets of practitioners.

Thus, career self-management interventions, including adaptability and proactivity interventions, appear to be effective in reducing unemployment and underemployment. However, there may be a need to investigate their effectiveness across cultures to a greater extent. A study by Smale et al. (2019) found that although career proactivity was related to subjective financial success, this was more important in cultures with high in-group collectivism, high power distance, and low uncertainty avoidance.

Future Research Directions

In this chapter, we have demonstrated that precarious underemployment has somewhat different antecedents and outcomes across different stages of one's career and life stage. We would encourage researchers in the future to take greater consideration of life and career stages in considering how to address underemployment. In particular, future research would do well to consider the fact that workers are more likely now than ever before to change careers, and so early-career stage is not necessarily associated with younger employees. Thus, conducting research which separates worker age effects and career stage would provide valuable insights into the nuances of these antecedents of precarious underemployment and its effects on workers.

Furthermore, longitudinal studies that look at continuous and discontinuous change patterns would be useful in terms of understanding the short- and long-term impacts of underemployment at different ages and career stages. Relatedly, considering the impact of underemployment at different life transitions (e.g., transition from school or university to work, and transition to parenthood) may help to provide a deeper understanding of when and how precarious underemployment has negative effects for employees.

Our chapter has also pointed to the importance of considering the impacts of macro-contextual factors on precarious underemployment. Future research would do well to consider interactions between career stage and macro-contextual factors in precarious underemployment, and in identifying how to support employees who find themselves in precarious underemployment in these different circumstances.

When employees find themselves in precarious underemployment because of macro-contextual factors (e.g., recessions and pandemics), their agency and ability to get themselves out of this situation is often extremely limited. As such, future research is needed to better understand how to support workers impacted by such macro-contextual factors, and particularly those cohorts of workers likely to be disproportionately affected (e.g., younger and older workers, women, ethnic minorities, and immigrants).

Employers have a significant role to play in the prevalence of precarious underemployment. A pressing issue for future research to investigate is how to motivate employers to provide high-quality, secure forms of employment that match the skills of employees. Government policy may have a role to play here, but this is an issue as much to do with the values of an organization, and so, research looking into developing corporate social responsibility, ethical leadership, and organizational ethics and values as they relate to providing quality employment is undoubtedly important.

Conclusion

In this chapter, we have demonstrated that underemployment as a form of precarious work can have different manifestations, antecedents, and outcomes for different cohorts of workers and across age and career stages. We map these in Figure 15.1, demonstrating that they also have an impact on employability dimensions for workers and the individual circumstances of workers. However, precarious underemployment is impacted by various macro-contextual factors, pointing to the multilevel nature of its occurrence and the fact that we need solutions and strategies to combat it across these levels. Thus, we suggest a range of interventions at the individual, organizational, and government-policy levels that are needed to tackle underemployment.

Notes

1 OECD.Stats. https://stats.oecd.org/glossary/detail.asp?ID=3539.
2 Principles for Responsible Management Education (PRME). https://www.unprme.org/about.

References

Albelda, R., Bell-Pasht, A., & Konstantinidis, C. (2020). Gender and precarious work in the United States: Evidence from the Contingent Work Supplement 1995–2017. *Review of Radical Political Economics, 52*(3), 542–563. https://doi.org/10.1177/0486613419891175

Alfes, K., Shantz, A., & van Baalen, S. (2016). Reducing perceptions of overqualification and its impact on job satisfaction: The dual roles of interpersonal relationships at work. *Human Resource Management Journal, 26*(1), 84–101. https://doi.org/10.1111/1748-8583.12094

Allan, B. A., Tay, L., & Sterling, H. M. (2017). Construction and validation of the Subjective Underemployment Scales (SUS). *Journal of Vocational Behavior, 99*, 93–106. https://doi.org/10.1016/j.jvb.2017.01.001

Andrei, D. M., & Parker, S. K. (2022). Organizational metastrategies for younger and older workers. In H. Zacher & C. W. Rudolph (Eds.), *Age and work: Advances in theory, methods, and practice* (pp. 310–327). Routledge. https://doi.org/10.4324/9781003089674

Ashford, S., George, E., & Blatt, R. (2007). Old assumptions, new work: the opportunities and challenges of research on nonstandard employment. *Academy of Management Annals, 1*(1), 65–117. https://doi.org/10.5465/078559807

Autor, D. (2019). *Work of the past, work of the future* (NBER Working Paper No. 25588). National Bureau of Economic Research. http://www.nber.org/papers/w25588

Barnard, C. (2014, November 27–28). *Non-standard employment: What can the EU do?* [Paper presentation]. European Labor Law Network 7th Annual Legal Seminar, New Forms of Employment and EU law, The Hague, Netherlands.

Benach, J., Vives, A., Amable, M., Vanroelen, C., Tarafa, G., & Muntaner, C. (2014). Precarious employment: Understanding an emerging social determinant of health. *Annual Review of Public Health, 35*, 229–253. https://doi.org/10.1146/annurev-publhealth-032013-182500

Betti, G., Bettio, F., Georgiadis, T., & Tinios, P. (2015). *Unequal ageing in Europe: Women's independence and pensions*. Springer.

Bolino, M. C., & Turnley, W. H. (2009). Relative deprivation among employees in lower-quality leader-member exchange relationships. *The Leadership Quarterly, 20*(3), 276–286. https://doi.org/10.1016/j.leaqua.2009.03.001

Bonnet, C., Buffeteau, S., & Godefroy, P. (2006). Les effets des réformes des retraites sur les inégalités de genre en France. *Population, 61*(1–2), 45–75. https://doi.org/10.3917/popu.601.0045

Brady, G. M., Truxillo, D. M., Cadiz, D. M., Rineer, J. R., Caughlin, D. E., & Bodner, T. (2020). Opening the black box: Examining the nomological network of work ability and its role in organizational research. *Journal of Applied Psychology, 105*(6), 637–670. https://doi.org/10.1037/apl0000454

Burgess, S., Propper, C., Rees, H., & Shearer, A. (2003). The class of 1981: The effects of early career unemployment on subsequent unemployment experiences. *Labour Economics, 10*(3), 291–309. https://doi.org/10.1016/S0927-5371(02)00138-0

Campbell, I., Tranfaglia, M. A., Tham, J. C., & Boese, M. (2019). Precarious work and the reluctance to complain: Italian temporary migrant workers in Australia. *Labour & Industry: A Journal of the Social and Economic Relations of Work, 29*(1), 98–117. https://doi.org/10.1080/10301763.2018.1558895

Cano Cano, E. (2000). Análisis de los procesos socioeconómicos de precarización laboral [Analysis of the socioeconomic processes of work precarization]. In E. Cano Cano, A. Bilbao, & G. Standing (Eds.), *Precariedad laboral, flexibilidad y desregulación [Precarious work, flexibility and deregulation]*. Germanía.

Crystal, S. (2021). Impact of economic shocks on cumulative advantage processes: Recession, recovery, and trajectories of inequality. *Innovation in Aging, 5*(Supplement 1), 508. https://doi.org/10.1093/geroni/igab046.1957

de Castro, A. B., Fujishiro, K., Sweitzer, E., & Oliva, J. (2006). How immigrant workers experience workplace problems: A qualitative study. *Archives of Environmental & Occupational Health, 61*(6), 249–258. https://doi.org/10.3200/AEOH.61.6.249-258

Dean Avila, D., & Lunsford, K. G. (2022). *Underemployment following the Great Recession and the COVID-19 Recession* (Economic Commentary2022-01). Federal Reserve Bank of Cleveland. https://doi.org/10.26509/frbc-ec-202201

Debus, M. E., Gross, C., & Kleinmann, M. (2020). The power of doing: How job crafting transmits the beneficial impact of autonomy among overqualified employees. *Journal of Business and Psychology, 35*(3), 317–331. https://doi.org/10.1007/s10869-019-09625-y

Deng, H., Guan, Y., Wu, C.-H., Erdogan, B., Bauer, T., & Yao, X. (2018). A relational model of perceived overqualification: The moderating role of interpersonal influence on social acceptance. *Journal of Management, 44*(8), 3288–3310. https://doi.org/10.1177/0149206316668237

Dooley, D., Prause, J., & Ham-Rowbottom, K. A. (2000). Underemployment and depression: Longitudinal relationships. *Journal of Health and Social Behavior, 41*(4), 421–436. https://doi.org/10.2307/2676295

Duggan, J., Sherman, U., Carbery, R., & McDonnell, A. (2020). Algorithmic management and app-work in the gig economy: A research agenda for employment relations and HRM. *Human Resource Management Journal, 30*(1), 114–132. https://doi.org/10.1111/1748-8583.12258

Erdogan, B., & Bauer, T. N. (2009). Perceived overqualification and its outcomes: The moderating role of empowerment. *Journal of Applied Psychology, 94*(2), 557. https://doi.org/10.1037/a0013528

Erdogan, B., & Bauer, T.N. (2021) Overqualification at work: A review and synthesis of the literature. *Annual Review of Organizational Psychology and Organizational Behavior, 8*(1), 259–283. https://doi.org/10.1146/annurev-orgpsych-012420-055831

Erdogan, B., Bauer, T. N., Peiró, J. M., & Truxillo, D. M. (2011a). Overqualification theory, research, and practice: Things that matter. *Industrial and Organizational Psychology, 4*(2), 260–267. https://doi.org/10.1111/j.1754-9434.2011.01339.x

Erdogan, B., Bauer, T. N., Peiró, J. M., & Truxillo, D. M. (2011b). Overqualified employees: Making the best of a potentially bad situation for individuals and organizations. *Industrial and Organizational Psychology, 4*(2), 215–232. https://doi.org/10.1111/j.1754-9434.2011.01330.x

Evans, G. (1915). The social aspects of the public regulation of wages. *The American Economic Review, 5*(1), 270–277. http://www.jstor.org/stable/1810789

Feldman, D. C. (1996). The nature, antecedents, and consequences of underemployment. *Journal of Management, 22*(3), 385–407. https://doi.org/10.1177/014920639602200302

Feldman, D. C. (2007). Career mobility and career stability among older workers. In K. S. Schultz & G. A. Adams (Eds.), *Aging and work in the 21st century* (pp. 179–197). Lawrence Erlbaum Associates.

Feldman, D. C., Leana, C. R., & Bolino, M. C. (2002). Underemployment and relative deprivation among re-employed executives. *Journal of Occupational and Organizational Psychology, 75*(4), 453–471. https://doi.org/10.1348/096317902321119682

Fisher, G. G., Stachowski, A., Infurna, F. J., Faul, J. D., Grosch, J., & Tetrick, L. E. (2014). Mental work demands, retirement, and longitudinal trajectories of cognitive functioning. *Journal of Occupational Health Psychology, 19*(2), 231–242. https://doi.org/10.1037/a0035724

Freeney, Y., van der Werff, L., & Collings, D. G. (2021). I left Venus and came back to Mars: Temporal focus congruence in dyadic relationships following maternity leave. *Organization Science, 33*(5), 1701–2083. https://doi.org/10.1287/orsc.2021.1508

Friedland, D. S., & Price, R. H. (2003). Underemployment: Consequences for the health and well-being of workers. *American Journal of Community Psychology, 32*(1), 33–45. https://doi.org/10.1023/A:1025638705649

Friedman, G. (2014). Workers without employers: Shadow corporations and the rise of the gig economy. *Review of Keynesian Economics, 2*(2), 171–188. https://doi.org/10.4337/roke.2014.02.03

Fugate, M., Kinicki, A. J., & Ashforth, B. E. (2004). Employability: A psycho-social construct, its dimensions, and applications. *Journal of Vocational Behavior, 65*(1), 14–38. http://doi.org/10.1016/j.jvb.2003.10.005

Gallup. (2018). *The gig economy and alternative work arrangements.* Gallup Inc.

García-Castro, L., Rocabert-Beut, E., Yeves, J., & Peiró, J. M. (2018). Modelo de medida del constructo 'subempleo' en jóvenes trabajadores en España [English translation]. *Revista Mexicana de Psicología, 35*(1), 26–37.

Ghilarducci, T., & Farmand, A. (2020). Older workers on the COVID-19-frontlines without paid sick leave. *Journal of Aging & Social Policy, 32*(4–5), 471–476. https://doi.org/10.1080/08959420.2020.1765685

Goda, G. S., Jackson, E., Nicholas, L. H., & Stith, S. S. (2021). *The impact of COVID-19 on older workers' employment and social security spillovers* (NBER Working Paper No. 29083). National Bureau of Economic Research. https://www.nber.org/system/files/working_papers/w29083/w29083.pdf

Griffin, M. A., Neal, A., & Parker, S. K. (2007). A new model of work role performance: Positive behavior in uncertain and interdependent contexts. *Academy of Management Journal, 50*(2), 327–347. https://doi.org/10.5465/amj.2007.24634438

Gubler, M., Arnold, J., & Coombs, C. (2014). Reassessing the protean career concept: Empirical findings, conceptual components, and measurement. *Journal of Organizational Behavior, 35*(S1), S23–S40. https://doi.org/10.1002/job.1908

Han, S. K., & Moen, P. (1999). Clocking out: Temporal patterning of retirement. *American Journal of Sociology, 105*(1), 191–236.

Harari, M. B., Manapragada, A., & Viswesvaran, C. (2017). Who thinks they're a big fish in a small pond and why does it matter? A meta-analysis of perceived overqualification. *Journal of Vocational Behavior, 102*, 28–47. https://doi.org/10.1016/j.jvb.2017.06.002

Heyes, J., Tomlinson, M., & Whitworth, A. (2017). Underemployment and well-being in the UK before and after the Great Recession. *Work, Employment and Society, 31*(1), 71–89. https://doi.org/10.1177/0950017016666199

Hille, K. (2010, May 24). Foxconn seeks suicide answers. *Financial Times.* https://www.ft.com/content/8a638d40-6698-11df-aeb1-00144feab49a

Howard, E., Luksyte, A., Amarnani, R. K., & Spitzmueller, C. (2022). Perceived overqualification and experiences of incivility: Can task i-deals help or hurt? *Journal of Occupational Health Psychology, 27*(1), 89–103. https://doi.org/10.1037/ocp0000304

International Labor Organization. (2012). *From precarious work to decent work: Outcome document to the workers' symposium on policies and regulations to combat precarious employment.*

Jagannathan, R., Kapoor, M., & Schaumburg, E. (2013). Causes of the Great Recession of 2007–2009: The financial crisis was the symptom not the disease! *Journal of Financial Intermediation, 22*(1), 4–29. https://doi.org/10.1016/j.jfi.2012.06.002

Johnson, J. (2011, February 28). 1 million workers. 90 million iPhones. 17 suicides. Who's to blame? *Wired*. https://www.wired.com/2011/02/ff-joelinchina/

Judge, T. A., Cable, D. M., Boudreau, J. W., & Bretz Jr, R. D. (1995). An empirical investigation of the predictors of executive career success. *Personnel Psychology, 48*(3), 485–519.

Jung, Y., & Takeuchi, N. (2018). A lifespan perspective for understanding career self-management and satisfaction: The role of developmental human resource practices and organizational support. *Human Relations, 71*(1), 73–102. https://doi.org/10.1177/0018726717715075

Kalleberg, A. L. (2009). Precarious work, insecure workers: Employment relations in transition. *American Sociological Review 74(1),* 1–22. https://doi.org/10.1177/000312240907400101

Kalleberg, A. L. (2011). *Good jobs, bad jobs: The rise of polarized and precarious employment systems in the United States, 1970s–2000s*. Russell Sage Foundation.

Kalleberg, A. L. (2016). Good jobs, bad jobs. In S. Edgell, H. Gottfried, & E. Granter (Eds.), *The Sage handbook of the sociology of work and employment* (pp. 129–147). Sage.

Kalleberg, A. L., Reskin, B. F., & Hudson, K. (2000). Bad jobs in America: Standard and nonstandard employment relations and job quality in the United States. *American Sociological Review, 65,* 256–278. https://doi.org/10.2307/2657440

Kamerāde, D., & Richardson, H. (2018). Gender segregation, underemployment, and subjective well-being in the UK labour market. *Human Relations, 71*(2), 285–309. https://doi.org/10.1177/0018726717713829

Keith, M. G., Harms, P. D., & Long, A. C. (2020). Worker health and well-being in the gig economy: A proposed framework and research agenda. In P. L. Perrewé, P. D. Harms, & C.-H. Chang (Eds.) *Entrepreneurial and small business stressors, experienced stress, and well-being* (pp. 1–33). Emerald Publishing. https://doi.org/10.1108/S1479-355520200000018002

Keller, B., & Seifert, H. (2006). Atypische Beschäftigungsverhältnisse: Flexibilität, soziale Sicherheit und Prekarität [Atypical employment relationships: Flexibility, social security and precarity]. *WSI Mitteilungen, 5*, 235–240. https://nbn-resolving.org/urn:nbn:de:0168-ssoar-154890

Klehe, U. -C., Zikic, J., van Vianen, A. E. M., Koen, J., & Buyken, M. (2012), Coping proactively with economic stress: Career adaptability in the face of job insecurity, job loss, unemployment, and underemployment. In P. L. Perrewé, J. R. B. Halbesleben, & C. C. Rosen (Eds.), *The role of the economic crisis on occupational stress and well being* (pp. 131–176). Emerald Group Publishing.

Konrad, A. M., Moore, M. E., Ng, E. S., Doherty, A. J., & Breward, K. (2013). Temporary work, underemployment, and workplace accommodations: Relationship to well-being for workers with disabilities. *British Journal of Management, 24*(3), 367–382. https://doi.org/10.1111/j.1467-8551.2011.00809.x

Kooij, D. T. (2020). The impact of the COVID-19 pandemic on older workers: The role of self-regulation and organizations. *Work, Aging and Retirement, 6*(4), 233–237. https://doi.org/10.1093/workar/waaa018

Kooij, D. T., van Woerkom, M., Wilkenloh, J., Dorenbosch, L., & Denissen, J. J. (2017). Job crafting towards strengths and interests: The effects of a job crafting intervention on person–job fit and the role of age. *Journal of Applied Psychology, 102*(6), 971–981. https://doi.org/10.1037/apl0000194

Krebs, N. (2021, December 24). COVID cases in meatpacking plants impacted workers and their rural communities. *NPR.* https://www.npr.org/2021/12/24/1067775073/covid-cases-in-meatpacking-plants-impacted-workers-and-their-rural-communities

Lee, J. O., Kapteyn, A., Clomax, A., & Jin, H. (2021). Estimating influences of unemployment and underemployment on mental health during the COVID-19 pandemic: Who suffers the most? *Public Health, 201(December),* 48–54. https://doi.org/10.1016/j.puhe.2021.09.038

Liu, S., & Wang, M. (2012). *Perceived overqualification: A review and recommendations for research and practice.* Emerald Group Publishing. https://doi.org/10.1108/S1479-3555(2012)0000010005

Losada-Baltar, A., Jiménez-Gonzalo, L., Gallego-Alberto, L., Pedroso- Chaparro, M. D. S., Fernandes-Pires, J., & Márquez-González, M. (2020). "We're staying at home." Association of self-perceptions of aging, personal and family resources and loneliness with psychological distress during the lock-down period of COVID-19. *The Journals of Gerontology: Series B, 76*(2), e10–e16. https://doi.org/10.1093/geronb/gbaa048

Luksyte, A., Bauer, T. N., Debus, M. E., Erdogan, B., & Wu, C. H. (2022). Perceived overqualification and collectivism orientation: Implications for work and nonwork outcomes. *Journal of Management, 48*(2), 319–349. https://doi.org/10.1177/0149206320948602

Mainiero, L. A., & Gibson, D. E. (2018). The kaleidoscope career model revisited: How midcareer men and women diverge on authenticity, balance, and challenge. *Journal of Career Development, 45*(4), 361–377. https://doi.org/10.1177/0894845317698223

Mainiero, L. A., & Sullivan, S. E. (2006). *The opt-out revolt: Why people are leaving companies to create kaleidoscope careers.* Davies-Black Publishing.

Maynard, D.C. (2011) Directions for future underemployment research: Measurement and practice. In D. Maynard & D. Feldman (Eds.), *Underemployment.* Springer. https://doi.org/10.1007/978-1-4419-9413-4_13

Maynard, D. C., Joseph, T. A., & Maynard, A. M. (2006). Underemployment, job attitudes, and turnover intentions. *Journal of Organizational Behavior, 27*(4), 509–536. https://doi.org/10.1002/job.389

McCarthy, J., Heraty, N., Cross, C., & Cleveland, J. N. (2014). Who is considered an 'older worker'? Extending our conceptualization of 'older' from an organizational decision maker perspective. *Human Resource Management Journal, 24*(4), 374–393. https://doi.org/10.1111/1748-8583.12041

McKee-Ryan, F. M., & Harvey, J. (2011). 'I have a job, but …': A review of underemployment. *Journal of Management, 37*(4), 962–996. https://doi.org/10.1177/0149206311398134

Miller, J. D., & Cepuran, C. (2019). The impact of the Great Recession on Generation X. *Longitudinal and Life Course Studies, 10*(2), 201–216. https://doi.org/10.1332/175795919X15514456677303

Milner, A., King, T. L., LaMontagne, A. D., Aitken, Z., Petrie, D., & Kavanagh, A. M. (2017). Underemployment and its impacts on mental health among those with disabilities: evidence from the HILDA cohort. *Journal of Epidemiology and Community Health, 71*(12), 1198–1202. https://doi.org/10.1136/jech-2017-209800

Mousteri, V., Daly, M., & Delaney, L. (2020). Underemployment and psychological distress: Propensity score and fixed effects estimates from two large UK samples. *Social Science & Medicine, 244,* Article 112641. https://doi.org/10.1016/j.socscimed.2019.112641

Munnell, A. H., Cannon Fraenkel, R. & Hurwitz, J. (2012). *The pension coverage problem in the private sector.* (Issue in Brief No. 12–16). Center for Retirement Research at Boston College. http://hdl.handle.net/2345/bc-ir:103935

Olsthoorn, M. (2014). Measuring precarious employment: A proposal for two indicators of precarious employment based on set-theory and tested with Dutch labor market-data. *Social Indicators Research, 119*(1), 421–441. https://doi.org/10.1007/s11205-013-0480-y

Organization for Economic Co-operation and Development (OECD). (2014, September 10–11). *Preventing unemployment and underemployment from becoming structural* [Paper presentation]. G20 Labour and Employment Ministerial Meeting Melbourne, Australia.

Organisation for Economic Co-operation and Development (OECD). (2018), *Productivity and jobs in a globalized world: (How) can all regions benefit?* https://doi.org/10.1787/9789264293137-en

Organisation for Economic Co-operation and Development (OECD). (2019), *OECD employment outlook 2019: The future of work.* https://doi.org/10.1787/9ee00155-en

Organisation for Economic Co-operation and Development (OECD). (2021), *OECD Employment Outlook 2021: Navigating the COVID-19 crisis and recovery.* https://doi.org/10.1787/5a700c4b-en

O'Sullivan, M. (2019). Zero hours and on-call work in Anglo-Saxon countries: A comparative review. In M. O'Sullivan, J. Lavelle, J. McMahon, L. Ryan, C. Murphy, T. Turner, & P. Gunnigle (Eds.), *Zero hours and on-call work in Anglo-Saxon countries* (pp. 159–178). Springer.

O'Sullivan, M., Turner, T., Lavelle, J., MacMahon, J., Murphy, C., Ryan, L., Gunnigle, P. & O'Brien, M. (2020). The role of the state in shaping zero hours work in an atypical liberal market economy. *Economic and Industrial Democracy, 41*(3), 652–671. https://doi.org/10.1177/0143831X17735181

Pak, K., Kooij, D. T., De Lange, A. H., & Van Veldhoven, M. J. (2019). Human resource management and the ability, motivation and opportunity to continue working: A review of quantitative studies. *Human Resource Management Review, 29*(3), 336–352. https://doi.org/10.1016/j.hrmr.2018.07.002

Peiró, J. M., Hernández, A., & Ramos, J. (2015). The challenge of building human capital and benefiting from it: A person-centric view of youth unemployment and underemployment. In L. Finkelstein, D. Truxillo, F. Fraccaroli and R. Kanfer (Eds.) *Facing the challenges of a multi-age workforce: A use inspired approach* (pp. 83–107). Routledge.

Pomfret, J. & Siu, T. (2010, May 26). Suicides expose stress of China factory life. *Reuters.* https://www.reuters.com/article/us-china-suicides-idUSTRE64O2CK20100525

Potočnik, K., Tordera, N., & Peiró, J. M. (2009). The role of human resource practices and group norms in the retirement process. *European Psychologist, 14*(13), 193–206. https://doi.org/10.1027/1016-9040.14.3.193

Potočnik, K., Tordera, N., & Peiró, J. M. (2010). The influence of the early retirement process on satisfaction with early retirement and psychological well-being. *International Journal of Aging and Human Development, 70*(3), 251–273. https://doi.org/10.2190/AG.70.3.e

Potočnik, K., Tordera, N., & Peiró, J. M. (2013). Truly satisfied with your retirement or just resigned? Pathways toward different patterns of retirement satisfaction. *Journal of Applied Gerontology, 32*(2) 164–187. https://doi.org/10.1177/0733464811405988

Raabe, B., Frese, M., & Beehr, T. A. (2007). Action regulation theory and career self-management. *Journal of Vocational Behavior, 70*(2), 297–311. https://doi.org/10.1016/j.jvb.2006.10.005

Russell, H., & McGinnity, F. (2014). Under Pressure: The impact of recession on employees in Ireland. *British Journal of Industrial Relations, 52*(2), 286–307. https://doi.org/10.1111/bjir.12018

Ryan, L., Lavelle, J., O'Sullivan, M., McMahon, J., Murphy, C., Turner, T., Gunnigle, P., & O'Brien, M. (2019). Defining and regulating zero hours work: Lessons from a liberal market economy. *Nordic Journal of Working Life Studies, 9,* 75–93. https://doi.org/10.18291/njwls.v9iS6.114692

Schoar, A., & Zuo, L. (2017). Shaped by booms and busts: How the economy impacts CEO careers and management styles. *The Review of Financial Studies, 30*(5), 1425–1456. https://doi.org/10.1093/rfs/hhw111

Schoon, I., & Bynner, J. (2019). Young people and the Great Recession: Variations in the school-to-work transition in Europe and the United States. *Longitudinal and Life Course Studies, 10*(2), 153–173. https://doi.org/10.1332/175795919X15514456677349

Shipp, A. J., Edwards, J. R., Lambert, L. S. (2009). Conceptualization and measurement of temporal focus: The subjective experience of the past, present, and future. *Organizational Behavior and Human Decision Processes, 110*(1), 1–22. https://doi.org/10.1016/j.obhdp.2009.05.001

Smale, A., Bagdadli, S., Cotton, R., Dello Russo, S., Dickmann, M., Dysvik, A., Gianecchini, M., Kaše, R., Lazarova, M., Reichel, A., Rozo, P., & Verbruggen, M. (2019). Proactive career behaviors and subjective career success: The moderating role of national culture. *Journal of Organizational Behavior, 40*(1), 105–122. https://doi.org/10.1002/job.2316

Spreitzer, G. M. (1995). Psychological empowerment in the workplace: Dimensions, measurement, and validation. *Academy of Management Journal, 38*(5), 1442–1465.

Spreitzer, G. M., Cameron, L., & Garrett, L. (2017). Alternative work arrangements: Two images of the new world of work. *Annual Review of Organizational Psychology and Organizational Behavior, 4,* 473–499. https://doi.org/10.1146/annurev-orgpsych-032516-113332

Standing, G. (2017). *The corruption of capitalism: Why rentiers thrive and work does not pay.* Biteback Publishing.

Standing, G. (2018, October). *The precariat: Today's transformative class?* Great Transition Initiative. https://www.greattransition.org/publication/precariat-transformative-class

Strauss, K., Griffin, M. A., & Parker, S. K. (2012). Future work selves: How salient hoped-for identities motivate proactive career behaviors. *Journal of Applied Psychology, 97*(3), 580–598. https://doi.org/10.1037/a0026423

Sylva, H., Mol, S. T., Den Hartog, D. N., & Dorenbosch, L. (2019). Person-job fit and proactive career behavior: A dynamic approach. *European Journal of Work and Organizational Psychology, 28*(5), 631–645. https://doi.org/10.1080/1359432X.2019.1580309

Todoli Signes A., Naji, M. J., & Llorens. J. (2020) *Riesgos laborales específicos del trabajo en plataformas digitales* [Specific occupational risks of digital platforms work]. Osalan.

Tordera, N., Peiró, J. M., Ayala, Y., Villajos, E., & Truxillo, D. (2020). The lagged influence of organizations' human resources practices on employees' career sustainability: The moderating role of age. *Journal of Vocational Behavior, 120,* Article 103444. https://doi.org/10.1016/j.jvb.2020.103444

Triana, M. D. C., Trzebiatowski, T., & Byun, S. Y. (2017). Lowering the threshold for feeling mistreated: Perceived overqualification moderates the effects of perceived age discrimination on job withdrawal and somatic symptoms. *Human Resource Management, 56*(6), 979–994. https://doi.org/10.1002/hrm.21812

Van Doorn, N., Ferrari, F., & Graham, M. (2020). *Migration and migrant labour in the gig economy: An intervention.* SSRN https://doi.org/10.2139/ssrn.3622589

Vanroelen, C., Julià, M., & Aerden, K. V. (2021). Precarious employment: An overlooked determinant of workers' health and well-being? In C. Korunka (Ed.), *Flexible working practices and approaches: Psychosocial and social implications* (pp. 231–255). Springer.

Vara, M. J. (2013). Gender inequality in the Spanish public pension system. *Feminist Economics, 19*(4), 136–159. https://doi.org/10.1080/13545701.2013.822525

Verd, J. M., Barranco, O., & Bolíbar, M. (2019). Youth unemployment and employment trajectories in Spain during the Great Recession: What are the determinants? *Journal for Labour Market Research, 53*(4), 1–20. https://doi.org/10.1186/s12651-019-0254-3

Vosko, L. (2010). *Managing the margins: Gender, citizenship, and the international regulation of precarious employment.* Oxford University Press.

Vuori, J., Toppinen-Tanner, S., & Mutanen, P. (2012). Effects of resource-building group intervention on career management and mental health in work organizations: Randomized controlled field trial. *Journal of Applied Psychology, 97*(2), 273–286. https://doi.org/10.1037/a0025584

Wanberg, C. R., Kanfer, R., Hamann, D. J., & Zhang, Z. (2016). Age and re-employment success after job loss: An integrative model and meta-analysis. *Psychological Bulletin, 142*(4), 400–426. https://doi.org/10.1037/bul0000019

Wassermann, M., Fujishiro, K., & Hoppe, A. (2017). The effect of perceived overqualification on job satisfaction and career satisfaction among immigrants: Does host national identity matter? *International Journal of Intercultural Relations, 61*, 77–87. https://doi.org/10.1016/j.ijintrel.2017.09.001

Wassermann, M., & Hoppe, A. (2019). Perceived overqualification and psychological well-being among immigrants: The moderating role of personal resources. *Journal of Personnel Psychology, 18,* 34–45, https://doi.org/10.1027/1866-5888/a000219

Waters, L., Briscoe, J. P., Hall, D. T., & Wang, L. (2014). Protean career attitudes during unemployment and re-employment: A longitudinal perspective. *Journal of Vocational Behavior, 84*(3), 405–419. https://doi.org/10.1016/j.jvb.2014.03.003

Watson, G. P., Kistler, L. D., Graham, B. A., & Sinclair, R. R. (2021). Looking at the gig picture: Defining gig work and explaining profile differences in gig workers' job demands and resources. *Group & Organization Management, 46*(2), 327–361. https://doi.org/10.1177/1059601121996548

Whelan, N. (2018). *Evaluating the effectiveness and implementation of new employment enhancement programmes in an Irish context: A focus on well-being and employability* [Unpublished PhDl dissertation]. National University of Ireland.

Whoriskey, P. (2017, December 23). 'I hope I can quit working in a few years': A preview of the U.S. without pensions. *The Washington Post.* https://www.washingpost.

com/business/economy/i-hope-i-can-quit-working-in-a-few-years-a-preview-of-the-us-without-pensions/2017/12/22/5cc9fdf6-cf09-11e7-81bc-c55a220c8cbe_story.html

Zacher, H. (2015). Daily manifestations of career adaptability: Relationships with job and career outcomes. *Journal of Vocational Behavior, 91*, 76–86. https://doi.org/10.1016/j.jvb.2015.09.003

Zacher, H., Ambiel, R. A., & Noronha, A. P. P. (2015). Career adaptability and career entrenchment. *Journal of Vocational Behavior, 88,* 164–173. https://doi.org/10.1016/j.jvb.2015.03.006

Zhang, F., Wang, B., Qian, J., & Parker, S. K. (2021). Job crafting towards strengths and job crafting towards interests in overqualified employees: Different outcomes and boundary effects. *Journal of Organizational Behavior, 42*(5), 587–603. https://doi.org/10.1002/job.2517

Zikic, J., & Klehe, U. C. (2021). Going against the grain: The role of skilled migrants' self-regulation in finding quality employment. *Journal of Organizational Behavior, 42*(8), 1023–1041. https://doi.org/10.1002/job.2550

16

CHALLENGES ASSOCIATED WITH REGULATING ZERO HOURS WORK

Jonathan Lavelle, Juliet McMahon, Caroline Murphy, Lorraine Ryan, Michelle O'Sullivan, Mike O'Brien, Patrick Gunnigle, and Thomas Turner.

The purpose of this chapter is to explore the role of the state in the regulation of precarious work, more specifically zero-hour work in Ireland. Zero-hour work is characterized by the non-guarantee of working hours; workers may or may not be required to be available for work, and their working hours are likely to be variable. Zero-hour work is precarious because its outcomes, in the main, include low pay, job insecurity, and very limited social and employment rights protection (Blanchflower et al., 2017; Broughton et al., 2016; Eurofound, 2015). Budd (2020) outlines that work and employment are very complicated subjects and stresses the need for a multidisciplinary approach to the many themes within the field, with precarious work being one of those themes. Precarious work has been a key interest within the field of I/O psychology and has been explored through such lenses as employee wellbeing and job design (Troth & Guest, 2021). However, Allan et al. (2021), whilst acknowledging the contribution of I/O psychology to the study of precarious work, call for greater interdisciplinary research adding that other fields have "important perspectives and expertise… that can complement and extend work and organizational psychology" (p. 9). Advocating for a similar multidisciplinary approach, Troth and Guest (2021) acknowledge the need for I/O psychologists to pay more attention to the external institutional contexts that can influence human resource activities. This chapter addresses that gap by exploring precarious work through an ER lens that draws attention to issues such as workers' collective action (mainly through trade unions) and public policies and institutions (Budd, 2020). Our focus is particularly on the role of the state. Martínez Lucio and MacKenzie (2018) outline that the state is critical to the public regulation and control of the contractual bases of ER. Yet, there is general agreement within the extant literature that there has

DOI: 10.4324/9781003440444-19

been a paucity of attention on the role of the state within ER, with some notable exceptions, including Hyman (2008), Meardi (2014), and Martínez Lucio and MacKenzie (2018). Kalleberg (2018) notes the relations between "the state and markets are central to explanations of differences among employment relations, and hence to variations in the experience of precarious work" (p. 243).

Ireland represents an interesting case with which to examine the relationship between the actions of the state and zero-hour work. Ireland is considered a liberal market economy (Hall & Soskice, 2001) and has a largely liberal welfare regime which differs from other liberal regimes by having higher welfare payments, more investment in active labor-market programs, and less sanctions and conditionality attached to benefits (Murphy, 2016). There have also been considerable indicators of precariousness in the labor market. Drawing on a range of sources, Nugent et al. (2019) estimate that between 31% and 51% of Irish employees are in employment, which is at medium- to high risk of precariousness.

The first section of this chapter sets the scene in terms of the role of the state, both in general terms and more specific to ER. The second section of the chapter focuses on evidence from a large-scale study of precarious work in Ireland. Our focus is on three sectors—health, education, and retail—illustrating the incidence and explanations for the emergence of zero-hour work in Ireland. This section also examines the implications of zero-hour work from a state perspective. The third and final section of the chapter critically examines more recent regulatory responses to regulating zero-hour work in Ireland and other liberal market regimes. In doing so, we analyze the state's response to zero-hour work in Ireland and point to the benefits, challenges, and limitations of legislation in regulating precarious work.

The State

Conceptually, it is very difficult to define what is meant by the state. One way to address this is to draw on assemblage theory (DeLanda, 2006, 2016). Savage (2020) notes that "framing assemblages as relational constructs, comprised of heterogeneous and emergent component parts that are arranged together toward certain strategic ends, in particular spaces and times, scholars have engaged assemblage thinking to make sense of an array of phenomena" (p. 319). An assemblage approach to the state therefore offers an opportunity to look at specific relations within the state (Dittmer, 2020). Often the state is conflated with or understood as the prevailing government of the day: largely because it is the most visible and active of institutions of the state. However, an assemblage approach to the state involves conceptualizing the state as comprising a "…complex of institutions that encompasses the legislature, the executive, the judiciary and the apparatus of central and local government" (Heyes & Clark, 2011, p. 70). The institutions and agencies of the state which have the most relevance for labor markets and industrial relations are the parliament, judiciary, and state agencies particularly dispute resolution bodies.

Understanding the state as an assemblage of institutions and agencies (Dundon et al., 2017) is important as it outlines that the state is not a monolithic actor (Martínez Lucio & MacKenzie, 2018) and thus we need to understand what makes up the state and explore how these institutions and agencies may interact with each other. Given the multitude of institutions and agencies, it cannot be assumed that the various institutions and agencies of the state all act in concert; indeed, we know that the different institutions and agencies may have divergent and competing interests and may act accordingly (Martínez Lucio & MacKenzie, 2018). Martínez Lucio and MacKenzie (2018) summarize that the state may not function in the manner in which it is intended, or even in the manner it espouses, and in terms of its reach and efficacy, the state may not be as omnipotent as sometimes assumed. What is more, the state may govern or regulate for a specific set of interests and enshrine or support the role and activities of certain actors and organizations over the interests of others. The state reflects the balance of power between capital and labor (Wallace et al., 2020). Thus, it is important to understand conceptually the meaning of the state as we separate out "the state" as a unitary abstraction and the state as a collection of institutions organized around various projects and potentially competing agendas (Martínez Lucio & Mackenzie, 2017).

The State and ER

The social relations of production create conflict between labor and capital, and an objective of the state is to provide for an "orderly operation of the employment relationship" (Treuren, 2000, p. 81). State policies in market societies are perennially confronted by the challenge to devise mechanisms and processes to ensure that the needs of labor and capital are mutually compatible, to a degree (Offe, 1984). The state influences ER (and by extension, precarious employment), through a number of paths (cf. Hyman, 2008): the first as an employer, both direct and indirect. The state is generally the largest direct employer in a country but also influences employment indirectly, as many public services such as health and education are provided by private actors. Thus, the state is well positioned to influence the employment relationship both directly and indirectly.

Indeed, the state has traditionally been viewed as a model employer—workers enjoy relatively good pay and terms and conditions of employment, including high levels of job security, job quality, and high levels of unionization. However, this characterization is being challenged, with claims that the state is moving toward a more restricted or "regressive" role as an employer, particularly in the aftermath of the Global Financial Crisis, and the many austerity programs governments have pursued (Hebdon & Kirkpatrick, 2005; Kirkpatrick et al., 2011; Stuart & Martínez Lucio, 2008).

The second way the state influences ER is as a legislator setting the rules of the game. Conventional wisdom is that employers enjoy the balance of power in the employment relationship and therefore the state needs to step in and provide protection for individuals in such a relationship. Thus, the state in effect sets the rules of the game for employers and workers within that employment relationship. In setting those rules of the game, the state may decide to introduce legislation that is collective in orientation (trade union rights and collective bargaining rights) or individual (e.g., protection against unfair dismissals, and for equality, and health and safety). For example, the state will define the status, rights, and obligations of labor market actors regarding compulsory employee representation and employee voice, legal status of collective agreements, resolution of disputes, health and safety, recruitment and selection, and pay and working hours (Hyman, 2008). The degree of legislation and the balance between collective and individual rights and obligations are dependent on the government. A key issue relates to the efficacy of the legislation.

The third way the state can influence ER is as a macroeconomic manager. Whilst this is a very broad role, the fiscal and monetary policies of a state can influence ER. For example, policies addressing issues such as price stability, full employment, economic growth (monetary policy), and taxation and spending (fiscal policy) can influence ER. This includes impacting the balance of power between capital and labor within the labor market and trade union membership.

A fourth way is through the provision of state welfare. The state also has a role in protecting citizens from over dependence on employers for survival. To protect against the commodification of labor, the state can provide a range of institutional supports. How the state protects workers via the welfare system may differ. For example, these protections may be provided by the state or private actors regulated by public policies. These welfare systems also differ in terms of their generosity, with some systems being more generous to citizens than others.

Given the number of ways that the state can influence ER, there are infinite possible permutations of the ways in which the state, directly or indirectly, shapes ER, and more specifically precarious work. For example, as a direct and indirect employer, the state can influence the use of precarious work. By reducing its role as employer, it has been argued that state policies of deregulation, privatization, and outsourcing have been a driver of precarious jobs (Carré et al., 2012; Kalleberg, 2012; Prosser, 2016). As a legislator, the state can set the coverage, scope, "exit options," enforcement, and interactions with other labor market institutions (Appelbaum & Schmitt, 2009; Prosser, 2016) around precarious work. The state can also influence the generosity of the welfare systems, and how that system interacts with employment institutions and policies. An assemblage approach to the study of the state provides a framework for analyzing the relationship between politics and economics (Dittmer, 2020).

Changing Role of the State

Forde and Slater (2016) argue that the role of the state is changing, a change driven by politics, economics, and dominant ideologies. Trends such as increased globalization, neoliberalism, and economic crises have been offered as potential reasons for a lesser role for the state (Martínez Lucio & MacKenzie, 2018). For example, as levels of globalization increases, the nation state is said to be withering away, creating a borderless world (Ohmae, 1995). Neoliberalism, sometimes referred to as market fundamentalism, is, according to Hopewell (2017), "…an ideology and policy paradigm, directed at reducing the role of the state in the economy by liberalizing trade and capital flows, privatizing state-owned enterprises, lowering taxes and public spending, and freeing business from government regulation" (p. 571). Neoliberal ideology advocates that free markets and little regulation are the best way to regulate both economic organization and human welfare. However, more recent critical thinking suggests that state intervention is a key characteristic of neoliberalism, in contrast to classical liberalism (Berry, 2022). The recent Global Financial Crisis (2008/2009) also witnessed many states implementing austerity programs with a reduced role for state intervention.

Opposite this are arguments that the role of the state has become even more important. For example, Heyes and Nolan (2010) argue that the state is extending its role in the regulation of work and employment. Post-2008 Global Financial crisis, Heyes and Clark (2011) point to a range of state initiatives designed to protect workers in the labor market, including policies to keep people in jobs; support the creation of new jobs; and increase unemployment benefits, activation measures, and targeted training programs. More recently, the COVID-19 pandemic has illustrated the necessity and importance of state intervention (Berry, 2022). Responding to the public health crisis in Ireland, the Irish Government announced a series of initiatives, including lockdowns to curb the spread of the virus. In order to support and protect affected workers and businesses during this period, a range of supports were introduced. For example, the Irish Government introduced a wage-subsidy scheme to support employers to continue to pay their employees during the pandemic. The first scheme was called the Temporary Wage Subsidy Scheme, which was then replaced by the Employment Wage Subsidy Scheme. A new Pandemic Unemployment Payment was also introduced to support employees and the self-employed who had lost their job (or in the case of self-employed ceased trading temporarily) due to the COVID-19 restrictions. Furthermore, other support initiatives such as loans, loan guarantees, and grants for small businesses were introduced, demonstrating how state intervention can be used to support workers, businesses, and the economy.

Forde and Slater (2016) similarly agree that the state is far from retreating, however, their summary of state intervention has a different orientation, characterizing recent state involvement as involving "market-orientated" approaches to the regulation of labor markets, underpinned by neoliberal ideology (Gamble & Kahn, 1998; Howell, 2006), for example, encouragement of more "individualized" employment contracts over collective agreements, or the amelioration of some negative consequences of flexibility through new rights and regulations (Gamble, 2010; MacKenzie & Martínez Lucio, 2014; Martínez Lucio & Stuart, 2011). Exploring this theme further, Howell (2021) identifies four categories of state roles in the regulation of class relations in what he terms the "neoliberal era." The first role is a market-making one, whereby the state intervenes in dismantling the old regulatory institutions and constructing new regulatory institutions appropriate to emerging growth models. A second major role of the state is to offer a modest level of protection and compensation to workers, but to do so in ways that still permit the liberalization of labor markets. The third state role in the neoliberal era has been to facilitate austerity, and to liberalize labor markets and ER through the use of a new type of social pact with the intention to legitimize and enable austerity and deregulation. The fourth role of the state involves embedding and naturalizing market behavior and disciplining and removing alternatives to it. Howell (2021) uses the example of precarious work as an illustration of these new roles of the state in a neoliberal era. For example, once precarious work becomes pervasive, it produces new demands for social protection (the flip side of flexicurity), for management of an underemployed labor force, and for disciplining the behavior of precarious workers themselves (Howell, 2021).

In summary, the state is a key actor within ER and through its assemblage of institutions and agencies can significantly impact the growth and regulation of precarious employment. In the next section, we draw on our empirical investigation of precarious work in Ireland, with a particular focus on the role of the state.

Zero-Hour Work in Ireland: An Empirical Investigation

In this section, we explore the development and regulation of zero-hour work in Ireland, with a particular focus on the role of the state, and also trade unions as representatives of the labor movement. In our empirical investigation, we found zero-hour work reflected in three different contract types:

1 Zero-hour contracts whereby an employee does not have guaranteed hours of work and is required to be available for work.
2 "If and when" contracts whereby an employee does not have guaranteed hours of work and is not required to be available for work.
3 Hybrid part-time/if and when contracts which is a hybrid of a part-time contract and an if and when contract with some guaranteed and some non-guaranteed hours.

Our analysis focused on three sectors: health, education, and retail. It involved in-depth interviews with key stakeholders, including employee representatives and employer representatives, as well as government agencies and departments, and was undertaken in 2015. The interviews (lasting 40–90 minutes on average) focused on gaining a greater understanding of workforce demographic characteristics, skill levels, working arrangements, and the extent of union power and influence in each sector. The qualitative data was supplemented with documentary evidence provided by stakeholders, such as examples of contracts and collective agreements. Furthermore, we drew on secondary documentary analysis of key reports, legislative developments, and media reports from "Industrial Relations News," a weekly periodical with information on collective agreements which has been used as a reliable source of information on industrial relations developments (Roche & Gormley, 2017).

Health Sector

The health and social care sector employs over a quarter of a million people in Ireland. The single largest employer is the Health Service Executive (HSE). In fact, the HSE is the largest employer in the state, with more than 67,000 direct employees, and a further 35,000 employed by agencies funded by the HSE (2022). As such, conditions of employment in the public health service act as a barometer for the performance of the state as an employer more broadly. The health sector has experienced significant changes over the last two decades, including the restructuring of local health boards to form the national-level HSE, new strategies for primary care delivery, increased regulation and inspection of care through the Health Information and Quality Authority (HIQA), and the introduction of the new funding arrangements for long-term residential care. The related employment consequences included employee pay cuts and productivity reforms under public service agreements reached after the onset of the Global Financial Crisis. Interviewees referred to the public-sector moratorium on recruitment which was put in place amid austerity policies and cuts to public spending during the financial crisis, along with the increase in community-care provision and increased subcontracting of community-care services by the HSE, as key drivers in the use of precarious "if and when" contracts and low-hour contracts in the sector.

Although the recruitment moratorium has since been lifted, certain sectors such as home care continue to see a rise in private-sector provision over direct state provision (Murphy & O'Sullivan, 2021). Zero-hour-type work emerged in the health service despite the fact that the health sector in the main is heavily unionized, although organizing lower level occupations continues to be challenging for unions (Murphy & O'Sullivan, 2021). Furthermore, the re-introduction of recruitment moratoriums in the public sector in the future cannot be ruled out (McConnell, 2020).

The ability of the unions to negotiate an agreement with the HSE largely stems from institutional conditions of high union membership rates, and a history of collective bargaining in the wider health sector. However, these features are largely absent in the private and not-for-profit sectors of healthcare, which are now the dominant providers of many forms of care services. In 2011, an agreement was concluded between the HSE and two of the largest unions (the largest general Services Industrial Professional and Technical Union [SIPTU] and the Irish Nurses and Midwives Organization) which stipulated that "if and when" contracts would only be used to provide short-term cover such as annual leave. While the agreement curtailed the potential growth in such contracts in HSE-operated establishments, among HSE-funded organizations a greater prevalence of "if and when" contracts was found. Despite legislation introduced in 2018 also curtailing the use of "if and when" contracts (discussed in more detail later in this chapter), it was suggested by interest groups in the home-care sector that the tendering process allows for the creation of casual contracts, since workers are not paid for contracted hours if their clients are admitted to hospital or go on holiday (Rogan, 2022).

Community care services are provided through a mix of public-sector provision, private agencies, and nonprofit organizations that receive public funding, referred to as "Section 39 agencies" (so-called because Section 39 of the Health Act 2004 allows the statutory health agency—HSE—to fund organizations to provide health and care services). The latter group is significant in size with approximately 1,900 such agencies, primarily in older people's care and disability/long-term care. Traditionally, these agencies received substantial funds from the HSE through a grant-based system; however, in the past decade or so this has changed to predominantly competitive tendering processes (McInerney & Finn, 2015; Mercille & O'Neill, 2021). The relationship between the state and nonprofit organizations has been described by one such organization as based on "command and control" principles and characterized by managerialism, a value-for-money ethos, accountability, compliance, and regulation (Rehab Group, 2018). This has resulted in the agencies themselves (both nonprofit and private profit making) increasing the use of flexible contracts. The effects of this on (the predominantly female) employees is financial precarity, lack of adequate notice of working hours, a lack of perceived fairness in the distribution of work, and difficulties in accessing state income supports (Murphy et al., 2019; Murphy & O'Sullivan, 2021).

The impact of the agreements made between unions and the HSE has been curtailed due to an increasing use of outsourcing and agency work in the sector. While agency work is low nationally (at less than 2% of employees), analysis of quarterly national household data from 2014 revealed that more than half of all agency workers are in the health sector. The HSE noted that agency work was necessary to fulfill staffing requirements, while the public-sector moratorium was in place. Agencies typically supply staff for a range of roles, including doctors, nurses, and healthcare assistants. The unions have expressed concern over the use of agency work in health because of the financial costs incurred by the state, and because of the lack of direct full-time positions being created.

While new regulations introduced in 2018 to curtail the use of "if and when" contracts may have been effective in improving the job security of many workers, the use of precarious contracts still remains a feature in the health sector. This was evidenced at the peak of the COVID-19 pandemic when the HSE recruited for 500 contact-tracing roles. The initial contracts stated that the workers were not guaranteed hours, would not be entitled to sick pay, and would not be protected under the Unfair Dismissal Act (Carswell, 2020). The HSE later claimed that the contracts were issued in error by a recruitment company and issued an amendment letter clarifying that the contact tracers would be offered contracts for working 37 hours a week for an 11-month period (Carswell, 2020). However, the debacle demonstrates the extent to which precarity becomes embedded in the system as the state's active role as a direct employer becomes eroded through the use of agencies and outsourced services.

Education Sector

Grummell and Lynch (2016) emphasize that successive Irish governments have attempted to change public services (health and education in particular) toward a marketable services model. The Irish education system comprises primary and secondary education, and tertiary and further education, governed by the Department of Education and Skills and the Higher Education Authority, respectively. Much like health, the sector is heavily unionized and ER within the sector are regulated both by legislation and collective agreements between government, employer bodies, and unions. Interviewees from across various parts of the education sector argued in 2015 that the resourcing model used by the state had increased precarious work in the sector. This translates into some occupations in secondary education not being funded as full-time jobs, and instead employees are more likely to have low hours and "if and when" hours. At tertiary institutions, a similar trend was evident, with some institutions claiming that the delivery of a wide range of programs was predicated on "flexible" employment contracts due to fluctuating demand and funding. Funding was seen as a key driver of "if and when" work, affecting the employment conditions and hours of teachers (particularly newly qualified), third-level lecturers, special needs assistants, adult education tutors, and ancillary staff (secretaries, caretakers, and cleaners).

Within the school setting, unions argued strongly that full-time work should be the "norm" and alternative arrangements should be exceptional. They were successful to an extent in this with the use of "if and when" contracts generally being regulated and restricted to covering leave arrangements. Teachers are under no obligation to accept hours offered and refusal generally does not rule them out of being offered hours again in the future. However, regular part-time contracts were used particularly at secondary level where a full teaching post (based on 22 hours per week) was not available. Schools must offer increased hours to an existing teacher with "less than full hours" before they can advertise for additional staff. At the time the research was conducted, interviewees reported a growing trend of teachers working in multiple schools to increase their hours. The Teacher Unions of Ireland (TUI) made reference to a growing trend of the fragmentation of hours, with hours being given to multiple teachers rather than one person. They believed this had the effect of creating competition among individuals. The vast majority of ancillary staff are employed via grant funding rather than the Department of Education and Skills; therefore, terms and conditions are effectively developed at local level between such staff and the school. It was common for ancillary staff to be employed on a hybrid "if and when" basis.

At tertiary level, employers stressed that the only way to meet diverse skill demands was through "atypical" employment arrangements. Furthermore, at tertiary level, where no teaching ratios exist, the Employment Control Framework (a policy document on employment numbers and terms and conditions of employment issued by the government to public-sector organizations) has led to an increase in hourly paid contracts. A report from Cush (2016) estimated that three quarters of lecturing staff in institutes of technology were permanent and full-time if they lectured on "core" state-funded programs mostly for daytime students. The Institutes of Technology Ireland (IoTI) stated that "zero-hour contracts" are not a feature in the sector, but there are two types of arrangements—a pro rata contract, and an hourly paid assistant lecturer (HPAL) contract. The unions argue that the number of people employed as hourly- paid assistant lecturers (HPALS) is growing and that little progress has been made on commitments for the phased conversion of HPALS to pro rata assistant lecturers. The significant concern expressed by unions in regard to HPALS is that they only get paid for time teaching and not for preparatory work. According to unions, they do not enjoy such benefits as annual leave, sick leave, or overtime pay, and they have no access to an incremental scale or pension. The IoTI acknowledged that the HPAL contract is underdeveloped but argued that the rationale for the difference between HPAL and pro rata contracts is that people on the pro rata contracts are expected to perform the full range of duties of a lecturer, whereas the HPALS do not. This, however, was contested by the trade unions. Whilst the Employment Control Framework was in place only from 2011 to 2014, the Irish

Government has not ruled out the re-introduction of such a framework in the future (McConnell, 2020).

Mercille and Murphy (2017) argue that the restructuring in the education sector has been shaped by forces originating from the European Union (EU) and global institutions, as well as the interests of Irish political and economic elites. Piasna and Myant (2017) emphasize that the Country-Specific Recommendations made by the European Commission to Member States (and particularly those termed Programme Countries, receiving aid with debt crises; Ireland being one) were to reduce employment protection, resulting in a reduction in the scope and effectiveness of collective bargaining. While trade unions and government did agree a number of pay and productivity deals (Croke Park and Haddington Road agreements), the scope of these agreements focused on those directly employed before the onset of the crisis, arguably allowing for a deterioration of job quality for new entrants and limiting the scope of protection for those indirectly employed. As evidenced in the health and education sectors, the Irish state as an employer allowed for a demonstrable deterioration in job quality in two of the sectors where it is the single largest employer. Without the state as guardian of employment conditions, an amelioration of conditions in the private sector is less likely, as we examine in the next section through a review of retail employment.

The Retail Sector

Outside of its role as an employer, there are a number of institutions and functions of the state that interact with employers, employees, and their employment relationships in the private sector. Here we examine the retail sector as one of the most significant private-sector employers in Ireland and a sector that has been considerably impacted by precarious work in recent years (Broughton et al., 2016). The Irish retail sector is the largest private-sector employer in Ireland, directly employing more than 300,000 people. It employs people in every region in the country, where its share of employment typically ranges from 12% to 15.5% (Central Statistics Office [CSO], 2022; Retail Ireland, 2022). Employment in the sector is predominantly female, with different forms of nonstandard work, including part-time work, low-hour work, and "if and when" contracts forming a key feature of employment within the sector. Numerous changes have occurred over the past number of years, however, that have accelerated employers' demands for ever-increasing levels of flexibility, particularly in relation to hours of work. Changing customer-spending patterns, increased competition, demographic changes, and technological advances have led to longer opening hours and increases in evening and weekend work.

Business groups such as the Irish Business and Employers Confederation (IBEC) and the National Recruitment Federation highlighted in interviews the need for flexibility for employers to operate within these changing patterns of consumer demand. Interviewees representing IBEC noted the importance for businesses to be able to "flex up and down" and to manage that flexibility and "be able to roster people more flexibly because it is a business demand." These demands for such high levels of flexibility have had significant implications for employment practices within the sector, leading to increasing numbers of "if and when" contracts, as well as a considerable shift toward nonstandard hours. However, the trade union Mandate, which represents over 40,000 workers across Ireland, has contested any justifications for the extent of non-guaranteed hours in the sector. It has claimed that there is no business need for "complete open-ended" flexibility, and that modern technology allows much more predictability in relation to customer-spending habits. Interviewees from Mandate argued that predictable customer-spending habits should enable predictable staffing requirements and thus more predictable hours for workers. Many workers in the sector are employed on hybrid "if and when" contracts that guarantee them 15 hours per week with any additional hours (possibly up to 40) scheduled as and when required by the employer, causing considerable difficulties for workers in terms of unpredictability and the inability to plan for financially and for childcare, and other needs (see O'Sullivan et al., 2019).

Both business and trade-union representatives from the sector noted in interviews that employees on full-time contracts tend to be those on older contracts who have long service. As these employees exit the sector, their replacements are not being employed on similar full-time contracts. Mandate has highlighted the declining possibilities for career progression and stability in retail jobs. It noted that despite retail not being a high-paying sector, in the past it was possible for workers to develop a career by progressing through service scales and supplementing income with overtime. However, the consequences of increased use of low hours, "if and when," and hybrid contracts are that for many, according to Mandate, retail jobs mean a lack of career prospects, poverty and welfare traps, and possibly underemployment. This occurs where workers are available and willing to work more hours, but hours are not available, or employers choose to allocate hours across larger numbers of employees rather than increasing hours of existing employees (O'Sullivan et al., 2019).

Implications for the State

The implications for the state of increased levels of "if and when" contracts, and other forms of precarious work within the retail sector, are numerous. Firstly, the industrial relations machinery of the state is employed to resolve industrial disputes that arise relating to these issues. A recent case in point was a long running dispute between the Mandate trade union and one of the largest retailers in the country, Dunnes Stores. The key issues raised by the union included the introduction of a minimum weekly hours threshold, a review of the number of pay scales/pay rates, a review of the use of temporary contracts, and wage increases and representation rights for union members (Prendergast, 2015). While the Labour Court recommended the company meet with the union to resolve the issues in dispute, the refusal of the company to engage in talks resulted in a ballot for industrial action and a one-day strike by up to 6,000 workers. Despite historically high levels of union membership in Dunnes, the company has consistently refused to recognize the trade union or engage in collective bargaining. In Ireland, while there is a constitutional right of association (Constitution Article 40.6.1), there is no right to trade-union recognition and employers are free to recognize a trade union or not. In the absence of effective collective bargaining, the union resorts to use of the state's dispute resolution institutions. Thus, the state intervenes to resolve employment-relations issues in the private sector through recommendations from the Labour Court, often with the employer refusing to attend such hearings, given the voluntarist nature of industrial relations in Ireland (see Wallace et al., 2020).

A second implication for the state stems from the extensive public and political support for workers during disputes and campaigns to improve workers' terms and conditions of employment. Such campaigns have included calls for decent work, elimination of precarious hourly employment, and demands for a living wage. Employee representatives and other advocacy groups have increasingly been campaigning for intervention from the state in its role as regulator to improve regulations around working hours, terms and conditions of employment, and collective bargaining rights. It has been argued that the actions of the state have created a weak regulatory environment that has facilitated the emergence of zero-hour work (see O'Sullivan et al., 2017).

One positive development in the sector has been the implementation of banded-hours agreements. Banded hours provide an element of certainty for workers by placing each employee within a set guaranteed "band" of hours, e.g., 15–19 hours. A review takes places on an annual basis, and if any employee continuously works above the band they are in, they are automatically lifted into the next band (i.e., the higher number of hours that they have actually been working now determines their new guaranteed band). Banded-hours agreements were voluntarily negotiated between Mandate and some retailers over the past number of years. However, rights to banded hours became formalized with the introduction of the Employment (Miscellaneous Provisions) Act 2018 following lengthy campaigns by trade unions and other advocacy groups. Thus, we see evidence of the importance of the state's role in tackling precarious work in the retail sector as a regulator and provider of employment rights as well as a provider of dispute resolution institutions.

A third and important implication for the state that results from the rise in precarious employment relates to the social-welfare support it provides to supplement the income of low-paid workers. The link between social welfare and low-hour work is an important factor when considering the interaction between the state and both public- and private-sector employment. The welfare system in Ireland provides financial and other supports to workers who earn below specified minimum-income-threshold levels. The low pay that is often associated with precarious or low-hour work is a concern for government and policy makers given that workers in such jobs often cannot earn a living wage, particularly those who have a family to support. Thus, such workers are compelled to supplement their income through social-welfare payments, although they may often be available and willing to work more hours.

During our research, the Department of Social Protection highlighted the rising cost to the state of such supports, particularly the Working Family Payment (WFP)—previously called Family Income Supplement (FIS). The WFP is a weekly tax-free payment to families at work on low pay. To qualify, an employee must be in a paid job expected to last at least three months, work at least 19-hour work per week (or 38 per fortnight), have at least one child and earn under specific income thresholds. Some employer organizations have argued that providing "if and when" hours and low-hour jobs saves the state money because organizations are employing people that would otherwise be fully unemployed and require larger social-welfare support. Alternatively, trade unions and NGOs have maintained that the state is subsidizing poor employment through the WFP and other welfare supports and compensating for the increasing erosion of pay and hours (see O'Sullivan et al., 2015). In interviews, the Department of Social Protection noted that 70% of those on WFP (FIS at the time) were working in the retail sector and commented that many recipients of WFP are lone parents. The large size of the industry offers some explanation for the high levels of WFP receipt, but it nonetheless gives an indication that many retail employees are reliant on the state to subsidize their earnings. This would indicate that many working in the retail sector are reliant on their job as a family income (or part of a family income).

The Department of Social Protection noted in interviews that the goal of social-welfare employment supports is to help to get people out of low-hour work, and that employment should be sustainable in the long term. However, the trade union Mandate has argued that many retail workers become trapped in low-paid jobs and reliant on welfare supports. It is not simply the number of hours of work that is important to consider when examining the links between precarious work and social welfare supports. The scheduling of hours is also a critical consideration with many workers trying to balance the number of hours they work across the week to ensure eligibility for welfare supports. Workers who work too many hours run the risk of exceeding the limit of eligibility for welfare supports such as WFP. As well as the financial implications, trade unions and advocacy groups have argued that such situations cause significant mental and emotional strain for workers as they must continuously balance their hours of work with their eligibility for welfare supports. It has also been argued by trade unions during our research that the interaction between hours of work and eligibility for welfare supports gives significant control to employers. This is because employees must rely on their employer to schedule their working hours in a way that does not interfere with their capacity to maximize their combined work and welfare earnings.

This section has examined the role of the state as an employer, as a provider of third-party dispute-resolution institutions, a regulator, and a provider of welfare support for low-paid workers. Each of these functions interacts with each other and is also shaped by the historical actions of the state and the broader political, employment, and economic environment. In the next section, we critically evaluate the actions of the state as a regulator of zero-hour work to date and highlight the remaining regulatory gaps.

Contemporary Developments in the Regulation of Precarious Work

The regulation of zero-hour work has come under political and public scrutiny in many countries globally in recent years and has engendered widespread debate within the broader narrative of precarious versus decent work (Adams & Prassl, 2018; Kalleberg, 2012; Rubery & Grimshaw, 2016; Vosko, 2010). Those who oppose regulation highlight the competitive imperative for flexibility of labor, and that such work suits many people. However, as stated earlier, many other commentators highlight the potential for exploitation of vulnerable workers and the consequent threat such fragmented work can pose to the human and citizenship rights of individuals. Ireland has often been cited as a state that was early and proactive in enacting legislation to limit the use of such contracts, with specific limitations on zero-hour contracts in existence since 1997 (Section 18 of the Organization of Working Time Act 1997). The 1997 Act contained compensatory rules for zero-hour employees who were required to be available for a specific job/shift but for whatever reason the work did not subsequently materialize.[1] However, over time the decisions in a number of cases resulted in the emergence of an Irish jurisprudence which generally held that the wording of the original 1997 Act only offered protection and compensation to zero-hour "employees," i.e., those people with contracts of employment. This occurred due to the wording of Section 18 which stated: "This section applies to an employee whose *contract of employment* operates to require the employee to make himself or herself available to work for the employer in a week." Section 18 also explicitly excluded those whose work was of a "casual nature."

Ireland has to all intents and purposes a binary employment-status legal regime. Those who are employees and employed under a contract of service are protected by the full swathe of employment law. Those who are not deemed to be employees are virtually unprotected. Thus, the legal effect of the Section 18 clause, as illustrated in a number of cases,[2] was that workers who could not prove the existence of an employment contract were excluded both from Section 18 and most other legislative protections.[3] One problem identified was that the Organisation of Working Time Act did not define "casual" and the interpretation in Irish Courts has been that a "casual worker" is not an employee. Research conducted in Ireland (O'Sullivan et al., 2015) found that while there was virtually no evidence of people being employed on zero-hour contracts, there was more widespread use of casually constructed arrangements, which in effect sidestepped the provisions of the Act and allowed for zero-hour work to be utilized by employers without penalty.

In 2018, following political and public pressure, new legislation was enacted.[4] This was hailed by the Government of the time as "banning zero hours contracts except in very limited circumstances" (O'Halloran, 2018), and "one of the most significant changes to working conditions in a generation" (O'Fátharta, 2018) which "crucially, will improve the security and predictability of working hours for employees on insecure contracts and those working variable hours" (O'Fátharta, 2018).

The Act has two key provisions in relation to zero- and variable-hour work. Firstly, there is a provision covering those people employed on low-hour contracts, i.e., where only a low number of hours (e.g., ten hours a week) are contractually guaranteed, but the employee may regularly work a greater number of non-guaranteed hours. This "banded hours" provision (Section 18A) identifies a series of 8 bands of hours (e.g. 6–11, 11–16, etc.). It has introduced an entitlement for zero-hour/low-hour employees to be placed into a higher band of hours where they can show that the hours they have been contracted for do not reflect the hours they actually work (within a reference period of 12 months from commencement of employment). The second provision has substantially increased the compensation owed to zero-hour employees when they are required to be available, but the work does not accrue. In such a situation, employees will be entitled to compensation of 15 hours pay, or 25% of the hours they had expected to work, whichever is the lesser. This provision was available under pre-existing legislation (Section 18 of the Organisation of Working Time Act, 1997) but the 2018 Act increases the rate of compensation to three times the rate of the national minimum wage (or three times the minimum hourly rate of remuneration established by an employment regulation order).

What has been the effect of the legislation? The effect of the banded-hours provision has not been widely tested in the Irish tribunals and courts system as of yet, but the few cases that have been heard have had positive outcomes for the employees concerned.[5] Thus, tentatively, it could be surmised that this provision seems to have more efficacy for those employees on low-hour contracts of employment. With respect to the zero-hour provision, sadly for those workers employed on a casual "if and when" basis, where there is no clear evidence of a contract of employment, not much has changed. Section 18 dealing with zero-hour work continues to utilize the term "employee" and exclude work of a casual nature from its ambit. Thus, while compensation for zero-hour employees may be enhanced, there is no rational or legal imperative for any employer to issue a zero-hour contract of employment when they can simply engage people on a zero-hour basis by inserting nonmutuality clauses within engagement agreements. Thus, this piece of legislation arguably does not address the prevalence of zero-hour work vis-à-vis "if and when" contracts and represents very little change from the previous piece of legislation (Organization of Working Time Act, 1997). Indeed, it could be argued that the increased compensation for zero-hour employees would cause employers to further shy away from considering contracts of employment. Thus, this provision of the Act could incentivize the use of precarious work arrangements rather than limit their use. This is a concern in sectors such as retail and hospitality, where, as we have noted above, there is a trend of replacing full-time contracts with more casual-type contracts.

The outcomes of cases heard since the introduction of the 2018 Act have demonstrated that employment status or the delineation between employee and nonemployee continues to be problematic for workers.[6] As the research outlined in this chapter illustrates, this issue affects workers across a range of sectors in the Irish context. Platform workers, an increasing cohort globally, are also impacted by the issue of employment status (De Stefano et al., 2021; Mangan, 2020). The situation is compounded by the fact that while workers are entitled to challenge their ascribed employment status through the courts, such challenges can be costly, and lengthy, and thus prohibitive for workers. Furthermore, as research worldwide illustrates (Barnard & Ludlow, 2016; Campbell et al., 2019; Vosko et al., 2019) many workers engaged on this basis can be vulnerable (migrants, younger workers, and lower skilled), lack access to support networks, face language barriers, and/or fear retribution.

In Ireland, as in many other countries, the question of the efficacy of labor law in protecting new and emerging forms of work has been the subject of discussion and reflection (Collins, 2018; Freedland, 2013; Keane, 2014). Much of this debate centers around the issue of status, given that this is the fulcrum around which access to rights revolves, and which is emerging as highly problematic for workers (alongside platform, gig, and zero-hour work). Legal experts have suggested such developments as redefining the law around the statutory definition of the "worker" (such as that in the UK) or a contract to perform work personally (Freedland & Contouris, 2011). Others have highlighted the possibility of a continuing relationship over time (Keane, 2014) giving rise to a contract of employment. Other authors call for the emphasis on subordination inherent in the classification of an employee-employer relationship to be amended (Perulli, 2020). Up to recently, however, and especially in neoliberal regimes, there seems to have been a reluctance on the part of the state to interfere in the operation of the free market, thus resulting in either no legislation or relatively low-impact legislation. In Ireland, for instance, when the 2018 Act was at bill stage and being debated in the Irish Parliament (Dail Eireann) and upper House (Seanad), there were attempts to introduce robust provisions that would deal with "bogus self-employment," and provisions that would introduce a statutory provision for the hardening of continuing work and reasonable expectation into a contract for casual-type workers. These propositions were rejected in favor of the provision outlined above.

However, the emergence of a human-rights perspective in relation to work quality (Bellace, 2011) and increased awareness around negative impacts of the proliferation of precarious work has been gaining traction worldwide (Campbell & Burgess, 2018; Kalleberg & Vallas, 2018, Rubery et al., 2018). This has been prompted to some extent by increased commentary on the negative impact of such work, not just in the general working community but its specific impact on black and ethnic minorities in the US and the UK, the impact on women, people with disabilities, migrants, young people, and other minority groups who are particularly vulnerable and at risk of poverty and exclusion. In 2020, an International Labor Organization committee of experts indicated that countries should potentially reconsider the criteria to determine the existence of an employment contract and move to placing the emphasis on the employer to prove that a contract did not exist, rather than placing the burden of proof on the worker (De Stefano et al., 2021) who is recognized as being in a position of unequal power (Davidov, 2011; Kahn-Freund, 1977).

Interestingly, this approach has already been utilized in that most liberal of regimes, the US, with the rise and codification into law in some states of the "ABC" test, whereby employers have to prove that a contract of employment does not exist in situations of dispute. The test is now being considered for enactment at federal level. However, this is set against a backdrop where the power of employers is being demonstrated in terms of their ability to utilize huge financial resources and political connections to influence public perceptions and resist any perceived interference in the status quo. One example is the recent situation in California whereby Uber, Lyft, and similar companies spent more than $200 million successfully persuading Californian voters in 2020 to support a ballot they wrote, which provides that app-based transportation and delivery drivers are classified as independent contractors. This was done as a counter reaction to the codification into law of the ABC test in that state. The result was Proposition 22 that effectively excluded Uber and Lyft drivers from coverage by the relevant statute.

Future Research

States are not monolithic actors, but rather it is best to conceptualize them as assemblages of institutions and agencies (Dundon et al., 2017). Yet very little research has explored the interactions of these various institutions and agencies within the field of ER/human resource management (HRM)/I/O psychology. Research tends to focus on these institutions and agencies as stand-alone entities rather than exploring their interactions with each other (Jyoti & Arora, Chapter 6; Saner & Saner, Chapter 5; Searle & McWha-Hermann, Chapter 4). Examining how a state's various institutions and agencies interact and influence outcomes, actions, and policies of the state and thus acquiring greater understanding of these interactions can help better inform outcomes for issues like precarious work. Above state level, supra-national organizations such as the EU are also important in impacting precarious work. In particular, research and analysis on actions by the EU, e.g., enacting legislation such as the Directive on Transparent and Predictable Working Conditions and economic and social policies, e.g., European Pillar of Social Rights, would help explore how supra-national organizations might regulate precarious work. Focusing on such institutions and agencies through a political-economic lens would support the interdisciplinarity of research on precarious work (Allan et al., 2021).

The role of the other key actors within ER—organizations, employer associations, and trade unions—and their influence on precarious work are also worthy of future research. For example, we need greater understanding of why organizations may or may not offer such precarious work. What are the benefits and challenges for organizations—do these differ depending on sector or organizational size? What internal and external influences impact organizational decision-making around the provision of precarious work? Have organizations considered the implications of such precarious work on their workers/employees and the organization? If so, what types of factors influenced this analysis? From a trade-union perspective, a key challenge is how to best represent labor in preventing precarious work. For example, what strategies and where best to target those strategies are key questions for trade unions. Finally, a key stakeholder in this is the worker—we need further research to explore the impact of precarious work on workers from a range of different perspectives (e.g., income, employment rights, and health and wellbeing). This research could draw on a range of different disciplines and theoretical frameworks to give us a much clearer understanding of the impact of such work. In particular, we need a greater focus on vulnerable groups as the voice of these groups is rarely captured (Jyoti & Arora, Chapter 6; Saxena & Tchangneno, Chapter 11; Searle & Mcwha-Hermann, Chapter 4).

A final area for further research draws on a concept which is the subject of a strong public campaign by the Living Wage Foundation in the UK which is focused on "living hours." Living hours, which sits alongside a living wage (Intraprasert et al., Chapter 9; Meyer & Maleka, Chapter 7; Teng-Calleja et al., Chapter 8), focuses on providing workers with enough hours to earn a decent standard of living—another element in responding to precarious work. The concept includes decent notice periods, contracts of employment, and a minimum number of hours per week (https://www.livingwage.org.uk/living-hours). Whilst many of these ideas have featured as policy responses to precarious work, further exploration of such initiatives, in particular their success, would help develop our understanding and response to precarious work.

Conclusion

Adopting an employment-relations lens, this chapter has focused on the role of the state in the development and regulation of precarious work, drawing on empirical work across health, education, and retail. Using assemblage theory to understand the role of the state, it illustrates how assemblages work in terms of how policy impacts with other parts of the assemblage, how policy may not have the desired effect, and the continuous movement and development of the different parts. The roles of the state as a direct and indirect employer, a legislator, economic manager, and provider of social welfare interact to create an environment that may facilitate, but also limit, the growth of precarious work.

In particular, the chapter has highlighted the use of state intervention via legislation to regulate precarious work, and the associated challenges and limitations with such regulation. The chapter has also demonstrated the role that trade unions may play in protecting workers from precarious work. Our empirical evidence provides examples where trade unions have secured agreements that prevent precarious work, such as in education whereby any new hours must be offered to existing teachers, which prevents the splitting of working hours among multiple people. Thus, stronger trade union and collective bargaining rights would appear to be one solution to stem the growth of precarious work and protect workers.

However, action by trade unions on their own may not be enough. There is also a role for employers and management. As key actors within the employment relationship, their decisions around the types of jobs they create impact on levels of precariousness. Benefits of precarious employment from an employer's perspective are often presented in the form of greater flexibility and reduced costs (Adams & Prassl, 2018). However, noted downsides for employers include lack of worker availability, loyalty, and retention; higher training costs and lower staff morale; and loss of trust and productivity (Adams & Prassl, 2018). Wiengarten et al.'s (2021) empirical analysis shows little benefits to employers of adopting precarious employment; indeed organizations really only benefit from low levels of adoption of precarious work.

The chapter illustrates how the wider institutional context can influence human-resource policies and practices within organizations and, in particular, precarious work. Whilst I/O psychologists' focus on precarious work has been on issues such as wellbeing and work design, there is a need for a stronger focus on context, which significantly influences the emergence of either decent or precarious work. In response to debates around different disciplinary perspectives on the world of work, Troth and Guest (2020, p. 43) call for greater multidisciplinary, multilevel, multistakeholder, and methodological plurality to advance HRM research:"[I/O] psychology can offer insights into the employee perspective and interests, but this has to be sit alongside the interests of other stake-holders, which can often more usefully be considered within other disciplinary frameworks of analysis" (Troth & Guest, 2020, p. 43). An example of this type of research is Allan et al. (2021), where the role of economic conditions is incorporated into their work precarity framework to explore precarious work and subsequent experiences of work precarity. By understanding and including context, I/O psychologists can better situate their theories and perspectives in addressing the challenges associated with precarious work.

Notes

1 Compensation to be paid amounted to 25% of the contract hours, or the hours they were required to be available or for 15 hours, whichever was the lesser.
2 Contract Personnel Marketing Ireland vs Marie Buckley (DWT1145), Sabina Murphy vs Grand Circle Travel [2014] IEHC 337 22/5/2014.
3 Employment (Miscellaneous Provisions) Act 2018.
4 The Employment (Miscellaneous Provisions) Act 2018.
5 Aer Lingus Ireland Ltd. vs Cliona O'Leary DWT207 30th November 2020.
6 Karshan (Midlands) Ltd. T/A Dominos Pizza Vs Revenue Commissioners [2022] IECA 124Appeal Number: 2020/53.

References

Adams, A., & Prassl, J. (2018). *Zero-hours work in the United Kingdom.* International Labour Organization. https://www.ilo.org/wcmsp5/groups/public/—ed_protect/—protrav/—travail/documents/publication/wcms_624965.pdf

Allan, B. A., Autin, K. L., & Wilkins-Yel, K. G. (2021). Precarious work in the 21st century: A psychological perspective. *Journal of Vocational Behavior, 126*, Article 103491. https://doi.org/10.1016/j.jvb.2020.103491

Appelbaum, E., & Schmitt, J. (2009). Low-wage work in high-income countries: Labor-market institutions and business strategy in the US and Europe. *Human Relations, 62*, 1907–1934.

Barnard, C., & Ludlow, A. (2016). Enforcement of employment rights by EU-8 migrant workers in employment tribunals. *Industrial Law Journal, 45*, 1–28.

Bellace, J. R. (2011). Achieving social justice: The nexus between the ILO's fundamental rights and decent work. *Employment Rights & Employment Policy Journal, 15*, 5–30.

Berry, C. (2022). The substitutive state? Neoliberal state interventionism across industrial, housing and private pensions policy in the UK. *Competition & Change, 26*, 242–265.

Blanchflower, D., Costa, R., & Machin, S. (2017). *The return of falling real wages* (Working Paper No. CEPRWU006). LSE Centre for Economic Performance. https://cep.lse.ac.uk/pubs/download/rwu006.pdf

Broughton, A., Green, M., Rickard, C., Swift, S., Eichhorst, W., Tobsch, V., Magda, I., Lewandowski, P., Keister, R., Jonaviciene, D., Ramos, Martin N.E., Valsamis, D., & Tros, F. (2016). *Precarious employment in Europe: Patterns, trends and policy strategies*. European Parliament.

Budd, J. W. (2020). The psychologisation of employment relations, alternative models of the employment relationship, and the OB turn. *Human Resource Management Journal, 30*, 73–83. https://doi.org/10.1111/1748-8583.12274

Campbell, I., Azzurra Tranfaglia, M., Tham, J. C., & Boese, M. (2019). Precarious work and the reluctance to Complain: Italian temporary migrant workers in Australia. *Labour & Industry: A Journal of the Social and Economic Relations of Work, 29*, 98–117.

Campbell, I., & Burgess, J. (2018). Patchy progress? Two decades of research on precariousness and precarious work in Australia. *Labour & Industry: A Journal of the Social and Economic Relations of Work, 28*, 48–67.

Carré, F., Findlay, P., Tilly, C., & Warhurst, C. (2012). Job quality: Scenarios, analysis and interventions. In C. Warhurst, F. Carré, P. Findlay, and C. Tilly (Eds.), *Are bad jobs inevitable?* (pp. 1–24). Palgrave Macmillan.

Carswell, S. (2020, October 14). HSE says zero-hour contracts issued to new COVID-19 contact tracers in error. *The Irish Times*. https://www.irishtimes.com/news/health/hse-says-zero-hour-contracts-issued-to-new-covid-19-contact-tracers-in-error-1.4381123

Central Statistics Office. (2022). *National Labour Force Survey*. Central Statistics Office.

Collins, H. (2018, July 31). A missed opportunity of a unified test for employment status. *UK Labour Law Blog*. https://uklabourlawblog.com/2018/07/31/a-missed-opportunity-of-a-unified-test-for-employment-status-hugh-collins/

Cush, M. (2016). *Report to the Minister for Education and Skills of the Chairperson of the Expert Group on Fixed-Term and Part-Time Employment in Third Level Education in Ireland.* Department of Education and Skills.

Davidov, G. (2011). Re-matching labour laws with their purpose. In G. Davidov & B. Langreille, B. (Eds.), *The idea of labour law.* Oxford University Press.

De Stefano, V., Durri, I., Stylogiannis, C., & Wouters, M. (2021). *Platform work and the employment relationship* (ILO Working Paper No. 27). International Labour Organization.

DeLanda, M. (2006). *A new philosophy of society: Assemblage theory and social complexity*. Continuum.

DeLanda, M. (2016). *Assemblage theory.* Edinburgh University Press.

Dittmer, J. (2020). Assemblage and the changing geographies of the State. In S. Moisio, N. Koch, A. E. G. Jonas, C. Lizotte, & J. Luukkonen (Eds.), *Handbook on the changing geographies of the state: New spaces of geopolitics.* Edward Elgar.

Dundon, T., Cullinane, N., &Wilkinson, A. (2017*) A very short, fairly interesting and reasonably cheap book about employment relations*. Sage Publications.
Dundon, T., & Rollinson, D. (2011). *Understanding employment relations* (2nd ed.). McGraw-Hill Higher Education.
Eurofound. (2015). *New forms of employment*. Publications Office of the European Union.
Forde, C., & Slater, G. (2016). Labour market regulation and the 'competition state': An analysis of the implementation of the Agency Working Regulations in the UK. *Work, Employment and Society, 30*, 590–606.
Freedland, M. (2013). Burying Caesar: What was the standard employment contract? In K. V. W. Stone and H. Arthurs (Eds.), *Rethinking workplace regulation: Beyond the standard contract of employment*. Russell Sage Foundation.
Freedland, M., & Countouris, N. (2011). *The legal construction of personal work relations*. Oxford University Press.
Gamble, A. (2010). New Labour and political change. *Parliamentary Affairs, 63*(4), 639–652.
Gamble, A., & Kahn, K. (1998). *The free economy and the strong state: The politics of Thatcherism*. MacMillan Education.
Grummell, B., & Lynch, K. (2016). New managerialism: A political project in Irish education. In M. Murphy, & F. Dukelow (Eds.), *The Irish welfare state in the twenty-first century*. Palgrave Macmillan.
Hall, P. A., & Soskice, D. (2001). *Varieties of capitalism: The institutional foundations of comparative advantage*. Oxford University Press.
Health Service Executive. (2022). *Human Resources Overview*. Retrieved June 4, 2022, from https://www.hse.ie/eng/about/who/hr/#:~:text=The%20HSE%20is%20the%20largest,in%20contributing%20to%20the%20HSE
Hebdon, R., & Kirkpatrick, I. (2005). Changes in the organization of public services and their consequences for employment relations. In S. Ackroyd, R. Batt, P. Thompson, & P. Tolbert (Eds.), *The Oxford handbook of work and organisation*. Oxford University Press.
Heyes, J., & Clark, I. (2011). The state and employment relations. In K. Townsend, & A. Wilkinson (Eds.), *Research handbook on the future of work and employment relations*. Edward Elgar Publishing.
Heyes, J., & Nolan, P. (2010). The state, capital and labour relations in crisis. In T. Colling & M. Terry (Eds.), *Industrial relations*. Wiley Blackwell.
Hopewell, K. (2017). When market fundamentalism and industrial policy collide: The Tea Party and the US Export–Import Bank. *Review of International Political Economy, 24*, 569–598.
Howell, C. (2006). *Trade unions and the state*. Princeton University Press.
Howell, C. (2021). Rethinking the role of the state in employment relations for a neoliberal era. *ILR Review, 74*, 739–772.
Hyman, R. (2008). The state in industrial relations. In P. Blyton, N. Bacon, and J. Fiorito (Eds.), *The Sage handbook of industrial relations*. Sage Publications.
Kahn-Freund, O. (1977). *Labour and the law*. Stevens and Sons.
Kalleberg, A. L. (2012). Job quality and precarious work: Clarifications, controversies, and challenges. *Work and Occupations, 39*, 427–448.

Kalleberg, A. L. (2018). Job insecurity and well-being in rich democracies. *The Economic and Social Review, 49*, 241–258.
Kalleberg, A. L., & Vallas, S. P. (2018). Probing precarious work: Theory, research, and politics. *Research in the Sociology of Work, 31*, 1–30.
Keane, E. (2014). Providing access to job security legislation for intermittent workers. *Kings Law Journal, 25*, 332–339.
Kirkpatrick, I., De Ruyter, A., Hoque, K., & Lonsdale, C. (2011). Practising what they preach? The disconnect between the state as regulator and user of employment agencies. *The International Journal of Human Resource Management, 22*, 3711–3726.
MacKenzie, R., & Martinez Lucio, M. (2014). The colonisation of employment regulation and industrial relations? Dynamics and developments over five decades of change. *Labor History, 55*, 189–207.
Mangan, D. (2020). Regulating for decent work: Reflections on classification of employees. *European Labour Law Journal, 11*, 111–116.
Martínez Lucio, M., & Stuart, M. (2011). The state, public policy and the renewal of HRM. *International Journal of Human Resource Management, 22*, 3661–3671.
Martínez Lucio, M., & MacKenzie, R. (2017). The state and the regulation of work and employment: Theoretical contributions, forgotten lessons and new forms of engagement. *The International Journal of Human Resource Management, 28*, 2983–3002.
Martínez Lucio, M., & MacKenzie, R. (2018). The state and employment relations: Continuity and change in the politics of regulation. In A. Wilkinson, T. Dundon, J. Donaghey, and A. Covin (Eds.), *The Routledge companion to employment relations*. Oxford University Press.
McConnell, D. (2020, August 2). Fresh public sector recruitment ban may be needed, minister told. *Irish Examiner*. https://www.irishexaminer.com/news/arid-40025909.html
McInerney, C., & Finn, C. (2015). *Caring—At what cost? Rebuilding and refinancing the community and voluntary sector.* IMPACT
Meardi, G. (2014). The state and employment relations. In A. Wilkinson, G. Wood, and R. Deeg (Eds.), *The Oxford handbook of employment relations: Comparative employment systems.* Oxford University Press.
Mercille, J., & Murphy, E. (2017). The neoliberalization of Irish higher education under austerity. *Critical Sociology, 43*, 371–387.
Mercille, J., & O'Neill, N. (2021). The growth of private home care providers in Europe: The case of Ireland. *Social Policy & Administration, 55*, 606–621.
Murphy, C., Lavelle, J., Turner, T., Ryan, L., McMahon, J., O'Sullivan, M., O'Brien, M, & Gunnigle, P. (2019). Zero hours work in Ireland. In M. O'Sullivan, J. Lavelle, J. McMahon, L. Ryan, C. Murphy, T. Turner, & P. Gunnigle (Eds.), *Zero hours and on-call work in Anglo-Saxon countries* (pp. 21–40). Springer.
Murphy, C., & O'Sullivan, M. (2021). Running to stand still? Two decades of trade union activity in the Irish long-term care sector. *Transfer: European Review of Labour and Research, 27*, 383–397.
Murphy, M. P. (2016). Low road or high road? The post-crisis trajectory of Irish activation. *Critical Social Policy, 36*, 1–21.

Nugent, C., Pembroke, S., & Taft, M. (2019). *Precarious work in the Republic of Ireland* (NERI WP 2019/No. 64). Nevin Economic Research Institute. https://www.nerinstitute.net/sites/default/files/research/2019/precarious_work_in_the_republic_of_ireland_july_19_final.pdf

O'Fátharta, C. (2018, December 20). Law banning zero hour contracts to come into force in March. *Irish Examiner*. https://www.irishexaminer.com/news/arid-30893410.html

Offe, C. (1984). *The contradictions of the welfare state*. Hutchinson & Co. Publishers.

O'Halloran, M. (2018, February 14). Minister says zero-hour contracts to be all but prohibited. *Irish Times*. https://www.irishtimes.com/news/politics/oireachtas/minister-says-zero-hour-contracts-to-be-all-but-prohibited-1.3392468

Ohmae, K. (1995). *The end of the nation state: The rise of regional economies*. Free Press.

O'Sullivan, M., Lavelle, J., McMahon, J., Ryan, L., Murphy, C., Turner, T., & Gunnigle, P. (Eds.). (2019). *Zero hours and on-call work in Anglo-Saxon Countries*. Springer.

Perulli, A. (2020). The legal and jurisprudential evolution of the notion of employee. *European Labour Law Journal, 11*, 117–130.

Piasna, A., & Myant, M. (2017). *Myths of employment deregulation: How it neither creates jobs nor reduces labour market segmentation*. European Trade Union Institute. https://www.etui.org/sites/default/files/17%20Piasna%20Myant%20Employment%20deregulation%20WEB.pdf

Prendergast, A. (2015, June 10). Dunnes unions cite improvements, but 'banded hours' still elusive. *Industrial Relations News, 22*.

Prosser, T. (2016). Dualization or liberalization? Investigating precarious work in eight European countries. *Work, Employment and Society, 30*, 949–965.

Rehab Group. (2018). *Who cares? Building a new relationship between the not-for-profit sector and the State 2018*. Rehab Group.

Retail Ireland. (2022). *Retail is at the heart of every Irish community: How the sector supports and improves life nationwide*. IBEC.

Roche, W. K., & Gormley, T. (2020). The durability of coordinated bargaining: Crisis, recovery and pay fixing in Ireland, *Economic and Industrial Democracy, 41*, 481–505.

Rogan, A. (2022, September 24). Home care providers threaten HSE with legal action over new tender process. *Business Post*. https://www.businesspost.ie/news/homecare-providers-threaten-hse-with-legal-action-over-new-tender-process/

Rubery, J., & Grimshaw, D. (2016). Precarious work and the commodification of the employment relationship: The case of zero hours in the UK and mini jobs in Germany. In G. Bäcker, S. Lehndorff, & C. Weinkopf (Eds.), *Den Arbeitsmarkt verstehen, um ihn zu gestalten*. Springer.

Rubery, J., Grimshaw, D., Keizer, A., & Johnson, M. (2018). Challenges and contradictions in the 'normalising' of precarious work. *Work, Employment and Society, 32*, 509–527.

Savage, G. C. (2020). What is policy assemblage? *Territory, Politics, Governance, 8*, 319–335.

Stuart, M., & Martinez Lucio, M. (2008). The new benchmarking and advisory state: The role of the British Advisory, Conciliation and Arbitration Service in facilitating labour management consultation in public sector transformation. *Journal of Industrial Relations, 50*, 736–751.

Treuren, G. (2000). The concept of the state in Australian industrial relations theory. *Labour and Industry, 11*, 75–98.

Troth, A. C., & Guest, D. E. (2020). The case for psychology in human resource management research. *Human Resource Management Journal, 30*, 34–48.

Vosko, L. F. (2010). *Managing the margins: Gender, citizenship, and the international regulation of precarious employment*. Oxford University Press.

Vosko, L. F., Tucker, E., & Casey, R. (2019). Enforcing employment standards for temporary migrant agricultural workers in Ontario, Canada: Exposing underexplored layers of vulnerability. *International Journal of Comparative Labour Law and Industrial Relations, 35*, 227–254.

Wallace, J., Gunnigle, P., & O'Sullivan, M. (2020). *Industrial relations in Ireland* (5th ed.). Institute of Public Administration.

Wiengarten, F., Pagell, M., Durach, C. F., & Humphreys, P. (2021). Exploring the performance implications of precarious work. *Journal of Operations Management, 67*, 926–963.

PART IV

Social Protection

17

IS WORK-LIFE BALANCE ONLY FOR SOME? A CASE FOR MORE LOW INCOME AND PRECARIAT SAMPLES

Jarrod Haar

The WLB literature shows that WLB is an important factor for many employees. It is linked with better workplace and wellbeing outcomes, and it also mediates many antecedents. However, there is an inherent bias in the WLB literature in its study of professions (e.g., skilled workers) and worker pay (salaried, higher paid). This bias leads to the question: Does WLB function similarly for low-paid, precariat workers? Are the antecedents and consequences of WLB replicable and robust? With precarious work now endemic across the working world (see, Carr, Hodgetts et al., Chapter 1), this chapter provides an overview of the WLB literature and then proceeds to argue the case not only for less WEIRD but also less POSH representation, within the WLB field (Gloss et al., 2017). The chapter provides examples of how researchers, even those researching within WEIRD but not POSH populations (many of whom are experience precarious work), might examine WLB to aid understanding, policy, and practice. It offers an integrated, inclusive model of WLB by suggesting how selected factors might be especially pertinent to acknowledge when exploring how to tackle precarious work. The aim of this chapter is to encourage WLB researchers to move their focus to more diverse samples and test WLB with populations that are largely missing in the field, thereby contributing to tackling precarious work by advancing WLB for all.

Haar (2013) defines WLB as "the extent to which an individual is able to adequately manage the multiple roles in their life, including work, family and other major responsibilities" (p. 3308). Importantly, the literature acknowledges that WLB is a personal perception and uses a person-centered approach, so WLB is very much about individual perceptions of balance (see Greenhaus & Allen, 2011; Haar, 2013; Haar et al., 2014). The original precursors to the field of WLB

DOI: 10.4324/9781003440444-21

focused on work and family roles only, and this was dominated initially by perceived work-family conflict (Greenhaus & Beutell, 1985), and then work-family enrichment was added three decades later (Greenhaus & Powell, 2006). Haar (2013) focused extending the focus of the WLB literature on work and family to the interface between work and nonwork. Importantly, WLB has been shown to be distinct from these earlier conceptualizations of work-family conflict and enrichment (Haar, 2013; Haar et al., 2014). Thus, it is a distinct way of looking at how workers can manage their work and nonwork commitments and pressures.

The attention given to WLB has broadened and it has become a frequent rally cry for workers when they are faced with high work pressures. For example, Elsworthy (2019) reports on a UK study of 2,000 employees who when asked why they had quit their jobs, cited WLB as the number one issue. Consequently, WLB has grown in importance and is viewed as a critical issue for organizations and employees, with some suggesting that WLB has become extremely challenging to achieve (see Giauque et al., 2019). In one extreme example of system-justification, a Fortune 500 CEO stated that, with respect to themselves, they see WLB as being a lie (Sahadi, 2021), that is, something unattainable. However, there is a wider question of how well WLB research and associated commentaries represent and reflect the entire workforce. For example, given the CEO's comment above, does this make WLB only an issue for professionals, at the exclusion of precarious workers?

Since 2010, more attention has been given to psychology research's focus on WEIRD populations (Henrich et al., 2010b). The argument is that by focusing research attention on students from such populations, we can fail to best understand effects across all populations. Indeed, analysis by Henrich et al. (2010b) concluded that there was "substantial variability in laboratory experimental results across populations and that WEIRD subjects are particularly unusual compared with the rest of the species—frequent outliers" (p. 61). This concept of WEIRD has limitations, however. Today, precarious work is endemic. As well as being commonplace in non-WEIRD countries, it is also found commonly within them (e.g., across rustbelts; see Chapter 1). Secondarily, much of the research in our field is not, and indeed never has been, "laboratory"-based (i.e., experimental). Nonetheless, as Gloss and colleagues (2017) have shown, I/O psychology in general has tended to stay focused on occupations that are relatively POSH. Thus, a key bias has been the relative exclusion of precarious work(ers), which in turn often *intersects* with cultural bias(es).

This intersectional focus on relatively privileged work populations limits our understanding of employee phenomena. This is certainly the case for WLB, where few cross-cultural, precarious work studies have been conducted (see Haar et al., 2014 for an exception). Across related topics like work-family conflict, there have been better studies across different cultures (see Spector et al., 2004) and work classes (Haar et al., 2018) providing insight and direction for future studies. However, rather than solely critiquing the WLB literature for its relatively privileged settings and work populations, the present chapter asks: *Is WLB similar for minority employees? And for low-paid and precariat workers?* The next section provides insight into why exploring unheard voices is needed.

Minority Employees

Henrich et al. (2010b) stated "Behavioral scientists routinely publish broad claims about human psychology and behavior in the world's top journals based on samples drawn entirely from Western, Educated, Industrialized, Rich, and Democratic (WEIRD) societies" (p. 61). Henrich et al. (2010a) note this is problematic because psychology research "assumes that everyone shares most fundamental cognitive and affective processes, and that findings from one population apply across the board" (p. 29). Hence, the bias within psychology and business research feeds the assumption that employees are a rather homogenous group, and extended to the WLB literature, suggests that the antecedents and consequences of WLB are typical for all employees. This is an important aspect to highlight, because analyses by Henrich et al. (2010b) suggest that WEIRD populations are the exception rather than the norm, whilst those by Gloss et al. (2017), focused on work, indicate a bias toward work that is more secure than precarious (Bergman & Jean, 2016; Smith, 2015).

The original WLB study was based in New Zealand, and that study included two distinct samples, with (1) older aged employees who are parents, and (2) younger aged employees who are nonparents (Haar, 2013). Similar effects were found across both samples. However, these samples still represent largely WEIRD and largely POSH populations. New Zealand is a Western industrialized democratic economy, and the study sample was of disproportionately highly educated workers. Although income was not disclosed, the assumption was that they were likely to be at least middle-income employees. While this is not problematic of itself, it does validate the call for greater diversity (Henrich et al., 2010a, 2010b). In another rare deviation from standard populations, Haar et al. (2014) did extend WLB research cross-culturally to include non-Western and less democratic economies. Again though, a bias toward WEIRD and POSH was likely, with respondents more likely to have been both educated and rich.

However, this study did include an indigenous population of New Zealand Māori employees, which provided the world's first sample of WLB amongst indigenous employees. This is important because Māori have previously been found to report unique differences at work when directly compared to New Zealand European employees (see Haar & Brougham, 2016). Aligned with Henrich et al. (2010b) and their WEIRD findings, Māori reported similar conceptualization of self-esteem from work, but it was found to be much more valuable to Māori compared to New Zealand European (white) employees (Haar &

Brougham, 2016). Further, Haar and Brougham (2022) collected two samples that included the indigenous population (New Zealand Māori employees), providing support for the antecedents and consequences of WLB applying beyond a typically "white" population. This might be seen as going somewhere toward representing a non-WEIRD population.

Given that Haar et al. (2014) found similar beneficial effects from WLB for an indigenous employee population (and for all other populations), this does strengthen their suggestion that WLB is widely beneficial. Aligned with the WEIRD dominance in psychology and POSH business psychology research, the most recent meta-analysis of WLB reported on 130 empirical studies with more than 220,000 employees (see Vaziri et al., 2022) but failed to acknowledge any sampling bias against precarious work, and workers, even though most studies could be characterized as conducted with relatively nonprecarious populations. As such, the replicability of effects can be challenged. This chapter encourages the bias to be addressed specifically in WLB research. However, it is important to acknowledge the challenge for researchers who are often located within WEIRD populations themselves, in relatively POSH research jobs: *How do I access precarious worker groups?* This chapter suggests that it is the precariousness component to which even Western and/or relatively job-secure researchers might be especially able to draw more attention.

And Those Who May Also Be Low-Paid and Precariat Workers

Hodgetts, Groot, and Garden (2017) noted that most Western workforces now have a precariat, which is defined as comprising people (including those in the workforce) who live insecure lives and have limited economic and social capital; Hodgetts et al. (2017) also noted that they have highly constrained social mobility. Standing (2011) argues that the precariat class reflects the undermining of work conditions and work securities that were traditional in the working middle classes. Of particular interest to WLB scholars is that the precariat worker is characterized by the dynamics of underemployment and unliveable wages (Hodgetts et al., 2017). Given that this reflects the reality of a new class of workers *within* WEIRD populations, extending studies to not only explore low-income workers but also those whose work situation fluctuates and is precarious would make an excellent addition to the WLB literature. Further, examining this precariat in relation to housing and food insecurities (Standing, 2011) and social exclusion (Boon & Farnsworth, 2011) would be useful for breaking the WEIRD and POSH focus, especially within Western, industrialized, and democratic populations (Gloss et al., 2017). Here the argument could be that nonrich workers might face unique challenges that currently remain underexplored.

In an illustration of this approach, Haar et al. (2018) explored the influence of pay fairness and WLB on job satisfaction amongst those with low education and below median-income earners in New Zealand. They found that WLB was a significant predictor of job satisfaction, aligning with other studies (e.g., Haar, 2013; Haar et al., 2014). Importantly, this clarified that WLB plays a significant role in shaping job satisfaction even within a precariously employed population, specifically noneducated and nonrich employees. Haar et al. (2018) stated "This finding also highlights that work–life balance is not only a middle-class or higher-earner phenomenon, but rather an issue that is universally important for all employees, including the working poor" (p. 10).

In another recent example, Carr et al. (2018) explored several outcomes, including WLB across a population of low-income workers in New Zealand and South Africa (Meyer & Maleka, Chapter 7). They assessed the influence of a living wage on employee outcomes and found a positive relationship between income and WLB as it approached this benchmark. Later in this chapter, these approaches are drawn on to provide insights into how WLB researchers can undertake WLB studies that are more inclusive, not only socioculturally but also socioeconomically. What these studies showed was that precarious workers were caught in working poverty traps that likely reflected work-life imbalance.

WLB Theory and Precarious Work

Historically, the first research explorations of WLB showed that researchers struggled initially to capture its dynamics. For example, early work suggested that balance was simply the absence of conflict (e.g., Clark, 2001; Premeaux et al., 2007; Saltzstein et al., 2001). Thus, employees with low levels of work-family conflict were in effect reporting better balance than those employees with higher conflict. Similarly, other researchers have suggested that balance reflects having higher levels of work-family enrichment than work-family conflict (e.g., Aryee et al., 2005; Frone, 2003). In this approach, researchers contended that balance was achieved when the beneficial effects of enrichment in effect cancelled out the detrimental effects of conflict (see Haar, 2013 for more details), creating higher levels of balance in employees. Further, while some contend they are measuring WLB (e.g., Hayman, 2005), they often conflate conflict and enrichment with WLB (as is the case in that measure, ibid). These studies are more aligned theoretically with work-family conflict and work-family enrichment and are not really a measure of WLB. It was not until Carlson, Grzywacz, and Zivnuska (2009) explored work-family balance that balance was considered a unique factor beyond conflict and enrichment. However, a criticism of all these approaches is the focus on work and family only. Indeed, researchers have often discussed WLB while only focusing on work and family. It was not until Haar (2013) that WLB was conceptualized and tested as being distinct from work-family conflict and enrichment and found to be important over and above the influences of work-family conflict and enrichment.

Overall, the WLB literature has captured distinct and unique forms of interactions between the work roles of employees and the *other* roles they are involved in, i.e., beyond paid work itself. Haar et al. (2018) stated that with WLB, "employees formulate a subjective appraisal of non-work and work roles, and thus, work–life balance represents the equilibrium and harmony between all of the roles that are perceived as being important to an employee" (p. 3). Yet, do those on minimum wage, often with far less choice, perceive WLB the same way as workers on median- or higher incomes? Maré and Hyslop (2021) reported, for example, that workers on the minimum wage in New Zealand represent about 9% of all employees. But we understood very little about their WLB perceptions and experiences. Heading in the direction of understanding requires us to first revisit psychological theory in more detail.

WLB Psychological Approaches

Several theoretical approaches have been used to understand and apply WLB in workplace settings. Haar (2013) offered role-balance theory, stating: "attaining a level of self-perceived balance between these roles…will enable employees to attain additional benefits from their roles through successful management of these roles" (p. 3308). Thus, WLB refers to an employee achieving harmony between their roles and, importantly, ways to do this are likely to vary between employees. Haar (2013) states: "balance is not assumed to be equality in time, engagement and satisfaction…but is a personal assessment of how employees balance multiple roles" (p. 3308). Hence, balance is not the most intuitive term because it is not around "balancing" work and life 50/50. In fact, WLB reflects the achievement of greater *harmony* between roles, at whatever levels those might be for individuals. Overall, role-balance theory is the most popular theoretical approach linked to WLB (for a theoretical review, see Casper et al., 2018).

One employee might spend more time working (50+ hours/week) because this helps them achieve the things they want. This might include the work itself or income to fund a lifestyle of choice, including time for leisure. For another employee, a 40-hour week might create too many tensions and role imbalance, and thus be detrimental. The theoretical approach of role balance aligns with work by Barnett and Hyde (2001) and their arguments that employees engaging in multiple roles are not the critical issue. Rather, it is the *combination* of roles that creates the challenge. Consequently, employees who perceive they have greater role balance demonstrate good management of their multiple roles and experience harmony between them, and thus higher WLB. For people who are working multiple low-paid jobs or gigs to make a living, this idea of role balancing implies that WLB might actually be more relevant to the precariat than to people who are less precariously employed (and overrepresented in the WLB literature corpus and quantum).

Related to and aligned with role-balance theory, a common theoretical approach used to understand how factors influence WLB and WLB influences outcomes is conservation of resources theory (COR; Hobfoll, 1989, 2002). For example, Haar and Brougham (2022) used conservation of resources (COR) theory to understand the influences of WLB on important work attitudes and behaviors. COR theory represents an integrated model of stress, which focuses on resources (Hobfoll, 1989), and the way that employees acquire, maintain, and potentially lose resources. In relation to antecedents of WLB, those that are detrimental such as long work hours (e.g., Haar et al., 2019) ultimately reflect a loss of resources because the excessive time spent working leaves less resources (e.g., time, energy, and attention; Hobfoll, 2002) to give to other roles. Conversely, potentially beneficial antecedents like supervisor support can increase WLB (e.g., Haar, Suñe et al., 2019) because this support provides the employee with additional resources, making their ability to balance roles easier. Again therefore, WLB might be not less but even *more* relevant to, and salient for precarious than nonprecarious workers.

Hobfoll et al. (2018) clarify understanding of several resources and highlight a few different categories, "[including] object resources (e.g., car, tools for work), condition resources (e.g., employment, tenure, and seniority), personal resources (e.g., key skills and personal traits such as self-efficacy and optimism), and energy resources (e.g., credit, knowledge, and money)" (p. 105). A good resource example, particularly relevant to precarious work, is time. Employees who lose time, due to overcommitment (e.g., having to work late in a workday, or leaving work early for a dependent/sport/charity commitment), have lost a valuable resource. In the first example, the employee cannot spend that lost time with family, while in the second example, the employee may be required to do additional work later in the week, cycling back and creating issues relating to the first example. Ultimately, this leads to a reduction in WLB. Further, resource supply can theoretically play a role in employee perceptions (Hobfoll, 2002) which aligns with WLB as a perception-based factor (Haar, 2013).

In summary, according to COR theory, employees with an abundance of resources (called a resource reservoir, Ghafoor & Haar, 2021) are more likely to have superior WLB. WLB in turn influences wellbeing. This creates the potential for WLB to be especially salient for the precarious working classes, whose material and temporal resources are likely to be less to begin with (because of indecent work conditions) and more strained thereafter.

Antecedents of WLB

The meta-analysis by Vaziri et al. (2022) focused only on antecedents. They identified many factors across six categories: (1) work-related demands, (2) personal characteristics with a negative view, (3) family-related demands, (4) work-related resources, (5) personal characteristics with a positive view, and (6) family-related resources. Interestingly, wage levels and income were not included. On the one hand, the meta-analysis found strong support for resource losses being detrimental to WLB, including work hours, job overload, and work-family conflict. On the other hand, job resources were beneficial, including support, autonomy, work-family enrichment, and family-friendly cultures and policies. Once more, this ledger of losses and gains would favor nonprecarious- over precarious-worker WLB. However, Vaziri et al. (2022) also noted that there were "insufficient studies to include family demands and resources" (p. 665). This is important because Haar, Suñe et al. (2019) found that family demands were significant and negatively related to WLB. Logically, one would expect that these family-related resources and demands would be psychologically more salient to people who are struggling to make ends in poorly paid, time-intensive, and insecure work roles.

Consequences of WLB

Here, the consequences of WLB are split into two groups: (1) wellbeing and (2) work outcomes; both include positive and negative outcomes. Regarding (1) wellbeing, WLB has been found to influence a range of outcomes. For example, Haar (2013) found that WLB was related negatively to job anxiety and job depression, and that this relationship was replicable cross-culturally, across seven samples (Haar et al., 2014). WLB is also linked to lower emotional exhaustion (Haar, 2013; Haar & Harris, 2021; Haar & Mowat, 2021), as well as cynicism and insomnia (Haar & Harris, 2021). More generally, Rashid et al. (2022) found that WLB was negatively related to negative affect. These findings as a set provide support for the idea that negative wellbeing outcomes are a consequence of poor WLB or work-life imbalance.

Looking toward the positive wellbeing outcomes, WLB is linked to higher life satisfaction in New Zealand (Haar, 2013), a relationship that again held cross-culturally (Haar et al., 2014). The positive links to life satisfaction have been replicated in a range of culturally diverse settings (Edgar et al., 2017; Schnettler et al., 2021; Talukder et al., 2018). Other types of positive wellbeing outcomes linked by WLB include family satisfaction (Chan et al., 2016), and Ejlertsson et al. (2018) found that WLB was linked beneficially to after-work recovery, energy at work, and reflection. Edgar et al. (2017) found that WLB was beneficially related to happiness and health, while Rashid et al. (2022) found that WLB was positively related to positive affect. Overall, this provides strong evidence that WLB is positively related to positive wellbeing outcomes.

In addition, there is evidence of WLB influencing key work outcomes, although the literature is dominated by a focus on largely positive types of outcome. These include organizational commitment (Talukder et al., 2018; Haar &

Brougham, 2022), and job satisfaction (Haar, 2013; Haar & Brougham, 2022), as well as work behaviors such as organizational citizenship behaviors (OCBs; Haar & Brougham, 2022). Edgar et al. (2017) found that WLB was positively related to task performance and contextual performance (nonmandatory helpful behaviors at work), as well as job satisfaction and trust. Haar, Di Fabio et al. (2019) also found support for WLB influencing organizational trust. Poulose and Dhal (2020) found that WLB was linked with career commitment, while Bansal and Agarwal (2020) found that WLB was linked with employees engaging in innovative work behaviors. Finally, Haar et al. (2017) found that WLB was positively related to individual dimensions of work engagement (vigor, dedication, and absorption). Overall, this provides strong evidence that WLB is positively related to positive work outcomes, for employers as well as employees.

As noted earlier, the links between WLB and negative work outcomes is limited. Currently, the literature has focused on turnover intentions (e.g., Brough et al., 2014; Haar & Brougham, 2022; Haar et al., 2021). The evidence here is that WLB is negatively related to turnover intentions. To date, the attention on WLB and negative work behaviors has been extremely limited. Only recently (see Becker et al., 2022) has a negative link between WLB and counterproductive work behaviors been found. Overall, there is some evidence that WLB is beneficially related to mitigating negative work outcomes, although clearly this area needs more attention. Again, therefore, both employer and employee can benefit from WLB. Put another way, enhancing WLB is in the best interests of employees and employers alike.

Finally, it is important to note that studies have found WLB to mediate the effects of other factors, including work-family conflict (Haar, 2013; Haar et al., 2014) and work-family enrichment (Haar, 2013). Haar et al. (2017) found that WLB mediated the positive influence of servant leadership on work engagement. Similarly, Haar and Brougham (2022) found that antecedents of WLB (e.g., job autonomy, job control) were also significant predictors of work outcomes (e.g., job satisfaction), with these direct effects being partially mediated by WLB. Overall, there are a wide range of wellbeing and work factors aligned with WLB.

But where does all this research quantum stand in relation to tackling precarious work?

Expanding WLB Research

Even within the WLB literature, there have been calls to expand the cultural scope to address issues around WLB being culturally embedded (Ollier-Malaterre & Foucreault, 2016). As noted earlier, there are many elements within the WLB field that remain unknown, even within work-secure populations. A theoretical model is offered in Figure 17.1 to represent where more inclusive

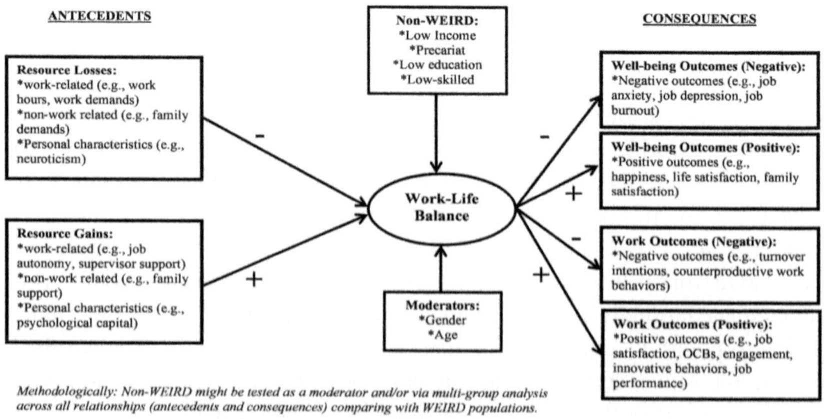

FIGURE 17.1 Theoretical Model of Antecedents and Consequences of WLB.

efforts might be focused regarding WLB. This theoretical model fully embraces the COR theoretical approach and builds on the WLB antecedents' model of Vaziri et al. (2022).

The model applies a strong COR theoretical framework because this also aligns well with role-balance theory. It is separated into antecedents of WLB, and the outcomes or consequences of WLB. On the antecedents' side of the model, the focus is solely on *resources*: those that represent losses and gains. These are typically viewed (see Vaziri et al., 2022) as work-related, family-related, and individual (e.g., personality, or dispositional characteristics). The model extends the family-related focus of Vaziri et al. (2022) and applies more to the recent conceptualizations of WLB (see Haar, 2013) which include nonwork-related factors (losses and gains). The focus is extended to beyond the family (Haar, 2013), although it is also acknowledged that family-related demands and resources are largely missing from the literature.

The focal part of Figure 17.1 for this chapter are the moderators in the middle of the diagram. This part of the model largely aligns with Vaziri et al. (2022) and includes the same two moderators of age and gender. While the evidence on the effects of these is limited (see Vaziri et al., 2022), the work did encourage further exploration of these effects. However, this focus might also reflect a bias against precarious work and workers. For example, in a study of low-income workers, Haar et al. (2018) found a small but positive and significant correlation between age and WLB. This also aligns with Haar, Suñe et al. (2019) in a study of WLB across New Zealand, France, Italy, and Spain, where a similar positive correlation was reported between age and WLB. This should encourage examination of these moderators within precariously employed populations (see Figure 17.1).

WLB Antecedents Example

Next, an example of a WLB antecedent is used to illustrate a more inclusive methodological approach. In Figure 17.1, and supported by meta-analysis, work hours have a significant and negative relationship ($r = -.18$, $p < .05$) with WLB (Vaziri et al., 2022). In their WLB study of low-income workers, Haar et al. (2018) reported a similar but smaller negative relationship between work hours and WLB ($r = -.11$, $p < .01$). Ganster et al. (2018) note that the evidence supports long work hours as being detrimental to wellbeing but acknowledged small effect sizes. Theoretically, this effect aligns with role-balance theory (Haar, 2013) and COR theory (Hobfoll et al., 2018), because time is viewed as a resource, and it is mainly an employee's ability to manage time that can be problematic: draining resources and lowering WLB. Indeed, beyond the WLB literature but within the work and family literature, evidence supports total work hours being detrimental to role functioning (Bruck et al., 2002; Spector et al., 2004; Sturges & Guest 2004). One possibility, based on COR, is that precarious work will exacerbate (strengthen) the negative link, in Figure 17.1, between hours and WLB (see, Lavelle et al., Chapter 16, on living hours).

For example, within New Zealand, 9% of the workforce is on the minimum wage (Maré & Hyslop, 2021). How do minimum-wage workers balance their work and nonwork roles? What role do work hours play for the lowest paid employees, who might need to work long hours to gain sufficient income to survive? Statistics New Zealand (2019) reported that 7.3% of the New Zealand workforce (those in paid employment) held two or more jobs. Related, The New Zealand attitudes and values study (2015) reported that the New Zealand workforce had an average commute time of between two and five hours per week. However, for those in Auckland, New Zealand's largest city, a quarter of the workforce were commuting over eight hours per week.

How does commuting time impact on WLB for multiple-job workers? Is it worse for those in larger cities? Low-income workers especially challenged by income demands (Carr et al., 2018) might have to work multiple part-time jobs to earn sufficient income. If they somehow averaged 40 hours/week (a standard working week), we might not expect them to report extraordinarily adverse levels of WLB. But what if each of the multiple jobs also required long commute times? Further, Statistics New Zealand (2014) reported that 75% of the urban New Zealand workforce commuted by car, but those using public transport reported twice the travel times. Imagine a low-income worker, who must work two jobs to earn sufficient money (and is paid minimum wage for 40 hours/week). Now factor in long commutes on public transport, including long trips between the two jobs on some days. What effects would this have on the workers' WLB?

The WLB literature would suggest that WLB for those working an "average working time" should be superior to those working longer hours just to make ends meet. But the literature does not acknowledge the long hours commuting for a low-income worker (potentially). Further, we know that job insecurity is broadly detrimental (Jiang & Lavaysse, 2018) including with WLB (Vaziri et al., 2022), but within the literature, exploration of the experience of precariat workers might provide a useful and socioeconomically more inclusive focus. Next in Figure 17.1, I explore a resource-gain factor and specifically relate this to the resource-loss factor of work hours. Workplace support is typically explored at either the supervisory or organizational level. In their meta-analysis, Kossek et al. (2011) showed that supervisory support perceptions were distinct from organizational level support. Importantly for WLB, ten Brummelhuis and Bakker (2012) have suggested that support can act as a critical resource providing employees with sufficient resources to manage their work and nonwork roles. Under COR theory, this should lead to positive WLB.

In a test of this possibility, Russo, Shteigman, and Carmeli (2016) found that supervisory support and perceived organizational support (Kurtessis et al., 2015) were related to WLB. However, what does such support look like for low-income workers? Indeed, might it be that workplace support is even more beneficial for low-income and precariat workers? Being a precariat worker but knowing your immediate supervisor is doing all they can to get you more work, more hours, more permanence in the role might be more valuable and lead to greater WLB. More precariat studies are needed; these might include conducting a WLB study comparing precariat and nonprecariat workers and exploring the role of supervisor support, which might be more salient when work is precarious.

WLB Consequences Example

Returning to Figure 17.1, the second half of the model explores the consequences of WLB. Consequences are separated into two broad groups: (1) wellbeing outcomes and (2) work outcomes; both include both negative and positive outcomes. Indeed, a wide range of outcomes have already been explored within the WLB literature, but few of these have been examined in conjunction with a precarious work population or context. However, evidence strongly shows that insecurity around work leads to poorer wellbeing (Jiang & Lavaysse, 2018). Studies have shown that mental health is affected by WLB (e.g., Haar, 2013; Haar et al., 2014; Haar & Harris, 2021; Haar & Mowat, 2021). However, we currently do not know whether this relationship between WLB and mental health differs for employees in more precarious work positions or by low-paid versus high-paid worker status.

The effects regarding work outcomes might be similar as for wellbeing outcomes. Again, when examining whether WLB has the same effect on turnover intentions for non-WEIRD populations, it is useful to compare findings in the existing literature (e.g., Brough et al., 2014; Haar & Brougham, 2022; Haar et al., 2021). For example, Haar (2022) found that burnout risk rates had grown through the COVID-19 period, and these had a massive influence on turnover, with workers at risk of burnout much more likely to quit. Exploring these relationships with the inclusion of WLB and focusing on precariat workers, gig workers, and low-paid workers would all provide much needed nuance for the broader research literature. Given the very precarious nature of work for some, exploring whether WLB provides more or less resources (under COR theory) for such employees, WLB perhaps provides greater drive to leave work in search of more abundant and less precarious work. For example, future studies might conduct multigroup analyses to confirm the psychometric properties of WLB, including metric invariance tests within precarious populations (see Haar et al., 2014). Exploring differences using WEIRD and non-WEIRD population status as a dichotomous moderator might, at the minimum, determine the universal benefits of WLB (if nonsignificant effects are found), or something else entirely. At the least, any such findings would provide greater research population diversity (Henrich et al., 2010a, 2010b) and provide new insights.

Summary

The WLB literature is popular but not robust. Indeed, a recent WLB meta-analysis reported 130 empirical studies with more than 220,000 employees (Vaziri et al., 2022). This suggests it is a growing phenomenon amongst researchers. Further, WLB remains a current issue for employees and is readily commented upon in the popular press. But, apart from a handful of studies, we do not know much about WLB in precarious work. In the workplace context, including digital platform work, researchers are especially encouraged to conduct research with and alongside populations of workers who are especially low paid, precariously employed, and indigenous or minority peoples. Such studies are likely to be especially fruitful, whether significant differences are found or not. Nonsignificant differences in antecedents or consequences of WLB would strengthen the argument that WLB is universally beneficial. Significant differences would provide new avenues for exploration that can only be beneficial for the WLB field. Most importantly of all, however, research needs to expand its own horizons to be more inclusive and reflective of the precarious work that most people in the global workforce—be they in an OECD or low-income country and economy—are caught in (Carr, Hodgetts et al., Chapter 1; Saltzman et al., Chapter 2): this is work that is likely to be relatively out of balance with the demands and needs of human relationships in everyday life.

References

Aryee, S., Srinivas, E. S., & Tan, H. H. (2005). Rhythms of life: Antecedents and outcomes of work-family balance in employed parents. *Journal of Applied Psychology, 90*(1), 132–146. https://doi.org/10.1037/0021-9010.90.1.132

Bansal, N., & Agarwal, U. A. (2020). Direct and indirect effects of work-family enrichment: role of gender role ideology. *International Journal of Productivity and Performance Management, 69*(5), 873–894. https://doi.org/10.1108/IJPPM-10-2018-0370

Barnett, R. C., & Hyde, J. S. (2001). Women, men, work, and family: An expansionist theory. *American Psychologist, 56*(10), 781–796. https://psycnet.apa.org/doi/10.1037/0003-066X.56.10.781

Becker, W. J., Belkin, L. Y., Tuskey, S. E., & Conroy, S. A. (2022). Surviving remotely: How job control and loneliness during a forced shift to remote work impacted employee work behaviors and well-being. *Human Resource Management, 61*(4), 449–464. https://doi.org/10.1002/hrm.22102

Bergman, M. E., & Jean, V. A. (2016). Where have all the workers gone? A critical analysis of the under-representativeness of our samples relative to the labor market in the industrial-organizational psychology literature. *Industrial and Organizational Psychology, 9*(1), 84–113.

Boon, B., & Farnsworth, J. (2011). Social exclusion and poverty: Translating social capital into accessible resources. *Social Policy & Administration, 45*(5), 507–524. https://doi.org/10.1111/j.1467-9515.2011.00792.x

Brough, P., Timms, C., O'Driscoll, M. P., Kalliath, T., Siu, O. L., Sit, C., & Lo, D. (2014). Work–life balance: A longitudinal evaluation of a new measure across Australia and New Zealand workers. *The International Journal of Human Resource Management, 25*(19), 2724–2744. https://doi.org/10.1080/09585192.2014.899262

Bruck, C. S., Allen, T. D., & Spector, P. E. (2002). The relation between work-family conflict and job satisfaction: A finer-grained analysis. *Journal of Vocational Behavior, 60*(3), 336–353. https://doi.org/10.1006/jvbe.2001.1836

Carlson, D. S., Grzywacz, J. G., & Zivnuska, S. (2009). Is work-family balance more than conflict and enrichment? *Human Relations, 62*(10), 1459–1486. https://doi.org/10.1177/0018726709336500

Carr, S., Maleka, M., Meyer, I., Barry, M. L., Haar, J., Parker, J., Arrowsmith, J., Yao, C., Hodgetts, D., Jones, H., Young-Hausner, A., Afeaki-Mafile'o, E., Rasmussen, A.-H., Alefaio-Tugia, S., Falealili, B., Mafile'o, K., Pikula, T., Wolfgramm, N., 'Uhila, H., … & Naithani, A. (2018). How can wages sustain a living? By getting ahead of the curve. *Sustainability Science, 13*(4), 901–917. https://doi.org/10.1007/s11625-018-0560-7

Casper, W. J., Vaziri, H., Wayne, J. H., DeHauw, S., & Greenhaus, J. (2018). The jingle-jangle of work–nonwork balance: A comprehensive and meta-analytic review of its meaning and measurement. *Journal of Applied Psychology, 103*(2), 182–214. http://dx.doi.org/10.1037/apl0000259

Chan, X. W., Kalliath, T., Brough, P., Siu, O. L., O'Driscoll, M. P., & Timms, C. (2016). Work–family enrichment and satisfaction: The mediating role of self-efficacy and work-life balance. *The International Journal of Human Resource Management, 27*(15), 1755–1776. https://doi.org/10.1080/09585192.2015.1075574

Clark, S. C. (2001). Work cultures and work/family balance. *Journal of Vocational Behavior, 58*(3), 348–365. https://doi.org/10.1006/jvbe.2000.1759

Edgar, F., Geare, A., & Zhang, J. A. (2017). A comprehensive concomitant analysis of service employees' well-being and performance. *Personnel Review, 46*(8), 1870–1889. https://doi.org/10.1108/PR-05-2016-0108

Ejlertsson, L., Heijbel, B., Ejlertsson, G., & Andersson, I. (2018). Recovery, work-life balance and work experiences important to self-rated health: A questionnaire study on salutogenic work factors among Swedish primary health care employees. *Work, 59*(1), 155–163. https://doi.org/10.3233/WOR-172659

Elsworthy, E. (2019, March 20). Employees think about leaving their job after three and a half years on average, survey claims. *Independent.* Retrieved March 22, from https://www.independent.co.uk/news/uk/home-news/employee-job-quit-pay-rise-survey-results-spana-a8829601.html

Frone, M. R. (2003). Work-family balance. In J. C. Quick & L. E. Tetrick (Eds.), *Handbook of occupational health psychology* (pp. 143–162). American Psychological Association.

Ganster, D. C., Rosen, C. C., & Fisher, G. G. (2018). Long working hours and well-being: What we know, what we do not know, and what we need to know. *Journal of Business and Psychology, 33,* 25–39. https://doi.org/10.1007/s10869-016-9478-1

Ghafoor, A., & Haar, J. (2021). Does job stress enhance employee creativity? Exploring the role of psychological capital. *Personnel Review 51*(2), 644–661. https://doi.org/10.1108/PR-08-2019-0443

Giauque, D., Anderfuhren-Biget, S., & Varone, F. (2019). Stress and turnover intents in international organizations: Social support and work–life balance as resources. *The International Journal of Human Resource Management, 30*(5), 879–901. https://doi.org/10.1080/09585192.2016.1254105

Gloss, A., Carr, S. C., Reichman, W., & Abdul-Nasiru, I. (2017). From handmaidens to POSH humanitarians. *Industrial & Organizational Psychology Journal, 10*, 1–41.

Greenhaus, J., & Allen, T. (2011). Work–family balance: A review and extension of the literature. In J. C. Quick, & L. E. Tetrick (Eds.), *Handbook of occupational health psychology* (2nd ed.). American Psychological Association.

Greenhaus, J. H., & Beutell, N. J. (1985). Sources of conflict between work and family roles. *Academy of Management Review, 10*(1), 76–88.

Greenhaus, J. H., & Powell, G. N. (2006). When work and family are allies: A theory of work-family enrichment. *Academy of Management Review, 31,* 72–92.

Haar, J. M. (2013). Testing a new measure of work-life balance: A study of parent and non-parent employees from New Zealand. *The International Journal of Human Resource Management, 24*, 3305–3324.

Haar, J. (2022). What are the odds of burnt-out risk and leaving the job? Turnover intent consequences of worker burnout using a two sample New Zealand study. *International Journal of Selection and Assessment.* https://doi.org/10.1111/ijsa.12393

Haar, J., & Brougham, D. (2016). Organizational-based self-esteem: A within country comparison of outcomes between Maori and New Zealand Europeans. *Journal of Management & Organization, 22*(5), 720–735. https://doi.org/10.1017/jmo.2015.59

Haar, J., & Brougham, D. (2022). Work antecedents and consequences of work-life balance: A two sample study within New Zealand. *The International Journal of Human Resource Management, 33*(4), 784–807. https://doi.org/10.1080/09585192.2020.1751238

Haar, J., Brougham, D., Roche, M., & Barney, A. (2017). Servant leadership and work engagement: The mediating role of work-life balance. *New Zealand Journal of Human Resource Management, 17*(2), 56–72.

Haar, J., Carr, S. C., Arrowsmith, J., Parker, J., Hodgetts, D., & Alefaio-Tugia, S. (2018). Escape from working poverty: Steps toward sustainable livelihood. *Sustainability, 10*(11), 4144. https://doi.org/10.3390/su10114144

Haar, J., Daellenbach, U., O'Kane, C., Ruckstuhl, K., & Davenport, S. (2021). Top executives work-life balance, job burnout and turnover intentions: Moderated-mediation with knowledge sharing culture. *New Zealand Journal of Employment Relations, 46*(1), 1–22. https://doi.org/10.24135/nzjer.v46i1.46

Haar, J., Di Fabio, A., & Daellenbach, U. (2019). Does positive relational management benefit managers higher up the hierarchy? A moderated mediation study of New Zealand *Managers. Sustainability, 11*(16), 4373. https://doi.org/10.3390/su11164373

Haar, J. M., & Harris, C. (2023). A moderated mediation study of high performance work systems and insomnia on New Zealand employees: Job burnout mediating and work-life balance moderating. *The International Journal of Human Resource Management, 34*(1), 68–91.https://doi.org/10.1080/09585192.2021.1961161

Haar, J., & Mowat, R. (2021). Are human resource practices the key to managing job burnout in New Zealand nurses? Testing a path model. *Journal of Clinical Nursing, 31*(17–18), 2574–2583. https://doi.org/10.1111/jocn.16077

Haar, J. M., Russo, M., Sune, A., & Ollier-Malaterre, A. (2014). Outcomes of work-life balance on job satisfaction, life satisfaction and mental health: A study across seven cultures. *Journal of Vocational Behavior, 85,* 361–373.

Haar, J. M., Suñe, A., Russo, M., & Ollier-Malaterre, A. (2019). A cross-national study on the antecedents of work-life balance from the fit and balance perspective. *Social Indicators Research, 142*, 261–282. https://doi.org/10.1007/s11205-018-1875-6

Hayman, J. (2005). Psychometric assessment of an instrument designed to measure work life balance. *Research and Practice in Human Resource Management, 13*(1), 85–91.

Henrich, J., Heine, S. J., & Norenzayan, A. (2010a). Most people are not WEIRD. *Nature, 466*(7302), 29. https://doi.org/10.1038/466029a

Henrich, J., Heine, S. J., & Norenzayan, A. (2010b). The weirdest people in the world? *Behavioral and Brain Sciences, 33*(2/3), 61–83. https://doi.org/10.1017/S0140525X0999152X

Hobfoll, S. E. (1989). Conservation of resources: A new attempt at conceptualizing stress. *American Psychologist, 44*(3), 513–524. https://psycnet.apa.org/doi/10.1037/0003-066X.44.3.513

Hobfoll, S. E. (2002). Social and psychological resources and adaptation. *Review of General Psychology, 6*(4), 307–324. https://doi.org/10.1037/1089-2680.6.4.307

Hobfoll, S. E., Halbesleben, J., Neveu, J. P., & Westman, M. (2018). Conservation of resources in the organizational context: The reality of resources and their consequences. *Annual Review of Organizational Psychology and Organizational Behavior, 5*(1), 103–128. https://doi.org/10.1146/annurev-orgpsych-032117-104640

Hodgetts, D., Groot, S., & Garden, E. (2017). The precariat, everyday life and objects of despair. In C. Howarth & E. Andreouli (Eds.), *The social psychology of everyday politics* (pp. 183–198). Routledge.

Jiang, L., & Lavaysse, L. M. (2018). Cognitive and affective job insecurity: A meta-analysis and a primary study. *Journal of Management, 44*(6), 2307–2342. https://doi.org/10.1177/0149206318773853

Kossek, E. E., Pichler, S., Bodner, T., & Hammer, L. B. (2011). Workplace social support and work-family conflict: A meta-analysis clarifying the influence of general and work-family-specific supervisor and organizational support. *Personnel Psychology, 64*(2), 289–313. https://doi.org/10.1111/j.1744-6570.2011.01211.x

Kurtessis, J. N., Eisenberger, R., Ford, M. T., Buffardi, L. C., Stewart, K. A., & Adis, C. S. (2015). Perceived organizational support: A meta-analytic evaluation of organizational support theory. *Journal of Management, 43*(6), 1854–1884. https://doi.org/10.1177/0149206315575554

Maré, D. C., & Hyslop, D. (2021). *Minimum wages in New Zealand: Policy and practice in the 21st century* (Motu Working Paper No. 21-03). Motu Economic and Public Policy Research.

Ollier-Malaterre, A., & Foucreault, A. (2017). Cross-national work-life research: Cultural and structural impacts for individuals and organizations. *Journal of Management, 43*(1), 111–136. https://doi.org/10.1177/0149206316655873

Poulose, S., & Dhal, M. (2020). Role of perceived work-life balance between work overload and career commitment. *Journal of Managerial Psychology, 35*(3), 169–183. https://doi.org/10.1108/JMP-03-2018-0117

Premeaux, S. F., Adkins, C. L., & Mossholder, K. W. (2007). Balancing work and family: A field study of multi-dimensional, multi-role work-family conflict. *Journal of Organizational Behavior, 28*(6), 705–727. https://doi.org/10.1002/job.439

Rashid, M. S., Haar, J., Rashid, M. S., & Shami, G. M. (2022). Work demands, work-life balance and affect: A study of Pakistan managers. *New Zealand Journal of Human Resources Management, 22*(1), 32–45.

Russo, M., Shteigman, A., & Carmeli, A. (2016). Workplace and family support and work–life balance: Implications for individual psychological availability and energy at work. *The Journal of Positive Psychology, 11*(2), 173–188. https://doi.org/10.1080/17439760.2015.1025424

Sahadi, J. (2021, October 21). Fortune 500 CEO: 'Work-life balance is a lie'. *CNN Business*. Retrieved November 24, 2021, from https://edition.cnn.com/2021/10/12/success/thasunda-brown-duckett-ceo-work-life-balance/index.html

Saltzstein, A. L., Ting, Y., & Saltzstein, G. H. (2001). Work-family balance and job satisfaction: The impact of family-friendly policies on attitudes of federal government employees. *Public Administration Review, 61*(4), 452–467. https://doi.org/10.1111/0033-3352.00049

Schnettler, B., Miranda-Zapata, E., Grunert, K. G., Lobos, G., Lapo, M., & Hueche, C. (2021). Testing the spillover-crossover model between work-life balance and satisfaction in different domains of life in dual-earner household. *Applied Research in Quality of Life, 16*(4), 1475–1501. https://doi.org/10.1007/s11482-020-09828-z

Smith, L. (2015). Reforming the minimum wage: Towards a psychological perspective. *American Psychologist, 70*(6), 557–565. https://psycnet.apa.org/doi/10.1037/a0039579

Spector, P. E., Cooper, C. L., Poelmans, S. A., Allen, T. D., O'Driscoll, M., Sanchez, J. I., Siu, O. L., Dewe, P., Hart, P., & Lu, L. (2004). A cross-national comparative study of work-family stressors, working hours, and well-being: China and Latin America versus the Anglo world. *Personnel Psychology, 57*(1), 119–142. https://doi.org/10.1111/j.1744-6570.2004.tb02486.x

Standing, G. (2011). The precariat—The new dangerous class. Bloomsbury.

Statistics New Zealand. (2014). *New Zealand household travel survey: Travel to work, by main urban area results (3-year moving average)*. Retrieved October 2, 2022, from https://nzdotstat.stats.govt.nz/wbos/Index.aspx?DataSetCode=TABLECODE7432

Statistics New Zealand. (2019). *Household labour force survey multiple job holders: June 2019 quarter.*

Sturges, J. & Guest, D. (2004). Working to live or living to work? Work/life balance early in the career. *Human Resource Management Journal, 14*(4), 5–20. https://doi.org/10.1111/j.1748-8583.2004.tb00130.x

Talukder, A. K. M., Vickers, M., & Khan, A. (2018). Supervisor support and work-life balance. *Personnel Review, 47*(3), 727–744. https://doi.org/10.1108/PR-12-2016-0314

ten Brummelhuis, L. L., & Bakker, A. B. (2012). A resource perspective on the work-home interface: The work-home resources model. *American Psychologist, 67*(7), 545–556. https://psycnet.apa.org/doi/10.1037/a0027974

The New Zealand Attitudes and Values Study. (2015). *Regional Commute Times for Adult New Zealanders, 2015.* Retrieved October 2, 2022, from https://cdn.auckland.ac.nz/assets/psych/about/our-research/nzavs/Feedback%20Reports/NZAVS-Policy-Brief-Regional-Commute-Times.pdf

Vaziri, H., Wayne, J. H., Casper, W. J., Lapierre, L., Greenhaus, J., Amirkamali, F., & Li, Y. (2022). A meta-analytic investigation of the personal and work-related antecedents of work-family balance. *Journal of Organizational Behavior, 43*(4), 662–692. https://doi.org/10.1002/job.2594

18

MULTILEVEL FACTORS COUNTERACTING THE ADVERSE EFFECTS OF JOB INSECURITY

Lixin Jiang, Katharina Naswall, and Xiaohong (Violet) Xu

We live in a transformational era. The changing world is having a profound impact on our working lives. Globalization, digitalization, and other megatrends are constantly and rapidly transforming the way we work. For example, automation is estimated to replace 14% of existing jobs and radically change another 32% of individual tasks in the next 15–20 years (Organisation for Economic Co-operation and Development [OECD], 2019). Recently, COVID-19-related restrictions have led to global working-hour losses that were equivalent to 255 million full-time jobs in 2020: approximately 4 times greater than during the Global Financial Crisis in 2009 (International Labour Organization, 2021).

Unsurprisingly, these changes create precarity at work, resulting in employees worrying about the outlook for their employment. Consequently, job insecurity is the new normal. Unfortunately, the very real concern over one's job prospects has devastating consequences for both the employees and their organization. For example, job insecurity is significantly related to 30 work-related outcomes (e.g., job satisfaction, organizational commitment, work engagement, burnout, and turnover intentions) and 10 individual outcomes (e.g., psychological and physical health, anxiety, depression, and work-life conflict; Jiang & Lavaysse, 2018). Given that the sources of job insecurity are sometimes beyond individual control (e.g., economic recession; Jiang et al., 2021), the main purpose of this chapter is to identify myriad variables operating at the individual, organizational, and societal levels that have been found to enable employees to remain healthy, happy, and productive, despite their job insecurity. Thus, these factors can serve as springboards for the development of intervention to alleviate the harmful impacts of job insecurity. Below, we start with the definition and

DOI: 10.4324/9781003440444-22

conceptualizations of job insecurity, followed by its outcomes and mechanisms. Then, we primarily focus on the moderators that alter people's reactions to job insecurity, and evidence-based interventions that target job insecurity and its outcomes.

Definitions and Conceptualizations of Job Insecurity

After reviewing various definitions of job insecurity, Shoss (2017) defined job insecurity as "a perceived threat to the continuity and stability of employment as it is currently experienced" (p. 1914). Three defining features of job insecurity are subjectivity, uncertainty, and vulnerability (Jiang et al., 2021). That is, as a subjective perception, job insecurity is characterized by uncertainty about the future and potential *un*desired changes to the job (Lee et al., 2018).

Job insecurity can be viewed as uni-dimensional or multidimensional. Uni-dimensional conceptualizations focus on global job insecurity (De Witte, 1999), while multidimensional conceptualizations differentiate between quantitative and qualitative job insecurity as well as between cognitive and affective job insecurity. Specifically, quantitative job insecurity is one's concerns relating to the continuation of the job itself, whereas qualitative job insecurity is one's concerns relating to the continuation of valued job features (Hellgren et al., 1999). However, cognitive job insecurity is described as perceptions of the likelihood that there might be detrimental changes to the job, either in terms of job loss or loss of valued job features (Lee et al., 2018), whereas affective job insecurity is described as the affective reactions to cognitive job insecurity (Jiang & Lavaysse, 2018), expressed as worry, anxiety, or fear. Interestingly, Jiang and Lavaysse's (2018) meta-analysis indicated that affective job insecurity acts as a transmitter of the effect of cognitive job insecurity to potential outcomes.

Outcomes and Mechanisms of Job Insecurity

Job insecurity has been shown to be associated with many negative outcomes in several meta-analyses (e.g., Jiang & Lavaysse, 2018; Sverke et al., 2019). These outcomes range from lower levels of health and wellbeing (e.g., poorer mental and physical health, higher levels of burnout, and lower work engagement) to job-related attitudinal variables (e.g., lower job satisfaction and commitment, and higher turnover intentions). Interestingly, a recent meta-analysis confirms that job insecurity displays a U-shaped relationship with task performance and organizational citizenship behaviors; yet the positive relationships of job insecurity with task performance and citizenship behaviors after inflection points are much weaker compared to their negative associations prior to the inflection points (Jiang et al., 2022). Moreover, a review of longitudinal studies shows strong evidence that job insecurity influences psychological wellbeing and somatic health over time, rather than the other way around (De Witte et al., 2016). Thus, it is widely accepted that job insecurity is a predictor of negative outcomes for both individuals and organizations.

As job insecurity is commonly conceptualized as a stressor, stress theories have been utilized to understand why job insecurity is associated with detrimental outcomes (Shoss, 2017). For example, appraisal theory of stress (Lazarus & Folkman, 1984) argues that stress perceptions and reactions will follow when a threat against an employee's job is perceived and coping strategies to counteract the threat are unknown or insufficient (De Witte, 1999). Conservation of resources theory argues that job insecurity threatens an employee's valuable resources at work (Hobfoll, 1989), such as manifest and latent benefits (Vander Elst et al., 2016), and therefore prompts strain reactions. The job demands-resources model views job insecurity as a demand that is associated with psychological costs for employees (Bakker & Demerouti, 2007). If the demand of job insecurity is not successfully met by resources, strain ensues.

These theoretical perspectives can be integrated to understand the adverse outcomes of job insecurity, as well as the moderators that may alter employees' reactions to job insecurity discussed below. That is, these stress perspectives predict that resources at the individual, organizational, and societal levels can be used to meet the demand and counteract the adverse effects of job insecurity.

Multilevel Moderators Counteracting the Adverse Effects of Job Insecurity

The aforementioned stress mechanisms are key to understanding under what circumstances outcomes of job insecurity are most likely to arise (i.e., boundary conditions). Doing so also sheds light on how the negative consequences of job insecurity can be prevented. Specifically, the stress perspective argues that to offset job insecurity, individuals can call on available resources. Thus, employees with adequate and effective coping resources that can help individuals to attain their goals are better equipped to prevent adverse effects of job insecurity. Based on their sources, resources can be categorized as personal, organizational, and societal resources (ten Brummelhuis & Bakker, 2012). Moreover, as mentioned above, job insecurity is characterized by subjectivity, uncertainty, and vulnerability (Jiang et al., 2021). The resources discussed below are highly relevant to one or more of these features. For example, work centrality may increase one's vulnerability to job insecurity, while emotional intelligence may reduce the subjectivity of job insecurity. However, job control and organizational communication may reduce uncertainty associated with job insecurity.

Resources at the Individual Level

Personal resources may enable employees to counteract the thwarting effects of job insecurity. Many studies have explored various personal resources moderating the relationships between job insecurity and outcomes. For example, personal resources such as an internal locus of control (Ito & Brotheridge, 2007), secure attachment (Jiang, 2017), and core self-evaluation (Li et al., 2022) have been associated with less negative reactions to job insecurity, while high negative affectivity exacerbates the associations between job insecurity and negative outcomes (Näswall et al., 2005). Nevertheless, these factors are relatively stable and therefore less modifiable through interventions. Thus, we intentionally restrict our discussion to individual-level moderators that are malleable. Moreover, training interventions are available to increase these personal resources and the effect of such training persists over time (e.g., Peterson et al., 2011).

Employability

Employability is someone's perception that they are able to get alternate employment should they need to (Berntson & Marklund, 2007). Employability may serve as a resource, influencing the appraisal process by helping employees feel they can handle the possible threat against their job. By feeling that they may be able to get new employment if the threat of job loss, or an undesirable change of working conditions, should be realized, those with high employability should react less negatively to job insecurity.

However, the relationship between job insecurity and employability is complicated. The evidence of employability as a predictor of job insecurity has received the most support (De Cuyper et al., 2008). Furthermore, recent research indicates that employability moderates the relationship between organizational change and job insecurity (Çalışkan & Özkoç, 2020), where those with high (vs. low) employability are less likely to report job insecurity in relation to organizational change. Research also suggests that employability and job insecurity are reciprocally related, where employability predicts lower job insecurity and job insecurity predicts lower employability (De Cuyper et al., 2012).

More relevantly, previous studies have indicated that employability is associated with less negative reactions to job insecurity in terms of life satisfaction (Silla et al., 2009) and commitment to change (Kalyal et al., 2010). Interestingly, because employability enables individuals to easily find an alternative job, those with high employability report stronger intentions to quit and lower loyalty resulting from job insecurity (Berntson et al., 2010). Thus, more research is needed to clarify the role of employability in the job insecurity process.

Emotional Intelligence

Emotional intelligence is the ability to detect and manage emotional cues and information (Mayer & Salovey, 1997). Emotional intelligence includes several abilities: the ability to be aware of one's own and others' emotions, the ability to manage these emotions, and the ability to understand the complex relationships between emotions and emotional transitions (i.e., emotion perception, assimilation, understanding, and management). Employees with high (vs. low) emotional intelligence may be better equipped to deal with negative consequences of job insecurity (Jordan et al., 2002). Indeed, Cheng et al. (2012) found that emotional intelligence weakened the relationship between job insecurity and somatic complaints.

Resilience

Resilience can be operationalized as both dispositional tendencies and coping strategies. That is, resilience can be an individual difference in the capacity to bounce back or recover from stress (Smith et al., 2008) or the tendency to "cope with stress in a highly adaptative manner" (Sinclair & Wallston, 2004, p. 94). Either way, resilience allows individuals to better cope with stressors, recover from workplace adversities, and grow and learn from those challenges, emerging stronger than before. Indeed, Shoss et al. (2018) supported the buffering effect of resilience during times of job insecurity.

Psychological Capital (PsyCap)

PsyCap includes hope, self-efficacy, resilience, and optimism. Individuals who are high in PsyCap can mobilize resources from their environment, thereby minimizing negative outcomes of job insecurity. Probst et al. (2017) found that the nonlinear relationships of job insecurity with in-role performance and organizational citizenship behaviors are largely attenuated among employees with high (vs. low) PsyCap. Similarly, PsyCap also weakens the association between job insecurity and subjective wellbeing (Darvishmotevali & Ali, 2020), and the indirect association between job insecurity and job satisfaction via anxiety (Cheung et al., 2019).

Trait Mindfulness

Trait mindfulness is a personal resource that shapes individuals' reactions to work stressors. High trait mindfulness interrupts automatic conditioned reactions, providing employees with a large "psychological space" to access new perspectives that allow them to constructively cope with job-insecure situations

(Brown & Ryan, 2003). Thus, mindful employees can be protected against the draining effects of job insecurity. Indeed, Montani et al. (2021) observed that high trait mindfulness attenuates the negative relationship of job insecurity with intrinsic motivation and, indirectly, with innovative behaviors.

Grit

Grit is perseverance in the face of obstacles. Probst et al. (2021) found that the indirect relationships of job insecurity with various outcomes via idiosyncratic deals (i-deal) with employers depend on employee grit (specifically, perseverance of effort), such that higher grit attenuates the negative relationship between job insecurity and the pursuit of I-Deals and the indirect relationships. Thus, grit might be an essential resource, enabling employees to optimize their work arrangements, improve the work process, and overcome the difficulties associated with high job insecurity.

Work Centrality

Work centrality refers to the importance that working has in one's life (Hirschfeld & Field, 2000). Those with high work centrality believe that work is the most important part of life. Thus, when their employment is under threat, employees who highly value their job may react more negatively. Indeed, Jiang and Lavaysse (2018) found that those high in work centrality are more likely to report affective job insecurity when experiencing cognitive job insecurity. However, Hu et al. (2021) found that the negative effect of qualitative job insecurity on subjective wellbeing is more pronounced among those with low (as opposite to high) work centrality. Thus, whether work centrality operates as a buffer or an exacerbator in the relationships between job insecurity and its outcomes requires further examinations.

Regulatory Focus

The regulatory focus theory (Higgins, 1997) posits that highly prevention-focused individuals are driven by security and safety needs, prefer vigilant and avoidant coping strategies, and are inclined to pursue the maintenance of routines and the status quo. Highly promotion-focused individuals, however, are driven by the nurturance need, prefer eager approach coping strategies, and are inclined to pursue development and change. Thus, prevention focus may be more suitable for coping with quantitative job insecurity, which primarily threatens one's security and safety needs, while promotion focus may be more suitable for coping with qualitative job insecurity, which primarily threatens one's development and growth needs. Tu et al. (2020) indeed found that prevention focus weakens the positive relationship between quantitative job insecurity and employee stress symptoms, whereas promotion focus weakens the negative relationship between qualitative job insecurity and work engagement.

Coping Styles

Coping styles present one's response to a threat or demand (Lazarus & Folkman, 1984). Coping styles have been categorized in various ways, with the main categorization being problem-focused vs. emotion-focused. Typically, problem-focused coping is directed at the source of the threat, to change the threat in some way. In the case of job insecurity where the source is often unclear and ambiguous (De Witte, 1999), addressing the problem may not be effective. Instead, emotion-focused coping, directed at lessening the worry or anxiety felt in relation to the threat, may be more effective in the case of job insecurity. Experimental research has indicated that emotion-focused coping can be more beneficial to prevent negative reactions to a less controllable threat (e.g., layoff events) than problem-focused coping (Probst & Jiang, 2016).

The Tendency to Gossip

Jiang et al. (2019) conceptualized one's tendency to gossip as an emotion-focused coping style and distinguished negative gossip (when talk about others is negative and judgmental) from positive gossip (when talk about others is positive and complimentary). Different types of gossip were hypothesized to moderate the negative impact of different types of job insecurity (i.e., quantitative vs. qualitative) on workplace friendship. They found that employees' tendency to positive gossip buffers the negative relationship between qualitative job insecurity (undesirable changes to one's job features while maintaining organizational membership) and friendships, while employees' tendency to negative gossip buffers the negative relationship between quantitative job insecurity (the possibility of losing organizational membership) and workplace friendships. It suggests that different types of job insecurity may require different types of coping strategies and personal resources.

Resources at the Organizational Level

Organizational resources relate to social relations in the workplace (e.g., social support) and factors relating to organizational conditions, policies, and practices (Jiang et al., 2021). Many empirical studies have examined the moderating role of organizational resources in mitigating the negative impacts of job insecurity.

Social Support

Social support from a variety of different sources, including work (e.g., organizational support, supervisor support, coworker, and peer support) and nonwork (e.g., family support, friend support) sources (Lim, 1996), may buffer against the negative impact of job insecurity on various job-related outcomes (e.g., job satisfaction, in-role performance, creativity, safety performance), as well as employee health and wellbeing (e.g., life satisfaction, mental health complaints, somatic complaints; Guo et al., 2019; Schreurs et al., 2012). For example, work-based support mitigates mental health complaints relating to job insecurity, and nonwork support attenuates carryover effects of job insecurity (worrying about work outside work hours; Näswall et al., 2005). Interestingly, Teng et al. (2019) supported the idea that both *giving* support and receiving support reduces the negative effect of job insecurity on creativity where they both weaken the positive effect of job insecurity on employee irritation—a mediator linking job insecurity and creativity. They argued that giving support can enhance one's self-esteem, sense of mastery, and autonomy: all of which equip employees with personal resources to offset against job insecurity.

Constructive Leadership

Leadership also plays an important role in the relationships between job insecurity and employee outcomes. In particular, constructive leadership provides employees with valuable resources to counteract the adverse effects of job insecurity. For example, Castanon (2006) found that transformational leadership attenuates the negative relationship between job insecurity and supervisor satisfaction. Similarly, ethical leadership may attenuate the positive effects of job insecurity on job stress (Kim & Kim, 2020) and turnover intentions (Addai et al., 2022).

Leader-Member Exchange (LMX) and Guanxi

High LMX features mutual respect, deep trust, and professional relationships and obligations (Graen & Uhl-Bien, 1995), thereby serving as a social resource in the workplace. High LMX may mitigate employees' negative reactions to job insecurity. For example, in Chinese samples, LMX was found to attenuate the negative effects of job insecurity on employee altruism (Loi et al., 2011), organizational commitment (Cheng et al., 2012; Hu & Zuo, 2007), and somatic complaints (Cheng et al., 2012). In an American sample, Probst et al. (2016) indicated that employees report higher supervisor satisfaction, less health ailments, and fewer workplace accidents relating to job insecurity when LMX is high.

Unique to China, subordinate-supervisor *guanxi*, or interpersonal relationships that contain implicit mutual obligations, assurances, and understanding, is an important resource for employees. Empirically, Lam et al. (2015) confirmed that the nonlinear relationship between job insecurity and organizational citizenship behavior is only observed among those with low (vs. high) *guanxi* in a Chinese sample.

Trust

Because trust in management and the organization may increase the predictability of an ambiguous situation, trust serves as a valuable resource that weakens the negative impact of job insecurity on employees. Indeed, both trust in management (Jiang & Probst, 2019) and trust in the organization (Wong et al., 2005) have been found to buffer against the negative impacts of job insecurity on various outcomes (see also Searle & McWha-Hermann on trust, Chapter 4). Likewise, with a large sample of employees from 1,149 organizations, Wang et al. (2018) found that collective trust in management (i.e., employees shared perceptions regarding management being reliable, fair, and honest) significantly attenuates the negative impact of job insecurity on organizational commitment and work-related anxiety.

Organizational Communication

Organizations can also improve communications to help employees navigate job-insecure situations, as information disseminated by the organization and managers is valuable, increasing the predictability of a work situation and rebuilding employees' sense of control. Research suggests that organizational communication not only reduces employee job insecurity (e.g., Bordia et al., 2004; Vander Elst et al., 2010) but also mitigates the negative impact of job insecurity on employee outcomes (Jiang & Probst, 2014), although the interaction between organizational communication and job insecurity was not found in an earlier study (Vander Elst et al., 2010).

Organizational Justice

Organizational justice, defined as employees' perceptions of fairness in the organization (i.e., a multidimensional construct consisting of distributive justice, procedural justice, informational justice, and interpersonal justice), could alleviate the negative consequences of job insecurity (Saltzman et al., Chapter 2). For instance, with Chinese samples, organizational justice was found to reduce the negative impact of job insecurity on employee psychological safety (Long et al., 2021) and job performance (Wang et al., 2015). Recently, De Angelis et al. (2021) revealed that organizational justice buffers the spillover effect of job insecurity on work-family conflict. Interestingly, the indirect relationship between job insecurity and work-family conflict via work withdrawal and emotional exhaustion was further alleviated by organizational justice (Nauman et al., 2020). Thus, the way that the organization manages, explains, and clarifies decisions to employees plays a crucial role in neutralizing the negative effects of job insecurity.

Job Control

Improving employee job control or autonomy (i.e., individuals' perceived freedom and discretion in scheduling their work and determining their work procedures) is another effective way to alleviate the negative consequences of job insecurity. For instance, Barling and Kelloway (1996) found that the significant negative relationships of job insecurity with somatic symptoms and blood pressure were only observed under low (vs. high) levels of job control. Similarly, Schreurs et al. (2010) demonstrated that job control alleviates the negative effects of job insecurity on employee need for recovery and general health. Notably, recent research has indicated that perceived control might instead serve as an underlying mechanism explaining why job insecurity may be detrimental (e.g., Vander Elst et al., 2016).

Participative Decision-making

A related concept is participative decision-making where employees are given opportunities to regain control over important aspects of their job. Because participative decision-making allows employees to have voice in job-related decisions, it may be effective in attenuating adverse consequences of job insecurity. For example, Bordia et al. (2004) found that participative decision-making significantly reduces employees' perceived uncertainty during organizational change as well as the negative impact of such uncertainty. Likewise, participative decision-making was found to buffer against the relationships of job insecurity with work engagement (Vander Elst et al., 2010), burnout, job satisfaction, job crafting (Urbanaviciute et al., 2021), work withdraw, and turnover intentions (Probst, 2005).

Organizational Climate

Organizational climate is a set of underlying values, beliefs, and principles that employees perceive are held within their organization. Organizational climate provides cues and signals regarding expected and valued employee behaviors. Facet-specific climates, such as safety and justice, have been examined in the context of job insecurity. For example, when employees perceive that their organization values and emphasizes safety (i.e., high organizational safety climate), the relationships of job insecurity with safety outcomes (e.g., safety knowledge, safety compliance, near misses, accidents, and injuries) are attenuated (Probst, 2004). Relatedly, Sora et al. (2010) found that an organizational justice climate buffers against the relationships of job insecurity with job satisfaction and turnover intentions above and beyond individual organizational justice. Thus, creating an organization that values safety and justice is crucial for employees to cope constructively with job insecurity.

Organizational Intervention Programs

In addition to improving the above-mentioned working conditions, organizations may offer intervention programs to enhance employee health and wellbeing. Employees may perceive such programs as signaling that the organization cares about their wellbeing (i.e., organizational support), thereby attenuating the damaging consequences of job insecurity. For example, people with job insecurity are likely to work despite feeling ill (i.e., presenteeism) as employees generally expect positive outcomes from good attendance. However, Schmidt and Pförtner (2020) found that the positive relationship between job insecurity and presenteeism only exists if companies have no workplace health promotion program. Similarly, Lee and Tsai (2022) found in a Chinese sample from 43 companies that the negative association between job insecurity and life satisfaction is weaker in companies with better work-life balance programs that allow employees to separate their work and life responsibilities. Thus, merely offering organizational intervention programs that do not necessarily target job insecurity can protect employees from detrimental outcomes of job insecurity, revealing the symbolic value of organizational support for employees to cope with work stressors.

Macro-moderators at the Societal Level

Macro-factors are defined as "characteristics of the larger economic, social, cultural system in which a person is embedded" (ten Brummelhuis & Bakker, 2012, p. 548). Macro-factors may serve as enablers or barriers signaling contextual opportunities or constraints (Johns, 2006). Individuals in an environment that fosters resource creation and sustenance (i.e., macro-opportunity) may react less negatively to job insecurity, whereas individuals in an environment that limits resource accumulation and maintenance (i.e., macro-constraint) may react more strongly to job insecurity. That is, macro-opportunities can enable individuals to better cope with job insecurity, whereas macro-constraints can create barriers for individuals to cope with job insecurity. Therefore, macro-opportunities and constraints may serve as cross-level moderators altering the relationships between job insecurity and its outcomes.

Cultural Contexts as Moderators

Culture, or a "collective programming of the mind" (Hofstede, 2001, p. 9), refers to shared sets of norms for behavior, preferred or proscribed roles for individuals within a larger social structure, and values commonly shared by societal members (Triandis, 1995). Thus, cultural values influence how people process information, specify what people may notice and how they evaluate events, and prescribe guiding principles and values (Haar, Chapter 17).

Individualism-Collectivism

People from collectivistic cultures tend to value job security more than their individualistic counterparts because security, conformity, and tradition are core values of collectivism (Triandis, 1995). Indeed, employees from China where people tend to be collectivists were found to react more negatively to job insecurity than employees from the US, where people tend to be individualists (Probst & Lawler, 2006).

Power Distance, Egalitarianism, and Hierarchy

Power distance, egalitarianism, and hierarchy all capture the extent to which resources are (un)equally distributed in a society, thereby having implications for employee reactions to job insecurity. High power-distance cultures, defined as "the extent to which a society accepts the fact that power in institutions and organizations is distributed unequally" (Hofstede, 1980, p. 45), hamper social progress, promote the misuse of power, and result in unequal divisions of wealth, as well as unfair procedures and practices that determine hiring, pay raises, promotion, and layoffs (Davis & Ruhe, 2003). However, individuals in egalitarian societies are treated more equally, regardless of their gender, socioeconomic status, and ethnic background, while hierarchy is the polar opposite of egalitarianism (Schwartz, 2013). Consequently, power distance and hierarchy may exacerbate, but egalitarianism may buffer against, the negative impacts of job insecurity. Indeed, Xu et al. (2022) found that the negative relationship between job insecurity and pay satisfaction is stronger in countries with high (vs. low) power distance, whereas egalitarianism diminishes the negative impacts of job insecurity on job satisfaction, pay satisfaction, and organizational commitment. The moderating role of hierarchy, however, was not significant.

Uncertainty Avoidance (UA) and Enacted UA

UA reflects the society's level of tolerance for uncertainty (i.e., unstructured, unknown, or surprising situations). High UA societies tend to be rigid and have a shared preference for clear rules, standardization of situations, as well as law and order, whereas low UA societies tend to accept ill-defined situations as something normal. Thus, in a high UA society, people may perceive job insecurity more threatening than those in low UA society. However, König et al. (2011) found the opposite; the relationships of job insecurity with job satisfaction, organizational commitment, and turnover intentions were stronger in the US (more tolerant of uncertainty) than in the Switzerland (less tolerant of uncertainty). It is plausible that high UA societies may try to minimize uncertainty through the enactment and strict enforcement of laws, rules, and other safety and security measures designed to reduce such uncertainty (Hofstede, 2001). Thus, the strong UA of the Swiss may be expressed in part through social policies that provide workers with greater security should they face job loss.

Enacted UA is a practical consequence of the tendency to avoid uncertainty, representing the extent to which people from a society rely on "social norms, rules and procedures to alleviate the unpredictability of future events" (House et al., 2004, p. 30). Thus, people from countries with high enacted UA emphasize structured lives with laws and rules covering the majority of situations. When confronted with job insecurity, employees in countries with high enacted UA are expected to have a clearer idea regarding what happens and how they are protected in the event of job loss, thereby having a weaker reaction to job insecurity than those in countries with low enacted UA. With employees from 24 countries, enacted UA was found to buffer the negative relationships of job insecurity with job satisfaction and affective commitment (Debus et al., 2012). Similarly, the relationship between quantitative job insecurity and turnover intentions is weaker in the German-speaking region (higher enacted UA) than in the French-speaking region (lower enacted UA) of Switzerland (Sender et al., 2017).

Masculinity

Masculinity refers to the extent to which individuals in a country show a traditionally more masculine interest pattern; people in masculine countries attribute a considerable amount of importance to status, success, assertiveness, and material things, which is expressed by the fact that work occupies a central place in people's lives (Hofstede, 2001). Thus, when employees in highly masculine countries perceive that their job is at stake, they may perceive the experience of job insecurity as a sign of weakness and failure, representing a threat to the material and nonmaterial things that they value, thereby aggravating their reactions to job insecurity. Indeed, Debus et al. (2020) found that individuals from countries with high (vs. low) masculinity report stronger decrements in job satisfaction relating to job insecurity. Interestingly, they also found that the moderating role of masculinity is transmitted through supervisor interpersonal justice and coworker support.

Societal Practice Performance Orientation

Societal practice performance orientation measures "the extent to which society is perceived to encourage and reward performance improvement" (House et al., 2004, p. 246). High performance-oriented cultures value training, development, and individual achievement and are more materialistic than less performance-oriented cultures. Additionally, people in such cultures believe that individuals are in control, have "can do" approaches, and value taking initiative. Thus, high societal practice performance orientation is likely to intensify employee reactions to job insecurity. Indeed, Sender et al. (2017) found that the negative relationship between qualitative job insecurity and job satisfaction is stronger for the German-speaking region of Switzerland (higher societal practice performance orientation) than for the French-speaking region (lower societal practice performance orientation).

Social Policies as Moderators

Countries also differ dramatically in other macro-factors such as "political, economic, and legal factors, educational systems, climate, resources, level of technological advancement, and demographic composition" (Gelfand et al., 2017, p. 497). Thus, these country-level differences may moderate the relationships between job insecurity and its outcomes.

Social Safety Net

A country's social safety net refers to the extent of government regulation of the labor market and governmental social protection programs designed to protect workers from job loss and significant income declines (Blank, 1994). Such safety net programs generally include (a) income-transfer programs, (b) in-kind programs providing access to health insurance or affordable housing, and (c) social insurance programs. They also encompass regulatory mechanisms that provide for continued job security or that mandate employer contributions to benefit programs such as unemployment insurance. With these essential resources associated with social safety net, Debus et al. (2012) found that a social safety net lessens the negative relationships of job insecurity with job satisfaction and organizational commitment. Similarly, Carr and Chung (2014) found that the negative association between employment insecurity and life satisfaction is weaker in countries with generous labor market policy measures, especially for the more vulnerable (i.e., blue collar, temporary workers in manufacturing sectors). Moreover, Sverke et al.'s (2019) meta-analysis found that the associations of job insecurity with task performance, contextual performance, and counterproductive work behavior are weaker in welfare regimes characterized by high (vs. low) social protection.

Flexicurity

Flexibility involves the combination of easing rules related to the hiring and firing of employees, and the development of more flexible work arrangements (e.g., contingent contracts). Security involves the utilization of proactive labor market policies that provide employees with marketable and up-to-date job skills and the provision of robust unemployment benefits (Carr, Hodgetts et al., Chapter 1). By combing these elements, employers have greater freedom to expand their workforce and employees have greater access to jobs with a robust social safety net and marketable job skills should they become unemployed in the future. Thus, flexicurity shifts the focus from providing employees with job security (i.e., retaining their current job) to enabling employment security (i.e., the ability to obtain employment).

Probst and Jiang (2017) examined the extent to which country-level flexicurity policies are effective in attenuating the adverse impacts of job insecurity. They found that workers in countries with high flexibility have different reactions to cognitive job insecurity as a function of country-level security. With high employment security, affective job insecurity and job stress relating to cognitive job insecurity are significantly attenuated, compared to countries with low employment security. Thus, flexicurity (high employment security coupled with high flexibility) weakens employee reactions to perceived job insecurity. However, low flexibility coupled with low security is generally related to the most negative employee outcomes. Interestingly, comparing high security-high flexibility countries to high security-low flexibility ones, Probst and Jiang's (2017) results suggest that high security coupled with low flexibility may result in exacerbated rather than attenuated reactions to perceived job insecurity. Thus, robust employment security protections only attenuate employee reactions to job insecurity when also accompanied by high flexibility policies.

Social (In)equality as Moderators

Social equality is another set of macro-resources that has implications for job insecurity as it is relevant to the distribution and availability of valuable social resources (ten Brummelhuis & Bakker, 2012).

Income Inequality

Country-level income inequality is the degree to which income is distributed unequally among citizens of a country (see, Carr, Hopner et al., Chapter 10). High income inequality represents a great gap between the "haves" and the "have nots." Therefore, individuals in high income-inequality countries are more likely to be deprived of desirable and valuable resources (Wilkinson & Pickett, 2009). Moreover, income inequality divides communities and decreases interpersonal trust (Ichida et al., 2009). Thus, country-level income inequality may threaten one's attainment of material and nonmaterial coping resources and exacerbate one's reactions to job insecurity. Indeed, country-level income inequality was found to compound the relationship between individual job insecurity and employee exhaustion (Jiang & Probst, 2017). The same pattern of results was replicated in another study by Taht et al. (2020) where both objective and subjective social inequality were examined (see also Carr, Hopner et al., Chapter 10).

National Corruption

National corruption is defined as the misuse of public power or authority for private gain or benefit via bribery, extortion, nepotism, and embezzlement (Gupta et al., 2002). Consequently, corruption results in the allocation and redistribution of resources from the general population to certain individuals, parties, or groups. Thus, the vulnerable in a society (e.g., the unemployed) are often not the ultimate beneficiaries of social programs. Indeed, national corruption was found to exacerbate the negative relationships between job insecurity and various employee outcomes (Xu et al., 2022). Interestingly, the above-mentioned moderating effects of egalitarianism and power distance on employees' reactions to job insecurity were explained by national corruption (Xu et al., 2022; on corruption, see also, Saltzman et al., Chapter 2; Saner & Yiu, Chapter 5; Kuhn, Chapter 12).

Evidence-Based Interventions to Reduce Job Insecurity and Its Outcomes

Although some of the moderators identified above (e.g., resilience, organizational climate, flexicurity) can be enhanced through interventions to attenuate the negative impacts of job insecurity, we were only able to identify four intervention studies directly relating to job insecurity. Schneider and DeNisi (1991) conducted one in which they examined the impact of a "realistic merger preview" involving a program of realistic communications providing detailed information regarding the merger, on employees of an organization with two manufacturing plants, that had just announced a merger. In one plant, employees received the realistic preview; however, in the control plant, employees received limited information on the merger. Although employees at both plants experienced initial negative effects following the announcement of the upcoming merger, the experimental plant rebounded more quickly from the negative effects; whereas employees in the control plant continued to report negative job attitudes, a lack of trust toward the company, and lower self-reported performance four months following the merger announcement. Although job insecurity was not measured (see, Seubert & Seubert, Chapter 14), this intervention revealed the importance of realistic communications as a means of reducing uncertainty and increasing employee commitment.

Recently, Barrech et al. (2018) conducted a supervisor-focused intervention to reduce employee job insecurity during organizational change. Supervisors were randomly assigned to either the intervention group or the control group. The intervention focused on factors that facilitate employee-supportive leadership during organizational change: (a) understanding their supervisory role as a resource for employees, (b) enhancing their ability to provide social support, (c) communicating effectively, and (d) improving their knowledge of work-related stress. Such an intervention was expected to reduce employee job insecurity and maintain their health in the long run. In the longitudinal intervention study at a work site with several organizational changes, job insecurity was reduced to a marginally significant degree post-intervention in the intervention group compared to the control group. Following the intervention, exhaustion among supervisors in the intervention group was significantly reduced. Overall, training supervisors to enhance their supportive leadership behavior during organizational change may reduce job insecurity among the team members.

Finally, Abildgaard et al. (2018) conducted an organizational-level intervention to prevent job insecurity caused by organizational restructuring and downsizing among postal delivery workers. The intervention was based on employee participation where employees were actively involved in planning and implementing the intervention and its activities. When job insecurity and restructuring were revealed to be substantial problems, managers and employees developed intervention activities (e.g., sharing consistent information) to address them. They found that the planned activities were implemented to a reasonable extent. Although qualitative job insecurity had a significant increase in the control group from the baseline survey to the follow-up survey one year later, employees in the intervention group reported a smaller increase in qualitative job insecurity. Overall, the study supports the use of participatory organizational-level interventions to reduce the inevitable increase of job insecurity during organizational restructuring.

Although important, the organizational-level interventions described above depend on organizational initiatives, thereby potentially lacking flexibility at the least. Therefore, Jiang (2018) developed a simple writing exercise that can be used to counteract the detrimental effect of job insecurity on creativity. Specifically, both work-affirmation manipulation (where participants were asked to write about a specific incident at work or something about their job in general that helped them feel good about themselves) and self-affirmation manipulation (where participants were asked to write an essay indicating why a particular value was important to them, and a time in their lives when this value had been especially important) were found to attenuate the negative relationship between job insecurity and creativity. Such writing exercises are promising for lifting employees up in the face of workplace challenges and setbacks.

Future Research Directions

Recent years have seen significant growth in job-insecurity research (Bazzoli & Probst, 2022). Despite progress made, there is still so much we do not know about job insecurity. Due to space limitations, we highlight three aspects that require researchers' attention, and that we believe will have the most impact on increasing our understanding of job insecurity.

Although the negative impacts of job insecurity on attitudinal and well-being-related outcomes have been well-documented (Jiang & Lavaysse, 2018), the relationships between job insecurity and behavioral outcomes (e.g., task performance and organizational citizenship behaviors) are less conclusive. A recent meta-analysis (Jiang et al., 2022) attempts to resolve this issue by contrasting two theoretical perspectives (an integrated perspective of social exchange theory and job preservation motivation vs. activation theory) and testing the curvilinear impacts of job insecurity on task performance, organizational citizenship behaviors, safety behaviors, creative performance, and counterproductive work behaviors. The confirmed U-shaped relationships between job insecurity with both task performance and organizational citizenship behavior toward organizations provide strong support for the integrated perspective of social exchange theory and job preservation motivation. Building on these findings, it is imperative to examine the underlying mechanisms explaining these relationships between job insecurity and performance-related behaviors at work. In addition to the proposed mechanisms (i.e., integrating social exchange theory and job preservation motivation), there might be other theoretical frameworks that help explain the impacts of job insecurity (e.g., affective events theory, uncertainty reduction theory).

Much research to date on job insecurity has looked at the differences between individuals to understand the negative consequences of job insecurity where it is considered a chronic working condition. That is, previous research has focused on relationships at the level of interpersonal difference (e.g., individuals with higher levels of job insecurity will have lower levels of job satisfaction), ignoring the temporal fluctuations of job insecurity and its within-person consequences (e.g., an individual experiencing a higher level of job insecurity on Day T may have a lower level of job satisfaction on Day $T + 1$). As job insecurity may vary from time to time within individuals, especially during the COVID-19 lockdown periods, overlooking its daily effects hinders our understanding of how employees may cope with job insecurity on a daily basis. To the best of our knowledge, there is only one daily diary study examining the effects of daily job insecurity (Garrido Vásquez et al., 2019), which finds that daily coworker conflict predicts the next day's job insecurity (but daily job insecurity does not predict the next day's coworker conflict). Thus, to supplement, complement, and extend the job insecurity literature, future research might adopt experience-sampling methodology to explore how and when job insecurity at the within-person level may impact employees' experiences at the within-person level.

The ongoing Fourth Technological Revolution features a fusion of technologies which are blurring the lines between physical and digital worlds and is marked by emerging technological breakthroughs in robotics and artificial intelligence. The rapid technological changes raise an important concern about human replacement by machines. Perhaps not surprisingly, the current research has mainly focused on the negative impacts of technological advancements on job insecurity (e.g., Lee et al., 2022; Yam et al., 2022). In addition to replacement, technology can also complement employee tasks and generate new tasks (Selenko et al., 2022). For example, it is estimated that 85% of jobs that will exist by 2030 have not been invented yet (Tencer, 2017). Therefore, it is important to examine how the bright and dark sides of Fourth Technological Revolution will impact on different types of job insecurity (e.g., quantitative vs. qualitative job insecurity) and how employees may cope with such changes.

Conclusion

Given the growing prevalence of job insecurity across the globe and its negative outcomes, this chapter identifies myriad variables operating at the individual, organizational, and societal levels that have been found to influence employee reactions to job insecurity. These factors can be developed into interventions to attenuate the adverse consequences of job insecurity. Indeed, the three aforementioned organizational-level interventions were based on the attenuating roles of organizational communication, constructive leadership behaviors, and employee participative decision-making to moderate effects of job insecurity. We hope that this chapter can inspire more intervention studies targeting multilevel moderators to alleviate the adverse outcomes of job insecurity.

References

Abildgaard, J. S., Nielsen, K., & Sverke, M. (2018). Can job insecurity be managed? Evaluating an organizational-level intervention addressing the negative effects of restructuring. *Work & Stress, 32*(2), 105–123. https://doi.org/10.1080/02678373.2017.1367735

Addai, P., Mottey, R., Afrifah, M., & Boakye, A. O. (2022). Job insecurity and turnover intentions among banking sector employees: The moderating role of organizational support and ethical leadership. *SEISENSE Journal of Management, 5*(1), 17–30. https://doi.org/10.33215/sjom.v5i1.736

Bakker, A. B., & Demerouti, E. (2007). The job demands-resources model: State of the art. *Journal of Managerial Psychology, 22*(3), 309–3028. https://doi.org/10.1108/02683940710733115

Barling, J., & Kelloway, E. K. (1996). Job insecurity and health: The moderating role of workplace control. *Stress Medicine, 12*(4), 253–259.

Barrech, A., Seubert, C., Glaser, J., & Gündel, H. (2018). Can a workplace leadership intervention reduce job insecurity and improve health? Results from a field study.

International Archives of Occupational and Environmental Health, 91(5), 547–557. https://doi.org/10.1007/s00420-018-1302-y

Bazzoli, A., & Probst, T. M. (2022). Taking stock and moving forward: A textual statistics approach to synthesizing four decades of job insecurity research. *Organizational Psychology Review, 12*(4), 507–544.

Berntson, E., & Marklund, S. (2007). The relationship between perceived employability and subsequent health. *Work and Stress, 21*(3), 279–292. https://doi.org/10.1080/02678370701659215

Berntson, E., Näswall, K., & Sverke, M. (2010). The moderating role of employability in the association between job insecurity and exit, voice, loyalty and neglect. *Economic and Industrial Democracy, 31*(2), 215–230. https://doi.org/10.1177/0143831X09358374

Blank, R. M. (1994). *Social protection versus economic flexibility: Is there a trade-off?* University of Chicago Press.

Bordia, P., Hobman, E., Jones, E., Gallois, C., & Callan, V. J. (2004). Uncertainty during organizational change: Types, consequences, and management strategies. *Journal of Business and Psychology, 18*(4), 507–532.

Brown, K. W., & Ryan, R. M. (2003). The benefits of being present: Mindfulness and its role in psychological well-being. *Journal of Personality and Social Psychology, 84*(4), 822–848. https://doi.org/10.1037/0022–3514.84.4.822

Çalışkan, N., & Özkoç, A. G. (2020). Organizational change and job insecurity: The moderating role of employability. *International Journal of Contemporary Hospitality Management, 32*(12), 3971–3990. https://doi.org/10.1108/IJCHM-05-2020-0387

Carr, E., & Chung, H. (2014). Employment insecurity and life satisfaction: The moderating influence of labour market policies across Europe. *Journal of European Social Policy, 24*(4), 383–399. https://doi.org/10.1177/0958928714538219

Castanon, A. (2006). *Managing traumatic change: The role of leadership as a buffer against the negative impact of job insecurity on employee outcomes*. Alliant International University.

Cheng, T., Huang, G. H., Lee, C., & Ren, X. (2012). Longitudinal effects of job insecurity on employee outcomes: The moderating role of emotional intelligence and the leader-member exchange. *Asia Pacific Journal of Management, 29*(3), 709–728. https://doi.org/10.1007/s10490-010-9227-3

Cheung, F. Y. L., Wu, A. M., & Ching Chi, L. (2019). Effect of job insecurity, anxiety and personal resources on job satisfaction among casino employees in Macau: A moderated mediation analysis. *Journal of Hospitality Marketing & Management, 28*(3), 379–396. https://doi.org/10.1080/19368623.2019.1525332

Darvishmotevali, M., & Ali, F. (2020). Job insecurity, subjective well-being and job performance: The moderating role of psychological capital. *International Journal of Hospitality Management, 87*, Article 102462. https://doi.org/10.1016/j.ijhm.2020.102462

Davis, J. H., & Ruhe, J. A. (2003). Perceptions of country corruption: Antecedents and outcomes. *Journal of Business Ethics, 43*, 275–288. https://doi.org/10.1023/A:1023038901080

De Angelis, M., Mazzetti, G., & Guglielmi, D. (2021). Job insecurity and job performance: A serial mediated relationship and the buffering effect of organizational justice. *Frontiers in Psychology, 12*. https://doi.org/10.3389/fpsyg.2021.694057

De Cuyper, N., Bernhard-Oettel, C., Berntson, E., De Witte, H., & Alarco, B. (2008). Employability and employees' well-being: Mediation by job insecurity. *Applied Psychology: An International Review, 57*(3), 488–485. https://doi.org/10.1111/j.1464-0597.2008.00332.x

De Cuyper, N., Mäkikangas, A., Kinnunen, U., Mauno, S., & Witte, H. D. (2012). Cross-lagged associations between perceived external employability, job insecurity, and exhaustion: Testing gain and loss spirals according to the conservation of resources theory. *Journal of Organizational Behavior, 33*(6), 770–788. https://doi.org/10.1002/job.1800

De Witte, H. (1999). Job insecurity and psychological well-being: Review of the literature and exploration of some unresolved issues. *European Journal of Work and Organizational Psychology, 8*(2), 155–177.

De Witte, H., Pienaar, J., & De Cuyper, N. (2016). Review of 30 years of longitudinal studies on the association between job insecurity and health and well-being: Is there causal evidence? *Australian Psychologist, 51*(1), 18–31. https://doi.org/10.1111/ap.12176

Debus, M. E., Kleinmann, M., König, C. J., & Winkler, S. (2020). Being tough versus tender: The impact of country-level and individual masculinity orientations as moderators of the relationship between job insecurity and job attitudes. *Applied Psychology=Psychologie Appliquee, 69*(3), 616–652. https://doi.org/10.1111/apps.12189

Debus, M. E., Probst, T. M., König, C. J., & Kleinmann, M. (2012). Catch me if I fall! Enacted uncertainty avoidance and the social safety net as country-level moderators in the job insecurity-job attitudes link. *The Journal of Applied Psychology, 97*(3), 690–698. https://doi.org/10.1037/a0027832

Garrido Vásquez, M. E., Kälin, W., Otto, K., Sadlowski, J., & Kottwitz, M. U. (2019). Do co-worker conflicts enhance daily worries about job insecurity: A diary study. *Applied Psychology, 68*(1), 26–52.

Gelfand, M. J., Aycan, Z., Erez, M., & Leung, K. (2017). Cross-cultural industrial organizational psychology and organizational behavior: A hundred-year journey. *Journal of Applied Psychology, 102(3)*, 514–529. https://doi.org/10.1037/apl0000186

Graen, G. B., & Uhl-Bien, M. (1995). Relationship-based approach to leadership: Development of leader-member exchange (LMX) theory of leadership over 25 years: Applying a multi-level multi-domain perspective. *The Leadership Quarterly, 6*(2), 219–247.

Guo, M., Liu, S., Chu, F., Ye, L., & Zhang, Q. (2019). Supervisory and co-worker support for safety: Buffers between job insecurity and safety performance of high-speed railway drivers in China. *Safety Science, 117,* 290–298. https://doi.org/10.1016/j.ssci.2019.04.017

Gupta, S., Davoodi, H., & Alonso-Terme, R. (2002). Does corruption affect income inequality and poverty?. *Economics of Governance, 3*(1), 23–45.

Hellgren, J., Sverke, M., & Isaksson, K. (1999). A two-dimensional approach to job insecurity: Consequences for employee attitudes and well-being. *European Journal of Work and Organizational Psychology, 8*(2), 179–195.

Higgins, E. T. (1997). Beyond pleasure and pain. *American Psychologist, 52*, 1280–1300.

Hirschfeld, R. R., & Feild, H. S. (2000). Work centrality and work alienation: Distinct aspects of a general commitment to work. *Journal of Organizational Behavior, 21*, 789–800.

Hobfoll, S. E. (1989). Conservation of resources: A new attempt at conceptualizing stress. *American Psychologist, 44*(3), 513–524.

Hofstede, G. (1980). *Culture's consequences: International differences in work-related values.* Sage.

Hofstede, G. (2001). *Culture's consequences: Comparing values, behaviors, institutions, and organizations across nations.* Sage.

House, R. J., Hanges, P. J., Javidan, M., Dorfman, P. W., & Gupta, V. (Eds.). (2004). *Culture, leadership, and organizations: The GLOBE study of 62 societies*. Sage Publications.

Hu, S., Jiang, L., Probst, T. M., & Liu, M. (2021). The relationship between qualitative job insecurity and subjective well-being in Chinese employees: The role of work-family conflict and work centrality. *Economic and Industrial Democracy, 42*(2), 203–225. https://doi.org/10.1177/0143831X18759793

Hu, S., & Zuo, B. (2007). The moderating effect of leader-member exchange on the job insecurity-organizational commitment relationship. In W. Wang, Y. Li, Z. Duan, L. Yan, H. Li, & X. Yang (Eds.), *Integration and innovation orient to e-society* (Vol. 2, pp. 505–513). Springer.

Ichida, Y., Kondo, K., Hirai, H., Hanibuchi, T., Yoshikawa, G., & Murata, C. (2009). Social capital, income inequality and self-rated health in Chita peninsula, Japan: A multilevel analysis of older people in 25 communities. *Social Science & Medicine, 69*(4), 489–499. https://doi.org/10.1016/j.socscimed.2009.05.006

International Labour Organization. (2020). *ILO Monitor: COVID-19 and the world of work. Updated estimates and analysis* (7th ed.). https://www.ilo.org/wcmsp5/groups/public/-dgreports/-dcomm/documents/briefingnote/wcms_767028.pdf

Ito, J. K., & Brotheridge, C. l. M. (2007). Exploring the predictors and consequences of job insecurity's components. *Journal of Managerial Psychology, 22*(1), 40–64. https://doi.org/10.1108/02683940710721938

Jiang, L. (2017). Perception of and reactions to job insecurity: The buffering effect of secure attachment. *Work & Stress, 31*(3), 256–275. https://doi.org/10.1080/02678373.2017.13050057.1305005

Jiang, L. (2018). Job insecurity and creativity: The buffering effect of self-affirmation and work-affirmation. *Journal of Applied Social Psychology, 48*(7), 388–397.

Jiang, L., & Lavaysse, L. M. (2018). Cognitive and affective job insecurity: A meta-analysis and a primary study. *Journal of Management, 44*(6), 2307–2342. https://doi.org/10.1177/0149206318773853

Jiang, L., Lawrence, A., & Xu, X. (2022). Does a stick work? A meta-analytic examination of curvilinear relationships between job insecurity and employee workplace behaviors. *Journal of Organizational Behavior, 43*(8), 1410–1445. https://doi.org/10.1002/job.2652

Jiang, L., & Probst, T. M. (2014). Organizational communication: A buffer in times of job insecurity? *Economic and Industrial Democracy, 35*(3). http://doi.org/10.1177/0143831X13489356

Jiang, L., & Probst, T. M. (2017). The rich get richer and the poor get poorer: Country- and state-level income inequality moderates the job insecurity-burnout relationship. *The Journal of Applied Psychology, 102*(4), 672–681. https://doi.org/10.1037/apl0000179

Jiang, L., & Probst, T. M. (2019). The moderating effect of trust in management on consequences of job insecurity. *Economic and Industrial Democracy, 40*(2), 409–433. https://doi.org/10.1177/0143831X16652945

Jiang, L., Xu, X., & Hu, X. (2019). Can gossip buffer the effect of job insecurity on workplace friendships? *International Journal of Environmental Research and Public Health, 16*(7), 1285–1299. http://doi.org/10.3390/ijerph16071285

Jiang, L., Xu, X., & Wang, H.-J. (2021). A resources-demands approach to sources of job insecurity: A multilevel meta-analytic investigation. *Journal of Occupational Health Psychology, 26*(2), 108–126. https://doi.org/10.1037/ocp0000267

Johns, G. (2006). The essential impact of context on organizational behavior. *The Academy of Management Review, 31*(2), 386–408. https://www.jstor.org/stable/20159208

Jordan, P. J., Ashkanasy, N. M., & Hartel, C. E. (2002). Emotional intelligence as a moderator of emotional and behavioral reactions to job insecurity. *Academy of Management Review, 27*(3), 361–372. https://doi.org/10.2307/4134384

Kalyal, H. J., Berntson, E., Baraldi, S., Näswall, K., & Sverke, M. (2010). The moderating role of employability on the relationship between job insecurity and commitment to change. *Economic and Industrial Democracy, 31*(3), 327–344. http://doi.org/10.1177/0143831X09351214

Kim, M. J., & Kim, B. J. (2020). The performance implications of job insecurity: The sequential mediating effect of job stress and organizational commitment, and the buffering role of ethical leadership. *International Journal of Environmental Research and Public Health, 17*(21), 7837–7852. https://doi.org/10.3390/ijerph17217837

König, C. J., Probst, T. M., Staffen, S., & Graso, M. (2011). A Swiss-US comparison of the correlates of job insecurity. *Applied Psychology, 60*(1), 141–159. https://doi.org/10.1111/j.1464-0597.2010.00430.x

Lam, C. F., Liang, J., Ashford, S. J., & Lee, C. (2015). Job insecurity and organizational citizenship behavior: Exploring curvilinear and moderated relationships. *Journal of Applied Psychology, 100*(2), 499–510. https://doi.org/10.1037/a0038659

Lazarus, R. S., & Folkman, S. (1984). *Stress, appraisal and coping*. Springer.

Lee, C., Huang, G.-H., & Ashford, S. J. (2018). Job insecurity and the changing workplace: Recent developments and the future trends in job insecurity research. *Annual Review of Organizational Psychology and Organizational Behavior, 5*(1), 335–359. https://doi.org/10.1146/annurev-orgpsych-032117-104651

Lee, M. H., & Tsai, H. Y. (2022). A study of job insecurity and life satisfaction in COVID-19: The multilevel moderating effect of perceived control and work–life balance programs. *Journal of Men's Health, 18*(1), 21. https://doi.org/10.31083/j.jomh1801021

Li, Z., Zou, H.-Y., Wang, H.-J., Jiang, L., & Zhao, Y. (2022). Qualitative job insecurity, negative work-related affect and work-to-family conflict: The moderating role of core self-evaluation. *Journal of Career Development, 50*(1), 216–233. https://doi.org/10.1177/08948453221090610

Lim, V. K. (1996). Job insecurity and its outcomes: Moderating effects of work-based and nonwork-based social support. *Human Relations, 49(2),* 171–194.

Loi, R., Ngo, H. Y., Zhang, L., & Lau, V. P. (2011). The interaction between leader–member exchange and perceived job security in predicting employee altruism and work performance. *Journal of Occupational and Organizational Psychology, 84*(4), 669–685. https://doi.org/10.1348/096317910X510468

Long, L. R., Tu, Y., Wang, H. J., & Jiang, L. (2021). The content of the threat matters: The differential effects of quantitative and qualitative job insecurity on different types of employee motivation. *Journal of Business and Psychology, 37,* 297–310. https://doi.org/10.1007/s10869-021-09746-31

Mayer, J. D., & Salovey, P. (1997). What is emotional intelligence? In P. Salovey & D. J. Sluyter (Eds.), *Emotional development and emotional intelligence: Educational implications* (pp. 3–31). Basic Books.

Montani, F., Courcy, F., Battistelli, A., & De Witte, H. (2021). Job insecurity and innovative work behaviour: A moderated mediation model of intrinsic motivation and trait mindfulness. *Stress and Health, 37*(4), 742–754. https://doi.org/10.1002/smi.3034

Näswall, K., Sverke, M., & Hellgren, J. (2005). The moderating role of personality characteristics on the relationship between job insecurity and strain. *Work & Stress, 19*(1), 37–49. https://doi.org/10.1080/02678370500057850

Nauman, S., Zheng, C., & Naseer, S. (2020). Job insecurity and work–family conflict: A moderated mediation model of perceived organizational justice, emotional exhaustion and work withdrawal. *International journal of conflict management, 31*(5), 729–751. https://doi.org/10.1108/IJCMA-09–2019–0159

Organisation for Economic Co-operation and Development. (2019). *The future of work: OECD employment outlook 2019.* https://www.oecd-ilibrary.org/employment/oecd-employment-outlook-2019_9ee00155-en

Peterson, S. J., Luthans, F., Avolio, B. J., Walumbwa, F. O., & Zhang, Z. (2011). Psychological capital and employee performance: A latent growth modeling approach. *Personnel Psychology, 64*(2), 427–450. https://doi.org/10.1111/j.1744-6570.2011.01215.x

Probst, T. M. (2004). Safety and insecurity: Exploring the moderating effect of organizational safety climate. *Journal of Occupational Health Psychology, 9*(1), 3–10. https://doi.org/10.1037/1076–8998.9.1.3

Probst, T. M. (2005). Countering the negative effects of job insecurity through participative decision making: Lessons from the demand-control model. *Journal of Occupational Health Psychology, 10*(4), 320–329. https://doi.org/10.1037/1076-8998.10.4.320

Probst, T. M., Bazzoli, A., Jenkins, M. R., Jiang, L., & López-Bohle, S. (2021). Coping with job insecurity: Employees with grit create I-Deals. *Journal of Occupational Health Psychology, 26*(5), 437–447. https://doi.org/10.1037/ocp0000220

Probst, T. M., Gailey, N. J., Jiang, L., & López Bohle, S. (2017). Psychological capital: Buffering the longitudinal curvilinear effects of job insecurity on performance. *Safety Science, 100(Part A),* 74–82. https://doi.org/10.1016/j.ssci.2017.02.002

Probst, T. M., & Jiang, L. (2016). Mitigating physiological responses to layoff threat: An experimental test of the efficacy of two coping interventions. *International Journal of Environmental Research and Public Health, 13*(3), 338–352. https://doi.org/10.3390/ijerph13030338

Probst, T. M., & Jiang, L. (2017). European flexicurity policies: Multilevel effects on employee psychosocial reactions to job insecurity. *Safety Science, 100*(Part A), 83–90. https://doi.org/10.1016/j.ssci.2017.03.010

Probst, T. M., Jiang, L., & Graso, M. (2016). Leader-member exchange: Moderating the health and safety outcomes of job insecurity. *Journal of Safety Research, 56,* 47–56. https://doi.org/10.1016/j.jsr.2015.11.003

Probst, T. M., & Lawler, J. (2006). Cultural values as moderators of employee reactions to job insecurity: The role of individualism and collectivism. *Applied Psychology, 55*(2), 234–254. https://doi.org/10.1111/j.1464-0597.2006.00239.x

Schmidt, K., & Pförtner, T. K. (2020). Job insecurity, sickness presenteeism and the moderating effect of workplace health promotion. *Journal of Occupational and Environmental Medicine, 62*(11), 937–942. https://doi.org/10.1097/JOM.0000000000001997

Schneider, B., & DeNisi, A. (1991). Communication with employees following a merger: A longitudinal experiment. *Academy of Management Journal, 34*(1), 110–135.

Schreurs, B. H., van Emmerik, I. J. H., Guenter, H., & Germeys, F. (2012). A weekly diary study on the buffering role of social support in the relationship between job insecurity and employee performance. *Human Resource Management, 51*(2). https://doi.org/10.1002/hrm.21465

Schreurs, B., van Emmerik, H., Notelaers, G., & De Witte, H. (2010). Job insecurity and employee health: The buffering potential of job control and job self-efficacy. *Work & Stress, 24*(1), 56–72. https://doi.org/10.1080/02678371003718733

Schwartz, S. H. (2013). Culture matters: National value cultures, sources, and consequences. In C.-Y. Chiu, Y. Y. Hong, S. Shavitt, & R. S. Wyer, Jr. (Eds.), *Problems and solutions in cross-cultural theory, research and application.* Psychology Press.

Selenko, E., Bankins, S., Shoss, M., Warburton, J., & Restubog, S. L. D. (2022). Artificial intelligence and the future of work: A functional-identity perspective. *Current Directions in Psychological Science, 31*(3), 272–279.

Sender, A., Arnold, A., & Staffelbach, B. (2017). Job security as a threatened resource: Reactions to job insecurity in culturally distinct regions. *The International Journal of Human Resource Management, 28*(17), 2403–2429. https://doi.org/10.1080/09585192.2015.1137615

Shoss, M. K. (2017). Job insecurity: An integrative review and agenda for future research. *Journal of Management, 43*(6), 1911–1939. https://doi.org/10.1177/0149206317691574

Shoss, M., Jiang, L., & Probst, T. M. (2018). Bending without breaking: A two-study examination of employee resilience in the face of job insecurity. *Journal of Occupational Health Psychology, 23*(1), 112–126. http://doi.org/10.1037/ocp0000060

Silla, I., De Cuyper, N., Gracia, F. J., Peiró, J. M., & De Witte, H. (2009). Job insecurity and well-being: Moderation by employability. *Journal of Happiness Studies, 10*(6), 739–751. https://doi.org/10.1007/s10902-008-9119-0

Sinclair, V. G., & Wallston, K. A. (2004). The development and psychometric evaluation of the Brief Resilient Coping Scale. *Assessment, 11(1)*, 94–101. https://doi.org/10.1177/1073191103258144

Smith, B. W., Dalen, J., Wiggins, K., Tooley, E., Christopher, P., & Bernard, J. (2008). The brief resilience scale: Assessing the ability to bounce back. *International Journal of Behavioral Medicine, 15,* 194–200. https://doi.org/10.1080/10705500802222972

Sora, B., Caballer, A., Peiró, J. M., Silla, I., & Gracia, F. J. (2010). Moderating influence of organizational justice on the relationship between job insecurity and its outcomes: A multilevel analysis. *Economic and Industrial Democracy, 31*(4), 613–637. https://doi.org/10.1177/0143831X10365924

Sverke, M., Låstad, L., Hellgren, J., Richter, A., & Näswall, K. (2019). A meta-analysis of job insecurity and employee performance: Testing temporal aspects, rating source, welfare regime, and union density as moderators. *International Journal of Environmental Research and Public Health, 16*(14). https://doi.org/10.3390/ijerph16142536

Taht, K., Xanthopoulou, D., Figgou, L., Kostouli, M., & Unt, M. (2020). The role of unemployment and job insecurity for the well-being of young Europeans: Social inequality as a macro-level moderator. *Journal of Happiness Studies, 21,* 2355–2375. https://doi.org/10.1007/s10902-019-00184-w

ten Brummelhuis, L. L., & Bakker, A. B. (2012). A resource perspective on the work–home interface: The work–home resources model. *American Psychologist, 67*(7), 545. https://doi.org/10.1037/a0027974

Tencer, D. (2017, July 14). 85% of jobs that will exist in 2030 haven't been invented yet: Dell. *Huffpost.* https://www.huffpost.com/archive/ca/entry/85-of-jobs-that-will-exist-in-2030-haven-t-been-invented-yet-d_ca_5cd4e7dae4b07bc72973112c

Teng, E., Zhang, L., & Qiu, Y. (2019). Always bad for creativity? An affect-based model of job insecurity and the moderating effects of giving support and receiving support. *Economic and Industrial Democracy, 40*(3), 803–829. https://doi.org/10.1177/0143831X17744026

Triandis, H. C. (1995). *Individualism and collectivism.* Westview Press.

Tu, Y., Long, L., Wang, H. J., & Jiang, L. (2020). To prevent or to promote: How regulatory focus moderates the differ-entiated effects of quantitative versus qualitative job insecurity on employee stress and motivation. *International Journal of Stress Management, 27*(2), 135–145. https://doi.org/10.1037/str0000139

Urbanaviciute, I., Roll, C. L., Tomas, J., & De Witte, H. (2021). Proactive strategies for countering the detrimental outcomes of qualitative job insecurity in academia. *Stress and Health, 37*(3), 557–571. https://doi.org/10.1002/smi.3023

Vander Elst, T., Baillien, E., De Cuyper, N., & De Witte, H. (2010). The role of organizational communication and participation in reducing job insecurity and its negative association with work-related well-being. *Economic and Industrial Democracy, 31*(2), 249–264. https://doi.org/10.1177/0143831X09358372

Vander Elst, T., Näswall, K., Bernhard-Oettel, C., De Witte, H., & Sverke, M. (2016). The effect of job insecurity on employee health complaints: A within-person analysis of the explanatory role of threats to the manifest and latent benefits of work. *Journal of Occupational Health Psychology, 21*(1), 65–76. https://doi.org/10.1037/a0039140

Wang, H.-J., Lu, C.-Q., & Siu, O.-I. (2015). Job insecurity and job performance: The moderating role of organizational justice and the mediating role of work engagement. *Journal of Applied Psychology, 100*(4), 1249–1258. https://doi.org/10.1037/a0038330

Wang, W., Mather, K., & Seifert, R. (2018). Job insecurity, employee anxiety, and commitment: The moderating role of collective trust in management. *Journal of Trust Research, 8*(2), 220–237. https://doi.org/10.1080/21515581.2018.1463229

Wilkinson, R. G., & Pickett, K. E. (2009). *The spirit level: Why more equal societies almost always do better.* Allen Lane.

Wong, Y. T., Wong, C. S., Ngo, H. Y., & Lui, H. K. (2005). Different responses to job insecurity of Chinese workers in joint ventures and state-owned enterprises. *Human Relations, 58*(11), 1391–1418. https://doi.org/10.1177/0018726705060243

Xu, X., Jiang, L., Probst, T. M., Shoss, M., & Jalil, D. (2022). How national culture shapes employee reactions to job insecurity: The role of national corruption. *European Journal of Work and Organizational Psychology.* 1–19. https://doi.org/10.1080/1359432X.2022.2090344

Yam, K. C., Tang, P. M., Jackson, J. C., Su, R., & Gray, K. (2022). The rise of robots increases job insecurity and maladaptive workplace behaviors: Multimethod evidence. *Journal of Applied Psychology*. Advance online publication. https://doi.org/10.1037/apl0001045

19

REVERSING JOB LOSS AND ENHANCING JOB-SEARCH

Edwin A. J. Van Hooft and Greet Van Hoye

Job loss and unemployment are major stressors in people's working lives, having negative financial and mental health consequences for the individuals themselves as well as their families (McKee-Ryan et al., 2005; Paul & Moser, 2009; Ström, 2003). Unemployment spells are also expensive for society, due to unemployment benefits and social services provided to individuals (Sinfield, 2018). Reversing job loss and finding suitable and sustainable employment is of utmost importance, not only financially but also because re-employment positively affects people's mental and physical health (McKee-Ryan et al., 2005; Paul & Moser, 2009; Zhou et al., 2019). Finding decent re-employment, however, is often not easy and is affected by many factors that are outside the individual's control (e.g., contextual factors such as labor market demand and employer discrimination; and individual factors such as age, ethnicity, and social class). To handle and reverse their precarious situation, unemployed individuals need to engage in self-regulatory coping behavior. Job search behavior is a coping strategy within individuals' control that is effective, as research suggests that the intensity and quality of people's job search positively affect re-employment success (Kanfer et al., 2001; van Hooft et al., 2021). Because job searching is difficult and comes with setbacks and rejections, unemployed individuals additionally need to engage in emotion-focused coping to support their mental health (Kreemers et al., 2018, 2020).

In this chapter, we first focus on the negative effects of job loss and unemployment on the health and wellbeing of individuals and their families. Second, we outline the benefits of returning to work, emphasizing the importance of suitable and sustainable re-employment. Third, we describe the process of re-employment, distinguishing between job search behavior (i.e., intensity and

DOI: 10.4324/9781003440444-23

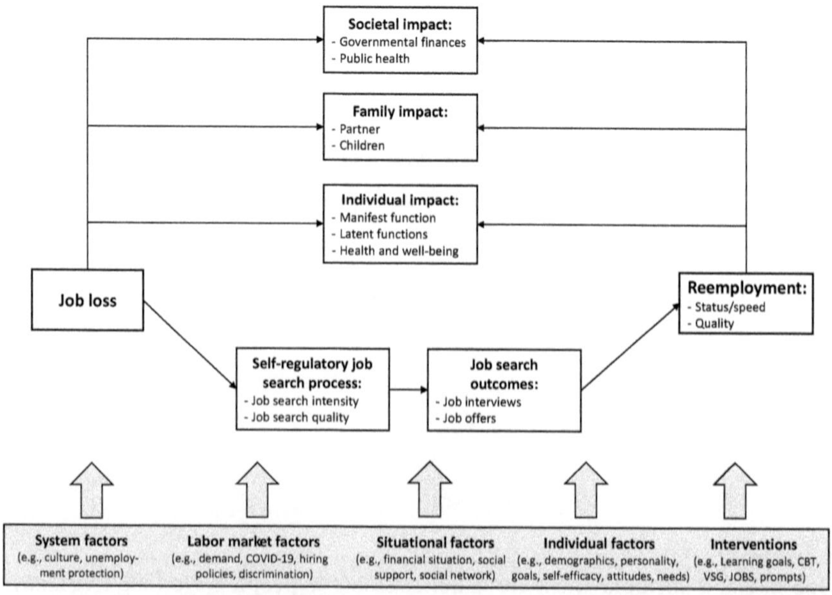

FIGURE 19.1 A Schematic Overview of the Factors and Processes Relevant to Job Loss and Job Search.

quality), proximal outcomes such as job interviews, and distal outcomes such as re-employment speed and quality. Third, we outline relevant systemic (e.g., national culture and unemployment benefits), labor market (e.g., unemployment rate and discrimination), situational (e.g., financial hardship and social support), and relatively stable individual factors (e.g., demographics and personality) in the context of health, job searching, and re-employment. These factors help identify specific groups that are hit harder by job loss and unemployment and target those who need help in the process of finding re-employment. Further, we identify malleable antecedent factors that facilitate job search motivation, intensity, and quality. Last, we discuss several individual-level interventions to foster self-regulation of affect and behavior during the job search process. Figure 19.1 presents a schematic overview.

Job Loss and Unemployment

Job loss and unemployment are omnipresent in the labor market. Unemployment is generally defined as being without a job and available for the labor market and actively seeking employment. In the first two decades of this millennium, the global unemployment rate varied between 5% and 6% (International Labour Organization [ILO], 2020). Unemployment rates typically increase after global crises, such as 9/11 in 2001, the financial crisis in 2008, and the COVID-19 pandemic in 2020. In 2019, an estimated 188 million individuals worldwide were unemployed (5.4%; ILO, 2020), which increased by 33 million in 2020 (to 6.5%; ILO, 2021). The COVID-19 pandemic led to unprecedented employment losses, amounting to 114 million fewer jobs worldwide in 2020 relative to 2019 (ILO, 2021). In addition to people losing their jobs, a substantial amount of people voluntarily quit their jobs in the aftermath of the COVID-19 pandemic: a trend sometimes labeled as "the great resignation" (Hirsch, 2021).

Societal Impact

Unemployment is expensive for society (e.g., Sinfield, 2018). On the one hand, governmental expenses increase due to unemployment insurance benefits and social services provided to unemployed individuals. On the other hand, governments face budgetary losses due to reduced income taxes and other taxes as unemployed people's spending drops. In addition to the monetary societal consequences, unemployment has negative consequences for public health. Many studies have been conducted on the relationships between unemployment, health outcomes, and health behaviors: as summarized in various narrative and quantitative reviews (e.g., Bambra & Eikemo, 2018; McKee-Ryan et al., 2005; Paul et al., 2018; Paul & Moser, 2009; Wanberg, 2012). Specifically, evidence is widely available indicating that unemployment correlates with reduced mental health (e.g., distress, anxiety, and depression) and wellbeing (reduced life satisfaction, family satisfaction, and self-esteem; for meta-analyses see McKee-Ryan et al., 2005; Paul & Moser, 2009). Unemployment has even been associated with increased mortality (Roelfs et al., 2011) and increased risks of suicide and suicide attempts (Milner et al., 2014), especially in the first five years of unemployment (Milner et al., 2013). Further, meta-analyses found correlations between unemployment and reduced physical health (McKee-Ryan et al., 2005; Paul & Moser, 2009). Although the directionality of these correlations has been debated, Wanberg (2012) concluded in her review that while poor physical health leads to increased risks of unemployment, there was solid evidence indicating that unemployment also leads to poorer physical health. Lastly, some studies linked unemployment to increases in hazardous health behaviors such as smoking or excessive drinking (Bambra & Eikemo, 2018). Because of these negative effects of unemployment on mental and physical health, higher unemployment rates likely have consequences for national health care systems.

Individual Impact

Job loss (and subsequent unemployment) represents one of the worst stressors that people encounter in their working lives. Some research even indicates that job loss ranks in the top five or ten of most stressful life events (Miller & Rahe, 1997). Deprivation theory (Jahoda, 1981) suggests that the distressing effects of unemployment are caused by losing the manifest and latent functions of employment. First, employment has the *manifest* function of earning a living, and job loss deprives individuals of a regular salary. Even in countries with generous unemployment insurance, job loss is usually accompanied by a substantial drop in income (e.g., 25%–30% in The Netherlands, 33%–40% in Germany, and 50% in the United States; Wanberg, van Hooft, Dossinger et al., 2020). Meta-analytic evidence supports the assumption that financial strain has a strong and negative impact on unemployed individuals' mental health ($r_c = -.45$; McKee-Ryan et al., 2005).

Second, employment serves several *latent* functions. In her deprivation theory, Jahoda (1981) identified five latent functions of employment: time structure (i.e., provision of structure and purposive time use), social contact (i.e., secure regular contact and shared experiences with people other than direct family), collective purpose (i.e., providing individuals with goals and purposes that transcend their own), personal status and identity (i.e., providing social status and identity), and activity (i.e., enforcing some level of activity). Creed and Bartrum's (2006) review of the literature showed that research generally supported the assumption that the five latent functions positively relate to mental health and wellbeing. McKee-Ryan et al. (2005) included time structure in their meta-analysis, showing that unemployed individuals' time structure was positively associated with mental health. Research by Van Hoye and Lootens (2013) indicates that the purposive time use component of time structure especially is related to mental health. Other theories complement and/or expand the latent functions as identified by Jahoda (1981). For example, in his agency theory, Fryer (1986) emphasized the role of personal agency and identified the loss of control when being unemployed as a predictor of mental health. In his vitamin model, Warr (1987) identified nine environmental features of employment that cause decrements in mental health after becoming unemployed. These features partially overlap with Jahoda's (1981) manifest and latent functions, with the addition that employment also provides opportunities for control, performance of skills, and variety. Self-determination theory (SDT) (Ryan & Deci, 2000) has also been proposed to explain the detrimental effects of unemployment on psychological wellbeing. Specifically, Vansteenkiste and Van den Broeck (2018) suggest that the frustration of the three universal human needs for autonomy, competence, and relatedness likely explains the negative effects of unemployment on mental health. However, research is needed to examine whether these three needs can capture the mental health effects of unemployment.

The loss of both manifest and latent functions of employment is a potentially traumatic experience, especially for mature-aged unemployed individuals (Gabriel et al., 2013; Kira & Klehe, 2016). Losing one's job may pose a threat to people's identity and self-definition. Specifically, job loss may cause people to lose their valued professional identity and status. Moreover, the unwanted new identity of being unemployed is perceived to be of low status and accompanied by stigma. Qualitative work has indicated that unemployed individuals experience feelings of shame and stigmatization based on their employment status, for example, when networking or applying for jobs (Wanberg et al., 2012). Experimental work attests to these perceptions, demonstrating that unemployed individuals are evaluated as less conscientious and emotionally stable, and lower on work competence and humaneness (Schofield et al., 2019). Further, research suggests that the anticipation of being stigmatized because of being unemployed is associated with reduced mental and physical health (Krug et al., 2019; O'Donnell et al., 2015; Rantakeisu et al., 1997). The loss of the manifest and latent functions that employment provides (e.g., income, social contact, purpose and meaning, and identity and self-definition) may also induce processes of grief (Albert et al., 2015; Vickers, 2009). Recent research has identified grief as an explanatory mechanism of the negative effects of job loss on mental health (Eersel et al., 2020).

Family Impact

Job loss and unemployment not only affect the individuals themselves but also their partners and children (McKee-Ryan & Maitoza, 2018; Ström, 2003). Because unemployment usually implies a reduction in family income, it may cause financial difficulties and financial strain. For example, based on a series of interviews, Wanberg et al. (2012) identified the impact of unemployment on family and finances as an important context-related demand. Respondents mentioned the fear about making ends meet and family pressures when having to cut back on spending, resulting in relational tensions. Quantitative research also found that financial hardship caused by unemployment induces anxiety and distress, with crossover effects between unemployed individuals and their partners (Song et al., 2011; Westman et al., 2004). Partners of unemployed individuals also report reduced life satisfaction after the job loss as compared to before the job loss of the individual (except when the partners themselves are unemployed; Luhmann et al., 2014). Furthermore, in her review, Ström (2003) concluded that there is relatively strong evidence that unemployment increases marital instability and risk of divorce, especially when limited financial resources are available.

In addition to relational effects, job loss has also been linked to children's health, problem behavior, and educational attainment (Kalil, 2009; McKee-Ryan & Maitoza, 2018; Ström, 2003). For example, using panel data from 1996 to 2012 in the US, Schaller and Zerpa (2019) found that paternal (but not maternal) job loss relates to a reduction in reported mental and physical health of children and an increase in mental health problems (e.g., anxiety and depression). Mari and Keizer (2021) reported evidence suggesting that especially paternal job loss links to increased problem behavior among young children (e.g., emotional symptoms, peer problems, conduct problems, and hyperactivity/inattention). Regarding educational attainment, Stevens and Schaller (2011) found that parental job loss links to a 15% higher probability of children having to repeat a grade. Andersen (2013) found that paternal unemployment is associated with children finding less interest in doing well in school in the first year after job loss. Of the potential mechanisms, Anderson (2013) concluded that the father's status loss especially may explain the effect.

Reversing the Negative Effects of Unemployment

Based on the idea that unemployment reduces mental health because of the loss of the latent functions that employment serves, several studies have examined if these latent functions can be provided by other activities. For example, Gowan et al. (1999) found that engagement in community and leisure activities reduces distress among unemployed job seekers. Goodman et al. (2017) concluded that exercise and social and self-focused leisure activities may reduce depressive symptoms among unemployed individuals if these activities provide time structure (i.e., structured and purposive time use). In a study among unemployed individuals, Van den Hee et al. (2022) found that challenging volunteering work positively relates to mental health by providing latent benefits (e.g., time structure and social contact).

However, the best way to counter the negative effects of unemployment is to return to work. In their meta-analysis of longitudinal studies, McKee-Ryan et al. (2005) reported a large improvement in the mental health of unemployed individuals after re-employment ($d_c = 0.89$). In a subsequent meta-analysis, Paul and Moser (2009) also found that re-employment leads to an increase in mental health, which is of a similar size to the reduction in mental health after job loss. These findings suggest that returning to work fully restores the deleterious mental health effects of job loss. This conclusion is corroborated by a study by Zhou et al. (2019), using data on reported life satisfaction from the annual British Household Panel Survey from 1991 to 2008. Specifically, Zhou et al. (2019) found that unemployed individuals experienced a boost in their life satisfaction after re-employment, which gradually returned to and stabilized at the pre-job loss level for those who remained employed.

Although one may think that any job is better than unemployment, research has shown that low-quality re-employment (e.g., underemployment, and insecure and precarious work) is negatively associated with psychological wellbeing, career attitudes, and career outcomes (e.g., McKee-Ryan & Harvey, 2011). Some studies found that unsatisfactory re-employment is not, or only slightly, better than unemployment for mental health (Leana & Feldman, 1995; Wanberg, 1995). In their systematic review, Kim and von dem Knesebeck (2015) concluded that insecure employment can be as harmful to health as unemployment. Grün et al. (2010) used several indicators of re-employment quality and examined their association with wellbeing (i.e., life satisfaction). For the re-employment quality indicator of job satisfaction, they also found that low-quality re-employment was not better than unemployment. However, for the other indicators (i.e., wage, job fit, occupational prestige, and working conditions), low-re-employment quality mostly resulted in better wellbeing than unemployment, but poorer wellbeing than high-quality re-employment (see Di Fabio et al., Chapter 3).

The mechanisms identified as drivers of the reduction in mental health after job loss also seem to explain the recovery of mental health after re-employment. Specifically, in their longitudinal study among unemployed individuals, Zechmann and Paul (2019) found that the improvement in mental health following re-employment can be explained by a reduction in financial strain (i.e., a manifest function) and increases in Jahoda's (1981) latent functions (i.e., time structure, social contact, status, collective purpose, and activity). Based on SDT, Zechmann and Paul (2019) also found that re-employment improves mental health through satisfaction of the need for competence (but not autonomy). Research examining whether the stigma attached to unemployment resolves after re-employment provides mixed results. For example, in two scenario studies, Norlander et al. (2020) asked people to evaluate the competence and warmth of a newly hired employee who was either employed or unemployed before starting the job, based on the employee's performance review report. Both competence and warmth were rated lower when the employee was previously unemployed rather than employed. In contrast, the findings of a series of vignette studies by Schofield et al. (2019) suggest that the unemployment stigma resolves after re-employment. Specifically, employed individuals with and without a history of unemployment were similarly evaluated in contrast to unemployed individuals on aspects such as conscientiousness, emotional stability, work competence, and humaneness. Further research is needed to examine if and under what conditions the unemployment stigma resolves after returning to work, if re-employed individuals themselves also experience stigma reduction after returning to work, and whether this explains mental health improvements.

The Process of Re-Employment

Re-employment thus is of utmost importance, not only because employment serves the manifest function of paying the bills, but also because of its latent functions such as providing meaning and structure, social involvement, status and identity, and personal development and growth. Theoretical frameworks typically describe re-employment as a motivational and self-regulatory process, distinguishing between antecedents (e.g., demographics, personality, and motivating factors), job search behavior (i.e., quantity and quality), and re-employment success outcomes (e.g., Kanfer et al., 2001; van Hooft, 2018a; van Hooft et al., 2021; Wanberg et al., 2002).

Re-Employment Success

Research has identified several important re-employment success outcomes, which can be classified into proximal and distal outcomes with quantitative and qualitative dimensions (e.g., Boswell et al., 2012; van Hooft et al., 2021, 2022). While proximal outcomes occur during the job-search process, distal outcomes occur after the completion of the job-search process. Specifically, distal quantitative outcomes include employment status (i.e., job attainment and re-employment) and the speed of re-employment. Such outcomes can be predicted by proximal quantitative outcomes such as number of job interviews and job offers. In addition to these quantitative outcomes, research has addressed more qualitative outcomes. A focal distal qualitative outcome is re-employment quality, which includes perceptions of salary, contract type, job improvement, absence of underemployment (O'Shea et al., Chapter 15), person-job or person-organization fit, job satisfaction, and intentions to stay (van Hooft et al., 2021). Similarly, proximal qualitative outcomes include, for example, the perceived fit with the jobs interviewed for and the jobs offered (e.g., van Hooft et al., 2022). Given the importance of the quality of re-employment for wellbeing and career outcomes, careful attention should be paid to promoting high-quality and sustainable re-employment to prevent unemployed people from ending up in a precarious labor-market position after re-employment.

Job Search Behavior

Theoretical models identify job search behavior as the core individually controllable determinant of re-employment success (e.g., Kanfer et al., 2001; van Hooft, 2018a; van Hooft et al., 2021). Most prior job-search studies have operationalized job-search behavior in terms of effort or intensity, referring to the amount of time and energy devoted to job search in general or to specific job-search activities (Van Hoye, 2018). Such activities include networking, searching online for job postings, visiting employment agencies, and submitting job applications. Meta-analyses suggest that job search effort and intensity significantly and positively relate to finding employment (Kanfer et al., 2001; van Hooft et al., 2021). People who invest more time and effort into their job search receive more job offers, are more likely to find a job, and become re-employed more quickly. However, the effect sizes of these relations are typically quite small. In addition, how hard individuals look for a job seems to be unrelated to re-employment quality (van Hooft et al., 2021).

Beyond the quantity of job search, several scholars have also argued for the need to consider the quality of job-search behaviors. Spending large amounts of time on job-search activities does not necessarily imply that it is done well. Based on total quality management and self-regulation theories, van Hooft et al. (2013) have proposed that a high-quality job search consists of a self-regulated process, starting with goal establishment and followed by planning, goal striving, and reflection. Regarding goal establishment, job seekers need to formulate clear search goals and commit to these goals. Next, job seekers should plan how to realize these goals. This involves selecting a systematic strategy and sources for identifying job opportunities, forming concrete intentions, setting deadlines, and thoroughly preparing for the planned activities. Then, as job seekers translate their plans into actual behaviors to strive for their goals, they need to apply self-regulatory techniques to facilitate sustained performance of the planned search behaviors, such as self-control, goal shielding, self-monitoring, and feedback-seeking. Finally, job seekers should reflect on how their job search is going, what they can learn from evaluating their performance, and whether any revisions are required. Cycling through these four phases enables job seekers to learn what employers want and align their search behaviors and job applications with employers' expectations, increasing their chances of success.

Despite this multidimensional conceptualization of job-search quality, prior research has often used a unidimensional measure of metacognitive activities (aggregating several self-regulatory job-search activities such as goal setting, planning, and monitoring progress; Turban et al., 2009). Findings suggest that engaging in such metacognitive activities relates positively to being invited for job interviews (Turban et al., 2009), becoming re-employed (Koen et al., 2016), re-employment speed, and re-employment quality (Wanberg, van Hooft, Dossinger et al., 2020). Although these findings demonstrate that unemployed individuals should not only invest time and effort in their job-search activities but also engage in a qualitative job-search process, they do not provide much insight into which aspects of the process are most crucial. To enhance our understanding of the different job-search quality dimensions, van Hooft et al. (2022) developed the multidimensional Job Search Quality Scale (JSQS). Extending van Hooft et al.'s (2013) prior conceptualization with preliminary findings and practitioner insights, factor analyses showed a four-factor structure for job search quality: goal establishment and planning (loading on a single factor), preparation and alignment, emotion regulation and persistence, and learning and improvement. Investigating the criterion validity of the JSQS in multiple samples of unemployed, they observed positive correlations between these job-search quality dimensions with a range of proximal and distal outcomes. Overall, goal establishment and planning seemed the most crucial factor, as it was the strongest predictor of the number and perceived fit of job interviews, database re-employment status, and re-employment quality (perceived job fit and job satisfaction). However, emotional regulation and persistence were the strongest predictors of self-reported re-employment, and preparation and alignment showed the strongest relationship with re-employment speed. This suggests that the relative importance of the job-search quality dimensions might depend on the specific context and criterion of interest.

This is further corroborated by research from Stremersch et al. (2021), using a slightly different scale to measure job search quality. Among graduating students making the school-to-work transition, they found that goal striving and, to a lesser extent, goal establishment were the main predictors of finding a job after graduation. Moreover, goal establishment was the strongest predictor of employment quality (perceived job fit). In the context of final-year students looking for an internship, reflection emerged as a key dimension, showing the strongest relationship with internship quality (perceived fit and satisfaction; Stremersch & Van Hoye, 2020). Planning was the strongest predictor of the speed of finding an internship. Interestingly, in this study, the job-search quality dimensions explained incremental variance in these outcomes not only beyond job-search intensity but also above the unidimensional measure of metacognitive job-search activities.

Altogether, these findings suggest that, to reverse job loss and enhance job search success, unemployed individuals should not only invest time and energy into their search but also engage in a high-quality self-regulatory job-search process. Taking the multiple dimensions of job-search quality into account likely increases our understanding of when and why a given job search in a particular context is effective or not. To this end, job seekers and job search counselors can use the JSQS (van Hooft et al., 2022) to assess job search quality and take remedial actions to enhance job search quality if needed.

Factors Related to the Unemployment Experience and Re-employment Process

A myriad of factors affect the unemployment experience and re-employment process (e.g., McKee-Ryan et al., 2005; Paul & Moser, 2009; van Hooft et al., 2021; Wanberg, 2012; Wanberg et al., 2002). Taking a multidisciplinary approach, these factors can be categorized as: (a) system factors such as national culture and regulations regarding unemployment benefits; (b) labor-market factors such as labor-market demand, employer hiring policies, and discrimination; (c) situational factors such as financial need, social support, and social networks; (d) relatively stable individual factors such as an individual's demographics and personality; and (e) malleable individual factors such as goals, attitudes, and self-efficacy. Below we discuss these categories of factors and their links with unemployed people's mental health, job-search behavior, and re-employment success.

System Factors

Countries differ in terms of culture, income inequality, economic development, and provisions for unemployment protection. In their meta-analysis on unemployment and mental health, Paul and Moser (2009) conducted moderator analyses to examine country differences. They found weaker negative effects of unemployment on mental health in more egalitarian countries (operationalized as smaller income inequality) than in less egalitarian countries. Furthermore, unemployment had stronger negative effects on mental health in economically less developed countries than in more developed countries. These country differences may be explained by differences in unemployment protection since countries with high levels of state-provided unemployment protection show weaker effects of unemployment on mental health than countries with medium or low levels of unemployment protection (Paul & Moser, 2009). In their multination study, Wanberg, van Hooft, Dossinger et al. (2020) found that the generosity of unemployment insurance (i.e., level and duration of unemployment benefits) positively predicts mental health among unemployed individuals via reduced financial strain. Thus, generous unemployment insurance benefits have the potential to somewhat alleviate unemployed people's financial concerns, which promotes their mental health (Searle & McWha-Hermann, Chapter 4; Teng-Calleja et al., Chapter 8).

Research on system-level effects and the process of re-employment has mostly focused on the role of unemployment protection. Studies comparing nations/states as well as studies following a system change mostly show that higher levels of unemployment insurance relate to slower re-employment (e.g., Lalive, 2008; Tatsiramos & van Ours, 2014; Wanberg, van Hooft, Dossinger et al., 2020). Wanberg, van Hooft, Dossinger et al., (2020) examined the mechanisms underlying this effect and found that more generous unemployment insurance relates to less perceived time pressure and lower priority given to finding a job, which links to lower job-search quality and subsequently reduced re-employment speed. Besides re-employment speed, research has examined the link between unemployment insurance and re-employment quality (e.g., wages and tenure in the new job), with some studies finding positive and others no effects (Tatsiramos & van Ours, 2014). Wanberg, van Hooft, Dossinger et al., (2020) theorized that these mixed findings might be due to different pathways from unemployment insurance to re-employment quality. Their findings across three countries (i.e., United States, Germany, and The Netherlands) indeed show that, on the one hand, more generous unemployment insurance related to less perceived time pressure and lower priority given to finding a job, which linked to lower job-search quality and subsequent reduced re-employment quality. On the other hand, more generous unemployment insurance led to improved mental health during unemployment which positively linked to re-employment quality. Importantly, the combined overall relationship between unemployment insurance generosity and re-employment quality was positive.

Altogether, unemployment protection seems to be a double-edged sword as it hinders re-employment speed but benefits re-employment quality and mental health during unemployment. However, weighing the pros and cons, generous unemployment insurance may be advisable because it immediately supports mental health and allows people to find higher quality, and therefore more sustainable, re-employment, which likely benefits long-term career development and health. Nevertheless, when the generosity of unemployment insurance is a given, Wanberg, van Hooft, Dossinger et al., (2020) findings point toward different interventions for countries with high versus low unemployment-protection systems. For example, generous unemployment-protection systems should be complemented with unemployment policies and counseling that help unemployed people prioritize their job search and improve the quality of their job search. In contrast, less generous unemployment-protection systems should be complemented with services focused on improving unemployed people's mental health.

Labor-Market Factors

Labor market factors such as labor-market demand, employer hiring policies, and discrimination have been studied in relation to mental health and the re-employment process. Labor-market demand can be thought to relate either positively or negatively to mental health among unemployed (Paul et al., 2018). Specifically, when unemployment rates are higher, the prospects of re-employment are reduced, which may negatively affect mental health. In contrast, when unemployment rates are higher, the stigma of being unemployed may be lower, positively affecting mental health. In line with these opposed theoretical positions, evidence has been mixed. In their meta-analyses, McKee-Ryan et al. (2005) did not find a moderating effect of unemployment rate in the relationship between employment status and mental health, while Paul and Moser (2009) found marginal support for the idea that the detrimental effects of unemployment on mental health are stronger in countries with high rather than low unemployment rates.

Regarding the relationship of labor-market demand with re-employment success, theoretical positions and empirical evidence have also been ambiguous. In their qualitative study, Wanberg et al. (2012) found that the economic situation in terms of the lack of jobs was an often-mentioned difficulty that impaired job seekers' re-employment success. In individual-level quantitative studies, labor-market demand is mostly measured by individual perceptions because objective indicators such as unemployment rates vary across regions and occupations and are therefore hard to match to the individual's situation. Meta-analytic results indicate that labor-market demand perceptions are only very weakly if at all related to re-employment success (van Hooft et al., 2021). A potential explanation is that individuals are not able to accurately self-report the demand in the labor market in their region and occupation. Alternatively, the mixed findings may reflect the opposing theoretical perspectives as identified in the literature (e.g., van Hooft, 2018a). Specifically, motivational theories such as expectancy-value theory and behavioral coping theory suggest a positive effect of labor-market demand on job search and re-employment success. This behavioral coping effect holds that high labor-market demand mobilizes energy and motivates people in their job search, whereas low labor-market demand demotivates people causing them to withdraw. In contrast, control theory and rational choice theory suggest a negative effect of labor-market demand on job search and re-employment success. This compensatory effect holds that high labor-market demand causes job seekers to perceive that re-employment is easy, resulting in less effort given to their job search and switching of attention to other goals, whereas low labor-market demand may lead job seekers to invest extra effort in their job search to compensate for the low likelihood of finding a job. van Hooft and Crossley (2008) theorized that whether perceived labor-market demand positively or negatively affects job search depends on situational strength, such that strong situations induce a compensatory (i.e., negative) effect while weak situations induce a behavioral coping (i.e., positive) effect. Using financial need as an indicator of situational strength, they indeed found a compensatory effect under conditions of high financial need.

Further, the instability in the global economy following the COVID-19 pandemic had consequences for the labor market and job seekers' mental health and behavior. For example, Stremersch and Van Hoye (2021) surveyed job seekers during the first lockdown in Flanders and found that their mental wellbeing was much lower compared to scores for the general population. They were much more worried than before the pandemic that they would not find a job and experienced severe stress levels. About half of the job seekers also experienced concrete changes in their job-search process due to the pandemic, such as fewer available job vacancies, canceled selection processes, and shifts to online interviews. Moreover, Gabriel et al. (2021) found that COVID-19-related job-search anxiety impacted job-search cognitions and behaviors. Specifically, when such anxiety led to adaptive problem-solving thoughts (e.g., thinking how to improve one's job search), it benefited job search intensity and quality, resulting in more job interviews. However, when such anxiety led to maladaptive rumination (e.g., recurrent negative thoughts about one's job search), it hindered job search, which occurred especially among those with stronger beliefs in conspiracy theories. In addition, the pandemic and subsequent restrictions and lockdowns may have generated constraints to job search (e.g., family responsibilities and financial troubles). Koopman et al. (2021) found that such COVID-19 job-search constraints led to unemployed people having less hope and more distress regarding their job search (especially for those who felt vulnerable to catching COVID-19). At the same time, when people felt invulnerable against COVID-19, job-search constraints stimulated them to increase their job-search intensity and quality, resulting in more job interviews. Lastly, COVID-19 not only impacted the intensity and quality of job search but also the characteristics people looked for in jobs. Several studies found that job seekers changed their job preferences, such that they attached greater importance to the possibility of working from home, work-life balance (Haar, Chapter 17), job security, and having a good manager (Hensvik et al., 2021; McFarland et al., 2020; Stremersch & Van Hoye, 2021).

Hiring policies of recruiting organizations are another labor market factor that affects unemployed job seekers. Based on interview data, Wanberg et al. (2012) identified several employer-related factors that impact job seekers. For example, the experience of employers insisting on a perfect match between applicant characteristics and the vacant job causes frustration and discouragement and complicates re-employment. Lack of professionalism by the organization (e.g., vague or dated job postings) and recruiters (e.g., lack of knowledge or skill and impolite behavior) also negatively impacts job seekers' wellbeing. Ali et al. (2016) specifically focused on experiences of rude and discourteous treatment (i.e., incivility) by recruiters or interviewers, showing that such treatment may undermine self-efficacy and job-search motivation for some job seekers. In contrast, when organizations provide job seekers with feedback of high informational value (e.g., on their application), this enhances job seekers' positive affect, which benefits their job search (Chawla et al., 2019).

Further, job-seekers experience that organizations have a preference for employees with certain demographic characteristics (Wanberg et al., 2012). Research has found evidence of hiring discrimination on the basis of ethnicity, age, unemployment status, sexual orientation, physical appearance, and disability/health status (for reviews see Derous & Ryan, 2018; Lippens et al., 2021; Wanberg, Ali, et al., 2020a). For example, a meta-analysis of field experiments in the US in which matched candidates from different ethnic groups applied for jobs showed that Whites received 36% more callbacks than African Americans and 24% more than Latinos (Quillian et al., 2017). In their meta-analysis of field experiments, Lippens et al. (2021) found that older, disabled, and less physically attractive job seekers are on average around 40% less likely to receive a positive response to a job application. Related to the unemployment stigma we discussed earlier, studies mostly find signs of hiring discrimination for longer term unemployed individuals. For example, in a field experiment, Trzebiatowski et al. (2020) found that long-term unemployed applicants were less likely to receive a job interview than short-term unemployed applicants. However, anti-discrimination legislation diminishes these effects. To counter hiring discrimination, we recommend that organizations use standardized and structured selection methods, screen their recruitment and selection staff on the propensity to discriminate, train them to avoid bias, and hold them accountable for their hiring decisions (cf. Derous & Ryan, 2018).

Situational Factors

The specific context of unemployed individuals can support or undermine their mental health and help or hinder the job search and re-employment process. An important factor is the financial situation during unemployment. Availability of financial resources relates positively to mental health and life satisfaction among unemployed individuals, while financial strain has a strong negative relationship with these outcomes (McKee-Ryan et al., 2005). While financial need serves as a motivator to invest time in seeking re-employment, meta-analytic evidence suggests that it is unrelated to finding re-employment and negatively related to re-employment quality (van Hooft, 2018a; van Hooft et al., 2021). A potential explanation for these findings may be that financial strain undermines people's mental health and the cognitive functioning that is needed to engage in a high-quality and effective job search.

Social support in terms of instrumental and emotional help and assistance is an important protective resource for unemployed individuals' mental health (McKee-Ryan et al., 2005). In contrast, social undermining in terms of negative affect, criticism, and hindrance of goal attainment is negatively linked to unemployed individuals' mental health (McKee-Ryan et al., 2005). While highly important for mental health, the relationships between social support with job search and re-employment success are weak (van Hooft et al., 2021). A potential explanation could be that social support may also divert attention away from job search. Future research is needed to further examine to what extent and for what components instrumental and emotional support are functional in the re-employment process.

In addition, one's social network can have important implications for job search and re-employment success. Social network theory suggests that actors are embedded within networks of interconnected relationships that provide opportunities for and constraints on behavior (Burt, 1997). Much of the literature has focused on the "strength-of-weak-ties" hypothesis, proposing that job seekers are more likely to find a job when they gather job information from people they are only weakly connected to (i.e., acquaintances rather than friends). Given that weak ties are more likely to move in other social circles, they are more likely to provide nonredundant information and resources (Granovetter, 1973). However, other studies also found benefits for strong ties in terms of more social support and access to job leads (Wanberg, Ali et al., 2020; Wanberg, van Hooft, Liu, et al, 2020). Other key characteristics of social networks are the size (i.e., total number of people one is connected to) and composition (i.e., status of the ties in one's network), with larger and higher status networks resulting in more positive outcomes (Adler & Kwon, 2002). Attesting to the importance of social networks for job search, empirical research shows that a considerable percentage of job seekers find employment through networking (Franzen & Hangartner, 2006).

Moreover, Van Hoye et al. (2009) found that unemployed job seekers reported higher re-employment quality when they networked with weaker ties. In addition, job seekers were more likely to become re-employed when the educational and occupation status of their network contacts was higher.

Stable Individual Factors

In addition to system, labor-market, and situational factors, relatively stable individual factors such as an individual's demographics and personality have been examined in relation to unemployed people's mental health and the re-employment process. Such factors are important in the diagnosis of unemployed individuals to identify those who are more likely to have poorer mental health and longer unemployment duration and therefore need extra help.

Regarding age, empirical findings tentatively suggest that unemployment has stronger effects on mental health for adolescents and older individuals (Paul & Moser, 2009). In line with discrimination research, meta-analytic studies have demonstrated that age negatively relates to re-employment success (van Hooft et al., 2021; Wanberg et al., 2016). Specifically, Wanberg et al. (2016) showed that age negatively relates to re-employment status and speed and that the strength of this negative relationship increases over the age of 50. Variables such as self-efficacy and job search intensity partially mediated this negative relationship. Watermann et al. (2021) found that the job-search process of older job seekers is facilitated when they adopt specific age-related strategies pertaining to flexibility in developing new goals or approaches in response to setbacks and obstacles during the job search. Similarly, among mostly older unemployed job seekers, Noordzij et al. (2013a) found that a learning-goal orientation training increased re-employment probability because participants were more open to learning from setbacks and became more aware that there are other strategies to try to obtain their goal. Altogether these findings suggest that training older unemployed individuals to increase their learning orientation and in strategies toward dealing with setbacks and job search self-efficacy may benefit their job-search behavior and re-employment success.

Meta-analytic findings show that ethnic minority job seekers have slightly lower mental health during unemployment (McKee-Ryan et al., 2005) and take longer to become re-employed (Kanfer et al., 2001). Furthermore, research suggests that the job search process may work differently depending on ethnicity. For example, van Hooft, Born, Taris, and van der Flier (2004) found that among ethnic minorities in The Netherlands, job-search motivation is more dependent on their social environment than on personal attitudes. van Hooft and De Jong's (2009) findings suggest that motivational differences may be explained by differences in cultural value orientations such as collectivism. In most studies "Whites" are compared to "non-Whites," so we need more research investigating the job search and re-employment of specific groups and ethnicities. For instance, Van Hoye et al. (2019) observed that ethnic minority women with more children received fewer job offers and were less likely to engage in proactive job-search behaviors such as networking and visiting employment agencies. Ethnic minority women who spent more time on visiting employment agencies and looking up job ads were more likely to receive job offers. Finally, ethnic minority women's networking behavior only resulted in more job offers when their networking self-efficacy was high. In a sample of skilled migrants, Zikic and Klehe (2021) found that social support, proactive personality, and the recognition of foreign credentials (i.e., education and experience) positively related to migrants' career planning, which predicted employment quality.

Regarding occupational and educational levels, meta-analyses suggest that the negative effects of unemployment on mental health are larger among blue-collar and less-educated individuals than among white-collar and more highly educated individuals (McKee-Ryan et al., 2005; Paul & Moser, 2009). When considering re-employment success, meta-analyses found overall relationships between educational level and indicators of re-employment success to be absent or weakly positive (Kanfer et al., 2001; van Hooft et al., 2021). However, the content of job search in terms of the strategies and channels people use might differ across occupational and educational levels. Research has also suggested potential differences in the re-employment process depending on social class (e.g., parental education, occupation, and income). For example, studies have found that labor-market entrants from higher social classes have more access to family-provided resources such as instrumental and social job-search support, lower financial hardship, and higher job-search self-efficacy (DeOrtentiis et al., 2021; Verhaeghe et al., 2013). Furthermore, job seekers from higher social classes seem to invest more time in their job search and conduct their job search in a more systematic manner (DeOrtentiis et al., 2021; Fang & Saks, 2021). Some evidence also suggests that they are more able to translate their job-search efforts into job interviews and offers (Fang & Saks, 2021). Future research is needed to examine whether these findings also apply to unemployed job seekers.

In addition to demographic factors, research has examined the role of personality in relation to unemployed people's mental health and the re-employment process. McKee-Ryan et al. (2005) found that core self-evaluations (i.e., self-esteem, locus of control, self-efficacy, and emotional stability) may serve as personal resources that protect wellbeing during unemployment. Kanfer et al. (2001) examined the role of the Big Five personality factors (i.e., Extraversion, Agreeableness, Openness to Experience, Conscientiousness, and Emotional Stability) in the re-employment process and found that Conscientiousness and Emotional Stability predict re-employment success. However, van Hooft et al. (2021) found only very weak relationships between the Big Five factors and re-employment success. In contrast, personality facet-trait self-regulation (i.e., relatively stable individual differences in the ability to guide goal-directed activities over time and across changing circumstances) was the only aspect of personality that consistently predicted job-search behavior and re-employment success. This finding can be explained by the theoretical notion that the re-employment process is an often difficult and lengthy process, which requires motivation and self-regulation over time. Therefore, it is important to understand the motivational and self-regulatory factors that facilitate the job search process toward re-employment.

Malleable Individual Factors

An important factor in reversing job loss and enhancing job search is people's motivation to search for jobs. Motivation theories that have been applied in the context of job search include goal-setting and goal-orientation theories (e.g., Latham et al., 2018), social cognitive theory (Bandura, 1991), the theory of planned behavior (Ajzen, 1991), and SDT (Deci & Ryan, 2000). These theories specify malleable individual factors that facilitate people's motivation and self-regulation. These factors are largely under the control of individuals, and as such are important focus areas during re-employment counseling and provide pointers for developing interventions and training programs to facilitate job search and re-employment success.

Goal setting theory posits that goals are important drivers of motivation and self-regulation (Latham et al., 2018). To enhance and direct motivation and self-regulation, people should not only select the goal content but also develop its dimensions, such as goal commitment (i.e., employment commitment or the importance placed on having a job; Kanfer et al., 2001), goal clarity (i.e., having clear job-search objectives; Wanberg et al., 2002), and goal proximity (i.e., break down a distal goal into more proximal goals; van Hooft et al., 2013). Regarding goal content, Van Hoye and Saks (2008) have distinguished different goals that may instigate a job search (e.g., finding a new job, staying aware of opportunities, and developing a professional network) and found that the goal content related to the type of job-search behaviors that people engaged in. Employment commitment is an often-studied variable, showing positive relations with job-search self-regulation and job-search behavior (van Hooft et al., 2021). Research on goal clarity typically finds that it is positively related to job search intensity and quality, employment status, and employment quality (van Hooft et al., 2021). Less research attention has been devoted to goal proximity in the context of job search. However, based on self-regulation theory (e.g., Bandura, 1991; van Hooft et al., 2013), the translation of the distal goal of finding employment into proximal goals in the intermediate steps is posited to be important for motivation, self-regulation, and persistence because attaining proximal goals leads to self-satisfaction and progressive mastery. Future research is needed to examine such processes in the context of job search and re-employment.

Goal setting theory further states that when people have yet to acquire or improve the knowledge and skills needed for goal attainment, setting learning goals is more effective than setting performance goals (Latham et al., 2018). In the context of job search, performance goals can even harm job-search behavior and induce procrastination in job-search activities (van Hooft, 2018b). In contrast, learning goals benefit job search self-regulation and behavior and through those increase the chances of finding employment (Creed et al., 2009; da Motta Veiga & Turban, 2014; Noordzij et al., 2013a; van Hooft & Noordzij, 2009). Re-employment counseling and interventions should therefore focus on providing a learning-oriented climate and stimulate job seekers to set learning goals for their job search.

Social cognitive theory (Bandura, 1991) highlights the role of self-efficacy in motivation and self-regulation. Higher self-efficacy (i.e., confidence in the ability to perform a specific activity) motivates people to set challenging goals, commit to these goals, and persevere in goal pursuit despite difficulties and setbacks. In addition, self-efficacy facilitates self-aiding thoughts and reduces self-hindering thoughts and vulnerability to depression (Bandura, 1991). Sources of self-efficacy include mastery experiences (i.e., having performed a task successfully or experienced success in proximal steps), social modeling (i.e., seeing similar others performing the task successfully), social persuasion (i.e., being persuaded to believe in oneself and measure one's success by self-improvement), and reducing anxiety (e.g., by correcting misreading of emotional states; Bandura, 2012). Research on self-efficacy has widely supported its role as a predictor of job-search self-regulation, job-search intensity and quality, and re-employment success (van Hooft et al., 2021). Intervention programs have further shown that job-search self-efficacy can be developed through training in job-search skills (modeling, practicing in role plays), encouragement (social persuasion), and inoculation against setbacks (e.g., Eden & Aviram, 1993; van Ryn & Vinokur, 1992).

Extending the theory of planned behavior (TPB; Saxena & Tchangneno, Chapter 11) to job search, van Hooft (2018a, 2018b) proposed a theory of planned job-search behavior, outlining motivational and self-regulatory factors and mechanisms that determine job-search behavior and re-employment success. The strength of people's motivation to engage in job search is captured by job-search intentions, referring to the type of job-search activities that people are planning to perform (i.e., motivational direction), and the time, effort, and energy that people plan to allocate to perform those activities (i.e., motivational intensity). Job-search intentions depend on three motivational factors. First, personal attitudes toward job search refer to people's positive or negative evaluations of engaging in job search, both affectively (i.e., whether people evaluate job seeking as enjoyable, pleasant, and interesting) and instrumentally (i.e., whether people evaluate job seeking as wise, beneficial, and useful; van Hooft, Born, Taris, van der Flier, & Blonk, 2004). Second, perceived social pressure to search reflects a more normative aspect, concerning the amount of social pressure that people feel to engage in job search. Third, perceived behavioral control over job search refers to the perceived ease or difficulty of performing job-search activities, including both control perceptions over external factors, such as the availability of opportunities and resources, and internal factors such as skills and abilities (i.e., job-search self-efficacy). In a review of job-search studies testing the TPB, van Hooft (2018a) concluded that the three factors relate mostly positively to job-search intentions. Further, meta-analytic findings show positive correlations of job-search attitudes, social pressure to search, and job-search self-efficacy with job-search self-regulation, job-search intensity, and employment status (van Hooft et al., 2021). Regarding re-employment quality, however, social pressure to search showed a small negative relationship. In re-employment guidance, counselors should therefore focus on enhancing job search attitudes and self-efficacy rather than increasing the social pressure to search. For example, counselors can elicit people's underlying salient beliefs about job seeking and finding employment, and intervene on these idiosyncratic beliefs (van Hooft, 2018a).

SDT (Deci & Ryan, 2000, 2008) focuses not only on motivational strength but also on motivational quality. SDT proposes that the quality of motivation depends on the degree to which the basic psychological needs for autonomy, competence, and relatedness are satisfied. When job seekers feel that they can make their own choices, are effective in what they do, and are connected to other people, they more likely develop and maintain autonomous motivation. When job seekers are autonomously motivated, they engage in job search because they find it interesting, meaningful, or relevant to reach important personal goals. In contrast, controlled motivation occurs when job seekers search for jobs because they feel pressured to do so, either internally (e.g., feelings of guilt and shame) or externally (e.g., loss of unemployment benefits). SDT suggests that job seekers who are more autonomously motivated (rather than controlled) are more likely to persist and succeed in their job search while maintaining their wellbeing. Research has generally supported these assumptions in a job search context (da Motta Veiga & Gabriel, 2016; Koen et al., 2015, 2016; Vansteenkiste et al., 2004, 2005; van Hooft et al., 2022). Specifically, autonomous job-search motivation relates positively to both job-search intensity and quality, and thus indirectly to finding employment. Controlled job-search motivation is mostly unrelated to job-search behavior and negatively related to wellbeing.

Importantly, job seekers' social contexts (e.g., family, employment counselor) can play an important role in shaping their motivation. From the SDT perspective, job-search guidance and interventions should aim at supporting job seekers' needs for autonomy, competence, and relatedness to develop autonomous motivation (Vansteenkiste & Van den Broeck, 2018). Being autonomy-supportive means providing choices and meaningful rationales (e.g., explain to job seekers why it is important to regularly revise their resume and provide options for doing so rather than simply oblige them to submit a revised resume once a month). The need for competence can be supported by creating a well-structured and encouraging environment in which expectations are clear, the focus is on proximal goals and mastery experiences, and help is offered when needed (Vansteenkiste & Van den Broeck, 2018). Satisfying the need for relatedness requires involvement, such as showing genuine concern for people's personal situations and making them feel understood (rather than being distant). Supporting these suggestions, Koen et al. (2016) found that unemployed job seekers who experienced more autonomy in their re-employment guidance reported higher autonomous and lower controlled job-search motivation. In another study, the perceived usefulness of a re-employment course positively related to developing autonomous job-search motivation (Koen et al., 2015).

Interventions to Facilitate the Re-Employment Process

While active, high-quality, and sustained job search is important for a successful re-employment process, it is also difficult for various reasons (van Hooft, 2018a). Specifically, job search is a rather novel, nonroutine activity for which people mostly have little skilled experience. Further, job search involves the use of a wide array of methods, channels, and activities, which demand a broad range of different skills. Also, the context in which job search occurs is characterized by low transparency and high heterogeneity, making it relatively unclear how to find job leads, obtain job interviews, and meet the expectations of recruiting organizations. Last, job search is often a lengthy process toward a distal goal (i.e., obtaining a job) with many obstacles, setbacks, and rejections along the way, which may distract job seekers' attention and undermine their motivation. In fact, engaging in job search negatively affects job seekers' emotions and mental health (McKee-Ryan et al., 2005), which can be explained by these difficulties and the setbacks and rejections that job seekers encounter (Kreemers et al., 2018; Song et al., 2009; Wanberg Zhu, et al., 2010). This poses an interesting dilemma; while re-employment is the best way to improve unemployed people's mental health and wellbeing, the necessary job search process toward re-employment challenges their mental health. Therefore, unemployed people not only need to self-regulate their job-search cognitions and behavior but also their emotions and mental health to facilitate the re-employment process (Kreemers et al., 2018, 2020; van Hooft, 2018b).

General Effects of Interventions

Although there are several factors affecting mental health and re-employment success that are beyond the job seeker's control (e.g., system and labor-market factors discussed above) and require system- or organization-level interventions, various individual-level intervention programs have been developed to support unemployed people with their job search and wellbeing, based on the principles of motivation and self-regulation theories (e.g., JOBS program, learning goal training, cognitive-behavioral therapy (CBT), verbal self-guidance (VSG), networking intervention, metacognitive prompting, mindfulness, and self-compassion). In a meta-analytic review of (quasi-)experimental studies, Liu et al. (2014) included 47 job search interventions and found that, overall, interventions lead to a 2.67 higher re-employment likelihood as well as to higher re-employment quality (e.g., salary). Path analyses suggest that the intervention effects on re-employment status are (partially) explained by increases in job-search skills, job-search self-efficacy, and job-search behavior. Importantly, only those interventions that focused on both developing job-search skills and enhancing job-search motivation were found to promote re-employment success.

In addition to facilitating re-employment success, interventions have the potential to improve unemployed job seekers' mental health. For example, Liu et al. (2014) found that interventions may reduce depression and anxiety. Hollederer (2019) reviewed 30 intervention programs among unemployed individuals and concluded that interventions based on CBT, the JOBS method, and the JobFit approach (i.e., health counseling using motivational interviewing) positively impacts mental health and health behavior. Similarly, in their review of 36 studies, Puig-Barrachina et al. (2020) concluded that job-search assistance interventions that include a psychological component (e.g., inoculation against setbacks, improving self-efficacy) have positive effects on mental health.

In terms of timing, intervention programs should be offered shortly after job loss. Paul and Moser (2009) found that mental health sharply decreases immediately after job loss, suggesting that mental-health-supporting interventions are most needed in the first months after job loss. Also, for re-employment success, research suggests that interventions should be provided shortly after job loss, as they are more effective in promoting re-employment success for short-term rather than long-term unemployed individuals (Liu et al., 2014). However, attention should be paid to the danger of locked-in effects (i.e., unemployed people participating in training may focus on the training for its duration rather than actively searching for re-employment). Therefore, intervention programs should not be spaced over a too long time period, and longer intervention programs should be designed such that participants are stimulated to actively engage in rather than pause their job search.

Instead of offering interventions and/or individual re-employment counseling to all unemployed individuals, re-employment agencies may use diagnostic inventories to identify those that are in most need of help (e.g., Wanberg, Zhang & Diehn, 2010; Wijnhoven & Havinga, 2014). Such inventories should be based on both stable and malleable individual factors as discussed above, mental health, job search skills, and job-search quality. Indeed, based on a qualitative study among re-employment counselors, Noordzij et al. (2013b) found that careful assessment of unemployed job seekers is one of the important success factors underlying effective re-employment counseling as this allows for targeted interventions.

Specific Interventions

The re-employment process is inherently a performance-focused and oftentimes competitive-achievement situation, evoking performance goals in people. Such performance goals are ego-threatening and induce anxiety, vulnerability to failure, and job-search procrastination (van Hooft, 2018b). In contrast, a focus on learning goals reduces anxiety, helps with interpreting failures as learning opportunities, and facilitates self-regulation. Building on goal setting and goal-orientation theory, van Hooft and Noordzij (2009) developed a training on learning-goal orientation in job search. Unemployed job seekers were instructed to set specific, attainable, and moderately difficult learning goals for their job search. They were further encouraged to identify possible obstacles, focus on different strategies, view errors and failures as learning opportunities, and look for ways to improve their job-search skills. The trainer created a climate of development and improvement by giving both positive and negative feedback. The training was found to increase people's learning-goal orientation toward job search and led to more learning from failure, increased awareness of alternative job-search strategies, higher job-search intentions, more job-search behavior, and higher re-employment probabilities (Noordzij et al., 2013a; van Hooft & Noordzij, 2009).

Many job seekers experience dysfunctional cognitions after job loss and during job search, e.g., self-defeating cognitions (Wanberg et al., 2012), unhelpful attributions (Proudfoot et al., 1997), negative self-talk (Latham et al., 2018), undermining their goal commitment, self-efficacy, motivation, and mental health. Proudfoot et al. (1997) examined the effects of a CBT intervention aimed at identifying and modifying unemployed job seekers' attributional style. In a field experimental design, they compared the CBT intervention with a social support program. They found that CBT improved people's adaptive attribution style and benefitted mental health and wellbeing as well as job search self-efficacy, employment commitment, and re-employment success. Latham and colleagues (2018) integrated principles from goal setting and social cognitive theory to develop VSG training. In the training, job seekers learned to change negative self-talk (e.g., "I am too old for the jobs I want") into positive self-guidance (e.g., "My age indicates that I have a lot of experience"). In two studies, support was found for VSG as it led to increased job-search self-efficacy, more intense job-search behavior, better job-interview performance, higher re-employment probabilities, and greater re-employment quality (Latham & Budworth, 2006; Yanar et al., 2009).

The most widely studied intervention is the JOBS program, which was designed to improve unemployed people's job search and re-employment success while at the same time protecting their mental health (Price & Vinokur, 2018). Building on social cognitive theory, the program uses active learning techniques (e.g., modeling, role-playing) to improve job-search skills, while simultaneously safeguarding self-efficacy and motivation by inoculation against setbacks and unconditional positive regard by the trainers. Through these mechanisms, the JOBS intervention aims to increase unemployed people's job-search self-efficacy, coping with setbacks, and persistence in job search. Various studies have indeed shown that the JOBS program positively affects mental health, self-efficacy, resilience, persistence in job search, re-employment probability, and re-employment quality (see Price & Vinokur, 2018).

While the JOBS program focuses on teaching general job-search skills and self-efficacy, Wanberg, Van Hooft, Liu, et al. (2020) have developed an online intervention specifically devoted to improving unemployed people's skills and efficacy in job-search networking (see https://learntonetworkwithbrio.csom.umn.edu/). Social contacts are beneficial in the job-search process not only for potential job leads and referrals but also for emotional support, reassurance, and encouragement. However, job seekers may be reluctant to network, for example, because they have misconceptions about networking or feel incompetent. Applying social cognitive theory and research to job-search networking, the intervention includes modules to alter job seekers' perceptions of networking, improve knowledge on the benefits of networking, develop and practice networking skills, and set networking goals. In their field experiment, Wanberg, van Hooft, Liu, et al. (2020) found that participation in the online intervention positively affected unemployed job seekers' networking self-efficacy and made them experience more benefits of networking. Furthermore, the intervention stimulated networking behavior and positively affected re-employment quality.

Self-regulation is important for sustained and high-quality job-search behavior (Kanfer et al., 2001; van Hooft et al., 2021, 2013). To support the self-regulation of job seekers throughout the job-search process, Kanar and Bouckenooghe (2021) developed and tested an intervention using weekly metacognitive prompts by email. These prompts aimed to stimulate self-regulation aspects of planning, prioritization, self-monitoring, self-control, and goal shielding. Among student job seekers, they found that such prompts improved job seekers' metacognitive activities, which related to higher job search effort and more job interviews. Although the effectiveness of metacognitive prompts should be further examined among unemployed job seekers, these findings are promising from a practical point of view, as they provide a relatively economical intervention to improve job-search quality.

Lastly, several interventions focus specifically on emotional regulation after job loss and during job search. As discussed, job loss is a traumatic event that may evoke strong negative emotions. Spera et al. (1994) assumed that job-loss trauma is something unemployed job seekers do not readily speak about and that such inhibition impedes the re-employment process. Therefore, they developed a disclosive writing intervention in which unemployed individuals were instructed to express their deepest thoughts and emotions regarding their job loss and how they affected their lives on five consecutive days. In a field experimental study, Spera et al. (1994) found that disclosive writing increased re-employment probabilities. However, they did not find effects on job search and health indicators. de Jong et al. (2013) tested the effects of a mindfulness training for unemployed job seekers. They found that an eight-week mindfulness-based stress-reduction program (incl. body scan, mindful yoga, and sitting meditation) reduced unemployed job seekers' stress levels and increased their self-efficacy. However, no effects were found on job-search motivation. Kreemers et al. (2020) further examined the role of reflective writing on job seekers' emotions regarding their job search. Based on self-compassion theory, they instructed job seekers to describe a negative job-search event and reflect on this with self-kindness, common humanity, and mindful acceptance. This self-compassionate reflective writing was compared to a control task of regular reflective writing (i.e., describing naturally occurring thoughts and feelings on the negative job-search event; cf. Spera et al., 1994). The self-compassionate writing was found to induce states of self-compassion toward job search, resulting in less self-criticism, and more balanced emotional responses regarding job-search experiences (i.e., reduced negative affect and increased positive affect). Future research is needed to examine more specifically what, if, and how emotional regulation training approaches such as disclosive writing, mindfulness, and self-compassionate reflection can be used to simultaneously benefit job seekers' emotional wellbeing, job-search motivation, and re-employment success.

Future Research

In addition to the specific suggestions for future research described in the previous sections, we identify five important areas for future research based on the literature review. First, most research on re-employment success has focused on the dichotomous outcomes of employment status, while less research attention has been devoted to the predictors of sustainable, high-quality employment. Because precarious employment poses a threat to wellbeing (e.g., Grün et al., 2010; Kim & von dem Knesebeck, 2015), future research should focus more on quality of re-employment, uncovering the mechanisms of finding suitable and sustainable re-employment. Second, while research has demonstrated the importance of a high-quality job-search process (Stremersch et al., 2021; Stremersch & Van Hoye, 2020; van Hooft et al., 2021, 2022), future research is needed to increase our insight into (a) the conditions (i.e., moderators) in which job-search quality is more (or less) important for re-employment success, (b) how job-search quality develops over time, and (c) to what extent job search quality can be improved. In addition, future research should focus on the specific dimensions of job-search quality to understand if, how, and when these are important (e.g., reflection may be only important for specific groups or under difficult labor-market conditions) and how these dimensions mutually evolve and affect each other over time. Third, more generally, future research should focus on uncovering interactions between individual factors and context-related factors (e.g., system, labor market, and situational; see Figure 19.1) in relation to mental health, job search, and re-employment success. Fourth, future research should focus on increasing our understanding on how we can stimulate unemployed individuals' job-search motivation and behavior while at the same time supporting their mental health in the process toward re-employment. There is a need for the development and testing of interventions that serve this dual goal. Lastly, the basic premise of job search and re-employment research often is the search for permanent, full-time employment. With the rise of flexible working arrangements (e.g., gig work, independent contracting, temp work, and freelancing), an important question for future research is if, and to what extent, the current theories, models, and findings on job search and re-employment success generalize to contemporary gig economies (Kuhn, Chapter 12; Toaddy, Crawford, et al., Chapter 22).

Conclusion

In conclusion, job loss severely harms people's health and has negative consequences for their families and society as a whole. Although unemployment benefits can somewhat alleviate the financial concerns, speedy and high-quality (i.e., decent, suitable, and sustainable) re-employment is the best medicine to alleviate unemployed people's precarious situation. The job search and re-employment process, however, is difficult and full of obstacles that further challenge unemployed job seekers' mental health and motivation. Therefore, engaging in self-regulatory coping behavior such as job-search intensity, job-search quality, and emotion-focused coping is crucial for re-employment success. Intervention programs have been shown to be effective in supporting mental health and facilitating the job search and re-employment process. Taking system, labor-market, situational, and stable individual factors into account helps to identify those groups and individuals most likely to benefit from such interventions and counseling.

References

Adler, P. S., & Kwon, S. W. (2002). Social capital: Prospects for a new concept. *Academy of Management Review, 27*(1), 17–40. https://doi.org/10.2307/4134367

Ajzen, I. (1991). The theory of planned behavior. *Organizational Behavior and Human Decision Processes, 50*(2), 179–211. https://doi.org/10.1016/0749-5978(91)90020-T

Albert, L. S., Allen, D. G., Biggane, J. E., & Ma, Q. (2015). Attachment and responses to employment dissolution. *Human Resource Management Review, 25*(1), 94–106. http://dx.doi.org/10.1016/j.hrmr.2014.06.004

Ali, A. A., Ryan, A. M., Lyons, B. J., Ehrhart, M. G., & Wessel, J. L. (2016). The long road to employment: Incivility experienced by job seekers. *Journal of Applied Psychology, 101*(3), 333–349. http://doi.org/10.1037/apl0000055

Andersen, S. H. (2013). Common genes or exogenous shock? Disentangling the causal effect of paternal unemployment on children's schooling efforts. *European Sociological Review, 29*(3), 477–488. https://doi.org/10.1093/esr/jcr088

Bambra, C., & Eikemo, T. A. (2018). Insecurity, unemployment, and health: A social epidemiological perspective. In U.-C. Klehe & E. A. J. van Hooft (Eds.), *The Oxford handbook on job loss and job search* (pp. 111–125). Oxford University Press. https://doi.org/10.1093/oxfordhb/9780199764921.013.019

Bandura, A. (1991). Social cognitive theory of self-regulation. *Organizational Behavior and Human Decision Processes, 50*(2), 248–287. https://doi.org/10.1016/0749-5978(91)90022-L

Bandura, A. (2012). On the functional properties of perceived self-efficacy revisited. *Journal of Management, 38*(1), 9–44. https://doi.org/10.1177/0149206311410606

Boswell, W. R., Zimmerman, R. D., & Swider, B. W. (2012). Employee job search: Toward an understanding of search context and search objectives. *Journal of Management, 38*(1), 129–163. https://doi.org/10.1177/0149206311421829

Burt, R. S. (1997). The contingent value of social capital. *Administrative Science Quarterly, 42*(2), 339–365. https://doi.org/10.2307/2393923

Chawla, N., Gabriel, A. S., da Motta Veiga, S. P., & Slaughter, J. E. (2019). Does feedback matter for job search self-regulation? It depends on feedback quality. *Personnel Psychology, 72*(4), 513–541. https://doi.org/10.1111/peps.12320

Creed, P. A., & Bartrum, D. (2006). Explanations for deteriorating well-being in unemployed people: Specific unemployment theories and beyond. In T. Kieselbach, A. H. Winefield, C. Boyd, & S. Anderson (Eds.), *Unemployment and health: International and interdisciplinary perspectives.* Australian Academic Press.

Creed, P. A., King, V., Hood, M., & McKenzie, R. (2009). Goal orientation, self-regulation strategies, and job-seeking intensity in unemployed adults. *Journal of Applied Psychology, 94*(3), 806–813. https://doi.org/10.1037/a0015518

da Motta Veiga, S. P., & Gabriel, A. S. (2016). The role of self-determined motivation in job search: A dynamic approach. *Journal of Applied Psychology, 101*(3), 350–361. https://doi.org/10.1037/apl0000070

da Motta Veiga, S. P., & Turban, D. B. (2014). Are affect and perceived stress detrimental or beneficial to job seekers? The role of learning goal orientation in job search self-regulation. *Organizational Behavior and Human Decision Processes, 125*(2), 193–203. https://doi.org/10.1016/j.obhdp.2014.09.007

de Jong, A., Hommes, M., Brouwers, A., & Tomic, W. (2013). Effects of mindfulness-based stress reduction course on stress, mindfulness, job self-efficacy and motivation among unemployed people. *Australian Journal of Career Development, 22*(2) 51–62. https://doi.org/10.1177/1038416213486095

Deci, E. L., & Ryan, R. M. (2000). The 'what' and 'why' of goal pursuits: Human needs and the self-determination of behavior. *Psychological Inquiry, 11*(4), 227–268. https://doi.org/10.1207/S15327965PLI1104_01

Deci, E. L., & Ryan, R. M. (2008). Self-determination theory: A macro-theory of human motivation, development, and health. *Canadian Psychology, 49*(3), 182–185. https://doi.org/10.1037/a0012801

DeOrtentiis, P. S., Van Iddekinge, C. H., & Wanberg, C. R. (2021). Different starting lines, different finish times: The role of social class in the job search process. *Journal of Applied Psychology, 107*(3), 444–457. https://doi.org/10.1037/apl0000915

Derous, E., & Ryan, A. M. (2018). By any other name: Discrimination in resume screening. In U.-C. Klehe, & E. A. J. van Hooft (Eds.), *The Oxford handbook on job loss and job search* (pp. 501–522). Oxford University Press. https://doi.org/10.1093/oxfordhb/9780199764921.013.017

Eden, D., & Aviram, A. (1993). Self-efficacy training to speed re-employment: Helping people to help themselves. *Journal of Applied Psychology, 78*(3), 352–360. https://doi.org/10.1037/0021-9010.78.3.352

Eersel, J. H. W., Taris, T. W., & Boelen, P. A. (2020). Reciprocal relations between symptoms of complicated grief, depression, and anxiety following job loss: A cross-lagged analysis. *Clinical Psychologist, 24*(3), 276–284. https://doi.org/10.1111/cp.12212

Fang, R. T., & Saks, A. M. (2021). Class advantage in the white-collar labor market: An investigation of social class background, job search strategies, and job search success. *Journal of Applied Psychology, 106*(11), 1695–1713. https://doi.org/10.1037/apl0000842

Franzen, A., & Hangartner, D. (2006). Social networks and labour market outcomes: The non-monetary benefits of social capital. *European Sociological Review, 22*(4), 353–368. https://doi.org/10.1093/esr/jcl001

Fryer, D. (1986). Employment deprivation and personal agency during unemployment: A critical discussion of Jahoda's explanation of the psychological effects of unemployment. *Social Behavior, 1*(1), 3–23.

Gabriel, A. S., MacGowan, R. L., Ganster, M. L., & Slaughter, J. E. (2021). The influence of COVID-induced job search anxiety and conspiracy beliefs on job search effort: A within-person investigation. *Journal of Applied Psychology, 106*(5), 657–673. https://doi.org/10.1037/apl0000926

Gabriel, Y., Gray, D. E., & Goregaokar, H. (2013). Job loss and its aftermath among managers and professionals: Wounded, fragmented and flexible. *Work, Employment and Society, 27*(1), 56–72. https://doi.org/10.1177/0950017012460326

Goodman, W. K., Geiger, A. M., & Wolf, J. M. (2017). Leisure activities are linked to mental health benefits by providing time structure: Comparing employed, unemployed and homemakers. *Journal of Epidemiology and Community Health, 71*(1), 4–11. https://doi.org/10.1136/jech-2016-207260

Gowan, M. A., Riordan, C. M., & Gatewood, R. D. (1999). Test of a model of coping with involuntary job loss following a company closing. *Journal of Applied Psychology, 84*(1), 75–86. https://doi.org/10.1037/0021-9010.84.1.75

Granovetter, M. S. (1973). The strength of weak ties. *American Journal of Sociology, 78*(6), 1360–1380. https://doi.org/10.1086/225469

Grün, C., Hauser, W., & Rhein, T. (2010). Is any job better than no job? Life satisfaction and re-employment. *Journal of Labor Research, 31*(3), 285–306. https://doi.org/10.1007/s12122-010-9093-2

Hensvik, L., Le Barbanchon, T., & Rathelot, R. (2021). Job search during the COVID-19 crisis. *Journal of Public Economics, 194*, Article 104349. https://doi.org/10.1016/j.jpubeco.2020.104349

Hirsch, P. B. (2021). The great discontent. *Journal of Business Strategy, 42*(6), 439–442. https://doi.org/10.1108/JBS-08-2021-0141

Hollederer, A. (2019). Health promotion and prevention among the unemployed: A systematic review. *Health Promotion International, 34*(6), 1078–1096. https://doi.org/10.1093/heapro/day069

International Labour Organization (ILO). (2020). *World employment and social outlook: Trends 2020*. International Labour Organization.

International Labour Organization (ILO). (2021). *ILO Monitor: COVID-19 and the world of work: Updated estimates and analysis* (7th ed.). International Labour Organization.

Jahoda, M. (1981). Work, employment, and unemployment: Values, theories, and approaches in social research. *American Psychologist, 36*(2), 184–191. https://doi.org/10.1037/0003-066X.36.2.184

Kanar, A. M., & Bouckenooghe, D. (2021). Prompting metacognition during a job search: Evidence from a randomized controlled trial with university job seekers. *Applied Psychology: An International Review, 70*(3), 955–985. https://doi.org/10.1111/apps.12255

Kanfer, R., Wanberg, C. R., & Kantrowitz, T. M. (2001). Job search and employment: A personality-motivational analysis and meta-analytic review. *Journal of Applied Psychology, 86*(5), 837–855. https://doi.org/10.1037/0021-9010.86.5.837

Kalil, A. (2009). Joblessness, family relations and children's development. *Family Matters, 83*, 15–22.

Kim, T. J., & von dem Knesebeck, O. (2015). Is an insecure job better for health than having no job at all? A systematic review of studies investigating the health-related risks of both job insecurity and unemployment. *BMC Public Health, 15,* Article 985. https://doi.org/10.1186/s12889-015-2313-1

Kira, M., & Klehe, U.-C. (2016). Self-definition threats and potential for growth among mature-aged job-loss victims. *Human Resource Management Review, 26*(3), 242–259. https://doi.org/10.1016/j.hrmr.2016.03.001

Koen, J., Klehe, U.-C., & van Vianen, A. E. M. (2015). Employability and job search after compulsory re-employment courses: The role of choice, usefulness, and motivation. *Applied Psychology: An International Review, 64*(4), 674–700. https://doi.org/10.1111/apps.12037

Koen, J., van Vianen, A. E. M., van Hooft, E. A. J., & Klehe, U.-C. (2016). How experienced autonomy can improve job seekers' motivation, job search, and chance of finding re-employment. *Journal of Vocational Behavior, 95–96*, 31–44. https://doi.org/10.1016/j.jvb.2016.07.003

Koopmann, J., Liu, Y., Liang, Y., & Liu, S. (2021). Job search self-regulation during COVID-19: Linking search constraints, health concerns, and invulnerability to job search processes and outcomes. *Journal of Applied Psychology, 106*(7), 975–989. https://doi.org/10.1037/apl0000938

Kreemers, L. M., van Hooft, E. A. J., & van Vianen, A. E. M. (2018). Dealing with negative job search experiences: The beneficial role of self-compassion for job seekers' affective responses. *Journal of Vocational Behavior, 106*, 165–179. https://doi.org/10.1016/j.jvb.2018.02.001

Kreemers, L. M., van Hooft, E. A. J., van Vianen, A. E. M., & De Zilwa, S. C. M. (2020). Testing a self-compassion intervention among job seekers: Self-compassion beneficially impacts affect through reduced self-criticism. *Frontiers in Psychology, 11*, 1371. https://doi.org/10.3389/fpsyg.2020.01371

Krug, G., Drasch, K., & Jungbauer-Gans, M. (2019). The social stigma of unemployment: Consequences of stigma consciousness on job search attitudes, behaviour and success. *Journal for Labour Market Research, 53,* Article 11. https://doi.org/10.1186/s12651-019-0261-4

Lalive, R. (2008). How do extended benefits affect unemployment duration? A regression discontinuity approach. *Journal of Econometrics, 142*(2), 785–806. http://doi.org/10.1016/j.jeconom.2007.05.013

Latham, G. P., & Budworth, M.-H. (2006). The effect of training in verbal self-guidance on the self-efficacy and performance of Native North Americans in the selection interview. *Journal of Vocational Behavior, 68*(3), 516–523. https://doi.org/10.1016/j.jvb.2005.11.005

Latham, G. P., Mawritz, M. B., & Locke, E. A. (2018). Goal setting and control theory: Implications for job search. In U.-C. Klehe, & E. A. J. van Hooft (Eds.), *The Oxford handbook on job loss and job search* (pp. 129–141). Oxford University Press. https://doi.org/10.1093/oxfordhb/9780199764921.013.003

Leana, C. R., & Feldman, D. C. (1995). Finding new jobs after a plant closing: Antecedents and outcomes of the occurrence and quality of re-employment. *Human Relations, 48*(12), 1381–1401. https://doi.org/10.1177/001872679504801201

Lippens, L., Vermeiren, S., & Baert S. (2021). *The state of hiring discrimination: An overview of (almost) all recent correspondence experiments* (Discussion Paper No. 14966). IZA Institute of Labor Economics. https://docs.iza.org/dp14966.pdf

Liu, S., Huang, J. L., &Wang, M. (2014). Effectiveness of job search interventions: A meta-analytic review. *Psychological Bulletin, 140*(4), 1009–1041. https://doi.org/10.1037/a0035923

Luhmann, M., Weiss, P., Hosoya, G., & Eid, M. (2014). Honey, I got fired! A longitudinal dyadic analysis of the effect of unemployment on life satisfaction in couples. *Journal of Personality and Social Psychology, 107*(1), 163–180. https://doi.org/10.1037/a0036394

Mari, G., & Keizer, R. (2021). Parental job loss and early child development in the Great Recession. *Child Development, 92*(5), 1698–1716. https://doi.org/10.1111/cdev.13517

McFarland, L. A., Reeves, S., Porr, W. B., & Ployhart, R. E. (2020). Impact of the COVID-19 pandemic on job search behavior: An event transition perspective. *Journal of Applied Psychology, 105*(11), 1207–1217. https://doi.org/10.1037/apl0000782

McKee-Ryan, F. M., & Harvey, J. (2011). "I have a job, but...": A review of underemployment. *Journal of Management, 37*(4), 962–996. https://doi.org/10.1177/0149206311398134

McKee-Ryan, F. M., & Maitoza, R. (2018). Job loss, unemployment, and families. In U.-C. Klehe, & E. A. J. van Hooft (Eds.), *The Oxford handbook on job loss and job search* (pp. 87–97). Oxford University Press. https://doi.org/10.1093/oxfordhb/9780199764921.013.027

McKee-Ryan, F. M., Song, Z., Wanberg, C. R., & Kinicki, A. J. (2005). Psychological and physical well-being during unemployment: A meta-analytic study. *Journal of Applied Psychology, 90*(1), 53–76. https://doi.org/10.1037/0021-9010.90.1.53

Miller, M. A., & Rahe, R. H. (1997). Life changes scaling for the 1990s. *Journal of Psychosomatic Research, 43*(3), 279–292. https://doi.org/10.1016/S0022-3999(97)00118-9

Milner, A., Page, A., & LaMontagne, A. D. (2013). Long-term unemployment and suicide: A systematic review and meta-analysis. *PLoS One, 8,* e51333. https://doi.org/10.1371/journal.pone.0051333

Milner, A., Page, A., & LaMontagne, A. D. (2014). Cause and effect in studies on unemployment, mental health and suicide: A meta-analytic and conceptual review. *Psychological Medicine, 44*(5), 909–917. https://doi.org/10.1017/S0033291713001621

Noordzij, G., van Hooft, E. A. J., van Mierlo, H., van Dam, A., & Born, M. Ph. (2013a). The effects of a learning-goal orientation training on self-regulation: A field experiment among unemployed job seekers. *Personnel Psychology, 66*(3), 723–755. https://doi.org/10.1111/peps.12011

Noordzij, G., van Hooft, E. A. J., van Mierlo, H., van Dam, A., & Born, M. Ph. (2013b). Getting unemployed job seekers back to work: The development of a process model of employment counseling behavior. *Career Development Quarterly, 61*(3), 256–275. https://doi.org/10.1002/j.2161-0045.2013.00054.x

Norlander, P., Ho, G. C., Shih, M., Walters, D. J., & Pittinsky, T. L. (2020). The role of psychological stigmatization in unemployment discrimination. *Basic and Applied Social Psychology, 42*(1), 29–49. https://doi.org/10.1080/01973533.2019.1689363

O'Donnell, A. T. Corrigan, F., & Gallagher, S. (2015). The impact of anticipated stigma on psychological and physical health problems in the unemployed group. *Frontiers in Psychology, 6*, Article 1263. https://doi.org/10.3389/fpsyg.2015.01263

Paul, K. I., Hassel, A., & Moser, K. (2018). Individual consequences of job loss and unemployment. In U.-C. Klehe, & E. A. J. van Hooft (Eds.), *The Oxford handbook on job loss and job search* (pp. 57–85). Oxford University Press. https://doi.org/10.1093/oxfordhb/9780199764921.013.028

Paul, K. I., & Moser, K. (2009). Unemployment impairs mental health: Meta-analyses. *Journal of Vocational Behavior, 74*(3), 264–282. https://doi.org/10.1016/j.jvb.2009.01.001

Price, R. H., & Vinokur, A. D. (2018). The JOBS program: Impact on job seeker motivation, re-employment, and mental health. In U.-C. Klehe, & E. A. J. van Hooft (Eds.), *The Oxford handbook on job loss and job search* (pp. 575–590). Oxford University Press. https://doi.org/10.1093/oxfordhb/9780199764921.013.006

Proudfoot, J., Guest, D., Carson, J., Dunn, G., & Gray, J. (1997). Effect of cognitive-behavioural training on job-finding among long-term unemployed people. *Lancet, 350*(9071), 96–100. https://doi.org/10.1016/S0140-6736(96)09097-6

Puig-Barrachina, V., Giró, P., Artazcoz, L., Bartoll, X., Cortés-Franch, I., Fernández, A., González-Marín, P., & Borrell, C. (2020). The impact of active labour market policies on health outcomes: A scoping review. *European Journal of Public Health, 30*(1), 36–42. https://doi.org/10.1093/eurpub/ckz026

Quillian, L., Pager, D., Hexel, O., & Midtbøen, A. H. (2017). Meta-analysis of field experiments shows no change in racial discrimination in hiring over time. *Proceeding of the National Academy of Sciences, 114*(41), 10870–10875. https://doi.org/10.1073/pnas.1706255114

Rantakeisu, U., Starrin, B., & Hagquist, C. (1997). Unemployment, shame and ill health—an exploratory study. *Scandinavian Journal of Social Welfare, 6*(1), 13–23. https://doi.org/10.1111/j.1468-2397.1997.tb00160.x

Roelfs, D. J., Shor, E., Davidson, K. W., Schwartz, J. E. (2011). Losing life and livelihood: A systematic review and meta-analysis of unemployment and all-cause mortality. *Social Science & Medicine, 72*(6), 840–854. https://doi.org/10.1016/j.socscimed.2011.01.005

Ryan, R. M., & Deci, E. L. (2000). Self-determination theory and the facilitation of intrinsic motivation, social development, and well-being. *American Psychologist, 55*(1), 68–78. https://doi.org/10.1037/0003-066X.55.1.68

Schaller, J., & Zerpa, M. (2019). Short-run effects of parental job loss on child health. *American Journal of Health Economics, 5*(1), 8–41. https://doi.org/10.1162/ajhe_a_00106

Schofield, T. P., Haslam, N., & Butterworth, P. (2019). The persistence of welfare stigma: Does the passing of time and subsequent employment moderate the negative perceptions associated with unemployment benefit receipt? *Journal of Applied Social Psychology, 49*(9), 563–574. https://doi.org/10.1111/jasp.12616

Sinfield, A. (2018). Unemployment and its wider impact. In U.-C. Klehe & E. A. J. van Hooft (Eds.), *The Oxford handbook on job loss and job search* (pp. 99–109). Oxford University Press. https://doi.org/10.1093/oxfordhb/9780199764921.013.030

Song, Z., Foo, M.-D., Uy, M. A., & Sun, S. (2011). Unraveling the daily stress crossover between unemployed individuals and their employed spouses. *Journal of Applied Psychology, 96*(1), 151–168. https://doi.org/10.1037/a0021035

Song, Z., Uy, M. A., Zhang, S., & Shi, K. (2009). Daily job search and psychological distress: Evidence from China. *Human Relations, 62*(8), 1171–1197. https://doi.org/10.1177/0018726709334883

Spera, S. P., Buhrfeind, E. D., & Pennebaker, J. W. (1994). Expressive writing and coping with job loss. *Academy of Management Journal, 37*(3), 722–733.

Stevens, A. H., & Schaller, J. (2011). Short-run effects of parental job loss on children's academic achievement. *Economics of Education Review, 30*(2), 289–299. https://doi.org/10.1016/j.econedurev.2010.10.002

Stremersch, J., & Van Hoye, G. (2020). Searching hard versus searching smart: The role of search process quality in an internship context. *International Journal of Selection and Assessment, 28*(1), 31–44. https://doi.org/10.1111/ijsa.12274

Stremersch, J., & Van Hoye, G. (2021). Werk zoeken tijdens de coronacrisis: Het werkzoekproces en psychisch welzijn van werkzoekenden tijdens de coronacrisis. *Tijdschrift voor HRM, 24*(1), 49–74. https://doi.org/10.5117/THRM2021.1.STRE

Stremersch, J., Van Hoye, G., & van Hooft, E. A. J. (2021). How to successfully manage the school-to-work transition: Integrating job search quality in the social cognitive model of career self-management. *Journal of Vocational Behavior, 131*, Article 103643. https://doi.org/10.1016/j.jvb.2021.103643

Ström, S. (2003). Unemployment and families: A review of research. *Social Service Review, 77*(3), 399–430. https://doi.org/10.1086/375791

Tatsiramos, K., & van Ours, J. (2014). Labor market effects of unemployment insurance design. *Journal of Economic Surveys, 28*(2), 284–311. https://doi.org/10.1111/joes.12005

Turban, D. B., Stevens, C. K., & Lee, F. K. (2009). Effects of conscientiousness and extraversion on new labor market entrants' job search: The mediating role of metacognitive activities and positive emotions. *Personnel Psychology, 62*(3), 553–573. https://doi.org/10.1111/j.1744-6570.2009.01148.x

Trzebiatowski, T. M., Wanberg, C. R., & Dossinger, K. (2020). Unemployed needn't apply: Unemployment status, legislation, and interview requests. *Journal of Management, 48*(8), 1380–1407. https://doi.org/10.1177/0149206318823952

Van den Hee, S. M., van Hooft, E. A. J., & Nevicka, B. (2022). *Volunteer work during unemployment: Does it pay off? A 5-wave longitudinal study among volunteering job seekers* [Paper presentation]. 82nd Annual Meeting of the Academy of Management, Seattle.

van Hooft, E. A. J. (2018a). Motivation and self-regulation in job search: A theory of planned job search behavior. In U.-C. Klehe, & E. A. J. van Hooft (Eds.), *The Oxford handbook on job loss and job search* (pp. 181–204). Oxford University Press. https://doi.org/10.1093/oxfordhb/9780199764921.013.010

van Hooft, E. A. J. (2018b). Self-regulatory perspectives in the theory of planned job search behavior: Deliberate and automatic self-regulation strategies to facilitate job seeking. In U.-C. Klehe, & E. A. J. van Hooft (Eds.), *The Oxford handbook on job loss and job search* (pp. 205–221). Oxford University Press. https://doi.org/10.1093/oxfordhb/9780199764921.013.31

van Hooft, E. A. J., Born, M. Ph., Taris, T. W., & van der Flier, H. (2004). Job search behavior and the theory of planned behavior: Minority-majority group differences in The Netherlands. *Journal of Vocational Behavior, 65*(3), 366–390. https://doi.org/10.1016/j.jvb.2003.09.001

van Hooft, E. A. J., Born, M. P., Taris, T. W., van der Flier, H., & Blonk, R. W. B. (2004). Predictors of job search behavior among employed and unemployed people. *Personnel Psychology, 57*(1), 25–59. https://doi.org/10.1111/j.1744-6570.2004.tb02483.x

van Hooft, E. A. J., & Crossley, C. D. (2008). The joint role of locus of control and perceived financial need in job search. *International Journal of Selection and Assessment, 16*(3), 258–271. https://doi.org/10.1111/j.1468-2389.2008.00432.x

van Hooft, E. A. J., & De Jong, M. (2009). Predicting job seeking for temporary employment using the theory of planned behaviour: The moderating role of individualism and collectivism. *Journal of Occupational and Organizational Psychology, 82*(2), 295–316. https://doi.org/10.1348/096317908X325322

van Hooft, E. A. J., Kammeyer-Mueller, J. D., Wanberg, C. R., Kanfer, R., & Basbug, G. (2021). Job search and employment success: A quantitative review and future research agenda. *Journal of Applied Psychology, 106*(5), 674–713. https://doi.org/10.1037/apl0000675

van Hooft, E. A. J., & Noordzij, G. (2009). The effects of goal orientation on job search and re-employment: A field experiment among unemployed job seekers. *Journal of Applied Psychology, 94*(6), 1581–1590. https://doi.org/10.1037/a0017592

van Hooft, E. A. J., Van Hoye, G., & Van den Hee, S. M. (2022). How to optimize the job search process: Development and validation of the job search quality scale. *Journal of Career Assessment, 30*(3), 474–505. https://doi.org/10.1177/10690727211052812

van Hooft, E. A. J., Wanberg, C. R., & Van Hoye, G. (2013). Moving beyond job search quantity: Towards a conceptualization and self-regulatory framework of job search quality. *Organizational Psychology Review, 3*(1), 3–40. https://doi.org/10.1177/2041386612456033

Van Hoye, G. (2018). Job-search behavior as a multidimensional construct: A review of different job-search behaviors. In U.-C. Klehe, & E. A. J. van Hooft (Eds.), *The Oxford handbook on job loss and job search* (pp. 259–274). Oxford University Press. https://doi.org/10.1093/oxfordhb/9780199764921.013.009

Van Hoye, G., & Lootens, H. (2013). Coping with unemployment: Personality, role demands, and time structure. *Journal of Vocational Behavior, 82*(2), 85–95. https://doi.org/10.1016/j.jvb.2013.01.004

Van Hoye, G., & Saks, A. M. (2008). Job search as goal-directed behavior: Objectives and methods. *Journal of Vocational Behavior, 73*(3), 358–367. https://doi.org/10.1016/j.jvb.2008.07.003

Van Hoye, G., van Hooft, E. A. J., & Lievens, F. (2009). Networking as a job search behaviour: A social network perspective. *Journal of Occupational and Organizational Psychology, 82*, 661–682. https://doi.org/10.1348/096317908X360675

Van Hoye, G., van Hooft, E. A. J., Stremersch, J., & Lievens, F. (2019). Specific job search self-efficacy beliefs and behaviors of unemployed ethnic minority women. *International Journal of Selection and Assessment, 27*(1), 9–20. http://doi.org/10.1111/ijsa.12231

van Ryn, M., & Vinokur, A. D. (1992). How did it work? An examination of the mechanisms through which an intervention for the unemployed promoted job-search behavior. *American Journal of Community Psychology, 20*(5), 577–597. https://doi.org/10.1007/BF00941773

Vansteenkiste, M., Lens, W., De Witte, S., De Witte, H., & Deci, E. L. (2004). The 'why' and 'why not' of job search behaviour: Their relation to searching, unemployment experience, and well-being. *European Journal of Social Psychology, 34*(3), 345–363. https://doi.org/10.1002/ejsp.202

Vansteenkiste, M., Lens, W., De Witte, H., & Feather, N. T. (2005). Understanding unemployed people's job search behaviour, unemployment experience and wellbeing: A comparison of expectancy-value theory and self-determination theory. *British Journal of Social Psychology, 44*(2), 269–287. https://doi.org/10.1348/014466604X17641

Vansteenkiste, M., & Van den Broeck, A. (2018). Understanding the motivational dynamics among unemployed individuals: Refreshing insights from the self-determination theory perspective. In U.-C. Klehe & E. A. J. van Hooft (Eds.), *The Oxford handbook of job loss and job search* (pp. 159–179). Oxford University Press. https://doi.org/10.1093/oxfordhb/9780199764921.013.005

Verhaeghe, P.-P., Li, Y., & Van de Putte, B. (2013). Socio-economic and ethnic inequalities in social capital from the family among labour market entrants. *European Sociological Review, 29*(4), 683–694. https://doi.org/10.1093/esr/jcs047

Vickers, M. H. (2009). Journeys into grief: Exploring redundancy for a new understanding of workplace grief. *Journal of Loss and Trauma, 14*(5), 401–419. https://doi.org/10.1080/15325020902724198

Wanberg, C. R. (1995). A longitudinal study of the effects of unemployment and quality of re-employment. *Journal of Vocational Behavior, 46*(1), 40–54. https://doi.org/10.1006/jvbe.1995.1003

Wanberg, C. R. (2012). The individual experience of unemployment. *Annual Review of Psychology, 63*, 369–396. https://doi.org/10.1146/annurev-psych-120710-100500
Wanberg, C. R., Ali, A. A., & Csillag, B. (2020). Job seeking: The process and experience of looking for a job. *Annual Review of Organizational Psychology and Organizational Behavior, 7*, 315–337. https://doi.org/10.1146/annurev-orgpsych-012119-044939
Wanberg, C. R., Basbug, G., van Hooft, E. A. J., & Samtani, A. (2012). Navigating the black hole: Explicating layers of job search context and adaptational responses. *Personnel Psychology, 65*(4), 887–926. https://doi.org/10.1111/peps.12005
Wanberg, C. R., Hough, L. M., & Song, Z. (2002). Predictive validity of a multidisciplinary model of re-employment success. *Journal of Applied Psychology, 87*(6), 1100–1120. https://doi.org/10.1037/0021-9010.87.6.1100
Wanberg, C. R., Kanfer, R., Hamann, D. J., & Zhang, Z. (2016). Age and re-employment success after job loss: An integrative model and meta-analysis. *Psychological Bulletin, 142*(4), 400–426. https://doi.org/10.1037/bul0000019
Wanberg, C. R., van Hooft, E. A. J., Dossinger, K., Van Vianen, A. E. M., & Klehe, U.-C. (2020). How strong is my safety net? Perceived unemployment insurance generosity and implications for job search, mental health, and re-employment. *Journal of Applied Psychology, 105*(3), 209–229. https://doi.org/10.1037/apl0000435
Wanberg, C. R., van Hooft, E. A. J., Liu, S., & Csillag, B. (2020). Can job seekers achieve more through networking? The role of networking intensity, self-efficacy, and proximal benefits. *Personnel Psychology, 73*(4), 559–585. https://doi.org/10.1111/peps.12380
Wanberg, C. R., Zhang, Z., & Diehn, E. W. (2010a). Development of the "getting ready for your next job" inventory for unemployed individuals. *Personnel Psychology, 63*(2), 439–478. https://doi.org/10.1111/j.1744-6570.2010.01177.x
Wanberg, C. R., Zhu, J., Kanfer, R., & Zhang, Z. (2012). After the pink slip: Applying dynamic motivation frameworks to the job search experience. *Academy of Management Journal, 55*(2), 261–284. https://doi.org/10.5465/amj.2010.0157
Wanberg, C. R., Zhu, J., & van Hooft, E. A. J. (2010). The job search grind: Perceived progress, self-reactions, and self-regulation of search effort. *Academy of Management Journal, 53*(4), 788–807. https://doi.org/10.5465/AMJ.2010.52814599
Warr, P. (1987). *Work, unemployment, and mental health.* Clarendon Press.
Watermann, H., Fasbender, U., & Klehe, U.-C. (2021). Predicting the self-regulated job search of mature-aged job seekers: The use of elective selection, loss-based selection, optimization, and compensation strategies. *Journal of Vocational Behavior, 128*, Article 103591. https://doi.org/10.1016/j.jvb.2021.103591
Westman, M., Etzion, D., & Horovitz, S. (2004). The toll of unemployment does not stop with the unemployed. *Human Relations, 57*(7), 823–844. https://doi.org/10.1177/0018726704045767
Wijnhoven, M. A., & Havinga, H. (2014). The work profiler: A digital instrument for selection and diagnosis of the unemployed. *Local Economy: The Journal of the Local Economy Policy Unit, 29*(6–7), 740–749. https://doi.org/10.1177/0269094214545045
Yanar, B., Budworth, M.-H., & Latham, G. P. (2009). The effect of verbal self-guidance training for overcoming employment barriers: A study of Turkish women. *Applied Psychology: An International Review, 58*(4), 586–601. https://doi.org/10.1111/j.1464-0597.2008.00366.x
Zechmann, A., & Paul, K. I. (2019). Why do individuals suffer during unemployment? Analyzing the role of deprived psychological needs in a six-wave longitudinal study.

Journal of Occupational Health Psychology, 24(6), 641–661. https://doi.org/10.1037/ocp0000154

Zikic, J., & Klehe, U.-C. (2021). Going against the grain: The role of skilled migrants' self-regulation in finding quality employment. *Journal of Organizational Behavior, 42*(8), 1023–1041. https://doi.org/10.1002/job.2550

Zhou, Y., Zou, N., Woods, S. A., & Wu, C. H. (2019). The restorative effect of work after unemployment: An intraindividual analysis of subjective well-being recovery through re-employment. *Journal of Applied Psychology, 104*(9). 1195–1206. https://doi.org/10.1037/apl0000393

20

"PERMANENT TEMPORARINESS"—THE CURRENT LANDSCAPE OF MIGRATION AND WORK?

Shemana Cassim

In 2019, there were 169 million migrant workers around the world (International Labour Organization [ILO], 2021a). Migration is increasingly being utilized by governments as a response to labor market gaps, and a contributor to economic growth in host nations. This focus on migrants as holding economic value that can be extracted for national prosperity is particularly the case in relation to temporary migration programs, such as those focused on labor migrants for instance, which differentiate social freedoms and rights and partition off access to public resources for all but the most "desired" migrants (Collins, 2023).

The ongoing effects of the COVID-19 pandemic have underscored the extent to which the global economy relies on migrant labor in certain job sectors while simultaneously compounding the insecurity and uncertainty faced by migrant workers. Yet, while the pandemic-related effects on migration and work are no doubt extraordinary, the insecurities in the landscape of migration and work have imposed a state of "permanent temporariness," particularly for migrant workers in low-skilled jobs, even prior to the pandemic. This chapter provides an overview of the complex layers of challenges faced by migrant workers, within the current and ongoing context of the COVID-19 pandemic. I pay particular attention to challenges that result from broader systemic issues within the host nation, alongside "local" workplace-related challenges. Current events, spurred on by the pandemic, have also ignited calls for immigrant rights and justice at a global scale. This chapter offers a snapshot of how nations are responding to these calls and discusses implications at both systemic and organizational levels to alleviate the perpetuating precarity and insecurity faced by migrant workers in the long run. The chapter concludes by offering an alternative lens of human security and relational ethics through which labor-migrant governance can be reimagined.

DOI: 10.4324/9781003440444-24

The International Labor Organization (ILO) estimates that in 2019, the number of international migrant workers (hereafter "migrant workers") was 169 million, an increase of 3% since 2017 (ILO, 2021a). Here, the term "migration worker" refers to workers who enter a country specifically to seek work through formal channels with specific visas and can also include labor migrants. The majority of migrant workers are based in the Arab States, North America, and Europe (ILO, 2021a). In many countries, migrant workers represent a majority share of the workforce, with labor-force participation rates of migrants being higher (at 69%) than that of nonmigrants (60.4%; Jones et al., 2021). Most migrant workers are situated within the service sector (66.2%), with 26.7% in industry and 7.1% in agriculture. These jobs involve, for instance, serving on the front lines carrying out essential services in healthcare and transport, as well as construction, agriculture, and agro-food processing (Jones et al., 2021). Yet, many of these roles are considered low skilled, and migrant workers are reported to be overrepresented in less desirable, low-skilled jobs and are thought to be more exposed to adverse working conditions compared to nonimmigrant workers (Benach et al., 2011; Sterud et al., 2018). Additionally, most migrant workers are concentrated in jobs that are characterized by precarity, based on visa categories, contracts, or both (Jones et al., 2021).

In nations such as Canada (Ellermann, 2020), Australia (Robertson, 2015), and Aotearoa New Zealand (Collins, 2019), temporary and neo-guest worker schemes have not only become more prominent but also have started to outnumber other migrant-admission streams (Terruhn, 2023). Therein, migration is increasingly being utilized by governments as a response to labor market gaps and as a contributor to economic growth in host nations (Collins, 2023). As such, in the last decade, European Union (EU) and national state policies have been introduced to open up labor markets in Europe in order to meet demands and demographic outlook. These policies are intended to stimulate new forms of labor migration that are driven by supply-and-demand (Sterud et al., 2018).

International migration then is an important part of global social and economic development (Moyce & Schenker, 2018), with migrant workers making vital and substantial contributions to the economies of host nations, as well as their countries of origin. Despite the clear benefits and opportunities that migration and work offer people and their communities, migrant workers are concentrated in jobs characterized by high levels of precarity relating to visa categories and contracts, as well as informal and unprotected work, low wages, and a lack of social protection (Jones et al., 2021; Moyce & Schenker, 2018; Sousa et al., 2010). Therein, migrant workers face many challenges, including exploitation, discrimination, modern slavery, and unsafe working conditions (Jamil & Dutta, 2021; Martin & Nakayama, 2018; Norredam & Agyemang, 2019). This is particularly the case for low-skilled migrant workers, compared to high-skilled migrant workers. Often, the challenges paired with the insecurities and uncertainties that migrant workers face reflect broader structural and systemic inequalities within the host country that have been building for years (Migration Policy Institute, n.d.). The ongoing effects of the COVID-19 pandemic have exacerbated the insecurity and uncertainty faced by migrant workers while simultaneously underscoring the extent to which the global economy relies on migrant labor in certain job sectors (Jones et al., 2021). Therein, for the purpose of this chapter, precariousness is understood in a broad sense, as including the various insecurities and uncertainty relating to visas and contracts, the workplace-related risks and challenges discussed in the ensuing sections of the chapter, and the resultant power imbalances that come along with such dynamics.

This chapter provides a contemporary overview of the complex layers of challenges faced by migrant workers that were accentuated due to the pandemic. First, the chapter discusses the challenges that existed prior to the pandemic, such as those occurring as a result of broader systemic issues within host nations, as well as the "local" workplace-related challenges experienced by migrant workers. Next, the chapter highlights the challenges as compounded by the COVID-19 pandemic and its ongoing effects. This chapter then offers a snapshot of how nations are responding to the recent calls to alleviate the challenges and perpetuating precarity and insecurity faced by migrant workers in the long run. Finally, the chapter concludes by considering possible ways forward with an alternative approach to labor migration governance that involves human security and relational ethics.

System-Generated Challenges

Immigrants, particularly those in precarious positions, are always subject to the political climate of host countries, which has a clear bearing on the treatment and experiences of migrant workers (Moyce & Schenker, 2018). Contemporary migration regimes and policy changes in many nations have actively and progressively stratified migrant workers into precarity, thus creating insecurity in migration trajectories, resulting in many challenges experienced by these groups. The following sections provide an overview of such challenges that occur as a consequence of systemic inequalities in the host nations, including issues relating to permanent temporariness and migrant rights and social freedoms.

Permanent Temporariness

Throughout the last two decades, migration policy changes in many nations around the globe, including Aotearoa New Zealand, Canada, and Australia, have progressively driven migrant workers into landscapes of precarity in host nations (Arkilic & Sardelic, 2023; Collins, 2023; Rajkumaret al., 2012; Simon-Kumar,

2020; Terruhn, 2023). Such landscapes involve precarious jobs, visas, and thus income and lives in host nations that are characterized by fewer rights and limited prospects for long-term settlement (e.g. Collins, 2023; Parreñas et al., 2021; Vora, 2013). This trend toward a state of "permanent temporariness" (Bailey et al., 2002) driven by neoliberalist ideologies allows host nations to meet their labor and economic demands with minimal accountability for the lifeworlds and wellbeing of the migrant workers themselves. In the Aotearoa New Zealand context for instance, at the time of writing this chapter, essential-skill visas are often tied to employment, where redundancy can result in the loss of a migrant worker's visa and thus their ability to stay in the host country. Obtaining a new visa is dependent on a new job offer. Likewise, seasonal-work visa holders are on seven-month visas with no rights to extend or apply for alternative visas, and post-study work visa holders' prospects of settlement in the host nation depends on a job offer (Arkilic & Sardelic, 2023; Collins, 2020; Collins & Shubin, 2015). Similar conditions are apparent in other nations such as the United States (US), where temporary labor migrants are denied labor market flexibility, as their legal residency is made contingent on their employers (Kößler et al., 2023; Parreñas et al., 2021; Strauss & McGrath, 2017).

In Canada, this precarity is seen to be stratified based on economic calculus (e.g., labor as determined by skill-level) as well as privilege (e.g., privilege associated with nationality). Here, privileged forms of temporariness are afforded to highly skilled migrant workers, whereas restrictive and restricting forms of temporariness are offered to the low-skilled (Rajkumar et al., 2012). More recently, while a policy review created a new "International Mobility Programme" that recruited migrant workers mainly from the Global North, they still retained their "Temporary Foreign Workers Programme" that primarily recruits migrant workers from the Global South (Helleiner, 2017). As Terruhn (2023) notes, the language itself of the different visa pathways positions migrant workers from the Global South as being perpetually "temporary" and "foreign," whereas those from the Global North are awarded the label "internationals." This is, of course, in addition to the differing rights afforded to these two groups (Carr, Hopner et al., Chapter 10).

Overall then, the precarious migrant worker (especially the low-skilled) is characterized by a fragile existence, with their lives exemplified by struggle, exploitation, and, at times, poverty (Padovan-Özdemir & Moldenhawer, 2017; Simon-Kumar, 2020). The challenges they face also then cascade out into their everyday lives in many ways. Media anecdotes and research highlight experiences relating to exploitative wages, dubious arrival pathways, extreme indebtedness both in host and home countries, uncertain legal statuses, untenable living and housing standards, discrimination, anxiety, and the social censure of failure if they return home (e.g. Bathgate, 2022; Collins & Stringer, 2019; Doherty, 2022; Simon-Kumar, 2020).

Migrant Rights and Social Freedoms

As Collins (2023) states, migrant workers are seen as "rational economic decision-makers, who should assess the conditions and be responsible for the consequences of their migration, even if that involves precarity, marginalization and exploitation." This direction of migration policy development is being progressively adopted by a number of host nations around the world, including Australia, Canada, and Aotearoa New Zealand (Collins, 2023; Robertson, 2015; Vosko, 2022), seemingly mimicking the well-established regimes in East and Southeast Asia (Yeoh, 2022). Such developments are particularly relevant to temporary migration programs focused on labor, for instance, which consequently differentiate social freedoms and rights, and partition off access to public resources for all but the most "desired" migrants (Collins, 2023).

As an example, Aotearoa New Zealand has adopted a managerial approach to temporary migration over the last two decades, which is further underpinned by a logic of extraction based on perceived efficiency and productivity (Collins, 2023). Here, migrant workers are measured by their ability to create value and economic profit for host nations (Aradau & Tazzioli, 2019; Collins, 2023). Consequently, temporary migrants such as migrant workers are subjected to forms of "social quarantining" (Collins, 2023; Horgan & Liinamaa, 2017), where they are excluded from everyday life and social freedoms and exist solely as economic agents.

The restrictions on social freedoms that migrant workers experience can include limited labor-market options due to their visa status. In the case of domestic workers and construction workers for instance, host countries often control their ability to transfer the sponsorship of their visas (Parreñas et al., 2021). In Singapore and the Arab States, migrant domestic workers have to secure the permission of their employer to transfer jobs. In Bahrain, they are ineligible to transfer jobs at all (Gardner, 2010; Parreñas et al., 2021). Temporary migrant workers are also often excluded from formal and informal access to state entitlements such as healthcare (Hennebry et al., 2016; Landolt, 2020; Mucci et al., 2020; Parreñas et al., 2021). While agricultural workers in the US have formal access to federal health insurance, they often encounter barriers to accessing healthcare and may be deported following a work-related injury (Hennebry et al., 2016).

Overall, the exclusionary systems used to manage migrant workers deny them a sense of dignity and perpetuate their permanent state of precarity, thereby affecting their sense of wellbeing. Such issues can also have a flow-on effect, creating a further layer of challenges within the workplace.

Workplace-Related Challenges

Adding to the differential rights experienced by migrant workers within the precarious landscape of migration and work, research also indicates that migrant workers are often engaged in what are now broadly known as "3-D jobs": dirty, dangerous, and demeaning (sometimes also degrading; Quandt et al., 2013). Precarious employment is associated with less pay, longer hours, higher rates of poverty, wage theft and a lack of overtime, and health or employment benefits (Hege et al., 2015; ILO, 2015; Moyce & Schenker, 2018; Reid & Schenker, 2016). Moreover, many migrant workers (such as seasonal workers) are not usually represented by unions and thus have fewer protections than nonmigrant and/or permanent workers (Dong & Platner, 2004; Moyce & Schenker, 2018). Such conditions that are faced by millions of migrant workers can lead to various challenges within the workplace. The next sections discuss the workplace-related challenges faced by migrant workers that range from exploitation to mental health and workplace-safety-related issues.

Exploitation

Current approaches to migration policy play a significant role in creating opportunities for the exploitation of people holding temporary work visas. Visa conditions that provide employers with greater power and influence over both the employment and immigration status of migrant workers have therefore been repeatedly identified as drivers for exploitation (Collins & Stringer, 2019). According to recent evidence from Aotearoa New Zealand, Australia, and Canada, the key areas in which exploitation occurs include underpayment or nonpayment of wages, employers not complying with employment contracts, employers not paying taxes, denial of leave, withholding holiday pay, and health and safety violations (Collins & Stringer, 2019).

Aotearoa New Zealand is a country where the rapid growth in temporary migration (particularly for labor) has been associated with growing evidence of labor-market abuse (Collins & Stringer, 2019; Stringer & Michailova, 2019; Wong, 2021). A recent report indicates that while employers may promise to assist workers within their immigration requirements, this tends to serve as a mechanism of exploitation as some migrant workers accept wages and conditions below minimum standards in order to receive the perceived benefits of another work visa, or support for a residence application (Collins & Stringer, 2019). Moreover, exploited temporary migrant workers are often fearful of reporting abuses due to fears of deportation, unemployment, or reprisal (Stringer & Michailova, 2019).

Mental Health and Wellbeing

Migrant workers (particularly low-skilled workers) can experience marginalization and differential treatment in the workplace due to prejudice and discrimination, which can directly compromise their mental health and wellbeing (Hajro et al., 2019; Liem et al., 2021; Mucci et al., 2020). An international review of the literature indicates that the prejudice and discrimination experienced by migrant workers is often based on race, ethnicity, and/or religious affiliation (Hajro et al., 2019; Liem et al., 2021). Migrant workers may also suffer verbal and/or physical abuse in the workplace (Mucci et al., 2020).

Additionally, migrant workers can experience higher levels of work-related psychophysical stress due to poor quality of employment (Grzywacz et al., 2009; Mucci et al., 2020). While this stress may be a result of the discrimination mentioned previously, it can also be a result of inequitable, exploitative, and exclusionary working conditions. This may include strenuous work, the dangerous and unhealthy nature of some jobs, and cross-cultural and/or acculturative stress (Mucci et al., 2020). Therein, migrant workers show a higher incidence of anxiety and depressive symptoms than nonmigrant workers (Tarsitani & Biondi, 2016).

Workplace-related stress can also be exacerbated by underemployment, when migrant workers experience a disparity between their own skills and the characteristics of the job (Dunlavy et al., 2016; Mucci et al., 2020; Sterud et al., 2018). Often migrant workers find themselves working in roles for which they are overqualified, for various reasons, including wanting to stay in a host country, a need to support family members, a lack of other opportunities, and overseas qualifications not being recognized in host countries (Kößler et al., 2023). Research from Australia and Europe indicates a high underemployment rate with migrant workers often experiencing anger, irritability, and emotional distress as a consequence (Aalto et al., 2014; Mucci et al., 2020; Reid, 2012).

In addition to challenges relating to mental health, migrant workers also experience various challenges relating to physical health within, and as a result of the workplace setting.

Workplace Safety and Injuries

Many of the health risks for migrant workers are due to hazards inherent in the occupational setting. Reflecting on the 3-D characteristic of the jobs in which many, particularly low-skilled, migrant workers are employed; they are often required to take on greater risks on the job, do work without adequate training or protective equipment, and do not (or cannot) complain about unsafe working conditions (Moyce & Schenker, 2018). Such conditions thereby put migrant workers at increased risk for occupational injuries and fatalities. As such, the proportion of workplace-related injuries experienced by migrant workers has been increasing, reflecting a shift of the most hazardous jobs to the immigrant workforce (Flynn, 2014; Moyce & Schenker, 2018). Multiple reviews carried out recently indicate that the global prevalence of occupational health outcomes, including high rates of injuries, mortality, and physical and psychiatric morbidity, was greatest among migrant workers (Hargreaves et al., 2019; Norredam & Agyemang, 2019; Sterud et al., 2018).

The situation is particularly concerning for migrant workers as, given their precarious positions, they may be at risk of losing their jobs or even being deported if they voice their concerns or raise complaints (Moyce & Schenker, 2018). To add to these already serious challenges, the current COVID-19 pandemic has added another layer of interrelated issues for migrant workers.

Challenges in the Context of COVID-19

The onset and widespread effects of the COVID-19 pandemic have had a devastating impact on migrant workers around the globe. Migrant workers have generally been at higher risk of contracting COVID-19 for many reasons, including disproportionate presence in frontline work with higher virus exposure, cramped or inadequate living conditions, and the inability to access healthcare (Migration Policy Institute, n.d.). Beyond the effects of the public-health crisis working its way around the world since early 2020, various national response measures, including lockdowns and border closures, have had added implications for migrant workers relating to global movement, access to decent work, and hiring and employment conditions (Jones et al., 2021). The various resulting challenges faced by migrant workers demonstrate clear linkages between pandemic-related issues and the structural causes of the inequalities and vulnerabilities embedded in many current labor-migration processes and practices (Collins, 2023; Jones et al., 2021; Terruhn, 2023).

The following sections will discuss these challenges particularly relating to, and exacerbated by, already precarious situations ranging from job and income losses, lack of access to social protection, differential rights, costs and debts, and roles in essential work (Carr, Hodgetts et al., Chapter 1; Satzman et al., Chapter 2).

Job and Income Losses

Many migrant workers had their employment in host nations suspended or terminated as the pandemic spread, leaving them without a source of income: especially those in hospitality and tourism industries (Collins, 2023; Jones et al., 2021). In the Persian Gulf, for instance, many migrant construction, domestic, and other workers lost their jobs during the early days of the onset of the pandemic in March 2020 (Migration Policy Institute, n.d.). Migrant workers are a group that have been especially vulnerable to the economic shocks caused by the pandemic, and as they are predominantly employed in precarious, low-wages sectors, were often among the first to experience job losses. Loss of jobs and income also had multiple flow-on effects.

Given that in most nations, the initial response to COVID-19 was sudden and immediate border closures, migrants scrambled to return to their countries of origin. In Russia, close to 5 million workers from former Soviet states found themselves without jobs and attempting to find spots on government-chartered flights back to their countries of origin. Thousands of unemployed migrant workers based in Thailand had to return to their countries of origin in nearby South-East Asia (Migration Policy Institute, n.d.). Yet many more migrant workers found themselves stranded in host nations, while others found themselves or their families caught offshore with limited exemptions for entry being granted (Collins, 2023; Nadkarni, 2021). While the assumption was that communities would respond to the crisis by going into lockdown with their families, very little consideration was given by governments to the implications of such restrictions on the transnational lifeworlds of migrant workers (Jones et al., 2021).

Consequently, compounded by the loss of jobs and income, some migrant workers also found themselves unable to afford to live, which in turn affected their living conditions (Jamil & Dutta, 2021; Jones et al., 2021). Research indicates that many migrant workers in the Middle East were forced into overcrowded living conditions or had to find alternative accommodation (Jamil & Dutta, 2021; Jones et al., 2021). This also affected the mental health and well-being of these groups, with the disconnection from family, an inability to send funds back home to provide for their families, and overall uncertainty causing increased stress and anxiety (Jamil & Dutta, 2021). Additionally, given that for many migrant workers, employment is also tied to their legality in the host country, a lack of employment compounded their precarious status.

Lack of Access to Social Welfare and Protection

Alongside this perpetual precarity, the pandemic context also shone a spotlight on the many forms of social welfare and protection that migrant workers are routinely excluded from (Jones et al., 2021). While this was a challenge that pre-dated the pandemic, the onset of COVID-19 increased the severity of such challenges. First, migrant workers in many nations found themselves experiencing unequal access to healthcare when they really needed it, highlighted by challenges and barriers to obtaining basic care throughout the pandemic (ILO, 2020; Jones et al., 2021). In Tunisia and Latin America, for instance, many migrant workers lacked access to medical care or adequate COVID-19 testing, whereas migrant workers in the Gulf states also reported being excluded from healthcare (Jones et al., 2021). In the US, migrant workers with precarious legal status had anxieties about accessing COVID-19 testing and other healthcare services due to the possible responses (such as deportation or discrimination) by the existent political regimes (Migration Policy Institute, n.d.).

Second, migrant workers were often ineligible for or excluded from income security protection against sudden job and wage losses (ILO, 2021b; Jones et al., 2021). This impacted females more than males, due to the existing wage gap. In such contexts, nongovernmental organizations (NGOs) and initiatives such as

Migrant Worker Resource Centres in Asia stepped in to assist migrants with social security and wage claims (Jones et al., 2021). Additionally, some countries of origin were able to offer cash support to returning migrants, with one example being the Philippines, which provided funds to returning workers through an Overseas Worker Welfare Administration calamity assistance or business loans (Jones et al., 2021).

Third, in nations like Aotearoa New Zealand, temporary migrants and migrant workers were made ineligible for social welfare (until December 2020 when limited access was provided) and were instead supported through foodbanks and other charitable sources until a Red-Cross–administered program was established to provide food vouchers and accommodation payments for those in most dire need (Collins, 2023). Overall, however, even where formal inclusion existed, evidence suggests that migrants faced numerous barriers to accessing social protection.

Differential Rights Based on Visas

Throughout the COVID-19 pandemic, the differential rights allowed to migrant workers based on their (often temporary) visa statuses became increasingly apparent. For instance, the Australian Working Holiday Programme covers migrant workers who often work in low-skilled jobs such as fruit picking, and their working situations are considered more vulnerable and precarious than those on "regular" working visas. Throughout the pandemic, these conditions were made worse as this group, along with other temporary visa holders, were excluded from the Australian COVID-19 stimulus package (Berg & Farbenblum, 2020). In Hong Kong, low-skilled migrant domestic workers were strongly advised by the Government to stay at home (with their employers and thus working) even on their days off, or risk being profiled by the police. In contrast, high-skilled migrant workers could choose to move around freely as they pleased (Summers 2020). Similarly in Singapore, low-wage migrant workers were perceived as a "high-risk community" and were compelled to quarantine in their densely populated dormitories which inevitably increased their risk of contracting COVID-19. Migrant workers earning a higher wage, and considered highly skilled, were considered residents and had the freedom to choose where they quarantined (Hui, 2020).

Added Costs, Debts, and Recruitment Issues

The pandemic has also increased the financial insecurities and debt burdens carried by migrant workers. Due to the COVID-19 situation, many prospective migrant workers who had taken on debt to travel were either unable to depart, obtain refunds, or earn income to repay their debts (Jones et al., 2021).

Furthermore, migrant workers also faced added recruitment-related costs for managed isolation or quarantine facilities, as well as the various COVID-19 tests required for overseas travel that were often not covered by recruiters (Jones et al., 2021). Despite growing commitment to the notion that workers should not pay recruitment fees or costs, the pandemic situation highlighted that workers in many parts of the world continue to incur debt to fund their cross-border movement for work (Jones et al., 2021).

Migrant workers stranded without employment incurred additional debts and lost savings in attempts to repay these debts, in addition to having to cover basic living costs for themselves and their families. Alternatively, if they were able to somehow work around the border closures and return home, they also had to shoulder the added costs of repatriation and return, including travel, quarantine, and COVID-19 tests (Jones et al., 2021).

Migrants in Essential Work

Revalidating the perception of migrant workers as a commodity that responds to labor-market supply-and-demand, the COVID-19 pandemic highlighted the extent to which the global economy relies on migrant labor in particular job sectors (Saltzman et al., Chapter 2), with many migrant workers in both low- and high-skilled jobs being declared "essential workers" throughout the public health crisis (Jones et al., 2021). In relation to low-skilled work, migrant workers form the backbone of the workforce in areas such as construction, agriculture, hospitality, healthcare, and other critical but less visible sectors of the economy (Jones et al., 2021). European Commission announced guidelines to ensure that migrant workers in Europe could move between countries to prevent lags in EU supply chains. Similarly, Germany and the United Kingdom allowed farmers to airlift in thousands of workers to uphold their industries. Similar patterns were seen in certain high-skilled sectors such as healthcare. Australia, for instance, lifted restrictions on 20,000 international nursing students in the early days of the pandemic (Jones et al., 2021).

The pandemic has drawn attention to the exploitative light in which migrant workers have often been seen, where they are positioned as the "other," on the peripheries of those "deserving" of care and protection, yet still performing services for them (for instance in the context of migrant "essential workers"; Collins, 2023). Overall, the challenges faced by migrant workers, combined with changes to international travel conditions that have increased the costs of migration, are likely to outlast the pandemic itself. Such realities have prompted calls for acknowledgment of the importance of immigrants in the workforce, alongside the need for better recognition of academic and professional credentials acquired abroad.

National Responses

The United Nations 2030 Agenda for Sustainable Development (Carr, Hodgetts, et al., Chapter 1; Saltzman et al., Chapter 2) recognizes the contribution of migration and migrants to sustainable development for the first time. Specifically, Target 8.8 of Sustainable Development Goal 8 calls to "Protect labour rights and promote safe and secure working environments for all workers, including migrant workers, in particular women migrants, and those in precarious employment" (ILO, n.d.). The building and construction sector, for instance, has a particular reputation for exploitation and migrant rights violations. In this regard, bloggers such as Malcolm Bidali (Business and Human Rights Resource Centre, 2021) had some success in moving the societal needle toward migrant-labor protection and rights prior to being imprisoned and eventually released after pressure from the NGO sector. Adding to such developments, current events such as the Black Lives Matter movement in the US, also about social and racial justice, have further ignited broader calls in the field of migration for immigrant rights and justice in multiple countries around the globe. Host countries have found themselves having to listen and respond to the challenges particularly relating to the permanent temporariness faced by migrant workers.

In Aotearoa New Zealand, the compounding challenges particularly relating to precarity as well as the exploitation faced by migrant workers resulted in a series of nationwide protests led by the Aotearoa Migrant Workers' Association in 2021. The Government's initial response to the building resistance alongside the large numbers of migrant workers facing visa expiry (due to pandemic-related border closures) was to universally extend work visas by six months, initially in March, then again in July and December 2020, and June 2021 (Collins, 2023). While this response not only delayed forced departures but also maintained the precarious legality of temporary work visa holders, it seemed to be a move influenced by economic calculus as the Government responded to employer concerns about labor shortages (Faafoi, 2021). This initiative then provided no security and disregarded the social needs and precarious situations of temporary visa holders (e.g., migrant workers). In September 2021, the Government announced the 2021 Resident Visa, which was a one-off pathway to residence for up to 165,000 temporary visa holders, based on various criteria. This visa was a welcome announcement and provided amnesty for a large number of temporary work visa holders and their families in 2022. As of the time of writing this chapter, the Aotearoa New Zealand Government has just announced a new visa category, the Green List, which targets highly skilled migrant workers in sectors like construction, engineering, trades, health, and technology, offering two-year work visas, following which they can be eligible to apply for residency (Radio New Zealand, 2022). Yet, this development still perpetuates the unequal preferential treatment imposed by the existing regime, by privileging the highly skilled migrant worker. Therein, the 2021 Resident Visa addresses the Government's problem of the number of temporary visa holders still in Aotearoa New Zealand two years into the pandemic, and the Green List is a way of rebuilding the nation's economy following the pandemic situation. However, it does not address the precarity experienced by an important, yet unconsidered, group of migrant workers—the low-skilled—nor does it transform the current lens of economic impetus and privilege that drives the current immigration regime.

Similar "temporary fixes" have been evident in other host nations across the globe, particularly in direct response to the pandemic and host nations' need for essential workers. The Italian government, for instance, approved legislation in 2021 to grant temporary work permits to thousands of irregular migrants (Jones et al., 2021; Migration Policy Institute, n.d.). In Germany and Ireland, carve-outs were created to license migrant and refugee healthcare workers. Similar efforts were undertaken by several US states. Elsewhere, the governments of Chile and Canada, among others, have taken steps to retain and integrate foreign-born professionals into their health sectors (Migration Policy Institute n.d.). Yet, once again, these initiatives maintain the status quo of permanent temporariness while also perpetuating the view of migrant workers as solely economic agents.

Implications and Recommendations

Within the workplace, there are increasing and urgent calls to move toward a clear commitment to an agenda for "decent work for migrant workers, alongside the institution of a socially fair, rights-based regulatory framework relating to migration and workplace conditions" (Jones et al., 2021, p. 2). Many of the workplace-related recommendations by researchers in this regard are individual-focused initiatives. For instance, one suggestion for such an approach involves mental health, suggesting workplace interventions intended to improve the psychological health of migrant workers (Di Fabio, 2017; Mucci et al., 2020). Such a focus is seen as necessary to improve workers' motivation, to provide feedback, and increase employee participation. This may entail a multilevel initiative based on the personal characteristics of the migrant worker for the prevention of anxiety and depressive symptoms (Mucci et al., 2020). Interventions aimed at improving psychological wellbeing are also intended to build strengths, enhance positive individual resources, and promote the overall wellbeing of migrant workers (Mucci et al., 2020).

Scholars in this space also advocate for favorable working conditions for migrant workers overall. Here, in addition to promoting psychological wellbeing, other considerations include issues of diversity and inclusion. For instance, the importance of creating an intercultural environment and preparing the entire workforce for interaction with diverse cultures has been discussed, to facilitate the inclusion of migrant workers and avoid discrimination. Recommendations for workplaces in this regard include increasing cultural exchange through the creation of networks and opportunities for dialog (Mucci et al., 2020).

On a broader scale, the ILO has taken the lead in calls to protect the rights and welfare of migrant workers through a social justice lens that aims to create fair labor practices in host countries to promote worker protection. Through a recognition that migrant workers make significant contributions to the economies of both host and home countries by accepting and shouldering great personal risk, the ILO advocates for collaboration between host and home countries to promote the safety of migrant workers (ILO, 2014; Jones et al., 2021). Proposed standards for promoting "safe migration and decent work" include policies to protect against forced labor and trafficking, ensuring that wages are paid regularly and directly to the worker, protecting social security benefits, promoting written employment contracts, and ensuring a mechanism for workers to register violations of fair practices (ILO, 2014). This initiative is particularly important as the boundaries between migrant workers being "documented" versus "undocumented" can be fluid, and legal status can change and thus can be an additional determinant of vulnerability, particularly in terms of access to formally regulated employment. In response to violations of worker rights, the ILO also launched the Fair Recruitment Initiative in 2014, designed to strengthen laws and policies around international labor recruitment, to promote fair business practices, and to empower workers with provision of channels to combat corruption (Andrees et al., 2015).

More recently, following a review of the challenges faced by migrant workers in the COVID-19 context, the ILO recommended including migrant workers in COVID-19–related welfare and recovery packages, inclusion in and access to other forms of social protection, including justice and protection from violence, equality of treatment and nondiscrimination, increased inspection and Government oversight of recruitment practices, and the introduction of guidelines for recruitment associations on monitoring, supporting, and coordinating migrant workers, to name a few (see page 35 onward of the report by Jones et al., 2021 for full list of recommendations). This report also links to an array of other existing resources of relevance to ensuring fair working conditions and rights and protections for migrant workers. The focus of the ILO then goes beyond the individual, to also acknowledge the broader sociopolitical contextual factors that create and contribute to the challenges faced by migrant workers, particularly within the context of the COVID-19 pandemic.

Fair labor practices can also be promoted through initiatives such as the Migrant Welfare Fund, operated by governments in home countries (Moyce & Schenker, 2018). The Philippines provides a good exemplar, where an agency in the Department of Labour and Employment operates the Overseas Workers Welfare Administration (https://owwa.gov.ph/). The fund is financed by migrant workers and recruitment agencies and protects the rights of workers emigrating from the Philippines by providing support such as predeparture orientation, loans to cover costs of migration, insurance, and immediate repatriation of workers in the event of illness (Moyce & Schenker, 2018; Ruiz & Rannveig, 2008). Similarly, recognizing the boost to their economy from remittances sent by emigrants, the Government of Bangladesh monitors the overseas recruitment of its citizens. Their Bureau of Manpower Employment and Training issues licenses to recruiting agencies and provides immigration clearance after reviewing employment contracts (Fee & Rahman, 2007).

In addition to state-funded support networks, the Fair Recruitment Initiative can be applied at an organizational level, by a concerned Human Resources manager or director, for instance. Moreover, organizations could consider signing up for decent work structures, such as the Global Compact initiative (https://www.unglobalcompact.org/), and Fair-Trade accreditation, which can be applied both in and across organizations along supply chains (Jyoit & Arora, Chapter 6; Meyer & Maleka, Chapter 7; Searle & McWha-Hermann, Chapter 4). Thereby, this precariousness can be "tackled" at various levels by the individual, organization, and state working together, as government-level initiatives alone do not suffice.

Overall, as vital as it is for workplaces and governments to learn from such examples, and/or take up and operationalize the above-mentioned guidelines and recommendations, it is important to note that most of these guidelines and suggestions are not particularly new. Rather, they have been in existence for some time, and so it is critical that workplaces, as well as governments recruiting migrant workers, consider the available guidelines and resources more seriously. That said, while these recommendations are certainly a step toward improving the wellbeing, and thereby the lifeworlds of migrant workers, they do not completely address the state of "permanent temporariness" that many migrant workers are experiencing.

A Step Further: Human Security and Relational Ethics

The structures of exploitative work and extractive economics that drive the enduring state of permanent temporariness experienced by most migrant workers, despite pandemic-related realizations of the importance of their contribution to host nations, are problematic. Such a lens perpetuates uneven distributions of power and privilege that deny migrant workers a sense of dignity. Thereby, Collins (2023) proposes that governments (through migration regimes and policy initiatives) adopt an approach to receiving and managing temporary migrants (such as migrant workers) that prioritizes interdependence and mutual empowerment and reciprocity, instead of control, marginalization, and exclusion. I argue that such an approach should not only be adopted at a national level but also at organizational levels, to also ensure ethical treatment of migrant workers within workplaces. Accordingly, I cast our net wider, to draw on the work of scholars in the fields of migration as well as psychology who discuss approaches involving human security (Hodgetts et al., 2022) and relational ethics (Collins, 2023) that prioritize a sense of dignity and can provide a more humanistic, humanitarian work psychology lens to the present context of migration and work.

The concept of human security has been recently explored within the field of psychology, as a notion that engages with personal understandings and reactions to situations of [in]security. Human security recognizes the need for changes to protect those in insecure material circumstances, many of which are beyond the control of individuals (Hodgetts et al., 2022). According to this approach, human security, or a "sense of security," is perceived as an absence of *in*security. The key to developing a sense of security is to ensure that people are treated with dignity, fairness, and respect and have the resources needed to allow them to flourish (Hodgetts et al., 2022). As the authors state, organizational psychologists are already active in promoting this sense of security, by advocating for decent work, job sustainability, income security, and healthcare, alongside inclusive organizational structures, practices, and efforts as a way of addressing the mounting insecurities that characterize precarious work (Carr et al., 2018, 2021; Hodgetts et al., 2022). Such considerations are equally relevant and vital to the context of migrant workers, directly addressing many of the challenges discussed throughout this chapter.

Also relevant is that the human security lens as developed by Hodgetts et al. (2022) goes beyond the focus on job and income [in]security, to incorporate a sense of security relating to lives and wellbeing. In the context of migration and work and related permanent temporariness, the challenges faced by migrant workers should be seen and addressed in relation to the complex and dynamic interrelationships of their transnational everyday lives. Such a lens also prompts us to acknowledge that migrant workers are necessarily situated within, and affected by, the various sociocultural and political contexts in both host and origin countries.

Complementing this human security lens is an approach underpinned by relational ethics that can address the other layer of challenges faced by migrant workers due to them being perceived solely as economic agents. Collins (2023) recently proposed a case for relational ethics in responses to mobility and migrant lives that recognizes co-becoming, where migrants (e.g., migrant workers) are seen as being embedded within particular social relations and contexts. Collins (2023) accordingly proposes three starting points for transforming processes of migration "management": (1) the consideration of migrant workers as full human beings, who are embedded within their transnational social lifeworlds and are able to make contributions alongside, in collaboration, and reciprocally with citizens and residents; (2) the recognition of the historical imbalances and at times exploitative relationships between host and origin countries; and

(3) the recognition of justice and inclusion in the host community as a due part of "being migrant." Thereby, combined, both a relational ethics approach and a human security lens can complement and enhance existing efforts by the ILO as discussed previously. This provides an alternative to current understandings, management, and treatment of migrant workers and moves us further toward ensuring the ethical treatment of and thereby dignity and flourishing for migrant workers in their lifeworlds, ultimately alleviating them from this perpetual cycle of permanent temporariness.

Key Considerations and Future Research Directions

The pressing priority for new scholars and future generations in this space then is to work toward alleviating the precarity and associated challenges faced by migrant workers in host nations that have been identified over the past few years, and especially through the COVID-19 pandemic. Issues of precarity should be considered both within workplaces and in relation to migrant workers' lifeworlds in the host nation, and at a policy level. It is crucial that these considerations are especially focused on low-skilled migrant workers. We need to learn from our experiences through the pandemic. Migrant workers need to be seen as human beings with complex transnational lives, and not simply as economic agents.

Therein, directions for future research could include the application and evaluation of an approach to tackling precarious work particularly relating to migrant workers that is informed by a human security lens complimented by relational ethics to provide an idea of what such an approach might look like in practice. Consideration should be paid to the key values that could underpin such an approach. As discussed previously, such an approach could be implemented initially at organizational level but later perhaps trialed at national and policy levels. Ultimately, however, these efforts need to go beyond "temporary fixes" to provide genuine and sustained pathways to support migrant workers.

Additionally, building on recommendations by the ILO, future research could explore the instances where host and home countries do collaborate to promote the safety, rights, and social needs of migrant workers. What are some of the learnings we can derive from these? What are some of the advantages and disadvantages? And how can we look toward facilitating and promoting future collaborations between other host and home countries in a way that supports the dignity and welfare of migrant workers as well as boosting the economies of these nations? Such an approach can also take into account the complex networks of transnational lifeworlds and workflows that these migrant workers are part of and are actively creating. A deeper awareness of the "bigger picture" that migrant workers are contributing to might help nations and organizations to appreciate the importance of this contribution.

Conclusion

Overall, international labor migration benefits the countries of origin and the host countries, the businesses that employ migrants, and the migrants and their families. Despite the social and economic advantages of migration, migrant workers face mounting challenges generated by current migration regimes that flow-on into the workplace, that enforce and perpetuate a state of permanent temporariness. The sudden and ongoing effects of the COVID-19 pandemic have provided a stark reminder of the urgent need to transform the processes and practices of labor migration governance. This chapter considers an alternative approach underpinned by relational ethics and human security that may help us move toward a fair, ethical, and just system that is free of exploitation and provides a sense of security and dignity for migrant workers.

References

Aalto, A. M., Heponiemi, T., Keskimäki, I., Kuusio, H., Hietapakka, L., Lämsä, R., Sinervo, T., & Elovainio, M. (2014). Employment, psychosocial work environment and well-being among migrant and native physicians in Finnish health care. *European Journal of Public Health, 24*(3), 445–451. https://doi.org/10.1093/eurpub/cku021

Andrees, B., Nasri, A., & Swiniarski, P. (2015). *Regulating labour recruitment to prevent human trafficking and to foster fair migration: Models, challenges and opportunities.* International Labour Organization. https://www.ilo.org/wcmsp5/groups/public/---ed_norm/---declaration/documents/publication/wcms_377813.pdf

Aradau, C., & Tazzioli, M. (2019). Biopolitics multiple: Migration, extraction, subtraction. *Millennium, 48*(2), 198–220. https://doi.org/10.1177/0305829819889139

Arkilic, A., & Sardelic, J. (2023). Activist citizenship and migrant rights in Aotearoa/New Zealand. In J. Terruhn & S. Cassim (Eds.), *Transforming the politics of mobility and migration in Aotearoa New Zealand.* Anthem Press.

Bailey, A. J., Wright, R. A., Mountz, A., & Miyares, I. M. (2002). (Re)producing Salvadoran transnational geographies. *Annals of the Association of American Geographers, 92*(1), 125–144. https://doi.org/10.1111/1467-8306.00283

Bathgate, B. (2022, January 9). Migrant exploitation complaints jump more than 250 per cent. *Stuff.* https://www.stuff.co.nz/national/127378821/migrant-exploitation-complaints-jump-more-than-250-per-cent

Benach, J., Muntaner, C., Delclos, C., Menéndez, M., & Ronquillo, C. (2011). Migration and "low-skilled" workers in destination countries. *PLoS Medicine, 8*(6), e1001043. https://doi.org/10.1371/journal.pmed.1001043

Berg, L., & Farbenblum, B. (2020). *As if we weren't humans: The abandonment of temporary migrants in Australia during COVID-19.* Migrant Worker Justice Initiative. https://apo.org.au/sites/default/files/resource-files/2020-09/apo-nid308305.pdf

Business and Human Rights Resource Centre. (2021). *Alarm after Kenyan migrant worker Malcolm Bidali arrested in Qatar.* https://www.business-humanrights.org/en/latest-news/alarm-after-kenyan-migrant-worker-malcolm-bidali-arrested-in-qatar/

Carr, S., Maleka, M., Meyer, I., Barry, M.-L., Haar, J., Parker, J., Arrowsmith, J., Yao, C., Hodgetts D., Jones, H., Young-Hausner, A., Afeaki-Mafile'o, E., Rasmussen, A.-H.,

Alefaio-Tugia, S., Falealili, B., Mafile'o, K., Pikula, T., Wolfgramm, N., 'Uhila, H., … & Naithani, A. (2018). How can wages sustain a living? By getting ahead of the curve. *Sustainability Science, 13*(4), 901–917. https://doi.org/10.1007/s11625-018-0560-7

Carr, S., Young-Hauser, A., Hodgetts, D., Schmidt, W., Moran, L., Haar, J., Parker, J., Arrowsmith, J., Jones, H., & Alefaio, S. (2021). Research update: How decent wages transform qualities of living—By affording escape from working poverty trap. *Journal of Sustainability Research, 3*(2), e210012. https://doi.org/10.20900/jsr20210012

Collins, F. L. (2019). Anxious desires: Temporary status and future prospects in migrant lives. *Emotion, Space and Society, 31*, 162–169. https://doi.org/10.1016/j.emospa.2017.10.004

Collins, F. L. (2020, March 23). Caring for 300,000 temporary migrants in New Zealand is a crucial missing link in our coronavirus response. *The Conversation.* https://theconversation.com/caring-for-300-000-temporary-migrants-in-new-zealand-is-a-crucial-missing-link-in-our-coronavirus-response-134152

Collins, F. L. (2023). Relational ethics, settler colonialism and the transformation of migration in Aotearoa New Zealand. In J. Terruhn & S. Cassim (Eds.), *Transforming the politics of mobility and migration in Aotearoa New Zealand.* Anthem Press.

Collins, F. L., & Shubin, S. (2015). Migrant times beyond the life course: The temporalities of foreign English teachers in South Korea. *Geoforum, 62*, 96–104. https://doi.org/10.1016/j.geoforum.2015.04.002

Collins, F. L., & Stringer, C. (2019). *Temporary migrant worker exploitation in New Zealand.* Ministry of Business, Innovation and Employment. https://www.mbie.govt.nz/dmsdocument/7109-temporary-migrant-worker-exploitation-in-new-zealand

Di Fabio, A. (2017). Positive healthy organizations: Promoting well-being, meaningfulness, and sustainability in organizations. *Frontiers in Psychology, 8*, 1938-1938. https://doi.org/10.3389/fpsyg.2017.01938

Doherty, B. (2022, February 23). Suffer in silence, or risk speaking up? Exploited migrant workers face perverse dilemma. *The Guardian.* https://www.theguardian.com/australia-news/2022/feb/23/suffer-in-silence-or-risk-speaking-up-exploited-migrant-workers-in-australia-face-perverse-dilemma

Dong, X., & Platner, J. W. (2004). Occupational fatalities of Hispanic construction workers from 1992 to 2000. *American Journal of Industrial Medicine, 45*(1), 45–54. https://doi.org/10.1002/ajim.10322

Dunlavy, A. C., Garcy, A. M., & Rostila, M. (2016). Educational mismatch and health status among foreign-born workers in Sweden. *Social Science & Medicine, 154,* 36–44. https://doi.org/10.1016/j.socscimed.2016.02.018

Ellermann, A. (2020). Human-capital citizenship and the changing logic of immigrant admissions. *Journal of Ethnic and Migration Studies, 46*(12), 2515–2532. https://doi.org/10.1080/1369183X.2018.1561062

Faafoi, K. (2021, June 10). *Visa extensions provide certainty to employers and 10,000 visa holders* [Press release]. https://www.beehive.govt.nz/release/visa-extensions-provide-certainty-employers-and-10000-visa-holders

Fee, L. K., & Rahman, M. (2007). International labour recruitment: Channelling Bangladeshi labour to East and South-East Asia. *Asia-Pacific Population Journal, 21*(1), 85–107. https://doi.org/10.18356/0e16674a-en

Flynn, M. A. (2014). Safety & the diverse workforce: Lessons from NIOSH's work with Latino immigrants. *Professional Safety, 59*(6), 52–57. https://www.ncbi.nlm.nih.gov/pmc/articles/PMC4641045/

Gardner, A. (2010). *City of strangers: Gulf migration and the Indian community in Bahrain.* Cornell University Press.

Grzywacz, J. G., Alterman, T., Muntaner, C., Gabbard, S., Nakamoto, J., & Carroll, D. J. (2009). Measuring job characteristics and mental health among Latino farmworkers: Results from cognitive testing. *Journal of Immigrant and Minority Health, 11*(2), 131–138. https://doi.org/10.1007/s10903-008-9170-2

Hajro, A., Stahl, G. K., Clegg, C. C., & Lazarova, M. B. (2019). Acculturation, coping, and integration success of international skilled migrants: An integrative review and multilevel framework. *Human Resource Management Journal, 29*(3), 328–352. https://doi.org/10.1111/1748-8583.12233

Hargreaves, S., Rustage, K., Nellums, L. B., McAlpine, A., Pocock, N., Devakumar, D., Aldridge, R. W., Abubakar, I., Kristensen, K. L., Himmels, J. W., Friedland, J. S., & Zimmerman, C. (2019). Occupational health outcomes among international migrant workers: A systematic review and meta-analysis. *The Lancet Global Health, 7*(7), e872-e882. https://doi.org/10.1016/S2214-109X(19)30204-9

Hege, A., Vallejos, Q. M., Apostolopoulos, Y., & Lemke, M. K. (2015). Health disparities of Latino immigrant workers in the United States. *International Journal of Migration, Health and Social Care, 11*(4), 282–298. https://doi.org/10.1108/IJMHSC-06-2014-0024

Helleiner, J. (2017). Recruiting the "culturally compatible" migrant: Irish working holiday migration and white settler Canadianness. *Ethnicities, 17*(3), 299–319. https://doi.org/10.1177/1468796815610354

Hennebry, J., McLaughlin, J., & Preibisch, K. (2016). Out of the loop: (In)access to health care for migrant workers in Canada. *Journal of International Migration and Integration, 17*(2), 521–538. https://doi.org/10.1007/s12134-015-0417-1

Hodgetts, D., Hopner, V., Carr, S., Bar-Tal, D., Lui, J., Saner, R., Yiu, L., Horgan, J., Searle, R.H., Massola, G., Hakim, M.A., Marai, L., King, P., & Moghaddam, F. 2022. Human security psychology: A linking construct for an eclectic discipline. *Review of General Psychology.* Advance online publication. https://doi.org/10.1177/10892680221109124

Horgan, M., & Liinamaa, S. (2017). The social quarantining of migrant labour: Everyday effects of temporary foreign worker regulation in Canada. *Journal of Ethnic and Migration Studies, 43*(5), 713–730. https://doi.org/10.1080/1369183X.2016.1202752

Hui, M. (2020, December 18). Singapore's migrant workers are basically in coronavirus jail. *Quartz Media.* https://qz.com/1947877/singapores-covid-19-reopening-plan-leaves-out-migrant-workers/

International Labour Organization (ILO). (n.d.). *Goal 8: Promote inclusive and sustainable economic growth, employment and decent work for all.* https://www.ilo.org/global/topics/dw4sd/theme-by-sdg-targets/WCMS_556964/lang--en/index.htm

International Labour Organization (ILO). (2014). *Promoting cooperation for safe migration and decent work.* ILO Country Office for Bangladesh. https://www.ilo.org/wcmsp5/groups/public/---ed_protect/---protrav/---migrant/documents/publication/wcms_248857.pdf

International Labour Organization (ILO). (2015). *ILO global estimates on migrant workers: Results and methodology—Special focus on migrant domestic workers.* https://www.ilo.org/wcmsp5/groups/public/@dgreports/@dcomm/documents/publication/wcms_436343.pdf

International Labour Organization (ILO). (2020). *Social protection for migrant workers: A necessary response to the COVID-19 crisis.* https://www.ilo.org/secsoc/information-resources/publications-and-tools/Brochures/WCMS_748979/lang--en/index.htm

International Labour Organization (ILO). (2021a). *ILO global estimates on international migrant workers: Results and methodology* (3rd ed.). https://www.ilo.org/wcmsp5/groups/public/---dgreports/---dcomm/---publ/documents/publication/wcms_808935.pdf

International Labour Organization (ILO). (2021b). *Leading business in times of Covid crisis: Analysis of the activities of employer and business membership organizations in the COVID-19 pandemic and what comes next.* https://www.ilo.org/actemp/publications/WCMS_766658/lang--en/index.htm

Jamil, R., & Dutta, U. (2021). Centering the margins: The precarity of Bangladeshi low-income migrant workers during the time of COVID-19. *American Behavioral Scientist, 65*(10), 1384–1405. https://doi.org/10.1177/00027642211000397

Jones, K., Mudaliar, S., & Piper, N. (2021). *Locked down and in limbo: The global impact of COVID-19 on migrant worker rights and recruitment.* International Labour Organization. https://www.ilo.org/wcmsp5/groups/public/---ed_protect/---protrav/---migrant/documents/publication/wcms_821985.pdf

Kößler, F. J., Wesche, J. S., & Hoppe, A. (2023). In a no-win situation: The employment–health dilemma. *Applied Psychology, 72*(1), 64–84. https://doi.org/10.1111/apps.12393

Landolt, P. (2020). Assembling the local politics of noncitizenship: Contesting access to healthcare in Toronto-Sanctuary City. *Social Problems, 69(*1), 74–90. https://doi.org/10.1093/socpro/spaa046

Liem, A., Renzaho, A. M. N., Hannam, K., Lam, A. I. F., & Hall, B. J. (2021). Acculturative stress and coping among migrant workers: A global mixed-methods systematic review. *Applied Psychology: Health and Well-Being, 13*(3), 491–517. https://doi.org/10.1111/aphw.12271

Martin, J. N., & Nakayama, T. K. (2018). *Intercultural communication in contexts.* McGraw-Hill.

Migration Policy Institute. (n.d.). Top 10 migration issues of 2020. *Migration Information Source.* https://www.migrationpolicy.org/programs/migration-information-source/top-10-migration-issues-2020

Moyce, S. C., & Schenker, M. (2018). Migrant workers and their occupational health and safety. *Annual Review of Public Health, 39*, 351–365. https://doi.org/10.1146/annurev-publhealth-040617-013714

Mucci, N., Traversini, V., Giorgi, G., Tommasi, E., De Sio, S., & Arcangeli, G. (2020). Migrant workers and psychological health: A systematic review. *Sustainability, 12*(1), Article 120. https://www.mdpi.com/2071-1050/12/1/120

Nadkarni, A. (2021, April 22). Priority visas for 450 family [sic] of high income workers. *Stuff.* https://www.stuff.co.nz/national/300283460/priority-visas-for-450-family-of-high-income-workers

Norredam, M., & Agyemang, C. (2019). Tackling the health challenges of international migrant workers. *Lancet Global Health, 7*(7), e813-e814. https://doi.org/10.1016/s2214-109x(19)30224-4

Padovan-Özdemir, M., & Moldenhawer, B. (2017). Making precarious immigrant families and weaving the Danish welfare nation-state fabric 1970–2010. *Race Ethnicity and Education, 20*(6), 723–736. https://doi.org/10.1080/13613324.2016.1195358

Parreñas, R., Landolt, P., Goldring, L., Golash-Boza, T., & Silvey, R. (2021). Mechanisms of migrant exclusion: Temporary labour, precarious noncitizenship, and technologies of detention. *Population, Space and Place, 27*(5), e2488. https://doi.org/10.1002/psp.2488

Quandt, S. A., Arcury-Quandt, A. E., Lawlor, E. J., Carrillo, L., Marín, A. J., Grzywacz, J. G., & Arcury, T. A. (2013). 3-D jobs and health disparities: The health implications of Latino chicken catchers' working conditions. *American Journal of Industrial Medicine, 56*(2), 206–215. https://doi.org/10.1002/ajim.22072

Radio New Zealand. (2022, May 12). Two-tier visa system a 'kick in the guts'. *RNZ Morning Report.* https://www.rnz.co.nz/news/national/466949/two-tier-visa-system-a-kick-in-the-guts

Rajkumar, D., Berkowitz, L., Vosko, L. F., Preston, V., & Latham, R. (2012). At the temporary–permanent divide: How Canada produces temporariness and makes citizens through its security, work, and settlement policies. *Citizenship Studies, 16*(3–4), 483–510. https://doi.org/10.1080/13621025.2012.683262

Reid, A. (2012). Under-use of migrants' employment skills linked to poorer mental health. *Australian and New Zealand Journal of Public Health, 36*(2), 120–125. https://doi.org/10.1111/j.1753-6405.2012.00842.x

Reid, A., & Schenker, M. B. (2016). Hired farmworkers in the US: Demographics, work organization, and services. *American Journal of Industrial Medicine, 59*(8), 644–655. https://doi.org/10.1002/ajim.22613

Robertson, S. (2015). Contractualization, depoliticization and the limits of solidarity: Noncitizens in contemporary Australia. *Citizenship Studies, 19*(8), 936–950. https://doi.org/10.1080/13621025.2015.1110286

Ruiz, N. G., & Rannveig, D. A. (2008). *Protecting temporary workers: Migrant welfare funds from developing countries* (Migration and Development Brief No. 7). World Bank. https://openknowledge.worldbank.org/handle/10986/11010

Simon-Kumar, R. (2020). Justifying inequalities: Multiculturalism and stratified migration in Aotearoa/New Zealand. In R. Simon-Kumar, F. L. Collins, & W. Friesen (Eds.), *Intersections of inequality, migration and diversification* (pp. 43–64). Palgrave.

Sousa, E., Agudelo-Suárez, A., Benavides, F. G., Schenker, M., García, A. M., Benach, J., Delclos, C., López-Jacob, M. J., Ruis-Frutos, C., Ronda-Pérez, E., & Porthé, V. (2010). Immigration, work and health in Spain: The influence of legal status and employment contract on reported health indicators. *International Journal of Public Health, 55*(5), 443–451. https://doi.org/10.1007/s00038-010-0141-8

Sterud, T., Tynes, T., Mehlum, I. S., Veiersted, K. B., Bergbom, B., Airila, A., Johansson, B., Brendler-Lindqvist, M., Hviid, K., & Flyvholm, M.-A. (2018). A systematic review of working conditions and occupational health among immigrants in Europe and Canada. *BMC Public Health, 18*(1), Article 770. https://doi.org/10.1186/s12889-018-5703-3

Strauss, K., & McGrath, S. (2017). Temporary migration, precarious employment and unfree labor relations: Exploring the 'continuum of exploitation' in Canada's Temporary Foreign Worker Program. *Geoforum, 78*, 199–208. https://doi.org/10.1016/j.geoforum.2016.01.008

Stringer, C., & Michailova, S. (2019). *Understanding the exploitation of temporary migrant workers: A comparison of Australia, Canada, New Zealand and the United Kingdom.* Ministry of Business, Innovation and Employment. https://www.mbie.govt.nz/dmsdocument/7110-understanding-the-exploitation-of-temporary-migrant-workers-a-comparison-of-australia-canada-new-zealand-and-the-united-kingdom

Summers, H. (2020, December 15). Day off denied: How Covid confined Hong Kong's domestic 'helpers'. *The Guardian.* https://www.theguardian.com/global-development/2020/dec/15/day-off-denied-how-covid-confined-hong-kongs-domestic-helpers

Tarsitani, L., & Biondi, M. (2016). Migration and mental health: New challenges. *Rivista Di Psichiatria, 51*(2), 45–46. https://doi.org/10.1708/2246.24192

Terruhn, J. (2023). Human capital privilege in the neoliberal politics of mobility and migration in Aotearoa. In J. Terruhn & S. Cassim (Eds.), *Transforming the Politics of Mobility and Migration in Aotearoa New Zealand.* Anthem Press.

Vora, N. (2013). *Impossible citizens: Dubai's Indian diaspora.* Duke University Press. https://doi.org/10.1215/9780822397533

Vosko, L. F. (2022). Temporary labour migration by any other name: Differential inclusion under Canada's 'new' international mobility regime. *Journal of Ethnic and Migration Studies, 48*(1), 129–152. https://doi.org/10.1080/1369183X.2020.1834839

Wong, G. (2021, March 2). 'Exploitation is my destiny': Migrant workers open up about 'modern slavery' in NZ. *Newshub.* https://www.newshub.co.nz/home/new-zealand/2021/03/exploitation-is-my-destiny-migrant-workers-open-up-about-modern-slavery-in-nz.html

Yeoh, B. S. A. (2022). Is the temporary migration regime in Asia future-ready? *Asian Population Studies, 18*(1), 1–5. https://doi.org/10.1080/17441730.2022.2029159

21

THE ELEPHANT IN THE ROOM? IMPLICATIONS OF ECONOMIC VULNERABILITY FOR A HEALTHY (WORKING) LIFE

Katharina Klug, Jean-Yves Gerlitz, and Eva Selenko

A basic tenet of modern welfare states is that a job should afford people economic security (Streeck, 2012), and popular narratives of meritocracy suggest to "work hard and you'll get ahead" (Ehrenreich, 2001, p. 220). However, for a substantial number of workers, their work is not rewarded with social advancement or even a decent living: about 9–10% of European workers are estimated to be at risk of in-work poverty, which means that their household income is below the poverty line despite being employed (Eurostat, n.d.). Around 15% of European workers are classified as low-wage earners (Eurostat, 2020). Many have faced income losses during the COVID-19 crisis, while more than a quarter (27%) of Europeans reported having no savings to buffer financial cuts (Eurofound, 2020). Globally, the share of workers living in extreme poverty is expected to rise (United Nations [UN], 2020). Adding fuel to the fire, surging inflation rates, and food and energy prices have made living worldwide much more expensive (OECD, 2022).

Jobs which do not keep up with the cost of living or protect from economic shocks clearly create financial stress for workers (Sinclair & Cheung, 2016). Furthermore, low earnings send the message that society does not value these workers' labor (Smith, 2015). The pandemic has made this issue all too salient; many "essential workers" are employed in low-paid precarious jobs, despite providing indispensable services (International Labour Organization [ILO], 2017). Unable to work from home, many found themselves between a rock and a hard place: having to choose between exposure to the virus versus losing earnings, the pandemic posed an extreme example of the "employment-health dilemma" that people with limited choices in the labor market were facing already

DOI: 10.4324/9781003440444-25

anyway (see Kößler et al., 2022). Many healthcare workers, bus drivers, and retail workers, to name a few, experienced moral injury on top of physical health risks (Gaitens et al., 2021). Even before the pandemic, nurses reported frequent financial stress and the perception that their work was underpaid (Broetje et al., 2020).

In work and organizational psychology, money has received relatively little research attention compared to other aspects of precarity such as job insecurity, despite being one of the most salient sources of stress in many workers' lives (American Psychological Association, 2017; Probst et al., 2017). This is striking for several reasons: first, money is arguably the most fundamental resource derived from work, as it ensures access to other resources essential for a safe and decent life (Sinclair & Cheung, 2016). Second, economic insecurity is a central characteristic of precarious work (Allan et al., 2021). If financial insecurity is overlooked as a stressor in its own right, work and organizational psychology risks neglecting an important part of the lived experience of many workers, rendering an incomplete picture of precarity and the understanding of stress.

The goal of this chapter is to shed light on low earnings as the "elephant in the room": an issue often ignored in psychological discussion of precarious work (Fryer & Fagan, 2003). We focus on the concept of individual economic vulnerability, defined as the risk to workers' self-sufficiency, which includes both objective and subjective aspects (see Klug et al., 2021). The chapter is structured as follows; first, we introduce the concept of economic vulnerability in relation to the broader framework of precarious work (Allan et al., 2021; Standing 2011); second, we discuss how psychological theories can be employed to explain the link between economic vulnerability and its outcomes, such as stress theories, social identity, and social exchange models; and third, we present a brief review of empirical findings on the consequences of economic vulnerability, from health and well-being and work behavior and careers to care arrangements and social participation. Figure 21.1 provides a conceptual model and overview of the concepts we discuss regarding individual consequences, in the context of workplace-, household- and macrolevel influences. We conclude this chapter with recommendations for future research and intervention strategies for organizations and policy makers.

Overall, the chapter highlights the importance of individual financial self-sufficiency for a healthy, meaningful, and productive working life. With this review, we hope to contribute to the emerging discussion of the financial side of precarity in work and organizational psychology (Searle & McWha-Hermann, 2020, Chapter 4; Seubert & Seubert, Chapter 14; Sinclair & Cheung, 2016; Smith, 2015).

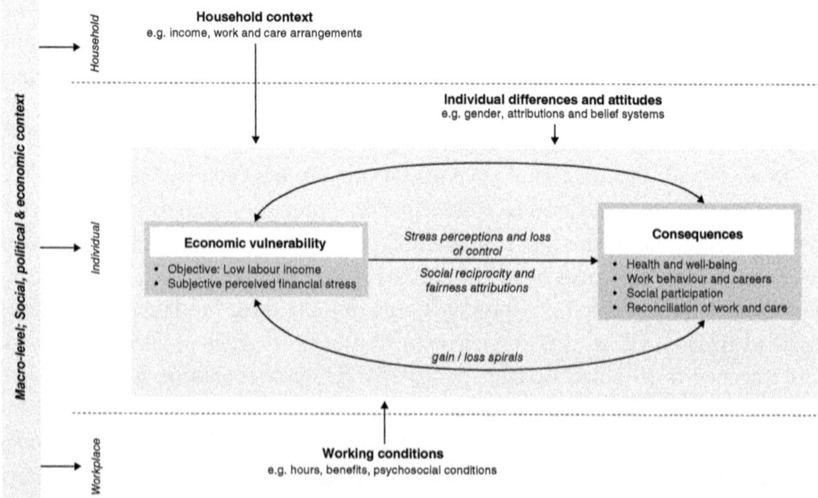

FIGURE 21.1 A Conceptual Model of Economic Vulnerability and its Consequences.

What Is Economic Vulnerability and How Does It Relate to Precarity?

Work precarity is a normative concept in two ways. It is a negative evaluation of a specific situation based on a set of social norms of how work should be organized. Some of its distinct features might be best described by contrasting precarity with another negatively connoted and related normative concept widely used in social sciences: the concept of poverty. While poverty refers to an *actually* problematic situation (lack of resources) at the *household level* (as the relevant economic unit; Atkinson et al., 2002, p. 27), work precarity focusses on an *individual-level, potentially* problematic state of work-related insecurity that puts an employee at risk (Allan et al., 2021; Kalleberg, 2009; Standing, 2011). The normative model that serves as a contrast to work precarity is the Standard Employment Relationship (SER; Mückenberger & Deakin, 1989), i.e., the permanent full-time employee who receives collectively set wages and enjoys full employment and the social protection that some modern welfare states provide. The SER is a multifaceted concept that comprises a variety of beneficial employment characteristics, depending on the legislative and country context. Work precarity describes the absence of one or more of the normative SER characteristics and can consequentially take on many different shapes (Rodgers, 1989), ranging from the lack of a single feature (e.g., in temporary employment) to the lack of all characteristics of the SER.

We can roughly distinguish between an objective dimension of *precarious work* and the subjective experience of *work precarity* (Allan et al., 2021). The *objective* dimension refers to the various aspects in which working conditions may deviate from the SER, such as temporary or low-wage employment. The *subjective* dimension refers to the psychological experience of precarity, in the form of cognitions, attitudes, and emotions which accompany the employment situation, such as job insecurity or a lack of psychosocial safety.

In this chapter, we focus on economic vulnerability mainly associated with remuneration (objective aspect) and perceived financial stress (subjective aspect). Economic vulnerability directly relates to financial resources and describes the fact or perception that one's own labor income is insufficient to afford a decent standard of living (Klug et al., 2021). It is important to highlight that economic vulnerability—like other forms of precarity—does not only capture actual states of insufficiency but also the enhanced risk of becoming financially insufficient. This means that someone can be economically vulnerable, even when the income of other household members or support by the welfare state allows for a decent standard of living. In this case, the person would be highly dependent on others and at risk if external income sources dry up (e.g., because of a divorce or the death of a spouse). At the core of the concept is *individual self-sufficiency*; feminist scholars especially (e.g., Daly, 2011; Lewis, 1992; Orloff, 1993) stress the importance of the individual capacity to form and maintain an autonomous household. This is also recognized in the UN Sustainable Development Goals (SDG), which explicitly include the reduction of income inequality and women's economic empowerment, and for which a focus solely on household income would be too narrow (UN, 2015).

As indicated above, measures of *objective economic vulnerability* put individual labor income in relation to average incomes of a society and thereby assess a state of resource-based deprivation. One indicator is *low wages*, usually defined as an hourly wage that lies below two thirds of the median wage of a country (Atkinson et al., 2002, p. 177–). Low wages first and foremost describe a position in the wage distribution of a society and are less informative with regard to actual earnings, because these depend on work intensity (i.e., hours worked), social contributions, and taxes. In contrast, *low labour income* refers to earnings over more meaningful time periods (e.g., a month or a year). It is defined as individual gross or net labor earnings below the national poverty line (Filandri & Struffolino, 2019; Peña-Casas & Ghailani, 2011; Ponthieux, 2018), usually marked at 60% of the median equivalized net household income in any society (Atkinson et al., 2002, p. 79). If we look at actual market outcomes over longer periods and the poverty line represents the minimum acceptable standard of living of a (single) household (Townsend, 1979), low labor income is seen to be more closely linked to the concept of individual economic self-sufficiency than low wages (Carr, Hodgetts et al., Chapter 1).

Subjective economic vulnerability tends to correlate modestly with people's objective financial situation (Klug et al., 2021; Selenko & Batinic, 2011).

Subjective indicators can be distinguished along the lines of whether they emphasize cognitive evaluations or affective reactions, absolute standards or relative comparisons to other people, the past or the future, or financial needs and wants (see Sinclair & Cheung, 2016 for a systematic review). In the context of precarity, we define subjective economic vulnerability in terms of financial stress, i.e., workers' perceptions of income insufficiency and worries related to their financial situation (Bjarnason & Sigurdardottir, 2003; Garðarsdóttir & Dittmar, 2012; Sears, 2008; Starrin et al., 2009). Financial stress comprises both a cognitive-evaluative component (e.g., perceived income inadequacy) and affective reactions, in the form of worries and negative emotions about money (Odle-Dusseau et al., 2018; Sears, 2008; Seubert & Seubert, Chapter 14; Sinclair & Cheung, 2016). By defining subjective economic vulnerability in terms of workers' perceived financial stress, we can create an analogy to job insecurity as an established concept of psychological precarity; while job insecurity refers to the perceived threat to the continuity of a job and is also comprised of cognitive evaluations and affective reactions (Shoss, 2017; Sverke & Hellgren, 2002), subjective economic vulnerability refers to the perceived threat to achieving or maintaining self-sufficiency through one's work (see also, Intraprasert et al., Chapter 9).

In the context of precarity, it is important to emphasize the threat to self-sufficiency to distinguish economic vulnerability from purely relative subjective measures such as pay dissatisfaction or perceived pay injustice (Till & Karren, 2011). For example, executive managers or physicians may feel that their pay is inadequate relative to their training and effort, but they are certainly not low earners by societal standards. Consequently, our understanding of economic vulnerability does not exactly map to distinctions between absolute (i.e., "context-free" direct measures of income) and relative measures (i.e., informed by social comparisons) other authors have made (Sinclair & Cheung, 2016).

We believe that it makes more sense to define subjective vulnerability in relation to perceptions of the ability to live self-sufficiently. Because economic risk is a core aspect of precarity, the threshold for maintaining self-sufficiency through one's earnings defines an absolute lower bound, while at the same time the threshold for a "decent" living itself is relative, and perceptions thereof are informed by social comparison (Carr, Hopner et al., Chapter 10). Even objective thresholds like the poverty line are defined relative to the total population in a given time and place (Carr, Hopner et al., Chapter 10).

In assessing the consequences of economic vulnerability, focusing on either the objective or subjective side both have their strengths and weaknesses: whereas objective income measures capture real access to financial resources, they omit people's subjective needs or experience of deprivation and consequently they relate less consistently to well-being outcomes than subjective indicators, and the underlying mechanisms are often unclear (Chan et al., 2002;

Ullah, 1990; Veenhoven, 2002). Subjective measures of financial stress capture exactly these psychological mechanisms, but tell us little about the source of stress, be it low income, debt, or high cost of living (Sinclair & Cheung, 2016). Each indicator provides only one piece of the puzzle (e.g., what people earn individually vs. what is available in their household, or what people can afford vs. how stressed they feel about it).

Theoretical Perspectives

Two reasons why economic vulnerability has been relatively neglected in work and organizational psychology might be the lack of agreement as yet on how to understand economic vulnerability theoretically and how to investigate it empirically. Recently, research seems to have rediscovered economic vulnerability, and the types of studies and the concepts seem to be proliferating (Allan et al., 2021; Jachimowicz et al., 2021; Schmalor & Heine, 2021). The following part aims to offer an overview over theoretical approaches that can help to understand economic vulnerability and its consequences better.

Explanations can be categorized using *stressor-based* and *cognitive* types of explanations. These do not exclude each other, and while stressor-based models might focus more on health outcomes of economic vulnerability than cognitive attribution focussed models, they can easily be applied to understanding behavioral and attitudinal outcomes, and vice versa.

Economic Vulnerability Leads to Stress

Most research on economic vulnerability agrees that a threat to financial self-sufficiency is a psychological stressor because (1) it indicates a threat to (often limited) resources, (2) it is appraised as a hindrance, and (3) lack of money comes with a significant loss of control.

Limited financial resources often form the starting point of threats to financial self-sufficiency. In order to feel economically vulnerable, a person usually has very few resources to start with. Limited and threatened resources are at the heart of stress experiences according to the conservation of resources (COR) theory (Hobfoll, 1989). Money in the understanding of COR theory functions as an "energy resource"; it is not necessarily valued for its intrinsic features but enables the acquisition of further resources. The model also states that not receiving enough in return for an investment (such as work effort) functions as a loss, because people lose out on an expectation they have (Hobfoll, 1989). Hence, economic vulnerability can be understood as stressful because it is a state of resources loss. People try to compensate this resources loss by investing additional resources. For example, people might work a second or third job and reduce their expenses, for example, on transport or food. These coping strategies come at the costs of other resources—reduced time for recovery, expenditure of physical health, time, etc. The loss and lack of financial resources hence can easily lead to further resource losses, leading to a so-called loss spiral and consequently to exhaustion (Hobfoll, 1989).

Economic vulnerability will also be perceived as stressful in itself, as it will lead to worrying. Low income is threatening, in that it prevents a person from making ends meet (primary appraisal). Furthermore, economic vulnerability ensures that this threat cannot be compensated by other means such as assets, savings, or other sources of income (secondary appraisal). This combination of a threat appraisal with insufficient coping resources is what results in feelings of stress, anxiety, and tension according to Lazarus and Folkman (1984).

Eventually, economic vulnerability is likely to cause stress, because it limits the degree of control people have over their direct circumstances and their future (Pepper & Nettle, 2017). One central aspect in the stress experience is the degree of control that people perceive themselves to have (e.g. Karasek, 1979). Money is essential for gaining control over key areas in life and it also protects against unforeseen misfortune. It enables people to make their life predictable and reduce the threat of uncertainty or future resource loss (Hobfoll, 1989). For example, money might allow ownership of one's house or flat, guarantees that one will eat regularly, that children are cared for, and that transport is ensured. Moreover, having money protects from and shortens the experience of daily unpleasantness. Jachimowicz et al. (2021) give the example of getting rained on while outside; a person with some level of income might be able to afford to spontaneously take a taxi, while an economically vulnerable person might not. Empirical evidence from longitudinal panel studies (Klug et al., 2021) and daily diary studies (Jachimowicz et al., 2021) support the assumption that economic vulnerability lowers a person's sense of control. Taken together, stress resulting from economic vulnerability will not only affect people's health but also their ability to think and perform, and the way they behave.

Economic Vulnerability Attributions

Aside from the direct stress-related consequences, being economically vulnerable will also affect fairness attributions, sensemaking, and identity. This is because money does not just have an instrumental value, but it also has multiple secondary functions, as it confers status and helps a person to define who they are in society (Hobfoll, 1989). Action research shows that people in poverty often report being socially excluded, isolated, and humiliated (Fryer & Fagan, 2003).

From a moral point of view, experiencing economic vulnerability while working runs against meritocratic societal exchange norms: at the heart of meritocratic societies lies the belief that hard work will be rewarded and that people are personally responsible for their own status and achievements. According to this logic, a person working hard but earning not enough would be in an unequal situation and feel unjustly treated. Perceived injustice, as in an imbalance between effort and reward (Siegrist, 1996), would be a driver of a multitude of different work behaviors and attitudes.

Interestingly, research shows that a disadvantageous situation is often—but not inevitably—judged as unjust (e.g., Mijs, 2021), for example, if people felt they were treated with respect and have procedures explained to them, they tend to judge their situation as less unjust and also less negatively (Fryer & Fagan, 2003). Also, the more people subscribe to meritocratic norms; the less likely they are to judge their own disadvantageous outcomes as unjust (McCoy & Major, 2007). One explanation for this could be the "belief in a just world" (Lerner, 1980; Mijs, 2021). This model posits that people hold an illusionary belief that the world is benevolent, that good things happen to good people and that they are in control of what happens to them. This belief is deemed enormously robust and functional for psychological health. Research confirms that people go out of their way to explain negative events according to this belief system, even if it means blaming themselves and others for things that were not under their control (Furnham, 2003). Earning below the poverty line despite hard work, being hindered in getting ahead in society would violate this belief system, and people would consequently try to protect it. Maybe this could explain why economically vulnerable people sometimes "reach low," because they think that they did not deserve any better (see Howard et al., 2011).

Eventually, economic vulnerability is going to have profoundly negative effects on a person's social identity, defined as the multitude of self-understandings a person has as a member of social groups, learned through enactment and fostered through social interaction (Turner et al., 1987). It does so in multiple ways: firstly, by undermining and bringing people's membership of certain identity categories into question. The money one earns and the living standard it affords serves a status function in society and acts as a measure of success within and beyond one's job. Being economically vulnerable hence questions people's belonging to mainstream society, or as representatives of their job. Humiliating procedures people have to endure to access state or charitable support further drive home the message that they are not fully respected members of society. Secondly, being economically vulnerable hinders the enactment of certain identities. Many social identity roles are coupled with prototypical expectations about behavior that requires money, for example, being a good parent means that someone can take care of their kids financially; being a good colleague means that someone will chip-in at a birthday fund-raiser. Lastly, economic vulnerability will hinder the social interactions needed for identity verification. Most social interactions in society involve the spending of some amount of money; not being able to partake in important social interactions questions one's belonging to associated social identity categories. For example, if one cannot participate in social activities with friends or colleagues, citizenship roles, or roles as a consumer, one might become uncertain about their belonging in these categories. Research shows that threatened and undermined identity comes with a host of very negative effects—not only on health and behavior but also on attitudes toward others (Selenko & De Witte, 2021).

Consequences of Economic Vulnerability

The consequences of economic vulnerability for workers and their families are far-reaching and diverse. In the following, we provide a brief overview of selected findings, focusing on mental health, work, and careers, as well as work care arrangements and social participation.

Economic Vulnerability Matters for Health

Low earnings and the associated financial strain can affect workers' health and mental well-being (Sinclair & Cheung, 2016). There is a consistent general association of income with health (Adler et al., 1994; Lund et al., 2010; Martikainen et al., 2003) and with subjective well-being indicators such as life satisfaction (Dolan et al., 2008; Hagerty & Veenhoven, 2003; Kahneman & Deaton, 2010). Regarding the specific experience of earning little despite being employed, existing evidence is less extensive and consistent. For example, a Swiss cross-sectional study investigated in-work household poverty and found that workers' material deprivation was related to reduced mental health, but not their income as such (Vetter et al., 2006). In our own research, we found that workers with low earnings did not differ in their mental health and life satisfaction from others once control variables such as education, occupational status, working conditions, and the household context were accounted for (Klug et al., 2021). These findings are in line with multidimensional approaches to poverty (Oshio & Kan, 2014) which suggest that it is the constellation of life circumstances that accompany low earnings rather than the earnings themselves that influence mental health.

However, our own longitudinal analysis also revealed that workers' well-being clearly responded to changes in their earnings; over time, when people fell below a certain low-earnings threshold, their sense of control and, in turn, their mental health and life satisfaction dropped and, vice versa, increased when earnings improved. These effects were independent of the household income and other socioeconomic conditions (Klug et al., 2021). The low sense of control and mental health associated with falling under the poverty line makes it harder to invest in strategies that may increase income—increasing the risk of economic vulnerability reinforcing itself (Haushofer & Fehr, 2014).

Similarly, a recent diary study showed that financial scarcity limits people's choices in coping with everyday stressors; individuals with low incomes show more intense stress reactions to daily hassles, lower control perceptions, and, in turn, lower life satisfaction (Jachimowicz et al., 2021). Other studies have shown both low wages and household poverty to contribute to workers' self-rated health (Pförtner et al., 2019; Pförtner & Schmidt-Catran, 2017).

With regard to subjective economic vulnerability, financial stress has consistently been linked to a range of physical and mental health outcomes; people who experience financial stress tend to experience poorer mental health (Aronsson et al., 2005; Dijkstra-Kersten et al., 2015; Rajani et al., 2016; Selenko & Batinic, 2011; Starrin et al., 2009), physical health (Aronsson et al., 2005; Price et al., 2002), and sleep quality (Hall et al., 2008) and are more likely to attempt suicide (Elbogen et al., 2020) than financially secure persons. Steptoe et al. (2005) have linked financial stress to elevated blood pressure and cortisol levels. Only few studies seem to take a closer look at the mechanisms that connect financial stress to health outcomes (Sinclair & Cheung, 2016). Our own research points to restricted agency, as employees' perceived financial stress was related to a lower sense of control (Klug et al., 2021). Limited control also plays a role in the work-family interface as financial stress reduces resources available for resolving conflicts between work and family roles; Odle-Dusseau et al. (2018) showed that workers' perceived financial insecurity was associated with increased distress and work-family conflict, which in turn related to physical health symptoms. Both ours and Odle-Dusseau et al.'s findings are in line with COR theory and the daily hassles hypothesis (Jachimowicz et al., 2021).

Economic Vulnerability Matters for (Working) Life

Given the severe consequences of economic vulnerability for people's physical and mental well-being, effects on work behavior and performance should not come as a surprise. The stressful experience of economic vulnerability and its identity undermining capacity will have consequences on wider work behaviors and career planning (e.g. Meuris & Gladstone, 2023). So rather than proposing that these consequences are due to a lack of knowledge, competence or motivation on the side of the economically vulnerable person (as often implied in neoliberal approaches to poverty alleviation), they are rather a consequence of the grave effects of poverty on well-being, stress levels, and identity. Likewise, supposedly irrational economic behavior (e.g., not saving and devaluing delayed financial rewards in favor of immediate gains) is a consequence rather than a cause of poverty—and may actually be a rational response to an uncertain future over which an economically vulnerable individual has little control (Haushofer & Fehr, 2014; Pepper & Nettle, 2017).

There is consistent evidence for the link between stress and lowered work performance, which has mostly been researched independently of economic vulnerability (e.g., Gilboa et al., 2008). More specifically, the stress of economic vulnerability and the loss of control over smaller and larger daily hassles it brings will affect people's resources to invest into work—be that health-wise, energy-wise or time-wise. People who have to work multiple jobs and have to save on costs to afford housing, reliable transport, and/or childcare will simply have less energy to invest into any particular employment. The link between recovery and work behavior is well-established in work and organizational psychology, and it is recognized that precarious workers are limited in their opportunity for recovery (e.g., Sonnentag et al., 2021). Seen from an identity perspective, the (work-related) identity-threatening effect of economic vulnerability will make it more difficult to strive for prototypical work-related identity goals; if one cannot be sure that they actually belong to that job, team, or organization (because they earn so little), how can they stand up for their profession, have the confidence to demand fair rewards, or aspire to the career paths of "normal" members of their organization? Indeed, there is evidence that people from precarious backgrounds often have lower aspirations and follow less ambitious educational or career goals (Howard et al., 2011). This can lead economic vulnerability to become fatalistically self-enforcing; because of the exhausting nature of economic vulnerability, and the reduced identification with inaccessible aspects of mainstream work and careers, people are less likely to be able to work well and aspire to seek better working conditions (Carr, Hodgetts et al., Chapter 1).

Social participation: financial resources and social participation are both linked in one of the most established poverty definitions. Townsend (1979) defines individuals, families, and groups as poor if they lack resources "to obtain the types of diet, participate in the activities and have the living conditions and amenities which are customary…in the societies which they belong [to]" (Townsend, 1979, p. 16). Although the correlations among income deprivation, deprivation in assets, and exclusion from customary activities are not as straightforward as one would think (Mack & Lansley, 1985), research shows that a persistent lack of income continuously limits assets (e.g., a car, a TV) and participation (e.g., having guests over for dinner, traveling; Whelan et al., 2003). Furthermore, while a clear link between *objective* (income-based) economic vulnerability and social participation has been established, this also holds true for *subjective* economic vulnerability in form of perceived economic strain (Whelan et al., 2001).

Social inclusion and exclusion can also be construed as gradual phenomena along the two dimensions of interdependence and participation (Kronauer, 2010). While participation is to a great deal enabled by resources (i.e., not being poor), interdependence refers to one's interconnectedness with the society that—in work societies—is achieved by employment. Following that logic, Kronauer

(2010) distinguishes four types of inclusiveness, where an individual who is poor and unemployed would be "twice excluded," while working individuals deprived in income would enjoy "exclusionary inclusion," that is, being included with regard to interdependence, but excluded with regard to participation.

This poses the question about the value of work itself. Is it better to have a bad job than no job at all? The answer to this question depends on the outcome in question; when looking at social participation, comparative studies lend some support to the idea that being unemployed is associated with a greater extent of social exclusion than having low earnings (Alber & Heisig, 2011; Blanchflower & Oswald, 2004; Di Tella et al., 2003; Winkelmann & Winkelmann, 1998). Looking at well-being, other research demonstrates that single and primary earners with low wages have lower job satisfaction than individuals with decent wages (Pohlig et al., 2020), and that employees with jobs of poor psychosocial quality have comparable or poorer mental health than the unemployed (Butterworth et al., 2011). Vice versa, the health effects of unemployment may not be as negative if people are let go from a low-quality, dissatisfying job but are financially secure (Fryer & Fagan, 2003). Thus, while access to employment as a social institution is important for identity formation and social participation (Hulin, 2002; Jahoda, 1982), the quality of the working conditions and pay matter for mental health (Fryer & Fagan, 2003). One should not go without the other. What is more, access to and quality of employment are connected, as unemployment increases people's risk to be reemployed in low-quality, lower paid jobs (Fryer & Fagan, 2003).

Issues of social participation seem particularly salient for marginalized groups in society. Specifically, ethnic minorities and immigrants face discrimination and structural barriers to high-quality employment are more vulnerable to exploitation and thus make up a large part of the population in low-paid and precarious jobs (Branyiczki, 2015; see also Chapter 20). In Germany, for instance, immigrants are more likely to work low-wage jobs, which benefits business models that take advantage of a steady supply of low-paid labor, leading in turn to a growth of low-paid jobs (see Krings 2021). Limited access to well-paid jobs, and in consequence to social participation, likely exacerbates the above-mentioned risks related to identity and belonging for those who are already construed as "others" by the majority in a society.

Work and care: precarity is not gender- or ethnicity-neutral. As feminist scholars (Fraser, 1994; Lewis, 1992; Orloff, 1993) point out, women are overrepresented in precarious jobs (Filandri & Struffolino, 2019; Peña-Casas & Ghailani, 2011; Ponthieux, 2018). The gendered nature of economic vulnerability implies (a) that women are disproportionately affected by economic dependency and the resulting psychological consequences (Arber et al., 2014; Ross & Mirowsky, 1992) and (b) that the consequences reach beyond the psychological and also include work and care arrangements in the household, family formation, and the division of paid and unpaid work between men and women in society (Daly, 2005; Hook, 2015). In fact, gender inequality is seen as a key factor contributing to poverty and preventing societies from reaching SDG-1, that is the eradication of poverty (UN Women, 2019).

The gendered nature of economic vulnerability stems from the traditional division of paid and unpaid (care)work between men and women; the gendered division of labor is strongly linked to the traditional male breadwinner and female homemaker model (Mückenberger, 1985). Within this paradigm, male employment is associated with family wages (labor earnings that support a family of four) and social protection covering all household members, while women are responsible for the reproductive labor within the household (i.e., care and housework) which is unpaid and unprotected.

While gender roles have become more egalitarian with increased economic development, there is still an imbalance, mainly connected to the question of reproductive work. The traditional gender division in household labor and childrearing hasn't shifted much and women still do the lion's share of care work in a household (Daly, 2005), which affords them less time for paid work. Not only does that create financial dependencies for women; but it also comes with the risk of serious financial vulnerabilities, particularly in old age (as earning less comes with lower pensions in old age) and in cases where women become separated from their partner (see Arber et al., 2014; Möhring, 2018).

Steadily growing female labor market participation has increased the demand for, and supply of paid care work, and to this day, a large number of women work in the care and service sector (Oesch, 2006; Streeck, 2012). This "commodification" of reproductive labor (Streeck, 2012) provides richer women with the opportunity to "outsource" their own care work, making themselves more independent, and providing other women (who do the care work) with paid jobs, but it comes with a catch; most paid care work is precarious—both in terms of working conditions (part-time, fixed-term, etc.) and remuneration (low wages and low labor income; Murphy & Oesch, 2016), and it is mostly done by women—often from migrant backgrounds, creating the phenomena of "global care chains" (Yeates, 2004).

This leads to the paradoxical situation that while well-paid women are able to achieve economic self-sufficiency and afford the external care needed to cover for the household labor they no longer have the time for (Hook, 2015), this is less the case for women working in precarious work, or for the women actually providing the outsourced household labor. These women's households also have to pay extra to cover the care work that they can no longer do, as men's share in household labor has not increased proportionately (Daly, 2005). The whole situation is further complicated by an increasing deterioration of working conditions and remuneration among (lower-skilled) men, meaning many no longer earn family wages (Gerlitz, 2023; Häusermann & Schwader, 2012; Lewis, 2001;

Streeck, 2012). For some couples it has become increasingly difficult to afford paid care work, for others it makes financially (almost) no difference if both partners work, as one partner's wage is fully used to cover externally paid care work.

The shift of modern welfare states toward the *adult worker model* (Lewis, 2001) as a guiding principle has increased the social pressure on women. As most welfare states fail to provide appropriate institutional settings (Daly, 2011), the freedom-turned-duty of female employment has resulted in the double burden of juggling care and work simultaneously. Not only do growing economic constraints exacerbate experiences of work-family conflict (Odle-Dusseau et al., 2018), but women are also increasingly remaining childless (Daly, 2005).

Conclusion: Where to From Here?

As we have shown, economic vulnerability in terms of risks to workers' self-sufficiency has repercussions for their individual well-being, work behavior, careers, and social participation. In the following, we sketch out a few recommendations, both for further scientific inquiry and for policy and practice to act.

Open Questions and Recommendations for Future Research

First, we recommend that work and organizational psychology pay more attention to economic vulnerability as a stressor in its own right, not just as a corollary of unemployment and job insecurity. In doing so, conceptual clarity is needed regarding definitions and measurement in order to separate characteristics of economic vulnerability from its outcomes (e.g., cognitive appraisals from strain reactions, Sinclair & Cheung, 2016). Referring to frameworks of precarity (Allan et al., 2021), we propose to use economic vulnerability as an umbrella term, the defining feature being the *threat to achieving or maintaining individual self-sufficiency* with one's earnings. Moreover, we want to reiterate previous calls to consider both objective and subjective operationalizations of economic vulnerability and their interrelations (Ullah, 1990; Veenhoven, 2002).

Second, economic vulnerability can have a wide range of consequences and the examples we have illustrated here are certainly not exhaustive. Sinclair and Cheung (2016) have provided a comprehensive review for the field of occupational health. Future research would benefit from extending the range of outcomes and providing further evidence of the effects of economic vulnerability on individuals, organizations, families, and communities. In doing so, economic vulnerability should be investigated in the context of other aspects of precarity to develop a clearer picture of separate effects on the one hand, and interrelationships with other factors such as job insecurity, mental health problems, and lack of safety at work on the other (see Blustein et al., 2020).

Third, to better understand its consequences, we need more research that can provide insight into *why* and *when* economic vulnerability leads to individual, organizational, and social consequences (Odle-Dusseau et al., 2018; Sinclair & Cheung, 2016). As for the why, existing research points to resource depletion and control as important mediators (Jachimowicz et al., 2021; Klug et al., 2021; Odle-Dusseau et al., 2018). Future research could delve deeper into the stress process, for example, by investigating the relationships between cognitive appraisals and affective stress reactions. Our reflections on attributions and social participation also point to justice perceptions as well as social identity and belonging as additional psychological mechanisms. As for the when, we also need more research to identify what exacerbates or attenuates the effects of economic vulnerability. Some mediators may also act as moderators, for example, a high sense of control has been shown to attenuate the relationship between income and health (Lachman & Weaver, 1998). Our reflections on work and care also suggest that the relationships between economic vulnerability and work-family conflict likely differ among mothers, fathers, and childless women and men (see Möhring et al., 2020). At the population level, a recent US study has shown that negative effects of economic vulnerability on individual well-being were weaker in counties with a more favorable socioeconomic profile and better access to healthcare (Probst et al., 2018). Cross-cultural investigations could also investigate the extent to which the psychological experience of economic vulnerability differs between more or less individualistic cultures; the salience of individual versus household self-sufficiency may be contingent on the extent to which people construe their self as independent or interdependent (Markus & Kitayama, 1991; Warmath et al., 2021). These examples illustrate a range of potential moderators, from traits and attitudes to the broader socioeconomic and cultural context, that could refine our understanding of when and for whom economic vulnerability is particularly harmful or less so.

In this chapter, we have focussed on the nature and consequences of economic vulnerability. Ultimately, researchers should strive to embed economic vulnerability in a nomological network of antecedents and consequences, and mediating and moderating factors, as has been suggested for precarious work as a whole (Allan et al., 2021). Developing integrated theoretical frameworks that show how poverty can be understood from the angle of specific psychological theories can guide further research and knowledge creation, as can more inductive, qualitative, participatory research that gives voice to the experiences of people living with poverty. Organizational psychologists may be particularly interested in job- and organization-level variables to identify levers for employers to use to alleviate negative effects. Nevertheless, the discussion on how to tackle economic vulnerability and address its root causes (i.e., pay and access to work) are one we need to have as a society (see Smith, 2015).

Implications for Policy and Practice

Alleviating economic vulnerability requires the political will to do so—by supporting people who are not financially self-sufficient. In the longer term, it is in the public interest to prevent economic vulnerability from occurring in the first place and ensure financial self-sufficiency for all citizens, including women and marginalized groups. On a global scale, efforts to eradicate economic vulnerability would contribute to the UN's right to work (quality, availability, and accessibility of employment) and several of the SDGs, such as ending poverty in all forms (SDG-1), gender equality (SDG-5), decent work and economic growth (SDG-8), and reducing inequalities (SDG-10; United Nations, 2015). The welfare state is a decisive player in the fight against economic vulnerability. There are at least two possible scenarios; if societies desire to remain centered around work, they should create institutional settings that fully facilitate the realization of the adult worker model. This means enabling and supporting vulnerable groups within the labor market to achieve individual economic self-sufficiency in good work environments. Measures would encompass general high labor standards that guarantee decent working conditions, i.e., permanent employment with full employment protections (e.g., against dismissal, maximum working hours), and social protections (e.g. in the case of unemployment, sickness, and old age), a decent income that allows for self-sufficient living (*quality of work*), and the creation of high-quality jobs that meet the demand for employment (*availability of work*). In order to guarantee decent incomes, governments must enforce wage-setting policies that are centered around living wages (Meyer & Maleka, Chapter 7). To ensure that people can actually work enough hours to achieve self-sufficiency, they need support in their caring and family duties, e.g., by providing universal free public childcare and elderly care, that allows caring responsibilities to be taken on outside the private home (*accessibility of work*). Certainly, vocational training and access to continuous learning opportunities are also essential in order to equip individuals with the necessary skills to work in occupations that match their interests and the demands of a changing labor market.

In the short term, organizations and policy makers should work on alleviating existing economic vulnerability and its consequences. This could include financial and tangible support for all those who are currently not financially self-sufficient. Measures could consist of a mix of financial support for individual households to subsidize the costs of daily living (e.g., public transport, health care, housing, and schooling) as well as directly regulating the prices of or limiting speculation on essential goods such as staple foods and energy. Many of the negative consequences of economic vulnerability are due to social exclusion and the impossibility of enacting important social roles (Fryer & Fagan, 2003). Regenerative city planning could help here, to offer contexts that allow for social interaction even without money. For example, well-kept and pleasant public spaces allow for free social interactions and participation as a citizen at a very low cost (e.g., public libraries, free internet, pay-as-you-feel restaurants). The important thing here is that public support needs to be understood and offered as a right that all citizens have, and not as a charity handout people have to apply for with evidence of their need, to prevent humiliation and barriers to access. As well as paying decent wages, organizations need to understand that economic vulnerability is likely going to affect the health and work behavior of employees. If raising earnings is not sufficient or possible (e.g., because people work part-time), employers might consider alternatives, for example, providing services people could usually not afford (e.g., free childcare, free transport, subsidized meals, etc.) as well as less tangible financial support (e.g., free tax advice, free advice on larger expenditures; see Teng-Calleja et al., Chapter 8).

More hypothetically, societies could loosen their strong focus on employment and decouple individual economic self-sufficiency from having a paid job. This could be realized through the provision of an unconditional basic income (Carr, Hodgetts et al., Chapter 1; Toaddy, Crawford et al., Chapter 22), probably combined with a strong reliance on automation and a considerable redistribution of labor, i.e., an increase in the number of employees and a decrease in individual working hours (see Bregman, 2016; Haagh, 2019). In this context, work and organizational psychology as a discipline could play a much more prominent role than it currently does in providing expertise about potential advantages and side effects for individuals and organizations of implementing a universal basic income (Hüffmeier & Zacher, 2021).

As our reflections throughout this chapter have shown, the nature of economic vulnerability is complex, and its consequences can be severe. We therefore want to reiterate calls that the onus for alleviating these consequences not to be put on the individual (Smith, 2015), but that employers and policy makers strive to improve access to financial resources to prevent economic vulnerability from occurring in the first place.

References

Adler, N. E., Boyce, T., Chesney, M. A., Cohen, S., Folkman, S., Kahn, R. L., & Syme, S. L. (1994). Socioeconomic status and health: The challenge of the gradient. *American Psychologist, 49*(1), 15–24.

Alber, J., & Heisig, J. P. (2011). *Do new labour activation policies work? A descriptive analysis of the German Hartz Reforms* (WZB Discussion Paper, Issue SP I 2011–211). Social Science Research Center Berlin.

Allan, B. A., Autin, K. L., & Wilkins-Yel, K. G. (2021). Precarious work in the 21st century: A psychological perspective. *Journal of Vocational Behavior, 126*, Article 103491.

American Psychological Association. (2017). *Stress in America: The state of our nation.* https://www.apa.org/news/press/releases/stress/2017/state-nation.pdf

Arber, S., Fenn, K., & Meadows, R. (2014). Subjective financial well-being, income and health inequalities in mid and later life in Britain. *Social Science and Medicine, 100*, 12–20.

Aronsson, G., Dallner, M., Lindh, T., & Göransson, S. (2005). Flexible pay but fixed expenses: Personal financial strain among on-call employees. *International Journal of Health Services, 35*(3), 499–528.

Atkinson, T., Cantillon, B., Marlier, E., & Nolan, B. (2002). *Social indicators: The EU and social inclusion*. Oxford University Press.

Bjarnason, T., & Sigurdardottir, T. J. (2003). Psychological distress during unemployment and beyond: Social support and material deprivation among youth in six northern European countries. *Social Science and Medicine, 56*(5), 973–985.

Blanchflower, D. G., & Oswald, A. J. (2004). Well-being over time in Britain and the USA. *Journal of Public Economics, 88*(7–8), 1359–1386.

Blustein, D. L., Perera, H. N., Diamonti, A. J., Gutowski, E., Meerkins, T., Davila, A., Erby, W., & Konowitz, L. (2020). The uncertain state of work in the U.S.: Profiles of decent work and precarious work. *Journal of Vocational Behavior, 122*, Article 103481.

Branyiczki, R. (2015). In-work poverty among immigrants in the EU. *Szociologiai Szemle, 25*(4), 86–106.

Bregman, R. (2016). Utopia for realists: The case for a universal basic income, open borders, and a 15-hour workweek. The Correspondent.

Broetje, S., Jenny, G. J., & Bauer, G. F. (2020). The key job demands and resources of nursing staff: An integrative review of reviews. *Frontiers in Psychology, 11*, 84.

Butterworth, P., Leach, L. S., Strazdins, L., Olesen, S. C., Rodgers, B., & Broom, D. H. (2011). The psychosocial quality of work determines whether employment has benefits for mental health: Results from a longitudinal national household panel survey. *Occupational and Environmental Medicine, 68*(11), 806–812.

Chan, A., Ofstedal, M. B., & Hermalin, A. I. (2002). Changes in subjective and objective measures of economic well-being and their interrelationship among the elderly in Singapore and Taiwan. *Social Indicators Research, 57*, 263–300.

Daly, M. (2005). Changing family life in Europe: Significance for state and society. *European Societies, 7*(3), 379–398.

Daly, M. (2011). What adult worker model? A critical look at recent social policy reform in Europe from a gender and family perspective. *Social Politics, 18*(1), 1–23.

Di Tella, R., MacCulloch, R. J., & Oswald, A. J. (2003). The macroeconomics of happiness. *The Review of Economics and Statistics, 85*(4), 809–827.

Dijkstra-Kersten, S. M. A., Biesheuvel-Leliefeld, K. E. M., van der Wouden, J. C., Penninx, B. W. J. H., & van Marwijk, H. W. J. (2015). Associations of financial strain and income with depressive and anxiety disorders. *Journal of Epidemiology and Community Health, 69*(7), 660–665.

Dolan, P., Peasgood, T., & White, M. (2008). Do we really know what makes us happy? A review of the economic literature on the factors associated with subjective well-being. *Journal of Economic Psychology, 29*(1), 94–122.

Ehrenreich, B. (2001). *Nickel and dimed: On (not) getting by in America*. Holt.

Elbogen, E. B., Lanier, M., Montgomery, A. E., Strickland, S., Ryan Wagner, H., & Tsai, J. (2020). Financial strain and suicide attempts in a nationally representative sample of US adults. *American Journal of Epidemiology, 189*(11), 1266–1274.

Eurofound. (2020). Living, working and COVID-19: First findings–April 2020. https://www.eurofound.europa.eu/sites/default/files/ef_publication/field_ef_document/ef20058en.pdf

Eurostat. (2020). *15% of all EU employees are low-wage earners*. https://ec.europa.eu/eurostat/en/web/products-eurostat-news/-/ddn-20201214-1

Eurostat. (n.d.). *In-work at-risk-of-poverty rate [Data set]*. Retrieved from https://ec.europa.eu/eurostat/databrowser/view/tespm070/default/table

Filandri, M., & Struffolino, E. (2019). Individual and household in-work poverty in Europe: Understanding the role of labor market characteristics. *European Societies, 21*(1), 130–157.

Fraser, N. (1994). After the family wage: Gender equity and the welfare state. *Political Theory, 22*(4), 591–618.

Fryer, D., & Fagan, R. (2003). Poverty and unemployment. In Carr, S. C. & Sloan, T. S. (Eds.), *Poverty and psychology. From global perspective to local practice* (pp. 87–102). Springer.

Furnham, A. (2003). Belief in a just world: Research progress over the past decade. *Personality and Individual Differences, 34*(5), 795–817.

Gaitens, J., Condon, M., Fernandes, E., & McDiarmid, M. (2021). COVID-19 and essential workers: A narrative review of health outcomes and moral injury. *International Journal of Environmental Research and Public Health, 18*(4), 1–16.

Garðarsdóttir, R. B., & Dittmar, H. (2012). The relationship of materialism to debt and financial well-being: The case of Iceland's perceived prosperity. *Journal of Economic Psychology, 33*(3), 471–481.

Gerlitz, J.-Y. (2023). The end of the golden age: on growing challenges for male workers and their partners to secure a family income. *European Sociological Review, 39*(2), 247–261.

Gilboa, S., Shirom, A., Fried, Y., & Cooper, C. (2008). A meta-analysis of work demand stressors and job performance: examining main and moderating effects. *Personnel Psychology, 61*(2), 227–271.

Haagh, L. (2019). *The case for universal basic income*. Polity Press.

Hagerty, M. R., & Veenhoven, R. (2003). Wealth and happiness revisited—Growing national income does go with greater happiness. *Social Indicators Research, 64*(1), 1–27.

Hall, M., Buysse, D. J., Nofzinger, E. A., Reynolds, C. F., Thompson, W., Mazumdar, S., & Monk, T. H. (2008). Financial strain is a significant correlate of sleep continuity disturbances in late-life. *Biological Psychology, 77*(2), 217–222.

Häusermann, S., & Schwader, H. (2012). Varieties of dualization? Labor market segmentation and insider-outsider divides across regimes. In P. Emmenegger, S. Häusermann, B. Palier, & M. Seeleib-Kaiser (Eds.), *The age of dualization* (pp. 27–51). Oxford University Press.

Haushofer, J., & Fehr, E. (2014). On the psychology of poverty. *Science, 344*(6186), 862–867.

Hobfoll, S. E. (1989). Conservation of resources: A new attempt at conceptualizing stress. *American Psychologist, 44*(3), 513–524.

Hook, J. L. (2015). Incorporating 'class' into work--family arrangements: Insights from and for Three Worlds. *Journal of European Social Policy, 25*(1), 14–31.

Howard, K. A. S., Carlstrom, A. H., Katz, A. D., Chew, A. Y., Ray, G. C., Laine, L., & Caulum, D. (2011). Career aspirations of youth: Untangling race/ethnicity, SES, and gender. *Journal of Vocational Behavior, 79*(1), 98–109.

Hüffmeier, J., & Zacher, H. (2021). The basic income: Initiating the needed discussion in industrial, work, and organizational psychology. *Industrial and Organizational Psychology: Perspectives on Science and Practice, 14*(4), 531–562.

Hulin, C. L. (2002). Lessons from industrial and organizational psychology. In J. M. Brett & F. Drasgow (Eds.), *The psychology of work* (pp. 3–22). Lawrence Erlbaum Associates.

International Labour Organization (ILO). (2017). *Labour legislation guidelines.*

Jachimowicz, J. M., Frey, E. L., Matz, S. C., Jeronimus, B. F., & Galinsky, A. D. (2021). The sharp spikes of poverty: Financial scarcity is related to higher levels of distress intensity in daily life. *Social Psychological and Personality Science 13*(3), 1187–1198. https://doi.org/10.1177/19485506211060115

Jahoda, M. (1982). *Employment and unemployment. A social-psychological analysis.* Cambridge University Press.

Kahneman, D., & Deaton, A. (2010). High income improves evaluation of life but not emotional well-being. *Proceedings of the National Academy of Sciences of the United States of America, 107*(38), 16489–16493.

Kalleberg, A. L. (2009). Precarious work, insecure workers: Employment relations in transition. *American Sociological Review, 74*(1), 1–22.

Karasek, R. A. (1979). Job demands, job decision latitude, and mental strain: Implications for job redesign. *Administrative Science Quarterly, 24*(2), 285–308.

Klug, K., Selenko, E., & Gerlitz, J.Y. (2021). Working, but not for a living: A longitudinal study on the psychological consequences of economic vulnerability among German employees. *European Journal of Work and Organizational Psychology, 30*(6), 790–807.

Kößler, F. J., Wesche, J. S., & Hoppe, A. (2022). In a no-win situation: The employment–health dilemma. *Applied Psychology, 72*(1), 64–84.

Krings, T. (2021). 'Good' Bad Jobs? The evolution of migrant low-wage employment in Germany (1985–2015). *Work, Employment and Society, 35*(3), 527–544.

Kronauer, M. (2010). *Exklusion: Die Gefährdung des Sozialen im hoch entwickelten Kapitalismus* (2nd ed.). Campus.

Lachman, M. E., & Weaver, S. L. (1998). The sense of control as a moderator of social class differences in health and well-being. *Journal of Personality and Social Psychology, 74*(3), 763–773.

Lazarus, R. S., & Folkman, S. (1984). *Stress, appraisal and coping.* Springer.

Lerner, M. J. (1980). The belief in a just world. In M. J. Lerner (Ed.), *The belief in a just world: A fundamental delusion* (pp. 9–30). Springer.

Lewis, J. (1992). Gender and the development of welfare regimes. *Journal of European Social Policy, 2*(3), 159–173.

Lewis, J. (2001). The decline of the male breadwinner model: Implications for work and care. *Social Politics, 8*(2), 152–169.

Lund, C., Breen, A., Flisher, A. J., Kakuma, R., Corrigall, J., Joska, J. A., Swartz, L., & Patel, V. (2010). Poverty and common mental disorders in low and middle income countries: A systematic review. *Social Science and Medicine, 71*(3), 517–528.

Mack, J., & Lansley, S. (1985). *Poor Britain.* George Allen and Unwin.

Markus, H. R., & Kitayama, S. (1991). Culture and the self: Implications for cognition, emotion and motivation. *Psychological Review, 98*(2), 224–253.

Martikainen, P., Adda, J., Ferrie, J. E., Davey Smith, G., & Marmot, M. G. (2003). Effects of income and wealth on GHQ depression and poor self rated health in white collar women and men in the Whitehall II study. *Journal of Epidemiology and Community Health, 57*(9), 718–723.

McCoy, S. K., & Major, B. (2007). Priming meritocracy and the psychological justification of inequality. *Journal of Experimental Social Psychology, 43*(3), 341–351.

Meuris, J., & Gladstone, J. (2023). Contextual Inequality in the Performance Costs of Financial Precarity. *Journal of Management*, online first. https://doi.org/10.1177/01492063231153136

Mijs, J. J. B. (2021). The paradox of inequality: income inequality and belief in meritocracy go hand in hand. *Socio-Economic Review, 19*(1), 7–35.

Möhring, K. (2018). Is there a motherhood penalty in retirement income in Europe? The role of lifecourse and institutional characteristics. *Ageing and Society, 38*(12), 2560–2589.

Möhring, K., Naumann, E., Reifenscheid, M., Wenz, A., Rettig, T., Krieger, U., Friedel, S., Finkel, M., Cornesse, C., & Blom, A. G. (2020). The COVID-19 pandemic and subjective well-being: Longitudinal evidence on satisfaction with work and family. *European Societies, 23*(4) 1–17.

Mückenberger, U. (1985). Die Krise des Normalarbeitsverhältnisses: Hat das Arbeitsrecht noch Zukunft? *Zeitschrift Für Sozialreform, 31*(7), 415–475.

Mückenberger, U., & Deakin, S. (1989). From deregulation to a European floor of rights: Labour law, flexibilisation and the European single market. *Zeitschrift Für Ausländisches und Internationales Arbeits- und Sozialrecht, 3,* 153–207.

Murphy, E., & Oesch, D. (2016). The feminization of occupations and change in wages: A panel analysis of Britain, Germany, and Switzerland. *Social Forces, 94*(3), 1221–1255.

Odle-Dusseau, H. N., Matthews, R. A., & Wayne, J. H. (2018). Employees' financial insecurity and health: The underlying role of stress and work–family conflict appraisals. *Journal of Occupational and Organizational Psychology, 91*(3), 546–568.

Oesch, D. (2006). *Redrawing the class map: Stratification and institutions in Britain, Germany, Sweden and Switzerland.* Palgrave Macmillan.

Organisation for Economic Co-operation and Development. (2022). *Consumer prices, OECD—Updated: 5 July 2022.* https://www.oecd.org/newsroom/consumer-prices-oecd-updated-5-july-2022.htm

Orloff, A. S. (1993). Gender and the social rights of citizenship: The comparative analysis of gender relations and welfare states. *American Sociological Review, 58*(3), 303–328.

Oshio, T., & Kan, M. (2014). Multidimensional poverty and health: Evidence from a nationwide survey in Japan. *International Journal for Equity in Health, 13*(1), 1–11.

Peña-Casas, R., & Ghailani, D. (2011). Towards individualizing gender in-work poverty risks. In N. Fraser, R. Gutiérrez, & R. Peña-Casas (Eds.), *Working poverty in Europe* (pp. 202–231). Palgrave Macmillan.

Pepper, G. V., & Nettle, D. (2017). The behavioural constellation of deprivation: Causes and consequences. *Behavioral and Brain Sciences, 40*, e314. https://doi.org/10.1017/S0140525X1600234X

Pförtner, T.-K., Pfaff, H., & Hower, K. I. (2019). Trends in the association of different forms of precarious employment and self-rated health in Germany. An analysis with the German Socio-Economic Panel between 1995 and 2015. *Journal of Epidemiology and Community Health, 73*(11), 1002–1011.

Pförtner, T.-K., & Schmidt-Catran, A. W. (2017). In-work poverty and self-rated health in a cohort of working Germans: A hybrid approach for decomposing within-person and between-persons estimates of in-work poverty status. *American Journal of Epidemiology, 185*(4), 274–282.

Pohlig, M., Israel, S., & Dingeldey, I. (2020). Does the household context matter for job satisfaction among low-wage workers? *Economic and Industrial Democracy, 43*(3), 1028–1058.

Ponthieux, S. (2018). Gender and in-work poverty. In H. Lohmann & I. Marx (Eds.), *Handbook on in-work poverty* (pp. 70–88). Edward Elgar.

Price, R. H., Choi, J. N., & Vinokur, A. D. (2002). Links in the chain of adversity following job loss: How financial strain and loss of personal control lead to depression, impaired functioning, and poor health. *Journal of Occupational Health Psychology, 7*(4), 302–312.

Probst, T. M., Sinclair, R. R., & Cheung, J. H. (2017). Economic stressors and wellbeing at work: Multilevel considerations. In C. L. Cooper & M. P. Leiter (Eds.), *The Routledge companion to wellbeing at work* (pp. 121–134). Routledge.

Probst, T. M., Sinclair, R. R., Sears, L. E., Gailey, N. J., Black, K. J., & Cheung, J. H. (2018). Economic stress and well-being: Does population health context matter? *Journal of Applied Psychology, 103*(9), 959–979.

Rajani, N. B., Giannakopoulos, G., & Filippidis, F. T. (2016). Job insecurity, financial difficulties and mental health in Europe. *Occupational Medicine, 66*(8), 681–683.

Rodgers, G. (1989). Precarious work in Western Europe: The state of the debate. In G. Rodgers & J. Rodgers (Eds.), *Precarious jobs in labour market regulation: The growth of atypical employment in Western Europe* (pp. 1–16). International Labour Organization.

Ross, C. E., & Mirowsky, J. (1992). Households, employment, and the sense of control. *Social Psychology Quarterly, 55*(3), 217.

Schmalor, A., & Heine, S. J. (2021). The construct of subjective economic inequality. *Social Psychological and Personality Science, 13*(1), 210–219.

Searle, R. H., & McWha-Hermann, I. (2020). "Money's too tight (to mention)": A review and psychological synthesis of living wage research. *European Journal of Work and Organizational Psychology, 30*(3), 428–443.

Sears, L. E. (2008). *Work-related outcomes of financial stress: Relating perceived income adequacy and financial strain to job performance and worker well-being* [Unpublished master's thesis]. Portland State University. https://pdxscholar.library.pdx.edu/open_access_etds/5295/

Selenko, E., & Batinic, B. (2011). Beyond debt. A moderator analysis of the relationship between perceived financial strain and mental health. *Social Science & Medicine, 73*, 1725–1732.

Selenko, E., & De Witte, H. (2021). How job insecurity affects political attitudes: Identity threat plays a role. *Applied Psychology, 70*(3), 1267–1294.

Shoss, M. K. (2017). Job insecurity: An integrative review and agenda for future research. *Journal of Management, 43*(6), 1911–1939.

Siegrist, J. (1996). Adverse health effects of high-effort/low-reward conditions. *Journal of Occupational Health Psychology, 1*(1), 27–41.

Sinclair, R. R., & Cheung, J. H. (2016). Money matters: Recommendations for financial stress research in Occupational Health Psychology. *Stress and Health, 32*(3), 181–193.

Smith, L. (2015). Reforming the minimum wage: Toward a psychological perspective. *American Psychologist, 70*(6), 557–565.

Sonnentag, S., Cheng, B. H., & Parker, S. L. (2021). Recovery from work: Advancing the field toward the future. *Annual Review of Organizational Psychology and Organizational Behavior, 9*, 33–60.

Standing, G. (2011). *The precariat: The new dangerous class.* Bloomsbury Academic.

Starrin, B., Åslund, C., & Nilsson, K. W. (2009). Financial stress, shaming experiences and psychosocial ill-health: Studies into the finances-shame model. *Social Indicators Research, 91*(2), 283–298.

Steptoe, A., Brydon, L., & Kunz-Ebrecht, S. (2005). Changes in financial strain over three years, ambulatory blood pressure, and cortisol responses to awakening. *Psychosomatic Medicine, 67*(2), 281–287.

Streeck, W. (2012). How to study contemporary capitalism? *European Journal of Sociology, 53*, 1–28.

Sverke, M., & Hellgren, J. (2002). The nature of job insecurity: Understanding employment uncertainty on the brink of a new millennium. *Applied Psychology: An International Review, 51*(1), 23–42.

Till, R. E., & Karren, R. (2011). Organizational justice perceptions and pay level satisfaction. *Journal of Managerial Psychology, 26*(1), 42–57.

Townsend, P. (1979). *Poverty in the United Kingdom: A survey of household resources and standards of living.* Penguin.

Turner, J. C., Hogg, M. A., Oakes, P. J., Reicher, S. D., & Wetherell, M. S. (1987). *Rediscovering the social group: A self-categorization theory.* Basil Blackwell.

Ullah, P. (1990). The association between income, financial strain and psychological well-being among unemployed youths. *Journal of Occupational Psychology, 63*(4), 317–330.

UN Women. (2019). *Annual Report 2018–2019.* https://www.unwomen.org/sites/default/files/Annual%20Report/Attachments/Sections/Library/2019/UN-Women-annual-report-2018-2019-en.pdf

United Nations. (2015). Transforming our world: The 2030 Agenda for Sustainable Development. In *Resolution adopted by the General Assembly on 25 September 2015.*

United Nations. (2020). *The sustainable development goals report 2020.* https://unstats.un.org/sdgs/report/2020/

Veenhoven, R. (2002). Why social policy needs subjective indicators. *Social Indicators Research, 58*, 33–45.

Vetter, S., Endrass, J., Schweizer, I., Teng, H. M., Rossler, W., & Gallo, W. T. (2006). The effects of economic deprivation on psychological well-being among the working population of Switzerland. *BMC Public Health, 6*, 1–10.

Warmath, D., Chen, P. J., Grable, J., & Kwak, E. J. (2021). Soft landings: Extending the cushion hypothesis to financial well-being in collectivistic cultures. *Journal of Consumer Affairs, 55*(4), 1563–1590.

Whelan, C. T., Layte, R., & Maître, B. (2003). Persistent income poverty and deprivation in the European Union: An analysis of the first three waves of the European Community Household Panel. *Journal of Social Policy, 32*(1), 1–18.

Whelan, C. T., Layte, R., Maître, B., & Nolan, B. (2001). Income, deprivation, and economic strain: An analysis of the European Community Household Panel. *European Sociological Review, 17*(4), 357–372.

Winkelmann, L., & Winkelmann, R. (1998). Why are the umemployed so unhappy? Evidence from panel data. *Economica, 65*(257), 1–15.

Yeates, N. (2004). Global care chains. *International Feminist Journal of Politics, 6*, 369–391.

22

THE JOBLESS FUTURE AND A WORLD WITHOUT PAID WORK?

./Steven Toaddy, Anna Crawford, J. Crentsil, J. Hernandez, S. Hohmann, A. F. Miles, J. R. Roman, and J. Tuason

In late April of 2022, at the Annual Conference of the Society for Industrial and Organizational Psychology (SIOP), ten individuals presented an Ignite session to over 100 attendees regarding the work that the field of I/O psychology had already done looking toward a future in which paid work is no more. The topics that those presenters put forward differed greatly from one to the next, but they all served a common purpose: to identify, acknowledge, share, and encourage further efforts in determining what, if anything, I/O psychology and its sibling fields can do to predict, explain, and even control our transition toward a future where human existence is not characterized by reliance on (or even availability of) paid work.

As an echo of that well-received session, the substance of this chapter is a series of segments that approach various aspects of this topic from those various perspectives, written by some of the presenters from that SIOP session. Notably, each segment focusses on a different point toward different potential paths to a future without paid work, from the near future to further down the line. They are perhaps best consumed as invitations to think about the topic from different perspectives, rather than as a single coherent model or narrative to guide us to or to help us understand such a future. In each case, they draw upon psychological thinking, in part to demonstrate what can be brought to bear on this issue and how it can be conceptualized.

The Connection to Precarious Work and to Psychology

On the one hand, this far-future focus diverts the reader's attention from the current pressing issues of precarious work addressed in this larger volume. On the

DOI: 10.4324/9781003440444-26

other hand, this focus converges clearly with conceptualizations of precarious work—it is an example of the current high global uncertainty regarding continued gainful employment. In terms of the four dimensions of precarious work addressed in this volume, it shows clear connections to each:

1 Sustainable livelihood: unemployment in this world could reach 100%, and some of the less desirable pathways to a world without paid work may lead to great differences between nations' experiences of unemployment as specific sectors are automated.
2 Fair incomes: questions of subsidies and of subsistence lie at the core of a world in which the current primary means of support (i.e., fair income from paid work) is potentially absent.
3 Security: automation is the beating heart at the core of the possible transition to a world free from paid employment, and the obsolescence of human labor is the necessary midwife of such a future. Additionally, as will be discussed briefly below, it is conceivable that the world can maneuver itself into a situation in which individuals continue to be occupied (even for pay), leading to a sense of decent work even if not of economic productiveness.
4 Social protection: questions of mental health and of work-family balance loom large and are, in the latter case, in need of radical reframing in the event that the "work" portion of the equation evaporates in this potential future.

As it pertains to precarious work, the purpose of this chapter is to invite the reader to step away from a fixation on "the job," not only in terms of a predetermined and prespecified role within a formal employment contract but also in the broader sense as employment, occupation, and labor. It is an attempt to cause us to lift our eyes from the (admittedly critical) issues addressed elsewhere in this volume to consider the possibility that even the days of work *not* characterized as precarious may be numbered, and that any solutions that we find to reduce the precarity of work may be sustainable only for a limited amount of time before the well of human employment dries up forever. It is targeted at those in I/O psychology (and any adjacent and even unrelated fields) in an effort to show that this is a worthwhile and not entirely unrealistic topic: to show that making meaningful contributions in this space is not a matter of reinventing the wheel and to lay the foundation of a role that such individuals and fields can play in actively improving the lives of humankind through preparatory work and in a future where assumptions about the daily activities of humans depart radically from where they stand today.

Along the way, we not only draw on I/O psychology research but also on work from other fields of psychology—counseling (vocational, political, and social)—and also more distant fields including career assessment and development, economics, management, robotics, food science, artificial intelligence, game design, electrical engineering, construction, and sustainability. Much of what is stated here is by its nature speculative, but it is theoretically and/or empirically grounded in varied literatures.

How Contingent Work Creates a Framework for Thriving in the Jobless Future

Jobs Today

When you think of a job, what comes to mind? What kinds of activities do you see yourself carrying out? Is the job repetitive or does it change day-to-day? Do you work mostly alone or with others? Do you see yourself staying at the job for more than three to five years or do you think it'll go away due to technology?

The prototypical example of a job is "something that is full-time, long term, with a steady paycheck that provides benefits and career growth" (Aronowitz & Difazio, 2010). And most importantly, a job meets your basic needs by providing an income for clothes, shelter, and food. In contrast, contingent work is defined as conditional working arrangements that are temporary—whether voluntarily or involuntarily (Barker & Christensen, 1998, pp. 1–2)—and according to the United States (US) General Accounting Office (2000) can often vary widely in the number of hours, pay structure, and benefits provided: in other words, often highly precarious (Carr, Hodgetts, et al., Chapter 1; Saltzman et al., Chapter 2).

Researchers have seen trends that contradict the seemingly "stable" nature of a job. Due to certain factors—such as recurring and frequent recessions, rapid automation, and technological advances, as well as an increase in the number of contingent and contract workers (both defined by their nonemployee status within an organization, and differing in terms of their specific relationship with the organization) being hired over full-time workers to fill knowledge and skill gap—society might be moving toward a future without permanent paid work, or to a jobless future. Fortunately, society might be more prepared for this jobless future than we think or know.

What Is the Jobless Future?

The jobless future is not a future without work (van Hooft & van Hoye, Chapter 19). Rather, it is a reality that doesn't require compensation due to relying primarily on universal basic income and automatons for repetitive or tedious tasks, and humans for work that requires nuance in judgment and creativity, such as law or education. In this reality, contingent, temporary, and part-time works are more commonplace than salaried jobs due to scientific and technological innovations (Mulcahy, 2016). Consequently, time is more abundant and flexible than under capitalism. Rather than work being organized into a list of tasks that must be performed within a 40-hour week, work is given on an assignment or on an as-needed basis, and how work gets done is decided by the individual worker rather than the organization or its representative.

Signs that We're Headed toward a Jobless Future

There are three factors or signals that indicate an imminent future of unpaid work: (1) increasingly frequent recessions, (2) technological automation, and (3) the growing demand for contingent workers over salaried ones.

Signal 1—Increasingly Frequent Recessions

Ever since the 1960s, recessions have become more frequent. In terms of the impact, this has on women and men, men tend to suffer the most job losses (nine times as often as women) due to their heavy participation in the goods-producing sector, which is more susceptible to the demands of the business cycle (Goodman et al., 1993). In contrast, while women make up less of the workforce overall, they are primarily employed in service-producing industries such as government, healthcare services, and retail trade, in which roles of this type have shown consistent growth before and during recessions (Goodman et al., 1993).

The Impact that Recessions Have on Workers

The Great Recession (2008–2009) was characterized by a staggering 8.8 million jobs lost and a very slow economic recovery; this resulted in a labor market in which US workers were faced with higher unemployment, challenging working conditions, and obstacles to economic mobility (Visser, 2019). With more frequent recessions and unpredictable impacts on certain sectors and contingent work opportunities, there is less job stability for workers (Goodman et al., 1993). However, there are some positives; following the recession that took place in 1990–1991, in which women suffered major job losses, there has been a steady uptick in women entering upper management positions, bringing innovative and diversified perspectives. This may indicate that during the transition period to a future of unpaid work, work may be highly gendered at least initially.

Signal 2—Technological Impacts on Workers

The idea of technological impacts conjures up the fear that "robots are coming for our jobs" and big waves of unemployment are imminent in society's future. However, sources on this are mixed (Aronowitz & Difazio, 2010; Vermeulen et al., 2018) and do not cleanly point to a direct increase in unemployment; instead, technology and automation have been found to bring down wages (augmenting work and wage precariousness), particularly in industries with common job classes and for roles with less in-demand skills, such as bookkeepers and executive assistants (Vermeulen et al., 2018).

Some industry sectors, such as manufacturing and retail, have already seen employment disruption and declines. These lost jobs appear to be compensated for with job growth in other industries, particularly in computer-based industries, though all-in-all the increase in full-time jobs in the private sector since the mid-1970s is marginal at best (Aronowitz & Difazio, 2010; Vermeulen et al., 2018). Rather, the private sector increasingly relies on hiring contingent workers to meet shorter term labor requirements.

Future Impact of Technology on Workers

With technology driving wages down and not generating many new full-time jobs, workers are further pushed into precarious territory. In order to stay marketable in an increasingly tech-dependent and specialized contingent workforce, workers will likely continue to expand their technological capabilities to maximize project opportunities.

The work already being replaced by technology is that which is filled with repetitive and rote tasks, like language translation and performing calculations. Work that is still safe contains more strategy, creativity, and nuance in judgment, such as practicing law or conducting end-to-end scientific experiments. So, while technology will drastically alter the landscape of paid work as society currently knows it today, not all work will be taken by robots.

Signal 3—The Rise in Contingent Workers

Organizations are incentivized to take on contingent, temporary workers to enhance flexibility, and reduce costs. Cost is reduced compared to full-time employees due to fewer or nonexistent benefits, training, and recruiting costs, as well as by only bringing in the talent at the exact time the work needs to be done (Matusik & Hill, 1998). With contingent workers, organizations can end contracts with very few exit costs, for example, when market conditions change, which cannot be done with full-time employees. Because of all of the above reasons and more, contingent workers are often targets of unjust treatment and tend to report lower job satisfaction than full-time employees (Wilkin, 2013).

Despite these downsides for workers, they may engage in contingent work for numerous reasons, sometimes due to its specific advantages. Women, for instance, tend to gravitate toward contingent work for schedule flexibility and the greater opportunity to work part-time hours, and they tend to make up the majority of contingent workers (Goodman et al., 1993). When men engage in contingent work, it is likely that they are looking to maximize the amount of work they can get, to boost their income (Amuedo-Dorantes & Kimmel, 2009). Whilst women are more likely to work one full-time job and one part-time role, men are more likely to work two full-time jobs (Amuedo-Dorates & Kimmel, 2009). Kosanovich (2018) suggested that approximately one third of all contingent workers were in the educational and health-services industries. Other popular industries included agriculture and construction, especially when compared to noncontingent workers (Kosanovich, 2018). Conversely, contingent workers were least represented in manufacturing and retail roles (Kosanovich, 2018).

Future Impact on Workers

It is difficult to accurately count the number of contingent workers, with most estimates focussed on digital "gig" workers (those whose work is mediated through a digital platform) with the US Bureau of Labor Statistics stating it made up 36% of the workforce in a 2019 survey (Risher, 2020), and the International Labour Organization stating in a 2021 report that around 22% of US workers were involved (International Labour Organization, 2021). One observation that both sources agree on is this; the number of workers belonging to this group is rising (Risher, 2020; International Labour Organization, 2021).

In the future, contingent work may very well become the standard "career," where workers focus on completing individual tasks and projects within a specialized skill set across organizations or industries, as opposed to remaining within one organization for multiple projects for long periods of time. Workers able to adapt to this shift most quickly will have the most autonomy and direction over the kinds of projects they take on, and there will be more individualized direction and creativity about what defines career success for contingent workers (van Hooft & van Hoye, Chapter 19).

The world already sees collectives and consultancies today that attract contingent workers by providing them access to projects—such as through online platforms like Upwork and Fiverr—but as contingent work continues to become the primary way of working, more communities will form where like-minded workers can develop, create, and network together in a more casual, fluid, and on-demand capacity.

What Does This Mean for the Individual?

In the jobless future, individuals will have more short-term and long-term occupational autonomy, meaning that from day to day they will have the ability to structure their day how they see fit (working independently or on a team, in a public or a private office, for a German client while in the Philippines) and, as a whole, they will decide what their careers will look like, what skill sets to develop, who they work with, and what market gaps they can fill (van Hooft & van Hoye, Chapter 19).

In terms of skill set, the worker will need to be enterprising and open to new challenges; aware of market gaps that they can fill with their own skill sets; comfortable structuring how, when, and where work gets done; and be able to exhibit deep expertise in a specific domain. The jobless future as a whole demands autonomy and flexibility via telework. Much as many members of society are working in the early 2020s, many will continue to work remotely and across time zones.

Due to the emphasis on adaptability and self-direction, workers outside of the traditional salaried-employee archetype, such as students, stay-at-home parents, the elderly, and retirees, are more likely to thrive in this world. Additionally, because of the flexibility (or precarity) that remote work permits, the authors predict that the need for affiliations and identification tied to organizations will be lessened, meaning employees or workers will feel less of a need to align with organizations: except, perhaps, the digital ones (Wiesenfeld et al., 2001). These same workers will find more meaning and value in other activities outside of paid work (Casey & Alach, 2004).

Making a Case for a World without Paid Work

Given a sufficient amount of time, humanity may move itself to a place in which human labor is neither required nor sought. In such a world, employment for pay could (but need not necessarily) be eliminated. The authors of this chapter are not interested in predicting whether, when, or how such a future will become the present; we are interested in setting resources in place to monitor, anticipate, and shape the transition should it occur, all with the twin objectives of landing in only the most desirable possible version of such a future and landing in that future only with the most peace and human flourishing as possible. The reader may find these words challenging to envision, or at least not sufficiently clear, so it may be worth taking the space here to provide a description of such a future. Let us briefly consider the basic but complex matter of feeding humans.

A Hypothetical Example of a (Corner of a) World That Does Not Require Human Labor

The following paragraph is a hypothetical description of a world that could come to pass (italicized), accompanied by actual supporting citations (not italicized) for the described technologies. Note the conspicuous lack of involvement of human labor in this description.

On the basis of an AI-powered predictive system that forecasts food needs for the nearby population, a fully automated "dark" warehouse (Hameed et al., 2020) *moves a store of a specific type of wheat seeds to an autonomous transport vehicle* (Badue et al., 2021), *which carries these to a preselected field in which robotic manipulators unload them into an autonomous combine (tractor system), which plants them. Automated irrigation* (Veerachamy et al., 2022) *and crop maintenance (fertilizer application, pest detection, weeding;* Hallik et al., 2022), *powered by an AI-controlled wind-power array* (Lipu et al., 2021) *supported by a smart-grid electrical-distribution system* (Zhang et al., 2021), *see the seeds sprout and grow to maturity. Come harvest time, the combine moves in concord with an autonomous tractor-trailer* (Shojaei, 2021) *to harvest the wheat, which is transported to a facility in which it is milled and baked (along with other, similarly obtained ingredients) into bread via automated systems* (Selişteanu et al., 2018). *The finished, packaged goods are shipped to unstaffed convenience stores* (Lee & Park, 2021) *based on local predictive needs modeling* (Ranjitha & Spandana, 2021).

Thus, a loaf of bread is planned, produced, transported, and presented before consumers, all without the active intervention of a single moment of human labor. Expansions of the example are, the authors argue, simply a matter of the extent of the application of similar technologies—for example, predicting not only *that* bread will be needed but predicting, a season in advance, *which type* of bread will be most desired and adjusting crop production accordingly is simply a matter of a more robust forecasting system; harvesting high-touch crops like saffron will require greater subtlety to mechanize (and efforts are underway; Nehvi et al., 2006).

Given sufficient space, the authors could assemble similar stories for personal transportation (Liang et al., 2016), education (Hao, 2019), home construction (Khoshnevis, 2004), entertainment like novel music production (Fernández & Vico, 2013) and video-game narrative-content production (Fernández-Vara & Thomson, 2012), and (close to home for some of us in the domain of selection assessment) test writing (Gierl & Haladyna, 2012). We believe that we could do so for each product and service consumed by humans today, excepting those that, by definition, require the involvement of humans—if you want your teacher or pharmacist or dog walker to be a human rather than an algorithm or robot, then it will be impossible by definition to automate this role (though if you want your newscaster to be a human, you could probably arrange to use deepfake technology to trick yourself sufficiently; Westerlund, 2019).

The authors acknowledge that each example covered is only a small fragment of the overall area being considered and that each example starts somewhere in the middle of the larger story it tells; supply chains are longer than seed to field to bakery to store, and they involve a myriad of interworking parts. Additionally, one may wonder who is supposed to have built such a system and who is expected to maintain it (to which the authors respond, "humans shall have" and "current efforts are underway to get the system to maintain itself; see Chenjie & Veres n.d.," respectively). Further exploration here is limited: largely by the restrictions in scope and space in this chapter, as well as the uncertainty about what will actually transpire in the future.

In time, some of these pathways and systems may be reflected upon as laughably quaint. For instance, if 3D-printer technology advances sufficiently along a specific course to include printing of food, the entire system of geographically dispersed growing, manufacturing, transport, and distribution of foodstuffs may be entirely obviated in favor of the ultra-local production of whatever food is desired, directly from vat-produced carbohydrates, proteins, and fats (wanting only for those pesky micronutrients, plus the substrates of the required macronutrients); in this case, concerns regarding the automation of bread baking and distribution are, of course, beside the point.

These observations not only attempt to absolve the authors of responsibility for the accuracy of any specific predictions regarding the development of such technologies and systems of technologies—by either these pathways or dozens of other possible pathways, the employment of humans in the task of providing food for humans is eliminated—but also to introduce us to another important point; if and when this transition occurs, it will likely occur in a piecemeal manner over a substantial period of time, with some types of human involvement disappearing significantly before others (vehicle washing is thought likely to be automated before, for example, legislation writing is; Josten & Lordan, 2020, pp. 1–24), some nations being converted earlier than others (consider Nii-Aponsah, 2022), and some intermediate steps occurring (e.g., humans working beside automated technologies; see Evjemo et al., 2020), for better or for worse. The examples presented above are congruent with this intermediate-steps characterization; we as a society did not reflect on the production of bread and set out to start deploying technologies toward the objective of automating this process from start to finish and perhaps, as a result, some of the described technologies (e.g., smart-grid electrical and networked wind-turbine systems, inventory-management predictive algorithms, and automated irrigation) are substantially more mature than others (e.g., automated delivery from distribution center to store and automated shelf stocking).

Though a world entirely without need for human labor is admittedly the stuff of science fiction at present, it was the authors' objective to demonstrate that, conceptually, it is *not* the stuff of fantasy (or, more specifically, it requires no magic to bring about), and that aspects of the processes are already in place today, although perhaps only in limited markets and not in a cost-effective manner. There are numerous barriers with foremost among them perhaps being the lack of widespread trust by humans of automated systems (see, e.g., Wojton et al., 2020); these issues may be reduced in time with the ongoing development and growing prevalence of such systems, however. The authors aim for the reader to be able to conceptualize, if not to believe in or to anticipate, a future in which all activities that today do or that historically have required human labor to no longer do so.

There are several topics that the discussions above and below conspicuously fail to address. This is not because these topics are not interesting; it is because, in some cases, we largely lack the expertise and grounded knowledge in these topics, and because the future is almost entirely unwritten, in others. For instance, questions arise of who (if anyone) will own the means of production; how (or whether) wealth will be distributed across and within populations; and where (or whether) the state and corporations will sit in the various steps along this transformation. Perhaps most conspicuously absent is the overall question of how (or whether) economies, as we currently understand them, will continue to operate, and, if so, who will pay for all of the technologies discussed here. The authors individually have opinions and predictions regarding these questions, and certainly preferences regarding them, but the call to action in this chapter echoes these uncertainties; unless scholars (and others) do work now to anticipate, understand, and seek to control the path to this future, it is possible that the future outlined in this chapter will be a calamitous one. The authors aim to make the case that such work is already underway, as incomplete as it may be.

Work Not Required, but Sought?

An earlier passage in this chapter mentioned human labor being neither required nor sought in this potential future. The distinction is important, as it differentiates between that which could be automated and that which will be. For example, at present, low- or no-labor manufacturing of foodstuffs is possible and underway, but consumers still seek high-labor, artisanal goods, for a variety of reasons, such as perceived quality, actual chemical differences between differently produced products, and desires to support family-owned businesses (Cirne et al., 2019). Should automated manufacturing advance to the point that its products are chemically and otherwise functionally identical to or superior (by whatever chosen metrics) to those produced by artisans, it remains an empirical question as to whether consumers will continue to seek products made in higher-labor processes; if so, human labor will be unnecessary but still sought by consumers, and at least some of the outcomes discussed in this chapter will be softened or eliminated entirely (van Hooft & van Hoye, Chapter 19). Even when the explicit expectation and objective is to enhance the quality of the service provided, such as in the case of automated driving (to avoid the ill-effects of human exhaustion, distraction, and proneness to errors), the question of trust for automated systems (e.g., Li et al., 2019) remains an important determinant of whether a widespread transition from human-staffed to autonomous transportation systems will be supported in relatively wealthy societies. Further, individuals currently employed in the transportation industry may lobby to prevent the deployment of automation technologies in their sector in an attempt to preserve their means of income. Again, even in the presence of the technology and resources to deploy a system that could replace a substantial segment of human labor, it is by no means a fait accompli that such a system will be so deployed.

Another way of thinking about the word "sought" in this context is by replacing it with the word "permitted"; in the example of transportation above, this could take the form of legislation that prevented the use of human labor in commercial transportation, should autonomous systems demonstrate themselves to be sufficiently more competent (i.e., safer) than even the most careful human drivers. Safety and critical precision are easy reasons to justify such restrictions; if a robotic surgeon or automated pharmaceutical-manufacturing system or intravenous drug-delivery system or lifeguard robot could be shown to be materially more safe and/or effective than its human counterpart, society may even tolerate the increased cost associated with such a system (both in terms of developing and deploying automated technologies and of displacing human workers) in order to reduce the potentially fatal mistakes made by each of their human counterparts. Prohibition is relatively easy for us to defend in the case of human involvement in activities that can, if executed imperfectly, lead to harm to the worker and/or those nearby, such as the use of heavy machinery, medical procedures, and similar. Prohibition of human involvement is (for the authors) much harder to imagine for checkout clerks, composers, poets, and (at least some) clerical workers, and prohibition is intermediately hard to imagine for teachers, childcare providers, and therapists (this latter group operating in an environment with intermediate potential for harm of self and/or others). As technologies advance that touch on each of these current professions, and as society encounters and makes decisions about individual domains, it is possible that human labor will be ensured (if, for instance, humanity collectively declares, perhaps via the UN, that they will in no situations permit the replacement of humans with automated systems, perhaps reversing changes already well underway, for instance) or eliminated (if humanity rallies behind the task of eliminating human labor and concertedly pursues such a future, for instance).

Employment With Pay, Employment Without Pay, or No Employment at All?

One loose end to tie up in this discussion is this: whether a world without the need for human labor equates to one without paid employment. It is straightforward to imagine a situation in which these two correspond—no labor is needed, so none is obtained and none is remunerated—but it is also possible to envision numerous options by which individuals could continue to be remunerated by governments or similar organizations for *some* kinds of activities, be it economically productive or not—for being engaged in the political system by voting and attending meetings to discuss policies and legislation, for instance (cf. Standing, 2017), or for participation in higher studies or artistic expression. In other words, it is not necessarily the case that the cessation of paid employment for the purpose of economic productivity means the end of individuals' *occupation*, and the psychological value associated therewith (Walia et al., 2021); humans may be occupied in systematic activities that do not correspond, for anyone in the system, directly to wages or remuneration of any kind. Movement from society's current system of paid work (for those fortunate enough to have work and to be paid for it) to this latter configuration is a greater leap than from society's current systems of work (formal or informal, paid or unpaid, volitional or compulsory) and the absence of paid work/occupation entirely, however, and would require additional effort to bring about.

The Objectives, Revisited and Expanded (and Pared Down)

What the authors aim to do in this chapter is to demonstrate that starting this journey looking at a future without paid work needs to begin now; indeed, whether they were aware of it or not, the work that contributors from various fields have been doing for years can be brought to bear productively on these activities—defining, contextualizing, anticipating, and integrating. Certainly, it would be convenient (and likely productive for this discussion) to initiate research explicitly oriented toward a future without paid work, but given other and more pressing issues, thinking in this area is largely a matter of riding on the backs of other studies, squinting at results and attempting to determine how they would apply to a future without paid work. There are some exceptions; work on universal basic income (see for example Langou & Forteza, 2012), for instance, can perhaps be claimed as falling within the scope of this larger project, but such research is limited in scope and in its direct relevance to an entire world without paid work. Thus, the state of this area of inquiry is largely one of contextualizing existing work to this hypothetical space, making predictions from what humanity knows from unrelated (or at least not tailored) studies, and building theoretical frameworks and directions for research of and in the future.

Cultural Values and the Future without Paid Work

Another dimension to consider is how culture impacts a possible shift to unpaid work. Transitioning to a world without paid work is not only a seismic shift for the economy, but it may also lead to changes in how work is viewed within different cultures. The value of work is intertwined with different cultural values including a pride in providing for your family (Schwartz, 1999). Work itself can be a status symbol to raise an individual's social standing (Mignonac et al., 2006). Taken together, the authors argue that it is imperative to investigate the role culture will play as society shifts to a future of unpaid work. This section will discuss how identity is tied to work, which countries might be more successful in a nonwork future, what meaningful work is, how individuals will transition to life beyond paid work, and how cultures will transition to life after work.

The authors argue that workers' identities are influenced by their job. According to social identity theory, people classify themselves into various social categories, such as organizational membership, which can be a foundational piece of one's identity (Tajfel & Turner, 2004; Thornborrow & Brown, 2009). Identities are important in that they provoke actions that are congruent with these identities (Ashforth & Mael, 1989). Therefore, one's job can be a catalyst for behaviors. For example, a medical doctor might be compelled to be extremely helpful and generous in their nonwork roles because they believe that is how they should act.

But what happens as society transitions to a jobless future? This transition can negatively impact the well-being of individuals because it is argued that exploring new identities can be stressful (Haslam & Reicher, 2006). Without paid jobs, individuals will need to seek other social categories they want to make foundational to their identity. This may be where culture plays a role as it can dictate what other social categories are valued.

Now the question is are there some underlying aspects of cultures that might better position some countries for a future with less emphasis on paid work? Rather than relying on speculation, there are indicators that some cultures are more likely than others to be better situated to embrace a future beyond paid work. Large-scale studies of culture (e.g., Hofstede model of cultural dimensions, the GLOBE Project) each have a measure to ascertain which cultures are collectivists versus those that are individualistic. Collectivism is the degree to which individuals from birth onward are integrated into strong, cohesive in-groups (Hofstede, 2011). Cultures in which individuals tend to value collectivism such as those in some Latin and South America, Southeast Asia, and African countries (Hofstede, 2001; Javidan et al., 2006) might embrace a future that moves beyond paid work due to tendencies for resource sharing at the societal level. Whereas, in cultures rated high in individualism such as those in the US, Australia, or the United Kingdom individuals are perhaps less likely to value and pursue endeavors that benefit society as a whole but are not tied to paid work due to the societal pressure to be self-reliant (Javidan et al., 2006).

Cultures consisting of individual members that tend toward gender equality and equity rights and opportunities for women (Javidan et al., 2006) are more likely to, in aggregate, embrace a future without paid work. Many countries that are rated as highly gender-egalitarian often have strong social programs in place to support families and people in general in times in which they may not be engaged in paid work. These cultures are prevalent in Scandinavian countries as well as some in Latin and South America and in Southeast Asia countries (Hofstede, 2001; Javidan et al., 2006). On the opposite end of the spectrum, countries rated as low on gender-egalitarianism such as Japan, Hungary, Austria, Venezuela, and Italy have high numbers of members demonstrating traits that include assertiveness, materialism, self-centeredness, and the desire for power, strength, and individual achievements. Material success and individual achievements are likely the opposite of what people engaging in a nonwork future might need for their success particularly as individuals seek meaning in their vocational endeavors (Di Fabio et al., Chapter 3).

Meaningful work is defined as work that is both personal and significant to people (Rosso et al., 2010). There are three main factors that contribute to meaningful work: Work Engagement (May et al., 2004), Job Satisfaction (Steger et al., 2012), and Career Development (Duffy & Dik, 2013). Within these three areas, there could be work that does not depend on monetary rewards to sustain a lifestyle. Therefore, in a jobless future, a financial salary may not be a necessity to maintain a day-to-day life. As meaningful work is both personal and significant to us, it must provide intrinsic value (Rosso et al., 2010). Thus, the emphasis must be on nonmonetary rewards and internal drivers. Examples include volunteering in programs that compensate workers through meals and shelter, instead of salary. In seeking long-term fulfillment, the worker's basic needs are satisfied. These factors contribute more things to meaningful work than financial benefits. Thus, for changes to occur on a cultural level, depends on the action of collective individuals (Vanhée & Dignum, 2018).

Vocational Interest and Job Placement

Given the limitations of their practical application in some economies, career interests have not received sufficient innovative attention (Mandelke et al., 2016). Specifically, strong abilities and the capacity to provide monetary value to corporations are likely to be more valuable in job placement than the pursuit of truly interesting work. If one considers interests as a driving force in career choice (or other life activity) instead of a luxury, there are three interesting ideas for the future of post-paid work.

First, interests are dynamic, and thus work can be too. If changing careers becomes less costly, society could see an increase in many alternative forms of traditional "jobs." For example, if financial barriers to entry are decreased as a function of universal basic income or other supportive structures making paid work ancillary to survival, entrepreneurial ventures aligned with an individual's interests, values, and strengths would thrive (Almeida et al., 2014). In the transition to a future with less or no paid work, career types within the confines of traditional employer-employee relationships could also be further expanded to include an emphasis on job placement from the lens of a protean career—one in which people, not organizations, lead their own career development toward success based on criteria which prioritizes psychological well-being over salary and rank (Hall, 2004). This emphasis on steering your own ship also lends itself to the perception that careers can be boundaryless at the organizational level (i.e., amenable to mobility both within and between organizations) and with respect to time (i.e., shorter term worker-interest-driven gigs; Oswald et al., 2019).

Second, if society prioritizes interests, society will also value their development at various stages of the lifespan. Interest development happens very early, well before one enters the workforce (Gottfredson, 1981; Low et al., 2005). In addition to I/O and vocational psychologists, any effort in this area needs to bring the educational psychologists who are also having their own conversations about interests into the fold (Su, 2020). In a world where making a career move is easier and quicker due to less financial constraints, the cultivation of personal interests and an emphasis on learning and growth is essential (Di Fabio et al., Chapter 3).

Finally, in the absence of pay-based work, interesting work is an equalizer. By increasing opportunities for career exploration and significantly cutting economic and societal pressures, pursuing interesting and meaningful work becomes an equal opportunity for everyone. In a society where people do not rely on work to sustain living, individuals and organizations can share the burden of establishing meaningful and interesting work.

There are plenty of concerning factors to consider in preparation for a future with unpaid work that has the potential to be more precarious, insecure, and uncertain. However, vocational-interests research is one positive area that could see a resurgence in practical application. Throughout history and as it currently stands, psychological assessments (e.g., interest inventories) meant to best place individuals in fulfilling careers that meet workforce demands are at the cross-section of vocational and I/O psychology. Although these two fields have essentially split off into semi-siloed research and practice areas, they study many of the same concepts, including vocational interests, but from different angles (Su, 2020).

Vocational psychologists might be perceived as serving the individual. Specifically, counselors are responsible for helping individuals in their great search for fulfillment by encouraging self-reflection on career interests and goals (McIlveen et al., 2021). They assess clients, guide them in career decision-making, monitor and explain barriers to career success and satisfaction, and manage expectations for bumps along the way. They direct jobseekers to the opportunities likely to lead to best fit, while experts in personnel selection open and close these doors based on the needs of organizations (Ryan & Ployhart, 2014). I/O psychologists also assess individuals and organizations; they guide organizational decision-making about selection, training, and career pathing and manage expectations about how quickly and with what level of impact these decisions can be made; and they monitor and explain barriers to an organization's performance and well-being goals for their workforce. Smoothing the transition to a post-work-for-pay future means rejoining these individual and organizational goals. This produces a dual-fit perspective for organizations and individuals. Finding purpose and meaningful work is much easier with environmental fit as opposed to economic necessity.

The research thus far regarding career interests can provide some insight into the priorities of these fields. I/O psychology has a heavy focus on defining and applying; and that is reflected in the literature. The structure and appropriate measurement of vocational interests has been well-debated and are established in the literature. Broad concepts like the realistic, investigative, artistic, social, enterprising, and conventional (RIASEC) model (Holland, 1959, 1997) and people, data, things, and ideas (Prediger, 1982; Prediger & Swaney, 2004) have created a strong foundation for vocational psychology and are widely used in both research and practice. Interest development is another major area of interest for researchers and practitioners. Social cognitive career theory proposes a continuous feedback loop based on experience (Lent et al., 1994). If someone has done something before and thinks that they are good at it, they will do more of the same; this is in essence a development of interest. In addition to conceptualization and development, the true application of interests is in fit with occupations. A large body of research over the last 50 years has supported that its contribution to performance and well-being is not insignificant. Person-environment fit, as seen through the lens of vocational interests' congruence with occupations, accounts for meaningful variance in both job performance and satisfaction (Nye et al., 2012, 2017). However, the conceptualization of career interests has been developed in a society where individuals' career decision-making is not in fact boundaryless and factors in more than just most preferred work activities (Brown & Lent, 1996; Tracey & Rounds, 1996).

With the current workforce demands and labor-market structure, interests actually play a very small role at the individual level (e.g., early career exploration, job search, first placement, career trajectories, career pivots). At the macro/meso level, selection and assessment practitioners rarely use interest inventories compared to measures of other individual differences like personality and cognitive ability (Nye et al., 2012). Even though they are underused by some standards, career interests play a substantial role in career choice. Interests affect the goals that individuals set for their career journeys and help them to sustain motivation for the long haul once they are on that journey (Lent et al., 1994). Reflecting on the current degree to which vocational interests play a role in employment decisions raises various inequities. Socioeconomic and individual factors (e.g., prior knowledge/experience, income, education level, self-efficacy), as well as negative feedback (family and friends, mentors, societal standards/norms), may stop someone from pursuing interesting work (Lent et al., 2000). Pursuing interesting work is a privilege for many. Due to a combination of the societal pressures to always be productive (i.e., "hustle culture" and workism; Thompson, 2019), financial precarity, and out of economic necessity, some individuals are forced to take every opportunity to transform their hobbies and other uses of their free time into income-producing ventures. Inequities are further extended considering which individuals are likely to even have the time to engage in interesting activities outside of (uninteresting) work or increase the value of their free time by monetizing hobbies. Clear gender differences also exist in measured career interests (Su et al., 2009); this, however, doesn't necessarily equate to some biological or innate difference. Interests, and thus career choices, are socially developed through experience, feedback, and social cognitive thought processes (Lent et al., 1994) and thus subject to gendered socialization and expectations (see role congruity theory; Diekman & Eagly, 2008).

Future-Research Directions

The breadth of and uncertainty surrounding the topics discussed in this chapter beget a list of recommended areas for future research that is diverse and inclusive on the one hand but that runs the risk of failing to yield a coherent knowledge base and/or set of technologies if not pursued in a systematic manner. To assuage this concern and to help indicate the specific value that each discrete unit of research would help to generate, the following section is subdivided into specific technologies and services that we could provide. Note that these technologies and services are a small subset of those that may, in time, become both useful and central to the function of I/O psychology; the interested reader is invited to follow a similar structure to the one demonstrated below in imagining technologies and services, and the research that would support them. Finally, these research domains are biased in favor of research that can be conducted in concord with other ongoing research that is designed to solve more immediate real-world problems, as promised earlier in the chapter; if unfettered by such practical constraints, research foci could expand into more dramatic and revolutionary areas.

Technology/Service 1: Avoiding Conflict during the Transition

- How has automation been introduced into workplaces, and what reactions have workers, industries, governments, and economies evidenced?
- What political and social movements have been attempted and/or envisioned when it comes to large-scale disruption of employment by automation? How did these movements succeed and fail and why?
- In what ways are economically vulnerable people treated differently when automation replaces jobs, and what controls could be put in place to avoid their mistreatment?
- Are there pathways whereby automation can be deployed whilst also improving the quality of life of those in the communities impacted by that automation? Adjacently, can income inequality be reduced rather than, as would be expected by default, exacerbated by deployment of automation technologies?

- What change-management techniques can be brought to bear such that replacement of human workers by automated systems is welcomed, by and large, by societies rather than resisted?
- How will work on large-scale reskilling/upskilling be phased out, as unnecessary, as the underlying promise of work for pay becomes (slowly or suddenly) untenable? How can these efforts be retooled to assist the same or similar populations in a world without paid work?

Technology/Service 2: Building a System that Permanently and Totally Replaces Human Work

- What key technologies are currently missing that would compromise an attempt to fully automate end-to-end manufacturing and product distribution, why are they missing or underdeveloped, and how can we divert resources toward developing these technologies?
- How mature are automated repair, optimization, and maintenance technologies? What are the major barriers to total dark-manufacturing systems when considered on a long-term-deployment basis?
- To encourage the start of the transition, how will incentives for human employment be attenuated and incentives for widespread automation be enhanced, all whilst avoiding economic inequality and the marginalization and loss of dignity of any individual people?
- What pathways between the world of economic productivity that we currently occupy and that without the involvement of human labor are practical and/or efficient? Is our current piecemeal automation approach likely to lead us to a completely automated world, or will industries and sectors need to be reinvented (or eliminated) entirely and rebuilt from the ground up?

Technology/Service 3: Maintaining all of the Advantages that Work Currently Provides

- How complete is our current understanding of the psychological advantages of employment? Do the assumptions of models need to be reexamined in light of the alternative being not temporary unemployment within a society where most are employed but rather a universal lack of human employment?
- What ancillary activities and systems have been and could conceivably be put into place to provide the same or greater levels of psychological health and well-being as those currently engaged in work for individuals no longer called upon or able to work? How does the tenability of such systems change from the current state of world economies to one in which human employment is no longer available?

- What system or systems for provision of human material needs (e.g., universal basic income; scarcity-free society) could serve humanity during the transition to and eventually in a steady-state world without human employment; how could these systems gain economic, social, and political support; and what intended and unintended changes from the current systems of wealth would accompany them, with what consequences?
- How might transitions to a world without human employment be facilitated and hampered by existing and likely future cultural contexts at the micro (e.g., individual, family) to macro (e.g., national, global) levels, and what extra efforts must needs be put in place to leverage (in the case of facilitation) and assuage (in the case of hampering) such influences?

Closing

As this chapter indicates, there are diverse ways of conceptualizing this future without paid employment, various tools and frameworks that can be brought to bear on the topic, and numerous foci—in terms of both processes and outcomes—that can be selected whilst doing so. Others may have occurred to the reader in the course of encountering these narratives, and the authors support this. There is not one correct way of thinking about a possible future without paid work; none of us would hazard a prediction as to how that future will, even in rough terms, actually look, and this is at present an opportunity (albeit a daunting one). The areas that are both ripe for exploration and well-served by existing work include those discussed above, as well as myriad others: from explorations of universal basic income as it pertains to (and facilitates) this transition, to explorations of changes in gender equality in the event of the automation of paid (and even unpaid) work, and so on.

Having set out to clarify a definition of a future without paid work and then to present narratives that show that investigation of this topic is not a hopeless endeavor, the authors have approached the topic from a variety of (sometimes quite nonoverlapping) angles, presenting both evidence and conjecture and tying together diverse areas of work with bearing on the topic at hand. It is our intention to leave the reader with an interest in this topic and ideas regarding how they can contribute to its exploration. This may include any and all of the following: reviewing past and ongoing work through this lens; adding research questions to ongoing, otherwise-unrelated, work; initiating entirely new lines of inquiry; beginning conversations about how to best move humanity toward this future (and how to best steer clear of undesirable paths adjacent to those), and of course building technologies that will help support humanity in the possible futures described in this chapter.

References

Almeida, P. I. L., Ahmetoglu, G., & Chamorro-Premuzic, T. (2014). Who wants to be an entrepreneur? The relationship between vocational interests and individual differences in entrepreneurship. *Journal of Career Assessment, 22*(1), 102–112. https://doi.org/10.1177/1069072713492923

Amuedo-Dorantes, C., & Kimmel, J. (2009). Moonlighting over the business cycle. *Economic Inquiry, 47*(4), 754–765. https://doi.org/10.1111/j.1465-7295.2008.00140.x

Aronowitz, S., & DiFazio, W. (2010). Facing the economic crisis of the twenty-first century: A new introduction to *The Jobless Future*. In S. Aronowitz, *The Jobless Future* (2nd ed., pp. xi–xxx). University of Minnesota Press.

Ashforth, B. E., & Mael, F. (1989). Social identity theory and the organization. *Academy of Management Review, 14*(1), 20–39.

Badue, C., Guidolini, R., Carneiro, R. V., Azevedo, P., Cardoso, V. B., Forechi, A., Jesus, L., Berriel, R., Paixão, T. M., Mutz, F., de Paula Veronese, L., Oliviera-Santos, T., & De Souza, A. F. (2021). Self-driving cars: A survey. *Expert Systems with Applications, 165*, Article 113816.

Barker, K., & Christensen, K. (1998). *Contingent work: American employment relations in transition.* Cornell University Press.

Brown, S. D., & Lent, R. W. (1996). A social cognitive framework for career choice counseling. *The Career Development Quarterly, 44*(4), 354–366. https://doi.org/10.1002/j.2161-0045.1996.tb00451.x

Casey, C., & Alach, P. (2004). 'Just a temp?' Women, temporary employment and lifestyle. *Work, Employment and Society, 18*(3), 459–480. https://doi.org/10.1177/0950017004045546

Chenjie, S. H. I., & Veres, S. M. (2021). *Concepts of self-maintaining robots and their design.* Arxiv. https://arxiv.org/abs/2110.05882

Cirne, C. T., Tunick, M. H., & Trout, R. E. (2019). The chemical and attitudinal differences between commercial and artisanal products. *NPJ Science of Food, 3*(1), 1–4.

Diekman, A. B., & Eagly, A. H. (2008). Of men, women, and motivation: A role congruity account. In J. Y. Shah & W. L. Gardner (Eds.), *Handbook of motivation science* (pp. 434–447). The Guilford Press.

Duffy, R. D., & Dik, B. J. (2013). Research on calling: What have we learned and where are we going? *Journal of Vocational Behavior, 83*(3), 428–436.

Evjemo, L. D., Gjerstad, T., Grøtli, E. I., & Sziebig, G. (2020). Trends in smart manufacturing: Role of humans and industrial robots in smart factories. *Current Robotics Reports, 1*(2), 35–41. https://doi.org/10.1007/s43154-020-00006-5

Fernández, J. D., & Vico, F. (2013). AI methods in algorithmic composition: A comprehensive survey. *Journal of Artificial Intelligence Research, 48,* 513–582. https://doi.org/10.1613/jair.3908

Fernández-Vara, C., & Thomson, A. (2012, May). Procedural generation of narrative puzzles in adventure games: The puzzle-dice system. In *Proceedings of the Third Workshop on Procedural Content Generation in Games* (pp. 1–6). Association for Computing Machinery.

Gierl, M. J., & Haladyna, T. M. (Eds.). (2012). *Automatic item generation: Theory and practice*. Routledge.

Goodman, W., Antczak, S., & Freeman, L. (1993). Women and jobs in recessions: 1969–92. *Monthly Labor Review, July,* 26–35. Retrieved March 10, 2023, from https://www.bls.gov/opub/mlr/1993/07/art3full.pdf

Gottfredson, L. S. (1981). Circumscription and compromise: A developmental theory of occupational aspirations. *Journal of Counseling Psychology, 28(*6), 545–579. https://doi.org/10.1037/0022-0167.28.6.545

Hall, D. T. (2004). The protean career: A quarter-century journey. *Journal of Vocational Behavior, 65*(1), 1–13. https://doi.org/10.1016/j.jvb.2003.10.006

Hallik, L., Šarauskis, E., Kazlauskas, M., Bručienė, I., Mozgeris, G., Steponavičius, D., & Tõrra, T. (2022). Proximal sensing sensors for monitoring crop growth. In D. D. Bochtis, M. Lampridi, G. P. Petropoulos, Y. Ampatzidis, & P. Pardalos (Eds.), *Information and communication technologies for agriculture—Theme I: Sensors* (pp. 43–97). Springer.

Hameed, H. M., Rashid, A. T., & Al Amry, K. A. (2020, June). Automatic storage and retrieval system using the optimal path algorithm *Iraqi Journal for Electrical and Electronic Engineering.* https://doi.org/10.37917/ijeee.sceeer.3rd.18

Hao, K. (2019, August 2). *China has started a grand experiment in AI education. It could reshape how the world learns.* MIT Technology Review. https://www.technologyreview.com/2019/08/02/131198/china-squirrel-has-started-a-grand-experiment-in-ai-education-it-could-reshape-how-the/

Haslam, S. A., & Reicher, S. (2006). Stressing the group: Social identity and the unfolding dynamics of responses to stress. *Journal of Applied Psychology, 91*(5), 1037–1052. https://doi.org/10.1037/0021-9010.91.5.1037

Hofstede, G. (2001). *Culture's consequences: Comparing values, behaviors, institutions, and organizations across nations*. Sage.

Hofstede, G. (2011). Dimensionalizing cultures: The Hofstede model in context. *Online Readings in Psychology and Culture, 2*(1), 2307-0919.

Holland, J. L. (1959). A theory of vocational choice. *Journal of Counseling Psychology, 6*(1), 35–45. https://doi.org/10.1037/h0040767

Holland, J. L. (1997). *Making vocational choices: A theory of vocational personalities and work environments* (3rd ed.). Psychological Assessment Resources.

International Labour Organization. (2021). *World employment and social outlook 2021: The role of digital labour platforms in transforming the world of work.* https://www.ilo.org/global/research/global-reports/weso/2021/WCMS_771749/lang--en/index.htm

Javidan, M., House, R. J., Dorfman, P. W., Hanges, P. J., & De Luquet, M. S. (2006). Conceptualizing and measuring cultures and their consequences: A comparative review of GLOBE's and Hofstede's approaches. *Journal of International Business Studies, 37*(6), 897–914. https://doi.org/10.1057/palgrave.jibs.8400234

Josten, C., & Lordan, G. (2020). *Robots at work: Automatable and non-automatable jobs*. Springer International Publishing.

Khoshnevis, B. (2004). Automated construction by contour crafting—Related robotics and information technologies. *Automation in Construction, 13*(1), 5–19. https://doi.org/10.1016/j.autcon.2003.08.012

Kosanovich, K. (2018) *A look at contingent workers.* U.S. Bureau of Labor Statistics. https://www.bls.gov/spotlight/2018/contingent-workers/home.htm

Langou, G. D., & Forteza, P. (2012). *Validating one of the world's largest conditional cash transfer programmes* (Working Paper No. 16). International Initiative for Impact Evaluation.

Lee, N., & Park, H. (2021). Key successful factors for unmanned convenience stores in the fourth industrial revolution: Case of E-Mart24 self-store. *Journal of the Korea Industrial Information Systems Research, 26*(2), 73–94.

Lent, R. W., Brown, S. D., & Hackett, G. (1994). Toward a unifying social cognitive theory of career and academic interest, choice, and performance. *Journal of Vocational Behavior, 45*(1), 79–122. https://doi.org/10.1006/jvbe.1994.1027

Lent, R. W., Brown, S. D., & Hackett, G. (2000). Contextual supports and barriers to career choice: A social cognitive analysis. *Journal of Counseling Psychology, 47*(1), 36–49. https://doi.org/10.1037/0022-0167.47.1.36

Li, M., Holthausen, B. E., Stuck, R. E., & Walker, B. N. (2019). No risk no trust: Investigating perceived risk in highly automated driving. In *Proceedings of the 11th International Conference on Automotive User Interfaces and Interactive Vehicular Applications* (pp. 177–185). Association for Computing Machinery.

Liang, X., de Almeida Correia, G. H., & Van Arem, B. (2016). Optimizing the service area and trip selection of an electric automated taxi system used for the last mile of train trips. *Transportation Research Part E: Logistics and Transportation Review, 93*, 115–129. https://doi.org/10.1016/j.tre.2016.05.006

Lipu, M. H., Miah, M. S., Hannan, M. A., Hussain, A., Sarker, M. R., Ayob, A., Saad, M. H. M., & Mahmud, M. S. (2021). Artificial intelligence based hybrid forecasting approaches for wind power generation: Progress, challenges and prospects. *IEEE Access, 9*, 102460–102489.

Low, K. S. D., Yoon, M., Roberts, B. W., & Rounds, J. (2005). The stability of vocational interests from early adolescence to middle adulthood: A quantitative review of longitudinal studies. *Psychological Bulletin, 131*(5), 713–737. https://doi.org/10.1037/0033-2909.131.5.713

Mandelke, A. J., Shoenfelt, E. L., & Brown, R. D. (2016). Expected utility of interest inventories in employee selection: Perceptions of industrial organizational psychology experts. *TIP: The Industrial-Organizational Psychologist, 54*(2), 1–7.

Matusik, S. F., & Hill, C. W. (1998). The utilization of contingent work, knowledge creation, and competitive advantage. *Academy of Management Review, 23*(4), 680–697. https://doi.org/10.5465/amr.1998.1255633

May, D. R., Gilson, R. L., & Harter, L. M. (2004). The psychological conditions of meaningfulness, safety and availability and the engagement of the human spirit at work. *Journal of Occupational and Organizational Psychology, 77*(1), 11–37. https://doi.org/10.1348/096317904322915892

McIlveen, P., Perera, H. N., Brown, J., Healy, M., & Hammer, S. (2021). Career Assessment. In P. J. Robertson, P. McCash, & T. Hooley (Eds.), *The Oxford handbook of career development*. Oxford University Press. https://doi.org/10.1093/oxfordhb/9780190069704.001.0001

Mignonac, K., Herrbach, O., & Guerrero, S. (2006). The interactive effects of perceived external prestige and need for organizational identification on turnover intentions. *Journal of Vocational Behavior, 69*(3), 477–493. https://doi.org/10.1016/j.jvb.2006.05.006

Mulcahy, D. (2016, October 27). Who wins in the gig economy, and who loses. *Harvard Business Review*. Retrieved March 15, 2022, from, https://hbr.org/2016/10/who-wins-in-the-gig-economy-and-who-loses

Nehvi, F. A., Wani, S. A., Dar, S. A., Makhdoomi, M. I., Allie, B. A., & Mir, Z. A. (2006). New emerging trends on production technology of saffron. In *II International Symposium on Saffron Biology and Technology* (pp. 375–381). ISHS.

Nii-Aponsah, H. (2022). *Automation exposure and implications in advanced and developing countries across gender, age and skills* (UNU-MERIT Working Paper Series No. 2022-021). Maastricht University, United Nations University. https://www.merit.unu.edu/publications/wppdf/2022/wp2022-021.pdf

Nye, C. D., Su, R., Rounds, J., & Drasgow, F. (2012). Vocational interests and performance: A quantitative summary of over 60 years of research. *Perspectives on Psychological Science, 7*(4), 384–403. https://doi.org/10.1177/1745691612449021

Nye, C. D., Su, R., Rounds, J., & Drasgow, F. (2017). Interest congruence and performance: Revisiting recent meta-analytic findings. *Journal of Vocational Behavior, 98*, 138–151. https://doi.org/10.1016/j.jvb.2016.11.002

Oswald, F. L., Hough, L. M., & Zuo, C. (2019). Personnel selection and vocational interests: Recent research and future directions. In C. D. Nye & J. Rounds (Eds.), *Vocational interests in the workplace: Rethinking behavior at work*. Routledge. https://doi.org/10.4324/9781315678924

Prediger, D. J. (1982). Dimensions underlying Holland's hexagon: Missing link between interests and occupations? *Journal of Vocational Behavior, 21*(3), 259–287. https://doi.org/10.1016/0001-8791(82)90036-7

Prediger, D. J., & Swaney, K. B. (2004). Work task dimensions underlying the world of work: Research results for diverse occupational databases. *Journal of Career Assessment, 12*(4), 440–459. https://doi.org/10.1177/1069072704267737

Ranjitha, P., & Spandana, M. (2021, May). Predictive analysis for big mart sales using machine learning algorithms. In *2021 5th International Conference on Intelligent Computing and Control Systems (ICICCS)* (pp. 1416–1421). IEEE.

Risher, H. (2021, April 13). *The gig economy and BLS surveys*. Government Executive. Retrieved March 13, 2023, from https://www.govexec.com/management/2020/02/gig-economy-and-bls-surveys/163089/

Rosso B.D., Dekas K.H., & Wrzesniewski A. (2010). On the meaning of work: A theoretical integration and review. *Research in Organizational Behavior, 30*(1), 91–127. https://doi.org/10.1016/j.riob.2010.09.001

Ryan, A. M., & Ployhart, R. E. (2014). A century of selection. *Annual Review of Psychology, 65*, 693–717. https://doi.org/10.1146/annurev-psych-010213-115134

Schwartz, S. H. (1999). A theory of cultural values and some implications for work. *Applied Psychology, 48*(1), 23–47.

Selişteanu, D., Roman, M., Şendrescu, D., Petre, E., & Popa, B. (2018). A distributed control system for processes in food industry: Architecture and implementation. In *2018 19th International Carpathian Control Conference (ICCC)* (pp. 128–133). IEEE.

Shojaei, K. (2021). Intelligent coordinated control of an autonomous tractor-trailer and a combine harvester. *European Journal of Control, 59*, 82–98.

Standing, G. (2017) *Universal Basic Income (UBI)* [Video]. Universal Basic Income. https://www.ubi.org/45/ubi-video-guy-standing

Steger, M. F., Dik, B. J., & Duffy, R. D. (2012). Measuring meaningful work: The work and meaning inventory (WAMI). *Journal of Career Assessment, 20*(3), 322–337. https://doi.org/10.1177/1069072711436160

Su, R. (2020). The three faces of interests: An integrative review of interest research in vocational, organizational, and educational psychology. *Journal of Vocational Behavior, 116*(Part B), Article 103240. https://doi.org/10.1016/j.jvb.2018.10.016

Su, R., Rounds, J., & Armstrong, P. I. (2009). Men and things, women and people: A meta-analysis of sex differences in interests. *Psychological Bulletin, 135*(6), 859–884. https://doi.org/10.1037/a0017364

Tajfel, H., & Turner, J. C. (2004). The social identity theory of intergroup behavior. In J. T. Jost & J. Sidanius (Eds.), *Political psychology: Key readings* (pp. 276–293). Psychology Press.

Thompson, D. (2019, February 25). Workism is making Americans miserable. *The Atlantic.* Retrieved March 13, 2023, from https://www.theatlantic.com/ideas/archive/2019/02/religion-workism-making-americans-miserable/583441/

Thornborrow, T., & Brown, A. D. (2009). 'Being regimented': Aspiration, discipline and identity work in the British parachute regiment. *Organization Studies, 30*(4), 355–376. https://doi.org/10.1177/0170840608101140

Tracey, T. J. G., & Rounds, J. (1996). The spherical representation of vocational interests. *Journal of Vocational Behavior, 48*(1), 3–41. https://doi.org/10.1006/jvbe.1996.0002

United States General Accounting Office (2000). *Contingent workers: Incomes and benefits lag behind those of rest of workforce.* https://www.gao.gov/assets/hehs-00-76.pdf

Vanhée, L., & Dignum, F. (2018). Explaining the emerging influence of culture, from individual influences to collective phenomena. *Journal of Artificial Societies and Social Simulation, 21*(4). https://www.jasss.org/21/4/11.html

Veerachamy, R., Ramar, R., Balaji, S., & Sharmila, L. (2022). Autonomous Application Controls on Smart Irrigation. *Computers and Electrical Engineering, 100*, Article 107855. https://doi.org/10.1016/j.compeleceng.2022.107855

Vermeulen, B., Kesselhut, J., Pyka, A., & Saviotti, P.P. (2018, May 21). The impact of automation on employment: Just the usual structure change? *Sustainability, 10,* 1661. https://doi.org/10.3390/su10051661

Visser, M. A. (2019). Restructuring opportunity: Employment change and job quality in the United States during the Great Recession. *Socio-Economic Review, 17*(3), 545–572. https://doi.org/10.1093/ser/mwy002

Walia, N., Bhetuwal, R., Acosta, L., Muddasani, S., Kamwal, C., Mishra, V. D., & Leszkowitz, D. (2021). Employment status and its association with psychological distress and alcohol consumption. *Cureus, 13*(6). https://doi.org/10.7759/cureus.16054

Westerlund, M. (2019). The emergence of deepfake technology: A review. *Technology Innovation Management Review, 9*(11), 39–52.

Wiesenfeld, B. M., Raghuram, S., & Garud, R. (2001). Organizational identification among virtual workers: The role of need for affiliation and perceived work-based social support. *Journal of Management, 27*(2), 213–229. https://doi.org/10.1177/014920630102700205

Wilkin, C. L. (2013). I can't get no job satisfaction: Meta-analysis comparing permanent and contingent workers. *Journal of Organizational Behavior, 34*(1), 47–64. https://doi.org/10.1002/job.1790

Wojton, H. M., Porter, D., T. Lane, S., Bieber, C., & Madhavan, P. (2020). Initial validation of the trust of automated systems test (TOAST). *The Journal of Social Psychology, 160*(6), 735–750. https://doi.org/10.1080/00224545.2020.1749020

Zhang, K., Xu, P., Gao, T., & Zhang, J. (2021, July). A trustworthy framework of artificial intelligence for power grid dispatching systems. In *2021 IEEE 1st international conference on digital twins and parallel intelligence (DTPI)* (pp. 418–421). IEEE.

INDEX

For Product Safety Concerns and Information please contact our EU representative GPSR@taylorandfrancis.com
Taylor & Francis Verlag GmbH, Kaufingerstraße 24, 80331 München, Germany

www.ingramcontent.com/pod-product-compliance
Ingram Content Group UK Ltd.
Pitfield, Milton Keynes, MK11 3LW, UK
UKHW022346190926
475702UK00015B/2125
9781032576633